Dynamic HTML

Peter Belesis

Arman Danesh

Rick Darnell

Craig Eddy

Brian A. Gallagher

John J. Kottler

Trevor Lohrbeer

Ryan Peters

Stephanos Piperoglou

Jeff Rouyer

William Randolph Royere III

David Wiley

Matthew Zandstra

sams.net

201 West 103rd Street
Indianapolis, IN 46290

UNLEASHED

International Standard Book Number: 0-57521-353-2

Library of Congress Catalog Card Number: 97-68546

2001   2000   99   98   4   3   2   1

Interpretation of the printing code: the rightmost double-digit number is the year of the book's printing; the rightmost single-digit, the number of the book's printing. For example, a printing code of 98-1 shows that the first printing of the book occurred in 1998.

Composed in AGaramond and MCPdigital by Macmillan Computer Publishing

Printed in the United States of America

Trademarks

President	*Richard K. Swadley*
Publisher	*Jordan Gold*
Executive Editor	*Mark Taber*
Managing Editor	*Patrick Kanouse*
Senior Indexer	*Ginny Bess*
Director of Software and User Services	*Cheryl Willoughby*
Brand Director	*Alan Bower*

Acquisitions Editor
Randi Roger

Development Editor
Bob Correll

Production Editor
Heather E. Butler

Copy Editors
Kris Simmons
Marilyn J. Stone

Indexer
Christine Nelsen

Technical Reviewer
Brett Bonenberger

Editorial Coordinators
Mandie Rowell
Katie Wise

Technical Edit Coordinator
Lorraine E. Schaffer

Resource Coordinators
Deborah Frisby
Charlotte Clapp

Editorial Assistants
Carol Ackerman
Andi Richter
Rhonda Tinch-Mize
Karen Williams

Cover Designer
Jason Grisham

Book Designer
Gary Adair

Copy Writer
David Reichwein

Production Team Supervisor
Andrew Stone

Production Team
Elizabeth Deeter
Shawn Ring

Dedications

For Des, who knows why, and Ion and Lena.
—Peter Belesis

Special thanks to my wife, Penny, for her love and encouragement, which is a continuous blessing. Thanks also to my parents for lovingly believing in me.
—Jay Kottler

Thanks to my girlfriend, Amanda, for her understanding and patience while I worked till 3 a.m., and to Susan for her support and constructive criticism of my writing.
—Ryan Peters

Special thanks to Peter Belesis.
—Stephanos Piperoglou

For Michelle.
—William Randolph Royere III

For David Enoch.
—David Wiley

To Louise. Thanks.
—Matt Zandstra

Contents

Part IV The Document Object Model

Part V Data Awareness

Acknowledgments

Brian Gallagher: I would like to recognize my family for the time and sacrifices they endured to allow me to participate in this project; Jen, Troy, and Sarge—thanks. Also, I would like to thank Jeff Rouyer, for his enthusiasm, creativity, and friendship.

Trevor Lohrbeer: I would like to thank Bob Ainsbury for giving me a chance in the computer industry and Glenn Anderson for showing me good programming and debugging practices.

Jeff Rouyer: All my Web-related projects start out as gray lumps of clay. I would like to thank my friends, Christina Baldi, Brian Gallagher, and Alice Rouyer for helping me form the lumps of clay into beautiful cobalt blue ashtrays.

William Royere: Thanks to the Sams.net editorial staff.

David Wiley: My thanks go to my wife, Elaine, for her support in terms of her encouragement, love, and extra time taking care of David Enoch. Ai shiteru!

Matthew Zandstra: I would like to thank Michael Morrison for his generous permission to use approaches and structures developed in his Java Sprite and SpriteVector classes. Thanks also to the Corrosive team for putting up with moments of madness and panic.

About the Authors

Peter Belesis resides in Greece with the sun, the sea, and his slow Internet connection. A pioneer in PC training, and old enough to know that "Moz" rhymes with "Woz," Peter presently maintains two popular online columns—CompuServe's Dynamic HTML 101 (`www.iehelp.com`) and WebReference's Dynamic HTML Lab (`www.webreference.com/dhtml/`). When not writing, Peter spends his time wondering what he would be doing had the Web not been invented.

Arman Danesh (`armand@landegg.com`) is the Director of Communications and Information Systems at Landegg Academy (`http://www.landegg.edu/`), an international university in Switzerland. He is also a consultant for "The Bahai World" Web site (`http://www.bahai.org/`) and a technology journalist, contributing regularly to the *South China Morning Post* in Hong Kong and other publications throughout Asia. He received his master's of science degree in mass communication from Boston University in 1990. Arman lives with his wife, Tahirih, in Switzerland.

Rick Darnell (`darnell@montana.com`) hails from the flatlands of Kansas, although he currently finds his view blocked by a bunch of mountains while living with his wife and two daughters in western Montana. He graduated from Kansas State University with a degree in broadcasting, after which he became confused, and started writing for two small energy industry magazines and a local weekly newspaper. While spending time as a freelance journalist and writer, Rick saw the full gamut of personal computers since starting out with a Radio Shack Model I in the late 1970s. When not in front of his computer, he serves as a volunteer firefighter/EMT and member of a regional hazardous materials response team. Rick has authored several books for Sams.net Publishing and Que Corporation, including *HTML Unleashed* and *Teach Yourself Dynamic HTML in a Week*. His Web page is located at `http://people.montana.com/darnell/`.

Craig Eddy (`craig.eddy@cyberdude.com`) resides in Richmond, Virginia with his wife and two children. Craig holds a bachelor of science degree in electrical engineering from Virginia Tech. He is currently employed as Senior Developer for Pipesteam Technologies, Inc., a leading developer of sales force automation and customer information management software. Craig specializes in Visual Basic, SQL Server, Access, and Active Server development. He contributed to *Access 97 Unleashed*, *VBScript Unleashed*, *Visual InterDev Unleashed*, *Teach Yourself Access 97 in 24 Hours*, and *Web Programming with Visual Basic*. Craig's outside interests include private business development and relaxing on the outer banks of North Carolina.

Brian Gallagher (`briang@spintheweb.com` or `briang@winntmag.com`) is a product reviewer in the *Windows NT Magazine* lab. He has been a writer/editor for numerous technology-focused publications.

John J. Kottler (jkottler@aol.com) has been programming for 14 years and has spent the past 6 years developing applications for the Windows platform. In addition to Windows development, John has been programming multimedia and Internet applications for more than three years. His knowledge includes C/C++, Visual Basic, multimedia and digital video production, and Internet application development. He has published numerous magazine articles on software development and programming techniques. John has been recently published in Sams.net's *Netscape Unleashed, Web Publishing Unleashed, Presenting ActiveX, Web Page Wizardry, Java Unleashed, Visual InterDev Unleashed*, and in Sams Publishing's *Programming Windows 95 Unleashed*. He was also a codeveloper of the shareware application Virtual Monitors. A graduate of Rutgers University with a degree in computer science, he enjoys in-line skating, cycling, and playing digital music in his spare time.

Trevor Lohrbeer began developing Web sites as a hobby in 1993. He joined Maximum Information two years later to develop database-driven interactive Web sites using WebC. After the company was sold to NetManage, he managed their Web team for five months before leaving the company to pursue work as a consultant. He now develops interactive Web sites using both database-driven dynamically generated Web pages and Dynamic HTML. In his spare time, he writes fiction, performs with fire and drums, and maintains several personal Web sites.

Ryan Peters (ryan@b29.com) lives in Rehoboth Beach, Delaware, with two cats, a dog, two computers, and a purple car. An accomplished Web developer specializing in Windows NT Web-based applications, he devotes an incredible amount of time to staying ahead of the curve in Internet development. One of the owners of B29 Development Corp. (http://www.b29.com), Ryan was awarded Best Overall Use of Dynamic HTML in the 1997 Netscape/Webmonkey Dynamic HTML Skill Contest for an interactive Dynamic HTML real estate kiosk. When not developing or experimenting with new ways to bring the Web to life, he enjoys personal watercraft, live music, and his ongoing quest for a 36-hour day.

Stephanos Piperoglou is currently a first-year undergraduate studying computer science at St. John's College, Cambridge University, in England. His professional experience includes work as a network administrator for Hellas On Line, one of Greece's largest Internet service providers, and recently as a Web developer for the Demokritos National Scientific Research Center, the largest scientific research institution in his home country.

Jeff Rouyer holds a degree in zoology from Oregon State University. He worked as a biologist for the National Marine Fisheries Service and Forest Service for several years. A blip in time finds Jeff currently residing with his wife in Lafayette, Colorado, where he builds Web pages for an Internet service provider. Jeff's Web projects and computer animations have bagged him several awards and Scooby snacks from publishers and the Internet community. While dreaming up his next Web project, he often reflects back to a time when he was counting whales off the coast of Alaska.

William Randolph Royere III is a southern California-based programmer in Internet security and secure Web development. He is a former systems administrator with programming expertise in the following platforms: Novell, SunOS, Solaris, LINUX, AIX, MS Windows 95 and NT. His preferred language (other than JavaScript) is Perl, but he also codes in C/C++, VB, BASIC, and various shells. He now heads an Internet security consulting firm. He has written for Sams.net in the past.

David Wiley is a graduate of Marshall University, where he received a bachelor of fine arts degree, with honors, in vocal performance. In addition to working as Marshall University's Web developer, teaching in the university's Computer Science department, and providing consulting support for a number of extra university projects such as Bell Atlantic's World School program, David tries to stay involved in his local fine arts community and church. He has served as music director for summer theater performances in addition to appearing in their leading roles, and served a two-year full-time mission for his church in Kyushu, Japan. Beyond DHTML, David's current projects include investigations of higher education policy governing online course delivery, Web publishing in Japanese, transmission of music via the Internet and creating free time for his family. David is married to Robina Elaine Wiley, and they have a one-year-old boy named David Enoch.

Matthew Zandstra is the creative director of Corrosive Web Design Ltd (`http://www.corrosive.co.uk/`), which he cofounded in 1996 after some years as a freelance designer and teacher. He codes in Perl, Java, Lingo, and JavaScript. In addition to teaching Web programming, creating Web environments, and acquiring Web skills, he masterminds occasional forays into the real world to read, write, and drink Guinness.

Tell Us What You Think!

As a reader, you are the most important critic and commentator of our books. We value your opinion and want to know what we're doing right, what we could do better, what areas you'd like to see us publish in, and any other words of wisdom you're willing to pass our way. You can help us make strong books that meet your needs and give you the computer guidance you require.

Do you have access to the World Wide Web? Then check out our site at http://www.mcp.com.

> **NOTE**
>
> If you have a technical question about this book, call the technical support line at 317-581-3833, or send e-mail to support@mcp.com.

As the team leader of the group that created this book, I welcome your comments. You can fax, e-mail, or write me directly to let me know what you did or didn't like about this book—as well as what we can do to make our books stronger. Here's the information:

Fax: 317-581-4669

E-mail: newtech_mgr@.mcp.com

Mail: Mark Taber
            Comments Department
            Sams.net Publishing
            201 W. 103rd Street
            Indianapolis, IN 46290

Introduction

Welcome to the world of Dynamic HTML, where the speed of the user's modem and the load on the host's server begin to become irrelevant. So what is Dynamic HTML (DHTML)? It's the world of point-and-click, drag-and-drop, instant gratification Web pages. It's about Web pages that can change themselves, and page elements with direct database connections. It's about the evolution from static page to interactive mini-applications. To be more specific, DHTML is an emerging Web standard that adds interactive features to Web pages while lightening the load on Web servers.

To accomplish all these feats of wonder, DHTML doesn't mandate your use of new tags, languages, or platforms. DHTML can be accomplished using existing technologies and features on the Web, including HTML, scripting, and object-oriented programming. You can go beyond this, of course, and experiment with the proprietary tags Microsoft and Netscape have developed for their latest generation of Web browsers. At its root, however, DHTML isn't a new version of HTML; it's a new way of tying the elements of a Web page together to create a page that crosses traditional static boundaries.

The combination of features and capabilities that become Dynamic HTML are working their way into the HTML standard through the primary standards-making body for the Web—the World Wide Web Consortium. At the same time, Microsoft and Netscape are both introducing browsers and add-ons to make DHTML possible for the user, while other developers are creating tools to author Web pages that include Dynamic HTML features. But, even with new browsers and tools in the offing, a strong understanding of the technical details will go a long way in helping you understand what's happening to your pages when the finished product hits the Web.

So, what are you required to know to enter this new arena in Web authoring and development? First, a solid knowledge of HTML. DHTML doesn't work without clean HTML, and we won't spend much time in this book reviewing how to assemble basic HTML pages. For that, you can check out *HTML 4 Unleashed* or *Teach Yourself HTML 4 in 24 Hours*. We will cover the rest of the details, including all the building blocks—style sheets, scripting, object models, events, and database handling.

When you're finished, you'll have all the information you need to build Web pages that change themselves without the help of the Web server receiving data from databases without CGI scripts. And, you'll have the information and resources that you need to stay on top of this evolving capability and standard.

Who Should Read This Book

Our primary audience is the readers who depend on the *Unleashed* series as both a learning tool and an indispensable reference. We're striving for this book to be the definitive work on the universe of Dynamic HTML. If you need information about philosophy, standards, and practical implementation, it's all under one roof in this book.

We wrote this book for the vast numbers of people who understand HTML and need an in-depth look at the new capabilities offered by Dynamic HTML. With the code listings and examples, you could probably get through this book without a working knowledge of HTML, but it's certainly going to make your life easier. If you have not read a technical book on HTML (standards 1.0, 2.0, 3.2, or 4.0), you might want to read one first.

What This Book Is

This book is a complete reference on fitting various technologies together to create Dynamic HTML. The caveat is that DHTML means different things to different companies: Netscape, Microsoft, and the W3C all have slightly different views and implementations, and they're not entirely compatible with each other. For that reason, we've tried to cover the nuances in implementation between browsers, and the work of W3C to bring everyone to a common ground. Where both browsers accomplish the same task with different means, we'll show you both ways of implementing the task.

This book covers every major feature of Dynamic HTML we have found. By following the sections of the book, you'll see where each feature of DHTML depends on the other features for the final result. By working with each feature separately and in concert with its companions, you'll add dynamically changing text, styles, and graphics; provide interactive access to a data source; and add animations to your Web pages—all of which readers can access through mouse- and keyboard-based events. You'll learn how to place text and graphics more precisely on a Web page as well as define a region on a Web page where your readers can drag and drop graphics themselves.

What You Need Before You Start

Because Dynamic HTML is a way of integrating existing HTML technologies, all you need to create Dynamic HTML files is a simple text editor (such as the Notepad application accessory provided with either the Windows or NT operating systems). You can use a word processor as well or a more sophisticated Integrated Development Environment (IDE) that comes with many of today's visual programming applications.

To see the Web pages you create in an interactive mode, you need either the Netscape Navigator 4.02 or Microsoft Internet Explorer 4.0 Web browser. To see all the examples in this book perform their dynamic features, you need both Navigator 4.02 and Internet Explorer 4.0. Both are available on the Web for download. Because Dynamic HTML is not implemented as a standard, Netscape and Microsoft present different implementations. We provide examples of each implementation.

A live Internet connection is not necessary for creating DHTML pages, although access to the Web will let you look up the many Web-based resources referenced throughout the text in this book.

Dynamic HTML Unleashed at a Glance

Part I is an introduction to Dynamic HTML concepts, including a more complete definition of DHTML and an overview of where it lies within the standards process with the World Wide Web Consortium and competitive implementation with Netscape and Microsoft.

Part II covers cascading style sheets, which comprise the first building block of DHTML. As HTML continues to move away from tag-based control over document appearance, knowledge and use of style sheets are necessary to implement visual changes in Web pages.

Part III gives a quick introduction and tutorial on scripting within Web pages. Scripting is required by DHTML to give "intelligence" to your Web pages by allowing decision making and processing to occur in reaction to user events. Although most of this book will utilize JavaScript for its examples, DHTML is not tied to a specific language.

Part IV is where DHTML-specific technologies really become apparent. This section includes evaluation and exploration of the different Document Object Models (DOM) available for DHTML. The DOM is what the scripting language uses to identify and manipulate virtually any element on the Web page.

Events are a cousin to scripting and the DOM, and are also covered in Part IV. Events are used by DHTML to "see" and "feel" its environment, including what the user is doing on the page— moving a mouse, clicking, typing, or moving on to a new page.

Part V explores a fledgling capability of DHTML which is currently limited to Internet Explorer. Data awareness allows a Web page to create a direct connection to a database, without the automatic dependence on CGI scripts. Once the connection is made, the page can display and manipulate data in a variety of ways, including inserting, deleting, and updating records. The result is a major breakthrough in creating Web pages that can interact with data by placing all the data functions within familiar HTML tags.

Part VI includes other options for Dynamic HTML, including animated transitions, layers, and Netscape Navigator's canvas mode. This section is primarily a collection of proprietary technologies that are only compatible with one browser or another, but they serve to give an indication of the different ways DHTML is evolving.

Part VII brings all the pieces of the first six sections together by looking at the practical application of DHTML on a Web page. This includes making a site for the 4.0 browsers, creating a site that will degrade gracefully, creating a Netcaster site, debugging strategies for DHTML pages, and publishing your content.

By the time you're done reading this book, we hope you'll have all the tools and information you need to use DHTML techniques in a responsible manner. The result should be pages that increase the effectiveness of your pages for your users, not drive them to distraction.

Because this is a reference book, we know you'll have additional questions about syntax and standards that aren't directly treated in the text of a chapter. Instead of keeping three or four books open at your side to look up information on HTML, style sheets, and scripting, we've provided a Companion Web site (http://www.mcp.com/info) and our Sams.net Dynamic HTML Guru site (http://www.htmlguru.com) that include a set of quick reference chapters that cover all the technologies we've implemented, plus a side-by-side reference of the different Document Object Models.

We're sure you'll be as excited as we are about Dynamic HTML by the time you've had a taste of the capabilities it offers for your Web pages. It opens a new way to communicate with your readers on the Web which provides practical tools and entertaining effects, so both you and your readers can have fun. And, isn't that what you're looking for? As we said earlier, welcome to Dynamic HTML. We think you'll like it here.

Getting Started with Dynamic HTML

I

PART

Introducing Dynamic HTML

by Rick Darnell

IN THIS CHAPTER

CHAPTER 1

Dynamic HTML (DHTML) is the latest big news on the World Wide Web since Java was introduced. It seems that with the advent of HTML 4, the new Document Object Model (DOM), ECMAScript, and a host of other new announcements from the gods who create standards for the World Wide Web, people can't get enough of DHTML.

So what's DHTML all about? Sometimes it's hard to tell, with all the drum beating from software developers and miscues from industry pundits. And that probably has something to do with why you bought this book. In a nutshell, DHTML is the interaction of existing Web technologies—primarily HTML, style sheets, and scripting—to create Web pages that can interact with the reader without depending on the Web server. In essence, DHTML is about creating mini-applications that run on the user's computer instead of a traditional static Web page that depends on a Web server for its updates.

The hard part of DHTML is sorting through all the options currently available to you. We'll sift through the hype in this book to let you know what can and can't be done with DHTML as it is currently implemented in Netscape Communicator and Microsoft Internet Explorer 4, and we'll tell you what's on the horizon from the World Wide Web Consortium (W3C). In short, we'll give you what you need to know to use DHTML now.

As you get started with DHTML, it helps to have a common terminology and frame of reference. That's what this chapter is for. DHTML is a moving target; everybody says DHTML is exciting, but not everyone is talking about the same technologies or capabilities. So take some time here to get a handle on the various terms so that you can get an idea of what you're in for.

This chapter introduces the concepts and possibilities that DHTML brings to the World Wide Web. I've included some examples to illustrate the basics of some important ideas. Don't worry too much about understanding how the examples work; those details are handled in other parts of the book. We're just giving you a "sneak peak" at what a DHTML page looks like.

The Current Approach to Dynamic Web Pages

Before the new developments with HTML 4 and the DOM, there were still a lot of ways to add dynamic features to a Web page. Here's an overview of some ways to add dynamic capability to a Web page using other technologies. Although these technologies are still viable solutions, we think you'll want to use DHTML as a quicker and easier way to implement dynamic Web pages.

CGI Scripts

Common gateway interface (CGI) scripts are still a favorite method for many Web developers, because this type of server-side script offers a lot of power and flexibility. After all, CGI is the standard that describes how Web servers connect to external programs, which in turn generate new Web pages. To change a page using CGI scripts, the user clicks a hyperlink or submits a form to connect the browser with the server, which contains a script that evaluates what happened and generates a new page in response. The new page might be a revised version of the current one or a completely new creation.

You can do a lot of interesting things with a CGI script, such as interact with databases or create Web pages with user-specific content. Other possibilities include creating sites that depend on various forms of information management, such as order processing or access to archives.

Although CGI scripts are powerful tools, they're still slow. In addition to the client/server transactions required for the original page, the script requires an additional interchange for the subsequent page, plus the additional processing time required to run the script. This probably is the biggest drawback to CGI scripts. The browser must send the input for the script—which is received by the Web server, evaluated, and processed—and then a new page is sent back to the browser. It's like browsing to a whole new page, except there's some additional processing time thrown in.

If only one user is connected to the server, server processing time probably isn't an issue. However, if the server is dealing with a lot of requests for other pages and script processing, the server's host computer can start to bog down with all the demands. This slows the process even more.

Another problem with CGI scripts is the time it takes to put one together. It involves writing a small program in one of the common scripting languages such as Perl, testing it with a variety of input, and then posting it to the Web site. The development process is long when compared with the time required to put together a Web page.

Java Applets

CGI scripts are neat, but using them requires some knowledge of client/server relations. Therefore, some bright people at Sun Microsystems developed a way to embed Web pages with programs that could run on any computer. This was accomplished with applets written in Java. Java applets have the capability to interact with the user and, in some cases, look at or modify various elements of the Web page.

The beauty of Sun's Java as a programming language is its "write once, run anywhere" capability. The same piece of Java code can run on any computer equipped with the Java Virtual Machine. Using Java, developers can write applets—applications such as spreadsheets or data processing that need a host program (like a browser) to run. For example, the little Microsoft Graph program packaged with Word or Excel works only within those programs. In turn, its output is displayed only within documents created by the parent program.

Applets offer a way to build applications customized to a Web page or site (see Figure 1.1). An applet can also be extended to recognize various elements on the Web page, such as the contents of form elements.

FIGURE 1.1.

*This Java applet from
c\net develops a
shopping list for
building a home
computer network.*

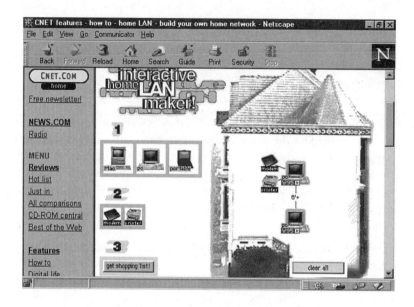

The c\net applet in Figure 1.1 is designed to gather information from the user, which is then passed along to a CGI script that generates the final results. This is typical of some of the more advanced Java applets. At some level, most require another connection with the server to generate a new page with updated information. The shopping list applet shows some of the power of Java to interact with the user and create a custom page in response. After all, Java is a full-featured programming language capable of great things. HotJava, for example, is a fully functional Web browser written entirely in Java.

Because applets behave just like programs, they're capable of a great deal. However, they still have some critical drawbacks. First, you must know how to program in Java. Java isn't the hardest language in the world to learn, but you still need to know about Web-based programming, and that's a level beyond most HTML authors. Then, like a CGI script, Java applets aren't able to update a Web page without reloading the entire page or referring back to a CGI script on the server.

Although designing the applet itself to interact with the user is a fairly simple and straightforward task, actually doing anything with the Web page in which the applet is located is more complicated. You can use scripting languages to help control the applet's behavior, and Netscape has provided an additional set of tools to help the applet look at the Web page. If the applet is going to start working with the contents of a form or other page elements, it is typically written for that specific page. You can probably start to see rather quickly the implications of customizing a program to fit every page where you want interaction with the Web page.

One other drawback to applets is the same as for other external content to a Web page: The download time for the page is increased because one more element on the page has to be loaded, initialized, and started. By the same token, the applet chews up some additional resources when you leave the host page. While you're waiting for a page to load, the Java Virtual Machine in the browser stops the applet's execution and releases all the resources it sucked up.

If the applet uses any images or other support files, the download times are extended that much more. Although Java transports well across computer platforms, it still has the big drawback of requiring additional bandwidth to copy a Java-powered page.

Plug-ins and ActiveX Controls

There are some very important differences between plug-ins and ActiveX controls, but their purpose on the page is basically the same. Like an applet, they add features and functionality to a Web page without directly affecting the host page. And, again like applets, creating interaction between the user and the plug-in is easier.

Plug-ins were initially developed by Netscape, and ActiveX controls are a Microsoft invention. The basic principle of both is that the controlling software is loaded onto the user's computer, and then the Web page contains another file that has the specific instructions or content. This type of interactive software can do all sorts of things, such as provide an interface to look at different types of graphic files (including movies and animations), listen to special sound files, view and edit spreadsheet and word processing files, or even play games.

However, like the applets, plug-ins and ActiveX controls also add to the download burden of a page. In addition to the time it takes to download and install the actual plug-in or control, there's the extra time to download the content files. Some ActiveX controls are used to provide features such as tool tips or pop-up menus, but, like plug-ins, these items are operated directly by the control, and their reach doesn't extend beyond the features.

Client-pull

Client-pull is how the vast majority of users get their content on the Web. They type a URL or click a hyperlink, which sends a request (the pull) for a page. There are other methods to implement this as dynamic behavior. One is to use a special tag called <META> in the header. Used with the HTTP-EQUIV=REFRESH attribute, the <META> tag causes the browser to reload the page from the server after a predetermined number of seconds, specified with CONTENT=*seconds*. If you wanted the browser to reload the current page in four seconds, you would add this tag to your HTML page:

```
<META HTTP-EQUIV="Refresh" CONTENT=4>
```

This starts the *client-pull* process, the mechanism for pages to automatically reload after a certain amount of time has passed or for a series of pages to automatically load themselves with a pause between them.

If the value of CONTENT is 0, the page is refreshed as fast as the browser can retrieve it, which can be rather slow if the user has a slow or poor-quality connection. It's definitely not fast enough for any sort of high-quality animation. When you add the REFRESH attribute to a page, the browser will reload it ad infinitum. To stop the process, you must provide a hyperlink to another page without a client-pull tag.

To be a dynamic process, client-pull needs something to change the page on the server between downloads. There are special programs designed to do this, usually from a database that is updated. This type of strategy is used by sites providing "live" updates of sports scores, stock quotes, and other information that changes on a steady basis.

However, client-pull is also used to load a different page. Continuing the process of loading a new page enables you to automatically lead a user through a series of slides or instructions, similar to a PowerPoint presentation. Modify the CONTENT attribute to provide this capability, like this:

```
<META HTTP-EQUIV="Refresh"
CONTENT="8;URL=http://www.mrfd.com/safety/tip2.html">
```

Inside another <META> tag on the target page, you can include a pointer to the next page, and so on. This technique allows any number of pages to load in sequence.

Server-push

The *server-push* technology, as you might have guessed from the name, is the opposite of client-pull. With push technology, the server doesn't wait for the request. When the content is ready, the server shoves it down the line to the user's browser so he or she can read it at his or her leisure.

The most common analogy of server-push is television. Broadcasters send out their signals to the viewers, who turn on their television sets to receive the signals. The television set doesn't request a program from the broadcaster; it only receives what's already out there.

Actually, push technology bears a closer resemblance to customized cable channels. The users are allowed to select the channels or specific programs that really interest them instead of surfing through the entire gamut of information. The other part of the analogy is the storage aspect. Your television can't store the broadcast signal as it passes through the air—that's the job of a VCR.

With server-push technology, you and your computer become the center of the process. You decide which portions of which channels you want to subscribe to, and the computer stands ready to receive the content and store it for future viewing when the material is broadcast.

Implementing Dynamic HTML with HTML 4

Dynamic HTML is a term that encompasses a lot of ground or very little, depending on whom you're talking to. *Dynamic* as it's used in *Dynamic HTML* doesn't follow the traditional dictionary definition of the word. In the real world, *dynamic* means "continual change." In the context of HTML, it means "subject to change at any time."

> **NOTE**
>
> Dynamic HTML isn't an official term on the Web—at least it hasn't yet been blessed by the World Wide Web Consortium (referred to as W3C—see Chapter 2, "Choosing a Standard," for more information about its work). However, the term is in common use by some vendors to describe the combination of HTML, style sheets, and scripts that let documents grow beyond their traditional lifeless behavior and appearance.

Traditional HTML is static. After it's loaded on a browser, it just sits there like a good dog. You can look at it all you want, but it's not going to change. You can click a hyperlink and then return to the starting page, but the page isn't going to change. You can stand on your head in a corner while moving the computer mouse, but the page still isn't going to change. You can pick up your monitor and shake it until the diodes fall out, and the page still isn't going to change.

Here's why. The HTML tags in a Web page are interpreted by the browser as the page loads. The tags tell the browser what kind of headings to use, where to place new paragraphs, which addresses to associate with hyperlinks, where to put images, and so on. When the browser is finished, the page is displayed and all processing stops until the browser sends a new request to the Web server. The only action allowed the user is to click a hyperlink, which tells the browser to load a new Web page, interpret it, and display it. This static behavior isn't much different from turning pages in book.

There have been advancements to the capabilities of HTML since its early days. One of the latest and most useful developments is the *style sheet*, an extension of HTML that allows greater control over how the browser interprets elements, resulting in more control over the appearance and placement of text and other objects on a Web page. However, even style sheets are static. After the style rules are defined and interpreted, the browser displays the page and there it sits, just like a good dog.

To be fair, there have been some advancements in trying to make HTML more interactive. Scripting languages, applets, plug-ins, and objects have all served a purpose in making HTML pages more dynamic for the user. The one thing these other technologies haven't been able to do is to change the page itself.

HTML has done everything expected of it. That's all well and good, but a discerning public demands more from their good dogs and from the pages on the World Wide Web. After all, they've paid a lot of money to buy a computer and hook up to the Internet, and they expect to see a little more than an electronic rendition of a book page. This type of demand leads us to DHTML—a page that can change after the server is finished delivering the page to the browser.

This is the concept we're tackling in this book. DHTML lets a Web page react to the user without relying on the server or depending on an embedded program. This is very important: *DHTML can change itself.* This is a big leap for the static Web page I mention at the beginning of this section.

Does this mean radically changing the old HTML we all know and love—the <H1>, the <STRONG>, and the <A HREF>? No, it means adding a way to control whether an element is displayed. This also includes how and where the element is displayed. To accomplish these tasks requires a few things: a way to get a handle on any element on the page and a way to control those elements with scripts.

The Document Object Model

First, DHTML needs a way to look at the document. When you work with static HTML, the browser looks at the entire document, interprets it, displays it, and is finished with it. It begins and ends life as a text file filled with display instructions. With DHTML, the document takes on a structure of its own, which is called the DOM.

The DOM works something like this: Although the page still exists as a text file, the browser now handles it differently. As the browser encounters each element on the page, it notes what the element is and where it is and places it in a stack with similar elements. In this way, it can keep track of everything on the page, from the smallest <H6> heading and <HR> horizontal rule to all the elements on a form. In essence, the browser creates a database each time a page is loaded, and each tag becomes a record in the database.

It's kind of like looking at a chessboard. Think of the board as the page and each of the pieces as elements on the page. There is a variety of pieces, and some duplication among all of them. However, each is handled and moved individually.

Controlling the Document with Scripts

Next, DHTML needs a way to control how the different elements of the document are controlled. This is accomplished through scripting languages, such as JavaScript or Visual Basic Scripting Edition (VBScript).

Scripting languages are specialized programming languages that are inserted on a Web page to control different elements of the page, including elements, frames, and the browser interface. They have fairly limited power because they can run only within a Web page on a browser compatible with a scripting language, such as Internet Explorer or Navigator.

In short, DHTML is not about server-side scripts, Java applets, or animated GIF images. All of these can accomplish nifty things on their own—except for changing the content of the Web page without a return trip to the server.

DHTML is about getting a handle on any element within the page at any time after the page has downloaded and changing its appearance, content, or location on the page. This includes a lot of neat things, such as dragging images from one place to another or expanding and collapsing documents that provide instant results to a user.

Although DHTML is just one more step in the natural evolution of the World Wide Web, it's an important one. It enables Web pages to act much more like computer programs and interactive CDs than the static book pages they've been limited to for so long.

Some Features of DHTML

The W3C has received several submissions from member companies on the ways in which an HTML document can attain dynamic behavior. The submissions to the W3C include offerings from both Netscape and Microsoft, which increases the importance and difficulty of the role of W3C as arbiter to make sure interoperable and scripting language–neutral solutions are the best for everyone, and not just one of the software developers' products.

With all of that preamble out of the way, it's time to take a closer look at some of the basic features of DHTML that have been identified by one or more of the players developing the standards.

Changing Tags and Content

This is the bit I was harping on just a few minutes ago. The capability to change tags and their content involves the DOM, which uncovers everything for change, including all tags and style sheet attributes. Figure 1.2 is a shot from Microsoft's overview of its version of DHTML. Note that it's just a bunch of headings.

FIGURE 1.2.

A Dynamic HTML Web page by Microsoft initially displays as a set of headings without much text.

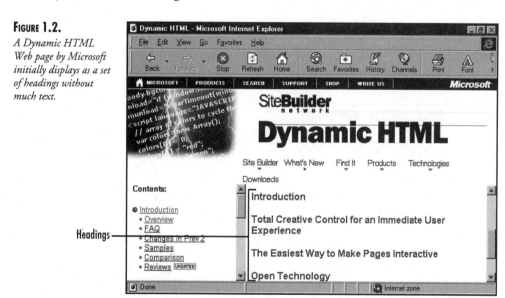

Each of the headings in Figure 1.2 is a special hyperlink that launches a script instead of loading another page. When you click a heading, the page changes. Figure 1.3 shows the same page, which now displays a paragraph of text under the heading. This is all accomplished with a little bit of JavaScript and an extra style tag or two.

Figure 1.3.

Clicking a heading reveals the text hidden underneath without any additional server interaction.

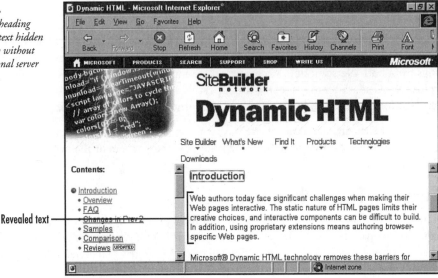

Revealed text

The headings are hyperlinks with the names of JavaScript functions as their URLs. The paragraph under each heading is marked with an inline style indicating that its contents should not be displayed. When the user clicks the heading, the JavaScript routine changes the no-show to show, and the browser updates the page to reflect the new status. It's that simple.

Live Positioning of Elements

Live element positioning can turn Web pages into an interactive playground. The term *interactive* once meant that the user was interacting with some embedded program or plug-in or he or she was filling out a form and clicking a submit button.

Both Microsoft and Netscape include this capability with their implementations of DHTML, although they accomplish it in different ways. Microsoft uses the style sheet <DIV> tag, whereas Netscape can use <DIV> or its own <LAYER> invention (layers are covered in Chapter 22, "Using Layers").

Between the two companies, there are several ways to move things around on the page after the page is loaded into the browser. First, the movement can happen automatically. Examples of this are illustrated with Netscape's layers, which make it possible to incorporate slides, fades, and other animated effects (see Figures 1.4 and 1.5). This is accomplished by hiding or moving each layer independently of the others to any position on the screen. They can overlap, let other layers show through, or hide everything underneath.

The process of layering, also referred to as z-ordering, makes it possible to download an entire site or section of a site at one time. The term *z-ordering* comes from the old x and y coordinate system you learned in high school geometry. Where x and y describe two dimensions (height and width), the *z* element describes the third dimension (depth). Each layer represents one page, and because all the layers are loaded into the user's browser to begin with, no additional requests to the server are needed. As the user requests additional pages, the browser simply passes the requested pages to the top of the stack for viewing. It's a lot like dealing from the bottom of the deck, except the recipient is on the winning side instead of the losing side.

FIGURE 1.4.

The main content of this page (below the selection box) is actually a layer.

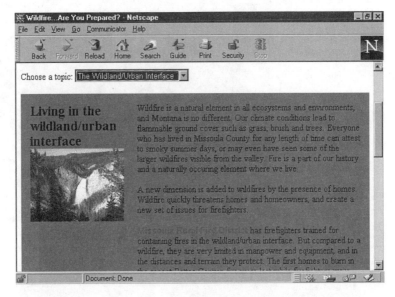

FIGURE 1.5.

Using the form element and a script, the first layer is hidden and a new layer is displayed without Web server processing.

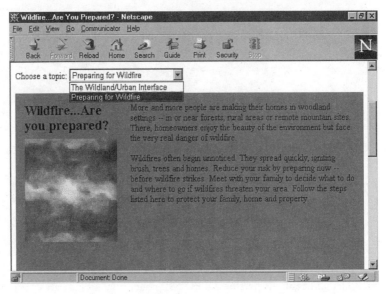

The Microsoft approach is capable of the same types of effects, plus the movement of specific elements on the screen. Instead of moving a section of the Web page, the user can click a single element, such as a graphic or plug-in, and drag it to a new location on the page (see Figures 1.6 and 1.7).

FIGURE 1.6.

Watch what happens to the position of the HTML text selected with the mouse pointer.

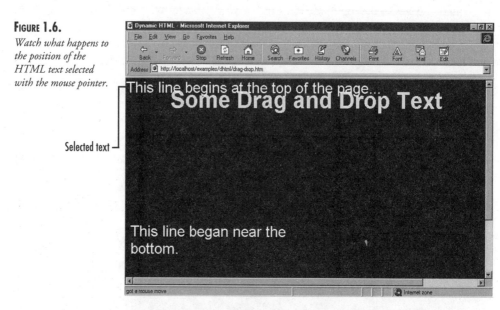

Selected text —

FIGURE 1.7.

The text is now relocated to the bottom of the screen after it was moved manually by the user.

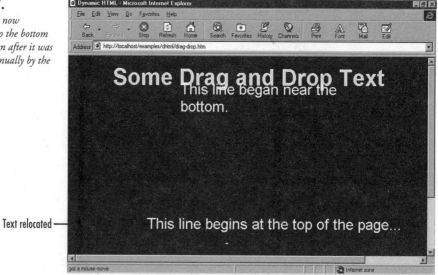

Text relocated —

Each element remains part of the HTML page; they aren't part of a plug-in or applet. The animation and movement are provided within the Web page itself and without additional communication with the server.

Dynamic Fonts

Netscape developed the idea of dynamic fonts, and it is hoped that it will catch on with other browsers. If you've worked with style sheets or the <FONT> command, you've probably become aware of a severe limitation: Just because you specify a font doesn't mean that the user has it on his or her machine. The end result is that the page developer just doesn't know how the page is going to appear.

You can try to work around the problem with style sheets or the <FONT> tag by providing a list of fonts in order of preference, followed by a general type such as sans serif. This works, but not very elegantly. Netscape's way around this uses TrueDoc technology from BitStream. The result is font information in a highly compressed format that is downloaded with the page. The details of the font are stored in vector format, which is assembled on-the-fly using common information from a library on the user's machine. This means the developer doesn't have to know what fonts are on the user's machine, and doesn't even have to guess. By using dynamic fonts, the necessary information is passed to the browser when the page is loaded, and all the user does is sit back and watch.

A vector format describes a picture—which includes individual letters—as a series of shapes. This comprises all the curves, lines, and other attributes of the shape, which is stored in a much smaller space than a similar image in a bitmapped format.

Data Binding

Data binding is one of the features Microsoft has worked hard to develop. Data binding enables page elements such as table cells to "attach" themselves to database records. This feature holds a great deal of promise for page authors and developers.

> **TIP**
>
> Currently, data binding is an exclusive Microsoft Internet Explorer 4 capability that relies on an ActiveX control for its functionality. If the data-binding attributes become a part of the W3C standard, you can expect Netscape Navigator to follow suit with direct database support.

Displaying database records currently requires advanced programming in a language such as C++ or Perl to access the database across a network connection and retrieve the desired information, which is virtually identical to using a CGI script for dynamic content. Other programs, such as Macromedia Backstage, have made this connection easier to create and manipulate. However, even using special authoring software requires the use of a special server and complicated instructions embedded on the page. In short, you can't just slap a database connection on a page and expect it to work.

With direct data binding, you can pass over this middle ground of database processing. Changes to a record are updated onscreen, while user modification of information is passed back to the database for updating. This is accomplished with a new attribute for the <TABLE> tag, which names the database to use for the contents of the table. By using the functions supported by Microsoft, authors now can connect to virtually any database, including comma-delimited, SQL, ODBC, and JDBC.

> **NOTE**
>
> *Comma-delimited, SQL, ODBC,* and *JDBC* represent types of databases. A comma-delimited database usually is represented by a text file, in which each field is separated by a comma and each record is separated by a carriage return. SQL stands for Structured Query Language and is the favorite choice of network programmers. It defines a common set of commands used for a variety of databases. ODBC and JDBC stand for open database connectivity and Java database connectivity, respectively. These two standards are similar to SQL in that they define common ground for a program to access a database without resorting to a bunch of commands that are specific to one database.

By allowing users to channel input directly back and forth between the browser and a database, the amount of time it takes to complete the interaction is shortened dramatically, because only the data or its display is changing, not the entire page.

Moving from Static to Dynamic HTML

The changeover from static HTML to DHTML will probably create more headaches than it should for many developers. This will be due in great part to the one overriding rule of the DOM: It must have correct HTML to work with from the beginning.

If you're creating a new site from scratch, you're more likely to work harder at creating technically accurate Web pages according to the HTML 4 Document Type Definition. With clean and solid HTML behind your page, the DHTML features will be a natural and easy extension.

> **NOTE**
>
> The Document Type Definition (DTD) is a set of rules written in Standard Generalized Markup Language (SGML) that outlines the syntax and structure of HTML documents. It is used by browsers and editors to determine how to interpret HTML documents. For more information about the HTML 4 DTD, take a look at the W3C site at www.w3.org.

Why is good HTML so important? There are a few good reasons. At the lowest level, there's the user. If your pages follow all the rules in the DTD, the browser never has to guess what you intended, and all users have a predictable experience with your pages. If you include inconsistent HTML, different browsers may try to interpret it in different ways so they can still present the page to the user.

Second, the DOM is not going to cut you any slack. One of the big points of discussion is how the DOM should handle incorrect or sloppy HTML, such as the following:

```
<DIV>Hello there <I>Bob</DIV>, how are you?</I>
```

When you attempt to use the DOM to access either element in this code, confusion reigns. Is the `<I>` tag a child of the `<DIV>` tag or not? When dynamically changing the content of either tag, which element should get priority over the overlapping material? The overriding opinion among the W3C DOM committee members is that the bad HTML will do one of two things, depending on the whims of the browser:

1. Disable the DOM for the affected elements, resulting in portions of the Web page that don't behave as expected.

2. Generate an error message for the user, letting him or her know the page contains invalid HTML and can't be displayed.

> **NOTE**
>
> The general trend with Web editors and browsers is to be less forgiving with invalid HTML. As HTML and its companion technologies evolve and become more powerful and flexible, it becomes increasingly harder for developers to write programs that allow for inconsistencies in the Web page. Let's face it, Internet Explorer and Navigator are already big enough downloads; if the software developers were to start writing exceptions to the established rules of HTML, the size and complexity of the applications would increase that much more.

If you're working with older pages, the chances for invalid HTML increase. After all, most of us weren't real purists when we started building Web pages. This is especially true of many of the more creative designers who exploited quirks in the way browsers interpreted some of the invalid HTML to achieve new design effects. Any Web page that is going to be converted to a DHTML page should at least be passed through an HTML 4 validator to ensure compliance.

As far as browsers go, the main two options for Dynamic HTML are Internet Explorer 4 and Navigator 4.02. As you read earlier in this chapter and will read about more in the next chapter, their approaches to DHTML are not all that compatible. You might want to pick one of the browsers to design for and leave the other one alone for a while, or you can work toward effects that are functional on both. Either way, you'll need to test your pages on both the Microsoft and Netscape products, in addition to a non-DHTML browser such as Mosaic, to make sure the page is still functional on a plain-HTML basis and doesn't exclude other readers.

This might sound like a bit more work than you had planned, but as a wise man once said, it's a lot easier to do a job right the first time.

Summary

Dynamic HTML is a new way of accomplishing an old task: making a Web page more interactive for the user. DHTML enables Web pages to change in reaction to user events without the need for additional support from the Web server, plug-ins, applets, or other programs and helpers embedded within the page.

The features enabled by DHTML include the capability to change the content and appearance of any item on the Web page, plus a mechanism for adding live data content directly to the page without using CGI scripts.

Rather than a new set of tags or a new programming language, DHTML is a new way of combining existing technologies—HTML and scripting languages—with a new way of looking at Web pages—the DOM. Using this set of features, Web authors and developers can extend their pages to look and act more like miniature computer programs than static book pages. It's an exciting new way to build Web pages and sites that promise to expand the way people use the World Wide Web.

Choosing a Standard

by Rick Darnell

IN THIS CHAPTER

Now that you're committed to learning about Dynamic HTML (DHTML) and how to use it, I must share a bit of bad news: The standards have not yet evolved to a mature level at which all the players can agree. This means you'll need to make some choices as to how you implement DHTML for your pages.

The problem is that Microsoft and Netscape both have their ideas about what DHTML should look like, even beginning with the name. Microsoft calls its implementation Dynamic HTML (with a capital "D"), and Netscape refers to its implementation as dynamic HTML (lowercase "d"). And it just gets worse from there.

Both Microsoft and Netscape are using a lot of the same terminology and are referring to the same set of published or proposed standards in their work toward interactive and dynamic Web pages. Both companies talk about the capability for pages to change without extra trips to the server and more extensive control of styles. However, the actual implementations aren't very compatible.

Netscape has added a new tag, and Microsoft has added new attributes for existing tags. Netscape added load-on-the-fly typefaces, and Microsoft added ActiveX controls for database access. Between the two, the water continues to get murkier.

Speaking of standards, now is a good time to mention the World Wide Web Consortium (W3C). The W3C is developing its own recommendation for DHTML. However, true to the spirit of working by committee, the W3C standard currently exists only as a list of capabilities that a DHTML document should have. The actual appearance and prescribed behavior are still under discussion.

NOTE

The World Wide Web Consortium, known as the W3C, is the recognized organization that is responsible for developing common standards for the World Wide Web. This includes updating HTML and HTTP standards and related issues, including new markup languages, accessibility, and recommended browser implementations. It also provides a repository of information about the Web for developers, users, and anyone else interested in long specification documents. The W3C is located at www.w3.org.

How does the W3C do its work? The first step is identifying an issue or technology that affects the World Wide Web. The W3C governing body, called the Advisory Committee, appoints a working group. This group of people consists of experts gathered to work together toward resolving a particular well-defined technical issue, such as HTML standards.

The working group develops a series of *working drafts* until they've reached a stable consensus and agreement. Then, if the W3C director approves, the draft is promoted to a *Proposed Recommendation*, also called a *Draft Recommendation*, which is sent to all W3C members for comment. Depending on the number and nature of the comments, the W3C director can issue the result as a *Recommendation* as is or with minor changes, return it to the working group, or scrap it altogether.

So, between W3C, Microsoft, and Netscape, where do you stand? In the same place you've probably been in before: trying to develop pages that are accessible to as many people as possible while working with implementations that, while not mutually exclusive, tend to be incompatible at the most inopportune times.

To help you understand where this whole technology is headed and how we got here in the first place, here's a description of the players and the rules we'll look at in this chapter:

- W3C has developed a wish list of some capabilities for DHTML, which they refer to as the *Document Object Model* (DOM). The DOM is a way for the browser to identify every markup tag and page element and make it accessible for inspection or change.

- Netscape created its own document object model a few years ago with Navigator 2.0. More recently, Netscape has tried other methods of creating dynamic behavior, primarily through the use of a nonstandard <LAYER> tag. In all fairness, Netscape is playing down the new tag and is working toward an implementation that expands on its original DOM. This approach brings Netscape closer in this aspect of DHTML with W3C and Microsoft.

- As part of the Internet Explorer 4.0 release, Microsoft has released its version of what its developers think the W3C DOM will look like. Microsoft's version appears to follow the wish list provided by W3C, but it's still only their best guess, because a standard doesn't exist yet.

NOTE

The process the two major browser companies are following is typical as they attempt to anticipate how the standards will develop. For instance, both Microsoft and Netscape released their respective version 3 browsers in 1996, which implemented an HTML standard that wasn't formally accepted until 1997.

In a word, there is no DHTML standard. But it appears that the W3C is leaning toward a DOM specification in which all elements on an HTML page would be accessible to the page developer through the scripting language of his or her choice. However, before we start getting into the nuts and bolts of DHTML in Chapter 3, "Dynamic HTML Fundamentals," we'll take some time in this chapter to explore the different visions of DHTML as it moves toward its first official standard.

World Wide Web Consortium

Even though it's not in anything resembling a final or usable form, the final word on the functionality of DHTML rests with the W3C and its DOM Working Group. There is a bit of irony in this situation because one of the first acts of the group's chair was to issue a statement that labeled the term *Dynamic HTML* as "just marketing."

NOTE

W3C doesn't work independent of the industry it affects. The W3C is hosted by the Massachusetts Institute of Technology, but the members of its various committees are representative of World Wide Web companies such as Microsoft, Netscape, Sun Microsystems, IBM, and others. It costs a significant sum of money for a company to join W3C, and once a member, no single organization or company has more influence in the W3C's final recommendation than any other.

The DOM Working Group issued a statement of purpose saying that its goal is not to extend HTML or develop a standard specific to any scripting language. The group is working on a "platform- and language-neutral interface which allows programs and scripts to dynamically access and update the content, structure and style of documents," according to a statement posted on its Web site.

HTML 4.0 AND DYNAMIC HTML

W3C is including several recommendations for more dynamic activity in its HTML 4.0 recommendation. This includes the DOM and scripting, mentioned at the beginning of this chapter.

Scripting bears further inspection. It has been a part of Navigator since version 2 and Microsoft since version 3 of their respective browsers. However, scripting still is not an accepted element with HTML standards. HTML 4.0 should change this.

The W3C proposal basically reflects the current practice on the Web for including scripts and doesn't make any suggestions as to how the scripting language is interpreted or how the script interacts with the document. Scripts can be embedded directly in the document or linked from a separate file.

W3C also takes no stance on which language should be used as a default, although it provides for a new META value to set the default for a specific page. For example, the following snippet sets the default for a Web page to JavaScript:

```
<META HTTP-EQUIV="Content-Script-Type" CONTENT="text/javascript">
```

If the META element is not included, the browser has the option of determining the default language. As a generally accepted implementation, script-compatible browsers use JavaScript as the default scripting language.

HTML 4.0 also includes several other items that, while not directly part of the DHTML discussed in this book, will help the page developer create less static documents.

First on the list are two new attributes: TITLE and TABINDEX. TITLE is added to existing elements and tags as a method for the user to request extra information or help. It includes a string of text that provides a note such as "Submit form to server." How the string is displayed is up to the browser, but on Windows you can expect an implementation using tool tips, and Macintosh versions will probably use help balloons. Another option for other platforms is the status bar. Implementing the title attribute would be similar to the following:

```
<A href="http://www.w3.org/" title="World Wide Web Consortium Home Page">
```

The TABINDEX attribute sets a specific tabbing order for traversing among interactive elements (hyperlinks, form fields, and so on) on the Web page using the Tab key. This is a way of explicitly deciding which element receives the next input from the keyboard. In the past, this was accomplished by giving focus to an element with the mouse or other pointing device and then clicking the object. The following example sets the second hyperlink to receive focus before the first by setting the second to 1 and the first to 2.

```
<a href="http://www.w3.org/" tabindex=2>
<a href="http://www.yahoo.com/" tabindex=1>
```

W3C has received several submissions from member companies, primarily Microsoft and Netscape, on how the various elements of HTML documents should be exposed to scripts. As mentioned at the beginning of this chapter, the W3C standard revolves around the DOM, which is discussed in greater detail in Part IV, "The Document Object Model." In a nutshell, the W3C model has two basic requirements:

- The document model can be used to take apart and build the document, even after it's loaded by the browser. Individual elements and their attributes can be added, removed, or changed within the document. This also includes a way to determine and change the content of a page, whether it's text, images, applets, or plug-ins. This is the dynamic part everyone is talking about.

- The DOM won't require a graphical user interface for implementation. This is part of the W3C's goal of establishing standards that provide access to Web content for all types of browsers, including those based on Braille and audio technologies. Remember, DOM is a way of opening the structure and contents of a Web page to the page developer so the page can interact with the user; it is not a standard for graphics or animation, although it can be utilized that way.

NOTE

The W3C is working very hard to develop standards that don't exclude any platform or browser. This is part of an ongoing goal to provide World Wide Web standards that support specialized browsers for disabled persons, such as the blind and deaf. For this reason, each new tag or way to manipulate a tag is being developed with an eye toward providing a textual substitute that can be interpreted by browsers for special needs.

To support this effort, W3C launched the Web Accessibility Initiative to promote and achieve Web functionality for people with disabilities. The initiative involves the establishment

continues

continued

of an International Program Office (IPO), which, according to a W3C press release, is responsible for "developing software protocols and technologies, creating guidelines for the use of technologies, educating the industry, and conducting research and development." Because the IPO office is contained within W3C, it will also ensure that all new W3C standards and technologies meet or exceed accessibility goals.

All other requirements of DOM follow from these two, including each of the major areas required by the DOM Working Group:

- Structure Navigation—This is the capability to locate elements in a document, such as the parents or children of an object. This is how Netscape started its document model in Navigator 2.0. It begins with `window`, then down to `document`, followed by the various children of `document`, including `form`, `link`, `applet`, and other page elements. Using the DOM model, all tags are exposed for the browser, including unknown tags and elements.

- Document Manipulation—The standard will provide a way to add, remove, or change elements and tags within the document. This also includes attributes of tags.

- Content Manipulation—This is the capability to add, change, or delete the content within a document or an individual tag. It also includes a requirement for determining which tag affects text from any part of the document.

- Event Model—The event model is comprehensive enough to generate completely interactive documents. It includes the capability to respond to any user action within the document, including moving in and out of form fields, detecting mouse movements and clicks, and determining individual keystrokes. Although W3C is committed to accessibility for disabled persons, some of the events will apply only to a graphical interface (such as Windows), which is designed for the average user.

- Style Sheet Object Model—This is similar to Document Manipulation, mentioned previously. Under DOM, cascading style sheet attributes are also exposed for modification. With an eye toward the future, W3C includes a provision to extend the style sheet model to other formats. This might be the loophole Netscape needs to include JavaScript Assisted Style Sheets while maintaining compliance with W3C standards.

- General Document and Browser Information—The W3C has left no stone unturned. Part of the DOM includes the capability to examine embedded objects such as cookies and the date a document was created. Other information available includes the user agent (browser) brand and version and the MIME types it supports.

The complete set of requirements for DOM runs about three pages and includes all the preceding items, plus document type definitions and error reporting. Essentially, all the requirements boil down to this: *Everything* within a document should be accessible for manipulation.

The first step toward creating the standard was determining the current object model utilizing the models implemented by Internet Explorer 3.0 and Navigator 3.0. This process resulted in the Level 0 standard. Then, the working group started toward its long-term goal of building a consensus of what should and shouldn't be part of the DOM standard, which will become version 1.0. Working Group Chair, Lauren Wood, says that a final version of DOM 1.0 could be released by early 1998.

Level 1 will cover the basics of the DOM, including document and content navigation and manipulation. Additional items, such as the event model and style sheet object model, will be the topic of the Level 2 implementation.

This leads us back to the original question: What's a developer to do? Our advice is to keep an eye on Microsoft and Netscape, as the developments within their browser products will be a pretty good indication of what's coming down the pike from W3C. Then, write your DHTML pages to the lowest common denominator of compatibility until the consensus begins to form. This is hard for developers to swallow, especially when they want to write with the "latest and greatest" tools on the Web.

If you're writing to a general audience, be wary of anything proprietary. This includes tags or attributes that are the sole domain of one browser or another. What you should probably start with is some combination of style sheets and JavaScript. To make sure your implementation is solid, test it with a wide variety of browsers—new and old versions of Navigator and Internet Explorer, no-frills versions such as Mosaic, and text-only applications such as Lynx. This is a reasonable precaution to take to ensure that your dynamic pages won't crater someone else's non-dynamic browser.

If you want to write to the evolving standard using the most advanced tools available, put it someplace separate on your Web site and mark it as "for demonstration only," along with a notation of which browser it was written for.

In short, it's still a long road to an implementation that is going to work well across all browsers, especially the major offerings from Netscape and Microsoft. If you write to the capabilities of a majority of your users and include safety nets for the rest, you won't go wrong.

Netscape

Netscape got the whole DHTML DOM rolling about 16 Internet years ago (that's 2 years on the Gregorian calendar) with its Navigator 2.0 release, which included a feature called JavaScript. JavaScript included a basic DOM that included access to elements such as forms, hyperlinks, colors, and various browser attributes.

That first object model was created with an instance hierarchy, which reflected the construction of the HTML page. At the top of the hierarchy was window—the parent of all other objects.

The window object included four children: location, history, frames, and document.

The document object included children representing selected information about the document: alinkColor, bgColor, fgColor, linkColor, vlinkColor, cookie, lastModified, location, anchors, referrer, forms, links, and title.

An *instance hierarchy* is built from actual instances of objects rather than general classes of objects. For example, suppose the only elements allowed on a page were headings, and a particular page included three H1s and an H4. A class hierarchy would include an object for each possible header—H1 through H6, including the unused H2, H3, H5, and H6. In an instance hierarchy, the same page would only include objects for the headings that actually appeared on the document—H1 and H4.

The first JavaScript DOM included a mishmash of page attributes (color settings), META information (last modified date and referring page), and physical elements on the page (anchors, forms, and links). In the next version of Navigator (3.0), the object model was extended to include applets and other embedded objects.

Netscape had the right idea, but it was still pretty limited in scope and usage. Only a few of the items, such as form elements and some of the colors, could be changed without reloading the document. It was also possible to modify the rest of a page's contents, but only by reloading it using the javascript protocol.

> **NOTE**
>
> The javascript protocol is used in the same way as other Internet protocols such as http or ftp. It enables the browser to reload a page by invoking a JavaScript method, which results in redefining the page's contents. The user still sees the page go blank and then reload. However, it's much faster than retrieving a new version from the server because the page is created by a process within the browser.

Of course, in addition to the DOM that JavaScript enabled, there is also the JavaScript language. JavaScript enables developers to write small applications that run on the user's browser, instead of processing through the server. The syntax was related to Java, and with Netscape 3.0, the two languages could talk back and forth across the Web page. This was also a big breakthrough, because it gave Java direct access to data on a Web page and provided a way to control Java from outside an applet.

In the early days of JavaScript, developers primarily used it and the Netscape DOM to verify form contents or make fun little 1040EZ calculators. A few hardy folks used it to create some neat effects, such as expanding and contracting outlines and Web sites with custom controls, but most of the uses were limited in scope and utility.

Netscape's Communicator release doesn't extend the DOM in any new and dramatic directions like its ancestors, but that doesn't mean Netscape doesn't have its eye on the DHTML bandwagon. Here are the three components of Netscape's vision of DHTML:

■ The use of layers to move, hide, and show blocks of HTML on the Web page—A Netscape layer is a set of HTML that is displayed, hidden, moved, and altered in various ways. Essentially, it converts your HTML document into a set of slides that you can shuffle and display in any order, singly or in combination. The layers can be manipulated in reaction to user events, making it the only portion of Netscape's solution that meets the definition of *dynamic* explained in Chapter 1, "Introducing Dynamic HTML."

■ Precise control over formatting, fonts, layout, and other aspects of page behavior through style sheets—Netscape includes support for the W3C CSS1 specification, which Microsoft uses, and JavaScript Style Sheets (JSSS). JSSS doesn't allow changes to the document after it's loaded, but it does allow the style sheet to ask the browser about its environment. The style sheet can then make changes to its implementation to match its specific situation.

NOTE

A JSSS working draft was posted at the W3C site by JavaScript developer Brendan Eich, although it appears to be languishing in obscurity while other technologies and issues are pursued.

Although JSSS isn't explicitly supported by W3C, part of W3C's position on the DOM is to extend the CSS1 style sheet model to other style sheet formats, of which the JSSS specification could eventually be a part.

■ Dynamic fonts, which are attached to a Web page rather than being dependent on the options available on a user's computer—In the past, developers have had to guess what typefaces are available on a user's machine and then provide a list of the preferred choices for a page in the style sheet font attribute or use the <FONT> tag. Dynamic fonts use a new method to check for the existence of the desired typeface and, if it's not found, download it from the server. This would eliminate some of the problems with font availability that have become more noticeable with style sheets.

A little more must be said about layers. With the initial betas of Navigator 4.0, Netscape decided to use a new tag to implement precise positioning of elements: <LAYER>. This caused a bit of a problem, because Microsoft wasn't going to include this tag on its browser, and the W3C decided not to develop the <LAYER> tag to work on other approaches to DHTML. Given a less-than-warm reception, Netscape is including more emphasis on layers implemented through the DOM with the <DIV> tag. Netscape is also downplaying the <LAYER> tag, although it is still part of the Netscape Communicator release.

The ultimate fate of Netscape's <LAYER> tag is unclear at this point. It doesn't appear as though W3C is including any support for it in its HTML 4.0 specification, although the tag seems to fulfill many of the features of the W3C draft on positioning HTML elements by using style sheets (www.w3.org/pub/WWW/TR/WD-positioning), which Netscape helped to develop in conjunction with Microsoft. You'll see a lot of neat examples of dynamic behavior in this book using the <LAYER> tag, so it's also safe to say that the jury has still not reached a final verdict on this one.

In DHTML, Netscape appears to be moving closer to working with the W3C rather than trying to set its own standards and have W3C follow its lead. Netscape Communicator is fully compatible with existing W3C recommendations or standards for HTML 3.2, plus some from HTML 4.0, Cascading Style Sheets 1, and JavaScript. It is also trying to maintain compatibility with working drafts on positioning, object models, and dynamic fonts.

Other than the implementation of the <LAYER> tag and JavaScript Accessible Style Sheets, covered on the Companion Web Site at http://www.mcp.com/info, Netscape seems to be working on a version of DHTML that doesn't depend exclusively on proprietary or platform-specific controls.

Does this mean that a DHTML page that works on Netscape will also work with Microsoft if both browsers are claiming to meet the upcoming standards? Not necessarily. There are several issues at work here. First, W3C is not tying DHTML to any specific scripting language. For example, suppose Microsoft makes VBScript and Netscape makes JavaScript completely compatible with the DHTML standard. If a Netscape browser loads a page made dynamic with VBScript, it's not going to work because Navigator still doesn't support that specific language.

Second, both companies view the standard in different ways and are claiming the exclusive privilege of being the only "real solution." This is why there's an expanded DOM on one side and layers on the other. These solutions are not compatible across the browsers, even if they both meet the letter or intent of the W3C's work. At this point, there is no official standard for the DOM or HTML 4, so claims that either browser is compatible with the W3C Dynamic HTML standard are inherently wrong.

Microsoft

As has become the standard operating practice in the ongoing browser battles, Microsoft is boldly going where no standard has gone before with its definition and implementation of DHTML in Internet Explorer 4.0. You can read all about Microsoft's vision of DHTML at www.microsoft.com/workshop/author/dhtml/.

Internet Explorer 4.0 (IE4) isn't just a collection of support for a few new tags and a new user interface. Microsoft has completely overhauled the HTML parsing engine.

The extended IE4 takes the individual tags and document elements and integrates them with a Scripting Object Model, which is supported by any scripting language available. As a matter of practicality, the two choices are JavaScript and VBScript, which are provided as components of IE4. The examples in this book are implemented in a variety of ways to show the variations that DHTML can support.

Microsoft's vision of DHTML includes four components, which are similar to Netscape's:

■ A DOM that enables any element on a page to be shown, hidden, changed, or rearranged without reloading the page from a server—One of the surprises in Microsoft's implementation of the DOM is that it isn't specific to Windows or ActiveX. The Microsoft model was completely built into the HTML parser as part of the browser. By implementing the DOM with JScript (Microsoft's version of JavaScript) and VBScript, developers can use the scripting languages to control page elements.

NOTE

Microsoft's IE4 component architecture allows for other software developers to add scripting language modules to IE4. This allows new scripting languages, such as Python and TCL, to become an option for controlling DHTML pages.

■ A way to control elements on a page through scripts, including JavaScript and VBScript—The scripting languages include objects that relate to the various elements on the page as defined by the DOM. Using the comparison and assignment features of the language, page developers can examine and change the attribute or content of any element on the page referenced by the DOM, including headings, links, text, and other items. This also includes control and manipulation of embedded Java applets, ActiveX controls, and plug-ins.

■ Multimedia controls for animation and other effects, such as filters and transitions, without relying on downloading large files or pages—These have been implemented through cascading style sheets with the use of filters for fade-in, fade-out, and other types of effects.

■ A way to bind data to an HTML page, including automatic generation of tables, sorting tabular data, and querying local tables—This uses a special set of HTML attributes to display "live" database records in the same way you would display an applet or plug-in. In the old HTML school, displaying database records required working with CGI scripts and advanced Perl, C, or Java programming. Because DHTML supports immediate changes to page content, the database can update automatically in reaction to user typing, or the table can display live updates from third-party changes to the database.

Like Netscape, Microsoft is working with W3C standards and proposals, trying to anticipate the future of DHTML through the work of the Consortium.

The Microsoft DOM is very similar to the Netscape Navigator 2.0 model. It begins with the core objects representing the page and browser (such as window and document) and then branches into more detail (such as form, applet, and link). Microsoft has further expanded the model to include every element on the page. From headings to paragraphs to images to tables to horizontal rules—it's no-holds-barred access to everything on the page.

One of the big strengths touted by Microsoft is compatibility with other browsers that don't support the Internet Explorer 4.0 DHTML implementation. Microsoft calls its compatibility with other browsers "graceful degradation." Developers and authors writing specifically to the Microsoft version of DHTML won't need to produce alternative versions for Netscape or anyone else, according to Microsoft (see the sidebar "The Reality of Graceful Degradation"). The scripting and tags used by Microsoft are accepted technologies in use by other browsers and are blessed by the W3C.

THE REALITY OF GRACEFUL DEGRADATION

Every silver lining has a dark cloud, and the DHTML story is no different. Microsoft DHTML doesn't gracefully degrade when placed on Navigator 4.0, especially when it depends on style sheets. Look at Figures 2.1 through 2.3. In Figure 2.1, you see the DHTML overview from Microsoft's site as viewed on Internet Explorer 4.0. Click a heading, and the contents underneath are displayed.

The first test of graceful degradation is NCSA Mosaic. The same page loaded on it (see Figure 2.2) degrades quite nicely. Mosaic doesn't understand style sheets or scripting, so it just ignores all the extra tags and attachments and displays the page in a clean, straightforward, and predictable manner.

In Figure 2.3, you see the same page on Navigator 4.0 (Preview Release 4). Microsoft uses the display:none attribute to hide the contents until the user clicks the heading, where it depends on a JavaScript method to remove the attribute so the contents can display. Here's the problem: Netscape doesn't support changing CSS1 style sheets with JavaScript, so there's no way to reveal the hidden elements without loading a new page from the server.

Why does the bulleted list display, even though it's associated with the content under the headings? Because Navigator doesn't think it belongs with the rest of the hidden text and assumes that the <UL> display attribute is set for display. The effect is a list without an explanation, which is still not an acceptable interpretation of the page.

FIGURE 2.1.

Click a heading in the Microsoft DHTML page, and the contents below it are displayed.

Previously hidden text —

There is hidden text associated with these — headings

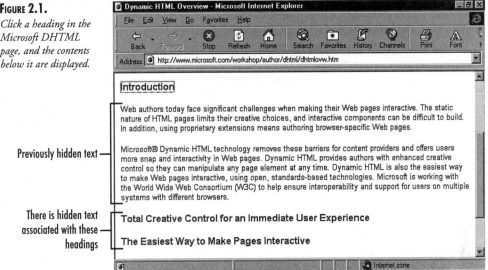

FIGURE 2.2.

Graceful degradation as Microsoft advertises— this non-style sheet browser displays the page according to the tags only.

All hidden text is shown —

FIGURE 2.3.

Because Netscape is compatible with CSS1 but not with JavaScript modification of CSS1, it doesn't degrade gracefully.

Hidden text associated with headings is inaccessible and not shown

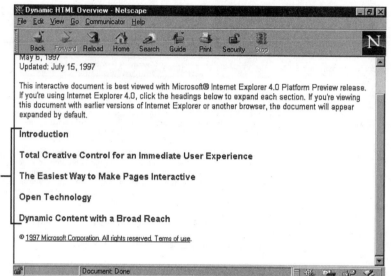

Summary

A DHTML standard implementation looks like it will remain a moving target for at least another year. There are three slightly different schools of thought on what it is, but the three main players—W3C, Netscape, and Microsoft—all seem to agree that an expanded DOM is at the center of the solution. The expanded document model will allow access to every element, its attributes, and content through a scripting language. With unbridled access and control over the contents, HTML pages will bear a closer semblance to Silly Putty than to tablets of stone.

Divergence begins with views about the DOM. W3C doesn't use DHTML as part of its vocabulary at all, except to acknowledge software vendors' use of the term. W3C's work is almost exclusively centered on developing the DOM and its relation to style sheets, scripting languages, and other existing technologies.

Netscape includes JavaScript Assisted Style Sheets and layers in its bundle of DHTML capabilities. Layers are the result of an implementation of the W3C working draft on positioning HTML elements, although the <LAYER> tag is not included as part of the proposed HTML 4.0 specification.

In addition to the DOM, Microsoft is also stressing multimedia effects and data awareness with its vision of DHTML while also relying on the object model and style sheet base similar to Netscape. However, the Microsoft solution also depends on proprietary items such as ActiveX controls to implement access to the DOM.

Unlike a year or two ago, when the two companies sought to build Web standards around their respective visions, both Netscape and Microsoft seem more eager to work with the W3C in the development of standards for their browsers. The days are gone, we hope, when each company created its own tags and technologies in an attempt to force standards to conform to its respective software. Although competition between the two remains fierce, the user is no longer subjected to getting caught between incompatibilities.

For the time being, I'd say W3C's final recommendation will be closer to Microsoft than Netscape, and the common areas between the two won't be completely compatible. At that point, each company will need to make sure its implementation of DHTML is in full compliance with the standard. However, W3C seldom moves quickly in comparison to the rest of the World Wide Web, so subsequent browser releases from Microsoft and Netscape should allow enough time for these companies to adjust to the W3C standard—whatever it looks like.

As you develop your DHTML pages, you'll probably need to write your pages specific to each browser. It's a pain, but remember, the standard is still evolving and is bound to change as the two competitors slug it out. It's still too early in the game to depend on anything that seems to be too proprietary.

2

CHOOSING A STANDARD

Dynamic HTML Fundamentals

by Rick Darnell

IN THIS CHAPTER

CHAPTER 3

In Chapters 1, "Introducing Dynamic HTML," and 2, "Choosing a Standard," you received a glimpse of the DHTML capabilities that are the current excitement on the World Wide Web. According to its promoters and supporters, DHTML will do just about everything except walk your dog and do your laundry. Obviously, something that's this powerful is going to be hard to create, right? Wrong. The fundamentals are really quite basic.

In this chapter, we're going to get a little closer look at how the pieces of DHTML fit together to create a Web page. We'll work through an example in this chapter to see how the components of DHTML fit together. We'll begin by building a page for Microsoft's version of DHTML, and then we'll expand the page to support Netscape's DHTML functionality as well. This should give you some idea of how the two compare.

Creating Dynamic Web Pages

Creating a new Web page with DHTML is a four-step process:

1. Planning your page. This step shouldn't be any different whether you're working with static HTML or dynamic content. If you don't know what you want to say or why you're saying it, you'll end up creating one of those "all-flash-and-no-substance" sites.

2. Creating the base HTML page. In essence, you begin with the lowest common denominator so that your page is accessible to the most browsers possible. Build the page as if the user didn't have DHTML capability. Remember, not everyone uses a Netscape or Microsoft product to browse the Web. There are still a great many people using Mosaic, Lynx, and other "bare-bones" browsers.

TIP

There's another reason to begin with solid and accurate HTML for your Web page: DHTML won't work well (if at all) unless it has solid HTML to work with. This means you must write clean and accurate pages that follow the rules of the HTML 4 Document Type Definition. To take advantage of DHTML features such as the Document Object Model (DOM), browsers such as Internet Explorer must have a technically accurate page to begin with.

If you use a good editor, such as FrontPage, Backstage, HomeSite, or PageMill, you shouldn't have any problems with this. If you still code your pages by hand, a little proofreading time now will save a lot of headaches and frustration later.

---

3. Adding a style sheet. This includes special color and font information, layers and divisions, and any other visual effects you're using to attract and help the reader through your page. If you're using a linked style sheet, most of this step is already completed. However, you might still need to embed styles necessary for the dynamic part of your page, such as attributes for visibility.

4. Making the page dynamic. This is when you add the scripts and attributes to make the content react to the user. Remember that your dynamic elements should have a

purpose in your plan at step 1. Adding a lot of special effects is fun, but if their only purpose is to show off your talent and the user's browser, there's not much point.

Except for all the details covered in the rest of the book, that's about all there is to it. For our first example, we'll begin with a page that uses both cascading style sheets and DHTML to offer an outline of things to remember when you're hiking in the woods.

We're planning this page to be a "quick reference" for hikers, hunters, and other folks who are headed to remote or wilderness areas. It's not a comprehensive course in wilderness survival; rather, it's intended to provide enough hints and clues to at least get people thinking in the right direction before they take the first step onto a trail.

Creating the Base HTML Page

Now that we've planned what we want to say and whom we're saying it to, it's time to put the page together. We could make life a lot easier and use a Web page editor, but that would take all the fun out of it.

Our base page results in a basic outline (see Listing 3.1 and Figure 3.1), which begins with an H1 for the main heading, and then descends into a series of H2 and H3 headings below. It includes paragraphs, block quotes and citations, and links for more information.

Listing 3.1. Our basic page is standard HTML. There's nothing fancy here.

```
<!doctype HTML PUBLIC "-//IETF//DTD HTML 4.0//EN">
<html>

<head>
<title>Traveling in the Backcountry</title>
</head>

<body>

<h1>Traveling in the Backcountry</h1>

<p>Walking in the woods, whether as a hiker, camper, backpacker or hunter,
 provides plenty of opportunities to practice the skills of a backcountry
 traveler. With the proper preparation, you'll have the knowledge and
 confidence to meet the challenges of a variety of outdoor adventures. This
 page is intended to provide you with some hints and tips to help you create
 a successful experience.</p>

<p>Before you read on, we'd like for you to hear a brief message from our
 lawyers....</p>

<blockquote>
 <p><strong>This is in no way intended to be a course in backcountry safety or
 survival. Information provided is from a variety of sources, and is to be
 accepted at the user's risk. The authors of this page assume no
 liability whatsoever as to the suitability of this information to any
 specific situation or person. It's you against the world, and
 we're not taking any responsibility for the outcome.</strong></p>
```

continues

Listing 3.1. continued

```
</blockquote>

<h2>Before you travel</h2>

<h3>How far can you go? </h3>

<p>When choosing a location and route, take into account your physical
   condition, the reason for hiking, and the terrain and weather you could
   possibly encounter. As a general rule, an average hiker can walk about 1 1/2
   to 2 miles an hour on level trails. Steep ascents require considerably
   greater time allowances. One hour for every 1,000 feet of elevation gain
   is a good rule of thumb.</p>

<h3>What should you wear?</h3>

<p>Proper foot gear is one of the most important parts of your journey.
   Sturdy running shoes are good for hiking on relatively smooth surfaces,
   such as maintained trails. You'll want something with a little more tread
   for rugged trails or cross-country travel. A ten mile hike in the woods is
   not the best place to break in new shoes.</p>

<p>You should also consider what clothes to wear. Your location and the time
   of year will be key factors, but a general rule of thumb is to have at least
   one layer available for each surface of your body -- a sweater if you're in
   a T-shirt, pants if you're in shorts, and gloves and a hat. The more
   versatile your clothing can be, the more comfortable you'll be. It should
   also fit your style. If you don't like a bunch of stuff banging around in
   your pockets, then consider wearing a fanny pack for essentials such as a
   compass, pocket knife, lighter or matches, and adhesive bandages.</p>

<h3>What should you carry?</h3>

<p>For short trips, a fanny pack or day pack should include at least one
   quart of water per person, map, flashlight, first aid kit, rain gear,
   high-energy snack, and toilet paper, in addition to any optional items
   such as sunglasses, camera, binoculars, and nature books.</p>

<h3>What else should you do?</h3>

<p>Make an itinerary and stick with it. Make sure someone knows when and where
   you're expected back, and how long they can allow. </p>

<h2>When things go wrong</h2>

<blockquote>
  <p>The worst thing you can do is to get frightened. The truly dangerous
  enemy is not the cold or the hunger, so much as the fear. It robs the
  wanderer of his judgement and of his limb power; it is fear that turns the
  passing experience into a final tragedy ... Keep cool and all will be well
  ... Use what you have, where you are, right now.</p>
  <p>Ernest Thompson Seton, 1906</p>
</blockquote>

<p>So you've planned, you've prepared, and now you're on the trail. And the
   worst part is, you don't know where you are. There's a four-step process to
   follow, and all you have to do is <em>STOP</em> -- <strong>S</strong>tay-
   <strong>T</strong>hink-<strong>O</strong>bserve-<strong>P</strong>lan.</p>
```

```
<h3>STAY!</h3>

<p>At the first sign of trouble, STAY WHERE YOU ARE! The urge to walk faster
or run blindly to escape the situation is difficult to resist, but rushing
about only leads to more confusion. Stopping helps you fight panic and
increases your chances of survival. If you're on foot, sit down. If you're
in a boat, get to shore. If anyone is injured, apply first aid and rest. It
may take a little bit for the panic to go away, but be patient. You probably
got yourself into this mess, you can certainly get yourself out of it.</p>

<h3>THINK!</h3>

<p>As you relax, think. If you're lost, study a map and look for landmarks.
How long ago did you know where you were? Are there footprints to show where
someone has gone before? Can you hear traffic from a highway? Do you see or
hear a river heading down stream? If you give all the clues time to sink in,
chances are you'll get yourself back on course. If you have any doubts, sit
still and observe.</p>

<p>...Yadda, yadda, yadda...More useful information here...</p>

</body>
</html>
```

FIGURE 3.1.

The base page for our DHTML page can stand alone without any other work. It's created according to HTML 4.0 standards.

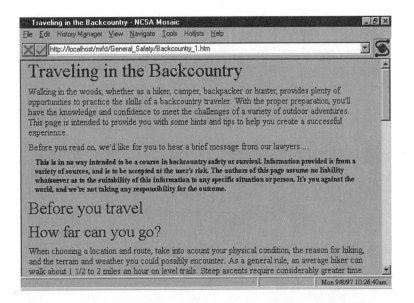

3

DYNAMIC HTML FUNDAMENTALS

TIP

If you need more help with HTML 4, take a look at *HTML 4 Unleashed* or *HTML 4 Unleashed, Professional Reference* from Sams Publishing. You'll find all the information you need on building solid Web pages with HTML 4.0.

As you can see in Figure 3.1, this page begins with basic HTML. It will display just as well on Internet Explorer as it will on Lynx or Mosaic. This type of approach is preferred at the outset for your DHTML pages—with a solid backbone that will translate well across as many browsers and platforms as possible.

> **TIP**
>
> For maximum compatibility, none of the HTML formatting tags (<B>, <U>, <STRIKE>, and so on) is used on the text. Instead, the page relies on the structure tags for its formatting, such as <STRONG> and <EM>.

A few other things become apparent on this page. First, as the information progresses, we can see that the page starts to get pretty long. The reader on a text-based browser could end up with a lot of scrolling to read the page.

Second, we can see that as it stands now, the page breaks into two parts. The first part is about preparing for a hike, and the second part is what to do if you get lost. We'll find some ways to address these two things in the section "Making the Page Dynamic."

Adding a Style Sheet

So far, our page is pure structural HTML. There are no formatting tags to control how the text is displayed, other than the tags that imply purpose (<H2>) rather than visual appearance (<FONT size=3><B>).

We'll address the vanilla state of the page now with a style sheet, which you can learn more about in Part II, "Cascading Style Sheets." There are a few things we want to accomplish with the style sheet. First, we want to give the document its basic appearance defaults: black text on a white background and a larger and more readable font. After inserting the <style> tags, the BODY element is added for overall page defaults, like this:

```
BODY { background-color: rgb(255,255,255); color: rgb(0,0,0);
➥font-family: Bookman Old Style, serif }
```

Next, let's work on the headings. To provide some contrast with the rest of the text, we'll set those in a sans serif face and provide some narrower margins for the H2 and H3 levels, like this:

```
H1, H2, H3 { font-family: Tahoma, sans-serif; font-weight: bold;
➥font-variant: small-caps }
H2 { margin-left: 20px }
H3 { margin-left: 60px }
```

We can start getting to work on the various text elements now. First is the text under the respective H2 and H3 elements. These elements should have narrower margins to reflect their parent headings. We'll accomplish this with two classes, which are named after their respective headings:

```
.h2 { margin-left: 20px }
.h3 { margin-left: 60px }
```

There's only one other item to address: the block quotes. We want these to stand out a little bit more, so we're going to apply them in italics. However, our chosen typeface (Bookman Old Style) doesn't look very good in italics, so we'll use a Times typeface instead. Also, if a citation is used within a block quote, we'll want it justified to the right margin. The code looks like this:

```
BLOCKQUOTE { font-family: Times New Roman, serif; font-style: italic }
.cite { text-align: right }
```

The last part is to integrate all our styles and classes with the rest of the text. This involves adding the `class` attribute to the appropriate tags. We're also going to separate our page into two broad divisions at this point using the `<DIV>` tag and add a unique `id` attribute to each division. To make the document easier to navigate, we've also added a table of contents with hyperlinks to anchors in the document. The result is Listing 3.2, and the results are displayed in Figure 3.2.

Listing 3.2. The third step of DHTML results in a page whose appearance is controlled by an embedded style sheet.

```
<!doctype HTML PUBLIC "-//IETF//DTD HTML 4.0//EN">
<html>

<head>
<title>Traveling in the Backcountry</title>
<style type="text/css">
<!--
BODY { background-color: rgb(255,255,255); color: rgb(0,0,0);
➥font-family: Bookman Old Style, serif }
H1, H2, H3 { font-family: Tahoma, sans-serif; font-weight: bold;
➥font-variant: small-caps }
H2 { margin-left: 20px }
H3 { margin-left: 60px }
.h2 { margin-left: 20px }
.h3 { margin-left: 60px }
BLOCKQUOTE { font-family: Times New Roman, serif; font-style: italic }
.cite { text-align: right }
-->
</style>
</head>

<body>

<h1>Traveling in the Backcountry</h1>

<ul>
<li><a href="#intro" alt="Introduction">Introduction</a></li>
<li><a href="#prepare" alt="Preparation">Before You Travel</a></li>
<li><a href="#lost" alt="In To Trouble">When Things Go Wrong</a></li>
</ul>
```

3

DYNAMIC HTML
FUNDAMENTALS

continues

Listing 3.2. continued

```
<p><a name=intro>Walking in the woods,</a> whether as a hiker, camper, backpacker
or hunter, provides plenty of opportunities to practice the skills of a backcountry
traveler. With the proper preparation, you'll have the knowledge and confidence to
meet the challenges of a variety of outdoor adventures. This page is intended to
provide you with some hints and tips to help you create a successful experience.
</p>

<p>Before you read on, we'd like for you to hear a brief message from our
lawyers....</p>

<blockquote>
  <p>This is in no way intended to be a course in backcountry safety or survival.
  Information provided is from a variety of sources, and is to be accepted at the
user's risk. <strong>The authors of this page assume no liability whatsoever as to
the suitability of this information to any specific situation or person</strong>.
It's you against the world, and we're not taking any responsibility for the
outcome. </p>
</blockquote>

<div id="div_0" title="Preparing">
<h2><a name="prepare">Before you travel</a></h2>

<h3>How far can you go? </h3>

<p class="h3">When choosing a location and route, take into account your physical
condition, the reason for hiking, and the terrain and weather you could possibly
encounter. As a general rule, an average hiker can walk about 1 1/2 to 2 miles an
hour on level trails. Steep ascents require considerably greater time allowances.
One hour for every 1,000 feet of elevation gain is a good rule of thumb.</p>

<h3>What should you wear?</h3>

<p class="h3">Proper foot gear is one of the most important parts of your journey.
Sturdy running shoes are good for hiking on relatively smooth surfaces, such as
maintained trails. You'll want something with a little more tread for rugged trails
or cross-country travel. A ten mile hike in the woods is not the best place to
break in new shoes.</p>

<p class="h3">You should also consider what clothes to wear. Your location and the
time of year will be key factors, but a general rule of thumb is to have at least
one layer available for each surface of your body -- a sweater if you're in a T-
shirt, pants if you're in shorts, and gloves and a hat. The more versatile your
clothing can be, the more comfortable you'll be. It should also fit your style. If
you don't like a bunch of stuff banging around in your pockets, then consider
wearing a fanny pack for essentials such as a compass, pocket knife, lighter or
matches, and adhesive bandages.</p>

<h3>What should you carry?</h3>

<p class="h3">For short trips, a fanny pack or day pack should include at least one
quart of water per person, map, flashlight, first aid kit, rain gear, high-energy
snack, and toilet paper, in addition to any optional items such as sunglasses,
camera, binoculars, and nature books.</p>

<h3>What else should you do?</h3>
```

```
<p class="h3">Make an itinerary and stick with it. Make sure someone knows when and
where you're expected back, and how long they can allow. </p>
</div>

<div id="div_1" title="Getting Lost">
<h2><a name=lost>When things go wrong</a></h2>

<blockquote>
  <p>The worst thing you can do is to get frightened. The truly dangerous enemy is
not the cold or the hunger, so much as the fear. It robs the wanderer of his
judgement and of his limb power; it is fear that turns the passing experience into
a final tragedy ... Keep cool and all will be well ... Use what you have, where you
are, right now. </p>
  <p class="cite">Ernest Thompson Seton, 1906</p>
</blockquote>

<p class="h2">So you've planned, you've prepared, and now you're on the trail. And
the worst part is, you don't know where you are. There's a four-step process to
follow, and all you have to do is <em>STOP</em> -- <strong>S</strong>tay<strong>T</
strong>hink-<strong>O</strong>bserve-<strong>P</strong>lan.</p>

<h3>STAY!</h3>

<p class="h3">At the first sign of trouble, STAY WHERE YOU ARE! The urge to walk
faster or run blindly to escape the situation is difficult to resist, but rushing
about only leads to more confusion. Stopping helps you fight panic and increases
your chances of survival. If you're on foot, sit down. If you're in a boat, get to
shore. If anyone is injured, apply first aid and rest. It may take a little bit for
the panic to go away, but be patient. You probably got yourself into this mess, you
can certainly get yourself out of it.</p>

<h3>THINK!</h3>

<p class="h3">As you relax, think. If you're lost, study a map and look for
landmarks. How long ago did you know where you were? Are there footprints to show
where someone has gone before? Can you hear traffic from a highway? Do you see or
hear a river heading down stream? If you give all the clues time to sink in,
chances are you'll get yourself back on course. If you have any doubts, sit still
and observe.</p>

<p>...Yadda, yadda, yadda...More useful information here...</p>

</div>
</body>
</html>
```

As we make the page dynamic, we'll return to the style sheet to include some additional features to help us. But for the time being, we have a page that has accurate HTML, whose appearance is further improved on compatible browsers with a style sheet. Step 3 of implementing DHTML is complete.

FIGURE 3.2.

The page is now a bit more interesting with a style sheet added on Internet Explorer.

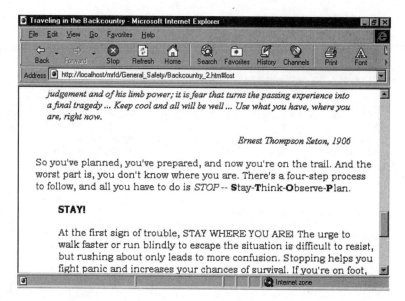

Making the Page Dynamic

To complete the loop for the creation of our page, we'll need to add two more elements. First are event handlers. These handy little items detect activity on the part of the user, such as mouse clicks and mouse movements.

Remember back in step 2 (creating the basic HTML page) when we said we'd address the fact the page was a little long and seemed to divide into two parts? We're going to take care of that now by displaying only one of the divisions at a time.

To do this, we need a way to control the `display` attribute to show or hide each division, depending on which hyperlink the user clicks. The `none` value for the `display` attribute causes the page to display as if the affected class didn't exist at all. (You'll learn more about style values and attributes in Part II.) The following code demonstrates the use of the `none` value:

```
<script language="JavaScript">
<!--
currentDiv = 0;

function showDiv ( aNum ) {
  setDisplay( nameDiv(currentDiv), "none");
  setDisplay( nameDiv(aNum), "");
  currentDiv = aNum;
}

function nameDiv( aNum ) {
  name = "div_" + aNum;
  return name;
}
```

```
function setDisplay( anId, aValue ) { //Line 49
  document.all(anId).style.display = aValue;
}
//-->
</script>
```

There's a lot going on in this script, so let's take it apart piece by piece to see what's happening. Right now it includes three different functions to make it more modular and reusable on this and other pages. Here's what each function does:

■ First, a global variable, currentDiv, is set, which identifies that the current section of the page is shown. We represent this only with a number, so we can change the naming scheme on the page without significantly changing the scripts. The default section to display is div_0, represented simply as 0.

■ Second, a function named showDiv accepts a parameter that is the number of the division to show. It calls the function setDisplay to set the display attribute of the current visible division to none; then it calls setDisplay again to set the new division's display to an empty string, which forces it to display. As its last step, it sets the currentDiv to the selected division now shown.

■ The nameDiv function is a utility function that builds the name of the division to pass to the showDiv function.

■ The last function is setDisplay, a generic piece of code that assigns a new value to the display attribute.

The script and new styles are all well and good, but we need a way to invoke the script when the user clicks the table of contents list. We'll do this by adding event handlers to the hyperlinks, like this:

```
<li><a href="#prepare" alt="Preparation" onClick="showDiv(0)">
Before You Travel</a></li>
<li><a href="#lost" alt="In To Trouble" onClick="showDiv(1)">
When Things Go Wrong</a></li>
```

Here's what happens when this page is loaded by a DHTML-enabled browser. The text in the hyperlink is still displayed as a hyperlink (typically blue underlined text). When the user clicks the link, the browser detects the mouse click and passes control to the showDiv function, which displays the appropriate part of the page. After the function is complete, page control passes back to the hyperlink, which moves the user down to the bookmark at the beginning of the selected area.

If this page were loaded on a noncompatible browser, the onClick event handler would be ignored, as would the styles, and the focus of the page would shift down to the appropriate section. This maintains downward compatibility, so this particular DHTML page should work equally well on Mosaic 2.0 and Internet Explorer 4.0.

3

DYNAMIC HTML
FUNDAMENTALS

We'll use one other event handler to hide all but one of the divisions when the page is first loaded. This utilizes the onLoad event in the <BODY> tag, which is triggered when the browser has received all the HTML for the page but has not yet begun to display it.

```
<body onLoad="initDisplay()">
```

The initDisplay function is a special one-use utility that uses a property of document.all to access each division in turn and set its display attribute to none. Then it calls the showDiv function to display the initial division. If you wanted to display the second division first, you would only need to change the value of currentDiv on the first line of the script to 1. The following code shows the display attribute set to none:

```
function initDisplay() {
  divColl = document.all.tags("DIV");
  if (divColl!=null) {
    for (i=0; i<divColl.length; i++) {
      divColl[i].style.display="none";
    }
  }
  showDiv(currentDiv);
}
```

The completed HTML for this page is shown in Listing 3.3. When it's initially displayed by Internet Explorer 4.0, it looks like Figure 3.3. Note the heading toward the bottom of the page that says, "Before You Travel."

Listing 3.3. The completed DHTML page includes basic HTML with style sheets, scripts, and event handling.

```
<!doctype HTML PUBLIC "-//IETF//DTD HTML 4.0//EN">
<html>

<head>
<title>Traveling in the Backcountry</title>
<style type="text/css">
<!--
BODY { background-color: rgb(255,255,255); color: rgb(0,0,0);
font-family: Bookman Old Style, serif }
H1, H2, H3 { font-family: Tahoma, sans-serif; font-weight: bold;
font-variant: small-caps }
H2 { margin-left: 20px }
H3 { margin-left: 60px }
.h2 { margin-left: 20px }
.h3 { margin-left: 60px }
BLOCKQUOTE { font-family: Times New Roman, serif; font-style: italic }
.cite { text-align: right }
-->
</style>
</head>

<script language="JavaScript">
<!--
currentDiv = 0;
```

```
function initDisplay() {
  divColl = document.all.tags("DIV");
  if (divColl!=null) {
    for (i=0; i<divColl.length; i++) {
      divColl[i].style.display="none";
    }
  }
  showDiv(currentDiv);
}

function showDiv ( aNum ) {
  setDisplay( nameDiv(currentDiv), "none");
  setDisplay( nameDiv(aNum), "");
  currentDiv = aNum;
}

function nameDiv( aNum ) {
  name = "div_" + aNum;
  return name;
}

function setDisplay( anId, aValue ) { //Line 49
  document.all(anId).style.display = aValue;
}
//-->
</script>

<body onLoad="initDisplay()">

<h1>Traveling in the Backcountry</h1>

<ul>
  <li><a href="#intro" alt="Introduction">Introduction</a></li>
  <li><a href="#prepare" alt="Preparation" onClick="showDiv(0)">Before You Travel</
a></li>
  <li><a href="#lost" alt="In To Trouble" onClick="showDiv(1)">When Things Go
Wrong</a></li>
</ul>

<p><a name="intro">Walking in the woods,</a> whether as a hiker, camper, backpacker
or hunter, provides plenty of opportunities to practice the skills of a backcountry
traveler. With the proper preparation, you'll have the knowledge and confidence to
meet the challenges of a variety of outdoor adventures. This page is intended to
provide you with some hints and tips to help you create a successful experience.
</p>

<p>Before you read on, we'd like for you to hear a brief message from our
lawyers....</p>

<blockquote>
  <p>This is in no way intended to be a course in backcountry safety or
  survival. Information provided is from a variety of sources and is to be
  accepted at the user's risk. <strong>The authors of this page assume no
  liability whatsoever as to the suitability of this information to any
  specific situation or person</strong>. It's you against the world, and
  we're not taking any responsibility for the outcome.</p>
</blockquote>
```

continues

Listing 3.3. continued

```
<div id="div_0" title="Preparing">
<h2>Before you travel</h2>

<h3>How far can you go? </h3>

<p class="h3">When choosing a location and route, take into account your
  physical condition, the reason for hiking, and the terrain and weather you
  could possibly encounter. As a general rule, an average hiker can walk about
  1 1/2 to 2 miles an hour on level trails. Steep ascents require considerably
  greater time allowances. One hour for every 1,000 feet of elevation gain
  is a good rule of thumb.</p>

<h3>What should you wear?</h3>

<p class="h3">Proper foot gear is one of the most important parts of your
  journey. Sturdy running shoes are good for hiking on relatively smooth
  surfaces, such as maintained trails. You'll want something with a little
  more tread for rugged trails or cross-country travel. A ten mile hike in the
  woods is not the best place to break in new shoes.</p>

<p class="h3">You should also consider what clothes to wear. Your location
  and the time of year will be key factors, but a general rule of thumb is to
  have at least one layer available for each surface of your body -- a sweater
  if you're in a T-shirt, pants if you're in shorts, and gloves and a hat. The
  more versatile your clothing can be, the more comfortable you'll be. It
  should also fit your style. If you don't like a bunch of stuff banging
  around in your pockets, then consider wearing a fanny pack for essentials
  such as a compass, pocket knife, lighter or matches, and adhesive bandages.</p>

<h3>What should you carry?</h3>

<p class="h3">For short trips, a fanny pack or day pack should include at
  least one quart of water per person, map, flashlight, first aid kit, rain
  gear, high-energy snack, and toilet paper, in addition to any optional items
  such as sunglasses, camera, binoculars, and nature books.</p>

<h3>What else should you do?</h3>

<p class="h3">Make an itinerary and stick with it. Make sure someone knows when and
where you're expected back, and how long they can allow. </p>

<div id="div_1" title="Getting Lost">
<h2><a name="lost">When things go wrong</a></h2>

<blockquote>
  <p>The worst thing you can do is to get frightened. The truly dangerous enemy is
not the cold or the hunger, so much as the fear. It robs the wanderer of his
judgement and of his limb power; it is fear that turns the passing experience into
a final tragedy ... Keep cool and all will be well ... Use what you have, where you
are, right now. </p>

  <p class="cite">Ernest Thompson Seton, 1906</p>
</blockquote>
```

```
<p class="h2">So you've planned, you've prepared, and now you're on the trail. And
the worst part is, you don't know where you are. There's a four-step process to
follow, and all you have to do is <em>STOP</em> -- <strong>S</strong>tay-
<strong>T</strong>hink-<strong>O</strong>bserve-<strong>P</strong>lan.</p>

<h3>STAY!</h3>

<p class="h3">At the first sign of trouble, STAY WHERE YOU ARE! The urge to walk
faster or run blindly to escape the situation is difficult to resist, but rushing
about only leads to more confusion. Stopping helps you fight panic and increases
your chances of survival. If you're on foot, sit down. If you're in a boat, get to
shore. If anyone is injured, apply first aid and rest. It may take a little bit for
the panic to go away, but be patient. You probably got yourself into this mess, you
can certainly get yourself out of it.</p>

<h3>THINK!</h3>

<p class="h3">As you relax, think. If you're lost, study a map and look for
landmarks. How long ago did you know where you were? Are there footprints to show
where someone has gone before? Can you hear traffic from a highway? Do you see or
hear a river heading down stream? If you give all the clues time to sink in,
chances are you'll get yourself back on course. If you have any doubts, sit still
and observe.</p>

<p>...Yadda, yadda, yadda...More useful information here... </p>
</div>

</body>
</html>
```

FIGURE 3.3.

This is our page as it displays initially on Internet Explorer 4.0.

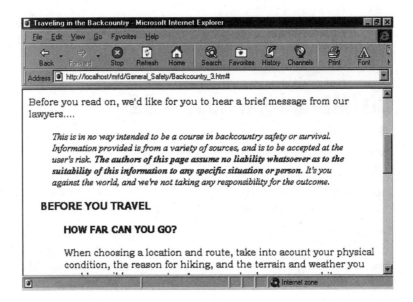

Clicking the third hyperlink (Getting Lost) at the top of the page hides the first division and displays the second division about "When Things Go Wrong," which is visible in Figure 3.4 in the place immediately after the introduction.

FIGURE 3.4.

Clicking the last hyperlink hides the first section about preparation and displays the second about getting lost.

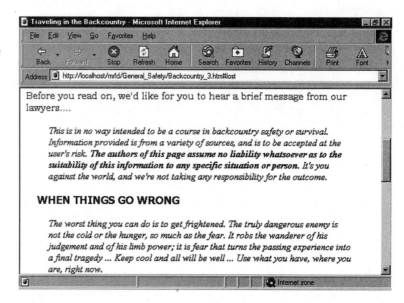

We could add more features to this page, such as making the legal disclaimer a pop-up message instead of part of the regular page, but we'll save those lessons for later, after you've had a chance to work back through some of the fundamentals. In the meantime, we'll take a look at this page and Navigator 4.02.

DHTML and Netscape 4.02

Take a look at Figure 3.5. This is our DHTML page on Navigator 4.02.

Welcome to the first DHTML incompatibility between Netscape and Microsoft. Microsoft uses the `all` object to reference the various page elements, whether they be paragraphs, headings, or forms. Because both Netscape and Microsoft support JavaScript, Netscape doesn't know that the `all` object is intended only for the Microsoft browser.

We need to create a new script that is specific to Navigator 4.02. This will utilize two features of HTML: More than one set of script tags can be placed on a page, and browsers will ignore script tags for languages they don't understand. We'll also need to add a new set of tags to the page to implement Netscape's layers for hiding and displaying the divisions.

FIGURE 3.5.

Our DHTML page on Navigator generates an error in the script.

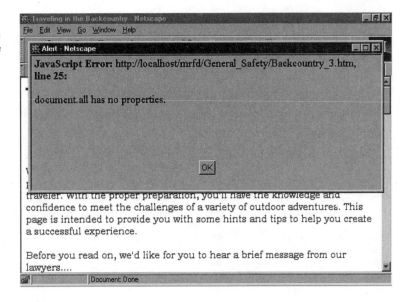

There are a few things that must happen with the new script. It must maintain the `initDisplay` and `showDiv` function names to retain compatibility with the rest of the page. The additional script for the page looks like this:

```
<script language="JavaScript1.2">
<!--
function initDisplay () {
  for (i=0; i<document.layers.length; i++) {
    setVisibility( nameLayer(i), "hide" );
  }
  showDiv(currentDiv);
}

function showDiv ( aNum ) {
  setVisibility( nameLayer(currentDiv), "hide");
  setVisibility( nameLayer(aNum), "show");
  currentDiv = aNum;
}

function nameLayer( aNum ) {
  name = "layer_" + aNum;
  return name;
}

function setVisibility( anId, aValue ) {
  document.layers[anId].visibility = aValue;
}
//-->
</script>
```

3

DYNAMIC HTML
FUNDAMENTALS

Notice the opening `<SCRIPT>` tag. This uses a language value of `JavaScript1.2`, which is the latest version of JavaScript supported by Netscape. This version is not recognized by Microsoft, so Internet Explorer will completely ignore this section.

Next, according to the hierarchy of scripts, the browser will use only the latest version of a function within a script. We now have two versions of `initDisplay` and `showDiv` appearing after the initial script, so the Netscape browser will use the new versions and ignore the prior two.

The actual work is accomplished by using the Netscape `layers` object to hide and display the sections by making use of the `visibility` attribute. Other than that, the scripts are essentially the same.

The only other matter left is to add the `<layer>` tags within the `<div>` tags with a background color attribute to make sure they remain opaque. The first layer tag looks like this:

```
<layer id="layer_0" bgcolor="white">
```

The second layer tag is identical except for the name. Listing 3.4 is the complete dual-DHTML-compatible page, which is shown on Navigator 4.02 in Figure 3.6.

Listing 3.4. The completed DHTML page, which is compatible on both Internet Explorer 4.0 and Navigator 4.02, and is backward compatible on other browsers.

```
<!doctype HTML PUBLIC "-//IETF//DTD HTML 4.0//EN">
<html>

<head>
<title>Traveling in the Backcountry</title>
<style type="text/css">
<!--
BODY { background-color: rgb(255,255,255); color: rgb(0,0,0);
➥font-family: Bookman Old Style, serif }
H1, H2, H3 { font-family: Tahoma, sans-serif; font-weight: bold;
➥font-variant: small-caps }
H2 { margin-left: 20px }
H3 { margin-left: 60px }
.h2 { margin-left: 20px }
.h3 { margin-left: 60px }
BLOCKQUOTE { font-family: Times New Roman, serif; font-style: italic }
.cite { text-align: right }

-->
</style>

</head>

<script language="JavaScript">
<!--
currentDiv = 0;
```

```
function initDisplay() {
  divColl = document.all.tags("DIV");
  if (divColl!=null) {
    for (i=0; i<divColl.length; i++) {
      divColl[i].style.display="none";
    }
  }
  showDiv(currentDiv);
}

function showDiv ( aNum ) {
  setDisplay( nameDiv(currentDiv), "none" );
  setDisplay( nameDiv(aNum), "" );
  currentDiv = aNum;
}

function nameDiv( aNum ) {
  name = "div_" + aNum;
  return name;
}

function setDisplay( anId, aValue ) { //Line 49
  document.all(anId).style.display = aValue;
}
//-->
</script>

<script language="JavaScript1.2">
<!--
function initDisplay () {
  for (i=0; i<document.layers.length; i++) {
    setVisibility( nameLayer(i), "hide" );
  }
  showDiv(currentDiv);
}

function showDiv ( aNum ) {
  setVisibility( nameLayer(currentDiv), "hide");
  setVisibility( nameLayer(aNum), "show" );
  currentDiv = aNum;
}

function nameLayer( aNum ) {
  name = "layer_" + aNum;
  return name;
}

function setVisibility( anId, aValue ) {
  document.layers[anId].visibility = aValue;
}
//-->
</script>

<body onLoad="initDisplay()">

<h1>Traveling in the Backcountry</h1>
```

continues

Listing 3.4. continued

```
<ul>
  <li><a href="#intro" alt="Introduction">Introduction</a></li>
  <li><a href="#prepare" alt="Preparation" onClick="showDiv(0)">Before You Travel</a></li>
  <li><a href="#lost" alt="In To Trouble" onClick="showDiv(1)">When Things Go
Wrong</a></li>
</ul>

<p><a name="intro">Walking in the woods,</a> whether as a hiker, camper,
backpacker, or hunter, provides plenty of opportunities to practice the skills of a
backcountry traveler. With the proper preparation, you'll have the knowledge and
confidence to meet the challenges of a variety of outdoor adventures. This page is
intended to provide you with some hints and tips to help you create a successful
experience.</p>

<p>Before you read on, we'd like for you to hear a brief message from our
lawyers....</p>

<blockquote>
  <p>This is in no way intended to be a course in backcountry safety or survival.
  Information provided is from a variety of sources and is to be accepted at the
user's risk. <strong>The authors of this page assume no liability whatsoever as to
the suitability of this information to any specific situation or person</strong>.
It's you against the world, and we're not taking any responsibility for the
outcome. </p>
</blockquote>

<div id="div_0" title="Preparing">
<layer id="layer_0" bgcolor="white">

<h2><a name="prepare">Before you travel</a></h2>

<h3>How far can you go? </h3>

<p class="h3">When choosing a location and route, take into account your physical
condition, the reason for hiking, and the terrain and weather you could possibly
encounter. As a general rule, an average hiker can walk about 1 1/2 to 2 miles an
hour on level trails. Steep ascents require considerably greater time allowances.
One hour for every 1,000 feet of elevation gain is a good rule of thumb.</p>

<h3>What should you wear?</h3>

<p class="h3">Proper foot gear is one of the most important parts of your journey.
Sturdy running shoes are good for hiking on relatively smooth surfaces, such as
maintained trails. You'll want something with a little more tread for rugged trails
or cross-country travel. A ten mile hike in the woods is not the best place to
break in new shoes.</p>

<p class="h3">You should also consider what clothes to wear. Your location and the
time of year will be key factors, but a general rule of thumb is to have at least
one layer available for each surface of your body -- a sweater if you're in a T-
shirt, pants if you're in shorts, and gloves and a hat. The more versatile your
clothing can be, the more comfortable you'll be. It should also fit your style. If
you don't like a bunch of stuff banging around in your pockets, then consider
wearing a fanny pack for essentials such as a compass, pocket knife, lighter or
matches, and adhesive bandages.</p>

<h3>What should you carry?</h3>
```

```
<p class="h3">For short trips, a fanny pack or day pack should include at least one
quart of water per person, map, flashlight, first aid kit, rain gear, high-energy
snack, and toilet paper, in addition to any optional items such as sunglasses,
camera, binoculars, and nature books.</p>

<h3>What else should you do?</h3>

<p class="h3">Make an itinerary and stick with it. Make sure someone knows when and
where you're expected back, and how long they can allow. </p>
</layer>
</div>

<div id="div_1" title="Getting Lost">
<layer id="layer_1" bgcolor="white">

<h2><a name="lost">When things go wrong</a></h2>

<blockquote>
  <p>The worst thing you can do is to get frightened. The truly dangerous enemy is
not the cold or the hunger, so much as the fear. It robs the wanderer of his
judgement and of his limb power; it is fear that turns the passing experience into
a final tragedy ... Keep cool and all will be well ... Use what you have, where you
are, right now. </p>

  <p class="cite">Ernest Thompson Seton, 1906</p>
</blockquote>

<p class="h2">So you've planned, you've prepared, and now you're on the trail. And
the worst part is, you don't know where you are. There's a four-step process to
follow, and all you have to do is <em>STOP</em> -- <strong>S</strong>tay-
<strong>T</strong>hink-<strong>O</strong>bserve-<strong>P</strong>lan.</p>

<h3>STAY!</h3>

<p class="h3">At the first sign of trouble, STAY WHERE YOU ARE! The urge to walk
faster or run blindly to escape the situation is difficult to resist, but rushing
about only leads to more confusion. Stopping helps you fight panic and increases
your chances of survival. If you're on foot, sit down. If you're in a boat, get to
shore. If anyone is injured, apply first aid and rest. It may take a little bit for
the panic to go away, but be patient. You probably got yourself into this mess, you
can certainly get yourself out of it.</p>

<h3>THINK!</h3>

<p class="h3">As you relax, think. If you're lost, study a map and look for
landmarks. How long ago did you know where you were? Are there footprints to show
where someone has gone before? Can you hear traffic from a highway? Do you see or
hear a river heading down stream? If you give all the clues time to sink in,
chances are you'll get yourself back on course. If you have any doubts, sit still
and observe.</p>

<p>...Yadda, yadda, yadda...More useful information here... </p>

</layer>

</body>
</html>
```

Standards Revisited for DHTML Fundamentals

After working through both examples, we're sure you're left with the original question we started with at the beginning of this book: What's a developer to do? The answer from the World Wide Web Consortium is to write your DHTML pages to the lowest common denominator of compatibility until the consensus begins to form. This is hard for developers to swallow, especially when you want to write with the "latest and greatest" tools on the Web. If you need more help on working through the maze of standards and implementations, see the preceding chapter, "Choosing a Standard."

FIGURE 3.6.

The Backcountry Travel page now appears correctly on Navigator without any scripting errors.

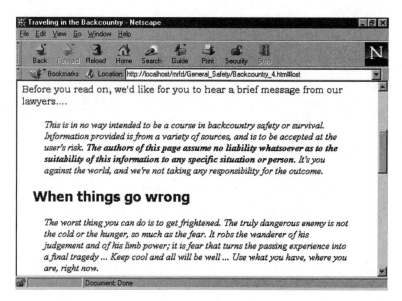

In short, it's still a long road to an implementation that is going to work well across all browsers, especially the major offerings from Netscape and Microsoft. If you write to the capabilities of a majority of your users and include safety nets for the rest, you won't go wrong.

Summary

Dynamic HTML is one of the best things to happen to HTML since HTML was blessed by the W3C. With DHTML, Web designers and authors can make their pages do the "song and dance" without relying on "click and sit." DHTML enables a page to change itself after it is loaded on the browser without any further input or guidance from the Web server.

Remember, HTML has never been interactive. It has hosted a great number of things that have been interactive, including plug-ins, applets, VRML, and other assorted adornments. DHTML makes the page itself interactive—a lot like some of those cool CD-ROMs you can buy that show you the cost of tea on Uranus or how to sweat a pipe while crammed under a crawl space.

DHTML might seem like smoke and mirrors, but it's really like old friends—the interaction of two features (documents and scripting) already available in rudimentary forms. By making every tag of a page identifiable (by using a DOM), the page developer can access and change virtually everything in reaction to the user's behavior (scripting).

You looked at a simple example in this chapter. Next, you'll take a step back and work your way into more complicated examples by beginning with style sheets and JavaScript.

IN THIS PART

Cascading Style Sheets

Cascading Style Sheets Basics

by David Wiley

IN THIS CHAPTER

CHAPTER 4

Every few years, something truly revolutionary happens to the Internet. As recently as 1993 the World Wide Web came into existence. A major leap forward came with the introduction of GUI browsers, which allow for the use of pictures and other types of media on Web pages. Another revolution is about to occur with Dynamic HTML, and cascading style sheets will be one of the technologies leading the way.

What Are Cascading Style Sheets?

Cascading style sheets (CSS) is the term used to describe a mechanism that applies a style across one or more Web pages. The so-called *sheets* are files or portions of files that reside on the Internet and are accessible by the World Wide Web. The *style* of cascading style sheets refers to a color scheme, layout, or other strategy for organizing the visual components of a document—in this case, a Web page. Work on CSS began at CERN (the European Laboratory for Particle Physics) in 1994. With the release of browsers from Microsoft (Internet Explorer 3 and higher) and Netscape (Navigator 4 and higher) that include support for CSS, cascading style sheets are finally here.

So What Can I Do with CSS?

You can use CSS to control every aspect of the graphic presentation of a Web page, including, but certainly not limited to, fonts (face, size, and color), background color and background image information for Web pages and any tables within them, the positioning of elements within the page, page margins, and text decoration such as italicizing and underlining. All these design elements are exposed to scripting as well (JavaScripting, for example) so that they can be modified after the document has been initially loaded. This scripting accessibility is what makes CSS an integral part of DHTML.

Why Would I Want to Use CSS?

The power of CSS comes with the explanation of the term *cascade* as used in the phrase "cascading style sheets." A potentially infinite number of style sheets can affect the appearance of a single Web page, giving Web page authors great flexibility in defining styles specific to certain parts of the presentation. Conversely, one cascading style sheet can be applied to a potentially infinite number of Web pages, giving Web page authors heretofore unknown ease of application of style across that potentially infinite number of pages. Perhaps more important, CSS allow a designer to update the style of all those pages by editing only one file: the style sheet. In this manner, maintainers of huge corporate or university Web sites, for example, could change the style of their entire site for Christmas, a black Monday, or any other occasion by simply modifying one file.

General Syntax

Getting started with style sheets is simple. Anyone who knows enough HTML to create a Web page can quickly master the basics of creating style sheets. The syntax of style sheet rules is as follows:

```
selector {declaration}
```

And each declaration follows the syntax, like this:

```
property: value
```

So, for example, to set the color of all second-level headings in a document to red, the following line would be included in a style sheet:

```
H2 { color: red }
```

To give you an idea of the amount of control designers now have over their Web sites, *every HTML element* is a potential CSS selector, and there are approximately 50 valid properties available for use with CSS. Many of these are explained in the other three chapters of Part II, "Cascading Style Sheets," and the comprehensive list can be found at the World Wide Web Consortium's official CSS Web site:

```
http://www.w3.org/pub/WWW/TR/REC-CSS1
```

Including CSS in HTML

Four ways to include style information within an HTML document are

- linking to an external style sheet
- importing a style sheet
- embedding a style sheet
- including style information inline

External style sheets and style sheets that will be imported should be plain text (ASCII) files including only the style rules (`selector {declaration}`). For example, HTML or other markup tags should not be within these external style sheets.

Linking to an External Style Sheet

Linking to an external style sheet is one of two methods for including style information that allows the cascade to occur. You reference an external style sheet in HTML as follows:

```
<HTML>
<HEAD>
<LINK REL=STYLESHEET TYPE="text/css" HREF=Ahttp://www.davidwiley.com/style1">
</HEAD>
```

REL=STYLESHEET tells the browser requesting this page that the *relation* of the information being linked to is STYLESHEET. TYPE discloses information about the MIME type of the information being passed, in this case a cascading style sheet. HREF contains the address of the link target just as if it had been used with the anchor tag. Information presented in externally linked style sheets will be used only if other style information is unavailable.

Importing a Style Sheet

Similarly, a style sheet can be imported for use in a Web page using the following syntax:

```
<HTML>
<HEAD>
<STYLE TYPE="text/css">
@import url(http://www.davidwiley.com/style2);
</STYLE>
</HEAD>
```

Style information imported in this way is automatically pulled into the document for use and can be overridden only by explicit style rules named within the document itself.

> **NOTE**
>
> Of the four techniques for including style information in a Web page, only linking to external style sheets and importing style sheets allow the style to cascade across multiple pages. Imported style information is automatically included in the document, whereas externally linked style information will be selected only if previously referenced style information is unavailable.

Embedding a Style Sheet

Style information can be embedded directly within the document by using the `<STYLE>` tag. The `<STYLE>` tag should always include the `TYPE=` declaration (in this case, `text/css`), and it should occur within the `<HEAD>` of the document. Most Web browsers will ignore tags that they do not know how to render, so the `<STYLE>` ... `</STYLE>` tags themselves will not be improperly displayed by older Web clients. However, it is good practice to comment out the style information designated between the tags. Often, `<SCRIPT>` information is treated the same way. Here is an example of an embedded style sheet:

```
<HTML>
<HEAD>
<STYLE TYPE="text/css">
<!-- // hide style information from older browsers

H1 {color: red};
H2 {color: blue};

// -->
<STYLE>
</HEAD>
```

Inlining Style Information

Finally, style information can be included *inline*, or within the tag of the HTML element itself. When style information is included within an HTML element's tag, the `TYPE=` declaration is omitted, and the {} (curly brackets) are replaced by quotes, as shown in the following example:

```
<BODY>
This text appears in the default font face.
<P STYLE="font-family: helvetica">This text appears in the Helvetica font face.</P>
</BODY>
```

Obviously, the power of the cascade is absent from this instance of the specific declaration of style.

Grouping Styles

To avoid redundancy in code, and because Web page designers are generally a lazy bunch, both selectors and declarations can be grouped together within style sheets. For example, say that Blue University wants all its headings to appear in blue. Developers could create a separate rule for each heading as follows:

```
<STYLE TYPE="text/css">
<!-- /* hide from old browsers */

H1 {color: blue};
H2 {color: blue};
H3 {color: blue};
H4 {color: blue};
H5 {color: blue};
H6 {color: blue};

/*stop hiding */ -->
</STYLE>
```

Or they could group the selectors into one larger rule, like this:

```
<STYLE TYPE="text/css">
<!-- /* hide from old browsers */

H1, H2, H3, H4, H5, H6 {color: blue}

/*stop hiding */ -->
</STYLE>
```

Likewise, declarations can be grouped. Say that Blue University wanted its first level headings always to display on a green background, in italics, and in an Arial font face.

Again, the developers could state each rule separately, like this:

```
<STYLE TYPE="text/css">
<!-- /* hide from old browsers */

H1 {background-color: green};
H1 {font-style: italic};
H1 {font-family: arial};

/*stop hiding */ -->
</STYLE>
```

Or they could lump them all into one larger rule:

```
<STYLE TYPE="text/css">
<!-- /* hide from old browsers */
```

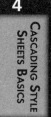

4

CASCADING STYLE
SHEETS BASICS

```
H1 {
background-color: green;
font-style: italic;
font-family: arial;
}

/*stop hiding */ -->
</STYLE>
```

Inheritance

Style properties are inherited by HTML elements that have no style rules that apply specifically to them. In the Blue University example, first level headings are set to be displayed in blue. Now, suppose that one of those headings contained text that is bold, like this:

```
<H1> Hi there. What a <b>statement</b> I'm making.</H1>
```

If no rule were declared regarding the color of text that displays in bold, the word *statement* in this example would be rendered blue. Default values for various selectors can be set document-wide by using the BODY element as a selector:

```
<STYLE TYPE="text/css">
<!-- /* hide from old browsers */

BODY {color: green};
/*stop hiding */ -->
</STYLE>
```

This sets the default text color for the document to green, just as if the declaration had been made within the <BODY> tag of the document using the TEXT= property, as can be done in standard HTML.

Taking Control

There are several ways in which designers can take advantage of the power of style sheets, and new selectors have been added to HTML to increase that number. These include CLASS and ID, as well as the capability to determine the context in which selectors occur.

The Class Selector

Any element that occurs inside the <BODY> of an HTML document may have a class associated with it. Classes give authors the ability to apply styles to specific parts of a document while not applying them to others. Figure 4.1 demonstrates this ability.

```
<HTML>
<STYLE type= "text/css">
P.makemered { color: red }
SPAN.highlighted {color: yellow }
</STYLE>
<BODY bgcolor="#000000" text="#FFFFFF">
<P class="makemered">
I must be brave, since I'm red. <SPAN class="highlighted">I'm scared
of CSS. <br>It's so complicated! That must be why I'm yellow.</SPAN></P>
</BODY>
</HTML>
```

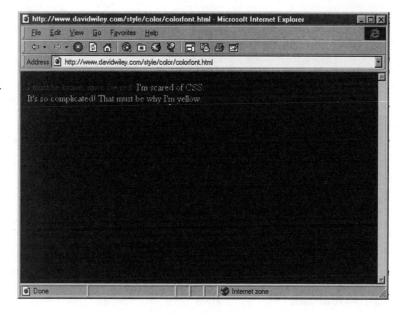

FIGURE 4.1.
Classes give authors the ability to apply styles to specific parts of a document while not applying them to others.

Rules for classes can also be declared that apply to all selectors:

```
<STYLE TYPE="text/css">
<!-- /* hide from old browsers */

.forge {color: green}

/*stop hiding */ -->
</STYLE>
```

Now, when a second level heading or paragraph, or any other selector that has color as a property, is declared to belong to the class froggy, it will be displayed in green.

```
<H1 CLASS="froggy">Green Heading</H1>
<H2>Normal Subheading</H2>
<P CLASS="froggy">All the text in this paragraph is green</P>
```

ID as a Selector

The new ID selector can be used in a way similar to the class element, except that the ID attribute has a unique value over the document. In the <STYLE> declaration, the ID name should be preceded by a #, like this:

```
<HTML>
<HEAD>
<STYLE TYPE="text/css">
<!-- /* hide from old browsers */

#1mei028 {text-transform: uppercase}
```

```
/*stop hiding */ -->
</STYLE>
</HEAD>
<BODY BGCOLOR="white">

<P ID=1mei028>This case will be displayed in all caps.</P>

</BODY>
</HTML>
```

Like CLASS, ID can be set to apply to all selectors, as in the previous example, or they can be bound to a specific one, like this:

```
<STYLE TYPE="text/css">
<!-- /* hide from old browsers */
A#0mei301 {background-color: orange}

/*stop hiding */ -->
</STYLE>


<A ID=0mei301 href="http://somwhere.com/">This link has an orange background.</A>
```

Contextual Selector

Style can also be determined by context. If Crimson, Inc. decides to set the text color within certain paragraphs to red for emphasis and to render all text in italics throughout the Web page to red, then italic words within the red paragraphs will be less emphasized.

```
<STYLE TYPE="text/css">
<!-- /* hide from old browsers */

P.red {color: red};
I {color: red};

/*stop hiding */ -->
</STYLE>
```

However, using context as a selector, a style sheet author could create a rule stating that all italicized text that appears within red paragraphs be rendered yellow, as in Figure 4.2.

```
<HTML>
<STYLE type= "text/css">
B { color: red }
I {color: yellow }
</STYLE>
<BODY bgcolor="#000000" text="#FFFFFF">
<B>
I feeling bold today,which explains why I'm red.<br>
<I>Suddenly I'm feeling yellow -- oh no!</I><br>
Whew! That's better!</B>
</BODY>
</HTML>
```

FIGURE 4.2.

*Property information
can be determined by
context or relationship
to other elements.*

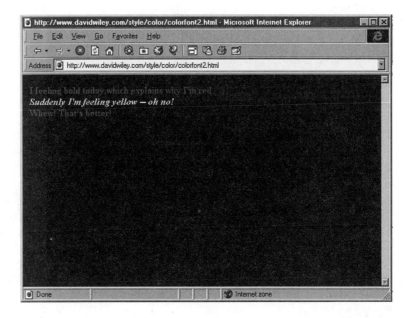

In the statement of context rules, the outer selector is named first, and the inner selector is
named second. So the preceding example would display as yellow all italicized text appearing
in paragraphs of class red. Contextual selectors can use standard HTML elements, class selectors, and ID selectors in any combination. Here are some examples:

```
DIV H1      {font-family: arial};
.butter P   {color: yellow};
#megu00 B   {text-align: center}
```

Contextual selectors can be grouped together in any way that stand-alone selectors can. This
means that you could write code this way:

```
H1 B  {color: purple};
H2 B  {color: black};
H1 I  {color: purple};
H2 I  {color: black};
```

Or you could write the code this way:

```
H1 B, H1 I      {color: purple};
H2 B, H2 I      {color: black};
```

Pseudo-Classes

Pseudo-classes allow style sheets to recognize different selector types. For example, the HTML
element <A> has three associated pseudo-classes whose property values can be accessed and set
in the following manner:

```
A:link      {font-size: 12pt};
A:visited   {font-size: 10pt};
A:active    {font-size: 14pt};
```

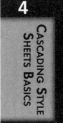

The anchor pseudo-classes are valid only for anchor tags that also include the HREF element. In other words, the following line would be unaffected by the three rules shown here:

```
<A CLASS=link NAME=target>Jump to here.</A>
```

As with normal selectors, pseudo-classes can be used as parts of contextual selectors.

```
A:link IMG {border: solid yellow};
```

This rule will cause all images that serve as links to unvisited locations to have a solid yellow border. Pseudo-classes can also be combined with other classes, like this:

```
A.menu1:link {color: green}
```

NOTE

Although pseudo-classes can be used with other classes, two standard classes *cannot* be used together. For example, P.menu1.Friday is not valid.

Pseudo-Elements

Pseudo-elements allow style sheets to access different subparts of elements. There are no HTML tags that represent these element subparts, but there are only two pseudo-elements currently supported by style sheets, so they shouldn't be too hard to remember: first-line and first-letter.

The first-line pseudo-element applies whatever styles you specify to text on the first line as displayed by the browser, as in the following example:

```
<HTML>
<HEAD>
<STYLE TYPE="text/css">
<!-- /* hide from old browsers */

P:first-line {font-style: italic};

/*stop hiding */ -->
</STYLE>

</HEAD>
<BODY BGCOLOR="white">
<P>This text will be rendered in italics until it line-wraps in the browser.
</BODY>
</HTML>
```

There are some restrictions on the use of the first-line pseudo-element. It can be used only with block-level elements and can access only the following properties: font properties, color and background properties, word-spacing, letter-spacing, text-decoration, vertical-align, text-transform, line-height, and clear.

As you've probably guessed, the first-letter pseudo-element is used to create drop caps in a document. The first-letter pseudo-element is a lot like the first-line pseudo-element in that it can be applied only to block level elements and has restrictions on the properties it can access. They are font properties, color and background properties, text-decoration, vertical-align (only if >float= is none), text-transform, line-height, margin properties, padding properties, border properties, float, and clear.

Creating a drop cap that works properly is slightly more involved than using the first-line pseudo-element. Here's an example:

```
<STYLE TYPE="text/css">
<!-- /* hide from old browsers */

P {font-size: 12pt; line-height: 12pt};
P:first-letter {font-style: italic};
SPAN {text-transform: uppercase};

/*stop hiding */ -->
</STYLE>

</HEAD>
<BODY>
<P>This text will have a drop cap which will float left, allowing the rest
➥of the text to snuggle right up against it.
```

When used in contextual selectors, pseudo-elements are only allowed as the final selector. For example:

```
SPAN BR:first-letter {color: blue}
```

As in the example with the first-line pseudo-element, first-letter can be combined with a class:

```
P.standout:first-letter {color: purple}
```

The pseudo-elements can be used together, even though they overlap each other:

```
P {color:black; font-size: 10pt};
P:first-letter {color: red; font-size: 20pt};
P:first-line {color: yellow; text-transform: uppercase}
```

Comments in CSS

If you want to include text comments in your style sheets, follow the conventions for using comments in the C programming language. Comments cannot be nested within comments; note what happens in the following code:

```
IMG.hidari {float: left} /* this image will align to the left */
```

Cascading

Using CSS, multiple style sheets can be used to affect the presentation of a single document. This is true for several reasons, probably the most important being that it reduces replication

4

of style information across style sheets. Instead of having several large sheets with only slightly different information (in one sheet H1s are red and in the other they are blue, in a third they are yellow, and so on), an author can create one CSS with all the unchanging information, and other shorter CSS with the different values for H1.

The person reading the document can also set up style sheets that affect the way they see documents displayed. Although these are handled in different ways in different browsers, most browsers allow the user to set the defaults for font face and size, background and text colors, and so on. The document's style rules override those which the reader has set up as defaults, and style rules named explicitly in the document (embedded style sheets) override those imported or linked to externally.

> **NOTE**
>
> All the `import` statements made in a document should come at the beginning of the style sheet to ensure that style rules named explicitly in the document take precedence over those from outside the document.

CSS authors can increase the weight of style rules by using the `! important` flag, like this:

```
IMG {border-top: solid green ! important}
```

This flag gives the style rule more weight in cases in which the browser might encounter a conflicting style rule. The algorithm used to determine precedence among rules is rather complex. Here is the explanation given in the Official W3C Recommendation:

1. Find all declarations that apply to the element or property in question: Declarations apply if the selector matches the element in question. If no declarations apply, the inherited value is used. If there is no inherited value (this is the case for the HTML element and for properties that do not inherit), the initial value is used.

2. Sort the declarations by explicit weight: Declarations marked `!important` carry more weight than unmarked (normal) declarations.

3. Sort by origin: The author's style sheets override the reader's style sheets which override the UA's default values. An imported style sheet has the same origin as the style sheet from which it is imported.

4. Sort by specificity of selector: More specific selectors will override more general ones. To find the specificity, count the number of ID attributes in the selector (a), the number of CLASS attributes in the selector (b), and the number of tag names in the selector (c). Concatenating the three numbers (in a number system with a large base) gives the specificity. Some examples:

```
LI            {...}  /* a=0 b=0 c=1 -> specificity =   1 */
UL LI         {...}  /* a=0 b=0 c=2 -> specificity =   2 */
UL OL LI      {...}  /* a=0 b=0 c=3 -> specificity =   3 */
```

```
LI.red              {...}  /* a=0 b=1 c=1 -> specificity =  11 */
UL OL LI.red        {...}  /* a=0 b=1 c=3 -> specificity =  13 */
#x34y               {...}  /* a=1 b=0 c=0 -> specificity = 100 */
```

Pseudo-elements and pseudo-classes are counted as normal elements and classes, respectively.

5. Sort by order specified: If two rules have the same weight, the latter specified wins. Rules in imported style sheets are considered to be before any rules in the style sheet itself.

Summary

CSS not only gives authors the power to control myriad design elements that they have never before been able to control (like the ability to absolutely position elements on the page), they also give authors the ability to manage those design elements for an entire Web site from a few small files, maybe even a single file. Details and the good stuff, like watermark backgrounds and sample JavaScript code to make your Web pages dynamic, are covered in the remaining chapters in this section.

Working with Color

by David Wiley

IN THIS CHAPTER

Perhaps the most easily noticed effects that can be rendered with style sheets are those dealing with color and background images. Their eye-catching nature also makes them some of the most hazardous elements with which a Web designer is forced to grapple. Persons with strictly technical background experience will do themselves (and the rest of us) a favor by gaining a rudimentary understanding of graphic design principles before unleashing a disaster of color on the unwary Web surfer. Of course, things like basic concepts of good taste are beyond the scope of this book.

Color and Background Colors

Before moving on to the more intricate "background image," Web authors should first understand the basics of handling plain-old solid colors, such as those that can be applied to both background and foreground.

Colors

Because text of all heading levels defaults to black, and backgrounds of pages and tables default to gray (or transparency), the appropriate use of color in these arenas is largely overlooked. With the advent of background images for Web pages with Netscape 2.0, an infinite number of psychedelically backgrounded pages sprang into existence, making Web pages harder to look at and all but impossible to read. Although cascading style sheets do not solve the problems of dark brown text on a camouflage background, they do make colors and background images easier to apply and manage. The `color` property applies to all HTML elements, including text, body backgrounds, and table backgrounds. The syntax follows:

```
selector {color: value}
```

The `value` can be one of many color words that the browser understands (for example, `red`, `blue`, `green`, `orange`) or a hexadecimal value. For example:

```
H1 { color: blue }
I {color: #FF0000 }
```

Text coloration is handled in a slightly different way in CSS from how it is in HTML. Instead of using a `<FONT>` tag to create arbitrary blocks of text with individual colors, CSS uses the parent element of the text. For example, if all the text in a document is to be rendered purple, one way to achieve the effect would be to set the `color` property for the paragraph element, as follows:

```
P { color: purple }
```

Doing so will cause all the text appearing between the `<P>` and the `</P>` to be rendered purple. Of course, when all else fails and you can find no parent element whose parent property of `color` can be set, the ubiquitous `<DIV>` or `<SPAN>` tags can be used. This is one way to highlight a single word in a paragraph. For example, say you want the text color for paragraphs of class `makemered` to be red but highlighted words to be yellow. The code would look like this:

```
<HTML>
<STYLE type= "text/css">
```

```
P.makemered { color: red }
SPAN.highlighted {color: yellow }
</STYLE>

<BODY bgcolor="#000000">
<P class="makemered">
I must be brave, since I'm red.
<SPAN class="highlighted">I'm scared of CSS.
It's so complicated! That must be why I'm yellow.
</SPAN>.
</P>
</BODY>
</HTML>
```

This would be rendered on the page in a way similar to Figure 5.1.

FIGURE 5.1.

You can use the SPAN *tag to change the color of words.*

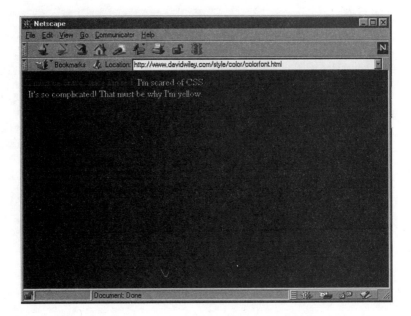

The color of any element without inherent color values (like an image, which contains its own color information) can be set by CSS. In other words, all HTML elements are potential selectors for the color property.

Background Colors

The promulgation of CSS will have a major effect on the Web similar in significance to the effect Netscape 2.0's background image capability had. Using CSS, background colors can be set for every HTML element—headings, paragraphs, links, even tables. One example might include inverting the background and foreground colors for links in order to make them stand out more. Highlighting this way could also replace the underlining that calls attention to link text. For example, the following code would be rendered as shown in Figure 5.2:

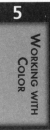

```
<HTML>
<STYLE TYPE="text/css">
A {
background-color: white;
color: black;
text-decoration: none;
}
</STYLE>

<BODY BGCOLOR= "black" TEXT= "white">
CSS can create all kinds of <a href=".">effects</a> including <a href=".">inverted
background links</a>
</BODY>
</HTML>
```

FIGURE 5.2.

With CSS, you can invert the background and foreground colors to call attention to links.

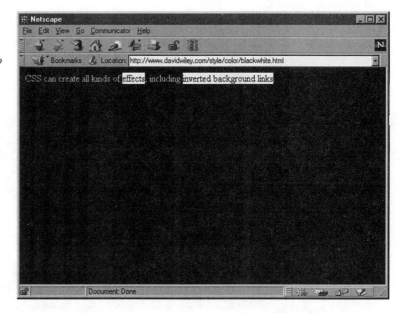

But CSS's decorative power doesn't end there. It also extends to background images, giving Web page authors extended capability they have always wanted.

Background Images and Their Properties

Now that you have a basic understanding of what cascading style sheets' color capabilities are, you're ready to dig in to the incredible things cascading style sheets can do with background images.

background-image

Background images can be applied to any HTML element, similar to the background-color property. The syntax is as follows:

```
selector { background-image: url(some_image.gif) }
```

or, optionally:

```
selector { background-image: none }
```

Until the advent of CSS, background images could only be applied to the <BODY> element of the HTML document. CSS allows tables, paragraphs, headings, and spans to have their own background images as well. As with background images applied to entire pages, Web page authors need to exercise caution when applying background images to other elements. Some examples of elements with background images assigned follow:

```
BODY { background-image: url(paper.gif) }
P { background-image: none }
TABLE { background-image: url(rock.gif) }
H2 { background-image: { url(dots.gif) }
```

The next few properties are the ones that really show some of the innovation of CSS's treatment of backgrounds. Consequently, they are the ones that designers seem to be getting the most excited about.

background-repeat

Every Web surfer has seen a background image that wrapped on the right when it wasn't supposed to. This is particularly annoying when the image is a slender column of color on the left (which may contain navigational aids or other information) and another, larger band of color on the right for the body of the page. Too many times the slender column of color shows up again on the right-hand side of the browser window, and in the most egregious cases, the color of the wider band may be present again as well. Until now, Web page authors have had few solutions to this problem, and all of them were workarounds: Create an image so long that, regardless of screen resolution, it will not wrap horizontally; write fairly advanced JavaScripts to detect the browser's window size and dynamically load the appropriate, properly sized, background image; and so on. However, the CSS property background-repeat finally gives authors a usable, sensible way to get around this problem. It gives Web authors the ability to control how (and if) their background images tile, how they are aligned, and even whether they scroll with the information on the page. Possible values for background-repeat are repeat (the default), repeat-x, repeat-y, and no-repeat. So, a Web page author can now use code similar to the following to get around this problem:

```
<HTML>
<STYLE TYPE="text/css">
BODY {
background-image: url(bluebox.gif);
background-repeat: repeat-y;
background-color: white;
}
P { color: C0C0C0 }
</STYLE>
```

This code will create, regardless of the resolution of the end user's monitor or size of the browser window, a blue column on the left (the square, blue image repeated vertically only) and the remainder of the body white. The screen will look like Figure 5.3.

FIGURE 5.3.

Using background-repeat *allows Web page authors to adjust to different monitor sizes.*

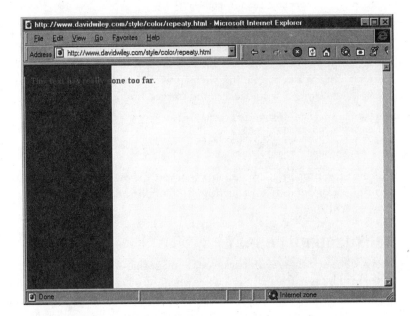

background-position

But wait—there's more! Using the property background-position, authors can do a number of other things they were never able to do before. This property actually gives authors control over where their background image is rendered. Valid values for background-position are percentages, length values, and the keywords top, middle, bottom, left, right, and center. Percentages are handled in the following ingenious manner: The height/width percentage position of the image is placed in the height/width percentage position of the browser window. So, for example, take 0% 0%. This would place the top left corner of the image (the 0% 0% position of the image) in the top left corner of the window (the 0% 0% position of the window). Likewise, 50% 50% would place the dead center of the image (the 50% 50% position of the image) in the dead center of the window (the 50% 50% position of the window). Length values such as cm, mm, em, ex, and others are valid (see the Companion Web site at http://www.mcp.com/info for a listing of valid units). Percentage and length values can be combined in declarations, such as 4em 25% (but cannot be combined with keywords) and should be listed horizontal value first, vertical value second. Keyword declarations can be made in either order, because three of the words are specific to vertical positions, and the other three are horizontal positions. For example, a valid declaration would look like this:

```
BODY { background-position: top left}
```

This would be equivalent to the percentage values 0% 0%. An example of how this CSS property could be used is a right-side navigation bar similar to the left-hand sidebar in the previous example. Before CSS, this was logistically impossible. An author could attempt to determine the window size and dynamically load a background, but he or she was then faced with the daunting task of creating a different image for every possible window width. Using CSS, the effect can be accomplished by adding one line of code to the previous example:

```
<HTML>
<STYLE TYPE="text/css">
BODY {
background-image: url(bluebox.gif);
background-position: top right;
background-repeat: repeat-y;
background-color: white;
}
P { color: C0C0C0 }
</STYLE>
```

This code creates a page that is white except for a column of blue flush up against the right side of the browser window—regardless of monitor resolution or window size (or resizing). It looks like Figure 5.4.

FIGURE 5.4.

Using background-position, *you can create a page that looks similar on all monitors, regardless of resolution or window size.*

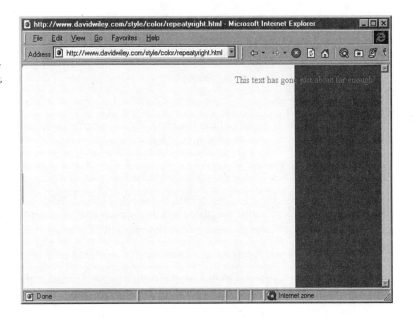

background-attachment

And now, the moment you've all been waiting for: one method for creating watermarks that will work across all CSS-compatible Web browsers. The background-attachment property tells the browser whether to let the background scroll along with the page (which is the default) or to keep it fixed relative to the page's contents. This is commonly known as a *watermark*. This effect can be achieved with code like this:

```
<HTML>
<STYLE TYPE="text/css">
BODY {
background-image: url(bluebox.gif);
background-position: 50% 50%;
background-repeat: no-repeat;
background-attachment: fixed;
background-color: white;
}
P { color: C0C0C0 }
</STYLE>

<BODY>
<CENTER>
<P>I'm really slick.</P>
<P>I can slide over this background!</P>
<P>I'm really slick.</P>
<P>I can slide over this background!</P>
<P>I'm really slick.</P>
<P>I can slide over this background!</P>
<P>I'm really slick.</P>
<P>I can slide over this background!</P>
<P>I'm really slick.</P>
<P>I can slide over this background!</P>
<P>I'm really slick.</P>
<P>I can slide over this background!</P>
<P>I'm really slick.</P>
<P>I can slide over this background!</P>
</BODY>
</HTML>
```

Figure 5.5 shows an example of how the page would initially load, and Figure 5.6 shows the page scrolled down (with the background image staying in place).

background

And last of all, of course, comes the shortcut. All the various background properties are accessible via the background property. Instead of listing each specific property separately, as in the previous examples, a Web page author can dump them all into one large listing, as follows:

```
BODY { background: url(bluebox.gif) 50% 50% no-repeat fixed white }
```

Because the various properties each have different acceptable values, they can be listed in any order. Properties that are omitted receive their default setting.

FIGURE 5.5.

When you use background-attachment, *the background image initially loads just like any other.*

FIGURE 5.6.

As the page scrolls down, the background image stays in place.

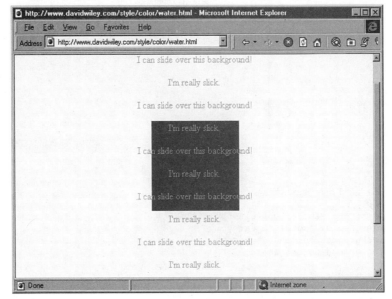

Cumulative Example

Here's a sample of a flip-flopped Web site. The navigation bar is on the right, and the entire page is flush right as well. Using the background `position` and `repeat` properties, the blue background follows the browser window, even when it is resized. By using a relative width for the table in the HTML, the "body" of the page can dynamically change width when the browser window changes size, but the absolute width of the second table cell keeps the white links in the blue area. I'll leave the table border on so that you can see the dynamic resizing; two different sample window widths are shown in Figures 5.7 and 5.8.

FIGURE 5.7.

Using the background *properties, you can accommodate different window widths.*

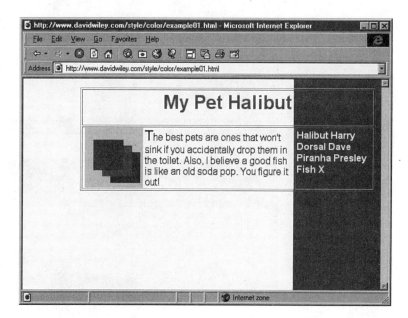

```
<HTML>
<STYLE TYPE="text/css">
BODY {
background-image: url(bluebox.gif);
background-repeat: repeat-y;
background-position: top right;
background-color: white;
}
```

This declaration sets up the background as a blue box, which will tile vertically only from the top right corner, on a white background. Because the position is `top right`, no matter how the window is resized, the blue column will follow.

```
H1{
font-family: arial;
color: red;
}
A {
color: white;
```

```
font-family: arial;
font-weight: bold;
text-decoration: none;
}
P.regular{
font-family: arial;
}
```

These declarations determine in which font face and color various elements of the document will be rendered.

```
</STYLE>
<BODY>
<table width=85% align=right border>
<tr><td colspan=2 align=center><h1>My Pet Halibut</h1></td></tr>
<tr><td valign=top>
<P class="regular"><img src = "./boxes.jpg" align=left>
<font size=+2>T</font>he best pets are ones that won't sink if you
accidentally drop them in the toilet. Also, I believe a good fish is like
an old soda pop. You figure it out!
</td><td width=130 align=left>
<P>
<a href =".">Halibut Harry</a><br>
<a href =".">Dorsal Dave</a><br>
<a href =".">Piranha Presley</a><br>
<a href =".">Fish X</a><br>
</P>
</td></tr>
</table>
</BODY>
</HTML>
```

Now see what happens when the browser window is resized and made more narrow. The positioning information is updated dynamically!

FIGURE 5.8.

A narrow window width is no obstacle when you use the background *properties.*

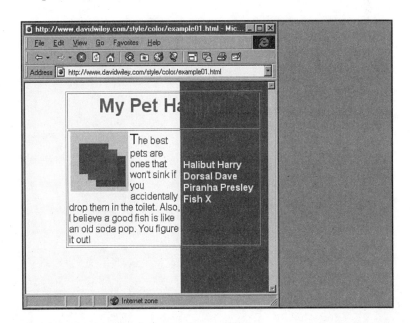

This is part of the reason cascading style sheets is included in this book on DHTML. It allows incredible flexibility for authors to make pages look the way they want them to look, and to keep looking that way, even when something changes on the users' end. Dynamic updating. It's about time.

Summary

This chapter demonstrated how to effectively use color to enhance your style sheets. Styling backgrounds with CSS is as important as using color in headings, paragraphs, and links. The next chapter focuses on the importance of using different fonts to design pages. Read on.

Text and Fonts with Style

by David Wiley

IN THIS CHAPTER

CHAPTER 6

As long as designers have been working on the Web, they have been clamoring for the ability to control the fonts in which their designs are ultimately rendered by the end user's client. At first, they had no choice at all, because early Web browsers rendered text in whatever font the telnet client or terminal emulator was set to use, and even this setting was unmodifiable by the user for a long time.

Then came a new generation of Web browsers, which exposed all the fonts installed on the user's system and made them available for use. But they were still inaccessible to the designer; the user chose which font to use for surfing the Web.

Finally, a new HTML tag, <FONT>, was introduced, which was to solve all designers' problems. Unfortunately, it didn't. Here are a few of the problems:

- Even though Web designers can define which font face they want the user's browser to display, they cannot control which fonts are installed on the user's system.

- Even if a designer chooses a font generic enough to be installed on most systems, the user can still set the browser to override the document's background and text color and/or font settings.

- Because the user can override either fonts *or* background and text colors, the chance exists that whichever element is overridden will have the same color value as that which is not; for example, the user could override the background color, setting it to white, only to find that the <FONT COLOR> is set to white, causing text to be transparent or invisible.

- Although the user can override the background and text color and font settings, he or she cannot override the <FONT COLOR="whatever"> tag itself. This can lead to situations in which the user keeps his or her specified background color only to have the <FONT COLOR="whatever"> tag set to the text to the same color.

Working with Fonts

The most basic of these problems is the way in which Web page designers are forced to attempt to "guess" which fonts end viewers will have installed on their systems. If a designer doesn't guess carefully, the text of the page he or she has designed will be rendered in Times New Roman or whatever font the user has set his or her browser to default to. CSS attempts to take the guesswork out of using fonts by doing the following:

- Applying an algorithm that makes judgments based on font properties to use the closest font possible when the requested font is not available.

- Providing a way for designers to name not only specific fonts in their pages, but also generic families of fonts (sans-serif, for example) from which the Web browser will find the closest match on the user's system.

The browser is able to make these judgments because CSS-compatible Web browsers keep a database of known fonts and their properties which it checks against. CSS defines five font-specific properties that can be set: `font-family`, `font-style`, `font-variant`, `font-weight`, and `font-size`.

font-family

The `font-family` property allows the Web page designer to designate which font family will be used. Specific font names can be designated (such as Arial) for display of text associated with the given selector, like this:

```
P.plain { font-family: Arial }
```

Font names that include spaces are given in quotes, like this:

```
P.fancy { font-family: "Times New Roman" }
```

> **NOTE**
>
> According to the official CSS1 specification, font names need to be included in quotes. Some browsers may work without the quotes, but regardless, font names should still be in quotes.

The value assigned the `font-family` property can, like the `<FONT>` tag, be a list of possible font faces, which the browser will attempt to locate and use in the order they are listed.

```
P.obscure { font-family: "Out There", Techie, "Really Cool Font" }
```

Generic font family names can also be given as values for the `font-family` property. CSS defines the following generic font families:

- `serif` (for example, Times)
- `sans-serif` (for example, Helvetica)
- `cursive` (for example, Zapf-Chauncery)
- `fantasy` (for example, Western)
- `monospace` (for example, Courier)

Although declaring a generic font family does not give the Web page designer as much control over the appearance of the page as the specific family name does, using a generic font family as the final list entry can help make the best out of a bad situation in which the user has none of the specific fonts you planned for.

```
P.lastditch { font-family: Arial, "Times New Roman", serif }
```

font-style

For you hard-core font fans out there, font-style differentiates between normal, italic, and oblique font faces. CSS-compatible Web browsers check for the given value in their font databases in order to decide which version of the font face to display. normal will only display the normal version of the font, oblique will only display the oblique version of the font, and italic will display the italic version or the oblique version when the italic one is unavailable. For example, the following code would be rendered as shown in Figure 6.1:

```html
<HTML>
<STYLE TYPE="text/css">
H1 { font-style: italic }
P { font-style: normal }
B { font-style: italic }
</STYLE>
<BODY>
<H1> Salon of Style</H1>
<P>
Some of the characters that hang out here have a pretty drab and awful outlook on
life. Others view it from a <B>different slant</B>.
</BODY>
</HTML>
```

Figure 6.1.

Using font-style, *you can differentiate among* normal, italic, *and* oblique *font faces.*

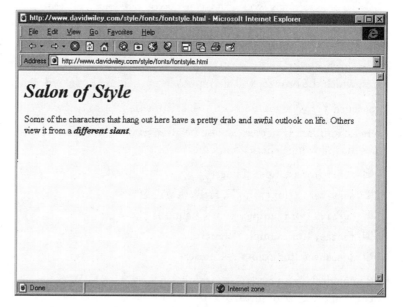

font-variant

The font-variant property refers to the small-caps variant of the font face. small-caps refers to fonts that have lowercase letters replaced by uppercase ones. These letters occur in slightly different proportions than the true uppercase letters in the small-caps variant. If no true small-caps version of the font is available, CSS-compatible browsers can replace lowercase letters with scaled-down versions of the uppercase letters. For example, the following code would look like Figure 6.2:

```
<html>
<STYLE TYPE="text/css">
.boohiss { font-variant: small-caps }
</STYLE>
<BODY>
<H1> Caution: Do Not Read</H1>
Did you hear about the font-variant who sponsored a fund raising drive?
It had a successful <SPAN CLASS="boohiss">Capital Campaign</SPAN>.
</BODY>
</HTML>
```

FIGURE 6.2.

Using font-variant, *you can make small caps.*

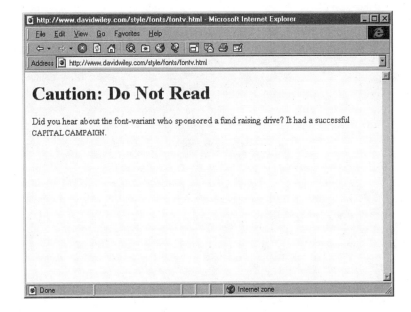

font-weight

CSS defines a new, sensible way of approaching the weight of fonts using the font-weight property. Because font names often include the words bold, dark, heavy, and so on, it is difficult to use these words to objectively describe font weight. Therefore, CSS uses a numeric scale of multiples of 100 ranging from 100 to 900. Within the scale, 400 is equivalent to "normal" font weight, and 700 is equivalent to "bold."

CSS defines a few keywords for use with the font-weight property: lighter, bolder, normal, and bold. lighter and bolder will select the next closest version of the font available—that is, if the font has only a normal and a bold version, the keyword bolder will display the bold version of the font when in a normal font context. It will continue to display the bold version of the font when already in the bold font context, because there is no "bolder" version available, as demonstrated in the following example and Figure 6.3:

```
<HTML>
<STYLE TYPE="text/css">
.dark {font-weight: bolder }
</STYLE>
<BODY>
<H1>Science</H1>
<P> Stars are large balls of glowing gass. You should avoid looking directly into
the sun because it is so bright. The sun isn't completely lit up, however. It has
<DIV CLASS="dark">spots</DIV></B>
</P>.
</BODY>
</HTML>
```

FIGURE 6.3.

Using font-weight, *you can make text look bold.*

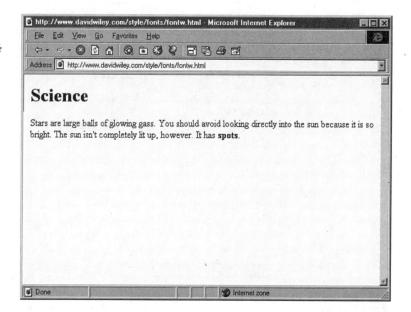

font-size

If you haven't guessed yet, the font-size property controls the size of the fonts displayed. Values are of four possible types: absolute size, relative size, percentage, and length.

CSS defines seven keywords as valid absolute size values: xx-small, x-small, small, medium, large, x-large, and xx-large. Although they may be of different sizes in different browsers, the following relationship will always exist between the sizes:

```
xx-small <= x-small <= small <= medium <= large <= x-large <= xx-large
```

The following example demonstrates some of these sizes, and the final product is shown in Figure 6.4:

```
<HTML>
<STYLE TYPE="text/css">
H1 { font-size: xx-large }
P { font-size: medium }
.legalstuff { font-size: xx-small }
</STYLE>
<BODY>
<H1>Eye Exam</H1>
<P>HTMLCSS1XML</P>
<P CLASS="legalstuff">insertotheracronymshere</P>
</BODY>
</HTML>
```

Figure 6.4.

Using font-size, *you can change the relative size of fonts, regardless of browser size.*

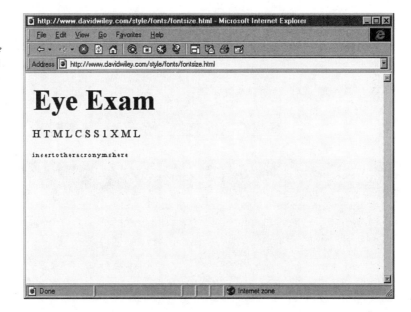

Relative size is also quite simple. There are only two valid values for relative size: larger and smaller. Size is determined using a comparison of the parent element or current context. The following example shows how this contextual usage works and is pictured in Figure 6.5:

```
<HTML>
<STYLE TYPE="text/css">
P { font-size: medium }
B { font-size: larger }
I { font-size: larger }
</STYLE>
<BODY>
<P> Once upon a time there were three font styles. A baby style,
<I>a mommy style, and
<B>a daddy style</B></I>. Even though they felt outraged at the way their sizes had
been stereo<B>typed</B>, they managed to live happily ever after.</P>
</BODY>
</HTML>
```

FIGURE 6.5.

You can also change the size of the font relative to the previous font using the keywords larger *and* smaller.

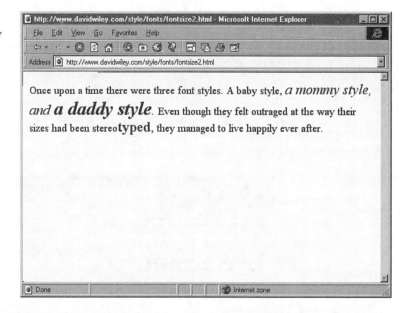

> **NOTE**
>
> Netscape Navigator 4 uses a scaling factor of 1.5 for larger and smaller sizes—that is, larger=150%. Internet Explorer uses a scaling factor of 1.35 for larger and smaller sizes—that is, larger=135%.

Percentage values work in a very intuitive way: Values such as 50% and 210% are valid. Length values (such as pt, px, em, and ex) are also valid methods for specifying font size.

> **NOTE**
>
> Length units em and ex are normally calculated using the current font size. However, for the font-size property, the sizes of em and ex are determined based on the font size of the parent element.

font Shortcut

As with every other category of properties that has several subproperties, the various font properties can all be accessed using the font shortcut property. Because each of the valid values are distinct, they can be included without explicit reference to whichever of the several font properties you are setting. For example:

```
P { font: larger italic small-caps Arial }
B { font: bold 138% }
I { font: x-small italic lighter Curly }
```

Working with Text

Aside from the myriad wonderful things CSS can do with fonts, there is an entirely separate group of properties that deal with text and are independent of the font involved. These include issues of leading and spacing. Although CSS defines the properties that follow, it also allows a browser to call itself CSS1 compliant while ignoring some of these properties. Often those that can be ignored are, so some of this functionality is available in neither of the current versions of Navigator or Internet Explorer.

word-spacing

The word-spacing property allows a Web page designer to control the amount of space between words on a page. Acceptable values for word-spacing are lengths given in pt, px, em, and normal. If a length value is given, the browser will increase the current space between words by the given amount (unless the value is negative, in which case it will decrease the space by the given amount). The official CSS1 specification states that browsers can render any word-spacing value as normal (that is, they can ignore the command).

```
H1 { word-spacing: 2em }
```

> **NOTE**
>
> Neither of the current versions of Navigator or IE interprets word-spacing. They render any setting as normal.

letter-spacing

letter-spacing controls the amount of space that the browser inserts between letters as it renders them on the page. It works in a manner similar to word-spacing in that it accepts the three length units and normal as values and adds (or subtracts, in the case of negative values) the given length unit to the current spacing context. The CSS specification also allows browsers to render any letter-spacing value as normal. The following code and Figure 6.6 show how this is rendered by Internet Explorer:

```
<HTML>
<STYLE TYPE="text/css">
P.loose { letter-spacing: 5pt}
</STYLE>
<BODY>
<P>Before exercising, it's a good idea to </P>
<SPAN CLASS="loose">warm up</SPAN></P>
</BODY>
</HTML>
```

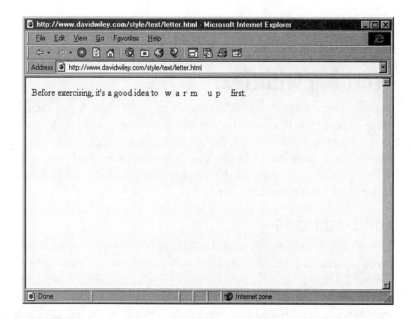

text-decoration

Have you guessed yet? The text-decoration property adds or removes decoration to the text on a Web page. The decorations supported by CSS are underline, overline, line-through, and (for some reason) blink. Obviously, when decoration is added, it must be rendered with a color (or it will "appear invisible"), so the value of the color property is used as the text-decoration color. By a stroke of genius, the authors of the CSS1 specification have determined that browsers can "ignore" the blink decoration as well. The following code and Figure 6.7 demonstrate this functionality:

```
<HTML>
<STYLE TYPE="text/css">
.inky { text-decoration: underline }
.blinky { text-decoration: blink }
.pinky { text-decoration: overline }
.clyde { text-decoration: line-through }
</STYLE>
<H1>Effects</H1>
<BODY>
<P CLASS ="inky">Underlined Text </P>
<P CLASS ="blinky">Blinking Text </P>
<P CLASS ="pinky">Overlined Text </P>
<P CLASS ="clyde">Line-through Text </P>
</BODY>
</HTML>
```

FIGURE 6.7.

You can use text-decoration *to create different effects for your text.*

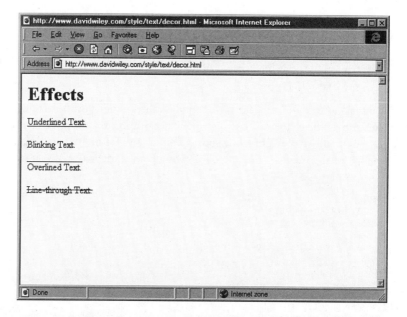

> **NOTE**
>
> Only Internet Explorer 4 (the final version) supports the overline property. Only Navigator 4 supports the blink value.

vertical-align

The vertical-align property wins the award for the CSS property with the greatest number of possible keyword values. vertical-align controls the way inline elements are placed in relation to other elements.

The list of nine keywords can be split up into two lists: keywords that align relative to the parent element, and keywords that align relative to the line which the inline element is in.

The following keywords align relative to the parent:

- baseline—Aligns the baseline of the element with the baseline of the parent
- middle—Aligns the vertical middle of the element with the vertical middle of the parent
- sub—Puts the element in subscript
- super—Puts the element in superscript
- text-top—Aligns the element's top with the top of the parent
- text-bottom—Aligns the element's bottom with the bottom of the parent

The following keywords are relative to the line:

- `top`—Aligns the top of the element with the top of the tallest element in the line
- `bottom`—Aligns the bottom of the element with the top of the lowest element in the line

`vertical-align` will also take a percentage value, either positive or negative. The percentage listed moves the element's baseline either that proportion above or, in the case of negative values, below the parent's baseline. For example, a value of `100%` will place the element on the baseline of the previous line. The following code and Figure 6.8 show examples of some of these properties:

```
<HTML>
<STYLE TYPE="text/css">
.kita { vertical-align: super }
.minami { vertical-align: sub }
.manaka { vertical-align: middle }
</STYLE>
<BODY>
<P>
<SPAN class="kita">
I'm above petty things like surfing.</SPAN>
I'm surf on occasion.
<SPAN class="minami">
I have sunk into a quagmire of internet addiction!</SPAN>
<br><br>
<img src = "./block.gif" class="manaka">
I'm the monkey in the middle.
</P>
</BODY>
</HTML>
```

FIGURE 6.8.

`vertical-align` *allows you to change alignment of text relative to the parent element or the line.*

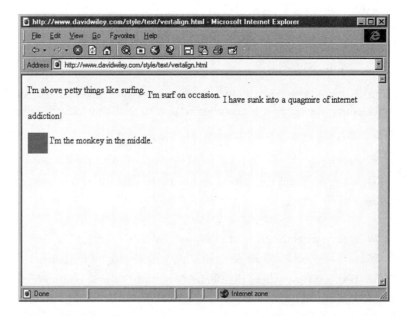

text-transform

The text-transform property allows Web page designers to transform the case of text on-the-fly. In other words, it can be used to convert to and from all uppercase (not to be confused with the font-variant value small-caps), all lowercase, or the capitalizing of the first letter of each word in the element. Valid values for text-transform are capitalize, uppercase, lowercase, and none. The following example and Figure 6.9 show some of these properties in action:

```
<HTML>
<STYLE TYPE="text/css">
P.ue { text-transform: uppercase }
P.shita { text-transform: lowercase }
P.dake { text-transform: capitalize }
</STYLE>
<BODY>
<P CLASS="ue">Look at me, I'm tall!</P>
<P CLASS="shita">Look at me, I'm short!</P>
<P CLASS="dake">Look at me, I'm an up-front kind of sentence!</P>
</BODY>
</HTML>
```

FIGURE 6.9.

You can use text-transform *to change capitalization of text on-the-fly.*

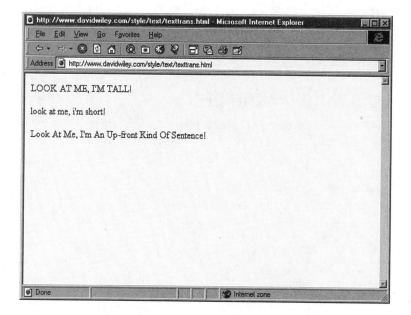

text-align

text-align is another of the "extremely intuitive" properties. Using this property, text can be aligned to the left, right, center, or even justified. Unfortunately, the CSS specification states that browsers can treat the value justify as either left or right (depending on which way the language runs by default), and both Navigator 4 and IE4 do treat it that way—that is, they both ignore the justify value.

text-indent

What can I say? The `text-indent` property controls the length of the indentation before the first character of the first line. Acceptable values are lengths and percentages, as follows:

```
P { text-indent: 3em }
P.half {text-indent: 50% }
```

line-height

The `line-height` property controls the amount of space between the baselines of two adjacent lines. Three different value types are accepted: numeric, length, and percentage values. Numeric values are multiplied by the size of the current element's font to produce the distance; length values give the length between the lines explicitly; and percentage values are multiplied by the parent element's font size to determine the distance.

> **NOTE**
>
> Although numeric and percentage values are calculated in the same way, they are inherited differently by child elements. The distance derived from percentage calculations is passed on directly to inheriting children, whereas the factor derived from a numeric value (and not the calculated value) is passed on.

Cumulative Example

The following cumulative example combines some of the font and text techniques discussed in this chapter. Figure 6.10 shows the finished product.

```
<HTML>
<HEAD>
<STYLE TYPE="text/css">

H1 {
background-color: blue;
color: white;
font-size: 30pt;
font-family: arial;
text-transform: uppercase;
text-align: right;
}
```

```
I {
font-style: italic;
text-transform: capitalize;
}

P {
text-indent: 2.5em;
font-size: 12pt;
font-family: tahoma;
}

BLOCKQUOTE {
letter-spacing: 0.2em;
font-size: 10pt;
font-family: arial;
}

</STYLE>
</HEAD>
<BODY>

<H1>The Story</H1>

<P>
It was a dark and stormy night. Channel 28
was showing <I>bill's gang</I> reruns again, channel
4 was <I>wide world of llamas</I>, and the
other channels had been unavailable since just
before 7:00. Tom brushed aside the torn paperback
copy of Edith Hamilton's <I>mythology</I> and
found the remote control. As he turned up the volume, he
distinctly heard the announcer say,</P>
<BLOCKQUOTE>
Llamas have long necks, fins for swimming and a beak for eating honey.
If you see llamas where people are swimming, shout out "Look out,
there are llamas!"
</BLOCKQUOTE>
<P>
The announcer then rattled off something that sounded like Spanish,
which Tom figured must be a translation of whatever he said about llamas.
Tom confusedly put the remote down, and lankily
lumbered off in search of Ethel, thinking she should
have returned from her surveying trip over an hour
ago.
</P>

</BODY>
</HTML>
```

FIGURE 6.10.

You can use many different text and font properties to achieve the effects you want.

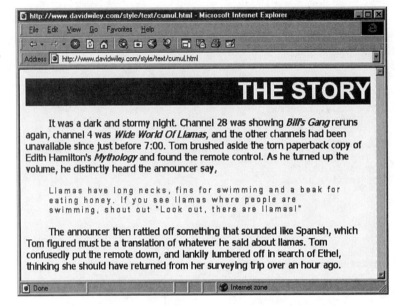

Summary

As you can see, cascading style sheets give designers a previously unavailable amount of flexibility and power to treat the text and fonts in their Web pages in almost any manner they desire. This expanded ability to manipulate the "wordy" part of Web pages brings us that much closer to being able to truly do whatever we want on our pages.

Formatting and Positioning

by David Wiley

IN THIS CHAPTER

CHAPTER 7

For years now, Web page designers have been clamoring for a universal method of controlling exactly where the elements they place on the canvas are displayed. Of course, there have been ways to assuage this desire for control: borderless tables tricks, the infamous single-pixel gif trick, and creating large background images with precisely placed elements, just to name a few. Now that support (in browsers as well as the HTML community at large) for CSS is becoming widespread, Web developers can comfortably rely on CSS to solve their page-layout woes.

Part of the problem that has given Web designers such grief is the way different browsers handle margins. For example, look at the screen captures of a square graphic in Netscape 4 (see Figure 7.1) and Internet Explorer 4 (see Figure 7.2) windows.

Figure 7.1.

Notice the top and left margins of a square graphic in Netscape.

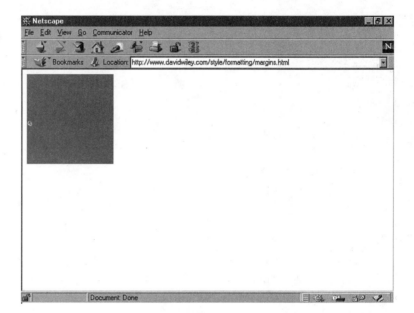

Netscape Communicator gives the document a default margin of 8 pixels on the top and the left, and Internet Explorer defaults to a margin 10 pixels wide on the left and 15 pixels down from the top. These may seem like minor details—what difference do a few pixels make? But many designers have worked long and hard to get foreground and background images to work together exactly as illustrated in Figure 7.3, only to find that the way the "finished product" looked on another browser was similar to what is shown in Figure 7.4. The image is pushed out of alignment by different margin defaults.

FIGURE 7.2.

Again, notice the top and left margins of a square graphic in Internet Explorer.

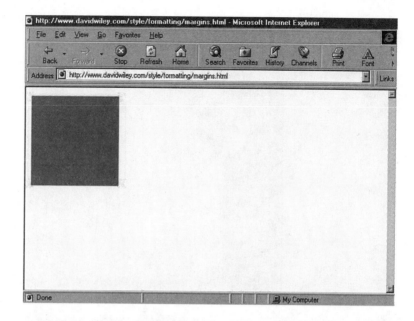

FIGURE 7.3.

Designers work long and hard to get foreground and background images such as these to align.

FIGURE 7.4.

*On a different browser,
the image may be out of
alignment.*

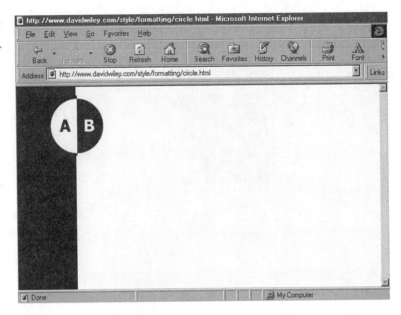

Another benefit of positioning elements absolutely on the canvas is that position information is exposed to scripting. This means that elements originally rendered in a certain position on the canvas can be moved dynamically through scripting.

The CSS Formatting Model

An understanding of how HTML elements can be positioned using CSS begins with an understanding of the CSS formatting model: CSS renders each element within a rectangular box. Each box is made up of the content region and (optionally) its padding, borders, and margins. Of course, the size and other properties of the padding, borders, and margins can be set by CSS properties that bear the same names. Figure 7.5 demonstrates the relationships among them.

> **NOTE**
>
> When the vertical margins of two elements are juxtaposed, the smaller of the two margins is omitted. This juxtaposition displays the larger of the two margins between the elements. Horizontal margins are *not* treated this way.

There are several types of elements to consider in this discussion of formatting, including block-level elements, inline elements, and replaced elements. Block-level elements are those whose display value is block or list item, such as <P>, <IMG>, and <UL>. Inline elements are those that occur within the line of text, such as `<BLINK>` or `<B>`. Finally, replaced elements are those tags that are replaced by some other content, such as the `<IMG>` tag, which is replaced with the image indicated in the `src=` declaration.

FIGURE 7.5.

The location of the padding, borders, and margins—and their spatial relationships.

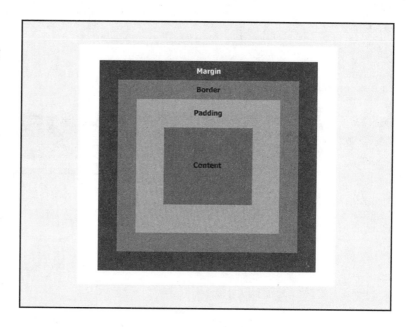

Block-Level Elements

Block-level elements are formatted as if they were large blocks, hence the name. Here's the nitty-gritty on how to format them.

List-item Elements

The way in which list items are displayed on the screen can be controlled to some degree with the CSS property `list-style`. The two valid values for `list-style` are `outside`, which is the default way in which list items are displayed, and `inside`. Here's an example:

```
<html>
<head>
<style type="text/css">
UL.normal {list-style: outside};
UL.flush {list-style: inside};
</style>
</head>
<body>
<table width=150>
<tr><td>
Sometimes you want your text to appear next to the bullet
<UL class="normal">
<li>with your bulleted text indenting as it wraps
```

```
</ul>
and other times,
<ul class="flush">
<li>you may want the bulleted text to wrap as if it were normal text.
</ul>
</td></tr>
</table>
</body>
</html>
```

This code would be rendered as shown in Figure 7.6.

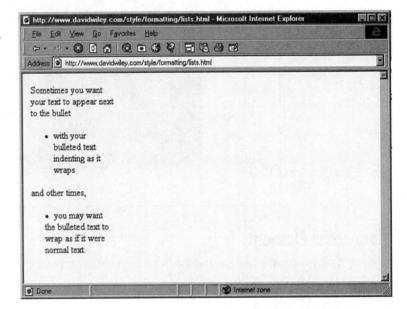

Floating Elements

As long as HTML has allowed the inclusion of images, Web page designers have been forced to rely on the align property when attempting to include them in the body of Web pages that also contain text. Even though it works well enough, *align* isn't really the proper term, and the functionality is rudimentary at best. The float property of CSS is a sensible, function-filled answer to this dilemma.

Using float, designers can push HTML elements to one side or the other and be assured that their padding, borders, and margins will stay intact. Unlike the padding, margins, and borders of other block-level elements, the surrounding space of elements that are floating is not collapsed. (See the note in the section "The CSS Formatting Model" on vertical formatting.) This unlocks some very powerful tools for designers, such as being able to float images (or other block-level elements) with negative margins. The following is an example of an image aligned left, and another floated left, taking advantage of the negative margin. Figure 7.7 shows the left-aligned image whereas Figure 7.8 shows a floating image.

```
<html>
<body>

<img src ="./box2.gif" align="left">
s long as I can remember, web pages have stood on a very
controversial side of the educational fence when it came
to images. Web pages had an unbending policy of total inclusion.
If you wanted to include an image on a page, it was all or nothing.
I appreciate this new flexibilty afforded me by <code>CSS1</code> and the
<code>float</code> to keep images on the page part of the time,
and off the page part of the time, and to be able to
partially include images whenever I want.

</body>
</html>
```

FIGURE 7.7.

An image placed using the align property of HTML.

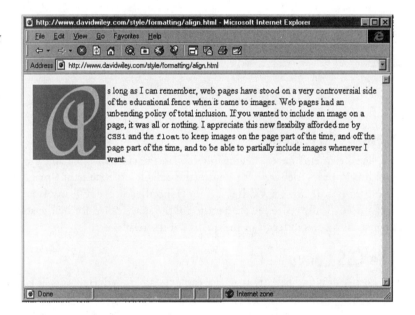

```
<html>
<body>

<img src ="./box2.gif" style="{float: left; margin-left: -75}">
s long as I can remember, web pages have stood on a very
controversial side of the educational fence when it came
to images. Web pages had an unbending policy of total inclusion.
If you wanted to include an image on a page, it was all or nothing.
I appreciate this new flexibilty afforded me by <code>CSS1</code> and the
<code>float</code> to keep images on the page part of the time,
and off the page part of the time, and to be able to
partially include images whenever I want.

</body>
</html>
```

Figure 7.8.

*An image placed using
the float and margin
properties of CSS.*

Image floats off page ──

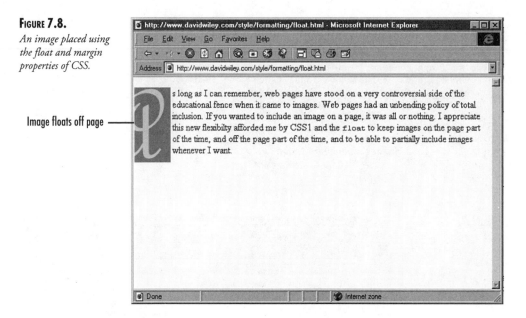

Replaced Elements

Replaced elements have a height inherent in the content replacing the HTML. If the width and height properties are left to auto (the default), the element (image, for example) will be rendered as is. If either a width or height is specified in the style information, the Web browser will automatically resize the element to fill the space called for by the style sheet, with varying degrees of success in terms of the quality of the result.

The CSS Canvas

Because widths and heights are changeable for all HTML elements, it is possible to restrict the dimensions of the BODY of a hypertext document using CSS. Because this is true, background information that is declared for an entire document could show through if the BODY of the document does not cover all the space rendered by the browser window. Using code like the following would create the potential for visitors to see something very different from what they are accustomed to—basically, two backgrounds:

```
<HTML STYLE="background: url(http://www.davidwiley.com/style/multi.gif)">
<BODY STYLE="background: green">
```

Box Properties

The boxes in which CSS renders all HTML elements have several properties that are mentioned previously—namely margins, padding, and borders. Each of the elements is accessible on a per-side basis (for example, margin-left, padding-bottom) so that the element's surroundings can be controlled exactly. Of course, all four sides can be manipulated at once, as well.

Margins

The individual margin properties are named `margin-top`, `margin-right`, `margin-bottom`, and `margin-left`. These all default to a value of `0` and will accept either absolute or percentage values as arguments. Margin values can also be negative. The ability to set the margin for each of the four sides of an object individually is extremely useful, but it should be remembered that vertical margins will be collapsed as mentioned in the note in the section "The CSS Formatting Model." All four margins can be accessed at once by using the "margin" property, like this:

```
H1 {margin: 7%}
```

If you can remember that the naming begins at the top and continues clockwise (that is, `margin-top`, `margin-right`, `margin-bottom`, `margin-left`), you can set individual margin sizes using the `margin` property as follows:

```
IMG {margin: 5em 2em 7em 1em}
```

This is equivalent to the following:

```
IMG {
Margin-top: 5em;
Margin-right: 2em;
Margin-bottom: 7em;
Margin-left: 1em;
}
```

If you declare margin widths this way and include two or three values, the widths for the sides that have been omitted will be obtained from the opposite side. For example, the following code explicitly sets the margin size for the top and right sides, so the browser will assume the bottom and left values based on the top and right ones:

```
IMG { margin: 5em 2em }
```

So, this declaration is equivalent to the following:

```
IMG {margin: 5em 2em 5em 2em }
```

or

```
IMG {
Margin-top: 5em;
Margin-right: 2em;
Margin-bottom: 5em;
Margin-left: 2em;
}
```

Padding

Padding and border share naming conventions in that the four sides are named beginning at the top and moving clockwise around the box: `padding-top`, `padding-right`, `padding-bottom`, and `padding-left`. The properties can be set individually or in a group using the padding property (the same way the `margin` property could be set), like this:

```
P { padding: 3px 4px 6px 2px }
```

This is equivalent to the following:

```
P {
padding-top: 3px;
padding-right: 4px;
padding-bottom: 6px;
padding-left: 2px;
}
```

Omitted padding size values are assumed in the same way that omitted border size values are. The main difference between borders and padding is that padding values cannot be negative.

Borders

Because the `border` property has more values than just `width`, it differs slightly from margins and padding. Borders have three values that can be set—width, color, and style—and there are individual property names that correspond appropriately. Brief descriptions follow:

- `Border-width`—Border width can be set for each side individually by a naming scheme that should be familiar: `border-top-width`, `border-right-width`, `border-bottom-width`, and `border-left-width`. The possible values for border width are thin, `medium`, `thick`, and `none`. Although they could be rendered different widths by different browsers, it will always be true that thin <= medium <= thick. All four border widths can be set with the `border-width` property using this syntax:

  ```
  UL {border-width: medium}
  ```

  Values for individual sides can be assigned using the `border-width` property just as they could for `margin` and `padding`, and omitted values are assumed based on opposite side values in the same way they are assumed for margins and padding. So, the following code:

  ```
  UL {border-width: thick thin medium }
  ```

  is equivalent to

  ```
  UL {border-width: thick thin medium thin }
  ```

- `Border-color`—Determines the color in which the border will be rendered. If no specific color is declared for the border, it will assume the color of the element it surrounds. For example, the following code will create a black border around the paragraph:

  ```
  P {
  color: black;
  background-color: red;
  border-width: thin;
  }
  ```

■ Border-style—Just as the name implies, `border-style` dictates the appearance of the border. Valid values are `none`, `dotted`, `dashed`, `solid`, `double`, `groove`, `ridge`, `inset`, and `outset`. The 3D effects used in `groove`, `ridge`, `inset`, and `outset` are based on the color of the border. And although this multiplicity of border types is fun, browsers could display all of the different types as simply `solid` and still meet CSS1 specifications.

■ Borders all at once—All three of a border side's values (`width`, `style`, and `color`) can be set at once using the following properties: `border-top`, `border-right`, `border-bottom`, and `border-left`. The value information should be stated in the order `width`, `style`, and `color`, like this:

```
P {border-top: medium solid purple}
```

By using the `border` property, all four `border-top` properties, for example, can be set in one fell swoop. Note the following code:

```
P {border: thin dotted green}
```

is equivalent to

```
P {
border-top: thin dotted green
border-right: thin dotted green
border-bottom: thin dotted green
border-left: thin dotted green
}
```

Width and Height

Although the `width` and `height` properties can be set for text elements, they are more commonly used on replaced elements such as images. The properties default to values of `auto` but will take absolute and percentage values as well. If only one value is set (and the other is left to `auto`) and scaling occurs, the replaced element's aspect ratio will be preserved. Negative values are not valid for the `width` and `height` properties. The following code shows `width` and `height` properties:

```
IMG {
width: 250px;
height: 200px;
}
```

Float

As mentioned in the section "Floating Elements," the `float` property provides functionality similar to that of the `align` property in HTML. It can be applied to text elements but, like `width` and `height`, is more often used with replaced elements. When an element is floated, it moves to the left or right of its parent element until the outside edge of its box meets the inside edge of its parent's box. Valid values are `left`, `right`, and `none`.

```
IMG {
float: left;
margin: 0;
```

```
padding: 0;
border: none;
}
```

This would float an image left until it met the inside edge of its parent element (a paragraph, for example). When elements are floated, text and other elements wrap around them on the page, as shown in the example in the "Floating Elements" section. This is similar to setting `align=left` inside an HTML `<img>` tag.

Clear

The `clear` property determines whether the element to which it applies allows other elements to float beside it. By setting `clear` to `left`, the element will be pushed beneath any elements floating on its left. Valid values are `right`, `left`, `none`, (floating objects are allowed on both sides) and `both` (floating objects are not allowed on either side). The syntax looks like this:

```
P { clear: both }
```

Positioning and Examples

Although the proposal to extend CSS to include the absolute positioning of HTML elements using properties such as top and `left` is still in an intermediate draft state, positive and negative margin values can be used to create some of the same positioning effects. When attempting to achieve positioning in this way, you should remember that z-ordering is accomplished based on a "last tag on top" principle. In other words, elements that appear later in the HTML of a page will be rendered "above" those that appear earlier. For example, a simple drop shadow effect could be achieved with code that looks like this:

```
<html>
<style type="text/css">

H1 {
font-size: 50pt;
font-family: arial;
}

.shadow {
color: black;
margin-top: 50;
margin-left: 50;
background-color: white;
}

.front {
color: red;
margin-top: -90;
margin-left: 52;
}
</style>

<body bgcolor="#000000">
```

```
<h1 class=shadow> Drop Shadow</h1>
<h1 class=front> Drop Shadow</h1>

</body>
</html>
```

The final result looks like what is shown in Figure 7.9.

FIGURE 7.9.

The drop shadow effect.

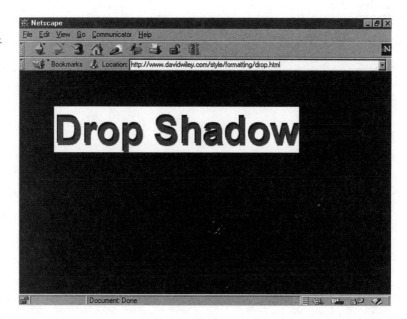

And, for a more complicated example, the following code and Figure 7.10 show a splash page done entirely in CSS and HTML.

```
<html>
<style type="text/css">

P {
color: white;
font-size: 80pt;
font-family: tahoma;
}

P.first {
background-color: red;
margin-top: -50;
margin-left: 50;
width: 150px;
float: left;
}

.second {
background-color: green;
margin-top: 65;
```

```
margin-left: 175;
width: 150px;
float: left;
}

.third {
background-color: blue;
margin-top: -50;
margin-left: 270;
width: 150px;
float: left;
}

.fourth {
background-color: orange;
margin-top: 100;
margin-left: 400;
width: 150px;
float: left;
}

.byline {
color: blue;
font-style: italic;
font-size: 14pt;
margin-top: 155;
margin-left: 83;
float: left;
}

</style>

<body bgcolor="#FFFFFF">


<P class="fourth"> S </P>
<P class="third"> W </P>
<P class="second"> E </P>
<P class="first"> N </P>
<P class="byline">A l l   t h e  
<font color="yellow">n e w s   t h a t ' s</font>
  f i t   t o   p r i n t</P>

</body>
</html>
```

FIGURE 7.10.

A splash page done entirely in CSS and HTML.

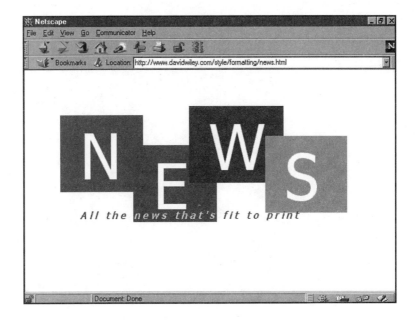

Summary

Even though the CSS1 specification is still in a draft state, and support for CSS1 in various browsers leaves a lot to be desired, it is one of the most exciting parts of the cascading style sheets. It empowers Web page authors to make things move around on the page, without creating huge, bandwidth-hogging, animated gifs. Stay tuned to the W3 Web site at `http://www.w3.org/` for the official version of this document, and check the DHTML Web site at `http://www.htmlguru.com` for "breaking coverage."

PART

IN THIS PART

Scripting Overview

by Ryan Peters

IN THIS CHAPTER

CHAPTER 8

This chapter is for those who haven't followed each and every development in the world of scripting and for those who want to make sure they have all the basics covered before advancing to the next round. You'll be able to amaze friends and family after learning and understanding these tidbits of information. You'll also be able to develop for more than one type of client by taking advantage of multiple scripting languages within one page. Although the examples in this chapter are simple, they provide a fast and easy way to build that foundation for the advanced topics and at the same time look at some simple ways to script your Web pages. In this chapter, you'll learn the following:

- Scripting basics
- Different scripting standards and the browsers they work with
- Scripting different languages and browsers on the same page

Scripting Basics

Scripting is not a new technology. Various types of scripting have existed for years, in a wide range of applications. One of the most important things to remember about scripting languages versus more mainstream programming environments: Scripts function within applications. One of the most popular tools on the Internet is the Web browser, an application that lets users access information rich in multimedia content. Now that these browsers are script enabled, scripts have come to play a pivotal role in the evolution of the Web.

In the Beginning...

Before the release of Netscape 2.0 in 1995, making the Internet interact with your average Web users required complex CGI scripting, more power on your server, and a knack for offbeat programming languages. Until Netscape 2.0, Web browsers did little more than show off static HTML pages, handle form input, and leave the growing online community thirsting for more. For the bulk of the content on the Web, the highest level of interaction was a graphical hit counter and possibly a noise or two.

Around this same time in 1995, Sun Microsystems was preparing the public release of its Java programming language, promising cross-platform network applications and a level of flexibility hitherto unheard of among the Web surfing minions. With little fanfare, a small startup company in Palo Alto, California, Netscape Communications Corporation, began developing Navigator 2.0. Buried within this release was the capability to include program scripts within regular Web pages. You no longer needed to purchase special editors or high-dollar compilers; the developer just included some extra text in the HTML source for a page, nested between special tags (`<script>` and `</script>`) that told this new browser "execute this script when loaded."

Breaking the chains of the standard "Hello World" example, try putting the Alert Box script shown in Listing 8.1 in one of your Web pages. It represents one of the most basic scripts available and serves as a doubly annoying reminder that before Dynamic HTML (DHMTL), some scripts were pretty much unnecessary baggage.

Listing 8.1. HTML source for the Alert Box.

```
<html>
<head>
<title>A Script!</title>
</head>
<script>
<!-- hide from old browsers --//

   //This line pops up a message box and
   //serves as a frightening reminder of
   //just how far we've come.
   alert('My First Script!');

   //changes the status bar in your Web
   //browser from the old "document done." To
   //a more personal note.
   window.status = ('My First Page With a Script!');

//-- end hiding -->
</script>
<body>
<h1>Got It?</h1>
</body>
</html>
```

LiveScript, as it was called back then, showed great promise. With it, developers could access, question, and even control certain aspects of the client's view of their creation. No more guessing about whether a form had the right type of data filled in or wondering what type of browser the user was running. From dynamic color changes to form validation, this new method of enhancing Web pages made for some pretty cool pages. JavaScript rapidly gained mainstream acceptance, partially because of the tremendous technological leaps made with Netscape Navigator 2.0 and also because it gave the capability to create interaction with the user to everyday people, not just system administrators. Simple applications like loan calculators no longer required executables stored on the server. What first started with often annoying scrolling messages and pop-up alerts ("Welcome to John's Page!") evolved into useful functionality. Forms were checked before even touching the server, documents were adjusted based on the client, and the Web became, well, simply cooler.

Advanced Web content, once a no-man's land of professionals requiring knowledge of CGI programming, was now open to everyone. These scripts required no formal training, were relatively simple to implement, and were quite a bit more informal than traditional languages. Novices found it simple to pick up the basics of the language and were quick to try the latest and greatest in development.

The new Netscape browser made it easy to add interactive elements to a Web page. By enclosing a script between the <script> and </script> tags, the developer's creation is executed by the client's browser, not the server, which makes for a faster ride to the Web user, as certain functionality was offloaded from the server to the client.

Fast forward two years. Sure, there's still the occasional tacky script hidden on an unknowing user's Web page, but things have moved forward at a tremendous pace. Scripting within Web pages has moved from an experiment in creativity to an exercise in ingenuity. Fly-over help, dynamic images, multimedia elements, and interactive pages have redefined the way we use the Web. 1997 has seen the rise of JavaScript, VBScript, JScript, and even the move for a standard scripting language with ECMAScript. With the exception of VBScript, these scripting languages roughly follow the same syntax, object, and event models, based loosely on an object-oriented, C-like syntax.

Getting the Objective: Programming with Objects

At first glance, object-oriented programming (OOP) can be an absolute nightmare to those more familiar with the straightforward syntax of common Internet languages like Perl. It helps to follow an easy-to-understand analogy when getting started, so I'll use this book.

This book is an object. If you were to program using that object, understand that the book object has what you call properties, events, and methods. *Properties* are things that describe the book, and *methods* are things you do to or with the book. In OOP you usually access an object's properties by using its name, a period, and then the property. So you might use something like `book.title` to get this book's title or `book.reader` to get your name. Certain properties, like the book's title, are marked as read-only, meaning that although you can access their values, you can't set them. For example, you really can't change the `book.title`, even if you wanted to. Read-only properties are a necessary evil, because certain things are just what they are. Imagine if you could change the title for the book; your peers wouldn't have any idea what you were talking about when you mentioned it. However, `book.reader` can change, so not only can you get a value from that property, you can also set it.

In JavaScript, objects have methods, or actions, that they perform. For example, `book.read()` might tell the browser to start reading the book. Some methods accept *arguments*, or parameters that control the action they perform. The `book.turnTo()` method would accept an argument of a page number, so running `book.turnTo(340)` tells the book object to turn to page number 340.

JavaScript is also an *event-driven programming language*, meaning that a program's code is executed when something happens. For the good old book here, you could have the `onFinish` event, which would contain program code that's executed when you've finished reading the book. Following the same rule of thumb, the book might have an `onPageTurn` event, as well as an `onPurchase` event.

Still a bit confused? Take a look at a quick rundown of some hypothetical properties, methods, and events of this book object in Tables 8.1, 8.2, and 8.3. You can see how each of these corresponds to something about this book. Scripting for Web pages acts the same way, with similar properties, methods, and events for the HTML document.

Table 8.1. The book object's properties.

Property	Value
book.currentpage	125
book.reader	(your name here)
book.chapter	8
book.title	*Dynamic HTML Unleashed*

Table 8.2. The book object's methods.

Method	Action
book.read()	Starts reading the book
book.turnTo(334)	Turns the book to page 334
book.dogEar()	Folds the corner of the current page
book.highlight()	Highlights a quote

Table 8.3. The book object's events.

Event	When
book.onPurchase	You buy this book
book.onFinish	You finish reading the book
book.onPageTurn	When a page is turned

Granted, the book object makes for a pretty simplified example of object-based programming, but it should give you enough of a foundation to follow along with the scripting concepts used to create high-impact Web documents with DHTML.

When we talk about being object based, it means looking at elements within an HTML page as objects, with different properties and methods. Just like the book object had a title property that reflects the title of the book, a Web document has a title, usually displayed at the top of the browser window. This property (window.title) is read-only; you can't change its value. Within a Web browser, that window object also has a location property that reflects where the current document is located, normally a URL. Because this property can be changed, you can simply assign a new value to the window.location property and make the browser load another page.

By accepting user input with a form and assigning data from that form to the window.location property, you can create a very simple means for the user to open another page on the Web.

Listing 8.2 shows a simple form that asks for a URL and then redirects based on what the user entered in a form.

Listing 8.2. Jumpin' Jack JavaScript.

```
<html>
<head>
<title>Where Do You Wanna Go?</title>
</head>
<script language="JavaScript">
<!--// hide the script from older browsers

//this is the 'jump' function, that we'll use to accept input from
//the form, and redirect the user to what the URL they entered
//this function is called with one argument (frm) which is a reference
//to the form that the user filled in.

function jump(frm){
    //the frm object has an element called URL, we'll use that value
    //for the new location for this window.
    window.location = frm.URL.value;
    }
}

// end hiding -->
</script>
<body bgcolor="#FFFFFF">
<center>
<form>
<h2>Where To?</h2>
<br>
<input type="text" name="URL" value="" size=35>
<br>
<input type="button" onClick="jump(this.form)" value="Jump!">
</form>
</center>
</body>
</html>
```

It all boils down to being able to visualize a Web page as an object. Just like any other programming object, scripting enables you to manipulate the Web page. Whether you're accessing a document object, a window object, a frame object, an image object, or even the layer object, many of them can be scripted, controlled, and manipulated to create interactive, dynamic Web pages.

The Scripting "Standards"

Not all scripting languages are created equal. Although Netscape started the trend with JavaScript, others soon followed suit and, in some cases, improved on Netscape's original vision. Each of these scripting specifications works with a particular browser or set of browsers and is often incompatible with others.

Although the browser wars have made for some intense market competition and brought us some of our most valuable tools and technologies, they have also created confusion because of the variety of scripting languages available. Understanding these languages and how to work around different versions is pretty much a prerequisite for any developer looking to develop some dynamic client-side content.

JavaScript

Netscape's Communicator 4.0 introduced JavaScript 1.2, the third major revision of Netscape's popular client-side scripting language. With each successive release, JavaScript has become more powerful and flexible. Each version of JavaScript builds on the previous one, extending its feature set, object model, and extensibility. Navigator 2.0 brought forth JavaScript 1.0, and Navigator 3.0 saw the rise of JavaScript 1.1. Table 8.4 lists the major changes from the initial version to version 1.2.

Table 8.4. Major JavaScript changes from version 1.0 to version 1.2.

Release Version	Major Changes
JavaScript 1.0	Initial Release
JavaScript 1.1	Capability to dynamically change the images within a document by accessing properties of that document's images array
	New, simplified array functions
	LiveConnect technology, allowing JavaScript, Java, and Plug-ins to interact
	Capability to use external script files
	New event handlers (`onMouseOut`, `onAbort`, `onReset`, `onError`)
JavaScript 1.2	Dynamic HTML functionality with the `document.layers` array
	New events, properties, and methods
	Signed scripts for greater security
	Event Capturing

Microsoft's JScript

JScript is Microsoft's implementation of JavaScript within its Internet Explorer browser. JScript versions 1 and 2 are compatible with Netscape's JavaScript 1.0 and therefore don't take advantage of the scripting capabilities incorporated into versions 2.0 and later of Netscape's software. The move in the release version of Internet Explorer 4.0 (IE4) is JScript 3.0, which fully supports the ECMA specification, encompassing JavaScript 1.1. Though not available at this date, there should be an update for Internet Explorer 3.*x* that enables support for JScript 3.0.

VBScript

The oddball language of the pack, VBScript is an Internet Explorer–only scripting platform. Designed as a small subset of Microsoft's Visual Basic programming language, the idea was to allow the massive installed base of Visual Basic programmers to get up to speed on Web scripting with little or no effort. Where the other languages have quite a few similarities and are even somewhat compatible with one another, VBScript extends the JavaScript object model and incorporates some proprietary VB functions in the mix. For example, to display a dialog box to the user, JavaScript-based languages would use a code similar to that shown in Listing 8.3.

Listing 8.3. Specifying JavaScript as the script language.

```
<script language="JavaScript">
<!---// hide script

function someFun() {
 var myMsg = 'Hello There!';
 alert(myMsg);
}

//--->
</script>
```

To accomplish a similar box in VBScript, you'd use a code fragment much like that shown in Listing 8.4. Those programmers familiar with Microsoft Visual Basic should be able to see VB heritage easily.

Listing 8.4. Specifying VBScript as the script language.

```
<script language="VBS">
<!---//

Sub someFun()
 dim myMsg As String
 myMsg = 'Hello There!'
 MsgBox(myMsg)
End Sub

//--->
</script>
```

When scripting exclusively for Internet Explorer, possibly on an intranet or a private Web site, combining VBScript with the power of ActiveX can make for some fairly powerful Web-based applications. The one downfall of scripting with VBScript is the lack of support for this technology outside Windows and Macintosh platforms. There is a plug-in available for Netscape Navigator that allows VBScript and ActiveX technologies to be used within Netscape browsers; but at this time it only works under Netscape 2.0 and 3.0 and requires modification to the scripts to function correctly under these browsers. For those interested in experimenting with this technology, the ScriptActive plug-in is available from NCompass Labs for download at http://www.ncompasslabs.com.

The Push for a True Standard: ECMA-262 Specification

It was bound to happen eventually. With as many different scripting platforms available to today's Web developer, a standard is under development. Based originally on Netscape's JavaScript, ECMAScript brings the promise of true cross-browser scripting to the ring. Beginning with the release of IE4, Microsoft has announced support for this specification. Based on JavaScript, Netscape support is somewhat obvious. It was submitted for adoption as a standard sometime in the fall of 1996, and as of now, has still not made it to the land of formal specifications.

For the time being, I suppose it's best to attack Web page development using whatever language you feel most comfortable with. Keeping in mind which browser the bulk of your target audience uses, you can make logical guesses as to where you should concentrate your efforts. Some people regularly examine their Web server's log files to get an idea of what this target platform is. Things should eventually settle down, and a standard scripting language will arise. Until then, we have to work around the differences in the various languages and optimize wherever appropriate.

Scripting Different Languages Together

The wide variety of scripting technologies out there is enough to make even the most courageous developer's head spin. What if you want or need to include some ultra-cool JavaScript image-swap routine, or a trick ActiveX control? Unlike HTML, scripting engines don't skip over a statement they don't recognize; they present the user with one or more ugly error boxes. Nothing deters traffic like errors.

There are ways around this incompatibility issue. As a content developer, you're regularly faced with deciding which browser to optimize your site for. In the first perfect model, incoming users are surfing the Web in two flavors: IE4 and Netscape Navigator 4.0. Let's say that you want to link from one page to another but control what the target page is, based on whether that client is IE4 or Netscape. Using the onClick event, which is accessible in either browser, you can redirect the person to the appropriate page by explicitly specifying the scripting language, as shown in Listing 8.5. This makes the other language pretty much invisible to the other browser, ensuring that your users get the right page.

Listing 8.5. Basic script language separation.

```
<html>
<head>
<title>Doorway</title>
</head>
<script language="JavaScript1.2">
<!---//
//by specifying 'JavaScript1.2' as the scripting
//language, only NS 4.0 and higher "sees" this script.
//the routeMe() function simply changes the current
```

continues

Listing 8.5. continued

```
//window's location to Netscape's page.
function routeMe() {
    self.location="http://www.netscape.com/";
    return false;
    //some people have asked why I use "return false"
    //on this script.  Simple... the onClick event is
    //setting netscape up to link to another page. By
    //returning "false", you're telling the browser not
    //to follow that link.
}
//--->
</script>
<script language="VBScript">
<!---//
//by specifying 'VBScript' as the scripting language for
//this block, only MSIE 3.0 and higher "sees" this script.
//again, the routeMe() sub changes the current
//window's location to Microsoft's page.
Sub routeMe()
    self.location="http://www.microsoft.com/"
End Sub
//--->
</script>
<body bgcolor="#ffffff">
<center>
<form>
<input type="button" onClick="routeMe()" value="Go Home!">
</form>
</center>
</body>
</html>
```

The reason the example shown in Listing 8.5 works is that we specified two completely separate scripting languages, designed to work exclusively with either Netscape 4.0 or IE 3.0+. Under Netscape 3.0 or Netscape 2.0, you get a pretty nasty error, telling you that `routeMe()` is not defined. Why? Because Netscape 2 and 3 don't read the JavaScript 1.2 script language. They simply bypass the `<script>` and `</script>` tags, ignoring everything in between. Specifying the script's language is a simple way to ensure that the correct browser interprets your scripts. Table 8.5 shows the current accepted languages and which browsers read them.

Table 8.5. Browser scripting compatibility.

Language	Supported Browsers
`<script language="JavaScript">`	Netscape Navigator 2.0x.
	Netscape Navigator 3.0x.
	Netscape Navigator 4.0x.
	Internet Explorer 3.0x.
	AOL v3 for Windows 95.

Language	Supported Browsers
`<script>` (no specified language)	Any Netscape or Microsoft browser will attempt to process a `<script>` tag with no specified language.
	AOL v3 for Windows 95.
`<script language="JavaScript1.1">`	Netscape Navigator 3.0*x.*
	Netscape Navigator 4.0*x.*
`<script language="JavaScript1.2">`	Netscape Navigator 4.0*x.*
`<script language="VBScript">`	Internet Explorer 3.0*x.*
	Internet Explorer 4.0*x.*
	AOL v3 for Windows 95.
`<script language="VBS">`	Internet Explorer 3.0*x.*
	Internet Explorer 4.0*x.*
	AOL v3 for Windows 95.
`<script language="JScript">`	Internet Explorer 3.0*x.*
	Internet Explorer 4.0*x.*
	AOL v3 for Windows 95.

My personal preference when it comes to scripting for several browsers involves reading the `navigator.userAgent` property and doing some quick checks to determine which browser the user has. To this end, I wrote a function called `whichVersion()` that returns a different string value based on the user's browser, shown in Listing 8.6.

Listing 8.6. The `whichVersion()` script.

```
<script language="JavaScript">
<!---//
function whichVersion() {
  var myBrowser = navigator.userAgent;
  if((myBrowser.lastIndexOf("MSIE") != -1) &&
    (myBrowser.lastIndexOf("4.0") != -1)) return "IE4"
  if((myBrowser.lastIndexOf("MSIE") != -1) &&
    (myBrowser.lastIndexOf("3.0") != -1)) return "IE3"
  if((myBrowser.lastIndexOf("2.0") != -1) return "NS2"
  if((myBrowser.lastIndexOf("3.0") != -1) &&
    (myBrowser.lastIndexOf("MSIE") == -1)) return "NS3"
  if((myBrowser.lastIndexOf("4.0") != -1) &&
    (myBrowser.lastIndexOf("MSIE") == -1)) return "NS4"
}
//--->
</script>
```

Using the whichVersion() function in your scripts is a breeze, provided you already have a handle on setting up if...else statements. Let's go back to the VBScript/JavaScript language scripts from Listing 8.5. Originally, we were just sending the user to either Netscape's or Microsoft's page. By incorporating the whichVersion() function, we can determine what version they're running, tell them to upgrade if necessary, and redirect them to the appropriate page, as shown in Listing 8.7.

Listing 8.7. Redirecting based on browser.

```
<html>
<head>
<title>Doorway</title>
</head>
<script language="JavaScript">
<!---//
//first set up a global variable to hold the result returned by
//the whichVersion() function
var b = whichVersion()
//the standard whichVersion function
function whichVersion() {
   var myBrowser = navigator.userAgent;
   if((myBrowser.lastIndexOf("MSIE") != -1) &&
      (myBrowser.lastIndexOf("4.0") != -1)) return "IE4"
   if((myBrowser.lastIndexOf("MSIE") != -1) &&
      (myBrowser.lastIndexOf("3.0") != -1)) return "IE3"
   if((myBrowser.lastIndexOf("2.0") != -1) return "NS2"
   if((myBrowser.lastIndexOf("3.0") != -1) &&
      (myBrowser.lastIndexOf("MSIE") == -1)) return "NS3"
   if((myBrowser.lastIndexOf("4.0") != -1) &&
      (myBrowser.lastIndexOf("MSIE") == -1)) return "NS4"
}
//this version of the  routeMe() function changes the current
//window's location to Netscape's page.
function routeMe() {
    var exitMsg = ''; //a placeholder for the exit message
    var exitURL = ''; //a placeholder for the exit URL
    //first check to see if "NS"is in the string b
    //which we assigned the result of whichVersion to
    if (b.lastIndexOf("NS" != -1)){
       exitURL = "http://www.netscape.com/";
    } else {
       exitURL = "http://www.microsoft.com/";
    }
    //now it's just simple string matching to check the
    //version and assign an exit message to the user
    if (b == "NS3") { exitMsg = 'Netscape 3.0? Upgrade to 4.0!'; }
    if (b == "NS2") { exitMsg = 'Netscape 2.0? Upgrade to 4.0!'; }
    if (b == "IE3") { exitMsg = 'Internet Explorer 3?  Try 4.0!'; }
    //one of my favorite tricks.  If the exitMsg variable
    //is not blank, then perform some action.  In this case
    //it's to alert the user to a possible upgrade
    if (exitMsg != '') {
       alert('An Upgrade Is Available!\n' + exitMsg);
    }
    self.location = exitURL;
}
//--->
```

```
</script>
<body bgcolor="#ffffff">
<center>
<form>
<input type="button" onClick="routeMe()" value="Go Home!">
</form>
</center>
</body>
</html>
```

The new `routeMe()` uses the `whichVersion()` function in the simplest manner possible—to perform pattern matching and do mild conditional redirection. There are almost an infinite number of ways to handle different browsers, and `whichVersion()` covers most of the mainstream browsers available today.

On many occasions, you'll find yourself optimizing a script for a particular browser version. Probably the most popular use of JavaScript is fly-over image rotation. It's done using the `onMouseOut` event and the `document.images` array, both of which premiered in Netscape Navigator 3.0. So the question usually is, What's the easiest way to make sure that other browsers (Netscape 2.0, Internet Explorer 3.0) don't blow up all over themselves when the script tries to execute a function?

Tune down the `whichVersion()` function! All it does is check for an x.x number in the `navigator.userAgent` string and reads into it a bit further to see whether there's an MSIE hidden someplace in there. MSIE is a dead giveaway for a Microsoft Internet Explorer browser, which will not handle image swapping. So let's do a quick rewrite of the script and just have it return 2 for a non-swappable browser and 3 for an image-changing one (see Listing 8.8).

Listing 8.8. The `whichVersion()` script (simplified).

```
<script language="JavaScript">
<!---//
//returns "2" for a JavaScript 1.0 compliant browser
//or "3" for a JavaScript 1.1 or higher browser
function whichVersion() {
   var myBrowser = navigator.userAgent;
   if(myBrowser.lastIndexOf("MSIE") != -1) return "2";
   if((myBrowser.lastIndexOf("4.0") != -1) ||
     (myBrowser.lastIndexOf("3.0") != -1)) {
     return "3";
     } else {
     return "2";
   }
}
//--->
</script>
```

That's it—plain, clean, and simple. Now with any function that uses JavaScript 1.1 specific language, simply check to see whether a quick call to the new `whichVersion()` function equals 3. By enclosing any of the potentially incompatible code within an `if` statement, you can circumvent code that could cause errors in older or noncapable browsers. This saves the trouble of writing double code or using more in-depth workarounds. Check out the example in Listing 8.9, which shows how you can hide this code within a conditional wrapper.

Listing 8.9. Using the new `whichVersion()` script.

```
<script language="JavaScript">
<!---//
//returns "2" for a JavaScript 1.0 compliant browser
//or "3" for a JavaScript 1.1 or higher browser
function whichVersion() {
    var myBrowser = navigator.userAgent;
    if(myBrowser.lastIndexOf("MSIE") != -1) return "2";
    if((myBrowser.lastIndexOf("4.0") != -1) ||
      (myBrowser.lastIndexOf("3.0") != -1)) {
      return "3";
      } else {
      return "2";
    }
}

function someFunction() {
    //wrap this function in a conditional whichVersion()
    if (whichVersion() == "3") {

    //JavaScript 1.1 specific code goes here....

    }

    //JavaScript 1.0 compatible code goes here....

}
//--->
</script>
```

By using functions that detect which browser the user is viewing your page with, you can enable or disable certain functions that could cause other browsers to generate a script error. Writing "smart" scripts allows you to take advantage of certain capabilities while maintaining some compatibility with older or incompatible browsers. In a perfect world or closed network, you can mandate which technology to optimize your pages for, but the nature of the Internet lends itself to diversity. Being prepared to write scripts that take advantage of that diversity sets the novices apart from the serious players.

Summary

I've only scratched the surface of Web scripting. With so many choices and uses when it comes to scripting Web pages, it's no wonder there are entire volumes dedicated to each specification. Whether your particular favorite flavor is VBScript, JavaScript, or ECMAScript, rest assured that DHTML and scripting go hand-in-hand for some powerful results. Throughout the rest of this book, you'll see how adding scripts to DHTML-enhanced Web pages can produce phenomenal results. So, buckle up and get ready for the ride...

Using JavaScript with Dynamic HTML

by Arman Danesh

IN THIS CHAPTER

CHAPTER 9

Dynamic HTML wouldn't be all that dynamic if it simply provided ways to define styles, choose fonts, and position page elements. What makes it dynamic is the ability—in both Netscape Communicator and Microsoft Internet Explorer 4—to programmatically manipulate all these fancy new features using scripts.

This is where you can move layers around, hide and display content, create drop-down menus, and change the style of type based on any number of factors from date to geographic location of the user.

To accomplish all this you need to understand exactly what can be manipulated, controlled, and monitored using scripting and Dynamic HTML. You've already seen the role that JavaScript, JScript, and VBScript have come to play in improving the interactive nature of Web pages.

In this chapter, we are going to take a general look at what features of DHTML are accessible to scripting in Netscape Communicator using JavaScript 1.2. In upcoming chapters, as you learn about specific features of DHTML, such as layers and dynamic fonts, you will learn the details of scripting these features. This chapter is not intended to teach JavaScript scripting from point zero. If you want a comprehensive introduction to JavaScript, consider *Teach Yourself JavaScript 1.1 in a Week* by Sams.net Publishing or visit Netscape's JavaScript documentation on the Web at `http://developer.netscape.com/library/documentation/javascript.html`.

In this chapter, we will cover

- New objects, properties, and methods made available to Web page creators in JavaScript 1.2 that can be used with DHTML
- How events work in JavaScript 1.2 and how they can be applied to DHTML
- How to use external scripts to create libraries of functions that can be reused in multiple pages
- What signed scripts are and what they can do to improve JavaScript security

What's New in JavaScript 1.2

With each release of Netscape Navigator since version 2.0, Netscape has included JavaScript and each release has seen additions, changes, and improvements in this versatile tool for creating interactive Web pages.

The latest version of JavaScript, referred to as version 1.2, is found in the Navigator 4 component of the Netscape Communicator Internet suite.

JavaScript 1.2 addresses several key issues:

- Additional objects, properties, and methods for handling DHTML elements such as layers and style sheets.
- An improved event handling model that allows programmers to create scripts that monitor and react to a wide range of actions including but not limited to,

double-clicking on page elements, dragging objects to resize, and moving windows and frames.

■ Regular expressions have been added to JavaScript in order to address its most serious limitation: Using a CGI script created in a language such as Perl, it was possible to perform sophisticated parsing of user input with little effort. With JavaScript this was a tedious and daunting task for most page creators—now JavaScript 1.2 includes regular expressions.

■ Security has been a problem with JavaScript—there have been cases of people's name and e-mail addresses being captured by JavaScript scripts in certain versions of Navigator, for instance—and this has meant severe limiting of the script's access to local information on a user's system. With signed scripts it becomes possible for a script to request expanded privileges from the user while the user can be sure of the origin and integrity of a script.

In addition, numerous new properties and methods of existing objects provide new functionality not directly related to DHTML:

■ Array—Methods are now available to combine two arrays into a single array, to extract part of an array into a new array, and to sort arrays effectively on all platforms where before sorting wasn't a universal function.

■ documents—It is now possible to get the text currently highlighted by the user and return it as a string.

■ navigator—It is now possible to check and set certain Navigator preferences including enabling and disabling Java. It is also possible to determine which language version of Navigator is being used and which platform it is running on without having to parse the User Agent property for the information.

■ string—Many new methods and properties are available for strings which include the ability to handle ISO-Latin-1 codeset values, concatenation, pattern matching using regular expressions, searching and replacing using regular expressions, extracting sections of a string as a new string, splitting a string at specified characters, and more.

■ window—With signed scripts, it is now possible, in a window with frames, to capture events in another frame displaying a page from another site. In addition, it is possible to find a text string displayed in the window, to move the window on the desktop to absolute or relative positions, and resize and scroll windows. Properties exist to determine and set the height and width of a window's content area, the status of the location, menu, personal, scroll, status, and toolbars, and the height and width of the window's outer boundary.

■ Shared methods—The most important shared method is the ability to print the contents of a frame or window. In addition, several methods exist for event capturing. Event capturing is discussed later in this chapter, in the section "Capturing Events."

> **NOTE**
>
> For an overview of new features in JavaScript 1.2, visit `http://developer.netscape.com/library/documentation/communicator/jsguide/js1_2.htm`.

New Objects in JavaScript 1.2

JavaScript 1.2 introduces four new objects to its object model: `layer`, `screen`, `RegExp`, and `event`.

Of these, the `layer` object, the `screen` object, and the `event` object are directly pertinent to DHTML. The `layer` object provides the methods and properties needed to manipulate layers. It allows layers to be hidden, resized, moved, and changed to produce pages that include animated text, overlapping text and images, drop-down menus, and more.

The `screen` object provides information previously inaccessible to the JavaScript programmer about the client's screen resolution and color depth. This is useful in order to ensure that your DHTML pages fit comfortably in a given user's browser window and allows you to adjust the size of type, the layout of pages, and the selection of images to match a user's system.

The `event` object has broad impact beyond the new DHTML features in Netscape Communicator. In combination with DHTML, though, it provides the means to take interactivity to a whole new level.

The `layer` Object

In order to understand the features provided by the `layer` object we need a basic understanding of how layers work. Layers are covered in more detail in Chapter 12, "Dynamic Positioning."

Let's start by looking at the general concept behind layers. Layers exist in a parent/child relationship. That is, one layer can act as a container for another layer. When you create a document with the `<BODY>` tag, that creates a container in which layers can be placed and manipulated.

When layers are created, they can be positioned based on the parent layer containing them or relative to the entire document window. When you create a layer that has no other layers, the entire document is treated as the container layer.

By way of example, Figure 9.1 shows how layers can be placed within each other in this parent/child relationship with the parent containing the child. In this case, Layer B is contained within Layer A, which is contained within the document. Layer B's positioning can be specified relative to Layer A or relative to the document window. Layer A can be positioned relative to the document window.

FIGURE 9.1.
An example of layers containing other layers.

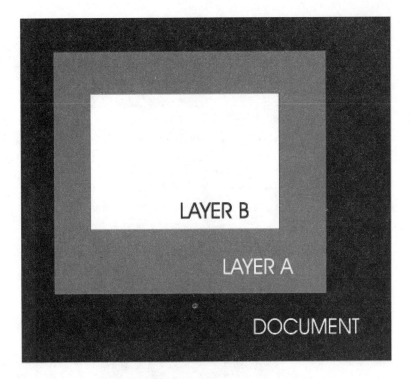

When layers are created, you can set their position relative to the top-left corner of the containing layer, their width and height, their background color or images, the presence or absence and style of borders, and their visibility (layers can initially be visible or hidden when they are created).

Another important aspect of layers is known as *Z-Order*. Z-order refers to the order in which layers are stacked. By default, new layers appear on top of all existing layers. However, this behavior changes when *Z-index*, or the layer's position in the existing Z-order, is explicitly assigned to a layer.

Netscape's Web site at `http://home.netscape.com/` provides an example of the effective use of layers and, specifically, Z-Orders and visibility. In Figure 9.2 we see Netscape's home page as it is displayed in Netscape Communicator. Here, we see the use of layers to produce the main menu in the top-left corner and the Netcenter panel in the bottom right, but underneath the menu. Their Z-Indexes define their relative positions.

In Figure 9.3, you can see how layers that were visible can be hidden—here the Netcenter panel has been hidden.

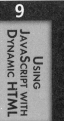

FIGURE 9.2.

Netscape's home page uses Z-Order to control the overlap of the menu and Netcenter panel.

FIGURE 9.3.

Netscape's home page with the Netcenter panel hidden.

Now that you understand the basic concept behind layers, let's take a look at how the `layer` object exposes layers to the programmer. The real power of using JavaScript with layers comes with being able to manipulate the layers. Each layer in a document is reflected as an instance of the `layer` object.

The `layer` object has several properties that reflect all the attributes of a `layer`. These are outlined in Table 9.1.

Table 9.1. Properties of the layer object.

Property	Description
name	The name of the layer. Reflects the NAME attribute.
left	The horizontal position of the left edge relative to the container layer. Reflects the LEFT attribute.
top	The vertical position of the top edge relative to the container layer. Reflects the TOP attribute.
pageX	The horizontal position of the left edge relative to the document window. Reflects the PAGEX attribute.
pageY	The vertical position of the top edge relative to the document window. Reflects the PAGEY attribute.
zIndex	The position of the layer in the Z-order as an integer.
visibility	Indicates if layer is visible. Reflects the VISIBILITY attribute and takes three possible values: show, hide, or inherit.
clip.top	The top of the layer's clipping rectangle in pixels as offset from the top of the layer.
clip.left	The left of the layer's clipping rectangle in pixels as offset from the left side of the layer.
clip.right	The right of the layer's clipping rectangle in pixels as offset from the left side of the layer.
clip.bottom	The bottom of the layer's clipping rectangle in pixels as offset from the top of the layer.
clip.width	The width of the layer's clipping rectangle in pixels.
clip.height.	The height of the layer's clipping rectangle in pixels.
background	The URL of the background image of a layer. Reflects the BACKGROUND attribute. Value is null if there is no background graphic.
bgColor	The color of the background of a layer. Reflects the BGCOLOR attribute. Value is null if the layer is transparent.
siblingAbove	The layer object for the layer above the current one in the Z-order. The value is null if there is no layer above the current one.
siblingBelow	The layer object for the layer below the current one in the Z-order. The value is null if there is no layer below the current one.
above	The layer object for the layer above the current one in the Z-order. The value is the window object if the layer is topmost.
below	The layer object for the layer below the current one in the Z-order. The value is null if there is no layer below the current one.

9

**USING
JAVASCRIPT WITH
DYNAMIC HTML**

continues

Table 9.1. continued

Property	Description
parentLayer	The layer object that contains this layer or the window object if the layer is not nested.
src	The URL of the source file for a layer. Reflects the SRC attribute.

All these properties can be altered by a script with the exception of name, siblingAbove, siblingBelow, above, and parentLayer.

Before going on to an example using a few of these properties, let's consider how to work with these properties. The document object in Communicator has a layers property that is an array of layer objects for all layers contained in the document window. We can use layer names as indexes to this array. So, to refer to a specific layer object, we refer to

```
document.layers["layerName"]
```

This means to refer to a specific property of a given layer we could use

```
document.layers["layerName"].propertyName
```

Now you are ready to do some work with these properties. Let's create a simple page that displays four color squares—each created by using layers of fixed size with different background colors. When the mouse is inside a given layer, you can make it display the color name in the layer and when the mouse moves out of the layer, you can make it remove the color name but leave the background color.

To start, create your layers document:

```
<HTML>
<HEAD>
<TITLE>Color name with Layers</TITLE>
</HEAD>
<BODY>
<LAYER NAME="red" BGCOLOR="red" TOP=10 LEFT=10 WIDTH=100 HEIGHT=100
onMouseOver="this.document.layers['redname'].visibility='show';"
onMouseOut="this.document.layers['redname'].visibility='hide';">
    <LAYER NAME="redname" TOP=10 LEFT=10 VISIBILITY="hide">
    <FONT COLOR=yellow>Red</FONT>
    </LAYER>
</LAYER>
<LAYER NAME="blue" BGCOLOR="blue" TOP=10 LEFT=120 WIDTH=100 HEIGHT=100
onMouseOver="this.document.layers['bluename'].visibility='show';"
onMouseOut="this.document.layers['bluename'].visibility='hide';">
    <LAYER NAME="bluename" TOP=10 LEFT=10 SRC="blue.html" VISIBILITY="hide">
    <FONT COLOR=yellow>Blue</FONT>
    </LAYER>
</LAYER>
<LAYER NAME="green" BGCOLOR="green" TOP=10 LEFT=230 WIDTH=100 HEIGHT=100
onMouseOver="this.document.layers['greenname'].visibility='show';"
onMouseOut="this.document.layers['greenname'].visibility='hide';">
```

```
    <LAYER NAME="greenname" TOP=10 LEFT=10 SRC="green.html" VISIBILITY="hide">
    <FONT COLOR=yellow>Green</FONT>
    </LAYER>
</LAYER>
<LAYER NAME="maroon" BGCOLOR="maroon" TOP=10 LEFT=340 WIDTH=100 HEIGHT=100
onMouseOver="this.document.layers['maroonname'].visibility='show';"
onMouseOut="this.document.layers['maroonname'].visibility='hide';">
    <LAYER NAME="maroonname" TOP=10 LEFT=10 SRC="maroon.html" VISIBILITY="hide">
    <FONT COLOR=yellow>Maroon</FONT>
    </LAYER>
</LAYER>
</BODY>
</HTML>
```

What exactly is going on here? Well, if you look carefully at the positioning of each layer, we have created one row of layers with each layer being a square 100 pixels by 100 pixels. The layers are spaced 10 pixels apart on all sides.

Each layer has a different background color and an embedded layer. The embedded layer is initially hidden and contains the name of the color to be displayed when the user points at the square.

In addition, each layer has two *event handlers.* Event handlers are covered in detail later in this chapter. For now, it's enough to understand that an event handler is used to indicate what JavaScript code to execute when an event occurs. For instance, onMouseOver is used to specify what to do when the user moves the mouse over an object while onMouseOut specifies actions to take when the mouse is moved off the object.

In this particular example, the onMouseOver event handler changes the visibility property for the current layer object to make the layer visible.

Notice that we use the special keyword this in each event handler to refer to the object for the current tag—in this case, the current layer object. This makes it easy to indicate the child layer relative to the parent layer.

Similar to the onMouseOver event handler, the onMouseOut event handler sets the visibility property to hide to hide the layer when the user removes the mouse from the layer.

When put all together, the results look like Figure 9.4.

In addition to all these properties, the layer object has several methods associated with it. These are listed in Table 9.2.

FIGURE 9.4.
With JavaScript we can manipulate the visibility of layers.

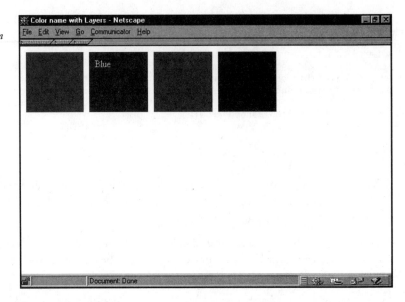

Table 9.2. Methods of the layer object.

Name	Description
moveBy(x,y)	Moves the layer by the number of pixels x and y. x and y can be negative or positive integers.
moveTo(x,y)	Moves the layer to the position indicated by x and y. This position is relative to the containing layer or, in the case of in-line layers, its natural position in the flow of the document.
moveToAbsolute(x,y)	Moves the layer to the position indicated by x and y relative to the document window instead of the container layer.
resizeBy(width,height)	Resizes the layer by the number of pixels provided as arguments. The content of the layer will not be relayed out, so this may clip some of the content if the size of a layer is reduced.
moveAbove(layer)	Moves the current layer above the layer provided as an argument.
moveBelow(layer)	Moves the current layer below the layer provided as an argument.
load(filename,width)	Loads filename in the layer and changes the width of the layer to width.

After seeing this table, you are probably wondering what exactly you could do with these methods. Here are two possibilities:

- Animate text—By moving a layer containing text across the page you can create the impression of animated, moving text.
- Transition effects—By moving non-transparent layers across lower layers you can create wipes or curtain effects for transitions between documents.

By way of example, let's create a page to display an in-line layer and then provide controls to animate the content of that layer. Users should be able to do the following:

- Determine the direction the layer should be moving
- Start and stop the animation

The page's source code would look like this:

```
<HTML>

  <HEAD>
  <TITLE>The Animated Word</TITLE>

  <SCRIPT LANGUAGE="JavaScript1.2">
  <!--

     var animate=true;
     var x=1;
     var y=0;

     function doMove() {

        if (animate) {
           document.layers["word"].moveBy(x,y);
           setTimeout("doMove()",300);
        }
     }

  //-->
  </SCRIPT>

  </HEAD>

  <BODY>

    <FORM>

       <TABLE WIDTH=100%><TR VALIGN=TOP>
       <TD WIDTH=25% ALIGN=LEFT>

          <INPUT TYPE=button VALUE="START" onClick="animate=true; doMove();"><BR>
          <INPUT TYPE=button VALUE="STOP" onClick="animate=false">

       </TD><TD WIDTH=50% ALIGN=CENTER>

          <INPUT TYPE=button VALUE="UP" onClick='x=0;y=-1'><BR>
          <INPUT TYPE=button VALUE="LEFT" onClick='x=-1;y=0'>
          <INPUT TYPE=button VALUE="RIGHT" onClick='x=1;y=0'><BR>
          <INPUT TYPE=button VALUE="DOWN" onClick='x=0;y=1'><BR>
```

```
        </TD>
        </TR></TABLE>

    </FORM>

    <HR>

    <H1><ILAYER VISIBILITY=SHOW NAME="word">Word</ILAYER></H1>

    </BODY>

</HTML>
```

This produces a simple interface like the one shown in Figure 9.5.

FIGURE 9.5.

A simple text animation program.

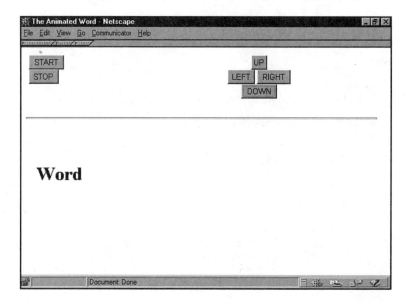

Here's how it works from the user's point of view: The default direction of motion is to the right. If the user clicks start, the word starts moving. If the user clicks a direction button, the word stops moving. The user can change speeds with the appropriate buttons and can stop the motion by clicking the stop button.

Underneath, there is a little more going on, but the program is surprisingly simple, thanks to layers.

There are three key variables:

- animate—This variable indicates whether the word is currently moving or stopped. Possible values are true and false.

- x—Indicates the direction of horizontal motion at any given time. A value of 1 indicates movement to the right, -1 to the left, and 0 vertical motion.

■ y—Indicates the direction of vertical motion at any given time. A value of 1 indicates movement down, -1 up, and 0 horizontal motion.

The other main component of the script is the function doMove(). This function is initially called when the user clicks the start button. The function does a few simple things. First, it checks the value of animate: if it is false, the function exits.

If animate is true, however, the function needs to move the word. The first thing that happens is the moveBy() method of the layer object moves the object in the direction indicated by x and y. Each time doMove() is called, the word is moved one pixel in a given direction. Finally, setTimeout() is used to schedule the next movement of the word, with speed indicating how long to wait before calling doMove() again. In this way, doMove() keeps getting called, at the intervals indicated by the value of the variable speed, until animate changes the value to false.

Now, let's look at what happens when the user clicks each button. The start and stop buttons are simple. Using the onClick event handler, the start button sets animate to true and calls doMove() to start the animation. Stop simply sets animate to false. If animate had been true, then doMove() will be called as scheduled by the last call and with animate set to false, motion will stop.

The direction buttons all do basically the same thing: They set the values of x and y as needed to change motion to the requested direction. If animate is true then the next scheduled call to doMove() will start animating with the new values of x and y.

There is one interesting point to note here. We use in-line layers so the layer simply sits on the line after the horizontal rule. (In-line layers are discussed later in Chapter 12.) There is no need for sizing or positioning the layer. Another interesting point is that the layer can move anywhere in the document window including up into the control area above the horizontal rule as shown in Figure 9.6.

The screen Object

Another new object in JavaScript 1.2 is the screen object. With the screen object, it's possible to ensure that your content fits on a user's screen without difficulty and to ensure that your layouts aren't altered by excessively large or small displays.

The screen object provides six properties for verifying the properties of the user's display but offers no methods, as outlined in Table 9.3.

Table 9.3. Properties of the screen object.

Name	Description
availHeight	Indicates the height of the screen in pixels after taking into account user interface features such as taskbars or menu bars displayed by the operating system.

continues

Table 9.3. continued

Name	Description
availWidth	Indicates the width of the screen in pixels after taking into account user interface features such as taskbars or menu bars displayed by the operating system.
height	Indicates the height of the screen in pixels without taking into account user interface features.
width	Indicates the width of the screen in pixels without taking into account user interface features.
pixelDepth	Indicates the number of bits per pixel—this generally correlates with colorDepth (for example, a pixelDepth of 8 matches a colorDepth of 256, a pixelDepth of 4 matches a colorDepth of 16, and so on).
colorDepth	Indicates the number of colors that can be displayed—this generally correlates with pixelDepth (for example, a colorDepth of 256 matches a pixelDepth of 8, a colorDepth of 16 matches a pixelDepth of 4, and so on).

FIGURE 9.6.

The layer can move anywhere in the window.

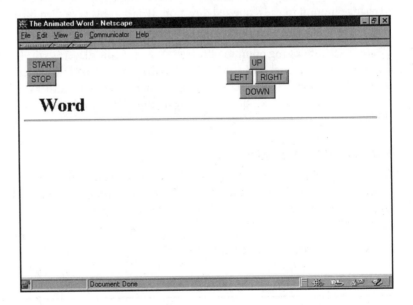

It's important to note that, unlike most properties of the layer object, the values of the properties of the screen object cannot be set by a script.

To show how to use these properties, we can create a simple HTML page that loads the correct version of a title image based on the width of a user's screen:

```
<HTML>
<HEAD>
<TITLE>screen Object Example</TITLE>
</HEAD>
<BODY>
<SCRIPT LANGUAGE="JavaScript1.2">
if (screen.availWidth <= 640) {
    document.writeln('<IMG SRC="small.gif">');
} else if (screen.availWidth <= 800) {
    document.writeln('<IMG SRC="medium.gif">');
} else {
    document.writlen('<IMG SRC="large.gif">');
}
</SCRIPT>
</BODY>
```

What this page does is really very simple. The script first checks if the available width is less than or equal to 640 pixels. If it is, then the smallest title image is used. Failing that, the script checks if the width is less than or equal to 800 pixels and if so loads the next largest title. Finally, if both conditions have failed, the largest image is loaded. This produces results similar to Figures 9.7 and 9.8.

FIGURE 9.7.

With a low screen resolution the smallest title is loaded.

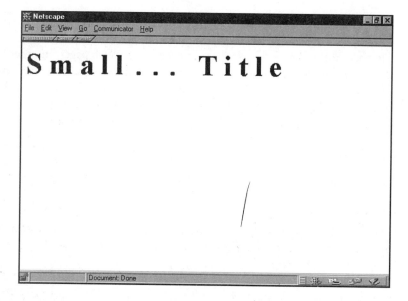

Events in JavaScript 1.2

Events are the key to making JavaScript such a useful tool. With the advent of JavaScript 1.2, the mechanisms for handling events has been greatly expanded and its flexibility and power increased. In this section, we are going to focus on several new features found in Netscape Communicator and particularly how they work with DHTML.

FIGURE 9.8.

*On an average 800 ×
600 pixel SVGA
display, the medium
title would be loaded.*

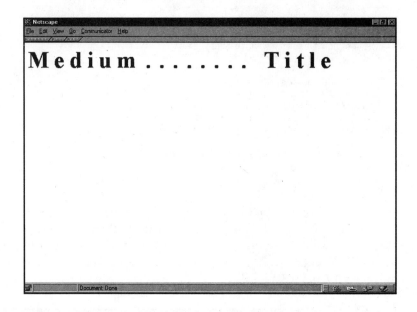

What Are Events?

The main role of JavaScript is to add interactivity to Web pages. In order for this to happen, scripts need to be written to react to actions the user makes. These actions can be anything from moving the mouse to typing on the keyboard to clicking a button. User actions create events and programmers can write event handlers—pieces of JavaScript code that run whenever a particular event occurs—to create interactivity when these actions occur.

For example, you find forms on the Web that tell you the data you entered is invalid before ever submitting the data to the server (as shown in Figure 9.9) or pages that pop up dialog boxes asking you for information before displaying the page.

Types of Events

Different objects or page elements can have different types of events associated with them and, by extension, different types of event handlers. Table 9.4 outlines the types of events that exist in JavaScript 1.2.

Table 9.4. Events in JavaScript 1.2.

Name	*When It Happens*
Abort	User aborts loading of an image
Blur	User or script removes focus from a form element, window, or frame
Change	User removes focus from a select, text, or textarea field and the content of the field has changed
Click	User clicks link or form element

Name	When It Happens
DblClick	User double-clicks link or form element
DragDrop	User drops object on a Navigator window
Error	Loading of a document or image causes an error
Focus	User or script gives focus to a form element, window, or frame
KeyDown	User presses a key
KeyPress	User presses and holds a key down
KeyUp	User releases a key
Load	A document or frameset completes loading
MouseDown	User presses a mouse button
MouseUp	User releases a mouse button
MouseMove	User moves the cursor
MouseOut	User moves the cursor out of an object
MouseOver	User moves the cursor over an object
Move	User or script moves a window or a frame
Reset	User resets a form
Resize	User or script resizes a window or frame
Select	User selects some text in a text or textarea field
Submit	User submits a form
Unload	User or script exits a document

FIGURE 9.9.

Using event handlers, it is possible to react to user actions, such as clicking a submit button.

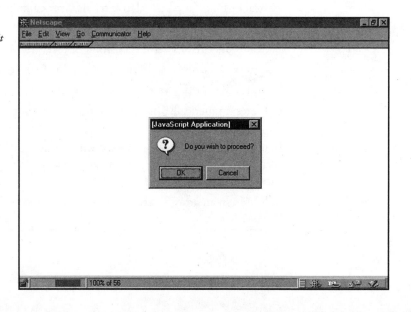

Each of these events has an event handler associated with it. The names of the event handlers are all of this form:

on*EventHandlerName*

Event handlers appear alongside attributes of HTML tags. For instance, to program an action for when the MouseDown event for an image occurs, you could use the following form:

```
<IMG SRC="some image file" onMouseDown="code to execute when the mouse is clicked
on the image">
```

The event Object

The event object is the core of events. The object provides information about the context within which an event occurred and this information can be used in the event handler to ensure that the correct action is taken.

Several properties are available in the event object and these are outlined in Table 9.5.

Table 9.5. Properties of the event object.

Name	Description
type	Indicates the type of event that occurred (for example, MouseDown, KeyPress, Abort, and so on)
target	Indicates the object to which the event was sent
layerX	Indicates the object's width when a resize event occurs or the cursor's horizontal position in pixels relative to the layer containing the object
layerY	Indicates the object's height when a resize event occurs or the cursor's vertical position in pixels relative to the layer containing the object
pageX	Indicates the cursor's horizontal position in pixels relative to the page
pageY	Indicates the cursor's vertical position in pixels relative to the page
screenX	Indicates the cursor's horizontal position in pixels relative to the screen
screenY	Indicates the cursor's vertical position in pixels relative to the screen
which	Indicates, numerically, the mouse button that was pressed or the ASCII value of a pressed key
modifiers	Indicates any modifier keys pressed when a mouse or key event occurs—possible modifier keys are ALT_MASK, CONTROL_MASK, SHIFT_MASK, and META_MASK
data	Indicates, in an array of strings, the URLs of objects dropped in a DragDrop event

It is important to note that the data property of the DragDrop event requires extended privileges granted by signing scripts. See the section on signing scripts later in this chapter for more about the role signed scripts play.

The use of the properties is numerous. To name just a few:

- Allow users to drag files into a Web page from Explorer (Windows 95 and NT) or Finder (Mac) and have that file uploaded to the server.

- Create multiple actions for clicks on a button—for instance, a standard left-click could cause a new page to load, a right-click could pop up another Window asking for information, and a shift-click could display help information.

- Allow the user to select and move layers around inside the Navigator window the way they would move icons around on a Windows 95 or Macintosh desktop.

In order to use the event object, we need to understand how to access it. In a script embedded in an event handler in an HTML tag, we can simply use the keyword event to access the object:

```
<A HREF="Some URL" onClick="alert(event.type)">
```

In addition, the event object is passed as an argument to event handlers.

For instance, in the following example, we create a function to do the same thing as just described, and then explicitly assign it as an event handler to a form button's onClick event:

```
<SCRIPT LANGUAGE="JavaScript1.2">
function type(e) {
    alert(e.type);
    return false;
}
document.testform.testbutton.onclick = type;
</SCRIPT>
<FORM NAME=testform>
<INPUT TYPE=submit NAME=testbutton VALUE="Click Me">
</FORM>
```

Capturing Events

JavaScript 1.2 introduces another capability that greatly extends the capability of JavaScript to deal with events in a robust, comprehensive, and easy to manage fashion. This feature is called event capturing.

Let's consider the following scenario: A Web designer wants to create a page where the user can only click in certain fields of a form and on the submit button. Other fields can't be clicked in and any attempt to do so should generate a warning message for the user.

One way to do this is to write an event handler for each field that you don't want the user to click in and have the handler generate the warning.

However, event capturing provides another alternative. If the window is designated to capture all Click events, then a click anywhere in the window will be handled by the window and its associated onClick event handler. Using a set of four methods, this event handler can determine whether a warning is needed and generate the warning. Table 9.6 describes the methods used for event capturing. Any window, document, or frame can capture events using these methods.

Table 9.6. Methods used in event capturing.

Name	Description
captureEvents(*event names*)	Indicates which events should be captured. Event names take the form Event.CLICK, EVENT.DRAGDROP, and so on. captureEvents can take a list of more than one event separated by |.
releaseEvents(*event names*)	Indicates that the named events should no longer be captured. Event names take the form Event.CLICK, EVENT.DRAGDROP, and so on. captureEvents can take a list of more than one event separated by |.
routeEvent(*event object*)	Indicates that an event handler for the event should be found and executed. If an appropriate handler is found, the handler is executed. The value returned by the handler is returned.
handleEvent(*event object*)	Used to bypass the normal event capturing hierarchy and causes an explicit object to handle the event. For instance, all Click events could be handled by the first link in a page: document.links[0].handleEvent(*captured event object*).

Using these methods for capturing events that occur in pages loaded from servers other than the one the script originates from requires that your script requests extended privileges by signing them appropriately. A discussion of signing scripts is provided later in this chapter.

As a small example of capturing events, the following script allows the window to capture the MouseMove event and use this to display the coordinates to the mouse in the status bar of the window (as shown in Figure 9.10):

```
<SCRIPT LANGUAGE="JavaScript1.2">
function stat(e) {
    self.status = "X: " + e.pageX + ", Y: " + e.pageY;
}
window.captureEvents(Event.MOUSEMOVE);
window.onmousemove = stat;
</SCRIPT>
```

Let's make sure we understand what's happening here. First, we define the stat() function. This function is what will be executed when the MouseMove event occurs. After we have the function defined, we call captureEvents() to capture the MouseMove event. Finally, we need to specify that the stat() function should be called when the event occurs by assigning the function to the event.

FIGURE 9.10.

The mouse coordinates are displayed in the status bar.

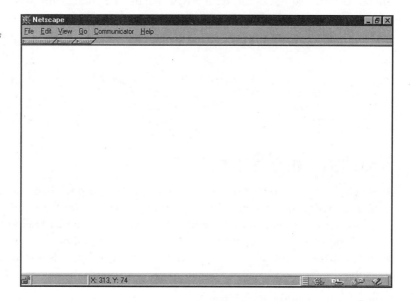

Using External Scripts

Increasingly, JavaScript is being used for more than simply creating forms that can check the data being entered for accuracy or perform simple visual tricks.

With the advent of layers and other components of DHTML and associated expansion of JavaScript in JavaScript 1.2, Web developers will need to—and want to—create sophisticated libraries of functions and objects for reuse in many pages and by many people.

In order for this to be effective, we need a way to maintain these libraries in separate files and then include them in as many pages as are needed. Since JavaScript 1.1, this has been possible using the SRC attribute of the <SCRIPT> tag.

In its simplest form, the SRC attribute can be used like this:

```
<SCRIPT LANGUAGE="Version of JavaScript" SRC="URL of JavaScript library file">
```

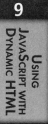

NOTE

For the SRC attribute to work, the name of the JavaScript source files should include the extension .js. In addition, your Web server needs to be configured with the correct file type for JavaScript files. Information about this is available on Netscape's Web site at http://home.netscape.com.

One of the benefits of this approach is that your scripts are automatically hidden from other browsers that don't support JavaScript. At the same time, though, this technique requires an additional server request and server access, which may be problematic on a slow server or across a slow connection to the Internet.

You can combine library files with the SRC attribute with your own scripts using a single <SCRIPT> tag:

```
<SCRIPT LANGUAGE="Version of JavaScript" SRC="URL of JavaScript library file">
<!-- HIDE FROM OTHER BROWSERS
    More JavaScript Code
// STOP HIDING -->
</SCRIPT>
```

Signing Your Scripts

Although the concept of signed scripts may be new in Netscape Communicator, the idea of signing pieces of code isn't. For instance, signing is the basis for the security mechanisms surrounding ActiveX components downloaded by Microsoft Internet Explorer. Using the signature, it is possible to identify the source of a component and determine whether it has been tampered with—possibly maliciously—before you give it permission to run amok on your computer.

Signing scripts requires several steps:

1. Request expanded privileges.
2. Use an ARCHIVE attribute in your <SCRIPT> tags.
3. Use an ID attribute in <SCRIPT> tags for in-line scripts and event handler scripts.
4. Sign your scripts.

Request Expanded Privileges

The whole point of signed scripts is that they can request expanded privileges from the client.

Among the actions you need privileges for are

- Setting properties of the event object
- Getting values of properties of the history object
- Getting the value of the data property from a DragDrop event
- Using the preference method of the navigator object
- Adding or removing directory bars, location bars, menu bars, and similar user interface features
- Capturing events from external pages displayed in a frame
- Moving or placing a window off the screen
- Resizing or creating a window smaller than 100 pixels by 100 pixels
- Generating a file upload

■ Submitting forms to `mailto:` or `news:` URLs

■ Using most `about:` URLs

In order to use these features you need to include an appropriate call to Navigator's Java security classes. This call takes the following form:

```
netscape.security.PrivilegeManager.enablePrivilege("a target");
```

What's important is that you choose the right target for the privilege you are requesting. Table 9.7 outlines the six targets you can request expanded privileges for and what they provide.

Table 9.7. Potential targets for expanded privileges.

Name	*What It Allows You to Do*
`UniversalBrowserRead`	Get the value of properties of the `history` object; get the value of the `data` property of the event object in a `DragDrop` event; use most `about:` URLs
`UniversalBrowserWrite`	Set values of properties of the event object; set values of properties of the `history` object; add or remove directory bars, location bars, menu bars, and similar user interface features; capture events from external pages displayed in a frame; move or place a window off the screen; resize or create a window smaller than 100 pixels by 100 pixels
`UniversalFileRead`	Generate a file upload
`UniversalPreferencesRead`	Get the value of a preference using the `preference` method of the `navigator` object
`UniversalPreferencesWrite`	Set the value of a preference using the `preference` method of the `navigator` object
`UniversalSendMail`	Submit forms to `mailto:` or `news:` URLs

Use ARCHIVE and ID Attributes

All signed scripts are stored in Java archive (JAR) files that include the digital signature. You use the ARCHIVE attribute to indicate the name of the JAR archive in the first <SCRIPT> tag in a page:

```
<SCRIPT ARCHIVE="some JAR file name">
Some JavaScript code
</SCRIPT>
```

This will tell the signing process where the JAR file should be stored.

You can include multiple scripts and event handlers in a page in a single JAR file by simply specifying the JAR file in the first <SCRIPT> tag using the ARCHIVE attribute and then assigning sequential ID values to <SCRIPT> tags and tags with event handlers:

```
<HTML>
<HEAD>
<SCRIPT ARCHIVE="some JAR file name" ID=1>
Some JavaScript code
</SCRIPT>
<SCRIPT ARCHIVE="the same JAR file name as before" SRC="some JavaScript file" ID=2>
</SCRIPT>
</HEAD>
<BODY onLoad="some event handler" onUnload="some event handler" ID=3>
Some HTML
</BODY>
</HTML>
```

Sign Your Scripts

Having made all these changes to a page with scripts in it, you are now ready to sign them. In order to sign a script or scripts, you need a signing tool that signs your script digitally and stores the results in a JAR file. To do this requires a little preparation the first time around:

1. Get an object signing certificate. You can get a certificate from a Certificate Authority or issue your own with Netscape's Certificate Server. Go to the site `http://developer.netscape.com/software/signedobj/jarpack.html` for more information.

2. Download a signing tool. Netscape makes the following tools available on its Web site: JAR Packager (a Java applet for signing Java applets, plug-ins, and other JAR files—see Figure 9.11), JAR Packager Command Line (a stand-alone signing tool), and Page Signer (a Perl script that uses JAR Packager Command Line). More information is available at `http://developer.netscape.com/software/signedobj/jarpack.html`.

FIGURE 9.11.
JAR Packager.

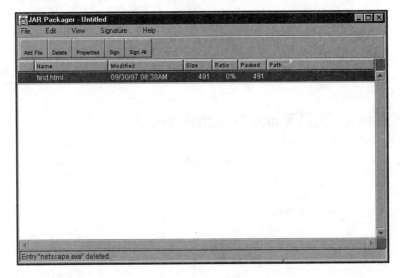

After you have these tools, you need to follow the enclosed instructions to sign the scripts and create the necessary JAR file. Signing scripts requires care to make sure you do it right and it is a good idea to read the overview provided by Netscape at `http://developer.netscape.com/library/documentation/communicator/jsguide/scripts.htm`.

Summary

In this chapter, you learned about just a few ways that JavaScript can be used in Netscape Communicator to work with Dynamic HTML. Most important, you have seen how you can manipulate layers to produce custom and complex visual effects and animation in Web pages. We have taken a look at how the wide range of events in Communicator can be leveraged with JavaScript, and finally how script signing can be used to gain added access to system resources for specialized applications.

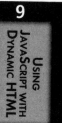

9

USING
JAVASCRIPT WITH
DYNAMIC HTML

CHAPTER 10

Using JavaScript for Internet Explorer Dynamic HTML

by Peter Belesis

IN THIS CHAPTER

If ever there was a classic love/hate relationship, it is that between Microsoft's Internet Explorer and JavaScript. On the love side, IE's major scripting engine, JScript, is a JavaScript parser and most examples on the Microsoft site use "JavaScript" as the scripting language identifier. Then the hate kicks in, and all references to JavaScript are omitted when the time comes for an official definition of JScript.

Such definitions of JScript are plentiful and diverse in the Microsoft documentation. One article describes JScript as "Microsoft's implementation of the ECMAScript scripting language…with some enhancements for Internet Explorer." In another, it is "a powerful scripting language…implemented as a fast, portable, lightweight interpreter for use in World Wide Web browsers and other applications that use ActiveX controls, OLE Automation servers, and Java applets."

Confusing? Very much so, but it doesn't have to be. In this chapter we will try to sift through the petty jargon of bad marketing and shed some light on using JavaScript with IE4.

Microsoft developed a JavaScript parser for Explorer without the assistance of Netscape, the JavaScript originators. Although the purpose of the development was to allow Navigator scripts to run on Explorer, the language that was being parsed was christened JScript.

Through common usage, "JavaScript" has come to mean both the scripting language of Netscape Navigator and the main scripting language of Explorer. "JScript" is regarded as nothing more than an alias for IE's implementation of JavaScript. Because IE's implementation is the topic at hand, the "JScript" identifier will be used in this chapter for IE-specific JavaScript and "JavaScript" for general cross-browser JavaScript.

A Brief History

Netscape introduced JavaScript in Navigator 2. Soon thereafter, JScript 1.0 was built into Explorer 3. Navigator 3 shipped with JavaScript 1.1. JScript 2.0, incorporating many of the JavaScript 1.1 features, became available as an upgrade to Explorer.

Today, Navigator 4 hosts JavaScript 1.2, and Explorer 4 hosts JScript 3.0. Table 10.1 illustrates this development.

JScript 3.0, arriving on the scene last, provides most of the JavaScript 1.2 features, but combined with Explorer's comprehensive Document Object Model (DOM) and CSS property reflection, JScript 3.0 has become a more powerful tool than JavaScript. Given the direction the World Wide Web Consortium (W3C) is taking with the DOM standard, it is likely that JScript's expanded properties and methods will be the model for the next version of JavaScript.

Table 10.1. JScript version history.

Version	JavaScript Compatibility	Shipped In
JScript 1.0	JavaScript 1.0 (NN2)	Explorer 3.0
JScript 2.0	JavaScript 1.1 (NN3)	Explorer 3.02 (some builds) available as upgrade module
JScript 3.0	JavaScript 1.2 (approx.) (NN4)	Explorer 4.0

Using JScript in the HTML Page

Explorer 4 recognizes the following SCRIPT tags as containing JavaScript statements, whether cross-browser or not:

```
<SCRIPT></SCRIPT>
<SCRIPT LANGUAGE="JScript"></SCRIPT>
<SCRIPT LANGUAGE="JavaScript"></SCRIPT>
<SCRIPT LANGUAGE="JavaScript1.1"></SCRIPT>
<SCRIPT LANGUAGE="JavaScript1.2"></SCRIPT>
```

As with JavaScript, JScript statements can be included anywhere on the page. The page position is at the author's discretion, depending on what prerequisites the script has. If the script, for example, refers to a collection outside a function, it is best included at the end, when the collection in question has been created and filled. Functions called after page load are best kept within the HEAD tag.

Unlike JavaScript, JScript has no version identifier available to the LANGUAGE= attribute. Authors can, however, dynamically check for version information with JScript proprietary functions. The next section, "The JScript Script Engine," describes these functions.

Using "JScript" as the LANGUAGE= value is useful for hiding script from Navigator, which does not recognize it. Use this value for Explorer-specific statements. Cross-browser statements should be enclosed in "JavaScript" SCRIPT containers, making it available to both browsers. Even though one is tempted to include DHTML-specific script with the "JavaScript1.2" value (allowing access only to fourth-generation browsers), it is not recommended because there might be popular JavaScript1.1/JScript 2 features—such as the Image object used for rollovers, for example—that may be inadvertently hidden from browsers that support it.

> **TIP**
>
> For cross-browser script, even if there are some code differences, use the LANGUAGE="JavaScript" attribute with browser detection and conditional execution. For Explorer-specific script, use the LANGUAGE="JScript" attribute. Be careful that calls to the functions in the script are not made available to Navigator so you can avoid errors.

Script is usually enclosed between the HTML start and end comment tags, `<!--` and `-->`, hiding it from non-JavaScript browsers. Position the closing identifier, to avoid generating a JavaScript error, after a JavaScript comment identifier:

```
<SCRIPT LANGUAGE="JavaScript">
<!-- hide from non-JavaScript browsers

...include script here...

//--> end hiding, but hide from JavaScript as well
</SCRIPT>
```

JScript does not require the final JavaScript comment. IE will parse the following correctly:

```
<SCRIPT LANGUAGE="JavaScript">
<!-- hide from non-JavaScript browsers

...include script here...

-->
</SCRIPT>
```

The second example generates an error in Navigator if `"JavaScript"` is the LANGUAGE value. With this attribute setting, the use of the JavaScript comments is mandatory. If the script uses `"JScript"`, no Navigator error is generated.

The JScript Script Engine

Unlike Netscape's JavaScript, the rendering engine of which is packaged as an inseparable part of the browser, JScript's engine exists as an external module. This allows for updates to the scripting engine without the need to upgrade the browser. Although we know that Navigator 3 supports JavaScript 1.1, we cannot be sure what version of JScript is supported by Explorer 3. The early releases shipped with JScript 1; the last release shipped with JScript 2. Early release owners had the option of upgrading their engines with a simple download.

Explorer 4, as previously mentioned, is shipped with the JScript 3 engine. Possible bug fixes might lead to a new JScript 3 build—one that would be made available for download. It is not only conceivable but probable that Explorer 4 users will soon be working with different script engines.

With this in mind, JScript, since version 2, has four unique built-in functions that enable authors to identify the exact version and build of the JScript engine used to view their page. The information retrieved from the functions can be used to conditionally execute script. These functions are

■ ScriptEngine() returns the scripting language in use as a string. The three possible values are JScript, VBA (Visual Basic for Applications), and VBScript.

In Explorer 4, if the LANGUAGE= attribute of <SCRIPT> has a value of a JavaScript version or JScript or is omitted completely, ScriptEngine() returns the string "JScript".

- ▪ ScriptEngineMajorVersion() returns the major version number of the script engine as an integer.

  In Explorer 4, this returns 3.

- ▪ ScriptEngineMinorVersion() returns the minor version number of the script engine (after the decimal) as an integer.

  The first release version of Explorer 4 returned 0.

- ▪ ScriptEngineBuildVersion() returns the build version number of the script engine as an integer.

  An October 1, 1997 version of Explorer 4 returned 2026.

The following script combines the four functions to obtain complete information on the engine in use. Because neither JScript 1 nor JavaScript supports these functions, we performed an additional check:

```
<SCRIPT LANGUAGE="JavaScript">
if (typeof(ScriptEngine) + "" != "undefined") {
    se = ScriptEngine();
    seMaj = ScriptEngineMajorVersion();
    seMin = ScriptEngineMinorVersion();
    seB = ScriptEngineBuildVersion();
    fullInfo = (se + " " + seMaj + "." + seMin + " " + seB);
    document.write(fullInfo);
}
else { document.write("JScript 1 or JavaScript") }
</SCRIPT>
```

Using the same sample engine as before, the result is JScript 3.0 2026.

The SRC= Attribute

Explorer 4 recognizes the SRC= attribute of the <SCRIPT> tag and reads and attempts to execute any JavaScript code in the external *.js file. One can assume then that the following tag safely isolates any JScript from parsing attempts by Navigator:

```
<SCRIPT LANGUAGE="Jscript" SRC="IEspec.js"></SCRIPT>
```

Not so. Navigator 4 does not attempt to load the file, true, but Navigator 3 does! Navigator 3 was, of course, the first and, at that time, only browser to recognize the SRC= attribute of <SCRIPT>. Somehow, the eventuality of other browsers, and even newer versions of their own browser, supporting the attribute escaped Netscape. Navigator 3 attempts to execute any external file whether it supports the language specified by the LANGUAGE= attribute or not!

Note the following HTML and the results it produces:

```
<HTML>
<HEAD>
<TITLE>Navigator 3 SRC Bug</TITLE>
</HEAD>
<BODY>
```

```
    <SCRIPT LANGUAGE="JavaScript1.2" SRC="javaExt.js"></SCRIPT>
    <SCRIPT LANGUAGE="JScript" SRC="jsExt.js"></SCRIPT>
    <SCRIPT LANGUAGE="Sanskrit" SRC="sanExt.js"></SCRIPT>
</BODY>
</HTML>
```

The preceding referenced external files each have one line of script:

The file, javaExt.js, has this line:

```
document.write("<BR>I am code in an external JavaScript 1.2 file");
```

The file, jsExt.js, contains this line:

```
document.write("<BR>I am code in an external JScript file");
```

Finally, sanExt.js, has this line:

```
document.write("<BR>I am code in an external Sanskrit file");
```

Explorer 4 produces the results illustrated in Figure 10.1.

FIGURE 10.1.

External JavaScript files—IE4.

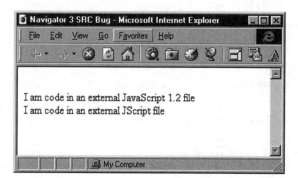

Figure 10.2 illustrates Navigator 4's rendering.

Finally, Navigator 3's erroneous display is visible in Figure 10.3.

TIP

When writing Internet Explorer-specific script in an external file, using the JScript language identifier, don't forget the undocumented Navigator 3 bug that causes that browser to read an external file, regardless of identifier. You must use other isolation techniques, such as browser-detection variables, within the external script.

FIGURE 10.2.

External JavaScript files—Netscape Navigator 4.

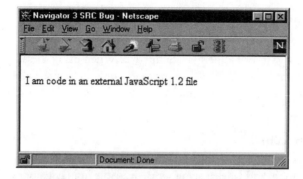

FIGURE 10.3.

External JavaScript files—Netscape Navigator 3.

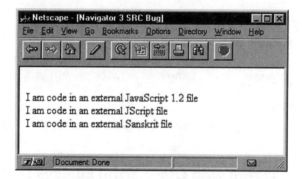

What's New in JScript for Explorer 4

In the Microsoft scheme of things, several scripting engines coexist in the same browser. The objects available to JScript are therefore split into two groups: those specific to JScript and those common to all scripting languages.

The former group has functions, operators, object constructors, statements, pre-DHTML objects, methods and properties, and the like.

The common group has most DHTML objects, object properties, many methods, events, collections, and so on.

Although this differentiation did not exist in older versions, the present division is described as "objects provided by the JScript engine" and "objects provided by Internet Explorer."

Netscape considers all properties, methods, and events as part of JavaScript proper, making the Microsoft dichotomy confusing to Navigator scripters.

New Features Unique to JScript (JavaScript 1.2 Compatible)

The new features that JScript 3.0 does not share with the other script engines are almost 100 percent compatible with Netscape's JavaScript 1.2. When using these features, either enclose the script with a JavaScript 1.2 identifier, or conditionally execute it after testing for DHTML browsers. Differences will be mentioned when we look at the features in detail later in this chapter.

Program Flow Control

JScript 3 provides several new tools for controlling statement execution in scripts. These are the switch, do… while, and labeled statements, available in Navigator as well.

New Properties and Methods for Existing Objects

The Date, Array, and String objects have been expanded. The Date object was expanded to provide better internationalization. The other two objects have new methods for improved manipulation. The string methods can now take regular expressions as arguments.

Regular Expressions

JScript has adapted Perl regular expressions to its own scripting engine for powerful string matching options.

New Features Shared with Other Script Engines (not JavaScript 1.2 Compatible)

As mentioned in the introduction, although the use of these features is attributed to JavaScript in the SCRIPT tag, they are not necessarily cross-browser. Some features, like the Document Object Model reflection properties, are IE-specific, making them available to JScript and the other IE scripting engines. Others, like CSS positioning and many events, are partly compatible with Netscape's version. If "JavaScript" is used as the language identifier, be sure to conditionally execute script after checking for browser compatibility.

Document Object Model

Explorer's comprehensive Document Object Model (DOM) is reflected into JScript with new collections, objects, properties, and methods. Hundreds of new properties and many new methods arise out of this reflection. A detailed discussion can be found in Part IV, "The Document Object Model."

CSS and CSS Positioning

All cascading style sheet properties are also reflected into JScript with the comparable scripting properties. Part II, "Cascading Style Sheets," explores this CSS reflection.

Expanded Event Model

New event reflection and expanded event handling apply to any page element. See Chapter 16, "The Internet Explorer 4.0 Event Model: Event Bubbling," for IE's unique approach to events.

The remainder of this chapter will concentrate on the new unique-to-JScript features, which are cross-browser JavaScript compatible.

Program Flow Control

More often than not, a script is called upon to execute a statement or group of statements only if certain conditions are met. Conditional statements such as if...else and loops such as for and while have been a mainstay of JScript since version 1. JScript 3 introduces the do...while, switch, and labeled statements.

do...while

Familiar from C, the do...while loop executes a block of statements once and then repeats the execution until a specified condition returns false. This obligatory run-through is the difference between it and the older, plain while loop. The following example demonstrates both loops. The do...while loop displays the value of counter once even though it is already out of the range of acceptable values (according to the while condition). The simple while loop does not display anything because it compares values on the first execution as well.

```
<HTML>
<HEAD>
<TITLE>while Test</TITLE>
<SCRIPT LANGUAGE="JavaScript">

if (!document.all) {return}

function loop() {
    counter = 1;
    do {
        first.insertAdjacentHTML("BeforeEnd",counter);
        counter++;
    } while (counter<1)

    counter = 1;
    while (counter<1) {
        second.insertAdjacentHTML("BeforeEnd",counter);
        counter++;
    }
}
```

```
</SCRIPT>
</HEAD>
<BODY>

<P><A HREF="javascript:loop()">while away</A></P>
<P ID="first">do...while: </P>
<P ID="second">while: </P>

</BODY>
</HTML>
```

> **NOTE**
>
> In the preceding example, a "JavaScript" identifier was used for the script. Even though the statements being demonstrated are cross-browser, the method used for displaying the results (`insertAdjacentHTML()`) is IE specific. Therefore, a check was performed that returned any non-IE4 browser, avoiding errors. This method of browser detection is discussed later in the section, "Scripting for Both Explorer and Navigator."

Labeled Statements

Any statement can have a label identifier. It can be a single-line statement or a compound statement enclosed in braces, such as `if` or `while` in the following example. Labels appear on the lines before the statements they identify and end with a colon.

```
1     abel :
2     if (brothersKeeper) {
3          ...statements...
4          cain :
5          while (marked) {
6               ...statements...
7               break abel;
8               ...statements...
9          }
10         ...statements...
11    }
12 ...rest of script...
```

In the example, the `abel` label is associated with the `if` conditional—that is, lines 2-11. Similarly, `cain` identifies the `while` loop, lines 5-9. The line execution proceeds as follows:

> If the `brothersKeeper` boolean evaluates to `true`, the `if` statements are executed line by line. The labeled `while` loop is entered if `marked` is `true`. When the `break abel` is encountered, program execution in `abel` is terminated and continues after the `if` closing brace. Therefore, lines 1, 2, 3, 4, 5, 6, 7, and 12 are executed.

> If `brothersKeeper` is `true` and `marked` is `false`, lines 1, 2, 3, 4, 5, 11, and 12 are executed.

Although you can use labeled statements in any if, while, do...while, and for group of statements, the most common use is with the new switch statement.

switch

Instead of using multiple if or nested if...else statements, authors can create a lookup table of sorts by matching a label to an expression's value. If the label preceded by the case identifier matches the expression, the statements immediately following are executed. Execution continues until a break statement is encountered. If no listed label matches the expression, then the default case is executed.

The following example assumes that three functions are accessible from the keyboard. A key press of "N" or "n" calls the goNext() function, "P" or "p" calls the goPrev() function, and "X" or "x" calls the exit() function. The document.onkeypress event handler calls the function getKey() to process the key press. After the passed ASCII integer value is converted to a string and made lowercase for easier lookup, the switch statement compares the string to a list of possible values and executes the corresponding code. If no comparison returns true, then the default code is executed. In this case, the default action is to break out of the lookup with no further processing.

```javascript
function getKey() {
    whichKey = String.fromCharCode(event.keyCode).toLowerCase();
    switch (whichKey) {
        case "n":
            goNext();
            break;
        case "p":
            goPrevious();
            break;
        case "x":
            exit();
            break;
        default:
            break;
    }
}

document.onkeypress = getKey;
```

Use switch when multiple values may exist for an expression, as in the key press example. If another key action is to be defined, simply insert another case statement.

New Properties and Methods for Existing Objects

The rapid internationalization of the Web has prompted the inclusion of new methods for the JavaScript Date object. At the same time, DHTML's need for improved string manipulation has led to the creation of new String methods.

10

USING
JAVASCRIPT FOR
IE DHTML

The Date Object

JScript 3 has expanded the Date object in accordance with ECMA and JavaScript 1.2, with several new methods.

To demonstrate the new methods, let us first create a sample Date object called samsDate. In our example the date is "December 1, 1997" and the time is 13:21:20. Our computer is in New York, keeping New York time, which is five hours earlier than Universal Coordinated Time (Greenwich mean time). The method arguments are self-explanatory with two exceptions: The second argument, the month, is 0-indexed, so the twelfth month, December, is 11. The final argument is a millisecond count, included for completeness.

```
samsDate = new Date(97,11,1,13,21,20,676);
```

The following table documents the changes in our samsDate object as we use the new methods:

Method	*Action*	*New Value of* samsDate
Local Date Methods		
samsDate.setFullYear(1966)	stores 1966 as year	December 1, 1966 13:21:20:676
samsDate.getFullYear()	returns 1966	
samsDate.setMilliseconds(898)	stores 898 as milliseconds	December 1, 1966 13:21:20:898
samsDate.getMilliseconds()	returns 898	
UTC (GMT) Methods		
samsDate.setUTCFullYear(1996)	stores 1996 as UTC year	December 1, 1996 18:21:20:898 UTC
samsDate.getUTCFullYear()	returns 1996	
samsDate.setUTCMonth(6)	stores 6 (July) as UTC month	July 1, 1996 18:21:20:898 UTC
samsDate.getUTCMonth()	returns 6	
samsDate.setUTCDate(4)	stores 4 as UTC date	July 4, 1996 18:21:20:898 UTC
samsDate.getUTCDate()	returns 4	
samsDate.setUTCHours(8)	stores 8 as UTC hour	July 4, 1996 09:21:20:898 UTC
samsDate.getUTCHours()	returns 8 (9 a.m.)	

Method	Action	New Value of samsDate
UTC (GMT) Methods		
samsDate.setUTCMinutes(55)	stores 55 as UTC minutes	July 4, 1996 09:55:20:898 UTC
samsDate.getUTCMinutes()	returns 55	
samsDate.setUTCSeconds(44)	stores 44 as UTC seconds	July 4, 1996 09:55:44:898 UTC
samsDate.getUTCSeconds()	returns 44	
samsDate.setUTCMilliseconds(989)	stores 989 as UTC milliseconds	July 4, 1996 09:55:44:989 UTC
samsDate.getUTCMilliseconds()	returns 989	
samsDate.getUTCDay()	returns 4 (Thursday)	
samsDate.toUTCString()	returns Thu, 04 Jul 1996 09:55:44 UTC	
Local Date/Time String (old feature, for comparison only)		
samsDate.toLocaleString()	returns 07/ 04/96 04:55:44	

JScript has one unique Date method, unsupported by JavaScript1.2. You can use the getVarDate() method with ActiveX or custom objects accepting date values in VT_DATE format. In the example, samsDate.getVarDate() returns "Thu, Jul 4 04:55:44 UTC-0500 1996".

The String Object

Explorer 4 provides many scripting objects, properties, and methods for manipulating text. Chapter 11, "Dynamically Changing Content," discusses several of these. Because text is nothing but a string, JScript 3 introduces new methods for the old String object, giving authors many tools for user-input interaction, conditional page updates, form-input verification, and many instances of dynamic decision-making and changes.

All the new methods are compatible with JavaScript 1.2.

Because all programmers are by now tired of the over-used "Hello World" sample string, the methods outlined in the following paragraphs use a new and unique string:

```
samsStr = "Hello There World"
```

charCodeAt()

A sibling of the old `charAt()` method, `charCodeAt()` returns the Unicode (ASCII) encoding of the character at the indexed location in the string.

```
stringReference.charCodeAt(index)
```

`samsStr.charCodeAt(0)` returns 72 (the encoding of H).

fromCharCode()

The `fromCharCode()` method takes one or more codes and creates a new `String` object. To use it, assign the new object to a variable.

```
String.fromCharCode(encoding1, encoding2, encodingn)
```

In the following example, `newStr` has a value of H:

```
newStr = String.fromCharCode(72);
```

Several codes, included as arguments, create a multicharacter string. In the next example, `newStr` has a value of `Hello`:

```
newStr = String.fromCharCode(72, 101, 108, 108, 111);
```

`fromCharCode()` is most often used with the new onkeypress event handler. The `switch` statement example in this chapter illustrates a real-world use.

concat()

`concat()` is a more efficient way to achieve string concatenation than the old `"string1 + string2"`. The following example combines a second string with an original string, changing the value of the original string. The syntax is

```
stringReference1 = stringReference1.concat(stringReference2)
```

Let's combine a new string with our `samsStr` example:

```
moreStr = " and Hockey Fans"
samsStr = samsStr.concat(moreStr)
```

The value of `samsStr` is now `"Hello There World and Hockey Fans"`.

You can also use the following, which creates a new third string with the concatenated first and second strings:

```
stringReference3 = stringReference1.concat(stringReference2)
```

Still using our `samsStr` example, the following code results in `newStr` having a value of `"Hello There World and Hockey Fans"` with `samsStr` retaining its original value of `"Hello There World"`.

```
newStr = samsStr.concat(moreStr)
```

slice()

The `slice()` method returns a new `String` object containing a substring of the original string, which can be assigned to a variable for later use. The syntax is

```
stringReference.slice(index)
```

With only one argument, the string section that is returned begins at the specified index and ends at the end of the string being sliced. In the following example, `newStr` is created with a value of `"There World"`.

```
newStr = samsStr.slice(6)
```

An optional second argument defines the endpoint of the section:

```
stringReference.slice(index1, index2)
```

In the following example, `newStr` has a value of `"There"`:

```
newStr = samsStr.slice(6,11);
```

The second argument may be a negative index, in which case the endpoint is found by offsetting from the string's termination. This integer is not zero based, so the first negative character accessible is the second-to-last one.

```
stringReference.slice(index1, -index2)
```

In this example, `newStr` has a value of `"There Worl"`:

```
newStr = samsStr.slice(6,-1)
```

And in this example, `newStr` has a value of `"There"`:

```
newStr = samsStr.slice(6,-6)
```

split()

If we need to create an array of strings out of a single string—to use in searches, for example—we provide `split` with a substring argument on which to divide the original string. The substring is replaced with the standard array comma delimiters. The `Array` object is created automatically. The substring argument can be a regular expression. The syntax is

```
arrayReference = stringReference.split(substring)
```

The following code creates an array named `newArray`, which contains three array elements, `"Hello"`, `"There"`, and `"World"`, since the string was broken on instances of the space character:

```
newArray = samsStr.split(" ")
```

`newArray[0]` has a value of `"Hello"`. `newArray[1]` is `"There"` and `newArray[2]` is `"World"`.

In the next example, where we split on the double "l", `newArray` has two elements, "He" and "o There World":

```
newArray = samsStr.split("ll")
```

Therefore, newArray[0] has a value of "He" and newArray[1] is "o There World".

We can also use a regular expression as the split() argument. Regular expressions are discussed later in the section "Regular Expressions."

The following assignment creates a regular expression for matching all instances of the letter "l" (g for global).

```
re = /l/g
```

We include the regular expression variable in our method, as we would any substring variable:

```
newArray = samsStr.split(re);
```

The preceding returns the array "He,o There Wor,d", where newArray[0] is "He", newArray[1] is "o There Wor", and newArray[2] is "d".

If we use the preceding example with a substring instead of a regular expression, the result is different. The second "l" in "Hello" creates an array element with a null value—that is, the following example returns an array of "He,,o There Wor,d".

```
newArray = samsStr.split("l")
```

In this case, newArray[0] is "He", newArray [1] has a value of null, newArray[2] is "o There Wor", and newArray[3] is "d".

Both examples have their uses. Keep in mind that a seemingly identical substring and regular expression can generate different results.

search()

Step aside, indexOf()! search() does everything this old method did and with regular expressions as well. The syntax options for this method are

stringReference.search(*substring*)

stringReference.search(*regExp*)

Like indexOf(), search returns the zero-based index of the substring's location in a successful search. In an unsuccessful search, it returns -1.

In the following example, newInd has a value of 2, the index of the double "l".

```
newInd = samsStr.search("ll")
```

The regular-expression version of the above also returns 2:

```
newInd = samsStr.search(/ll/)
```

Searching for a nonexistent substring returns -1, as in the following:

```
newInd = samsStr.search("oo")
```

replace()

The `replace()` method, of course, replaces a portion of a string with new text. It finds the portion to be replaced through a string or regular-expression argument. The power of this method is demonstrated only if a regular expression is used, simply because the substring argument cannot specify a complex search string or global and conditional replacements. The two syntax options are

```
stringReference.replace(findString,replaceString)
```

```
stringReference.replace(regExp,replaceString)
```

Using a substring argument, we will have only the first instance replaced. In this example, `newStr` is "Herlo There World":

```
newStr = samsStr.replace("l","r");
```

With a regular-expression argument, we can replace all instances of a substring. In the following example, `newStr` is "Herro There Worrd":

```
newStr = samsStr.replace(/l/g,"r");
```

match()

The `match()` method, like `split()`, returns an array of values corresponding to the matches found of a substring or regular expression in a target string.

The following example, using a substring argument, returns a single-array element with a value of "l", the matched substring:

```
newArray = samsStr.match("l");
```

In IE4, three additional, nonindexed, named elements are also created, providing useful information about the match. The complete `newArray` would be

```
newArray[input] = "Hello There World"
newArray[index] = 2
newArray[lastIndex] = 3
newArray[0] = "l"
```

`newArray[input]` stores the string on which the match was performed. `newArray[index]` is the *inclusive start index* of the match. Because we are dealing with a zero-based index, the first occurrence of "l", the third letter, is 2. `newArray[lastIndex]` is the noninclusive end index of the match—in our case the very next letter, the second "l".

NOTE

Only the indexed array elements are compatible with JavaScript 1.2. The three additional named elements are JScript specific.

If we use a global regular expression as an argument, `newArray` will have three indexed elements, the three occurrences of "1":

```
newArray = samsStr.match(/1/g);
```

`newArray` has the following elements:

```
newArray[input] = "Hello There World"
newArray[index] = 15
newArray[lastIndex] = 16
newArray[0] = "1"
newArray[1] = "1"
newArray[2] = "1"
```

Because we have more than one match, `newArray[index]` and `newArray[lastIndex]` now store the inclusive start and noninclusive end indices of the *final* match, respectively.

Let's use a slightly more complex regular expression in another match. This time we will match any "1" that is followed by any word character:

```
newArray = samsStr.match(/1\w/g)
```

This time `newArray` has the following elements:

```
newArray[input] = "Hello There World"
newArray[index] = 15
newArray[lastIndex] = 17
newArray[0] = "11"
newArray[1] = "1d"
```

The new `String` methods combined with the power of regular expressions give the Web page author unprecedented flexibility over page presentation. Unfortunately, this power is taking a back seat to WOW! features of DHTML, such as element animation.

The next section illustrates a simple, timesaving, resource-efficient application.

Regular Expressions

JScript 3 introduces, parallel with JavaScript 1.2, the powerful regular expression tool for string matching, replacing, and manipulation. JScript regular expressions are based on the Perl model, and those familiar with Perl will come up to speed immediately and notice very few differences.

A complete examination of regular expressions is beyond the scope of this chapter. Regular expressions have an extensive library of pattern identifiers, metacharacters, and modifiers. Here we provide a short introduction that lets you immediately begin using regular expressions.

A regular expression string "pattern" is delimited by forward slashes without the normal string-enclosing quotes. If you want to match the string `"Static HTML"`, you can create a regular expression by simple pattern enclosure:

```
samsOrig = "Static HTML is here and static HTML will last forever";
samsPattern = /Static HTML/;
```

```
samsNew = "Dynamic HTML";
samsOrig = samsOrig.replace(samsPattern, samsNew);
```

Our string, `samsOrig`, now has the value of "`Dynamic HTML is here and static HTML will last forever`".

A pattern can have modifiers. Two of the most often used are `g` for global matching and `i` for case-insensitive matching. They are simply appended after the slashes in the regular expression:

```
samsOrig = "Static HTML is here and static HTML will last forever";
samsPattern = /static hTmL/gi;
samsNew = "Dynamic HTML";
samsOrig = samsOrig.replace(samsPattern, samsNew);
```

`samsOrig` is now "`Dynamic HTML is here and Dynamic HTML will last forever`".

You can add metacharacters inside the slashes. Escape these characters with backslashes to avoid confusion with regular text:

> `\w` matches only letters, numbers, or underscores. It was demonstrated previously in the `match()` example.
>
> `\b` matches a word boundary (space, period, and so on).

In the following example, "st" will be matched only if it begins a word:

```
samsOrig = "Static HTML is here and static HTML will last forever";
samsPattern = /\bst/gi;
samsNew = "Acrob";
samsOrig = samsOrig.replace(samsPattern, samsNew);
```

The two instances of "st" beginning a word are replaced, but the "st" in the word "last" is not. `samsOrig` is now "`Acrobatic HTML is here and Acrobatic HTML will last forever`".

In the same way, we can match instances of "st" that occur at the end of a word:

```
samsPattern = /st\b/gi;
samsNew = "Acrob";
samsOrig = samsOrig.replace(samsPattern, samsNew);
```

`samsOrig` now has a value of: "`Static HTML is here and static HTML will laAcrob forever`".

Many more modifiers, metacharacters, and special characters exist. Complete documentation of the JavaScript implementation can be found on both the JavaScript 1.2 site at `http://developer.netscape.com/library/documentation/communicator/jsguide/js1_2.htm`, and the JScript site at `http://www.microsoft.com/jscript/`.

In addition to the literal representation of the regular-expression pattern, JScript lets you create an instance of the new object `RegExp` to contain the pattern. This is a good idea if the code repeatedly uses the pattern.

The following example demonstrates simple regular-expression use combined with the new string methods to dynamically add links to a Web page.

Consider this probable real-world scenario: A large educational, commercial, or technical site needs many in-page links to other pages—some on other servers, others on the same server. Keywords identify these links in the page proper. For example, a reference to Microsoft certainly gets a `<A HREF="www.microsoft.com">Microsoft</A>` link. This is a well-known URL that is not about to change. Other URLs might change. How do you change all links on all pages? A new URL appears and should get linked from many of the pages already posted. How can you change or append them quickly and efficiently?

The example has a simple English course outline snippet from a university. Several authors are mentioned in the course blurb. These authors might have pages to be linked in the bibliography page of the site. To avoid constantly updating the course page if new information is added to the bibliography page, you create a routine to dynamically create links each time the page is loaded, reflecting all changes and additions.

The whole script or just the referenced string can be in an external file. Making adjustments to the single string in the one external JScript file changes the links on possibly hundreds of Web pages:

```
<HTML>
<HEAD>

<SCRIPT LANGUAGE="JScript" SRC="authList.js"></SCRIPT>

<SCRIPT LANGUAGE="JScript">

// begin contents of minimum possible external file

    authLinked = "Roth, Dickens"

// end contents of possible external file

    function makeLinks() {

        allText = document.body.innerHTML;
        URLText = "bibliography.html#"

    pattern = /\s*,\s*/
    arAuthLink = authLinked.split(pattern);

    for (count=0; count<arAuthLink.length; count++) {

        searchStr = arAuthLink[count];
            URLText = URLText.concat(searchStr.charAt(0));

            replaceStr = searchStr.link(URLText);

        patternSearch = new RegExp(searchStr, "g");
            allText = allText.replace(patternSearch, replaceStr);
        }

        document.body.innerHTML = allText;

    }
```

```
</SCRIPT>
</HEAD>
<BODY onLoad="makeLinks()">

<P>English Literature 101 will introduce you to the pantheon of British
and American writers. Among the many masterpieces to be studied will be
works by Charles Dickens, Herman Melville, Martin Amis, Norman Mailer, and
Philip Roth.</P>

</BODY>
</HTML>
```

Step by Step

The SCRIPT, which could be contained completely in an external file, has a string assignment and the makeLinks() function. The string assignment should be in an external file, allowing it to be referenced by multiple pages.

A string therefore hosts the names of the authors the bibliography page has references to. In the example, it contains "Roth" and "Dickens."

The body HTML has no links, just the plain text. Figure 10.4 illustrates the display of the body HTML, before our script is run.

FIGURE 10.4.

The non-dynamic display.

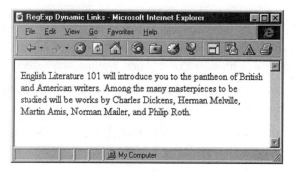

When the page loads, the onLoad event handler of the BODY tag calls the one and only function: makeLinks().

The function immediately stores all the page HTML (all the HTML between <BODY> and </BODY>, that is) in a string variable.

It also initializes a string variable containing the bibliography page URL. This string ends with a hash. Assume that the bibliography page has named anchors for each letter of the alphabet. The created link takes the user straight to the named anchor.

A regular-expression pattern is assigned to the variable `pattern`. This regular expression uses the `\s` metacharacter, which matches any white space. White space can be a space, line feed, form feed, tab, and so on. It also uses the special character `*`, which matches zero or more occurrences of the preceding character. Therefore, the regular expression matches any comma that may or may not be preceded by some white space and may or may not be followed by some white space.

This pattern is then used to create an array from the author string using the `split()` method. The array now has the following elements:

```
arAuthLink[0] = "Roth"
arAuthLink[1] = "Dickens"
```

Using the `for` loop, the script cycles through the array one element at a time. First, the element (author's name) is assigned to the variable `searchStr`.

The next line uses the old string method `charAt()` to isolate the first character of the author's name. This letter is then appended to the `URLtext` variable with the new `concat()` method. In the case of the first author, Roth, `URLtext` now contains `bibliography.html#R`.

The very powerful, but rarely used, old JScript and JavaScript method `link()` is then used to create the appropriate HTML link text. This text is stored in the `replaceStr` variable.

`replaceStr` contains `"<A HREF='bibliography.html#R'>Roth</A>"`.

An instance of the `RegExp` object is created to be used in the search. The object takes two arguments—the string pattern and any modifiers. The author's name of course, is the string to be searched for, and the search must be global. These arguments are the same as using `/Roth/g`.

Finally, the script searches for the unlinked author's name throughout the body HTML variable and replaces it with the linked version.

The new body HTML is displayed on the page when it is assigned back to the body's `innerHTML` property. Figure 10.5 illustrates the updated display:

FIGURE 10.5.

The dynamic display.

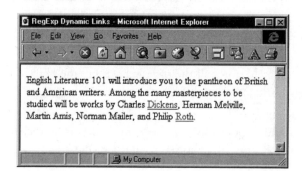

This routine demonstrates many of the new string methods with regular expressions. It can be modified to include multidimensional arrays with different links for different source text. It might not move anything across the page, but it is an example of the timesaving and resource-saving power of Dynamic HTML.

Scripting for Both Explorer and Navigator

It is not always possible to script for both dynamic browsers. The core operators, statements, and methods in JScript 3 and JavaScript 1.2 are more or less the same. JScript's capability to access the complete Document Object Model and CSS property values, however, gives it a power that JavaScript has yet to achieve. Unless you are writing for a controlled environment, such as an intranet, there should be considerations for both browsers.

Determining the Script to Be Exposed

Conditional exposure of script should not be based on browser identification or browser version. Unfortunately, most browser-detection scripts suggest this approach. Consider its weaknesses: If a script is exposed only to a certain browser version, what happens when a browser by a different vendor adopts support for the features in question? One must go back and change every page to accommodate the new browser as well—certainly not the most efficient coding technique.

The Image Object Example

Navigator 3 introduced the Image object and the document.images array. This allowed for image swapping on-the-fly and led to the creation of many image rollovers. Because Navigator 3 was the only browser supporting it, many authors used properties of the Navigator object to identify the browser being used and hide the code from all but Navigator 3.

The JScript 2 engine supports the Image object, and it shipped in some later builds of Explorer 3.02. What does one do—go back and check for Explorer 3.02 and accommodate that browser as well? The module concept in Internet Explorer lets you have the JScript 2 engine with Explorer 3.0 or 3.01, so what should have been done in the first place?

The answer, of course, is that you should have detected support of the Image object by checking for the existence of the document.images array:

```
if (document.images) {

...image object script goes here...

}
```

Any browser version that appears with support for this feature will see the script.

Version 4 Browsers

We, as authors, do not care what vendor manufactured our client's browser, nor do we care what the version number is. We care that whatever browser is visiting our page sees only script that it understands.

Avoid using names and version numbers. Can anyone guarantee that in version 5, Explorer won't support present Navigator-specific code, or vice versa? Because the two browsers have different DOMs, they each have unique arrays or collections to host properties of the model. Navigator 4 has a unique `document.layers` array and Explorer 4 has a unique `document.all` collection. The most efficient dynamic browser-detection script then becomes

```
IE4 = (document.all) ? 1 : 0;
NN4 = (document.layers) ? 1 : 0;
ver4 = (IE4 ¦¦ NN4) ? 1 : 0;
```

Three variables are created: `IE4`, which is `true` if the `document.all` collection exists; `NN4`, which is `true` if the `document.layers` array exists; and `ver4`, which is `true` if either of the previous two variables is true. (The names `IE4` and `NN4` are used for clarity. They could just as easily have been `allBrowser` and `layerBrowser`.)

In the future, if Navigator adopts the Explorer DOM or a third browser appears that supports one of the two models, the detection script will still work.

Using the Browser Variables

Some JScript is impossible to translate. The `TextRange` object and its properties and methods provide an example. Such code should be completely hidden from Navigator.

```
if (IE4) {

...Explorer-specific script...

}
```

If the script is in a function, use a single-line conditional to return the incompatible browser. This way, there is less chance of brace-matching errors:

```
function navStuff() {
    if (!NN4) {return};

    ...Navigator-specific script...

}
```

Many times, both browsers support the required result but need to go about it differently, as in positioning an element, for instance. If you have an element named `elMoveMe` and you need to move it 100 pixels to the right and 150 pixels down on the page, Explorer would require one of the two following sets of code:

```
document.all.elMoveMe.style.pixelLeft += 100;
document.all.elMoveMe.style.pixelTop +=150;

elMoveMe.style.pixelLeft += 100;
elMoveMe.style.pixelTop += 150;
```

To accomplish the same in Navigator, either one of the two following lines will suffice:

```
document.elMoveMe.moveBy(100,150);
```

```
document.elMoveMe.offset(100,150);
```

Both Navigator script snippets are more efficient than the Explorer versions because a single method is used. You can, however, create a script that will work on both equally well.

Explorer does not have a two-argument method for moving elements. Navigator elements do not have a `pixelLeft` or `pixelTop` property.

Both browsers, however, supply their positioned elements with a `left` and `top` property. The Explorer versions are strings reflecting the CSS property declaration (such as `240px`). Navigator's properties are integers (such as Explorer's `pixelLeft` and `Top`). Explorer accepts an integer as a property assignment and then internally converts it to a string. The following code works on both browsers:

```
if (ver4) {
    elToMove = (IE4) ? elMoveMe.style : document.elMoveMe;
    elToMove.left = parseInt(elToMove.left) + 100;
    elToMove.top = parseInt(elToMove.top) + 150;
}
```

This is a lowest common denominator approach. It makes no difference to browser performance and sacrifices browser-specific features for less elegant but compatible features.

Summary

Explorer 4 introduces a major new update to its primary scripting engine, JScript 3. Starting life as a one-step-behind JavaScript clone, JScript has grown to be completely compatible with the latest JavaScript version (1.2). In addition, it can also manipulate the new properties and methods generated by Explorer's comprehensive DOM and all CSS properties.

You have taken a detailed look at the different ways to include JScript in Web pages, with reference to browser-specific and cross-browser applications. JScript provides new statements for controlling program flow, such as `do...while` and `switch`. It has also added new internationalization methods for the `Date` object and powerful retrieval and manipulation methods for the `String` object. The latter, with its new capability to use Perl-like regular expressions, has perhaps become the most useful object for Dynamic HTML.

Dynamically Changing Content

by Peter Belesis

IN THIS CHAPTER

The term Dynamic HTML (DHTML), as mentioned in earlier chapters, has been bounced around for years, always in reference to on-demand pages built on the server before client download. Today, DHTML reduces the server workload by allowing content change after the page has been downloaded. This capability greatly increases update speed and expands the potential for interactive pages.

In this chapter, we will look at the tools offered by the document object models (DOMs) and scripting engines in Netscape Navigator 4 and Microsoft Internet Explorer 4 (IE4) for changing page content on the client side. We will conclude with the DHTML Author Quiz, a simple question-and-answer session with a student, demonstrating a real-life application of dynamic content change in IE4. This example can be easily expanded with the tools we will discuss to create a full-blown educational application.

Previous versions of JavaScript allowed you to dynamically change the values of form elements, but it was not until JavaScript 1.1 and the introduction of the image object that you got a taste of what has become today's DOM. The capability to change the source file (src property) of an already displayed image, combined with event handlers, has provided the tool for image display on demand, rollover effects, and simple animations.

Although the browser manufacturers have agreed to abide by the emerging standards, their implementations of dynamic content change capabilities differ. Netscape has expanded the concept of frames to include positioning, whereas Microsoft has attempted to expose every element of the document to change. The scripting methods are similar, fortunately, but most object properties are unique to each browser.

Changing Content in Netscape Navigator

Netscape Navigator 4 introduced a new HTML tag, <LAYER>, and adopted the W3C's *Positioning HTML Elements with Cascading Style Sheets*. Both of these features are discussed in great detail in Part II, "Cascading Style Sheets," and Chapter 22, "Using Layers." In this section we concern ourselves with using these new features to dynamically change page content.

The LAYER Tag

To properly envision the LAYER concept, consider this simplified definition:

- A layer is nothing more than a frame that can be absolutely positioned and can exist in 2.5 dimensions—that is, it can occupy the same 2D space as another frame.

- Layers, like frames, are documents unto themselves, with a document property that is in turn an object, with all the properties of the top-level document object. They capture events in the same way as the top-level window or document.

Consequently, to change content in a layer, you follow the same procedures used to change content in any regular HTML page:

■ Change the source HTML file or

■ Use the `write()` method of its document object

Changing a LAYER's Source HTML File

When the page is displayed, regardless of whether a layer has been defined with an SRC= attribute, changing its src property will load a new HTML page into the layer. Also, if the SRC attribute has a value, any in-page HTML between the LAYER start and end tags is ignored.

In the following example, the file `book1.html` is displayed in the layer in response to a link click:

```
<HTML>
<HEAD><TITLE>src Change 1</TITLE>

<SCRIPT LANGUAGE="JavaScript">
  function change(which) {
    document.goodRead.src="book1.html"
  }
</SCRIPT>

</HEAD>
<BODY>

<P><A HREF="javascript:change()">Good Read</A></P>

<LAYER
ID = "goodRead"
PAGEX = 120
PAGEY = 50
WIDTH = 300
CLIP = 400,150
BGCOLOR = "palegreen">
    <CENTER>Click on the link above for a Good Read!</CENTER>
</LAYER>

</BODY>
</HTML>
```

Corresponding to the different ways of referencing a layer are the respective ways to set its properties. We could have changed the src property in any of the following ways:

```
document.layers["goodRead"].src = "book1.html"  or
```

```
document.layers.goodRead.src = "book1.html" or
```

```
document.layers[0].src = "book1.html" or
```

```
document.goodRead.src = "book1.html"
```

The external file, `book1.html`, has a BODY tag with this attribute:

```
<BODY BGCOLOR=lightgrey>
```

In our example, the layer properties set by the HTML attributes in its start tag are maintained. The external file will wrap at 300 pixels, and the display will be clipped at 400 × 150 pixels.

Note that any attributes in the external file's BODY tag that correspond to possible LAYER attributes will override those of LAYER if set. In the code listed previously, the external file has the BGCOLOR attribute set to lightgrey. The background color of the layer will seem to be light grey. Although the HTML content of the external file wraps at 300 pixels, the layer's width property, the background colors, and background images expand to the clip margins.

The ILAYER Problem

If you need to create an in-flow layer that will require updating, do not use the ILAYER tag. The results, although fun to witness, will probably not relate in any way to your intentions.

TIP

To create an in-flow (that is, relatively positioned) layer, use the LAYER tag with no values for its LEFT, TOP, PAGEX, or PAGEY attributes. *Omit these attributes altogether.* The layer will position itself relative to the flow of the page HTML and will be properly changeable. The page HTML will not continue, however, after the end of the layer, because it is not a true ILAYER. If all your HTML is in LAYER tags, it is easy to position the other layers accordingly.

CAUTION

Don't forget, changing the content of a layer wipes out all previous content. This includes any nested layers the changed layer might have contained.

Using the load() Method

Changing the src property of a LAYER keeps the width property intact. There are times when the new content warrants changing the width property. For this we have the load() method, whose syntax looks like this:

```
layerReference.load(filename, width)
```

The argument for the name of the external file is given, of course, as a string; the width in pixels.

This example has two links that load two different external files. The first wraps at 300, the other at 400:

```
<HTML>
<HEAD><TITLE>load() Change2</TITLE>

<SCRIPT>

  function change(which) {
      howWide = (which == 1) ? 300 : 400
```

```
        document.goodRead.load("book" + which + ".html", howWide)
  }

</SCRIPT>

</HEAD>

<BODY>
<P><A HREF="javascript:change(1)">Good Read 1</A><BR>
   <A HREF="javascript:change(2)">Good Read 2</A></P>

<LAYER ID = "goodRead"
PAGEX = 100
PAGEY = 50
WIDTH = 250
CLIP = 400,150
BGCOLOR = palegreen>
    <CENTER>Good Reads</CENTER>
</LAYER>

</BODY>
</HTML>
```

Using the `document.write()` Method

Every layer defines a new x-y coordinate system for all its contained HTML. This contained HTML is reflected into the layer's `document` property, which is, in turn, itself an object. A layer's content can be changed by writing directly to this document using the `open()`, `write()`, and `close()` methods. For example, to display the tired phrase "Hello World" in a layer, we would use the following code:

```
layerReference.document.open();
layerReference.document.write("Hello World");
layerReference.document.close();
```

All the layer-addressing methods in this code are valid. If our layer were named `"tiredPhrase"`, the following pairs would all produce the same result:

```
document.layers["tiredPhrase"].document.write("Hello World");
document.layers["tiredPhrase"].document.close();

document.layers.tiredPhrase.document.write("Hello World");
document.layers.tiredPhrase.document.close();

document.layers[index].document.write("Hello World");
document.layers[index].document.close();

document.tiredPhrase.document.write("Hello World");
document.tiredPhrase.document.close();
```

NOTE

The `document.open()` method may be omitted. A direct `document.write()` implicitly opens a new document. The `close()` method, however, must be used to force a display of the layer's new content.

Every layer's `document` property has a `layers` array that contains all child layers nested within the parent. Each child layer has its own `document` property, which has an array of nested layers, and so on. The following HTML defines several nested layers:

```
<LAYER ID="grGrandDad">
    <LAYER ID="grandDad">
        …content to change is here…
    </LAYER>
    <LAYER ID="grandMa">
        <LAYER ID="ma">
            <LAYER ID="sis">
                …content to change is also here…
            </LAYER>
        </LAYER>
    </LAYER>
</LAYER>
```

If we needed to change the content of `grandDad` with `document.write()`, we would need to reference it as a child of `grGrandDad`. That is

```
document.layers["grGrandDad"].document.layers["grandDad"].document.write(new HTML);
document.layers["grGrandDad"].document.layers["grandDad"].document.close();
```

The `"sis"` layer, which is nested even deeper, would need a much longer reference:

```
document.layers["grGrandDad"].document.layers["grandMa"].document.layers["ma"].
➥document.layers["sis"].document.write(new HTML);
document.layers["grGrandDad"].document.layers["grandMa"].document.layers["ma"].
➥document.layers["sis"].document.close();
```

Any number of `document.write()` statements can be used to build the new content of a layer. The layer will be redrawn once the `close()` method is used. Successive writes to the same layer will, of course, erase all previous content.

Changing Content in Elements Positioned with Cascading Style Sheets

Netscape's underlying engine for cascading style sheets (CSS)–positioned elements is the same as the LAYER engine, so all the rules mentioned in the previous section apply. To flesh out omissions in the CSS specification that correspond to LAYER attributes, Netscape has introduced several proprietary CSS properties:

```
layer-background-color
```

```
layer-background-image
```

```
include-source
```

These extend CSS to support the LAYER attributes of BGCOLOR, BACKGROUND, and SRC, respectively. If the layer in the first code snippet were to have an external source upon declaration, it would be defined in Netscape-CSS as follows:

```
#goodRead {
    position: absolute;
    left: 120;
    top: 50;
    width: 300;
    clip: rect(0 150 400 0);
    layer-background-color: palegreen;
    include-source: url("book2.html")
}
```

It would be defined in the HTML page as follows:

```
<DIV
ID = "goodRead">
    <CENTER>Click on the link above for a Good Read!</CENTER>
</DIV>
```

or

```
<SPAN
ID = "goodRead">
    <CENTER>Click on the link above for a Good Read!</CENTER>
</SPAN>
```

CAUTION

All CSS-positioned elements that will have content changes cannot have a value of relative for the position property (see the section "The ILAYER Problem" earlier in this chapter).

Using document.write() in CSS Elements

The procedure for changing the contents of a CSS-positioned element with the write() method is exactly the same as that for a layer.

It is worth noting here, however, that a standard has emerged in layer and CSS element referencing. For no reason other than clarity, authors are using the layers array method for referring to a LAYER and the direct object name method for referring to a CSS element.

Our page HTML defines the following LAYER:

```
<LAYER ID="headHoncho">
</LAYER>
```

Most authors would use this code for the layer reference:

```
document.layers["headHoncho"];
```

Conversely, our HTML may contain the following CSS-positioned element:

```
<DIV ID="headHoncho">
</DIV>
```

In this case, the reference most often seen is the following:

```
document.headHoncho;
```

Changing Content in Internet Explorer

IE4's expanded DOM has exposed not only every element, but—using the tools available to us—every single letter, comma, and period in a document.

With scripting, the author can isolate any part of a document and add, modify, or delete it dynamically. In this section, we will look at the various ways Explorer allows us to achieve client-side content change.

We begin with author-scripted style changes and then proceed to text and HTML modifica-tions. Outside the scope of this section, however, lies the all-powerful `TextRange` object, which can allow the user to decide what to change and where.

NOTE

The IE4 DOM is discussed elsewhere in this book, as are cascading style sheets, event models, and the JavaScript language. A familiarity with these four is assumed.

Changing CSS Property Values

More often than not, the first experiments with dynamic content change in IE4 revolve around CSS styles. A complete exploration of IE4's dynamic styles can be found in Chapter 6, "Text and Fonts with Style," but no self-respecting chapter devoted to content dynamics can pro-ceed without at least a quick overview.

The Text Link Rollover

Problem: Text links should change color when the mouse passes over them and return to their original color when the mouse leaves.

Solution 1: In-line style property change:

```
I am a
<A
```

```
HREF = "linkOne.html"
STYLE = "color: red"
onMouseOver = "this.style.color = 'blue'"
onMouseOut = "this.style.color = 'red'">red</A> link.
```

The this keyword is reserved by JavaScript to refer to the object at hand, in this case the link. We simply change the color property of the object's style declaration.

Solution 2: In-line class change:

```
.red { color: red }
.blue { color: blue }

I am a
<A
HREF = "linkOne.html"
CLASS = red
onMouseOver = "this.className = 'blue'"
onMouseOut = "this.className = 'red'">red</A> link.
```

TIP

Although obvious strings do not need quotation containers in HTML, it is a must in scripts. A good practice is to always use them, avoiding any possible omissions that can generate errors.

In this example we used className, which is a direct property of the object, because it is created by the CLASS= attribute and not by STYLE=.

Any combination of properties can be modified with this method. But what if we have two or more types of links, with many classes to choose from?

Solution 3: Function-generated class change:

```
<HTML>
<HEAD><TITLE></TITLE>

<STYLE TYPE="text/css">

    .red { color: red }
    .yellow { color: yellow }
    .blue { color: blue }
    .weirdname { color: cornflowerblue }

</STYLE>

<SCRIPT LANGUAGE="JavaScript">

    var origClass = null;

    function swapClass(whichClass) {
        whichEl = event.srcElement;
```

```
            origClass = whichEl.className;
            whichEl.className = whichClass;
            whichEl.onmouseout = changeBack;
    }

    function changeBack() {
        whichEl = event.srcElement;
        whichEl.className = origClass;
    }

</SCRIPT>
</HEAD>
<BODY>

    <P>I am a
    <A
    HREF = "linkOne.html"
    CLASS = "red"
    onMouseOver = "swapClass('blue')">red</A> link.</P>
    <P>I am a
    <A
    HREF = "linkTwo.html"
    CLASS = "yellow"
    onMouseOver = "swapClass('blue')">yellow</A> link.</P>
    <P>I am a
    <A
    HREF = "linkThree.html"
    CLASS = "weirdname"
    onMouseOver = "swapClass('yellow')">cornflowerblue</A> link.</P>

</BODY>
</HTML>
```

Here we keep the body HTML typing to a minimum and let the script gather its own information through the event object. In the HTML element, we define only the action for the mouseover event: to call the swapClass() function, passing with it the name of the class to switch to.

The swapClass() function uses the event object generated by the mouseover to identify the element that fired the event. When the element is identified, the function places the present class name of the object in the origClass variable, which has been initialized outside the function, making it globally available.

Using the passed argument, a new class name is applied to the object. This done, it defines the onmouseout event handler for the object: Go to the changeBack() function.

The changeBack() function uses the event object in the same way as swapClass() and restores the original class name of the object.

This example introduces several good scripting techniques:

■ Keep the HTML to a minimum
■ Let the script gather as much information to use as arguments as possible
■ Make functions globally available, without need for changes if HTML is changed

Dynamically Changing Text and HTML

IE4 provides two new object properties and one method for dynamically changing text after initial browser formatting and display:

```
objectReference.innerText
```

```
objectReference.outerText
```

```
objectReference.insertAdjacentText()
```

The following properties are for changing HTML:

```
objectReference.innerHTML
```

```
objectReference.outerHTML
```

```
objectReference.insertAdjacentHTML()
```

All of these can be properties or methods of the following HTML elements:

A	ADDRESS	B	BIG	BLOCKQUOTE
BODY	BUTTON	CAPTION	CENTER	CITE
CODE	DD	DFN	DIR	DIV
DL	DT	EM	FIELDSET	FONT
FORM	H1	H2	H3	H4
H5	H6	I	IFRAME	KBD
LABEL	LEGEND	LI	LISTING	MARQUEE
MENU	OL	P	PLAINTEXT	PRE
S	SAMP	SMALL	SPAN	STRIKE
STRONG	SUB	SUP	TD	TH
TT	U	UL	VAR	XMP

In other words, they are element dependent.

To best illustrate the differences of these properties, let's apply them to the following text passage:

> Call me Ishmael. Some years ago—never mind how long precisely—having little or no money in my purse, and nothing particular to interest me on shore, I thought I would sail about a little and see the watery part of the world.

The HTML for this passage follows:

```
<P> Call me <B ID="moniker">Ishmael</B>. Some years ago - <SPAN
ID="howlong">never mind how long precisely</SPAN> - having little
or no money in my purse, and <I ID="nothing">nothing particular
to interest me on shore,</I> I thought I would sail about a
little and see the watery part of the world.</P>
```

.innerText

This value of the .innerText property must be both retrieved and set (read/write).

The inner text of the B element with the "moniker" ID can be referenced as follows:

```
document.all.moniker.innerText
```

```
moniker.innerText
```

In the present example, this inner text has a value of "Ishmael" because "Ishmael" is the text *within* the named tag. It is the *inner text.*

In this case, because we know the element ID, the comprehensive all collection (containing every element in the page) is redundant, much like referring to a human being as an "inhabitant of Earth."

Retrieve the value of moniker.innerText and assign it to a variable like this:

```
var narrator = moniker.innerText
```

Change the value of moniker.innerText like this:

```
moniker.innerText = "Barney"
```

When changed, the HTML of the passage would read as follows:

```
<P> Call me <B ID="moniker">Barney</B>. Some years ago...
```

Explorer would reformat all affected layout to accommodate the new text, which is one letter shorter than the original. In this case, the paragraph would be reformatted.

The following code can be used to experiment with the innerText property. It demonstrates retrieval and setting of the property with a toggle function:

```
<HTML>
<HEAD><TITLE>innerText</TITLE>

<SCRIPT LANGUAGE="JavaScript">

    var isOrig = true;

    function chgInnerTxt(){
        if (isOrig) {
            origName = moniker.innerText;
        moniker.innerText = "Barney";
        }
        else {
            moniker.innerText = origName;
        }

        isOrig = !isOrig;
    }
```

```
</SCRIPT>
</HEAD>
<BODY>
<P>
Call me <B ID="moniker">Ishmael</B>. Some years ago - <SPAN
ID="howlong">never mind how long precisely</SPAN> - having little
or no money in my purse, and <I ID="nothing">nothing particular
to interest me on shore,</I> I thought I would sail about a
little and see the watery part of the world.
</P>
<BUTTON onClick="chgInnerTxt()">Change Name (.innerText)</BUTTON>
</BODY>
</HTML>
```

Even though HTML is text as well, the innerText property will strip any HTML upon retrieval. Suppose the example read as follows:

```
Call me <B ID="moniker">Ish<I>m</I>ael</B>.
```

moniker.innerText would still be "Ishmael" and the formatting would be lost forever.

Now suppose we tried to change moniker with the following:

```
moniker.innerText = "<I>Barn</I>ey"
```

Our screen display looks like this:

```
Call me <I>Barn</I>ey.
```

That is, Explorer would process this as if the HTML were as follows:

```
Call me <B ID="moniker">&lt;I&gt;Barn&lt;/I&gt;ney</B>
```

.outerText

The value of the .outerText property can be both retrieved and set (read/write).

The *outer text* of the B element with the "moniker" ID can be referenced as follows:

```
moniker.outerText
```

It has a value of "Ishmael". Even though the outer text of the element includes the element tags, they will be stripped from the string.

CAUTION

Use outerText with caution, as it will strip the tag with the ID attribute and you will no longer be able to reference it. It is best used when you have no more call to use the formatting or ID of the enclosing tag.

The following code has a good reason to use `outerText`: We are not swapping proper names, as in the previous example. On the toggle, however, it generates an error because the tag no longer exists:

```
<HTML>
<HEAD><TITLE>innerText</TITLE>

<SCRIPT LANGUAGE="JavaScript">

    var isOrig = true;

    function chgOuterTxt(){
        if (isOrig) {
            origName = moniker.outerText;
        moniker.outerText = "anything you want";
        }
        else {
            moniker.outerText = origName;
        }

        isOrig = !isOrig;
    }

</SCRIPT>
</HEAD>
<BODY>

<P>Call me <B ID="moniker">Ishmael</B>. Some years ago - <SPAN
ID="howlong">never mind how long precisely</SPAN> - having little
or no money in my purse, and <I ID="nothing">nothing particular
to interest me on shore,</I> I thought I would sail about a
little and see the watery part of the world.</P>
<BUTTON onClick="chgOuterTxt()">Change Name (.outerText)</BUTTON>
</BODY>
</HTML>
```

The passage HTML has now been changed to the following:

```
<P>Call me anything you want. Some years ago...
```

.insertAdjacentText()

This method takes two parameters and inserts the `textstring` into the element object at the specified position:

```
objectReference.insertAdjacentText(position, textstring)
```

Because it *inserts* text, it is nondestructive.

The position string can have one of four values: `"BeforeBegin"`, `"AfterBegin"`, `"BeforeEnd"`, and `"AfterEnd"`. These values are explained in the sections that follow.

"BeforeBegin"

If we use the `"BeforeBegin"` position variable, the text in the `textstring` variable is inserted immediately before the element. It resides outside the element's enclosing tags, so it is not affected by any formatting the element generates.

For example, say we have the following code:

```
nothing.insertAdjacentText("BeforeBegin", "absolutely ")
```

It would generate this HTML:

```
absolutely <I ID="nothing">nothing particular to interest me on shore,</I>
```

"AfterBegin"

The "AfterBegin" position variable causes the text in the textstring variable to be inserted after the element starting tag but before any other enclosed content, like this:

```
nothing.insertAdjacentText("AfterBegin", "absolutely ")
```

This code gives us the following (our inserted text will be italicized):

```
<I ID="nothing">absolutely nothing particular to interest me on shore,</I>
```

"BeforeEnd"

"BeforeEnd" inserts the text before the element closing tag and after any other enclosed content. For example, say we have the following code:

```
nothing.insertAdjacentText("BeforeEnd", " or anywhere else, for that matter, ")
```

This produces the following HTML (our inserted text will be italicized):

```
<I ID="nothing">nothing particular to interest me on shore, or anywhere else,
for that matter, </I>
```

"AfterEnd"

"AfterEnd" inserts the text immediately after the element and is unaffected by element formatting. Say we have the following code:

```
nothing.insertAdjacentText("BeforeEnd", " or anywhere else, for that matter, ")
```

This results in the following:

```
<I ID="nothing">nothing particular to interest me on shore,</I> or anywhere else,
for that matter,
```

This code will help you visualize these differences. Use the reset button to restore the original formatting of the paragraph, like this:

```
<HTML>
<HEAD><TITLE>insertAdjacentText</TITLE>

<SCRIPT LANGUAGE="JavaScript">

    function doMoby() { passage.innerHTML = moby }

    function insAdjTxtBB() {
        insText = "absolutely ";
        nothing.insertAdjacentText("BeforeBegin", insText)
    }
```

```
        function insAdjTxtAB() {
            insText = "absolutely ";
            nothing.insertAdjacentText("AfterBegin", insText)
        }

        function insAdjTxtBE() {
            insText = " or anywhere else, for that matter, ";
            nothing.insertAdjacentText("BeforeEnd", insText);
        }

        function insAdjTxtAE() {
            insText = " or anywhere else, for that matter, ";
            nothing.insertAdjacentText("AfterEnd", insText);
        }
</SCRIPT>
</HEAD>

<BODY onLoad="moby = passage.innerHTML">

<P ID="passage">
Call me <B ID="moniker">Ishmael</B>. Some years ago - <SPAN
ID="howlong">never mind how long precisely</SPAN> - having little
or no money in my purse, and <I ID="nothing">nothing particular
to interest me on shore,</I> I thought I would sail about a
little and see the watery part of the world.
</P>

<CENTER>
<BUTTON onClick="doMoby()">Reset</BUTTON><BR>
<BUTTON onClick="insAdjTxtBB()">.insertAdjacentText("BeforeBegin")</BUTTON><BR>
<BUTTON onClick="insAdjTxtAB()">.insertAdjacentText("AfterBegin")</BUTTON><BR>
<BUTTON onClick="insAdjTxtBE()">.insertAdjacentText("BeforeEnd")</BUTTON><BR>
<BUTTON onClick="insAdjTxtAE()">.insertAdjacentText("AfterEnd")</BUTTON>
</CENTER>

</BODY>
</HTML>
```

.innerHTML

In the immediately preceding code, the innerHTML property is used to reset the paragraph to its original formatting. It is also used to assign the paragraph's content to a variable when the page loads. Consequently, the value of this property can be both retrieved and set (read/write).

> **NOTE**
>
> If there are no HTML tags in the string returned, the value of innerHTML is the same as innerText.

This property will probably be the one used most often, because when applied to a positioned element, it is similar to Navigator's document.write() method and is useful in minimizing cross-browser scripting.

Dynamically Changing Content

CHAPTER 11

203

11

DYNAMICALLY
CHANGING
CONTENT

Here is an example of using innerHTML to both replace content and add formatting through tags:

```
<HTML>
<HEAD><TITLE>innerHTML</TITLE>

<SCRIPT LANGUAGE="JavaScript">

    isOrig = true;

    function chgInnerHtml(){
        if (isOrig) {
            origTime = howlong.innerHTML;
            howlong.innerHTML = "<I><B>20</B> to be exact</I>";
        }
        else {
            howlong.innerHTML = origTime;
        }

        isOrig = !isOrig;
    }

</SCRIPT>
</HEAD>

<BODY>

<P ID="passage">
Call me <B ID="moniker">Ishmael</B>. Some years ago - <SPAN
ID="howlong">never mind how long precisely</SPAN> - having little
or no money in my purse, and <I ID="nothing">nothing particular
to interest me on shore,</I> I thought I would sail about a
little and see the watery part of the world.

</P>

<CENTER>
<BUTTON onClick="chgInnerHtml()">Change Time (.innerHTML)</BUTTON>
</CENTER>

</BODY>
</HTML>
```

.outerHTML

The value of the .outerHTML property can be both retrieved and set (read/write).

Like its text counterpart, this property can be destructive, because it replaces the start and end element tags. Conversely, this feature can be used to replace tags to change formatting. If the tags are changed and we need to maintain a reference to the element, the ID attribute must be included in the start tag. If we needed to change the moniker to "Barney", change the bold to italic, and maintain the reference, we would use the following script:

```
moniker.innerHTML = <I ID="moniker">Barney</I>
```

Unlike outerText, if we assign the value of outerHTML to a variable, the HTML remains intact and can be used. We cannot use it in a toggle function, however, unless we have maintained the ID, as in the previous line of code. The following code generates an error:

```
<HTML>
<HEAD><TITLE>outerHTML</TITLE>

<SCRIPT LANGUAGE="JavaScript">

    isOrig = true;

    function chgOuterHtml(){
        if (isOrig) {
            origTime = howlong.outerHTML;
            howlong.outerHTML = "<I><B>20</B> to be exact</I>";
        }
        else {
            howlong.outerHTML = origTime;
        }

        isOrig = !isOrig;
    }

</SCRIPT>
</HEAD>

<BODY>

<P ID="passage">
Call me <B ID="moniker">Ishmael</B>. Some years ago - <SPAN
ID="howlong">never mind how long precisely</SPAN> - having little
or no money in my purse, and <I ID="nothing">nothing particular
to interest me on shore,</I> I thought I would sail about a
little and see the watery part of the world.

</P>

<CENTER>
<BUTTON onClick="chgOuterHtml()">Change Time (.outerHTML)</BUTTON>
</CENTER>

</BODY>
</HTML>
```

.insertAdjacentHTML()

The .insertAdjacentHTML() method is the same as insertAdjacentText(), except it parses any HTML included.

Let's use the same examples we used to illustrate .insertAdjacentText.

The following code

```
nothing.insertAdjacentHTML("BeforeBegin", "<B>absolutely</B> ")
```

results in this HTML:

```
<B>absolutely</B> <I ID="nothing">nothing particular to interest me on shore,</I>
```

Because the HTML has been inserted before the start of the I tag, the resulting display has just bolded text.

This code

```
nothing.insertAdjacentHTML("AfterBegin", "<B>absolutely</B> ")
```

results in text that is both bold and italic, because the insertion is done after the start of the I tag:

```
<I ID="nothing"><B>absolutely</B> nothing particular to interest me on shore,</I>
```

Inserting with the "Before End" position variable

```
nothing.insertAdjacentHTML("BeforeEnd", " <B>or anywhere else,
 for that matter,</B> ")
```

again results in bold-italic text because we are still within the I tag:

```
<I ID="nothing">nothing particular to interest me on shore, <B>or anywhere else,
 for that matter,</B> </I>
```

"AfterEnd", of course, places our HTML after the I tag end:

```
nothing.insertAdjacentHTML("AfterEnd", " <B>or anywhere else,
 for that matter,</B> ")
```

so our text is again just bold:

```
<I ID="nothing">nothing particular to interest me on shore,</I>
<B>or anywhere else, for that matter,</B>
```

The following code combines the four methods and adds a different way of assigning the innerHTML value:

```
<HTML>
<HEAD><TITLE>insertAdjacentHTML</TITLE>

<SCRIPT LANGUAGE="JavaScript">

    function doMoby() { passage.innerHTML = moby }

    function insAdjHtmlBB() {
        insHtm = "<B>absolutely </B>";
        nothing.insertAdjacentHTML("BeforeBegin", insHtm)
    }

    function insAdjHtmlAB() {
        insHtm = "<B>absolutely </B>";
        nothing.insertAdjacentHTML("AfterBegin", insHtm)
    }

    function insAdjHtmlBE() {
        insHtm = "<B> or anywhere else, for that matter, </B>";
        nothing.insertAdjacentHTML("BeforeEnd", insHtm )
    }
```

```
        function insAdjHtmlAE() {
            insHtm = "<B> or anywhere else, for that matter, </B>"
            nothing.insertAdjacentHTML("AfterEnd", insHtm)
        }

</SCRIPT>
</HEAD>

<BODY>

<P ID="passage">
Call me <B ID="moniker">Ishmael</B>. Some years ago - <SPAN
ID="howlong">never mind how long precisely</SPAN> - having little
or no money in my purse, and <I ID="nothing">nothing particular
to interest me on shore,</I> I thought I would sail about a
little and see the watery part of the world.
</P>

<CENTER>
<BUTTON onClick="doMoby()">Reset</BUTTON><BR>
<BUTTON onClick="insAdjHtmlBB()">.insertAdjacentHTML("BeforeBegin")</BUTTON><BR>
<BUTTON onClick="insAdjHtmlAB()">.insertAdjacentHTML("AfterBegin")</BUTTON><BR>
<BUTTON onClick="insAdjHtmlBE()">.insertAdjacentHTML("BeforeEnd")</BUTTON><BR>
<BUTTON onClick="insAdjHtmlAE()">.insertAdjacentHTML("AfterEnd")</BUTTON>
</CENTER>

<SCRIPT LANGUAGE="JavaScript">moby = passage.innerHTML</SCRIPT>
</BODY>
</HTML>
```

NOTE

The three HTML techniques are much more powerful than our examples demonstrate. Because they contain HTML to be inserted into or set in an element, they can contain everything that an HTML page contains, including images, scripts, applets, and controls.

TIP

If innerHTML is used with the body object, it will replace the contents of the whole page. This can be useful as a response screen after form processing or to provide feedback in interactive applications.

There are a few things to remember when replacing HTML:

■ *HTML to be inserted must be valid in the context of the full page.* For example, we cannot replace "passage" in our example with: "<P>This is the first paragraph </P>", because the HTML page result would look like this: <P ID=passage><P>This is the first paragraph</P></P> with invalid nested P tags. Attempting this will generate an error.

Dynamically Changing Content

CHAPTER 11

207

11

DYNAMICALLY
CHANGING
CONTENT

■ *HTML to be inserted must be valid when standing alone.* It cannot be fragmented: `"<I>This has no end tag"` will have an end tag appended automatically by Explorer to avoid conflicts with later elements, resulting in `"<I>This has no end tag</I>"`. Attempting this will not generate an error.

■ *No insertions can be made while the page is loading.* (This also applies to text.) We can retrieve the value of the `inner-outer` properties while the page loads, but only after the elements referenced have been created and closed. The last code snippet in the previous example demonstrates this. We cannot, however, make any changes until the page has fully loaded. The earliest change is made through the `onLoad` event handler.

■ *Collections will be updated.* At least the `all` collection will be updated to reflect the new HTML layout. Other collections could be affected as well. Keep this in mind if referencing by index value; it might need updating.

■ *Overlapping elements will be modified.* If the element content you are replacing contains an overlap from another element, the start or end tag of one of the elements will be moved to avoid a double overlap.

Example 1:

```
<B ID="boldguy">This is bold <I> this is bold-italic</B>
 this is Italic</I>.
```

Say we used the following script:

```
boldguy.innerHTML = "<BIG>I am big</BIG>"
```

The result would look like this:

```
<B ID="boldguy"><BIG>I am big</BIG></B><I>this is Italic</I>.
```

Example 2:

```
<B>This is bold <I ID="italicguy"> this is bold-italic</B>
this is Italic</I>.
```

Say we have the following code:

```
italicguy.innerHTML = "<BIG>I am big</BIG>"
```

This produces the following:

```
<B>This is bold</B> <I ID="italicguy"><BIG>I am big</BIG></I>.
```

■ *Setting property with empty string deletes content/element.* Pasting an empty string deletes the element's content (`innerText`, `innerHTML`) or the element itself (`outerText`, `outerHTML`).

Binding Content Change to Elapsed Time

All the examples shown in this chapter bind content change to events. Even link selections are events (click events), and more often than not, content change will be the result of an event.

We can also script a change to occur after a certain period of time has elapsed or have the change occur at regular intervals.

The very first version of JavaScript introduced the `setTimeout()` method of the `window` object. It is used to evaluate a script expression, passed as a string, after a specified number of milliseconds:

```
setTimeout(expression, msecs);
```

The evaluation can be canceled before it occurs, if we first assign the identifier returned by the method to a variable and then pass that variable as an argument in the `clearTimeout()` method, like this:

```
var timerID = setTimeout(expression, msecs);
clearTimeout(timerID);
```

More often than not, the expression passed is a function call, with or without arguments. Both Navigator and Explorer support a new method: `setInterval()`. This replaces the oft-used hack of recursive `setTimeout()` calls by evaluating an expression or calling a function repeatedly, every specified number of milliseconds, like this:

```
var timerID = setInterval(expression, msecs);
clearInterval(timerID);
```

Navigator extends the two methods by offering a function-only syntax option:

```
var timerID = setTimeout(functionName, msecs, [arg1, arg2...]);
var timerID = setInterval(functionName, msecs, [arg1, arg2...]);
```

It does nothing different from the old version, except that it allows one to pass arguments in a slightly easier fashion, especially if variables are being passed.

Explorer extends the two methods as well. Its third, optional parameter is `language`, a string specifying which script language the code should be executed in:

```
var timerID = setTimeout(functionName, msecs, [language]);
var timerID = setInterval(functionName, msecs, [language]);
```

To achieve cross-browser compatibility, it is best to use the nonextended compatible methods.

Using the Timer Methods

The following code uses both methods. The only content of the SPAN element with an ID of purse is the word *purse*. When the Time-out button is clicked, the `setTimeout()` method is invoked, which calls the function `snatchPurse()` in three seconds. This function simply changes the HTML in purse to `<I>Gucci hand bag</I>`.

The Interval button calls the `start()` function. This in turn initializes a counter and uses the `setInterval()` method to call the `rotateNames()` function every second. `rotateNames()` saves the inner text of the `moniker` element for reinsertion later and replaces the content of `moniker` with a name from the array previously initialized. The counter is incremented, and a second later the next name is substituted, until the end of the array when the repeated calls are canceled with `clearInterval()` and the original name is placed back in the element.

```
<HTML>
<HEAD><TITLE>time methods</TITLE>

<SCRIPT LANGUAGE="JavaScript">

arMoniker = new Array(
    "Raskolnikof",
    "Portnoy",
    "Yossarian",
    "Fagin",
    "Alyosha",
    "Tartuffe",
    "Spock",
    "Bond, James Bond"
)

function start() {
    pointer = 0;
    naming = setInterval("rotateNames()",1000)
}

function rotateNames(){
    if (pointer == 0) { origName = moniker.innerText };
    if (pointer < arMoniker.length) {
    moniker.innerText = arMoniker[pointer];
    pointer++;
    }
    else {
    moniker.innerText = origName;
    clearInterval(naming);
    }
}

function snatchPurse() {
    purse.innerHTML = "<I>Gucci hand bag</I>";
}

</SCRIPT>

</HEAD>
<BODY>

<P>
Call me <B ID="moniker">Ishmael</B>. Some years ago - <SPAN
ID="howlong">never mind how long precisely</SPAN> - having little or nomoney in my
➥<SPAN
ID="purse">purse</SPAN>, and <I ID="nothing">nothing
particular to interest me on shore,</I> I thought I would sail
about a little and see the watery part of the world.
</P>

<BUTTON onClick="setTimeout('start()',3000)">Timeout</BUTTON>
<BUTTON onClick="switchNames()">Interval</BUTTON>

</P>

</BODY>
</HTML>
```

The *Dynamic HTML Unleashed* Author Quiz

The best way to appreciate real-world uses for all the content change techniques we've discussed is, obviously, to witness them in action in a useful page.

To this end, we have combined many of IE4–relevant properties and methods and developed this short quiz script. A discussion follows.

```
<HTML>
<HEAD><TITLE>DHTML Unleashed Author Quiz</TITLE>

<STYLE TYPE="text/css">

    #quiz {
        position: absolute;
        visibility: hidden;
        text-align: center;
        width: 400;
        background-color: lightgrey;
        border: thick gray ridge;
        margin: 10px;
    }

</STYLE>
<SCRIPT LANGUAGE="JavaScript">

    arQuestions = new Array();
    arrayCounter = questCounter = reviewCounter = 1;
    wrongAns = rightAns = lateAns = 0;

    function newQA(question,fName,lName) {
        arQuestions[arrayCounter] = new Array();
        arQuestions[arrayCounter][0] = question;
        arQuestions[arrayCounter][1] = fName;
        arQuestions[arrayCounter][2] = lName;
        arrayCounter++;
    }

    newQA("Who wrote the book we have been quoting from?","Herman ","Melville");
    newQA("Which author began a book \"It was the best of times...?\"",
    ➥"Charles ","Dickens");
    newQA("Who coined the term 'Catch-22'?","Joseph ","Heller");
    newQA("Who wrote over 1000 pages about an Idiot?","Fyodor ","Dostoyevsky");
    newQA("Who placed a Catcher in a grain type?","J.D. ","Salinger");

    totQuestions = (arrayCounter - 1);

    function startIt(first) {
        if (questCounter > totQuestions) {
            questCounter = 1;
            wrongAns = rightAns = lateAns = 0;
        }
        quizQuest.innerText = arQuestions[questCounter][0];
        if (first) {
            startLink.outerText="";
            quiz.style.left = ((document.body.clientWidth - quiz.offsetWidth) / 2);
            quiz.style.visibility = "visible";
        }
```

```
        else {
            quizEntry.innerHTML = origEntry
        }
        document.forms.test.elements[0].focus();
        ticker = setTimeout("tooLate()", 10000);
    }

function answered() {
    clearTimeout(ticker);
    studentAnswer = document.forms.test.elements[0].value.toLowerCase();
    authLName = arQuestions[questCounter][2].toLowerCase()
    if (studentAnswer.indexOf(authLName ) != -1) {
        correctAns();
    }
    else {
        dummy();
    }
}

function tooLate(){
    lateAns++;
    respTxt = "<BR><B>Sorry, your time is up.</B><BR>"
    response(respTxt);
}

function dummy(){
    wrongAns++;
    respTxt = "<BR><B>Sorry, your answer is incorrect.</B><BR>"
    response(respTxt);
}

function correctAns() {
    rightAns++;
    respTxt = "<BR><B>You are right!</B><BR>"
    response(respTxt);
}

function response() {
    quizEntry.innerHTML = respTxt + respDisplay();
    questCounter++;
}

function respDisplay(respTxt){
    respString = "The correct answer is: "
                + "<B>" + arQuestions[questCounter][1]
                + arQuestions[questCounter][2]+ "</B>";
    if (questCounter == totQuestions) {
        respString += "<BR><BR><B>QUIZ Score:</B><BR>"
                + " Correct Answers: " + rightAns.toString().bold()
                + "<BR> Not-so-correct Answers: "
                + wrongAns.toString().bold()
                + "<BR> No Response: " + lateAns.toString().bold()
                + "<BR>You got " + rightAns + " out of "
                + totQuestions + " correct.<BR><B>"
                + rightAns + "/" + totQuestions
                + " = " + ((rightAns/totQuestions)*100) + "%</B>"
                + "<BR><BR><BUTTON onClick='listThem()'>"
                + "Review Questions</BUTTON>"
                + "<BR><P><BUTTON onClick='startIt()'>"
                + "Start Over</BUTTON></P>";
```

```
        }
        else {
            respString += "<BR><P><BUTTON onClick='startIt()'>"
                    + "Go on to Question " + (questCounter+1) + "</BUTTON></P>"
        }
        return respString;
    }

    function listThem() {
        quiz.innerHTML = "";
        reviewCounter = 1;
        showQuest();
        flipThrough = setInterval("showQuest()",2000);
    }

    function showQuest(){
        if (reviewCounter == arQuestions.length) {
            clearInterval(flipThrough);
            revQuest = "<P><BUTTON onClick='location.reload()'>"
                    + "Next Quiz</BUTTON></P>";
        }
        else {
            revQuest = "<P><I>" + arQuestions[reviewCounter][0] + "</I><BR><B>"
                    + arQuestions[reviewCounter][1]
                    + arQuestions[reviewCounter][2]
                    + "</B></P>";
            reviewCounter++;
        }
        quiz.insertAdjacentHTML("BeforeEnd", revQuest);
    }

</SCRIPT>

</HEAD>
<BODY onLoad="origEntry = quizEntry.innerHTML">

<DIV ID="startLink" ALIGN=CENTER>
<P><BIG><B>Welcome to DHTML Unleashed's<BR>Author Quiz</B></BIG></P>

<P>For each of the 5 questions, enter the name of an author in the field
provided and click the <B>Submit Question</B> button.
You have 10 seconds for each question.</P>
<BUTTON onClick="startIt(true)">Start Quiz</BUTTON></DIV>

<DIV
ID="quiz">

<I ID="quizQuest"></I><BR>

<SPAN ID="quizEntry">
    <FORM NAME="test" onSubmit="answered()">
        <INPUT TYPE=TEXT SIZE=30><BR>
        <INPUT TYPE=SUBMIT VALUE="Submit Answer">
    </FORM>
</SPAN>

</DIV>

</BODY>
</HTML>
```

How Does the Quiz Work?

The students or users are welcomed by an introduction screen, stating the rules of the quiz and warning them about the time limit for each question—in this case, ten seconds. Figure 11.1 illustrates this opening screen.

FIGURE 11.1.

The Quiz Welcome screen.

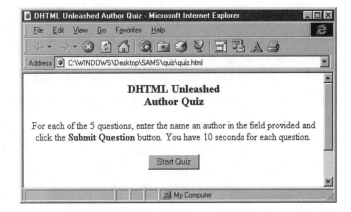

When the students press the Start Quiz button, the screen is replaced by the first question with a form entry field for the answer. See Figure 11.2 for an illustration of the first question.

FIGURE 11.2.

The Quiz Question screen.

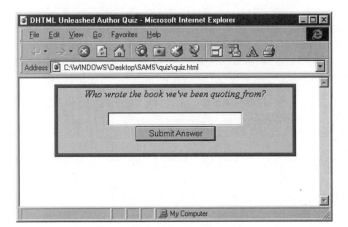

If the students answer by filling in the form and clicking the Submit Answer button or if their ten seconds elapse, a reply screen is displayed, informing the students of whether their answer was correct or if they were late in responding. See Figure 11.3 for a sample timed-out answer screen. In every case, the correct answer is supplied along with a button to proceed to the next question.

FIGURE 11.3.

The Quiz Answer screen.

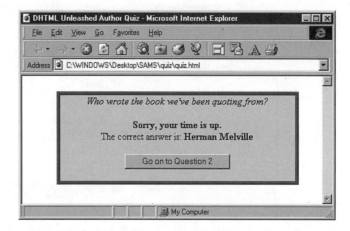

This routine is repeated until all questions have been displayed. On the final reply screen, a tabulation of results is also presented, along with a percentage grade, illustrated in Figure 11.4.

The students are presented with two options: to start again, in which case the first question is displayed and the quiz proceeds as before; or to review the questions, in which case a new screen presents each question with its answer, appending them one by one every two seconds. Figure 11.5 shows this screen after all questions have been appended.

At the end of the review, the students press a button to exit the Quiz.

The Code

We now go through the code step by step, as the rendering engine of Internet Explorer would.

A CSS-positioned element is defined in our STYLE tag: #quiz. This element will later contain the main Q&A screens. Although a position is defined, the actual pixel positioning is omitted. We will position it on the page later.

In our JavaScript, we create an array for our questions and answers and declare some global variables. The counter variables are initialized with a value of 1, for easier human-like counting. Variables for the different kinds of answers (wrong, right, and late) are of course initialized with 0. Next, we have our first function, newQA(). (We will discuss all functions in the code when they are actually used, not when they are displayed on the page; it will be easier to follow.)

FIGURE 11.4.
*The Quiz Results
screen.*

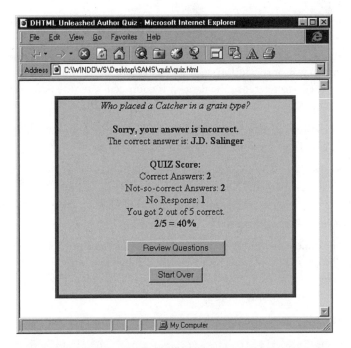

FIGURE 11.5.
*The Quiz Review
screen.*

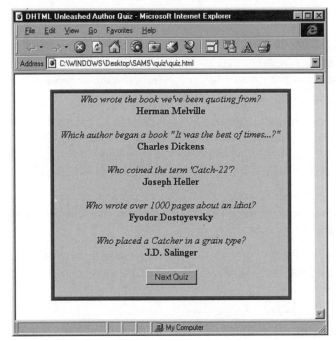

Next, we have five consecutive calls to the newQA() function with three arguments each. Every time newQA() is called, it takes an element in the arQuestions array, starting with element 1, and creates a new array off each element. These new arrays are populated with the question, the first name of the author, and the last name. This multidimensional array structure makes it easy for us to reference the data with counters. After the new array is created, arrayCounter is incremented, pointing to the next array element to be filled.

We initialize a variable to remember the total number of questions, and the remainder of the script contains functions to be compiled and put aside for later.

Our BODY tag has an onLoad event handler, which we'll get to when the page has finished loading. The first element on our page is a DIV container, aligned in the center of the page, named startScreen. It contains straightforward HTML with the welcome information and the Start Quiz button.

The next element, which contains all the remainder of the page elements, is the DIV defined in our STYLE. Presently it is hidden, so the students see only the welcome screen. In this hidden container we have an empty I named element (quizQuest) and a BR for formatting. quizQuest will later host our questions.

quizEntry, a SPAN container, holds the answer-insertion FORM.

That's it for the HTML. The rest is performed dynamically with Explorer's content-changing properties and methods.

The Script in Action

When the page loads, the onLoad event handler fires and assigns the HTML contained in our still-hidden SPAN to a variable, origEntry. Now our answer form, to be used for each question, is just a variable away.

When the students have read the welcome and are ready to proceed, the script springs back into action. The Start Quiz button calls startIt(), with one argument: true. Although startIt() will be called every time we go to a new question, this is the only time an argument will be included. We are telling startIt() that we are just coming off the welcome screen.

The first thing startIt() does is to check whether our question counter is more than our total questions. In other words, it checks to see whether the quiz is being repeated or is in progress—if repeated, the variables are reset.

Using the question counter, the current question is retrieved from the array and placed in our italicized element quizQuest. The question contains no HTML, so the innerText property is used.

startIt() now checks to see whether we are starting for the first time, using our passed argument. If we are, it deletes the startScreen DIV completely, by assigning an empty string to its outerText property. The students' welcome screens disappear from their monitors, and our hidden DIV moves up on the screen. It is centered horizontally by accessing the document.body.clientWidth property, which stores the pixel width of the browser window, and is made visible. The students see the first question. Before startIt() returns, it quickly gives focus to the form field, to save the students a mouse click, and starts counting off the ten seconds with the setTimeout() method. In ten seconds, the tooLate() function will be called.

If the students reply in the allotted time, the function answered() is called by the FORMs onSubmit handler. Immediately, the time-out is cleared, canceling the call to the tooLate() function. answered() converts the answer to lowercase and compares it to a lowercase version of the author's surname. *The surname suffices as an answer.* If the answer is correct, the correctAns() function is called; if not, dummy() is called.

If the students do not reply in ten seconds, control is passed to tooLate(). This function is similar to correctAns() and dummy(). In fact, they can be combined into one. They all increment their respective answer counters and provide a custom string to be used in the upcoming screen response. Then they pass that string to the response() function.

In response(), this string is combined with another string: the return value of the function respDisplay(). respDisplay() creates a string with the correct answer and, if the student is not at the last question, a button to navigate to the next question. This string is passed back to response() when the function returns. Back in response(), the innerHTML property of quizEntry is invoked to display the combined string on the screen in place of the entry form.

The students continue to the second question, but this time startIt() does not find a passed argument, so it retrieves the stored HTML from our onLoad call and reassigns it to quizEntry, creating a new answer entry form identical to the original.

This cycle is repeated until the students reach the last question. RespDisplay() will create a longer string with an appended tabulation of results and two buttons: one to review all the questions and one to start the quiz again.

If the quiz is restarted, startIt() will first reset relevant variables before proceeding. The script will cycle through as before.

If the students choose to review the questions, the listThem() function deletes the content of the main DIV by assigning a blank string to its innerHTML property. innerText would have done the same, of course. Our reviewCounter is set to 1, and we call the function showQuest() to display the first question and answer set. Using the setInterval() method, we place additional calls to showQuest() every two seconds until all our questions have been reviewed.

Every time showQuest() is called, it checks to see if the questions are finished. If they are not, it assigns a question and the appropriate answer to a string and uses the insertAdjacentHTML() method to update the quiz DIV, one question at a time. This method of appending HTML to the end of an element gives the impression on screen of a scrolling, expanding container. When the questions are finished, the clearInterval() method cancels the function calls and an Exit button is displayed. In our example, the Exit button reloads the page, but that is just a placeholder.

The quiz has been purposely written in a not-so-efficient manner. This gives it modularity and makes it easier to explain. Many variables and functions can be combined. Some redundancies could be omitted. It demonstrates, however, many of the Explorer properties and methods for changing content dynamically—albeit with text examples—but image, applet, and control manipulation follows exactly the same rules.

Summary

Although the browser vendors are moving toward a common standard, currently the procedure for changing content dynamically in Navigator and IE4 still differs greatly.

Navigator's LAYER tag and its handling of positioned CSS elements continues the tradition of the FRAME tag. Change is based on the replacement of the contents of the layer/element document property, either through the document.write() method or by loading a new external HTML page.

IE4's comprehensive DOM and its reflection into JavaScript allows for the addition, insertion, replacement, and deletion of any element with instant page redraw. To this end, four powerful properties and two methods have been introduced: innerText, outerText, innerHTML, outerHTML, insertAdjacentText(), and insertAdjacentHTML().

This chapter provided examples of changing content in both browsers with all the tools provided. A script for a simple Q&A quiz was developed for IE4, illustrating a real-life application for the new properties and methods.

Content change alone does not a DHTML page make. However, when content change is combined with the techniques discussed in Chapter 12, "Dynamic Positioning," your pages will truly come alive.

Dynamic Positioning

by Matthew Zandstra

IN THIS CHAPTER

The fourth-generation browsers give the coder nearly total control over page layout at last. Even better, their extensions to JavaScript introduce movement, depth, and even rudimentary intelligence to page elements.

This is a chapter about scripted positioning. It is also in part about objects and how object-oriented programming techniques can help you to breed smart page elements.

With Internet Explorer 4.0 (IE4) and Netscape Communicator 4.0, browser scripting has come of age, and Web pages will never be the same again.

In this chapter you will learn about:

- The basic cascading style sheet (CSS) properties for dynamic positioning
- Automatic cross-browser scripting
- Scripting position, movement, and depth
- Image maps with Dynamic HTML (DHTML)
- Object-oriented JavaScript techniques

Cross-Browser Issues

How many times have you produced an exciting Web environment, only to find that another browser rejects your script or interprets it eccentrically? It's a fact of life for Web publishers that various browsers behave differently, and it's our responsibility to compensate accordingly.

Almost all the examples in these pages will work on both IE4 and Netscape Communicator 4.0, thanks to code designed to compensate for scripting differences and browser quirks.

Occasionally, though, irreconcilable differences are impossible to avoid. Explorer does not support the CSS `clip` property, for example. If you don't explicitly set the width property of an element, it will default to fill all available horizontal space from the left of the element to the right margin of the parent element.

Communicator's support for the CSS `width` and `height` properties is not reliable; most of the time an element will shrink to the width and height of its contents. The `clip` property is partially supported. If `clip` is set within the style declaration, Communicator will ignore it. If it is set by a script, Communicator will clip the element accordingly.

There are some key differences in JavaScript syntax that are less problematic. We will automate a fix for these differences in this chapter.

Web coding is the art of the possible, and rather than halve your audience at a stroke, we concentrate in this chapter on the shared features of the fourth-generation browsers, compensating for and working around differences where necessary.

Positioning: The Basics

Cascading style sheets allow the coder unprecedented control over page elements. He or she can animate elements, change their relative depths, and make them appear or disappear. Before we can explore this level of dynamism, however, we must first assemble our page elements and assign styles to them. Some impressive effects are possible without writing even a line of JavaScript.

Absolute and Relative Positioning

One of the great frustrations for the Web designer has always been the inability to place page elements accurately.

DHTML gives the coder much greater control over layout, allowing him or her to place elements on the page with pixel accuracy. Alternatively, he or she can allow the browser to flow elements, placing them relative to one another in the traditional manner.

Cascading style sheets (CSS) allow for this control through the position property, which can be initialized in the style definition. The position property defaults to static if left uninitialized. Otherwise, you have a choice of two values: relative or absolute.

Going with the Flow: Relative Positioning

Very often, you'll want your CSS elements to be positioned conventionally in relation to other elements on the page. When the browser window is resized, your page will be reflowed as normal and your elements positioned accordingly.

This is easy to set up in your style definition by setting the position property to relative. Listing 12.1 shows the code for a relatively positioned element.

Listing 12.1. Relative positioning.

```
<HTML>
<HEAD>
<TITLE>relative positioning</TITLE>
</HEAD>
<STYLE TYPE="text/css">
.myClass{
    POSITION: relative;
    COLOR: red;
    FONT-SIZE: 40pt;
    FONT-FAMILY: sans-serif
    }
</STYLE>
<BODY>
Some standard text before the element
<DIV CLASS="myClass">
hello you
</DIV>
Some standard text after the element
</BODY>
</HTML>
```

As you can see in Figure 12.1, the style is applied, and the element is positioned with the document flow—that is, sandwiched between the starting and finishing text.

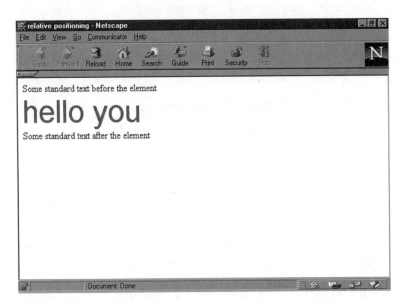

You can control this to some extent through your choice of tag. Applying a relatively positioned style to a <DIV> tag, as in Figure 12.1, will result in the element being treated as a block, sitting in its own space. For inline placement, use the <SPAN> tag. This will align your element as if it belonged within a line of text. Figure 12.2 shows the same example as Figure 12.1, using <SPAN> rather than <DIV>.

Relatively positioned elements are not simply at the mercy of the browser, however. You can exercise quite a lot of control through the top and left properties. With the position property set to relative, these will act as offsets. By initializing the top property, for example, you shift your element by that many pixels from its default top edge. So we can make text sink below or, if we use a negative value, float serenely above its line:

```
.myClass{
    POSITION: relative;
    COLOR: red;
    TOP: 30px;
    LEFT: 0px;
    FONT-SIZE: 40pt;
    FONT-FAMILY: sans-serif
    }
```

Notice that the top and left properties both require the addition of code that defines their units—pixels in this case—like this:

```
TOP: 30px;
LEFT: 0px;
```

FIGURE 12.2.

Relative positioning with the <SPAN> element.

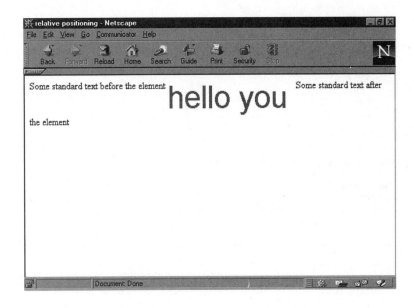

It is also possible to define the `left` and `top` properties in percentages. The element will be offset by the given proportion of its parent element's width.

```
TOP: 10%;
LEFT: 0%;
```

On the Nail: Absolute Positioning

There are times when you will need to take control of your page elements and tell them exactly where to go. You can do this by setting the `position` property to `absolute` in your style definition, like this:

```
.myClass{
    POSITION: absolute;
    //.. etc
    }
```

We can then use the `top` and `left` properties to force an element to a particular point on the page. Unless our element is nested within another, the element will take the top-left corner of the browser window (or, more properly, the `<BODY>` element) as its referent. Listing 12.2 demonstrates the code for an absolutely positioned element.

Listing 12.2. Absolute positioning.

```
<HTML>
<HEAD>
<TITLE>absolute positioning</TITLE>
</HEAD>
<STYLE TYPE="text/css">
```

continues

Listing 12.2. continued

```
.myClass{
    POSITION: absolute;
    COLOR: red;
    TOP: 100px;
    LEFT: 100px;
    FONT-SIZE: 40pt;
    FONT-FAMILY: sans-serif
    }
</STYLE>
<BODY>
Some standard text before the element
<SPAN CLASS="myClass">
hello you
</SPAN>
Some standard text after the element
</BODY>
</HTML>
```

You can see in Figure 12.3 that our element no longer has any real relationship with the surrounding text. Other elements will not make room for it, and it won't respect their space.

FIGURE 12.3.

An absolutely positioned element.

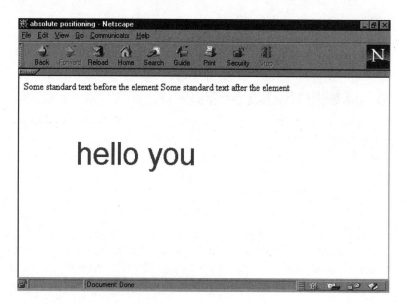

This fact can be used to achieve some interesting effects (not to mention some that are just plain ugly). How about a nice drop shadow, for example? In Listing 12.3 we create a shadow and place it three pixels to the left of and above another element.

Listing 12.3. Using absolute positioning to create drop shadows.

```html
<HTML>
<HEAD>
<TITLE>drop shadows with positioning</TITLE>
</HEAD>
<STYLE TYPE="text/css">
.myClass{
    POSITION: absolute;
    COLOR: red;
    FONT-SIZE: 40pt;
    FONT-FAMILY: sans-serif;
    Z-INDEX:2;
    }
.container{
    POSITION: absolute;
    TOP: 100px;
    LEFT: 100px;
    }
#shadow{
    COLOR: #aaaaaa;
    TOP: -3px;
    LEFT: -3px;
    Z-INDEX:1;
    }
</STYLE>
<BODY BGCOLOR="#ffffff">
Some standard text before the element
<DIV CLASS="container">
    <SPAN CLASS="myClass">
    hello you
    </SPAN>
    <SPAN ID="shadow" CLASS="myClass">
    hello you
    </SPAN>
</DIV>
Some standard text after the element
</BODY>
</HTML>
```

This code introduces a new property: z-index. This determines which element will be upper-most; we will deal with it more fully in the section titled "z-index." Notice that we have used nesting in Listing 12.3. The container element is absolutely positioned in relation to the BODY element. In their turn, the child elements are absolutely positioned in relation to the parent. We have used negative values for the top and left properties of the shadow element. Using this technique you only need worry about the positioning of the parent element on the page. Note also that the parent element could be relatively positioned.

Figure 12.4 shows the code in action.

Before CSS came along, our drop shadow effect would have required an image and the over-head of a new connection to the server.

Figure 12.4.

A drop shadow with absolute positioning and nesting.

height and width

Officially, CSS allows you to set both the height and the width of your elements. In practice, however, you should be cautious of this feature. At the moment, Netscape Navigator 4.0 is unreliable at best in its implementation of the width property. Its support for the height property is effectively nonexistent. To confuse matters even further, IE4 sets the width property of an element to the space available in the enclosing element by default, so it's a good idea to explicitly set this property—especially if you are going to set a background property as well.

The height and width properties can be specified in either pixels or percentages.

overflow

The overflow property should work only with elements whose position property is set to absolute. It determines what should happen if the width or height of an element is less than that of the content. The possible values of the overflow property include none, clip, and scroll. The default is none, which allows content that exceeds an element's dimensions to be displayed.

Because of the erratic behavior of the height and width properties, this property is probably best avoided for the present. It should be borne in mind, however, that both Microsoft and Netscape are committed to implementing the full CSS specification.

visibility

Visibility is a more reliable property than overflow and comes in very handy when scripting CSS elements. It accepts three values: visible, hidden, and inherit. If this property is not initialized, it defaults to inherit; that is, any element using it will take on the visibility of its parent element. The `visibility` property is fully accessible to scripting in both Communicator and Internet Explorer, and we use it in the examples demonstrated in this chapter. Its syntax looks like this:

```
#youWontSeeMe{
    VISIBILITY:hidden
    }
```

z-index

The drop shadow code in Listing 12.3 shows a good example of `z-index` in action. We wanted the shadow to appear behind the display text, no matter what order our elements were read by the browser. `z-index` gives us that control. `z-index` accepts an integer. Elements with higher `z-index` properties will display in front of those with lower ones. `z-index` is measured in relation to the parent element.

clip

`clip` is patchily implemented at present by Communicator and not at all by Explorer. It allows you to mask areas of an element. In Communicator, it is accessible to browser scripts and is therefore an excellent tool for creating low-overhead dynamic image maps. Officially, one should be able to clip an element from a CSS declaration with this syntax:

```
CLIP: rect (top right bottom left)
```

This should not be trusted, however. In practice, it is better to clip elements from a script. We deal with this in the section "Cutting Corners: Dynamic Image Maps Using Only Two Images."

Scripting Dynamic Elements

This is a chapter about dynamic positioning, and there's little dynamism without scripting. Luckily, both of the fourth-generation browsers allow the control of many CSS properties through JavaScript (or JScript, Internet Explorer's JavaScript implementation). The scripting model used by each browser differs somewhat from that of the other, but not so much that cross-browser code isn't possible.

To access a CSS element or one of its properties, you first need to assign it a unique name, using the ID argument of the element tag, like this:

```
<DIV ID="layerID" class="layerStyle">
...
</DIV>
```

In Netscape 4.0, you can now refer to your element as follows:

```
document.layers['layerID']
```

The code for IE4 is a little different:

```
document.all['layerID']
```

Unfortunately, the waters are muddied even further if you need to access one of the element's properties. Let's take the example of the top property. With Netscape 4.0, you can go right ahead:

```
document.layers['layerID'].top
```

With IE4, however, there's just a little more work to do:

```
document.all['layerID'].style.top
```

Where CSS properties use a hyphen, the JavaScript syntax differs slightly. JavaScript does not allow the use of hyphens for variables or property names, so it supports interCap notation instead. z-index, for example, becomes zIndex.

We have enough now to set the position of an element dynamically in each of the fourth-generation browsers. In Listing 12.4 we create an example that will work with Netscape 4.0.

Listing 12.4. Communicator-specific code for dynamic positioning.

```
<HTML>
<HEAD>
<TITLE>scripting position - communicator</TITLE>
</HEAD>
<SCRIPT LANGUAGE="JavaScript">
function random (limit)
    {
     return (Math.round(((Math.random())*1000))%limit)+1;
    }
function moveElement()
    {
    document.layers['movingElement'].left=random(300);
    document.layers['movingElement'].top=random(300);
    }
</SCRIPT>
<STYLE TYPE="text/css">
.comeAlong{
    POSITION: absolute;
    TOP: 100px;
    LEFT: 100px;
    }
</STYLE>
<BODY BGCOLOR="#ffffff">

<DIV ID="movingElement" CLASS="comeAlong">
<FORM>
<INPUT TYPE=BUTTON VALUE="you move me" ONCLICK="moveElement()">
</FORM>
</DIV>
</BODY>
</HTML>
```

This code creates a singularly annoying form button, which leaps to a random location when clicked.

In the style definition we have set up a basic class called `comeAlong`, initializing the `position`, `top`, and `left` properties. It is important to establish that we will be working with an absolutely positioned element. If we had omitted this, our element would have defaulted to `position: static`, and we would not have been able to change its location.

In the body of our document, we have applied this class to a `<DIV>`, or block-level, element with the unique name `movingElement`. This element holds only a simple form button, which calls a JavaScript function, `moveElement()`, when clicked.

`moveElement()` sets the top property of `comeAlong` to a random number and then does the same to the `left` property; our button then jumps to its new location.

To make this work in Internet Explorer 4.0, we need change only two lines:

```
document.layers['movingElement'].left=random(300);
document.layers['movingElement'].top=random(300);
```

These lines should become the following:

```
document.all['movingElement'].style.left=random(300);
document.all['movingElement'].style.top=random(300);
```

How about making the code work on both browsers? Well, we could set a switch in our `moveElement()` function so that the correct code is executed for the correct browser, like this:

```
function moveElement()
{
if (navigator.appName=="Netscape"
    {
    document.layers['movingElement'].left=random(300);
    document.layers['movingElement'].top=random(300);
    }
else
    {
    document.all['movingElement'].style.left=random(300);
    document.all['movingElement'].style.top=random(300);
    }
}
```

This may not seem like a clumsy solution at first glance. After all, it certainly works. Consider, though, a large script—a game, for instance. You would have to use a browser test similar to the one listed here every time you needed to access or set an element's properties. Your code would soon become ugly and confusing.

In the next section we define a neat way of overcoming the browsers' differences.

Entente in the Browser War: The `layerTool` Object

The `layerTool` object is designed to take the hard work out of cross-browser coding. Its constructor performs a browser test and then assigns different functions to an object method, `layerProp()`, according to the result. Its syntax looks like this:

```
var L=new layerTool();
function layerTool()
    {
    if (navigator.appName=="Netscape")
        this.layerProp=navProp;
    else
        this.layerProp=exProp;
    }
function exProp()
    {
    return document.all[arguments[arguments.length-1]].style;
    }
function navProp()
    {
    retVal="";
    for (var x=0;x<arguments.length;x++)
        {
        retVal+="document.layers[\'"+arguments[x]+"\']";
        if (x!=arguments.length-1)
        retVal+=".";
        }
return eval(retVal);
}
```

Later on, if we need to set a layer property, we need only call the `layerProp()` method, like this:

```
L.layerProp('myLayer').top=100;
```

In Listing 12.5 we re-create our annoying button example, this time using the `layerTool` object.

Listing 12.5. Cross-browser code for dynamic position.

```
<HTML>
<HEAD>
<TITLE> scripting position - cross browser</TITLE>
</HEAD>
<SCRIPT LANGUAGE="javascript">

var L=new layerTool();
function layerTool()
    {
    if (navigator.appName=="Netscape")
        this.layerProp=navProp;
    else
        this.layerProp=exProp;
    }
function exProp()
    {
    return document.all[arguments[arguments.length-1]].style;
    }
function navProp()
    {
    retVal="";
    for (var x=0;x<arguments.length;x++)
        {
        retVal+="document.layers[\'"+arguments[x]+"\']";
        if (x!=arguments.length-1)
```

```
                retVal+=".";
            }
      return eval(retVal);
      }
function random (limit)
      {
       return (Math.round(((Math.random())*1000))%limit)+1;
      }
function moveElement()
      {
      L.layerProp('movingElement').left=random(300);
      L.layerProp('movingElement').top=random(300);
      }
</SCRIPT>
<STYLE TYPE="text/css">
.comeAlong{
      POSITION: absolute;
      TOP: 100px;
      LEFT: 100px;
      }
</STYLE>
<BODY BGCOLOR="#ffffff">
<DIV ID="movingElement" CLASS="comeAlong">
<FORM>
<INPUT TYPE=BUTTON VALUE="you move me" ONCLICK="moveElement()">
</FORM>
</DIV>
</BODY>
</HTML>
```

The only real changes in this example are the addition of the layerTool object and the calls to its layerProp() method in moveElement().

One feature of the layerTool object worth mentioning is its support for nesting. Contrary to some reports, it is possible to access nested <DIV> elements in Communicator. The code is a little tortuous, however. To refer to an element called inner nested within another called outer, the Communicator code might look like this:

```
document.outer.document.inner
```

or

```
document.layers['outer'].document.layers['inner']
```

The navProp() function, which is associated with the layerProp() object method, deals with this property by testing for the number of arguments passed to it. It loops through the arguments using concatenation to build a string similar to the code listed previously. It then uses eval() to create a usable return value. To access a nested element in both browsers, therefore, is simple:

```
L.layerProp('outer','inner')
```

Now that we have a layerTool class in place, we can move on to create some real cross-browser code.

Shuffling the Pack: Dynamically Changing `z-index`

One of the greatest advantages of CSS is the power to exploit a new dimension in the document object. Not only can layers be made to overlap one another, but the coder can exert dynamic control over his or her ordering with the JavaScript `zIndex` property. Remember that hyphenated CSS elements cannot be accessed by JavaScript using the same syntax. You must use InterCap notation to dispense with the hyphen. In JavaScript, therefore, `z-index` becomes `zIndex`.

So why is this feature so useful? Why should we want to be able to control the relative depth of layers? Consider a simple animation. A spaceship is approaching a planet, passing in front of it. A quick switch of `zIndex` and it disappears behind it, giving the powerful illusion of depth on the page. Depth is also useful as a way of organizing information. The card file metaphor has been implemented in many programs and CD-ROM environments. Figure 12.5 shows a simple Web implementation.

FIGURE 12.5.

Using `z-index` *to create a simple card file effect.*

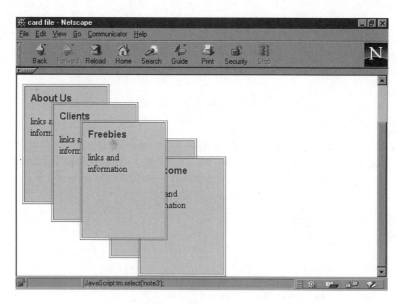

First we should create five "cards," all implementing a style called `shuffleClass`, like this:

```
.shuffleClass{
    POSITION: absolute;
    VISIBILITY: visible;
    LEFT: 10px;
    WIDTH:150px
    }
```

Each card will have its own ID property running from note1 to note5. This kind of naming is very useful for scripting, because we can use loops to refer to each card in turn. shuffleClass establishes absolute positioning and left, background, and width properties. The cards' dimensions are set again within the elements themselves using the width and height arguments of a table cell tag. Without the tables, Netscape would collapse each element to the size of its contents. The IDs override the shuffleClass's left property and initialize a top property, setting each element 30 pixels below and 50 pixels to the right of the last. z-index is established in ascending order, like this:

```
#note2{
    TOP: 130px;
    LEFT: 60px;
    Z-ORDER: 2
    }
#note2{
    TOP: 160px;
    LEFT: 110px;
    Z-ORDER: 3
    }
```

To control these layers, we should create a layerObject object to manage the layer properties. This in turn will make use of the layerTools object to ensure cross-browser compatibility. The layerObject object syntax looks like this:

```
function layerObject(layerID,z)
    {
    this.layerID=layerID;
    this.depth=z;
    this.oldDepth=z;
    this.draw=drawLayer;
    this.setZorder=setZorder;
    }
function setZorder(z)
    {
    this.depth=z;
    }
function drawLayer()
    {
    L.layerProp(this.layerID).zIndex=this.depth;
    }
```

This class takes two parameters in its constructor, the ID of the layer and its current z-index. It has two methods: setZorder() accepts an integer and applies it to the layerObject object's depth property; and the drawLayer() function (or draw() method) uses the layerTool object to apply the depth property to the layer, changing the elements' ordering on the page.

The structure of this class raises several questions with regard to style. Why have we used our own property for z-index, rather than simply interrogating the element's z-index property directly? Well, IE4 will not always return values for CSS properties unless they have first been set within the script, so we have to ask for z-index as a parameter.

Why does setZorder() merely change the depth property of the layerObject object and not apply the new value to the layer itself? In the section "A Smart layerObject," we'll be extending the `layerObject` to handle other behaviors, including movement. It makes sense, therefore, to change our various object properties and then apply these changes to the layer in one go, using the `drawLayer()` method. In some circumstances we might want to make more changes before we apply them all.

The `layerObject` object is a powerful way of maintaining control of page elements, so much so that we will be extending it as the chapter progresses. However, none of the elements have any knowledge of any of the others, which leaves us with a problem. How can we bring one of our layers to the front if we have no way of knowing the depth of all the others? Clearly we need to write some code to manage our `layerObject` objects, such as the following:

```
function noteManager()
    {
    this.LayerList=new Array();
    this.add=addLayer;
    this.select=select;
    }
function addLayer(layerObject)
    {
    this.LayerList[this.LayerList.length]=layerObject;
    }
function select(LayerName)
    {
    for (x=0;x<this.LayerList.length;x++)
        {
        if (this.LayerList[x].layerID==LayerName)
            {
            if (this.LayerList[x].depth==100)
                {
                this.LayerList[x].setZorder(this.LayerList[x].oldDepth);
                }
            else
                {
                this.LayerList[x].setZorder(100);
                }
            }
        else
            {
            this.LayerList[x].setZorder(this.LayerList[x].oldDepth);
            }
        this.LayerList[x].draw();
        }
    }
```

The `noteManager` object has only two methods, `addLayer()` and `select()`. `addLayer()` expects a `layerObject` object, which it adds to its `layerList` property. `select()` is called from a hyperlink with the containing element's ID as a parameter.

`select()` iterates through the `layerList` array looking for a match. If it finds one, it tests for the `layerObject` object's depth property, setting it either to `100` if the element is not already selected or to its default depth (stored in the `layerObject`'s `defaultDepth` property) if it is. In this way a user can click to bring an element to the front and click again to send it back to its usual place in the stack of elements. If no match is found on an iteration, the layerObject's depth property is set to its defaultDepth. The last line in the loop calls the draw() method of the layerObject, finally applying the value of the depth property to the layer's z-index property.

The noteManager is the organizing force of the script, overseeing the interrelation of all layerObject objects, which in turn set the properties for their corresponding page elements. This structure is a useful one for creating interactive pages, and we will be returning to it in the section "Making It Move."

In the meantime, there are two more steps to complete: First, we must actually create our objects; and second, we must make sure that the select() method of the noteManager class can be called from the page.

To create the layerObject objects, we should create an init() function that can be called from the document's onLoad handler, like this:

```
function init()
    {
    tm=new noteManager();
    for (x=1;x<=5;x++)
        {
        tm.add(new layerObject("note"+x,x));
        }
    }
```

Our noteManager is set up first and assigned to the variable tm. Then we use a loop to create five layerObject objects, passing up a string corresponding to each element's ID property and an integer that will become the layerObject object's depth (and the element's z-index) property. Each object is passed to the noteManager object via the noteManager class add() method. Note that the layerObject objects are not assigned to their own variables even temporarily; our noteManager object will store them for us in its layerList property.

Finally, we need to add hyperlinks to our elements. Because this is a chapter about positioning, we've used simple JavaScript calls, rather than get bogged down by the respective event models implemented by the fourth-generation browsers. See Part IV, "The Document Object Model," for more information about event models. We add the hyperlinks like this:

```
<div id="note1" class="shuffleClass">
<table height=200 width=150 bgcolor=green cellpadding=10 border=1>
<tr><td valign=top>
<a href="JavaScript:tm.select('note1');">About Us</A>
<p>
links and information
</p>
</td></tr>
</table>
</div>
```

The hyperlink passes the value of the element's ID property to noteManager's select method. Listing 12.6 shows the complete code for this script.

Listing 12.6. The complete card file script.

```html
<HTML>
<HEAD>
<TITLE>card file</TITLE>
</HEAD>

<SCRIPT LANGUAGE="JavaScript">

var L=new layerTool();
function layerTool()
    {
    if (navigator.appName=="Netscape")
        this.layerProp=navProp;
    else
        this.layerProp=exProp;
    }
function exProp()
    {
    return document.all[arguments[arguments.length-1]].style;
    }
function navProp()
    {
    retVal="";
    for (var x=0;x<arguments.length;x++)
        {
        retVal+="document.layers[\'"+arguments[x]+"\']";
        if (x!=arguments.length-1)
            retVal+=".";
        }
    return eval(retVal);
    }
function layerObject(layerID,z)
    {
    this.layerID=layerID;
    this.depth=z;
    this.oldDepth=z;
    this.draw=drawLayer;
    this.setZorder=setZorder;
    }
function setZorder(z)
    {
    this.depth=z;
    }
function drawLayer()
    {
    L.layerProp(this.layerID).zIndex=this.depth;
    }
function noteManager()
    {
    this.LayerList=new Array();
    this.add=addLayer;
    this.select=select;
    }
function addLayer(layerObject)
    {
    this.LayerList[this.LayerList.length]=layerObject;
    }
```

```
function select(LayerName)
    {
    for (x=0;x<this.LayerList.length;x++)
        {
        if (this.LayerList[x].layerID==LayerName)
            {
            if (this.LayerList[x].depth==100)
                {
                this.LayerList[x].setZorder(this.LayerList[x].oldDepth);
                }
            else
                {
                this.LayerList[x].setZorder(100);          .
                }
            }
        else
            {
            this.LayerList[x].setZorder(this.LayerList[x].oldDepth);
            }
        this.LayerList[x].draw();
        }
    }
function init()
    {
    tm=new noteManager();
    for (x=1;x<=5;x++)
        {
        tm.add(new layerObject("note"+x,x));
        }
    }
</SCRIPT>
<STYLE TYPE="text/css">
#note1{
    TOP: 100px;
    Z-ORDER: 1
    }
#note2{
    TOP: 130px;
    LEFT: 60px;
    Z-ORDER: 2
    }
#note3{
    TOP: 160px;
    LEFT: 110px;
    Z-ORDER: 3
    }
#note4{
    TOP: 190px;
    LEFT: 160px;
    Z-ORDER: 4
    }
#note5{
    TOP: 220px;
    LEFT: 210px;
    Z-ORDER: 5
    }
```

12

DYNAMIC POSITIONING

continues

Listing 12.6. continued

```
.shuffleClass{
    POSITION: absolute;
    BACKGROUND: green;
    VISIBILITY: visible;
    LEFT: 10px;
    WIDTH:150px
    }
A:link, A:visited, A:active {
    COLOR:blue;
    FONT-WEIGHT:bold;
    FONT-FAMILY: sans-serif;
    TEXT-DECORATION: none
    }

</STYLE>
<BODY BGCOLOR="#000000" ONLOAD="init()">

<DIV ID="note1" CLASS="shuffleClass">
<TABLE HEIGHT=200 WIDTH=150 BGCOLOR=GREEN CELLPADDING=10 BORDER=1>
<TR><TD VALIGN=TOP>
<A HREF="JavaScript:tm.select('note1');">About Us</A>
<P>
links and information
</P>
</TD></TR>
</TABLE>
</DIV>

<DIV ID="note2" CLASS="shuffleClass">
<TABLE HEIGHT=200 WIDTH=150 BGCOLOR=GREEN CELLPADDING=10 BORDER=1>
<TR><TD VALIGN=TOP>
<A HREF="JavaScript:tm.select('note2');">Clients</A>
<P>
links and information
</P>
</TD></TR>
</TABLE>
</DIV>

<DIV ID="note3" CLASS="shuffleClass">
<TABLE HEIGHT=200 WIDTH=150 BGCOLOR=GREEN CELLPADDING=10 BORDER=1>
<TR><TD VALIGN=TOP>
<A HREF="JavaScript:tm.select('note3');">Freebies</A>
<P>
links and information
</P>
</TD></TR>
</TABLE>
</DIV>

<DIV ID="note4" CLASS="shuffleClass">
<TABLE HEIGHT=200 WIDTH=150 BGCOLOR=GREEN CELLPADDING=10 BORDER=1>
<TR><TD VALIGN=TOP>
<A HREF="JavaScript:tm.select('note4');">Links</A>
<P>
```

```
links and information
</P>
</TD></TR>
</TABLE>
</DIV>

<DIV ID="note5" CLASS="shuffleClass">
<TABLE HEIGHT=200 WIDTH=150 BGCOLOR=GREEN CELLPADDING=10 BORDER=1>
<TR><TD VALIGN=TOP>
<A HREF="JavaScript:tm.select('note1');">Welcome</A>
<P>
links and information
</P>
</TD></TR>
</TABLE>
</DIV>

</BODY>
</HTML>
```

Cutting Corners: Dynamic Image Maps Using Only Two Images

In the days of Netscape 2.0 and Internet Explorer 3.0, dynamic image maps could only be achieved with an applet or a plug-in element. Then Netscape 3.0 heralded the JavaScript image object, allowing the coder to produce crude animations and effective mouseovers. While impressive, this technique involved the preloading of many images, slowing down access.

DHTML offers an elegant solution to this problem: the clip property. clip allows the coder to restrict the portion of a CSS element displayed. Creating image maps, therefore, is simply a matter of creating a highlight image, with all the hotspot areas active, placing it above another image with the hotspots in their default state, and then clipping the top image to show individual highlights as the mouse traverses the map. In Communicator, JavaScript can change the clipping of an element simply by accessing its clip property and setting top, left, bottom, or right to the desired integer, like this:

```
document['layer'].clip.top=25
```

That's the good news. The bad news is that at the time of this writing, IE4, PR2 does not support the clip property. It is likely that this will be fixed in the final release.

Figure 12.6 shows a dynamic image map running on Communicator 4.0 with one of its hotspots activated.

To create our image map, we first need to define our style sheet and create the elements, like this:

```
<STYLE TYPE="text/css">
.maps{
    POSITION:absolute
    }
#container{
    POSITION:relative
    }
#topLayer{
    VISIBILITY:hidden
    }
</STYLE>
<SCRIPT>
    m.writeMap("myMap");
</SCRIPT>

</HEAD>
<BODY BGCOLOR="#FFFFFF">

<DIV ID="container">
    <DIV ID="bottomLayer" CLASS="maps">
    <IMG SRC="res/apple1.gif" USEMAP="#myMap" BORDER=0>
    </DIV>
    <DIV ID="topLayer" CLASS="maps">
    <IMG NAME=TEST SRC="res/apple2.gif" USEMAP="#myMap" BORDER=0>
    </DIV>
</DIV>
```

The two map elements, topLayer and bottomLayer, are nested within a container element. Both are given absolute positions, which default to the top left-hand corner of the parent. Because of this structure, all coordinates will be calculated relative to the container element rather than the document. Note that the `topLayer` element's visibility property is set to `hidden`. The clipping will be applied by our script, so we need not worry about it yet.

As with a traditional image map, we need to define hotspots. In this case, however, the coordinates will fulfill a dual function. In addition to determining the reactive areas of the images, they will also form the basis of the `clip` property of the `topLayer` element. To manage this data, we will create an `Area` object, like this:

```
function Area(X1,Y1,X2,Y2,url)
    {
    this.left=X1;
    this.top=Y1;
    this.right=X2;
    this.bottom=Y2;
    this.url=url;
    }
```

The `Area` object expects five parameters: coordinates for top, left, bottom, and right locations of the hotspot as well as a string containing the target URL. The following array will serve to store all the map's areas:

```
p=new Array();
p[0]=new Area(25,30,125,75,"http://www.corrosive.co.uk/");
p[1]=new Area(5,125,130,175,"http://www.corrosive.co.uk/");
p[2]=new Area(115,100,225,126,"http://www.corrosive.co.uk/");
```

A map object is needed to work with these `Area` objects. The `map` object has three methods: a `writeMap()` method will write the traditional HTML for an image map, saving the coder the bother of pasting in the map coordinates twice; a `highlight()` method will handle the clipping; and a `reset()` method will restore the map to its `mouseOut` appearance:

```
function map(name,container,top,areas)
    {
    this.name=name;
    this.top=top;
    this.container=container;
    this.areas=areas;
    this.writeMap=writeMap;
    this. highlight=highlight;
    this.reset=reset;
    this.timeout=null;
    }
function writeMap (mapName)
    {
    document.write("<map name="+mapName+">");
    for (var x=0;x<this.areas.length;x++)
        {
        document.write("<area shape=\"RECT\" href='"+this.areas[x].url+"'
onMouseOver='"+this.name+".highlight("+x+")' ");
        document.write("onMouseOut='"+this.name+".reset()' ");
        document.write("COORDS=\""+this.areas[x].left+","+this.areas[x].top+"
"+this.areas[x].right+","+this.areas[x].bottom+"\">");
        }
    document.write("</map>");
    }
```

```
function highlight(num)
    {
    clearTimeout(this.timeout);
    this.timeout=setTimeout(this.name+".reset()",5000);
    L.layerProp(this.container,this.top).visibility="visible";
    L.layerProp(this.container,this.top).clip.top=this.areas[num].top;
    L.layerProp(this.container,this.top).clip.left=this.areas[num].left;
    L.layerProp(this.container,this.top).clip.bottom=this.areas[num].bottom;
    L.layerProp(this.container,this.top).clip.right=this.areas[num].right;
    }
function reset()
    {
    L.layerProp(this.container,this.top).visibility="hidden";
    }
```

The map class's constructor expects four parameters: a string representing the object's name (a string version of the variable to which the object is assigned), the ID property of the container element, the ID property of the topLayer element, and the array of Area objects that we set up earlier.

The writeMap() method iterates through the Area array, using the coordinate and url properties of each Area object to write the <AREA> tags to the page. It also uses the map object's name property to write mouseOver and mouseOut calls to the highlight() and reset() methods. If the writeMap() method is to be used, it must be as the page loads. The call should be placed in the body of the document, like this:

```
<SCRIPT>
    m.writeMap("myMap");
</SCRIPT>
```

The highlight() method does all the serious work. It accepts the index number of the Area object associated with a hotspot. The topLayer element is then clipped according to the Area object's coordinate properties. Finally, the clipped element is made visible. Note the use of the layerTool object. Because the topLayer element is nested within the container element, Netscape needs a reference to both layers in order to access the topLayer element's properties. The syntax looks like this:

```
document.layers['container'].document.layers['topLayer'].clip.left=25;
```

or, in brief:

```
document.container.document.topLayer.clip.left=25;
```

The layerTool object will handle all that for you. Internet Explorer can directly access any layer, nested or not; again the layerTool object will handle this, extracting only the last parameter passed to its layerProp() method and returning the correct code, like this:

```
document.all['topLayer'].style.clip.left=25;
```

The reset() method is called onMouseOut and simply hides the topLayer element. The PowerPC version of Communicator occasionally loses the mouseOut event, so setTimeout() is used to call reset() after five seconds.

Listing 12.7 shows the script in its entirety.

Listing 12.7. Dynamic image map script.

```
<HTML>
<HEAD>
<TITLE>Dynamic image map</TITLE>
<SCRIPT LANGUAGE="JavaScript">
var L=new layerTool();
function layerTool()
    {
    if (navigator.appName=="Netscape")
        this.layerProp=navProp;
    else
        this.layerProp=exProp;
    }
function exProp()
    {
    return document.all[arguments[arguments.length-1]].style;
    }
function navProp()
    {
    retVal="";
    for (x=0;x<arguments.length;x++)
        {
        retVal+="document.layers[\'"+arguments[x]+"\']";
        if (x!=arguments.length-1)
            retVal+=".";
        }
    return eval(retVal);
    }

p=new Array();
p[0]=new Area(25,30,125,75,"http://www.corrosive.co.uk/");
p[1]=new Area(5,125,130,175,"http://www.corrosive.co.uk/");
p[2]=new Area(115,100,225,126,"http://www.corrosive.co.uk/");

var cyc=0;
m=new map("m","container","topLayer",p);
function Area(X1,Y1,X2,Y2,url)
    {
    this.left=X1;
    this.top=Y1;
    this.right=X2;
    this.bottom=Y2;
    this.url=url;
    }
function map(name,container,top,areas)
    {
    this.name=name;
    this.top=top;
    this.container=container;
    this.areas=areas;
    this.writeMap=writeMap;
    this. highlight=highlight;
    this.reset=reset;
    this.timeout=null;
    }
```

continues

Listing 12.7. continued

```
function writeMap (mapName)
    {
    document.write("<map name="+mapName+">");
    for (x=0;x<this.areas.length;x++)
        {
        document.write("<area shape=\"RECT\" href='"+this.areas[x].url+"'
onMouseOver='"+this.name+".highlight("+x+")' ");
        document.write("onMouseOut='"+this.name+".reset()' ");
        document.write("COORDS=\""+this.areas[x].left+","+this.areas[x].top+"
"+this.areas[x].right+","+this.areas[x].bottom+"\">");
        }
    document.write("</map>");
    }
function highlight(num)
    {
    clearTimeout(this.timeout);
    this.timeout=setTimeout(this.name+".reset()",5000);
    L.layerProp(this.container,this.top).visibility="visible";
    L.layerProp(this.container,this.top).clip.top=this.areas[num].top;
    L.layerProp(this.container,this.top).clip.left=this.areas[num].left;
    L.layerProp(this.container,this.top).clip.bottom=this.areas[num].bottom;
    L.layerProp(this.container,this.top).clip.right=this.areas[num].right;
    }
function reset()
    {
    L.layerProp(this.container,this.top).visibility="hidden";
    }
</SCRIPT>
<STYLE TYPE="text/css">
.maps{
    POSITION:absolute
    }
#container{
    POSITION:relative
    }
#topLayer{
    VISIBILITY:hidden
    }
</STYLE>
<SCRIPT>
    m.writeMap("myMap");
</SCRIPT>

</HEAD>
<BODY BGCOLOR="#FFFFFF">

<DIV ID="container">
    <DIV ID="bottomLayer" CLASS="maps">
    <IMG SRC="res/apple1.gif" USEMAP="#myMap" BORDER=0>
    </DIV>
    <DIV ID="topLayer" CLASS="maps">
    <IMG NAME=TEST SRC="res/apple2.gif" USEMAP="#myMap" BORDER=0>
    </DIV>
</DIV>

</BODY>
</HTML>
```

(Nearly) Object-Oriented Code in JavaScript

So far in this chapter we have used and reused several techniques that bear closer examination. JavaScript is not strictly an object-oriented language; crucially, there is no built-in support for inheritance (although we will be working around this in the section "The JavaScript Inheritance"). Nevertheless, it is perfectly possible to create objects and to employ some object-oriented techniques.

An object is simply a bundle of properties and methods. As such, it's an excellent way of organizing information. Consider the image map example from Listing 12.7. The map object needed to keep track of the image map's hotspots. For each hotspot we simply bundled all the relevant information into an Area object and placed the object into an array. The map object could get at five separate pieces of information from each of the Area objects to which it had a reference. Of course, we could have achieved the same effect by passing a two-dimensional array to the map object, but such arrays tend to be confusing and difficult to read. Even worse, we would have to write five lines of code for each hotspot, whereas with an object, only one line is necessary after the class has been created.

In addition to storing information, objects can contain their own functionality. So, in the z-index example we were able to do more than just access information from an array of objects; we could instruct the objects to act based on that information. The noteManager object contained a list of layerObject objects in a property called layerList. noteManager's select method could invoke the setZorder() and draw() methods of all the objects in its list.

We have seen another interesting facet of JavaScript in our layerTool object. Take another look at the constructor:

```
function layerTool()
    {
    if (navigator.appName=="Netscape")
        this.layerProp=navProp;
    else
        this.layerProp=exProp;
    }
```

There is a certain amount of magic in operation here. According to the user's browser type, one of two functions is assigned to the layerTool's layerProp method. The coder who uses this object need never know anything about that, though; all he or she needs to do is call the layerProp() method, and the correct function will be invoked. This is one reason that object methods and the functions to which they refer are often given different names. We will be extending this crude form of polymorphism substantially later in the section "Bringing It All Together."

Making It Move

Dynamism implies movement, but in the examples so far, little has moved. In the annoying button example we demonstrated that it is possible to set the top and left properties of an element with JavaScript; it is a relatively small step from there to create the illusion of continuous movement. In the section on z-index we built a layerObject that managed the depth of layers. We can expand that now to deal with motion.

Much of the code for sprite movement and management owes its inspiration to Michael Morrison's Java sprite classes. It says a lot for JavaScript's evolution that it's possible now to port Java sprite classes to simplified JavaScript versions.

What would a layerObject need to know about in order to move itself around the page? A starting position is essential.

We could simply demand two more integers in the layerObject class's parameter list, one for top and one for left. The coordinate combination is so common, however, it might be as well to combine both parameters in a separate Point class, similar to the ones defined in Java and Macromedia's Lingo. Combining both parameters looks like this:

```
function Point(X,Y)
    {
    this.x=X;
    this.y=Y;
    }
```

That takes care of the sprite's initial position and helps us as well with the next parameter the layerObject object will be needing. The sprite will need to be told in which direction to move and the speed at which it should do it. A Point object will do this job, determining an increment for the x and y axes.

Let's extend the layerObject's constructor:

```
function layerObject(layerID,pos,vel,z)
    {
    // properties
    this.layerID=layerID;
    this.position=pos;
    this.velocity=vel;
    this.depth=z;
    this.visibility="visible";
    // methods
    this.draw=drawLayer;
    this.setZorder=setZorder;
    }
```

The layerObject class now requires two new parameters: pos and vel. These should be Point objects and are assigned to the properties position and velocity, respectively.

Remember, it's safest to let your object assign element properties and to store its own version of those that it's interested in. Why is this? Isn't it just a matter of duplication? Possibly, but it can save you an awful lot of trouble. In both browsers it is often easier to set than to test CSS properties. In Netscape, for example, the following test will return an integer:

```
document.layers['myLayer'].top;
```

In Internet Explorer, however, the equivalent test will return a string including the px characters at the end of the numerical value:

```
document.all['myLayer'].style.top
```

To use this, you would have to strip off the px and use parseInt() to convert the resultant string. It's much easier to avoid this and other quirks and incompatibilities by setting object properties that in turn set element properties.

To make the sprite move, the object will need some more code—a setPosition() method to change the position property, for example, and an extended draw() method to apply the position to the relevant CSS properties. The syntax looks like this:

```
function drawLayer()
    {
    L.layerProp(this.layerID).zIndex=this.depth;
    L.layerProp(this.layerID).left=(this.position).x;
    L.layerProp(this.layerID).top=(this.position).y;
    }
function setPosition(pos)
    {
    this.position=pos;
    }
```

How will the velocity property be applied to the sprite's current position? An update() method will do this, and a lot more if we need it to. Its syntax looks like this:

```
function layerUpdate()
    {
    var newPos=new Point(this.position.x+this.velocity.x,
this.position.y+this.velocity.y);
    this.setPosition(newPos);
    }
```

The update() method creates a temporary Point object, adding the velocity property's x and y properties to those of the layerObject object's position property. The new Point object is then passed to the setPosition() method.

That's enough to create a basic layer sprite. Listing 12.8 shows a script that applies the class, with a few useful new methods thrown in, and Figure 12.7 shows our element as it floats across the page.

FIGURE 12.7.

A single layer on the move.

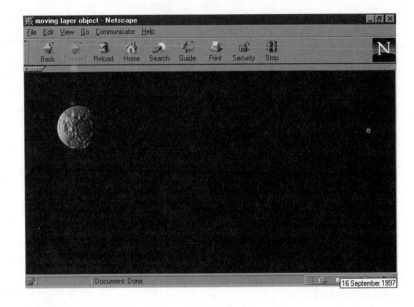

Listing 12.8. A layer in motion.

```
<HTML>
<HEAD>
<TITLE>moving layer object</TITLE>
</HEAD>

<SCRIPT LANGUAGE="JavaScript">
var L=new layerTool();
function layerTool()
    {
    if (navigator.appName=="Netscape")
        this.layerProp=navProp;
    else
        this.layerProp=exProp;
    }
function exProp()
    {
    return document.all[arguments[arguments.length-1]].style;
    }
function navProp()
    {
    retVal="";
    for (var x=0;x<arguments.length;x++)
        {
        retVal+="document.layers[\'"+arguments[x]+"\']";
        if (x!=arguments.length-1)
            retVal+=".";
        }
    return eval(retVal);
    }
function Point(X,Y)
    {
    this.x=X;
    this.y=Y;
```

```
    }
function layerObject(layerID,pos,vel,z)
    {
    // properties
    this.layerID=layerID;
    this.position=pos;
    this.velocity=vel;
    this.depth=z;
    this.visibility="visible";
    // methods
    this.show=showLayer;
    this.hide=hideLayer;
    this.setPosition=setPosition;
    this.draw=drawLayer;
    this.update=layerUpdate;
    this.show();
    }
function setZorder(z)
    {
    this.depth=z;
    }
function showLayer()
    {
    L.layerProp(this.layerID).visibility="visible";
    }
function hideLayer()
    {
    L.layerProp(this.layerID).visibility="hidden";
    }
function drawLayer()
    {
    L.layerProp(this.layerID).zIndex=this.depth;
    L.layerProp(this.layerID).left=(this.position).x;
    L.layerProp(this.layerID).top=(this.position).y;
    }
function setPosition(pos)
    {
    this.position=pos;
    }
function layerUpdate()
    {
    var newPos=new Point(this.position.x+this.velocity.x,
                         this.position.y+this.velocity.y);
    this.setPosition(newPos);
    }
function init()
    {
    mySprite=new layerObject("sprite1",new Point(0,0),new Point(5,5),1);
    cycle();
    }
function cycle()
    {
    mySprite.update();
    mySprite.draw();
    setTimeout("cycle()",30);
    }
</SCRIPT>
<STYLE>
```

12

DYNAMIC
POSITIONING

continues

Listing 12.8. continued

```
#sprite1{
    POSITION: absolute;
    VISIBILITY: hidden
    }

</STYLE>
<BODY BGCOLOR="#000000" onLoad="init()">
<DIV ID="sprite1">
<IMG SRC="rock.gif">
</DIV>
</BODY>
</HTML>
```

The layer element is given an `absolute` position property and starts out `hidden`. This is because the `layerObject` should control the element's location and `visibility`. A `layerObject` object is created, passing up the element's ID property, an initial location at the top left-hand corner of the browser window, a velocity, and an integer to control the sprite's depth. The `cycle()` method simply calls the `layerObject` object's `update()` and `draw()` methods over and over again. You can exert some control over tempo by changing the delay parameter in `setTimeout()`. A certain amount of trial and error will be necessary to balance tempo and velocity, although you should bear in mind that different machines, platforms, and browsers will affect the speed and smoothness of your sprite.

The `layerObject` sprite floats serenely from one corner of the screen to the other, disappearing into virtual space. A smarter object would know when to stop…

A Smart `layerObject`

It is possible to add a certain amount of bounce to a moving element, simply by extending the `update()` method and introducing a few new parameters. First, it will be necessary to define the sprite's boundaries. Once again, an object is the easiest way of doing this:

```
function rect(X1,Y1,X2,Y2)
    {
    this.left=X1;
    this.top=Y1;
    this.right=X2;
    this.bottom=Y2;
    }
```

You might notice that this class is similar to the `Area` class we created in the dynamic image map example. It simply defines the boundaries of a rectangle.

Next, the `layerObject` object will need to be instructed about whether to bounce when it hits a boundary. We can achieve this with a boolean parameter. Our constructor has now grown yet again:

```
function layerObject(layerID,pos,vel,z,bounds,bounce)
```

The object instantiation must now also change to create a rect object and pass up a boolean value to confirm that the sprite should bounce when it reaches its boundary—the bounds and bounce parameters, respectively:

```
mySprite=new layerObject("sprite1",
                          new Point(0,0),
                          new Point(5,3),
                          1,
                          new rect(0,0,400,400),
                          true);
```

The update() method will need to be extended to handle boundary collisions, like this:

```
function layerUpdate()
    {
    var newPos=new Point(this.position.x+this.velocity.x,
                          this.position.y+this.velocity.y);
    if (this.bounce)
        {
        if (newPos.x>this.boundsRect.right ¦¦ newPos.x<this.boundsRect.left)
            {
            this.velocity.x = this.velocity.x*-1;
            newPos.x += (this.velocity.x *2);
            }
        if (newPos.y>this.boundsRect.bottom ¦¦ newPos.y<this.boundsRect.top)
            {
            this.velocity.y=this.velocity.y*-1;
            newPos.y+= (this.velocity.y *2);
            }
        }
    this.setPosition(newPos);
    }
```

A temporary Point object is created as before. However, before the object is passed on to setPosition(), it is tested against the boundsRect property. If the newPos.x exceeds boundsRect.right, for example, the velocity.x is inverted. newPos is amended to reflect the change. The sprite will remain within its invisible prison, bouncing from wall to wall.

Getting to the Point

Our sprite is very independent just now—and sometimes that will be what you want. Occasionally, though, you will want it to be a little more obedient. With just a few more methods we can exert more control over layerObject objects.

To effect this, the layerObject object will need a journey() method, which will start the sprite moving in a given direction, and a courseCorrect() method, which will tweak the sprite's velocity as it moves. They look like this:

```
function journey(target,jumps)
    {
    this.leaps=jumps;//number of jumps
    this.target=target;
    this.isGoing=true;
    }
```

```
function courseCorrect()
    {
    var xDist=(this.target.x-this.position.x);
    var yDist=(this.target.y-this.position.y);
    if (this.leaps>1)
        {
        this.leaps--;
        this.velocity.x=Math.round( xDist/(this.leaps) ) ;
        this.velocity.y=Math.round( yDist/(this.leaps) );
        }
    else
        {
        this.isGoing=false;
        this.velocity=new Point(0,0);
        }
    }
```

The `journey()` method expects two parameters: a `Point` object, which defines the sprite's objective, and an integer for the number of hops the sprite should take on its way. The parameters are assigned to object properties, and a boolean flag, `isGoing`, is set to signal that the sprite is underway.

The `courseCorrect()` function is called by `update()`. It simply calculates the remaining distance to travel along both axes, decrements the number of leaps still to take, and calculates new values for velocity using these numbers.

`update()` must be amended to call `courseCorrect()`, like this:

```
function layerUpdate()
    {
    if (this.isGoing)
        this.courseCorrect();
    var newPos=new Point(this.position.x+this.velocity.x,
                         this.position.y+this.velocity.y);
    if (this.bounce && ! this.isGoing)
        {
        if (newPos.x>this.boundsRect.right || newPos.x<this.boundsRect.left)
            {
            this.velocity.x = this.velocity.x*-1;
            newPos.x += (this.velocity.x *2);
            }
        if (newPos.y>this.boundsRect.bottom || newPos.y<this.boundsRect.top)
            {
            this.velocity.y=this.velocity.y*-1;
            newPos.y+= (this.velocity.y *2);
            }
        }
    this.setPosition(newPos);
    }
```

`update()` now checks for the `isGoing` property and calls `courseCorrect()` if appropriate. The only other change here is an additional check for `isGoing`. If `isGoing` returns `true`, the bounds checking is not implemented. In this way, an order to travel to a particular location takes precedence over a sprite's constraints.

After amending the `layerObject` constructor to reflect the new functions and properties, we can test the code, using a simple form interface in the body of the document:

```
<FORM NAME="myForm">
<INPUT TYPE=TEXT NAME="xVal" SIZE=4>
<INPUT TYPE=TEXT NAME="yVal" SIZE=4>
<INPUT TYPE=BUTTON VALUE="send it"
onClick="mySprite.journey(new Point(this.form.xVal.value,
➥this.form.yVal.value),10)">
</FORM>
```

This form accepts numerical input and uses it to build a `Point` object. This is passed up to the `layerObject` object's `journey()` method, along with an integer representing the number of jumps to take. In Figure 12.8 you can see our well-behaved sprite.

FIGURE 12.8.

This well-behaved element goes where it's told.

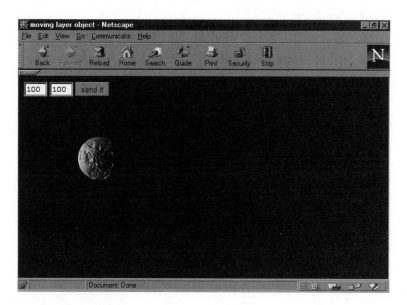

Managing Movement

So far we have seen only one moving `layerObject` object at a time. Usually, though, you will want to control more than one at any time. At first sight, the obvious way of doing this is simply to expand the `cycle()` method we defined in the section "Making It Move" to call the `update()` and `draw()` methods of more `layerObject` objects. With lots of objects, however, that would soon become unwieldy. Luckily, we've already defined a way of managing multiple sprite objects. In the section "Shuffling the Pack: Dynamically Changing z-index," we created a `noteManager` object to organize `layerObjects`. This is a model we can extend:

```
function layerManager()
    {
    this.update=managerUpdate;
    this.add=managerAdd;
```

```
        this.draw=managerDraw;
        this.layerList=new Array();
        }
function managerAdd(l)
        {
        this.layerList[this.layerList.length]=l;
        l.draw();
        l.show();
        }
function managerUpdate()
        {
        for (x=0;x<this.layerList.length;x++)
            {
            this.layerList[x].update();
            }
        }
function managerDraw()
        {
        for (x=0;x<this.layerList.length;x++)
            {
            this.layerList[x].draw();
            }
        }
```

The layerManager object is very simple. It defines only one property—layerList, an array that stores references to all layerObjects passed to the add() method. The update() method iterates through the layerList, calling each layerObject object's update() method. The draw() method does the same for each layerObject object's draw() method.

With a few loops we can create lots of sprites very simply. We will create a new function, writeLayers(), and call it from the Web page. The init() function will initialize a layerManager object and add all our layerObject objects to it. The syntax looks like this:

```
function random (limit)
        {
         return (Math.round(((Math.random())*1000))%limit);
        }
var num_of_sprites=random(10)+3;
function init()
        {
        layerMan=new layerManager();
        for (var x=1;x<=num_of_sprites;x++)
            {
            layerMan.add(
                new layerObject(
                    "sprite"+x,
                    new Point (random(400),random(400)),
                    new Point (random(20),random(20)),
                    x,
                    new rect(0,0,400,400),
                    true
                    )
                );
            }
        cycle();
```

```
    }
function cycle()
    {
    layerMan.update();
    layerMan.draw();
    setTimeout("cycle()",30);
    }
function writeSprites()
    {
    for (var x=1;x<=num_of_sprites;x++)
        {
        document.writeln ("<div id='sprite"+x+"' class='sprites'>");
        document.writeln ("<img src='res/rock2.gif'></div>");
        }
    }
```

First, a global variable called num_of_sprites is created, and a random integer between 2 and 10 is assigned to it. This total is used by both writeSprites() and init() in a for loop. writeSprites() writes each CSS element to the Web page, giving each an ID property. All the elements share a sprite class, which sets a position property of absolute.

Figure 12.9 shows the script in action.

12

DYNAMIC
POSITIONING

FIGURE 12.9.

Company at last. The layerManager *object handles multiple layers on the move.*

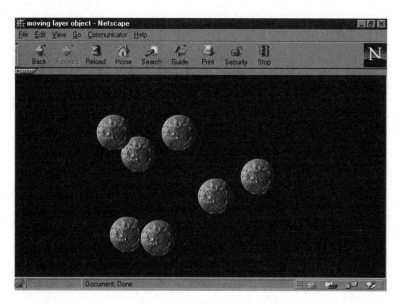

The onLoad handler calls init(), which first creates a layerManager object, layerMan. Another loop initializes the layerObject objects, randomizing the position and vector parameters. Each layerObject object is added to the layerManager's layerList.

The cycle() function repeatedly calls the layerManager object's update() and draw() methods.

Bringing It All Together

It's time to create a single page that combines some of the techniques that we have covered in this chapter. Take a look through the code in Listing 12.9. All the code will work happily in both fourth-generation browsers, apart from the image map we first looked at in the section "Cutting Corners: Dynamic Image Maps Using Only Two Images." In IE4, all the hotspots will activate at once when the pointer passes over a link. This is not ideal, but the effect is not unpleasing, so maybe we can call it a feature rather than a bug. We'll examine some of the code's features in more detail afterward.

Listing 12.9. Bringing it all together.

```
<HTML>
<HEAD>
<TITLE>Bringing it all together</TITLE>
</HEAD>

<SCRIPT LANGUAGE="JavaScript">
var L=new layerTool();
function layerTool()
    {
    if (navigator.appName=="Netscape")
        this.layerProp=navProp;
    else
        this.layerProp=exProp;
    }
function exProp()
    {
    return document.all[arguments[arguments.length-1]].style;
    }
function navProp()
    {
    retVal="";
    for (var x=0;x<arguments.length;x++)
        {
        retVal+="document.layers[\'"+arguments[x]+"\']";
        if (x!=arguments.length-1)
            retVal+=".";
        }
    return eval(retVal);
    }
function Point(X,Y)
    {
    this.x=X;
    this.y=Y;
    }
function rect(X1,Y1,X2,Y2)
    {
    this.left=X1;
    this.top=Y1;
    this.right=X2;
    this.bottom=Y2;
    }
function foster(child,ancestor)
```

```
        {
    for (x in ancestor)
            {
        if (!(child [x.toString()]))
                child [x.toString()]=ancestor[x];
            }
        }
function random (limit)
        {
         return (Math.round(((Math.random())*1000))%limit);
        }

function layerObject(layerID,pos,vel,z,bounds,bounce)
        {
        // properties
        this.layerID=layerID;
        this.position=pos;
        this.velocity=vel;
        this.boundsRect=bounds;
        this.depth=z;
        this.bounce=bounce;
        this.visibility="visible";
        this.isGoing=false;
        this.active=true;
        // methods
        this.show=showLayer;
        this.setZorder=setZorder;
        this.hide=hideLayer;
        this.setPosition=setPosition;
        this.draw=drawLayer;
        this.update=updateLayer;
        this.journey=journey;
        this.courseCorrect=courseCorrect;
        this.show();
        }

function setZorder(z)
        {
        this.depth=z;
        }
function showLayer()
        {
        L.layerProp(this.layerID).visibility="visible";
        }
function hideLayer()
        {
        L.layerProp(this.layerID).visibility="hidden";
        }
function drawLayer()
        {
        L.layerProp(this.layerID).zIndex=this.depth;
        L.layerProp(this.layerID).left=(this.position).x;
        L.layerProp(this.layerID).top=(this.position).y;
        }
function setPosition(pos)
        {
        this.position=pos;
        }
```

Listing 12.9. continued

```
function journey(target,jumps)
    {
    this.leaps=jumps;//number of jumps
    this.target=target;
    this.isGoing=true;
    this.active=true;
    }
function courseCorrect()
    {
    var xDist=(this.target.x-this.position.x);
    var yDist=(this.target.y-this.position.y);
    if (this.leaps>1)
        {
        this.leaps--;
        this.velocity.x=Math.round( xDist/(this.leaps) ) ;
        this.velocity.y=Math.round( yDist/(this.leaps) );
        }
    else
        {
        this.isGoing=false;
        this.velocity=new Point(0,0);
        }
    }
function updateLayer()
    {
    if (this.isGoing)
        this.courseCorrect();
    if (this.velocity.x==0 && this.velocity.y==0)
        this.active=false;
    else
        this.active=true;
    var newPos=new Point(this.position.x+this.velocity.x,
                         this.position.y+this.velocity.y);
    if (this.bounce
&& ! this.isGoing)
        {
        if (newPos.x>this.boundsRect.right ¦¦ newPos.x<this.boundsRect.left)
            {
            this.velocity.x = this.velocity.x*-1;
            newPos.x += (this.velocity.x *2);
            }
        if (newPos.y>this.boundsRect.bottom ¦¦ newPos.y<this.boundsRect.top)
            {
            this.velocity.y=this.velocity.y*-1;
            newPos.y+= (this.velocity.y *2);
            }
        }
    this.setPosition(newPos);
    }

function noteObject(layerID,pos,z)
    {
    this.ancestor=new layerObject(layerID,
                                  pos,
                                  new Point(0,0),
                                  z,
                                  new rect(0,0,1000,1000),
                                  false);
```

```
        foster(this,this.ancestor);
        this.defaultDepth=z;
        this.home=pos;
        }

function noteManager()
    {
    this.LayerList=new Array();
    this.add=noteAdd;
    this.select=noteSelect;
    }

function noteAdd(LayerObj)
    {
    this.LayerList[this.LayerList.length]=LayerObj;
    this.zone=new Point(LayerObj.position.x+160,LayerObj.position.y);
    }

function noteSelect(LayerName)
    {
    for (var x=0;x<this.LayerList.length;x++)
        {
        if (this.LayerList[x].layerID==LayerName)
            {
            if (this.LayerList[x].depth==100)
                {
                this.LayerList[x].setZorder(this.LayerList[x].defaultDepth);
                this.LayerList[x].journey(this.LayerList[x].home,6);
                }
            else
                {
                this.LayerList[x].setZorder(100);
                this.LayerList[x].journey(this.zone,6);
                }
            }
        else
            {
            this.LayerList[x].setZorder(this.LayerList[x].defaultDepth);
            this.LayerList[x].journey(this.LayerList[x].home,6);
            }
        this.LayerList[x].draw();
        }
    }

function layerManager()
    {
    this.update=managerUpdate;
    this.add=managerAdd;
    this.draw=managerDraw;
    this.layerList=new Array();
    }
function managerAdd(l)
    {
    this.layerList[this.layerList.length]=l;
    l.draw();
    l.show();
    }
```

continues

12

DYNAMIC
POSITIONING

Listing 12.9. continued

```
function managerUpdate()
    {
    for (x=0;x<this.layerList.length;x++)
        {
        if (this.layerList[x].active)
            this.layerList[x].update();
        }
    }
function managerDraw()
    {
    for (x=0;x<this.layerList.length;x++)
        {
        if (this.layerList[x].active)
            this.layerList[x].draw();
        }
    }

p=new Array();
p[0]=new Area(25,30,125,75,"http://www.corrosive.co.uk/");
p[1]=new Area(5,125,130,175,"http://www.corrosive.co.uk/");
p[2]=new Area(115,100,225,126,"http://www.corrosive.co.uk/");

m=new map("m","container","topLayer",p);
function Area(X1,Y1,X2,Y2,url)
    {
    this.left=X1;
    this.top=Y1;
    this.right=X2;
    this.bottom=Y2;
    this.url=url;
    }

function map(name,container,top,areas)
    {
    this.name=name;
    this.top=top;
    this.container=container;
    this.areas=areas;
    this.writeMap=writeMap;
    this. highlight=highlight;
    this.reset=reset;
    this.timeout=null;
    }
function writeMap (mapName)
    {
    document.write("<map name="+mapName+">");
    for (x=0;x<this.areas.length;x++)
        {
        document.write("<area shape=\"RECT\" href='"+this.areas[x].url+"'
onMouseOver='"+this.name+".highlight("+x+")' ");
        document.write("onMouseOut='"+this.name+".reset()' ");
        document.write("COORDS=\""+this.areas[x].left+","+this.areas[x].top+"
"+this.areas[x].right+","+this.areas[x].bottom+"\">");
        }
    document.write("</map>");
    }
```

```
function highlight(num)
    {
    clearTimeout(this.timeout);
    this.timeout=setTimeout(this.name+".reset()",5000);
    L.layerProp(this.container,this.top).visibility="visible";
    L.layerProp(this.container,this.top).clip.top=this.areas[num].top;
    L.layerProp(this.container,this.top).clip.left=this.areas[num].left;
    L.layerProp(this.container,this.top).clip.bottom=this.areas[num].bottom;
    L.layerProp(this.container,this.top).clip.right=this.areas[num].right;
    }
function reset()
    {
    L.layerProp(this.container,this.top).visibility="hidden";
    }

function init()
    {
    layerMan=new layerManager();
    noteMan=new noteManager();
    var yPos=30;
    for (var x=1;x<=5;x++)
        {
        note=new noteObject("note"+x,new Point(10,yPos),x);
        layerMan.add(note);
        noteMan.add(note);
        yPos+=30;
        }
    var xPos=200;
    for (var y=1;y<=3;y++)
        {
        temp=new layerObject(
            "heading"+y,
            new Point (xPos,300),
            new Point (random(30)-15,random(30)-15),
            200,
            new rect(180,30,500,400),
            true
            )
        layerMan.add(temp);
        xPos+=150;
        }
    cycle();
    }
function cycle()
    {
    layerMan.update();
    layerMan.draw();
    setTimeout("cycle()",20);
    }
</SCRIPT>

<STYLE TYPE="text/css">
.shuffleClass{
    POSITION: absolute;
    WIDTH: 150px;
    VISIBILITY: hidden;
    }
```

continues

Listing 12.9. continued

```
.headings{
    POSITION:absolute;
    FONT-WEIGHT:100;
    FONT-FAMILY:sans-serif;
    COLOR:#0066cc;
    FONT-SIZE:24pt;
    VISIBILITY:hidden;
    }
.maps{
    POSITION:absolute;
    }
#container{
    POSITION:absolute;
    TOP: 130;
    LEFT:250;
    VISIBILITY: visible;
    }
#topLayer{
    VISIBILITY:hidden;
    }
A:link, A:visited, A:active{
    COLOR:#0D20AE;
    FONT-WEIGHT:bold;
    FONT-FAMILY: sans-serif;
    TEXT-DECORATION: none
    }
</STYLE>

<BODY BGCOLOR="#ffffff" onLoad="init()">
<SCRIPT>
m.writeMap("myMap");
</SCRIPT>
<DIV ID="note1" CLASS="shuffleClass">
<TABLE HEIGHT=200 WIDTH=150 BGCOLOR=#CBD5FF CELLPADDING=10 BORDER=1>
<TR><TD VALIGN=TOP>
<A HREF="JavaScript:noteMan.select('note1');">About Us</A>
<P>
links and information
</P>
</TD></TR>
</TABLE>
</DIV>

<DIV ID="note2" CLASS="shuffleClass">
<TABLE HEIGHT=200 WIDTH=150 BGCOLOR=#CBD5FF CELLPADDING=10 BORDER=1>
<TR><TD VALIGN=TOP>
<A HREF="JavaScript:noteMan.select('note2');">Clients</A>
<P>
links and information
</P>
</TD></TR>
</TABLE>
</DIV>

<DIV ID="note3" CLASS="shuffleClass">
<TABLE HEIGHT=200 WIDTH=150 BGCOLOR=#CBD5FF CELLPADDING=10 BORDER=1>
<TR><TD VALIGN=TOP>
```

```
<A HREF="JavaScript:noteMan.select('note3');">Freebies</A>
<P>
links and information
</P>
</TD></TR>
</TABLE>
</DIV>

<DIV ID="note4" CLASS="shuffleClass">
<TABLE HEIGHT=200 WIDTH=150 BGCOLOR=#CBD5FF CELLPADDING=10 BORDER=1>
<TR><TD VALIGN=TOP>
<A HREF="JavaScript:noteMan.select('note4');">Links</A>
<P>
links and information
</P>
</TD></TR>
</TABLE>
</DIV>

<DIV ID="note5" CLASS="shuffleClass">
<TABLE HEIGHT=200 WIDTH=150 BGCOLOR=#CBD5FF CELLPADDING=10 BORDER=1>
<TR><TD VALIGN=TOP>
<A HREF="JavaScript:noteMan.select('note5');">Welcome</A>
<P>
links and information
</P>
</TD></TR>
</TABLE>
</DIV>

<DIV ID="container">
    <DIV ID="bottomLayer" CLASS="maps">
    <IMG SRC="res/apple1.gif" USEMAP="#myMap" BORDER=0>
    </DIV>
    <DIV ID="topLayer" CLASS="maps">
    <IMG NAME=TEST SRC="res/apple2.gif" USEMAP="#myMap" BORDER=0>
    </DIV>
</DIV>

<DIV ID="heading1" CLASS="headings">
Dynamic
</DIV>
<DIV ID="heading2" CLASS="headings">
Web
</DIV>
<DIV ID="heading3" CLASS="headings">
Design
</DIV>
</BODY>
</HTML>
```

You can see this script in action in Figure 12.10. The words "Dynamic," "Web," and "Design" float independently around the page. The image map works as before, with worms popping from the apple as the mouse traverses hotspots. The card file is a little more sophisticated than before: Selected cards leap to the front and float to the right as if pulled from the pack.

FIGURE 12.10.

Movement, depth, and an image map. All our techniques on one page.

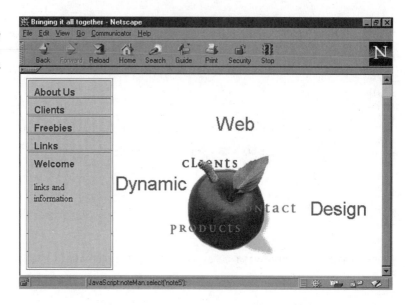

The example shown in Figure 12.10 and Listing 12.9 might look like lots of work, but in reality, most of the code consists of the classes that we've already created. In particular, the `map`, `layerObject`, and `layerManager` classes are implemented.

The floating text elements are controlled by simple instantiations of our traditional `layerObject` class. The class itself has been changed in one important respect: A new property—`active`—has been added to the constructor and set by default to `true`. The `update()` method now tests the object's `velocity` property: If both its x and y properties are at 0, the `active` property is set to `false`. What's this all about? Well, the `layerManager` object used to call the `update()` and `draw()` methods of all the `layerObject`s to which it had a reference. For objects that are not moving, like the card file elements for example, an awful lot of effort was being wasted every cycle, slowing down the script noticeably. Now the `layerManager` object checks the `active` property of all its `layerObject` objects. It will only call `update()` or `draw()` if the object is currently `active`.

The instantiation of the `layerObject` objects is affected in the `init()` function, using a loop. The loop creates each object, randomizing its `vector` property and incrementing its starting position along the x axis.

The image map is entirely unchanged. Note that on IE4, the clipping will not work. If a hotspot is activated, the entire top element will be shown.

There are, however, some interesting differences in our card file. We have introduced movement so that the selected card floats to one side of the pack in addition to jumping to the front. What makes this new code worth some analysis, furthermore, is the use of inheritance, perhaps JavaScript's most underrated feature and an important tool for Dynamic HTML coding.

The JavaScript Inheritance

It has often been written that JavaScript differs from Java in that it is not possible for one JavaScript class to inherit properties and functions from another. Although it is true that inheritance is not built into the language, it is a simple matter to implement it. But why would you want to? There are at least two good reasons: reusability and polymorphism.

Inheritance enables you to lay down functionality in a base class and build new features onto it with derived classes. This means that you can create many objects that share core functionality, without having to duplicate code. Furthermore, you can override the superclass's methods so that different child objects will behave differently to one another when their respective methods are called. This is known as polymorphism. Consider our `layerManager` object. It holds an array of `layerObject` objects and calls the `update()` method of each in turn. If some of these objects are, in fact, initialized from classes that override the `layerObject` class, they may behave differently from conventional `layerObject` objects when their `update()` method is called, but still have access to all the other methods of the `layerObject` class. If you were writing a game, for example, you might create `asteroid` and `spaceship` objects—both inheriting from `layerObject`. The `asteroid` objects could override the `update()` method in one way, and the `spaceship` objects in others. All would have access to other `layerObject` methods but would behave differently when their `update()` methods were called by the `layerManager`. And all without having to duplicate any of the `layerObject` code.

So, how is inheritance implemented in JavaScript? In fact, as the code below shows, it's very easy indeed:

```
function base()
    {
    this.whoAreYou=baseWho;
    this.identity="I am a base class";
    }
function baseWho()
    {
    alert (this.identity);
    }

function child()
    {
    this.ancestor=new base()
    foster(this,this.ancestor);
    this.identity="I am a child"; // overriding name property
    }

function foster(child,ancestor)
    {
    for (x in ancestor)
        {
        if (!(child [x.toString()]))
        child [x.toString()]=ancestor[x];
        }
    }
```

```
obj=new child();
obj.whoAreYou();
obj.ancestor.whoAreYou();
```

All the magic is in the foster() method, which should be globally available. It uses the fact that every object automatically creates an associative array of its properties. A child object should first initialize its ancestor, passing any necessary parameters to it. To inherit the ancestor's functionality, the child must call foster() with a reference to itself and its parent as parameters. The foster() function iterates through each of the ancestor's properties, and assigns it to the child (as long as the child has not defined its own version of that property). In our example above, the child object overrides the ancestor's identity property. When whoAreYou() is called, therefore, it is the child's identity property that is returned. The child can still access its parent's properties, however, simply by using the ancestor property.

We can see an example of this in action in our card file code:

```
function noteObject(layerID,pos,z)
    {
    this.ancestor=new layerObject(layerID,
                                  pos,
                                  new Point(0,0),
                                  z,
                                  new rect(0,0,1000,1000),
                                  false);
    foster(this,this.ancestor);
    this.defaultDepth=z;
    this.home=pos;
    }

function noteManager()
    {
    this.LayerList=new Array();
    this.add=noteAdd;
    this.select=noteSelect;
    }

function noteAdd(LayerObj)
    {
    this.LayerList[this.LayerList.length]=LayerObj;
    this.zone=new Point(LayerObj.position.x+160,LayerObj.position.y);
    }

function noteSelect(LayerName)
    {
    for (var x=0;x<this.LayerList.length;x++)
        {
        if (this.LayerList[x].layerID==LayerName)
            {
            if (this.LayerList[x].depth==100)
                {
                this.LayerList[x].setZorder(this.LayerList[x].defaultDepth);
                this.LayerList[x].journey(this.LayerList[x].home,6);
                }
            else
```

```
                    {
                    this.LayerList[x].setZorder(100);
                    this.LayerList[x].journey(this.zone,6);
                    }
            }
        else
            {
            this.LayerList[x].setZorder(this.LayerList[x].defaultDepth);
            this.LayerList[x].journey(this.LayerList[x].home,6);
            }
        this.LayerList[x].draw();
        }
    }
```

The `noteManager` object is similar to the version demonstrated in the section on `z-index`. One difference is that it calls the `journey()` method of the `noteObject` objects it stores. It can do this because the `noteObject` objects inherit from the `layerObject` class. Additionally, the `noteObject` class has some properties not included in `layerObject`. The `defaultDepth` and `home` properties allow each object to return to a specific `depth` and `position` when they are deselected. To include these extra properties without inheritance would have meant hacking the `layerObject` class itself. `layerObject` would be less reusable as a utility class in that it would have application-specific features that would need to be removed the next time you used it.

Take a look at the code that instantiates the `noteObject` objects:

```
for (var x=1;x<=5;x++)
    {
    note=new noteObject("note"+x,new Point(10,yPos),x);
    layerMan.add(note);
    noteMan.add(note);
    yPos+=30;
    }
```

`noteObject` requires only three parameters because many of the parameters required by `layerObject` are the same for each `noteObject` object. It's much easier to let the `noteObject` class deal with these, demanding only those parameters that are likely to change from object to object.

Summary

In this chapter we have developed several tools that can be reused and developed in your games or environments. In particular, the `layerObject` class is a useful way of controlling CSS elements. Not only can the class itself be developed further, but with the help of the inheritance techniques we have covered, child classes with widely differing functionality can be produced to build upon its features. `layerObject` objects are easy to control with the `layerManager` class.

The `layerTool` object is a handy class for cross-browser scripting, and could be developed to deal with other browser differences.

Despite Internet Explorer's present inability to handle the `clip` property, the `map` class is a useful means of creating easy and low-overhead `mouseOver` page elements.

This chapter has not completely filled your dynamic positioning toolbox, but the utilities and techniques presented here should form a good basis for your own work.

Possible Further Applications

So where now? Well, that's only limited by your imagination (and the occasional bug or incompatibility). Dynamic positioning heralds the possibility of genuine multimedia on a Web page, without a plug-in in sight.

In terms of the scripts we've examined, `layerManager` and `layerObject` are crying out for at least a couple of new features. One possibility you might consider in your development is some code to handle collisions between sprites. The `layerManager` class's `update()` method would have to handle this. What about some code to create sprites made up of multiple layers or images?

Useful Resources

The Internet is an excellent teacher, and there are some extremely useful sites around already to help you with your development once you've exhausted the online resources available from Microsoft and Netscape.

You should definitely check out the latest on CSS at W3C, in particular the W3C Working Draft on Positioning HTML Elements with cascading style sheets at `http://www.w3.org/TR/WD-positioning`.

Perhaps the best tutorial site around at the moment is Macromedia's DHTML Zone at `http://www.dhtmlzone.com/`. A complete dynamic environment is presented, and tutorials tell you how it was done.

Also excellent is the tip-based DHTML section of The WebMaster's Reference Library at `http://www.webreference.com/dhtml/`. This site is particularly useful for issues of backward compatibility and cross-browser coding.

If it's just a good reference you need, then `http://www.htmlhelp.com/` is certainly worth a look.

Using VBScript as an Alternative Language

by John J. Kottler

IN THIS CHAPTER

CHAPTER

13

Dynamic HTML is a powerful tool that enables developers to create more interactive and intriguing Web pages. However as you have seen throughout this book, Dynamic HTML alone does not make a great Web site. It is the scripting routines tied to the HTML Web pages that make a truly dynamic experience. Most of the examples you have seen in this book were written using JavaScript. This language is powerful and is completely capable of handling DHTML in your Web pages. However, it is not the only language available.

JavaScript is a popular choice for client Web page scripts, mainly because it is the only language that is compatible with both popular Web browsers on the market: Netscape Navigator 3.0/Communicator 4.0 and Microsoft Internet Explorer 3.0/4.0. If you have created Web pages for the Internet, chances are you have run across the issue of optimizing your site for one browser or the other. Since each browser has its own unique capabilities, it is difficult to create a single site that truly uses the unique capabilities of one browser. To make use of the most innovative features of each browser you would have to create separate versions of your Web pages optimized for each one. This of course becomes time consuming and is very labor intensive.

Currently the VBScript scripting language is only available in Microsoft Internet Explorer and not implemented in Netscape's products. The only way Netscape comes close to implementing a version of VBScript is via a special plug-in, which every user may not have installed on their desktop. Therefore many Web page authors choose to use JavaScript, since it has been implemented in both browsers.

Although both browsers support JavaScript, JavaScript has just recently become been a standardized language. Because JavaScript wasn't a standardized language before now, Microsoft implemented the language in its browsers as best it could without any specifications for the language. Though both browsers supported JavaScript, they both supported different implementations of the language and object model. This slight difference caused some compatibility issues on the browsers for sites using JavaScript. Some things written for Netscape's version of JavaScript worked perfectly, but did not translate in Microsoft's implementation.

In an attempt to finally standardize on a truly universal JavaScript language, a coalition of software developers standardized on one model. ECMA-262 is the most recent name for a standard JavaScript/JScript. It is named after the European Computer Manufacturers Association, which facilitated the process of setting a single implementation for the language.

In certain circumstances, you may still want to use VBScript and there are several good reasons to use this language. You may simply have more experience with Visual Basic and the BASIC language, the origins of VBScript. Or, you may have standardized on Internet Explorer within an intranet environment. If this is the case, you can be assured that all the potential users of your intranet site will also have VBScript and be able to fully utilize your site.

Whatever your reason, there will be times when you may prefer to use VBScript as your primary scripting language with Dynamic HTML. In this chapter, you will be introduced to Dynamic HTML and how VBScript can be used with DHTML to create the same interactive Web pages that you have seen in other sections of this book. Since VBScript is so tightly integrated with Microsoft Internet Explorer, you will also learn about this browser's implementation of the Document Object Model (DOM). You must understand this model to write VBScript that interacts with objects on a Web page.

Unfortunately, Dynamic HTML and the Document Object Model are new technologies that have been supplied to the World Wide Web Consortium (`http://www.w3c.org`) for standardization. You may experience some difficulty in implementing DHTML on your site because the Document Object Model may differ slightly between browsers. In this chapter, we will concentrate solely on the Microsoft Internet Explorer 4.0 browser, since currently it is the only browser that works well with VBScript.

Document Object Model

Document Object Model can be a scary term, particularly to those developers who are not seasoned programmers. In reality, the Document Object Model, or DOM for short, is a relatively simple concept. As a Web page designer, you are already familiar with an HTML page (or document) and the items that make up that page. You're familiar with the concept of setting certain attributes or properties for particular HTML tags within a document. You are also familiar with the scripting capabilities that allow you to cause those scripts to execute upon certain actions, such as `onClick`.

The Document Object Model, exposed by Microsoft Internet Explorer 4.0, basically expands upon these principles that you are already familiar with. In a sense, each object on a Web page document, including the actual document itself, is exposed as an object that can be manipulated by script commands. If you are already familiar with object-oriented programming, you will quickly realize that each of these HTML objects contain properties and events of their own.

HTML tags allow you to mark up items within a Web document, but in Dynamic HTML they also serve as definitions for objects on that HTML page. Any bit of information that exists between the open and close HTML tags in a document can now be treated as an object. If those HTML tags contain attributes or properties that you usually set within the opening HTML tag, you can reference those same properties within your script to change them on-the-fly.

To finish explaining the Document Object Model, let's take a quick look at events. When you define tags with attributes in HTML, you notice that some HTML tag attributes allow you to handle actions such as clicking the mouse. For example, with the INPUT tag you can specify that particular script commands be run whenever anyone clicks on that HTML object. Usually you can put this action in effect by adding the `onClick` attribute to the INPUT tag.

As powerful as this is, you are restricted to only being able to capture events on very specific objects. With Dynamic HTML and the Document Object Model, it is possible to create scripts that are triggered when *any* object on a page causes an action to occur. With this type of capability, it is now possible to add `onClick` or other events to objects such as heading tags (<H1>, <H2>, <H3>, and so on), paragraph tags (<P>), or other formatting tags.

In this chapter, you will be introduced to the Document Object Model as it applies specifically to Internet Explorer 4.0 using VBScript as the language. To learn additional information about how Microsoft and Netscape have implemented the Document Object Model, consult Chapter 15, "Document Object Model Comparison."

Elements and Collections

As we have already discussed, it is possible to treat each element on a Web Page as an object. You can also access properties and set attributes on each of those Web page elements. There are two ways you can address elements or objects on an HTML page: by unique name or by a collection.

Naming HTML Elements

The easier approach for using Dynamic HTML objects in your VBScript is to uniquely name each object that you want to reference in your scripts. By doing this, you can quickly and easily identify that element by the name you assign it. Assigning a name to an element in Dynamic HTML is easy, you simply use the ID= attribute with *any* opening tag and follow it with the name that you would like to use to identify that element.

To understand this more fully, let's take a look at a very simple example. Listing 13.1 shows a very short HTML document that uses a combination of Dynamic HTML and VBScript to create a more dynamic application. The results of this example can be found in Figure 13.1.

Listing 13.1. By naming HTML elements, you can reference those elements in your Dynamic HTML scripts.

```
<HTML>
<TITLE>Dynamic HTML Unleashed</TITLE>
<BODY>

<SCRIPT LANGUAGE="VBScript">
sub changeFont(newSize)
    myFont.size=newSize
end sub
</SCRIPT>

<FONT ID=myFont COLOR=#FF0000 SIZE=-3>Dynamic HTML and VBScript is fun!</FONT>

<P>
<INPUT SIZE=2 TYPE=TEXT NAME=fontSize VALUE="-3">
<INPUT TYPE=BUTTON VALUE="Change Font Size" onClick="changeFont(fontSize.value)">

</BODY>
</HTML>
```

FIGURE 13.1.

*With Dynamic
HTML, you can
change properties of
elements on-the-fly such
as the size of the font.*

> **NOTE**
>
> In Dynamic HTML, the attribute ID is used to assign names to HTML elements within the Web page. You may be more familiar with using the NAME attribute for naming elements. However, remember that when you define input tags on an HTML page within a form, the names of those tags are used to set name-value pairs of data that are sent to the server when the form is submitted. To avoid sending name-value pair data for all elements of a dynamic Web page, the ID attribute is used. This attribute still allows you to name elements on an HTML page without including them as form data objects.

As you can see in Listing 13.1, the FONT tag was used to create an object on the page named myFont. That font tag was then referenced in the VBScript routine to change the size of the font based on a value passed to the routine.

Element Properties

Each HTML element has its own set of properties, unique to that object. For example, you know that the <FONT> tag has SIZE, COLOR, and FACE attributes. You are aware that the <BODY> tag contains BACKGROUND and BGCOLOR attributes. To use these objects in Dynamic HTML, you can reference any attribute of an HTML element as a property of the object. You can retrieve these properties for analysis or modification. For instance, the following syntax is legal for these HTML elements:

```
myImage.src="newpic.gif"
myFont.size=myFont.size+1
oldColor=Document.bgcolor
```

> **TIP**
>
> Although you can reference a document page by using the Document object, there is no reason why you can't assign an ID to a document as well. This can be accomplished by adding the ID attribute to the <BODY> tag for the Web page. With an ID, you can reference the document using your own name.

It's important to notice, however, that although almost every tag exposes its attributes as properties to be accessed via script, there are some attributes that may not be accessible directly as named. Some names of attributes for HTML tags are the same names as reserved words within scripting languages. If this is the case, the property name will be confused with the scripting command in the script.

An example of this is the CLASS attribute for objects. Class is also a reserved word in scripting languages to create new objects. To avoid ambiguity, the property for accessing the CLASS attribute is className. There are few exceptions, but it is important to realize that they exist.

Sub-Object Properties

Although the direct relationship between properties in scripting and attributes in HTML tags is fairly obvious, sometimes properties of objects lead to sub-objects. This is usually the case for objects that can contain additional objects within them. In the world of HTML documents, this occurs fairly frequently, particularly with the use of cascading style sheets (CSS).

In Dynamic HTML, style sheets allow the Web page developer the flexibility to create objects on the page at exact pixel locations and at varying levels behind or in front of other objects on the page. With style sheets, it's possible to create very interactive applications by modifying these values to create motion or other effects. (To learn more about motion with Dynamic HTML and VBScript, see Chapter 24, "IE 4.0 Multimedia Effects with Dynamic HTML.")

The power of style sheets is actually encapsulated in a second object, embedded within the page object. For instance, the <DIV> tag can be used to define regions of grouped items on a Web page. Within a <DIV> tag, you can specify several attributes including a STYLE attribute. However the STYLE attribute can have numerous attributes of its own. For example, you can set the style's color, position, or filter effects. Therefore the STYLE attribute can be thought of logically as a sub-object of the original <DIV> object.

In this case, it's just as easy to define or access properties for a sub-object. You can still use the same syntax as before, but simply include all objects and sub-objects along the object hierarchy, separated by a period ("."). For example to change the left position of a <DIV> object, you could use the following syntax:

```
<DIV ID=myDiv STYLE="left:320;position:absolute">Some Text</DIV>
<SCRIPT LANGUAGE="VBScript">
    myDiv.style.left=120
</SCRIPT>
```

As you can see, the original object `myDiv` is referenced first, followed by the sub-object `style`, finishing with the actual property to change `left`.

Using Collections

In addition to retrieving information about HTML elements by name, you can traverse through all the objects on a page. All elements on a Web page are stored in arrays of objects referred to as *collections*. With these collections you can reference any item on the page, even those that you have not named. This can be particularly useful for scripts that add or modify the contents of a Web page. As items are removed or added to a page, you may need to reference the new items by this method. You can also use scripts in conjunction with collections to learn how objects are related to each other or to display statistics about a page. There are two types of collections that can be accessed: the `all` collection and the `children` collection.

all Collections

To find out about all of the tags on a page, you can use the `all` collection. This collection can be referenced in relation to an object to find *all* of the tags or elements that exist within that object. For instance, many tags in HTML are embedded within other tags. The `<BODY>` tag does not function by itself unless there are numerous display tags embedded within that tag. Likewise, the `<TABLE>` tag requires that `<TD>` or `<TR>` tags exist within that object in order to display table cells. Of course you may have embedded tags nested within other embedded tags, such as a `<TD>` tag within a `<TABLE>` tag that is within a `<BODY>` element.

To retrieve all of the elements no matter how deep within a collection associated with a particular HTML element, you can use the `all` collection with an initial object. Listing 13.2 shows how to display all of the elements on an HTML page using VBScript and the `all` collection. The page that is generated by the HTML and script in Listing 13.2 can be found in Figure 13.2.

Listing 13.2. The `all` collection can be used to display all items associated with an HTML element or page.

```
<HTML>
<TITLE>
Dynamic HTML - Collections
</TITLE>

<BODY>
<H1>Dynamic HTML is Fun!</H1>
Why?
<UL ID=myTag>
    <LI>Because of script interaction</LI>
    <LI>Dynamic positioning and properties</LI>
    <LI>It just is!</LI>
</UL>

<SCRIPT LANGUAGE="VBScript">
for l=0 to document.all.length
```

continues

Listing 13.2. continued

```
    document.write document.all(1).tagName & "<BR>"
next
</SCRIPT>

</BODY>
</HTML>
```

FIGURE 13.2.

Each document's collection holds a list of all the elements found on the page.

As you can see from Figure 13.2, the `all` collection returns a list of all elements found on the HTML page. By performing a simple loop, we can iterate through all the items in the collection and write out their respective tag names. The `all` collection contains only a few properties and methods that you can use, some of which we will cover shortly. These properties include:

- `length`—Determines the number of elements that exist in that collection.
- `tagName`—Returns the HTML tag that is found for the element you request.
- `item()`—References each item in the collection. This method expects an integer value to specify which numbered item in the collection you want to act upon. If you have named your elements on the Web page with the `ID` attribute, you can pass the `ID` name for the element into this method to identify that item.

■ tags()—Traverses the collection for elements of a particular tag type and returns the list of elements as another collection that you can act upon. This is helpful when you want to find elements in a collection by their HTML tag type.

NOTE

Collections are built from the beginning of an HTML document. Each tag in the document is then added to the collection in the order in which it appears within the document. Notice that the respective closing tags are not recorded in the collections built for a page.

Also, as a page is dynamically updated, so is the collection. So even if a document changes on-the-fly to add or subtract list items from the page, the page's collection is updated accordingly.

Tags and Items

You may also have noticed that you can index each element of the all collection by supplying an integer index value within parenthesis. For example, you will find that document.all(2).tagName is equivalent to document.all.item(2).tagName. As shown previously, there are two additional methods provided for collections: item() and tags(). You can use the item method to retrieve a particular element from the collection by index or ID, or the tags method to retrieve a group of elements from the collection.

NOTE

Items within a collection can be referenced by an index value for the collection via the item method. In either case, items are numbered in sequential order starting at 0. Although it is common for arrays to begin with 1 in VBScript, collection arrays begin at 0 to maintain compatibility with ECMA-262 languages.

To illustrate further, let's take a look at a modified version of Listing 13.2. Listing 13.3 shows a modified <SCRIPT> section for the HTML page listed in Listing 13.2.

Listing 13.3. You can also use the tags() and items() methods to access data in collections.

```
<SCRIPT LANGUAGE="VBScript">
for l=0 to document.all.length-1
    document.write document.all(l).tagName+"   "
next

document.write "<P>There are " & document.all.tags("LI").length-1 & _
               " &lt;LI&gt; tags on this page.<P>"
document.write "The first tag on this page is: " & _
```

continues

Listing 13.3. continued

```
                document.all.item(0).tagName & "<P>"
document.write "The 'myTag' element is a: " & _
                document.all.item("myTag").tagName & "<P>"

</SCRIPT>
```

The basic difference between Listing 13.3 and Listing 13.2 is the addition of the last three document.write statements. The first write statement invokes the tags method to collect all of the elements in the HTML page that are <LI> tags. Because the tags method returns a collection, it is then possible to use some properties or methods on the collection, such as length. This will count the number of <LI> tags on the page and write the result. The second and third write statements illustrate how to display information in the collection by calling the item method with an integer index and named ID respectively.

You'll recall in Listing 13.2 that the ID myTag is associated with the <UL> tag in the HTML. As you can see, it is possible to retrieve collections for the entire HTML document as well as other elements in the HTML page that can have embedded elements. In this case, the unsigned list element contains three additional list index elements that are retrieved by scripting code.

Children Collections

For many reasons, you will want to retrieve all of the embedded elements for any given element, no matter how deeply embedded. You can see that the all collection allows you to do that; it returns all elements related to the element you specify as well as any elements within those that are returned. In some circumstances, you may need to simply return the list of all elements *directly* related to an individual element. If you think of this hierarchically, you are then asking for information on only the children of an element or *parent*. In this case, you do not want to see the children's children or other descendants.

Fortunately, it is quite easy to return solely the *direct* descendant of an element using the children collection. This method returns the immediate HTML tags within a single HTML element. For instance if there were a <TABLE> tag within a <BODY> tag in an HTML document, only the <TABLE> element would appear in the children collection. The table's <TD> and <TR> tags would only be revealed using the all collection. Listing 13.4 shows the same Web page as originally displayed in Figure 13.2, however this time we will display only the children tags of the <BODY> tag instead of all tags for the document. The final result of this script is illustrated in Figure 13.3.

Listing 13.4. The children collection returns only HTML elements directly related to an element.

```
<HTML>
<TITLE>
Dynamic HTML - Collections
</TITLE>

<BODY ID=myDocument>
```

```
<H1>Dynamic HTML is Fun!</H1>
Why?
<UL>
    <LI>Because of script interaction</LI>
    <LI>Dynamic positioning and properties</LI>
    <LI>It just is!</LI>
</UL>

<SCRIPT LANGUAGE="VBScript">
msgbox myDocument.children.length
for l=0 to myDocument.children.length-1
    document.write myDocument.children(l).tagName & "<BR>"
next
</SCRIPT>

</BODY>
</HTML>
```

FIGURE 13.3.

Listing 13.4 displays fewer HTML documents because the children *collection is used.*

NOTE

Notice that the children collection in Listing 13.4 is based off of the <BODY> tag. The children collection must be used in conjunction with an element on the Web page that can be identified by a name. It does not function properly with some internal scripting elements such as document. If instead you want to create the children collection for the entire document, create an ID for the <HTML> tag and use that name when creating the collection.

Triggering Events

In the world of object-oriented programming, setting properties and invoking methods is only one part of creating applications. To create truly dynamic applications, it is essential that your program can trap particular events that may occur on the Web page. If you have been programming Web pages with scripts at all, you are familiar with the concept of adding event handlers such as onClick to individual HTML elements such as <INPUT> tags. With this capability, it is possible to invoke a script based on an event that occurred for an object on the Web page.

In the world of Dynamic HTML and the Document Object Model however, this concept of event handling has been expanded. Now you can place event handlers on any object of the Web page. You can describe events using more logical mechanisms and even create shared event handlers that can be triggered for multiple objects on a page.

This chapter introduces you to the basics of event handling within Internet Explorer 4.0 using VBScript. For additional information on event handling in VBScript, see Chapter 16, "The Internet Explorer 4.0 Event Model: Event Bubbling." For examples using JavaScript or Netscape, please see Chapter 17, "The Communicator 4.0 Event Model: Event Capturing."

Basic Event Handling

You are already familiar with basic event handling such as the onClick event. With tags such as the <INPUT> tag, you could trap a mouse click event to perform some type of action. For instance, the following sample creates a basic button and displays a message box when it is clicked.

```
<INPUT TYPE=BUTTON
       VALUE="Click Me"
       OnClick="msgbox 'You clicked me!'"
       LANGUAGE="VBScript"
>
```

In the past, the onClick event was handled by very few HTML objects. With Dynamic HTML however, it is possible to trap this event on *any* HTML object. Listing 13.5 illustrates this by placing an onClick on a bold line of text and a heading.

Listing 13.5. With Dynamic HTML, events can be added to any HTML tag.

```
<HTML>
<BODY>

<H1 onclick="msgbox 'Stop clicking on me!'" LANGUAGE="VBScript">
This is a Heading
</H1>

This is <B onclick="msgbox 'Be bold.'" LANGUAGE="VBScript">
BOLD</B> text.

</BODY>
</HTML>
```

NOTE

Make sure that you define the LANGUAGE attribute as "VBScript" if you create events like those in Listing 13.5. If not, the browser will be confused as to which language to use.

If you view this page in Internet Explorer 4.0, you will see that you can click on the word "BOLD" or anywhere on the heading line to reveal two different message boxes. If it's possible to add click events to the most basic of tags, you can apply them to *any* formatting tag. There are some exceptions to this; for instance, you cannot create a click event for the <TITLE> tag since that information is not displayed within the body of the Web browser. But most any tag is capable of triggering events.

Creating Specific Event Scripts

Listing 13.5 earlier in this chapter demonstrated a very simple example. A single line of source code was executed for each event that was handled. Although simple, it wasn't a very practical example. Usually you will want to perform numerous options based on an event that is triggered. To perform multiple operations at once, you should combine script commands into a function or subroutine. One method for handling this is to create specific script elements for an object and event using the <SCRIPT> tag.

In Dynamic HTML, the <SCRIPT> tag has been extended somewhat to accept two new parameters: FOR and EVENT. These two attributes together allow you to specify which object and event you want to run script for on a Web page. The following list describes each of these properties:

- ■ FOR—The FOR property within the <SCRIPT> tag is used to designate which object is to use the code between the <SCRIPT> and </SCRIPT> tags. Usually this property is set to the ID name of another object on the Web page.

- ■ EVENT—After determining which object the script is written for, the EVENT attribute specifies which event you want the script to handle. This tag usually simply contains the name of the event to trap, such as onClick.

Listing 13.6 illustrates the use of the FOR and EVENT attributes to create a script that adjusts the size of a font block on the page. Whenever you click on the glowing, bold text within the document it will grow in size.

Listing 13.6. The <SCRIPT> tag has been expanded to handle events.

```
<HTML>
<BODY id=DocBody BGCOLOR=#C0C0C0>

<SCRIPT FOR="myBold" EVENT="onClick" LANGUAGE="VBScript">
    msgbox myStyle.style.filter
```

continues

Listing 13.6. continued

```
    myFont.size=myFont.size+1
</SCRIPT>

<SPAN id=myStyle STYLE="filter:glow;width:100;height:50">
<FONT id=myFont size=1>
<B ID=myBold>text</B>
</FONT>
</SPAN>

</BODY>
</HTML>
```

In this example, any code that exists between the <SCRIPT> and </SCRIPT> tags is executed whenever the bold text is clicked. This is because the <SCRIPT> tag defines the FOR and EVENT tags as myBold for the bold object and onClick for the click event.

> **NOTE**
>
> Although compatible, using the FOR and EVENT tags with VBScript is not necessary. This format was written primarily for compatibility with other languages, which do not use the event model found in VBScript.

VBScript Event Handling

VBScript was designed to handle events easily that are generated by actions in controls such as ActiveX objects. To create an event handler for an ActiveX control, it is possible to simply create functions or subroutines within your Web page that are named *objectName_objectEvent*. For instance, if a control named "myControl" created an onClick event that could be handled by VBScript, you would simply need to create a subroutine called myControl_onClick.

In Dynamic HTML, the same capabilities are available with VBScript. In this case, the objects are HTML elements not just ActiveX controls. Listing 13.7 demonstrates the same Web page as the one created in Listing 13.6, except this time the event is trapped by a properly named subroutine.

> **NOTE**
>
> When using either the VBScript event handling model or the FOR and EVENT attributes of the <SCRIPT> tag, notice that you do *not* use the onClick attribute within the actual HTML object defined in the page.

Listing 13.7. VBScript allows you to create event handlers by naming the function by the object name, followed by an "_" and the event to trap for that object.

```
<HTML>
<BODY id=DocBody BGCOLOR=#C0C0C0>

<SCRIPT LANGUAGE="VBScript">
sub myBold_onClick
    msgbox myStyle.style.filter
    myFont.size=myFont.size+1
end sub
</SCRIPT>

<SPAN id=myStyle STYLE="filter:glow;width:100;height:50"><FONT id=myFont size=1>
<B ID=myBold>text</B>
</FONT></SPAN>

</BODY>
</HTML>
```

As you can see by viewing the HTML page in Listing 13.7, the results are identical to Listing 13.6. However, one advantage to this approach is that you can create all of your event handler routines without the burden of constantly using the <SCRIPT> tags.

Event Bubbling

By now you can clearly see the power of creating event handlers for any object on a Web page. There is also a minor drawback. What if you are creating a large number of objects on a Web page for which you want to trap events? You could group all of those items into a <DIV> tag or other grouping tag and then create events for that tag. But what if you want to share events across multiple HTML elements without necessarily grouping them together? If this is the case, you will have to rely on a new feature in Dynamic HTML called *event bubbling*.

With event bubbling, it is possible to define an event on an object and have that event be triggered whenever that object invokes the event or additional elements within that object invoke the event. For instance when multiple HTML events are embedded within a <DIV> tag and that <DIV> tag contains an onClick event handler, clicking on the <DIV> tag or on any object within the <DIV> tag will trigger the event.

Listing 13.8 demonstrates simple event bubbling by creating a DIV with bold and italic text lines within that DIV. The DIV and each bold and italic line are assigned IDs that are displayed in the myDiv_onClick subroutine. This subroutine is invoked whenever you click on the DIV, the line of bold text, or the line of italic text. Clicking on each of these three elements yields different results in the onClick event for the Web page, however.

Listing 13.8. Event bubbling allows you to trap events for multiple elements on a page.

```
<HTML>
<BODY>

<SCRIPT LANGUAGE="VBScript">
sub myDiv_onClick
    msgbox window.event.srcElement.id
end sub
</SCRIPT>

<DIV ID=myDiv LANGUAGE="VBScript">
<B ID=myBold>This is Bold Text</B><BR>
<I ID=myItalic>This is Italic Text</I>
</DIV>
</BODY>
</HTML>
```

If you examine the page listed in Listing 13.8, you will see that clicking on the blank area of the DIV causes the onClick event to display "myDiv". If you click on either the bold or italic lines however, you will see that the onClick event displays "myBold" or "myItalic." This example clearly demonstrates that you can bubble-up the click event from sub-elements into the main element for handing. Yet, you can easily distinguish which objects are being clicked. This creates a generic event handler that you can use for multiple objects or the entire Web page.

Multiple Events

When you work with bubbling events, you will quickly realize that multiple event handlers may fire when an event is triggered. This is due to the fact that events explicitly developed for an element fire first, then the event chain is bubbled-up and the element above in the hierarchy has its event fired. In our example in Listing 13.8, we created a single event for the DIV element. Let's also add an event for the bold (<B>) element. To accomplish this we can add the following three lines after the end sub in the myDiv_onClick subroutine, but before the closing </SCRIPT> tag:

```
sub myBold_onClick
    msgbox "BOLD!"
end sub
```

Now, whenever the user clicks on the bold line of text, the message box "BOLD!" will appear. This is what you logically would expect to happen. However, although this event is indeed triggered when a user clicks on the bold line, another event is fired. Because the line of bold text and thus the <B> tag are embedded within a DIV tag, event bubbling also triggers the event for the DIV. Therefore, clicking on the line of bold text will reveal two message boxes: the "BOLD!" message box and the "myBold" message box.

Canceling Bubbling Events

Obviously you can see a subtle problem with event bubbling. Although in most cases you will want events to bubble upward through the hierarchy chain, there will be some occasions when this is not desirable. In this case, you need to prevent event bubbling. To prevent events from triggering parent object events, you can simply use the expression:

```
window.event.cancelBubble = true
```

This will cancel the event bubbling process as soon as this line is interpreted. So, if we wanted to change Listing 13.8 so that only the message box "BOLD!" appeared, we could simply insert the `cancelBubble` line into the `myBold_onClick` event handler:

```
sub myBold_onClick
    msgbox "BOLD!"
    window.event.cancelBubble = true
end sub
```

> **NOTE**
>
> In VBScript, it is important that you use the `window` object to clarify the event object. You should never use word event by itself to set properties such as `cancelBubble`. VBScript reserves the word event for another action in its language; therefore, to avoid ambiguity always include the `window` object when referencing the event object.

Canceling Default Events

Although not as common as canceling bubbling events, it is possible to disable default events for HTML elements. For instance, the anchor element (`<A HREF>`) allows you to create hot spots or hypertext links on your page that cause the browser to jump to another location in your site or on the Web. If, however, you wanted to change the action of this element to display a message box and *not* jump to a page, you would essentially disable the default action for that element.

You can disable default actions for elements in Dynamic HTML by simply setting the return value of an event handler's function to `false`. In languages such as JScript where you can return values from a function via the `return` keyword, this is a simple addition. In other languages such as VBScript, the `return` keyword does not exist. Therefore to return a `false` value in VBScript, you can use the following line:

```
window.event.returnValue=false
```

Listing 13.9 demonstrates how to cancel a default event for an HTML element by using the `returnValue` property.

Listing 13.9. Default events for elements can be canceled by setting `returnValue` **to false at the end of your custom event handler.**

```
<HTML>
<BODY>

<SCRIPT LANGUAGE="VBScript">
sub myDiv_onClick
    msgbox window.event.srcElement.id
end sub

sub myBold_onClick
    msgbox "BOLD!"
    window.event.cancelBubble=true
end sub

sub myRef_onClick
    msgbox "Whoa!  Can't let you go there!"
    window.event.cancelBubble=true
    window.event.returnValue=false
end sub
</SCRIPT>

<DIV ID=myDiv LANGUAGE="VBScript">
<B ID=myBold>This is Bold Text</B><BR>
<I ID=myItalic>This is Italic Text</I><BR>
<A ID=myRef HREF="http://www.microsoft.com/ie/ie40">
This is a link to Microsoft</A>
</DIV>
</BODY>
</HTML>
```

NOTE

There have been references to the event object in this section of the chapter. This object allows you to set numerous properties for event handling as you have seen, as well as receive information about other events in the system such as keyboard state, browser size, and others. For more information on this event, it is recommended that you examine the Internet client SDK that is available at Microsoft's Web site (http://www.microsoft.com/ie/ie40).

Valid Events

There are a number of valid events that can be handled by Dynamic HTML and VBScript. The list has grown substantially since previous versions of HTML. Table 13.1 lists all of these events as well as their appropriate actions.

Table 13.1. Several new events are available in Dynamic HTML.

Event Name	Applies To	Action
onabort	IMG	This event is triggered when a user interrupts the loading of an image.
onafterupdate	APPLET, BODY, BUTTON, CAPTION, DIV, EMBED, IMG, INPUT, MAP, MARQUEE, OBJECT, SELECT, TABLE, TD, TEXTAREA, TR	This event fires after data-bound information has been updated.
onbeforeunload	FRAMESET, window	Before the page is unloaded, this event is triggered.
onbeforeupdate	APPLET, BODY, BUTTON, CAPTION, DIV, EMBED, HR, IMG, INPUT, MAP, OBJECT, SELECT, TABLE, TD, TEXTAREA, TR	Triggered before databound information is passed to the provider.
onblur	A, APPLET, AREA, BUTTON, DIV, EMBED, HR, IMG, INPUT, MARQUEE, OBJECT, SELECT, SPAN, TABLE, TD, TEXTAREA, TR, window	Whenever an object loses focus, this event is triggered.
onbounce	MARQUEE	When the text within a scrolling MARQUEE reaches the side, this event is fired.
onchange	INPUT, SELECT, TEXTAREA	This event fires when the contents of an entry field are committed by pressing Enter or losing focus.

13

VBSCRIPT AS AN
ALTERNATIVE
LANGUAGE

continues

Table 13.1. continued

Event Name	Applies To	Action
onclick	A, ADDRESS, APPLET, AREA, B, BIG, BLOCKQUOTE, BODY, BUTTON, CAPTION, CENTER, CITE, CODE, DD, DFN, DIR, DIV, DL, DT, EM, EMBED, FIELDSET, FONT, H1, H2, H3, H4, H5, H6, HR, I, IMG, INPUT, KBD, LABEL, LEGEND, LI, LISTING, MAP, MARQUEE, MENU, OBJECT, OL, OPTION, P, PLAINTEXT, PRE, S, SAMP, SELECT, SMALL, SPAN, STRIKE, STRONG, SUB, SUP, TABLE, TBODY, TD, TEXTAREA, TFOOT, TH, THEAD, TR, TT, U, UL, VAR, XMP, FORM, document	If a user clicks with the left mouse button on any clickable item or presses the Enter key to select that item, this event is fired.
ondataavailable	APPLET, IMG, MAP, OBJECT	As data arrives to data source objects, this event is triggered so that data can be delivered asynchronously.
ondatasetchanged	APPLET, IMG, MAP, OBJECT	Whenever data source objects change their information because of filtering or other processes, this event is fired.
ondatasetcomplete	APPLET, IMG, MAP, OBJECT	Once all data has become available in a data source object, this event is triggered.
ondblclick	Same as onclick event	Fired whenever a user double-clicks on a listed, valid object.
ondragstart	Same as onclick event	When a user begins the operation of dragging an element, this event is triggered.

Event Name	Applies To	Action
onerror	window	Whenever an error occurs on a page, it is trappable by the onerror event. Your event handler can capture the incoming message, URL, and line number.
onerrorupdate	A, APPLET, MAP, OBJECT, SELECT, TEXTAREA	After data has been transferred down to a data source object, this event is triggered in the event of an error.
onfilterchange	BODY, BUTTON, CAPTION, DIV, HR, IMG, INPUT, MARQUEE, OBJECT, SPAN, TABLE, TD, TEXTAREA, TR	Once a multimedia transition filter has completed, this event will fire.
onfinish	MARQUEE	If a Marquee has been established with looping parameters, this event is fired once the looping has completed.
onfocus	Same as onblur event	When an object receives focus, this event is fired.
onhelp	Same as onclick event	If the user presses the help key (F1) or clicks the browser's Help button, this event is triggered.
onkeydown	A, ACRONYM, ADDRESS, APPLET, AREA, B, BIG, BLOCKQUOTE, BODY, BUTTON, CAPTION, CENTER, CITE, CODE, DD, DEL, DFN, DIR, DIV, DT, EM, FIELDSET, FONT, FORM, H1, H2, H3, H4, H5, H6, HR, I, IMG, INPUT, KBD, LABEL, LEGEND, LI, LISTING, MAP, MARQUEE, MENU, OBJECT, OL, P, PLAINTEXT, PRE, Q, S,	This event is triggered whenever the user presses and holds a key on the keyboard for one of the listed objects. The keycode of the key pressed down is returned.

13

VBSCRIPT AS AN ALTERNATIVE LANGUAGE

continues

Table 13.1. continued

Event Name	Applies To	Action
	SAMP, SELECT, SMALL, SPAN, STRIKE, STRONG, SUB, SUP, TABLE, TBODY, TD, TEXTAREA, TFOOT, TH, THEAD, TR, TT, U, UL, VAR, XMP, document	
onkeypress	Same as onkeydown event	Whenever a user presses down and releases a key on the keyboard, this event is fired and the keycode of the key pressed it returned.
onkeyup	Same as onkeydown event	Opposite to onkeydown, this event is fired only when the user releases a key. The keycode of the key released is returned.
onload	APPLET, BODY, EMBED, FRAMESET, IMG, LINK, SCRIPT, STYLE, window	Fires immediately after a valid, listed object has successfully loaded.
onmousedown	Same as onclick event	This event is fired when a user presses down and holds the mouse button.
onmousemove	Same as onclick event	As the user moves the mouse, this event is fired.
onmouseout	Same as onclick event	After the user moves the mouse off an object, this event is triggered.
onmouseover	Same as onclick event	The opposite of onmouseout, onmouseover is triggered only when the user first moves the mouse pointer over an object. It does not fire while the mouse is moved over the object, unless it is moved off the object and then back into the object.
onmouseup	Same as onclick event	The opposite of onmousedown, this event is fired when the user releases the mouse button.

Event Name	Applies To	Action
onreadystatechange	APPLET, EMBED, FRAME, FRAMESET, IFRAME, IMG, LINK, OBJECT, SCRIPT, STYLE, document	If the readyState property for an object changes, this event is fired. Valid readyState's include: complete, interactive, loading, uninitialized.
onreset	FORM	When the user clicks the "Reset" button on a form, this event is triggered.
onresize	APPLET, BUTTON, CAPTION, DIV, EMBED, FRAMESET, HR, IMG, MARQUEE, SELECT, TABLE, TD, TR, TEXTAREA, window	Whenever a valid, listed object changes size, this event is fired.
onrowenter	APPLET, BODY, BUTTON, CAPTION, DIV, EMBED, HR, IMG, MAP, MARQUEE, OBJECT, SELECT, TABLE, TD, TEXTAREA, TR	Indicates that new data is available which has changed the current row's information.
onrowexit	Same as onrowenter event	Just before a data source object changes its row information, this event is fired.
onscroll	BODY, DIV, FIELDSET, IMG, MARQUEE, SPAN, TEXTAREA, window	Whenever the scrollbar's position changes, this event fires.
onselect	INPUT, TEXTAREA	As a user drags the mouse across text in INPUT or TEXTAREA tags to select text, this event is triggered.
onselectstart	A, ACRONYM, ADDRESS, AREA, B, BIG, BLOCKQUOTE, BODY, BUTTON, CAPTION, CENTER, CITE, CODE, DD, DEL, DFN, DIR, DIV, DL, DT, EM, FONT, FORM, H1, H2, H3, H4, H5, H6, HR, I, IMG, INPUT, KBD, LABEL,	Whenever a user drags the mouse across multiple elements on a Web page to select those elements, this event is triggered.

13

VBSCRIPT AS AN ALTERNATIVE LANGUAGE

continues

Table 13.1. continued

Event Name	Applies To	Action
	LI, LISTING, MAP, MARQUEE, MENU, OBJECT, OL, OPTION, P, PLAINTEXT, PRE, Q, S, SAMP, SELECT, SMALL, SPAN, STRIKE, STRONG, SUB, SUP, TABLE, TBODY, TD, TEXTAREA, TFOOT, TH, THEAD, TR, TT, U, UL, VAR, XMP	
onstart	MARQUEE	When using the looping parameters of the MARQUEE tag, this event is fired at the beginning of each loop.
onsubmit	FORM	After a user clicks the "Submit" button on a form, this event fires. This event can return true or false. If false is returned, then the submission process is canceled and the data is not sent to the server.
onunload	BODY, FRAMESET, window	Whenever a page is unloaded to present another page, this event is fired.

Summary

In this chapter you were introduced to Dynamic HTML programming with VBScript. You had the opportunity to learn how to implement typical object-oriented programming and how to use some of the capabilities offered only in VBScript. You also saw how it differs slightly in use and function from other developer languages such as JavaScript. This chapter has helped you learn how to implement the functionality of Dynamic HTML within a VBScript environment. With this knowledge, you can create some truly dynamic sites of your own.

IV
PART

The Document Object Model

CHAPTER 14

What Is a Document Object Model?

by Trevor Lohrbeer

IN THIS CHAPTER

The term Document Object Model (DOM) has become a buzzword used to describe the features of Dynamic HTML (DHTML). But what exactly is a DOM, and where did it come from? Although a DOM has been a part of Web design for some time, it has only recently been given a name. The desire to make HTML more dynamic has fueled a systematic rethinking of the definition and implementation of the DOMs in browsers. These broader, more complete DOMs implemented in Communicator 4.0 and Internet Explorer 4.0 (IE4) are the engines behind DHTML.

A DOM is a way of describing an HTML document to a scripting language by representing HTML page elements as objects in the scripting language. An HTML *page element* can be any piece of HTML on the page, including hidden tags (for example, META) and implied tags (for example, HEAD). The objects representing these HTML page elements enable them to be accessed by a scripting language. When they are accessible, the attributes of the page elements can be retrieved, modified, added, and deleted; events triggered on these elements can be reacted to; and the page elements themselves can be added to or deleted from the document structure. A DOM also provides models for representing and manipulating style sheets, for generating and reacting to user- and system-generated events, and for accessing document meta- and user-agent information.

History of the DOM

DOMs have existed since the first days of scripting on the Web, when Netscape introduced JavaScript into Navigator 2.0. Although primitive compared with the DOMs of today, the original DOM allowed for the representation of form elements, frames, links, and user-agent information in JavaScript. As scripting developed as a technology, simple form validation wasn't enough. The addition of the Image object to the Navigator 3.0 DOM started the evolution toward DHTML, with image rollovers appearing all over the Web. Today, with the development of a formal DOM specification, you have the capability to make your Web pages more dynamic than you may have imagined.

The DOMs currently implemented in Communicator 4.0 and IE4 allow for a greater level of interactivity on the client side than ever before seen on the Web. Communicator 4.0 extends the Navigator 3.0 DOM with new objects for layers, events, and screen resolution; a new event model; and a new style sheet object model. IE4 features a full DOM with every HTML page element reflected into scripting. It adds support for document navigation and modification, a new event model, and a new style sheet object model. In addition, it now supports instantaneous page updating.

Although both Communicator 4.0 and IE4 bring new levels of interactivity to the Web with new and improved DOMs, the DOM implementations each uses are not fully compatible with each other. Working to help rectify this situation, the World Wide Web Consortium's DOM Working Group is creating a recommendation for a standard to which both Netscape and Microsoft have promised to adhere. When fully implemented in both browsers, the level of interactivity a fully defined DOM promises will become widespread.

Why Is a DOM Useful?

A DOM introduces a whole new level of interactivity to a Web page by allowing the Web designer to manipulate the individual HTML elements through scripting. By scripting elements to move, change size and color, and disappear and reappear, the Web designer can create dynamic elements such as tickers, scrolling news, and interactive menus without Java applets or Shockwave plug-ins. Complex animations that used to require Shockwave or a GIF animation can now be done with a few lines of code, thereby greatly reducing bandwidth. And by making the client side more dynamic, the amount of processing needed on the server is reduced proportionally.

The Object Model

HTML page elements are represented in a scripting language through objects. The Object Model determines how a page element is reflected into the scripting language and where in the object hierarchy of the scripting language it is reflected. Specifically, the Object Model defines the following:

- How page elements are exposed
- How page elements are navigated
- How page elements are modified
- How user-agent and meta information are exposed

Exposing Page Elements

For page elements to be accessible in a scripting language, they must be exposed in some way. The object-oriented approach (the approach used by JavaScript and VBScript) is to create an object in the scripting language for each page element that is to be exposed. The object represents the page element in the scripting language with the attributes of the element reflected as the properties of the object. Methods can be added to the object, allowing for the manipulation of the page element. Figure 14.1 shows how an <IMG> tag is exposed as an object in JavaScript.

FIGURE 14.1.

How an <IMG> tag is exposed as an object in JavaScript.

```
HTML Source:
<IMG NAME=homeButton SRC="home.gif" WIDTH=50 HEIGHT=35 BORDER=1>

Object:
homeButton

Properties:
name            'homeButton'
src             'home.gif'
width           50
height          35
border          1
```

Not all object models reflect all page elements and their attributes, though. Which page elements and their respective attributes are reflected in the scripting language is determined by the object model being implemented. For most object models, only a subset of the page elements is reflected as objects (the exceptions being the IE4 and W3C object models). Likewise, even if a page element is reflected, often only a portion of the element's attributes are reflected as object properties. Figure 14.2 shows that some of the attributes of the <INPUT> tag are not reflected into JavaScript in Netscape 2.0.

FIGURE 14.2.

Some attributes of the <INPUT> *tag are undefined in JavaScript.*

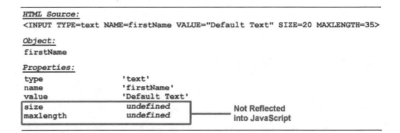

```
HTML Source:
<INPUT TYPE=text NAME=firstName VALUE="Default Text" SIZE=20 MAXLENGTH=35>

Object:
firstName

Properties:
type              'text'
name              'firstName'
value             'Default Text'
size              undefined          ─── Not Reflected
maxlength         undefined              Into JavaScript
```

> **NOTE**
>
> When only some page elements or attributes are reflected into a scripting language, the object model is said to be a *partial* object model. When all page elements and all their attributes, whether recognized by the browser or not, are reflected as objects in a scripting language, the object model is said to be a *complete* or *full* object model.

In addition to specifying *whether* a page element is reflected in the scripting language, the Object Model also defines *how* it is reflected. Where the page element is reflected in the object hierarchy and whether the element's attributes are reflected as read/write or read-only are important parts of the Object Model.

Objects exist within a scripting language in an object hierarchy. The object hierarchy logically organizes objects, determining how they are accessed by a script and scoping them into their proper contexts. Because the Object Model defines where objects exist within the object hierarchy, it also defines how scripts access those objects. Figure 14.3 shows the object hierarchy of IE4. The IE4 Object Model defines that the links collection exists as a child of the document object, which in turn exists as a child of the window object. To access a link in JavaScript in IE4, you would need to use the notation window.document.links[index].

After an object has been exposed in the object hierarchy, the Object Model defines how the properties of that object are reflected. Whether a page element's attributes are reflected as read/write or read-only determines the level of interaction available with that element. Attributes that are reflected as read-only can be used only for informational purposes, whereas read/write properties can affect how the element is rendered in the browser window.

FIGURE 14.3.
The IE4 object hierarchy.

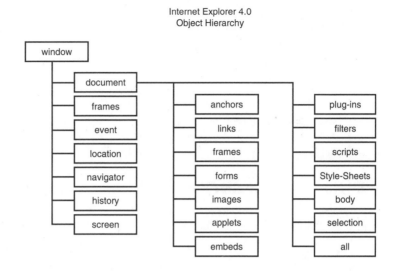

Navigating Page Elements

Because of the nature of HTML, all page elements within a document, except the root HTML element, are contained by other page elements. Page elements inherit attributes from their parent elements, which inherit attributes from *their* parent elements. This hierarchical document structure determines how the document is rendered in the browser window.

Figure 14.4 shows a sample HTML page and its document structure. The I element in the middle of a Shakespeare quote is contained by the P element, which in turn is contained by the BLOCKQUOTE element, the BODY element, and the HTML element. The P element inherits the margins of the BLOCKQUOTE element, and both elements inherit their background color from the BODY element.

FIGURE 14.4.
A sample HTML page and its document structure.

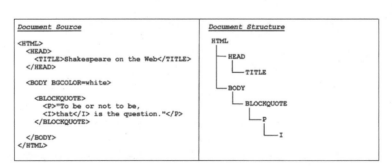

Because the document structure determines the inheritance of page element attributes, it is important to be able to navigate among the objects representing parent and child page elements. This capability to navigate the document structure allows the script to modify not only individual page elements, but elements that are visually and logically related. The Object Model defines how the document structure is represented in a scripting language and the methods by which it is navigated.

The techniques used to reflect the document structure into a scripting language vary. In Navigator 3.0 and Internet Explorer 3.0, only certain elements of the document structure (such as frames) are reflected directly into the object hierarchy. Navigation among frames is done by querying the object hierarchy directly through the frames array. IE4 reflects all page elements into its scripting languages and uses the parentElement property and the contains() method to navigate between a page element's object and its parent and child, respectively.

Manipulating Page Elements

Exposing page elements and navigating among them provide a way for the scripting language to gather information about the document. But without a way to manipulate those elements, DHTML remains relatively static.

As discussed in the section "Exposing Page Elements," the Object Model defines how page elements are exposed to the scripting language. By exposing certain page element attributes as read/write, these attributes can be modified and the rendering of their page elements changed dynamically through scripting. This, however, is only one way in which page elements can be manipulated through scripting.

By providing a series of properties and methods for page element objects and the capability to create new objects, the Object Model defines ways to change not only individual page element characteristics, but the document structure itself. The Object Model defines techniques both for adding and deleting attributes to page elements and for adding and deleting page elements from the document structure itself. Because these techniques differ greatly between IE4 and Communicator 4.0, further in-depth discussion will wait until Chapter 15, "Document Object Model Comparison."

Exposing User-Agent and Meta Information

In addition to exposing the HTML page elements as objects in the scripting language, the Object Model also describes how relevant information not explicitly part of the HTML of a document is reflected into the scripting language. This information falls into two main categories: user-agent information and meta information.

User-agent information includes relevant information about the browser and its environment, including the browser name and version, screen resolution, color depth, and browsing history. *Meta information* includes information about the document that is not directly represented in the document, including the URL, any cookies sent with the document, and the date it was last modified.

User-agent and meta information are represented in the scripting language by a series of objects. In IE4 and Communicator 4.0, these objects are navigator, window, document, location, history, and screen. These objects contain properties that represent user-agent and meta information to the scripting language. They also provide methods for window and document management, such as opening new windows and loading new documents.

The Style Sheet Object Model

Style sheets have become an important part of Web design because they provide fine control over the presentation of everything from individual page elements to the entire page. Because style sheets are not strictly part of HTML, they are not represented by the Object Model. Instead, the Style Sheet Object Model defines how style sheets are exposed and manipulated in a scripting language.

Exposing Style Sheets

Style sheets can be exposed in two different ways: At the individual element level, styles applying to a page element can be reflected in that page element's object; and with multiple related page elements, the styles can be reflected in an object that represents the entire group of elements. Both methods of exposing style sheets are useful in different scenarios.

The Individual Element Level

At the individual element level, each page element has a style associated with it. This style can be explicitly defined through a style sheet or the STYLE attribute or can be implied through default settings or inheritance from a parent element. An individual element's style can be exposed as an independent style object, a child style object of the page element's object, or a set of properties of the page element's object. Often, styles for an individual page element are exposed in more than one of these ways.

When the style for a page element is exposed as an independent style object, the style properties become the properties of a new object that represents the style for that page element. This object, although often named the same as the page element's object, contains only style properties and exists at a different place in the object hierarchy. See Figure 14.5 for an example of how Communicator 4.0 places such objects under the ids collection.

14

WHAT IS A
DOCUMENT
OBJECT MODEL?

FIGURE 14.5.

The style of a page element is reflected in the ids *collection in Communicator 4.0.*

```
HTML Source:
<H1 ID=pageTitle STYLE="color: blue; text-align: center;">
    What is a Document Object Model?
</H1>

Object:
document.ids.pageTitle

Properties:
color          'blue'
textAlign      'center'
```

Another method of exposing the style for an individual page element is as a child object of the page element's object. This object is exactly like the independent style object, except that it exists at a different place in the object hierarchy—namely, as a child of the page element's object. This approach is taken by IE4, which creates a `style` object as a child object of every page element object. Figure 14.6 shows the same piece of HTML as in Figure 14.5, but in IE4 it is reflected as a `style` object under the page element object.

FIGURE 14.6.

The style of a page element is reflected as a style *object under the page element's object in IE4.*

```
HTML Source:
<H1 ID=pageTitle STYLE="color: blue; text-align: center;">
    What is a Document Object Model?
</H1>

Object:
pageTitle.style

Properties:
color               'blue'
textAlign           'center'
```

In cases in which a style property is the same as one of the page element's attributes, the style property might be reflected as a property of the page element's object directly. This helps to maintain backward compatibility with older HTML in which the style was incorporated as attributes of the HTML tag. Figure 14.7 shows how a border specified as a style in the `<IMG>` tag is reflected in the image object for that tag in Communicator 4.0.

FIGURE 14.7.

A border specified as a style in the <IMG> *tag is reflected into the image object for that tag in Communicator 4.0.*

```
HTML Source:
<IMG NAME=homeButton SRC="home.gif" STYLE="border: 1;">

Object:
homeButton

Properties:
name                'homeButton'
src                 'home.gif'
border              1
```

The Group Element Level

Although exposing styles at the individual element level has its advantages, it lacks flexibility. Styles rarely apply to only one page element; they usually apply to entire groups of page elements. By defining how styles can be exposed at the group element level as well, the Style Sheet Object Model increases the functionality of style sheet manipulation.

One technique for exposing styles at the group element level is to expose a single object for each group of elements. For instance, one object is created for each class and tag existing in a document, and because style sheets can specify combinations of a class and a tag, one object is created for each combination of class and tag. Each object represents all the styles that apply to that group, whether default styles or styles specified by rules in a style sheet.

Communicator 4.0 takes this approach by providing the `tags` and `classes` collections. The `tags` collection contains a style object for each tag in a document, whereas the `classes` collection contains a style object for each class in the document as well as for each combination of tag and class. Figure 14.8 demonstrates how the styles of different tags and classes can be accessed in Communicator 4.0.

FIGURE 14.8.

The classes *and* tags *collections reflect the styles of all the classes and tags in a document.*

```
HTML Source:
<STYLE>
    BLOCKQUOTE        { font-style: italic; }
    .warning          { color: red; }
    IMG.screenshot    { border-width: 2; }
</STYLE>

Objects & Properties:
tags.BLOCKQUOTE.fontStyle              'italic'
classes.warning.all.color             'red'
classes.screenshot.IMG.borderWidth    2
```

Manipulating Style Sheets

By manipulating the styles of a document, the rendering of individual page elements or of an entire Web page can be dynamically changed. The Style Sheet Object Model defines how these manipulations occur within a scripting language and includes how styles on individual elements and groups of elements are modified as well as how entire style sheets are associated and disassociated with an HTML document.

The styles of individual elements and groups of elements are modified by changing the properties of the style object that represents that element or group of elements. Although the properties of style objects are rarely read-only, whether the rendering of the page element is updated to reflect the change in style is subject to how the browser has implemented page updating.

Depending on the style sheet object model implemented, methods can exist for associating and disassociating a style sheet with an HTML document. This allows for the script to attach style sheets to a document that were not specified in the original HTML and to detach style sheets that were originally attached. With this functionality, developers can provide the user the option to dynamically change the look and feel of a document through a choice of available style sheets.

The Event Model

The Event Model is an important part of the DOM, defining how a user's actions activate the scripts in a document. It determines not only which events are generated, but how they are delivered to an event handler and what information is available to that event handler to process the event. The Event Model enables the DOM to create Web pages that are not only dynamic but interactive.

NOTE

The event models of Communicator 4.0 and IE4 differ significantly and are not compatible beyond the functionality available in Navigator 3.0. For detailed information about the Communicator 4.0 and IE4 event models, see Chapter 16, "The Internet Explorer 4.0 Event Model: Event Bubbling" and Chapter 17, "The Communicator 4.0 Event Model: Event Capturing."

Generating Events

Events can be generated in two ways: by the user and by the system. *User-generated events* occur when the user performs an action with the mouse or keyboard within a certain context, such as clicking a mouse button while the cursor is positioned over a link. *System-generated events* occur when the state of the system changes, such as when an error occurs or when a page finishes loading. The context of both user- and system-generated events determines the target of the event.

The Event Model defines under which contexts an event can be generated from an action and what the target under that context is. For user-generated events, the Event Model defines a certain subset of possible events that can be generated for any page element. If an action falls within the subset of valid events for a page element, an event is generated and the target page element is said to have generated the event. The A element, for instance, can generate click, dblClick, mouseOver, and mouseOut events, among others.

For system-generated events, the event is triggered by a change in the state of the system. System-generated events often do not have a target element but are captured by event handlers defined by a global script on a page. The Event Model defines when system-generated events occur and which ones have a target element. For instance, the load and unload events target the BODY element, whereas the error and scroll events have no specific target.

Delivering Events

The process by which an event is delivered to the code that reacts to the event is called *event delivery*. Event delivery occurs in different ways depending upon the type of event and the event model being implemented. Traditionally, all events have target page elements that specify the code for the event handler as an attribute of the page element. For instance, the following code uses the onMouseOver attribute to specify the code for handling a mouseOver event on the link:

```
<A HREF="home.html"
    onMouseOver="window.status='Return To The Home Page';">Home</A>
```

Internet Explorer 3.0 introduced the idea of binding an event handler to a page element by using a special name for the function that handles the event. By using the NAME attribute and naming the event handler *name_onEvent,* Listing 14.1 produces the same effect as the preceding example but uses VBScript to handle the event and stores the script farther down the page.

By binding to the event from a script external to the page element, you can use languages other than JavaScript to handle events and can group all the event handlers together.

Listing 14.1. Binding an event elsewhere on the page.

```
<A NAME=homeLink HREF="home.html">Home</A>

...rest of HTML code...

<SCRIPT LANGUAGE="VBScript">
sub homeLink_onMouseOver
    window.status = "Return To The Home Page"
end sub
</SCRIPT>
```

Although having events delivered to the target page element is no doubt useful, advanced event-handling techniques require events to be handled by page elements other than the target element. Instead, events travel through the document structure being handled by the page elements most relevant to the event. You can write event handlers to be generic and reusable, which reduces the amount of scripting necessary when creating new pages and adding new elements to pages.

The Event Model enables advanced event delivery by defining how events travel along the document structure, when page elements intercept events, and how they release events to continue traveling the document structure. Communicator 4.0 and IE4 each implement different techniques for enabling advanced event delivery. The details of these techniques are discussed in Chapters 16 and 17.

Exposing Event Attributes

The Event Model defines an event object that exposes relevant information about the event. Information such as the type of event, the event's target, the location of any mouse clicks, and any keys that were pressed is stored in the properties of the event object. Event handlers access this information to determine how to correctly react to the event.

Page Updates

Although not technically part of the DOM, a browser's implementation of page updating determines how useful the DOM is in creating dynamic Web pages. As you have seen, the DOM makes page elements, style sheets, and events accessible to the scripting language. But without regular page updates, the changes made by scripts to these objects are never seen.

When a page element is manipulated in some way, the results of that manipulation must be rendered in the browser. What sort of page updating is implemented by a browser determines when and how often the results of scripts are rendered in the browser window. In older browsers, a page is rendered once during load time and never again. Scripting that affects how an HTML page is rendered had to appear earlier on the page than the HTML it affected.

With the newer browsers, page updating occurs a lot more often. Communicator 4.0 not only renders the page during load time, but also updates the page whenever the position, clipping, or visibility of a layer or absolutely positioned page element is changed. IE4 goes one step further and updates the page whenever *anything* that affects the layout or display of the page is changed. These new page updating schemes finally allow truly dynamic HTML pages to be created using a DOM.

Summary

DOMs have evolved into the driving force behind DHTML in IE4 and Communicator 4.0. A DOM defines how page elements are exposed, navigated, and manipulated within a scripting language. It also defines how additional information such as user-agent and meta information is exposed. By defining a style sheet object model to expose, navigate, and manipulate style sheets, a DOM provides an interface not only to HTML but to cascading style sheets. A DOM also defines an event model, which determines events that are generated in response to a user's actions and how those events are delivered to the proper event handlers.

By allowing page elements and style sheets to be exposed, navigated, and manipulated by the scripting language, a DOM defines the interaction between the page elements and the scripts of a document. With the addition of an event model, the DOM also defines the interaction between a document and the user. When they are combined, the DOM enables you to design Web pages that are both dynamic and interactive. And with advanced DOMs implemented in both Communicator 4.0 and IE4, designing dynamic Web pages is now easier than ever.

CHAPTER 15

Document Object Model Comparison

by Trevor Lohrbeer

IN THIS CHAPTER

A Document Object Model (DOM) defines how an HTML document is exposed to a scripting language. It allows a document to interact and respond to a user dynamically through scripting. Although both Communicator 4.0 and Internet Explorer 4.0 (IE4) have developed new DOMs that are more powerful and complete than the DOMs of the past, these DOMs are not fully compatible with each other. The incompatibilities that exist between the Communicator 4.0 and IE4 DOMs greatly reduce the cross-browser functionality of Dynamic HTML (DHTML). However, obtaining a deeper understanding of how each browser has implemented its DOM and what commonality exists between the two DOMs can help you develop robust dynamic cross-browser scripts.

Why Different Models?

The first Communicator 4.0 beta was released in December 1996. At that time, the idea of a formal DOM specification was still in its infancy. The Communicator 4.0 DOM was developed as a natural extension to the Navigator 3.0 DOM to enable HTML documents to become more dynamic. As Communicator 4.0 progressed through its beta cycle, the idea of a DOM solidified. Although the Communicator 4.0 DOM was updated, many new features of a DOM could not be incorporated into the final release.

By the time the first IE4 Platform Preview was released in May 1997, general requirements for a DOM had been published by the World Wide Web Consortium's DOM Working Group (W3C DOM-WG) and work on developing a recommendation for a standard DOM for the Web had begun. Due to its longer development cycle, IE4 was able to incorporate many of the newer ideas of what a DOM should consist of.

Although Netscape could have extended its development cycle to implement more features and Microsoft could have expanded their DOM to include the features in the Communicator 4.0 DOM, each company chose not to. The result is two separate DOMs that provide powerful new features for each browser alone, but little compatibility for advanced cross-browser DHTML.

How Does This Affect Development?

Due to the separate, incompatible DOMs in Communicator 4.0 and IE4, cross-browser scripts developed to take advantage of the new features of DHTML will have to make compromises. They won't be able to take advantage of many of the advanced features each browser provides. And extra code will need to be written to accommodate the different approaches for achieving the same effect in each browser. This extra code will make the scripts longer, slower, and more complex.

Looking toward the future, the W3C will recommend a formal DOM specification sometime in 1998. Both Microsoft and Netscape have stated that they will fully support this specification in future versions of their browsers. In fact, Microsoft has already taken many steps to incorporating the features of the preliminary specification into IE4. However, until a common DOM is supported in both browsers, extra coding and avoidance of advanced features will be necessary in the development of cross-browser DHTML pages.

Organization of This Chapter

This chapter is a companion chapter to Chapter 14, "What Is a Document Object Model?" Whereas Chapter 14 discusses the theory behind a DOM, this chapter discusses the implementation of the DOM in each browser and how these implementations can be reconciled. Each section of this chapter contains the following three subsections:

- The Communicator 4.0 Approach—Describes the Communicator 4.0 implementation of the DOM feature
- The Internet Explorer 4.0 Approach—Describes the IE4 implementation of the DOM feature
- Making Them Work Together—Describes the compatibility of the DOM feature in the Communicator 4.0 and IE4 DOMs and techniques for reconciling the two DOMs to develop cross-browser code

The Object Model

The Object Model defines how the scripting language accesses page elements and their attributes as well as user agent and document meta information. By defining how page elements are exposed, navigated, and manipulated, the Object Model determines how scripts can change the characteristics of any element on a Web page.

Exposing Page Elements

The Object Model determines how page elements are exposed to a scripting language. A page element can be any piece of HTML on the page, including hidden tags (for example, META) and implied tags (for example, HEAD). Both Communicator 4.0 and IE4 expose page elements into their scripting languages, but which page elements are exposed and where they are exposed into the object hierarchy differ between the two browsers.

The Communicator 4.0 Approach

Communicator 4.0 exposes only a limited subset of the page elements in a document. Elements previously exposed in Navigator 3.0 in the `forms`, `anchors`, `links`, `applets`, `embeds`, `images` and `frames` arrays continue to be exposed in those arrays. Forms and images also continue to be reflected by name underneath the `document` object.

Layers and absolutely positioned page elements are exposed in the `layers` array, and also by name or ID under the `document` object. For layers, an additional `document` object is reflected under each layer object, and all page elements contained within a layer are reflected in their respective arrays under this `document` object instead of the main `document` object.

Figure 15.1 and Listing 15.1 show how the DIV element is exposed as both `document.layers['layerID']` and `document.layerID`, while the IMG element is exposed as both `document.images['name']` and `document.name`. The FONT element is not exposed in Communicator 4.0.

15

DOCUMENT OBJECT MODEL COMPARISON

FIGURE 15.1.

Exposing the DIV *and* IMG *elements in Communicator 4.0.*

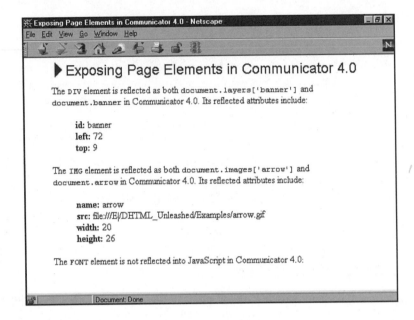

FIGURE 15.1.

Exposing the DIV *and* IMG *elements in Communicator 4.0.*

Listing 15.1. HTML source for Figure 15.1.

```
<IMG NAME=arrow SRC="arrow.gif" ALIGN=left>

<DIV ID=banner STYLE="position: absolute; left: 72; top: 9;">
  <FONT FACE="Arial, Helvetica" SIZE=+2>
    Exposing Page Elements in Communicator 4.0
  </FONT>
</DIV>

<BR><BR>
<P>The <TT>DIV</TT> element is reflected as both
<TT>document.layers['banner']</TT> and <TT>document.banner</TT> in
Communicator 4.0. Its reflected attributes include:</P>

<BLOCKQUOTE>
<SCRIPT>
  document.writeln("<B>id:</B> " + document.banner.id + "<BR>");
  document.writeln("<B>left:</B> " + document.layers['banner'].left +
                  "<BR>");
  document.writeln("<B>top:</B> " + document.layers['banner'].top +
                  "<BR>");
</SCRIPT>
</BLOCKQUOTE>

<P>The <TT>IMG</TT> element is reflected as both
<TT>document.images['arrow']</TT> and <TT>document.arrow</TT> in
Communicator 4.0.  Its reflected attributes include:</P>

<BLOCKQUOTE>
<SCRIPT>
  document.writeln("<B>name:</B> " + document.images['arrow'].name +
                  "<BR>");
```

```
     document.writeln("<B>src:</B> " + document.images['arrow'].src +
                        "<BR>");
     document.writeln("<B>width:</B> " + document.arrow.width + "<BR>");
     document.writeln("<B>height:</B> " + document.arrow.height + "<BR>");
</SCRIPT>
</BLOCKQUOTE>

<P>The <TT>FONT</TT> element is not reflected into JavaScript in
Communicator 4.0.</P>
```

Figure 15.2 and Listing 15.2 demonstrate how, by placing an IMG element within the DIV positioned page element, it is exposed at a different place in the object hierarchy. Instead of being exposed as document.*name*, the IMG element is now exposed as document.*layerID*.document.*name* and as document.*layerID*.document.images['*name*']. All elements contained within layer page elements in Communicator 4.0 are exposed in the layer's document object, not the main document object.

FIGURE 15.2.

Exposing the IMG *element under the* DIV *element's document object in Communicator 4.0.*

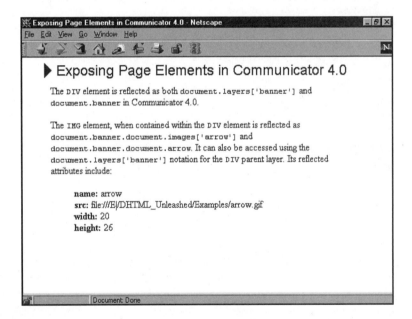

Listing 15.2. HTML source for Figure 15.2.

```
<DIV ID=banner STYLE="position: absolute; left: 32; top: 9;">
  <IMG NAME=arrow SRC="arrow.gif" ALIGN=left>
  <FONT FACE="Arial, Helvetica" SIZE=+2>
    Exposing Page Elements in Communicator 4.0
  </FONT>
</DIV>
```

continues

Listing 15.2. continued

```
<BR><BR>
<P>The <TT>DIV</TT> element is reflected as both
<TT>document.layers['banner']</TT> and <TT>document.banner</TT> in
Communicator 4.0.</P>

<P>The <TT>IMG</TT> element, when contained within the <TT>DIV</TT>
element is reflected as <TT>document.banner.document.images['arrow']</TT>
and <TT>document.banner.document.arrow</TT>.  It can also be accessed
using the <TT>document.layers['banner']</TT> notation for the
<TT>DIV</TT> parent layer.  Its reflected attributes include:</P>

<BLOCKQUOTE>
<SCRIPT>
   document.writeln("<B>name:</B> ");
   document.writeln(document.banner.document.images['arrow'].name);
   document.writeln("<BR>");
   document.writeln("<B>src:</B> ");
   document.writeln(document.layers['banner'].document.images['arrow'].src);
   document.writeln("<BR>");
   document.writeln("<B>width:</B> ");
   document.writeln(document.banner.document.arrow.width);
   document.writeln("<BR>");
   document.writeln("<B>height:</B> ");
   document.writeln(document.layers['banner'].document.arrow.height);
   document.writeln("<BR>");
</SCRIPT>
</BLOCKQUOTE>
```

The IE4 Approach

IE4 exposes all valid page elements into the all collection under the document object. All known attributes for each page element are reflected as properties of that page element's object. Unrecognized elements are not reflected into the scripting languages in IE4; however, unknown attributes can be accessed using the getAttribute(), setAttribute(), and removeAttribute() methods.

Each page element object has a set of common properties and methods that it shares with all other page elements. Common properties owned by every page element object are detailed in Table 15.1, and Table 15.2 details the common methods owned by every element object. The parentElement property is discussed in more detail in the section "Navigating Page Elements," and the insertAdjacentHTML() and insertAdjacentText() methods are discussed in the section "Manipulating Page Elements."

Table 15.1. Properties of every page element object.

Property	Value
document	References the document object within whose hierarchy the element exists
id	Reflects the element's ID attribute

Property	*Value*
offsetHeight	Contains the height of the element measured in the offsetParent element's coordinate system
offsetWidth	Contains the width of the element measured in the offsetParent element's coordinate system
offsetLeft	Contains the left offset of the element's position on the page relative to the offsetParent element
offsetTop	Contains the top offset of the element's position on the page relative to the offsetParent element
offsetParent	References the parent element whose coordinate system is used to determine offsetTop and offsetLeft
sourceIndex	Contains the index into the all collection of the element object
style	References the style object containing the style properties of the element's in-line styles
tagName	Reflects the tag of the page element
parentElement	References the parent element one level higher in the document structure

Table 15.2. Methods of every page element object.

Method	*Action*
getAttribute(*name*, [*caseSensitive*])	Returns the value of the attribute whose name matches *name*. *caseSensitive* is a boolean value determining whether the match is case sensitive.
setAttribute(*name*, *value*, [*caseSensitive*])	Sets the value of the attribute whose name matches *name* to the string *value*. *caseSensitive* is a boolean value determining whether the match is case sensitive.
removeAttribute(*name*, [*caseSensitive*])	Removes the attribute whose name matches *name* from the element. *caseSensitive* is a boolean value determining whether the match is case sensitive.
insertAdjacentHTML (*where*, *text*)	Inserts HTML before or after either the opening or closing tag of an element. *where* is a string specifying where to insert the text, and *text* is the HTML to insert. *text* must be valid HTML and is parsed into the document structure.
insertAdjacentText (*where*, *text*)	Inserts text before or after either the opening or closing tag of an element. *where* is a string specifying where to insert the text, and *text* is the text to insert.

Page elements are also exposed into special collections under the document object. In IE4 page elements are exposed into the frames, links, anchors, images, forms, applets, embeds, plugins, scripts, and styleSheets collections. In addition, each frame object in the frames collection contains a document object that contains each of the special collections and the all collection. Page elements contained within a frame are exposed in the collections under the frame's document object rather than the main document object.

IE4 does not have a special layers collection for a positioned page element. Instead, all positioned page elements are accessed from the all collection like other page elements.

Figure 15.3 and Listing 15.3 show how the same elements in Figure 15.1 are exposed in IE4. The DIV element is exposed into the document.all collection and is referenced using the notation document.all['banner'] or document.all.banner. The IMG element is exposed by name directly under the document object, in the document.images collection and in the document.all collection. In IE4, the FONT element is exposed under the all collection. Because the FONT element has no NAME or ID attribute, it is referenced using its position in the source document.

> **NOTE**
>
> The all collection stores all elements in source order, disregarding unknown tags and end tags. Comment tags are counted as page elements even though they do not display in the rendering of the document. The sourceIndex property of a page element object contains the index of that element in the all collection.

FIGURE 15.3.

Exposing the DIV, IMG, *and* FONT *elements in IE4.*

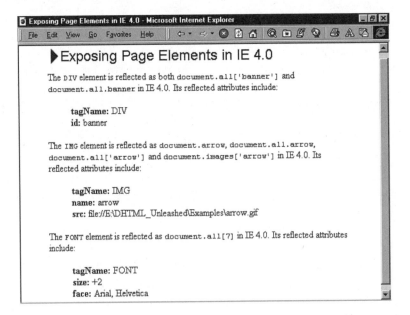

Listing 15.3. Source HTML for Figure 15.3.

```
<HTML>
<HEAD>
  <TITLE>Exposing Page Elements in IE4</TITLE>
</HEAD>

<BODY BGCOLOR=white>
  <BLOCKQUOTE>

  <IMG NAME=arrow SRC="arrow.gif" ALIGN=left>

  <DIV ID=banner STYLE="position: absolute; left: 72; top: 15;">
    <FONT FACE="Arial, Helvetica" SIZE=+2>
        Exposing Page Elements in IE4
    </FONT>
  </DIV>

  <BR><BR>
  <P>The <TT>DIV</TT> element is reflected as both
  <TT>document.all['banner']</TT> and <TT>document.all.banner</TT> in
  IE4. Its reflected attributes include:</P>

  <BLOCKQUOTE>
  <SCRIPT>
    document.writeln("<B>tagName:</B> " + document.all['banner'].tagName +
                     "<BR>");
    document.writeln("<B>id:</B> " + document.all.banner.id + "<BR>");
  </SCRIPT>
  </BLOCKQUOTE>

  <P>The <TT>IMG</TT> element is reflected as <TT>document.arrow</TT>,
  <TT>document.all.arrow</TT>, <TT>document.all['arrow']</TT> and
  <TT>document.images['arrow']</TT> in IE4. Its reflected attributes
  include:</P>

  <BLOCKQUOTE>
  <SCRIPT>
    document.writeln("<B>tagName:</B> " + document.all['arrow'].tagName +
                     "<BR>");
    document.writeln("<B>name:</B> " + document.images['arrow'].name +
                     "<BR>");
    document.writeln("<B>src:</B> " + document.all.arrow.src + "<BR>");
  </SCRIPT>
  </BLOCKQUOTE>

  <P>The <TT>FONT</TT> element is reflected as <TT>document.all[7]</TT>
  in IE4. Its reflected attributes include:</P>

  <BLOCKQUOTE>
  <SCRIPT>
    document.writeln("<B>tagName:</B> " + document.all[7].tagName + "<BR>");
    document.writeln("<B>size:</B> " + document.all[7].size + "<BR>");
    document.writeln("<B>face:</B> " + document.all[7].face + "<BR>");
  </SCRIPT>
  </BLOCKQUOTE>

  </BLOCKQUOTE>
</BODY>
</HTML>
```

Making Them Work Together

Because Communicator 4.0 does not expose all page elements, scripts designed for IE4 might never work in Communicator 4.0. However, by scripting only page elements exposed in Communicator 4.0 and programmatically correcting for the differences between the two browsers' object hierarchies, you can write cross-browser scripts.

Many of the element arrays existing under the document object are present in both browsers' object model, so elements such as forms, images, anchors, links, frames, embeds, and applets are easily scripted for cross-browser compatibility. Arrays for scripts, filters, and style sheets exist only in IE4 and so cannot be scripted to be cross-browser. Likewise, the layers array can only be used in Communicator 4.0, although some of the elements in the layers array can be accessed in both browsers.

Positioned page elements in Communicator 4.0 are primarily reflected in the layers array but, when named, are also reflected directly under the document object. In IE4, positioned page elements are reflected under the all collection. By programmatically reflecting the page element objects in IE4 to the document object, cross-browser scripts can be written using the same notation to access positioned page element objects in both browsers.

Listing 15.4 contains a generic function called reflectElements() that does just this. It performs a browser detect and, if the browser is IE4, reflects all named page elements from the all collection to the document object. The DIV element accessed elsewhere in the script is then referenced using the same notation for both IE4 and Communicator 4.0.

Listing 15.4. Using a generic function called reflectElements() to correct for differences in the object hierarchies of IE4 and Communicator 4.0.

```
<IMG NAME=arrow SRC="arrow.gif" ALIGN=left>

<DIV ID=banner STYLE="position: absolute; left: 72; top: 15;">
  <FONT FACE="Arial, Helvetica" SIZE=+2>
     Exposing Page Elements Cross-Browser
  </FONT>
</DIV>


<SCRIPT>
// reflectElements:
//
//   Reflects elements from the document.all collection up one
//   level to underneath the document object.
//
function reflectElements()
{
  for (var i=0; i<document.all.length; i++)
  {
    // If an element has an id and does not already exist
    // under the document object, reflect the element object
    // underneath the document object.
```

```
    if (document.all[i].id != "" &&
        !eval("document." + document.all[i].id))
    {
       eval("document." + document.all[i].id +
            " = document.all[" + i + "];");
    }
  }
}

// Detect if browser is IE4 and if so, reflect page elements up
// to document object.
//
if (navigator.appName.indexOf("Internet Explorer") != -1 &&
    navigator.appVersion.charAt(0) == '4')
      reflectElements();
</SCRIPT>


<BR><BR>
<P>The <TT>DIV</TT> element is normally reflected as
<TT>document.banner</TT> in Communicator 4.0 and
<TT>document.all['banner']</TT> in IE4.  Using this script to
manually reflect all named page elements beneath the document
object allows both browsers to access the <TT>DIV</TT> element using
<TT>document.banner</TT>.</P>

<P>The attributes of the <TT>DIV</TT> element that are reflected in both
browsers include:</P>

<BLOCKQUOTE>
<SCRIPT>
  document.writeln("<B>id:</B> " + document.banner.id + "<BR>");
</SCRIPT>
</BLOCKQUOTE>

<P>The <TT>IMG</TT> element is normally reflected as
<TT>document.arrow</TT> and <TT>document.images['arrow']</TT> in both
Communicator 4.0 and IE4.</P>

<P>The attributes of the <TT>IMG</TT> element that are reflected in both
browsers include:</P>

<BLOCKQUOTE>
<SCRIPT>
   document.writeln("<B>name:</B> " + document.arrow.name + "<BR>");
   document.writeln("<B>src:</B> " + document.arrow.src + "<BR>");
   document.writeln("<B>width:</B> " + document.images['arrow'].width +
                    "<BR>");
   document.writeln("<B>height:</B> " + document.images['arrow'].height +
                    "<BR>");
</SCRIPT>
</BLOCKQUOTE>
```

Although convenient for correcting the object hierarchy differences for positioned page elements while maintaining readable code, this approach is inefficient. An alternate approach is
to write statements within the language differently. Listing 15.5 demonstrates another method
of correcting for the differences in the object hierarchies of the two browsers.

**Listing 15.5. Correcting for the differences in the object hierarchies of the two browsers using the eval()
function.**

```
<IMG NAME=arrow SRC="arrow.gif" ALIGN=left>

<DIV ID=banner STYLE="position: absolute; left: 72; top: 15;">
  <FONT FACE="Arial, Helvetica" SIZE=+2>
    Exposing Page Elements Cross-Browser
  </FONT>
</DIV>


<SCRIPT>
  // Detect if browser is IE4 and if so, assign objectRoot to contain
  // 'document.all' instead of 'document'
  //
  objectRoot = "document";
  if (navigator.appName.indexOf("Internet Explorer") != -1 &&
      navigator.appVersion.charAt(0) == '4')
        objectRoot = "document.all";
</SCRIPT>


<BR><BR>
<P>The <TT>DIV</TT> element is normally reflected as
<TT>document.banner</TT> in Communicator 4.0 and
<TT>document.all.banner</TT> in IE4.  By assigning
<TT>objectRoot</TT> to contain the differences in the object hierarchy,
the <TT>eval()</TT> function can be used to dynamically access the
<TT>DIV</TT> element using the correct notation for each browser.</P>

<P>The attributes of the <TT>DIV</TT> element that are reflected in both
browsers include:</P>

<BLOCKQUOTE>
<SCRIPT>
  document.writeln("<B>id:</B> " + eval(objectRoot + ".banner.id"));
  document.writeln("<BR>");
</SCRIPT>
</BLOCKQUOTE>

<P>The <TT>IMG</TT> element is dynamically accessed as
<TT>document.arrow</TT> in Communicator 4.0 and
<TT>document.all.arrow</TT> in IE4 using the <TT>objectRoot</TT>
variable and the <TT>eval()</TT> function.  </P>

<P>The attributes of the <TT>IMG</TT> element that are reflected in both
browsers include:</P>
```

```
<BLOCKQUOTE>
<SCRIPT>
   document.writeln("<B>name:</B> " + eval(objectRoot + ".arrow.name"));
   document.writeln("<BR>");
   document.writeln("<B>src:</B> " + eval(objectRoot + ".arrow.src"));
   document.writeln("<BR>");
</SCRIPT>
</BLOCKQUOTE>
```

In the beginning of the script a browser detect is performed, and the `objectRoot` variable assigned specifying how the object hierarchy is altered. Whenever a positioned page element needs to be accessed, `objectRoot` is used in conjunction with the `eval()` function to dynamically reference the object. This allows the DIV element to be accessed in both browsers without the preliminary processing required to correct the object hierarchy through manual reflection. The disadvantage of this method is that the code becomes harder to read.

Navigating Page Elements

Page elements within a document exist in a hierarchy known as the *document structure*. Every page element in a document, except the HTML element, has a parent element and may or may not have child elements. The document structure determines attribute inheritance and is important in event delivery. By defining methods for navigating the document structure, the Object Model allows an element to determine its parent element and any child elements it may contain. Both Communicator 4.0 and IE4 provide some level of page element navigation, but to varying degrees.

The Communicator 4.0 Approach

Navigation of page elements in Communicator 4.0 is limited. Because all page elements are not reflected into scripting, information on the document structure as a whole is not available. Instead, structural information is available only for frames, layers, and positioned page elements by reflecting it directly into the object hierarchy.

For layers and positioned page elements, the `parentLayer` property of the layer object contains a reference to the parent layer object. The `layers` array of a layer's `document` object contains the layer objects of any child layers. Similarly, for frames, the `parent` property of a frame object contains a reference to the parent frame object, and the `frames` array of a frame's `document` object contains the frame objects of any child frames. Using this information, nested frames and layers in a document can be navigated in script.

In Listing 15.6, several nested layers have been created using absolutely and relatively positioned page elements and the `<LAYER>` tag. JavaScript code then queries the layer structure by accessing the `parentLayer` property to obtain a reference to the parent layer. Child layers are enumerated by looping through the `layers` array under the `layerA1` document object. Figure 15.4 shows the results of this page when displayed in the browser.

FIGURE 15.4.

Navigating the layer structure using nested layers.

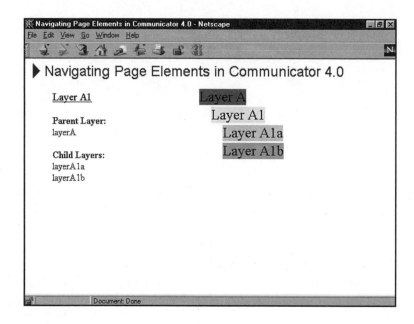

Listing 15.6. HTML source for Figure 15.4.

```
<DIV ID=layerA STYLE="position: absolute; left: 300; top: 50;
  background-color: red;">
  <P><FONT SIZE=+2>Layer A</FONT></P>

  <BLOCKQUOTE ID=layerA1 STYLE="position: absolute; left: 20; top: 30;
    background-color: yellow">
    <P><FONT SIZE=+2>Layer A1</FONT></P>

    <P ID=layerA1a STYLE="position: relative; left: 20; top: -24;
     background-color: lightGreen">
    <FONT SIZE=+2>Layer A1a</FONT></P>

    <LAYER ID=layerA1b LEFT=20 TOP=60 STYLE="background-color: orange;">
      <P><FONT SIZE=+2>Layer A1b</FONT></P>
    </LAYER>
  </BLOCKQUOTE>
</DIV>

<BLOCKQUOTE>
<P><FONT SIZE=+1><U>Layer A1</U></FONT></P>
<P><B>Parent Layer:</B><BR>

  <SCRIPT>
document.writeln(document.layers[0].document.layers['layerA1'].
➥parentLayer.name);
  </SCRIPT>
</P>

<P><B>Child Layers:</B><BR>
```

```
    <SCRIPT>
      function printChildLayers(rootDocument)
      {
        for (var i=0; i<rootDocument.layers.length; i++)
        {
          document.writeln(rootDocument.layers[i].name);
          document.writeln("<BR>");
        }
      }

      printChildLayers(document.layers[0].document.layers['layerA1'].document);
    </SCRIPT>
</P>
</BLOCKQUOTE>
```

The IE4 Approach

IE4 allows for complete navigation of the document structure through the inclusion of the parentElement property, the contains() method and the children collection in most page element objects. The parentElement property contains a reference to the object of an element's parent page element, and the contains() method is used to determine if a page element is contained within another element. The children collection contains references to the objects of the child elements contained within the current element.

Using the parentElement and the contains() methods in conjunction, Figure 15.5 and Listing 15.7 demonstrate how the entire structure of a document can be dynamically displayed through scripting. By looping through page elements with a higher index in the all collection, the enumerateChildElements() function displays the tags for all elements contained by the page element passed to it as a parameter. The result is an enumeration of the same elements contained in the children collection of the page element object. The parentLayer property is used to navigate up the document structure to determine how much to indent the tag displayed.

Listing 15.7. Source HTML for Figure 15.5.

```
<HTML>
<HEAD>
  <TITLE>Navigating Page Elements in IE4</TITLE>
</HEAD>

<BODY BGCOLOR=white>

<P>
  <IMG ID=arrow SRC="arrow.gif" ALIGN=left">
  <FONT FACE="Arial, Helvetica" SIZE=+2>
    Navigating Page Elements in IE4
  </FONT>
</P>

<P>The following is the document structure of this Web page:
```

continues

Listing 15.7. continued

```
<BLOCKQUOTE>
<PRE><SCRIPT>
  function enumerateChildElements(pageElement)
  {
    var i = pageElement.sourceIndex + 1;

    // Display the root element
    document.writeln(pageElement.tagName);

    // Display elements sequentially while they
    // are still contained by pageElement.
    //
    while (i < document.all.length &&
          pageElement.contains(document.all[i]))
    {
      // Indent the element three spaces for each
      // parent between the current element and
      // root element
      //
      parentElement = document.all[i].parentElement;
      while (parentElement != pageElement && parentElement != null)
      {
        parentElement = parentElement.parentElement;
        document.write("   ");
      }

      // Display the tag name and move to the next element
      document.writeln("   " + document.all[i].tagName);
      i++;
    }
  }

  enumerateChildElements(document.all[0]);
</SCRIPT></PRE>
</BLOCKQUOTE>
</P>

</BODY>
</HTML>
```

In addition to supporting the parentElement property, the contains() method and the children collection for document structure navigation, IE4 supports navigation of frames through the frames array and parent property.

Making Them Work Together

Because Communicator 4.0 does not support the parentElement property, the contains() method or the children collection, and IE4 does not support the layers array, the only page element navigation available cross-browser is frame navigation.

Navigation of frame objects is performed in the same way as navigation of layer objects in Communicator 4.0. The parent frame object is referenced through the parent property, and child frames are referenced by looping through the frames array of the frame's document object. For more information, see Listing 15.6, which demonstrates navigation between layer objects.

Figure 15.5.

A document structure dynamically generated using the contains() *method and the* parentElement *property.*

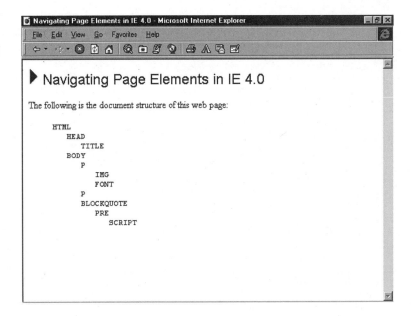

Manipulating Page Elements

Page elements must be exposed to the scripting language to be manipulated. The Object Model, by defining which page elements are exposed, determines which elements can be manipulated. By determining which attributes are exposed and how they are exposed, the Object Model also determines how the page elements can be manipulated.

The Object Model can also define methods of adding and deleting attributes to a page element, content within a page element, and entire page elements to and from the document structure. These methods of manipulation exist separately from the determination of which page elements are exposed.

The Communicator 4.0 Approach

Communicator 4.0 reflects only a subset of the page elements in a document. These elements can be manipulated through scripting by retrieving and modifying the properties of the object representing each page element. Which attributes are reflected and whether they are reflected as read/write or read-only is determined by the HTML tag of a page element.

Communicator 4.0 has limited support for advanced page element modification. There is no method for adding or deleting page elements or their attributes. Content of a document can be changed only if it is contained within a positioned page element or layer and if the page containing the page element or layer has finished loading.

Listing 15.8 demonstrates how the contents of a layer can be rewritten using JavaScript. Clicking the link opens the document object of the banner layer, writes to it, and closes it. Once closed, the content of the layer is updated in the browser window.

15

DOCUMENT OBJECT MODEL COMPARISON

Listing 15.8. Rewriting the contents of a layer in Communicator 4.0.

```
<IMG NAME=arrow SRC="arrow.gif" ALIGN=left>

<DIV ID=banner STYLE="position: absolute; left: 72; top: 9;">
  <FONT FACE="Arial, Helvetica" SIZE=+2>
    Manipulating Page Elements in Communicator 4.0
  </FONT>
</DIV>

<BR><BR><BR><BR>
<P ALIGN=center>
  <A HREF="" onClick="changeBanner(); return false;">
    Click Here To Change Banner
  </A>
</P>

<SCRIPT>
function changeBanner()
{
  document.banner.document.writeln("<FONT SIZE=+2>");
  document.banner.document.writeln("Re-Writing The Content of Layers");
  document.banner.document.writeln("in Communicator 4.0");
  document.banner.document.writeln("</FONT>");
  document.banner.document.close();
}
</SCRIPT>
```

The IE4 Approach

IE4 reflects all valid page elements and all attributes within a document. Every page element in a document can be modified through scripting by retrieving and modifying the properties of its object. Which properties are accessible as read/write and which properties are read-only is determined by the type of page element.

IE4 provides support for adding, removing, and retrieving page element attributes through the setAttribute(), getAttribute(), and removeAttribute() methods belonging to every page element object. Although similar to accessing attributes directly through the properties of the page element object, these methods provide access to unknown page element attributes that are not normally reflected as properties of an element object.

Page content can be modified in IE4 using the insertAdjacentHTML()and insertAdjacentText() methods that exist in every page element object. In addition, many page element objects have innerHTML, outerHTML, innerText, and outerText properties that allow for the modification of both the content of and the elements contained within a page element.

The insertAdjacentHTML() and insertAdjacentText() methods are used to insert content into a document before or after the beginning or ending tag of a page element. The syntax of these methods follows:

```
document.all.pageElement.insertAdjacentHTML(where, text);
document.all.pageElement.insertAdjacentText(where, text);
```

The *where* parameter is a string specifying where the text should be inserted relative to the page element's tags. Its possible values are BeforeBegin, AfterBegin, BeforeEnd, and AfterEnd. The *text* parameter is a string to insert into the document. If the insertAdjacentHTML() method is used, the text is parsed as HTML, and any new elements are added to the document structure. If the insertAdjacentText() method is used, no parsing is performed, and the text is inserted as is into the document.

To modify the contents of an element, the innerHTML, innerText, outerHTML, and outerText properties are used. These properties reflect the contents of an element and can be assigned new values to change those contents. The innerHTML and innerText properties affect the text contained within an element, and the outerHTML and outerText properties include the element in the change. Likewise, the innerHTML and outerHTML properties are parsed, and any new HTML is added to the document structure. The innerText and outerText simply replace the text of the element with no parsing.

Listing 15.9 demonstrates the use of the innerHTML, innerText, outerHTML, and outerText properties. Four FONT elements initially contain the text "Generic Content That Will Be Replaced". When the link is clicked, the changeContent() function replaces this text using a different text property for each FONT element. Both the internal document structure and the rendering of the page in the browser are instantly updated. The resulting page is shown in Figure 15.6.

FIGURE 15.6.

Replacing text with the innerHTML, innerText, outerHTML, *and* outerText *properties.*

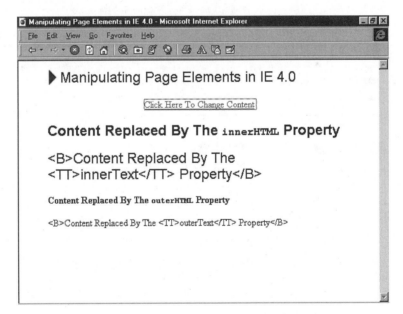

Listing 15.9. HTML source for Figure 15.6.

```
<P ALIGN=center>
  <A HREF="" onClick="changeContent(); return false;">
    Click Here To Change Content
  </A>
</P>

<P><FONT ID=first FACE="Arial, Helvetica" SIZE=+2">
  Generic Content That Will Be Replaced
</FONT></P>

<P><FONT ID=second FACE="Arial, Helvetica" SIZE=+2">
  Generic Content That Will Be Replaced
</FONT></P>

<P><FONT ID=third FACE="Arial, Helvetica" SIZE=+2">
  Generic Content That Will Be Replaced
</FONT></P>

<P><FONT ID=fourth FACE="Arial, Helvetica" SIZE=+2">
  Generic Content That Will Be Replaced
</FONT></P>

<SCRIPT>
function changeContent()
{
  beginText = "<B>Content Replaced By The <TT>";
  endText = "</TT> Property</B>";

  document.all.first.innerHTML = beginText + "innerHTML" + endText;
  document.all.second.innerText = beginText + "innerText" + endText;
  document.all.third.outerHTML = beginText + "outerHTML" + endText;
  document.all.fourth.outerText = beginText + "outerText" + endText;
}
</SCRIPT>
```

Making Them Work Together

As discussed in the section "Exposing Page Elements," objects are exposed at a different level in the object hierarchy between IE4 and Communicator 4.0. When this difference has been corrected for programmatically, accessing a page element's attributes is the same between both browsers. Because Communicator 4.0 does not expose all elements or attributes, cross-browser scripts are limited to modifying the elements exposed in it.

Page elements exposed in the forms, images, anchors, links, frames, embeds, or applets arrays existing under the document object can be accessed in both browsers using the same notation. However, which properties are exposed in both browsers depends upon the type of page element being accessed.

Advanced page element manipulation—such as adding and deleting page elements, page element attributes, and element content—is not compatible between Communicator 4.0 and IE4.

Exposing User Agent and Meta Information

The Object Model defines how user agent information about the browser and meta information about the document is reflected into the scripting languages of the browser. In Navigator 3.0 and Internet Explorer 3.0 these objects are window, document, navigator, history, and location. Both Communicator 4.0 and IE4 have updated these objects and added a new screen object.

The Communicator 4.0 Approach

Communicator 4.0 has updated the window, document, and navigator objects to provide even more information about the document and the browser. In addition, a new screen object has been added that exposes the characteristics of the user's screen to JavaScript. Details about both the updated objects and the new screen object are available in Chapter 9, "Using JavaScript with Dynamic HTML."

The IE4 Approach

IE4 has updated the window, document, navigator, and location objects to provide functionality almost equivalent to the corresponding Navigator 3.0 objects. The window and document objects have also been updated with several new properties and methods that extend beyond the Navigator 3.0 functionality. A new screen object allows access to the resolution and color depth of the user's screen, while a new external object provides access to document object models that are external to the current DOM.

Making Them Work Together

Although both Communicator 4.0 and IE4 expose the same objects for user agent and meta information, the properties those objects contain differ slightly between the two browsers. The user agent and meta information objects in Communicator 4.0 and IE4 implement most of the methods and properties of the Navigator 3.0 objects; however, some functions and properties of the history and navigator objects have not been implemented in IE4.

IE4 does not implement the mimeTypes and plugins arrays of the navigator object or the current, next, and previous properties of the history object. IE4 also does not implement the javaEnabled() and the taintEnabled() methods of the navigator object, although it does implement a javaEnabled property that provides the same functionality as javaEnabled().

Because both Communicator 4.0 and IE4 have added new properties and methods to the user agent and meta information objects that do not exist in the other browser, cross-browser scripts should use only the methods and properties available to the Navigator 3.0 objects. The exception to this rule is the new screen object, which supports the width, height, and colorDepth properties in both Communicator 4.0 and IE4.

The Style Sheet Object Model

The Style Sheet Object Model defines how style sheets and their corresponding style rules are exposed and manipulated. The method by which the style sheet has been attached to the document determines which type of style sheet it is. Different types of style sheets are exposed and manipulated in different ways depending upon the browser. The four types of style sheets are as follows:

- *Defined style sheets* that are defined within a document by the STYLE element. They usually are displayed in the head of a document.
- *Linked style sheets* that exist external to the document and are attached to the document using the LINK element.
- *Imported style sheets* that exist external to the document and are attached to the document using the @import statement from within another style sheet.
- *Inline style sheets* that define styles for an individual page element using the STYLE attribute.

Exposing Style Sheets

Style sheets can be exposed in three different ways. First, at the individual element level, styles of individual page elements are exposed into style objects reflecting the style properties for that element. Second, the styles for an entire group of elements are exposed at the group element level into a single style object representing that group. Finally, style sheets and their associated style rules can be exposed at the style sheet level into styleSheet objects representing each instance of a linked, imported, or defined style sheet.

The Communicator 4.0 Approach

The Communicator 4.0 Style Sheet Object Model exposes the cumulative style of all style sheets attached to a document. Individual style sheets and style rules are not exposed; instead, the composite styles for each class, tag, and ID are exposed into style objects representing that class, tag, or ID. The composite style is the result of applying each applicable style rule to the properties of the style object. Style rules later in the source code override the default properties or properties set by earlier style rules. The resultant style object determines how its associated page elements are displayed.

Style objects in Communicator 4.0 are stored in three arrays, depending on which set of page elements they are associated with. The ids array contains the style objects of all page elements with the ID attribute, and the tags array contains the style objects of all tags in a document. Both exist under the document object and can be referenced using the notations document.ids.*elementID* for the ids array and document.tags.*tagName* for the tags array.

The classes array represents the styles applying to classes in a document and contains a separate child array for each class. This child array contains a style object both for the class in general and for each tag that might be associated with that class. This allows rules specifying both a class and a tag such as the following to be represented as a style in JavaScript:

```
LI.important    { font-weight: 900; }
```

The notation for referencing a style object for a particular tag in the `classes` array is `document.classes.`*`className`*`.`*`tagName`*. To reference the style object for the class in general, use the notation `document.classes.`*`className`*`.all`.

Figure 15.7 and Listing 15.10 demonstrate the use of the `ids`, `tags`, and `classes` arrays in accessing style objects in Communicator 4.0.

FIGURE 15.7.

Using the `ids`, `tags`, *and* `classes` *arrays to access style objects in Communicator 4.0.*

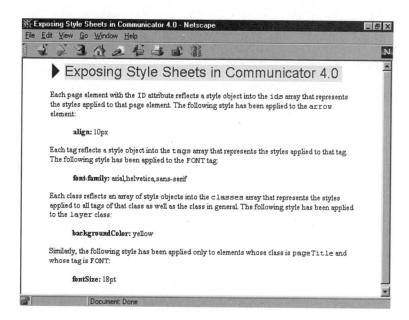

Listing 15.10. Source HTML for Figure 15.7.

```
<HTML>
<HEAD>
  <TITLE>Exposing Style Sheets in Communicator 4.0</TITLE>

  <STYLE>
    BODY            { background-color: white; font-size: 10pt; }
    FONT            { font-family: arial, helvetica, sans-serif; }
    FONT.pageTitle  { font-size: 18pt; }
    .layer          { background-color: yellow; }
    #arrow          { padding-right: 10px; }
    #banner         { position: absolute; left: 72; top: 8; }
  </STYLE>
</HEAD>
```

continues

15

DOCUMENT
OBJECT MODEL
COMPARISON

Listing 15.10. continued

```
<BODY>
  <BLOCKQUOTE>

  <IMG ID=arrow SRC="arrow.gif">

  <DIV ID=banner CLASS=layer STYLE="color: blue;">
    <FONT CLASS=pageTitle>
      Exposing Style Sheets in Communicator 4.0
    </FONT>
  </DIV>

  <P>Each page element with the <TT>ID</TT> attribute reflects a
  style object into the <TT>ids</TT> array that represents the
  styles applied to that page element.  The following style has
  been applied to the <TT>arrow</TT> element:</P>

  <BLOCKQUOTE>
  <SCRIPT>
    document.writeln("<B>align:</B> ");
    document.writeln(document.ids.arrow.paddingRight);
    document.writeln("<BR>");
  </SCRIPT>
  </BLOCKQUOTE>

  <P>Each tag reflects a style object into the <TT>tags</TT> array
  that represents the styles applied to that tag.  The following
  style has been applied to the <TT>FONT</TT> tag:</P>

  <BLOCKQUOTE>
  <SCRIPT>
    document.writeln("<B>font-family:</B> ");
    document.writeln(document.tags.FONT.fontFamily);
    document.writeln("<BR>");
  </SCRIPT>
  </BLOCKQUOTE>

  <P>Each class reflects an array of style objects into the
  <TT>classes</TT> array that represents the styles applied to
  all tags of that class as well as the class in general.  The
  following style has been applied to the <TT>layer</TT> class:</P>

  <BLOCKQUOTE>
  <SCRIPT>
    document.writeln("<B>backgroundColor:</B> ");
    document.writeln(document.classes.layer.all.backgroundColor);
    document.writeln("<BR>");
  </SCRIPT>
  </BLOCKQUOTE>

  <P>Similarly, the following style has been applied only to elements
  whose class is <TT>pageTitle</TT> and whose tag is <TT>FONT</TT>:</P>

  <BLOCKQUOTE>
  <SCRIPT>
    document.writeln("<B>fontSize:</B> ");
    document.writeln(document.classes.pageTitle.FONT.fontSize);
```

```
    document.writeln("<BR>");
  </SCRIPT>
  </BLOCKQUOTE>

  </BLOCKQUOTE>
</BODY>
</HTML>
```

The IE4 Approach

The IE4 Style Sheet Object Model exposes inline styles attached to individual page elements, style rules applying to groups of elements, and style sheets as a whole. *Inline styles* are styles defined by the STYLE attribute of a page element. They are exposed through the style object that exists as a property under most page element objects. The properties of the style object reflect the style properties defined in the STYLE attribute for a page element. Figure 15.8 and Listing 15.11 demonstrate the use of a page element's style object to expose style properties.

> **NOTE**
>
> Styles defined in imported, linked, and defined style sheets, although affecting the appearance of a page element, are not reflected in the style object. Instead, these styles are available through separate style objects existing for each rule in the rules collection of each styleSheet object.

FIGURE 15.8.

Exposing styles through the style *object in IE4.*

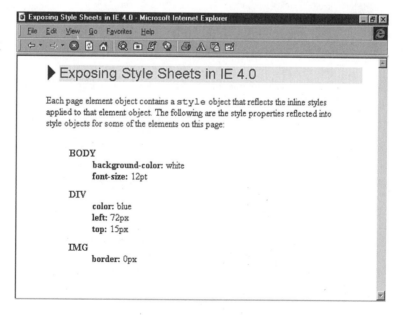

Listing 15.11. HTML source for Figure 15.8.

```
<HTML>
<HEAD>
  <TITLE>Exposing Style Sheets in IE4</TITLE>

  <STYLE>
    DT              { padding-top: 12; }
    FONT            { font-family: arial, helvetica, sans-serif; }
    .layer          { position: absolute; }
    #banner         { background-color: yellow; }
  </STYLE>
</HEAD>

<BODY ID=body STYLE="background-color: white; font-size: 12pt;">
  <BLOCKQUOTE>

  <P><IMG ID=arrow SRC="arrow.gif" STYLE="border: 0;">

  <DIV ID=banner CLASS=layer STYLE="color: blue; left: 72; top: 15;">
    <FONT CLASS=pageTitle SIZE=+2>
      Exposing Style Sheets in IE4
    </FONT>
  </DIV>

  <BR><BR>
  Each page element object contains a <TT>style</TT> object
  that reflects the inline styles applied to that element object.
  The following are the style properties reflected into style
  objects for some of the elements on this page:</P>

  <BLOCKQUOTE><DL>
  <SCRIPT>
    document.writeln("<DT><B>BODY</B></DT>");
    document.writeln("<DD><B>background-color:</B> ");
    document.writeln(document.all.body.style.backgroundColor);
    document.writeln("</DD>");
    document.writeln("<DD><B>font-size:</B> ");
    document.writeln(document.all.body.style.fontSize);
    document.writeln("</DD>");

    document.writeln("<DT><B>DIV</B></DT>");
    document.writeln("<DD><B>color:</B> ");
    document.writeln(document.all.banner.style.color);
    document.writeln("</DD>");
    document.writeln("<DD><B>left:</B> ");
    document.writeln(document.all.banner.style.left);
    document.writeln("</DD>");
    document.writeln("<DD><B>top:</B> ");
    document.writeln(document.all.banner.style.top);
    document.writeln("</DD>");

    document.writeln("<DT><B>IMG</B></DT>");
    document.writeln("<DD><B>border:</B> ");
```

```
        document.writeln(document.all.arrow.style.border);
        document.writeln("</DD>");

    </SCRIPT>
    </DL></BLOCKQUOTE>

    </BLOCKQUOTE>
</BODY>
</HTML>
```

Linked style sheets are style sheets defined through the LINK element, and *imported style sheets* are style sheets attached to a document using the @import statement. Linked style sheets, imported style sheets, and style sheets defined through the STYLE element are exposed as styleSheet objects into the document.styleSheets collection. In addition, imported style sheets are exposed into the imports collection existing under the styleSheet object associated with the STYLE element that imported the style sheet. The properties of styleSheet objects are listed in Table 15.3. Figure 15.9 and Listing 15.12 demonstrate how to access these properties from styleSheet objects in the styleSheets collection.

Table 15.3. Properties of `styleSheet` objects.

Property	Value
id	Contains the value of the ID attribute of the STYLE or LINK element that attached the style sheet
disabled	Contains a boolean value specifying whether the style sheet is affecting the styles of the document
href	Contains the URL of the source file for style sheets attached from an external file
owningElement	References the STYLE or LINK element object used to attach the style sheet
parentStyleSheet	References the styleSheet object associated with the STYLE element that imported an imported style sheet
title	Contains the value of the TITLE attribute of the STYLE or LINK element that attached the style sheet
type	Contains the value of the TYPE attribute of the STYLE or LINK element that attached the style sheet
readOnly	Contains a boolean value specifying whether the style sheet can be modified

FIGURE 15.9.

Exposing style sheets in IE4.

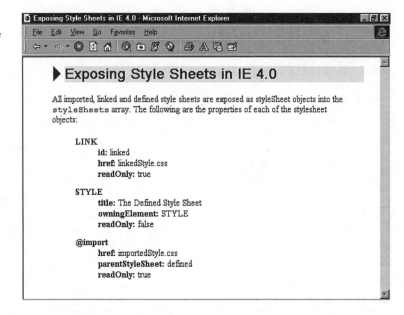

Listing 15.12. HTML source for Figure 15.9.

```
<HTML>
<HEAD>
  <TITLE>Exposing Style Sheets in IE4</TITLE>

  <LINK ID=linked REL=STYLESHEET TYPE="text/css" HREF="linkedStyle.css">

  <STYLE ID=defined TITLE="The Defined Style Sheet">
    @import url(importedStyle.css);

    H1              { color: darkBlue; margin: 0px; }
    .layer          { position: absolute; }
    #banner         { background-color: yellow; }
  </STYLE>
</HEAD>

<BODY>
  <BLOCKQUOTE>

  <P><IMG ID=arrow SRC="arrow.gif">

  <DIV ID=banner CLASS=layer STYLE="color: blue; left: 72; top: 15;">
    <H1>
      Exposing Style Sheets in IE4
    </H1>
  </DIV>
```

```
<BR><BR>
All imported, linked, and defined style sheets are exposed as
styleSheet objects into the <TT>styleSheets</TT> array.  The
following are the properties of each of the stylesheet objects:

<BLOCKQUOTE><DL>
<SCRIPT>
  document.writeln("<DT CLASS=first><B>LINK</B></DT>");
  document.writeln("<DD><B>id:</B> ");
  document.writeln(document.styleSheets.linked.id);
  document.writeln("</DD>");
  document.writeln("<DD><B>href:</B> ");
  document.writeln(document.styleSheets.linked.href);
  document.writeln("</DD>");
  document.writeln("<DD><B>readOnly:</B> ");
  document.writeln(document.styleSheets.linked.readOnly);
  document.writeln("</DD>");

  document.writeln("<DT><B>STYLE</B></DT>");
  document.writeln("<DD><B>title:</B> ");
  document.writeln(document.styleSheets.defined.title);
  document.writeln("</DD>");
  document.writeln("<DD><B>owningElement:</B> ");
  document.writeln(document.styleSheets.defined.owningElement.tagName);
  document.writeln("</DD>");
  document.writeln("<DD><B>readOnly:</B> ");
  document.writeln(document.styleSheets.defined.readOnly);
  document.writeln("</DD>");

  document.writeln("<DT><B>@import</B></DT>");
  document.writeln("<DD><B>href:</B> ");
  document.writeln(document.styleSheets.defined.imports[0].href);
  document.writeln("</DD>");
  document.writeln("<DD><B>parentStyleSheet:</B> ");
  document.writeln(document.styleSheets[1].imports[0].parentStyleSheet.id);
  document.writeln("</DD>");
  document.writeln("<DD><B>readOnly:</B> ");
  document.writeln(document.styleSheets.defined.imports[0].readOnly);
  document.writeln("</DD>");
</SCRIPT>
</DL></BLOCKQUOTE>

</BLOCKQUOTE>
</BODY>
</HTML>
```

Individual style rules of a style sheet are exposed into the rules collection underneath the styleSheet object. Each rule in a style sheet is exposed as a separate rule object containing a style object and the properties selectorText and readOnly. The style object contains the styles declared by that rule in the style sheet. Its usage is the same as the style object existing underneath a page element object for inline style sheets. The selectorText property contains a string specifying the tag, class, or ID to which the rule applies, while the readOnly property is set to true for rules that belong to read-only style sheets, such as imported and linked style sheets.

15

DOCUMENT
OBJECT MODEL
COMPARISON

> **NOTE**
>
> The style rules exposed through the rules collection underneath each styleSheet object represent the actual rules defined by a style sheet and do not necessarily reflect what is displayed by the browser. The application of a rule to the type of elements specified by its selector can be overridden by rules existing later in the source order of the file, by the style sheet containing the rule being disabled, or by a script changing the style by adding new rules or modifying the style object for an element. There is no way to access the cumulative applied style for all elements of a certain class or tag in IE4.

Making Them Work Together

Communicator 4.0 and IE4 expose style sheets in different ways, with differing degrees of functionality. Whereas Communicator 4.0 exposes the *cumulative* styles defined by the style rules for individual elements and groups of elements, IE4 exposes actual style rules and style sheets. Nowhere does IE4 expose the cumulative style for a group of elements. This difference in functionality allows only styles defined using the inline STYLE attribute, or styles defined by only one style rule in a style sheet, to be accessed in both browsers.

To complicate the situation more, in Communicator 4.0, individual page elements must have an unique ID attribute to be reflected into JavaScript. But assuming that inline styles are used only on page elements with an ID attribute and other styles are defined using a single style rule, cross-browser code can be written by manually reflecting all style objects in IE4 from document.all.*elementID*.style to document.ids.*elementID* and from document.styleSheets.*styleSheetID*.rules.item(*tagName*) to document.tags.*tagName*. This allows style objects to be accessed the same in both browsers. See the section "Exposing Page Elements" for an example of manually reflecting objects within JavaScript.

Manipulating Style Sheets

Manipulating style sheets can involve changing either the styles that apply to elements or the style sheets themselves. Modifying styles allows for the appearance of a document to be changed one aspect at a time, whereas modifying the style sheets themselves allows the style of the entire document to be changed at once by applying and removing style sheets from the document.

The Communicator 4.0 Approach

By exposing styles as style objects into the ids, tags, and classes arrays, Communicator 4.0 provides the capability to manipulate the styles of a document. These styles are changed by modifying the properties of the style object that represent the element or group of elements to which the styles apply. Although Communicator 4.0 provides the capability to change the style properties of any page element, these changes may not be rendered in the browser window. See the section "Page Updates" for more information about when the browser window is updated.

The IE4 Approach

In IE4, style sheets can be manipulated at the style sheet level, the group element level or the individual page element level. Styles applied to individual page elements through inline style sheets are easily changed by modifying the properties of the `style` object residing underneath the page element object. Styles of groups of elements are changed by modifying the properties of the `style` object residing underneath the rule object contained within the `rules` collection for a `styleSheet` object. The manipulation of entire style sheets is done by changing the properties of the `styleSheet` object representing that style sheet and by using the `addRule()`, `removeRule()`, and `addImport()` methods.

The `addRule()` and `removeRule()` methods are methods of the `styleSheet` object that allow rules to be added to and deleted from existing style sheets. The `addRule()` function adds a style rule to the `rules` collection of the `styleSheet` object just as if the rule appeared in the original style sheet. It follows the this notation:

```
styleSheet.addRule(selector, style, [index])
```

styleSheet is the `styleSheet` object representing the style sheet containing the `rules` collection to add the rule to. The *selector* parameter is a string representing which ID, tag, or class the rule applies to. It is equivalent to the string before the opening brace in normal style sheet notation. The *style* parameter is a string containing the rule declaration and defines which style properties are being added to the selector and their values. The *index* parameter is an optional parameter that specifies at which position within the `rules` collection the rule should be added.

The `removeRule()` function complements the `addRule()` function by providing a method for removing rules from the `rules` collection of a `styleSheet` object. The notation for the `removeRule()` function is

```
styleSheet.removeRule(index)
```

styleSheet once again is the `styleSheet` object representing the style sheet containing the `rules` collection to remove the rule from, and *index* is a numerical index into the `rules` collection specifying which rule should be removed.

The `addImport()` function attaches an imported style sheet to a `styleSheet` object. This imported style sheet is then added to the `imports` array of the `styleSheet` object that imported it and, if that `styleSheet` object is active, participates in affecting the styles of page elements. Listing 15.13 shows how the `addImport()` and `addRule()` functions can be used with the `disabled` property to attach, detach, and modify the style sheets of a document.

Listing 15.13. Attaching, detaching, and modifying style sheets.

```
<HTML>
<HEAD>
  <TITLE>Manipulating Style Sheets in IE4</TITLE>
```

15

DOCUMENT
OBJECT MODEL
COMPARISON

continues

Listing 15.13. continued

```
<LINK ID=linked REL=STYLESHEET TYPE="text/css" HREF="linkedStyle.css">

<STYLE ID=defined TITLE="The Defined Style Sheet">
   H1              { color: darkBlue; margin: 0px; font-size: 18pt; }
   .layer          { position: absolute; }
   #banner         { background-color: yellow; }
</STYLE>
</HEAD>

<BODY>
  <BLOCKQUOTE>

  <P><IMG ID=arrow SRC="arrow.gif">

  <DIV ID=banner CLASS=layer STYLE="color: blue; left: 72; top: 15;">
    <H1>
      Manipulating Style Sheets in IE4
    </H1>
  </DIV>

  <BR><BR>
  Style sheets in IE 4 can be manipulated by adding new rules
  to specific style sheets, importing new style sheets and disabling
  existing style sheets.  Click on the links below to manipulate the
  style sheets attached to this document.</P>

  <P ALIGN=center>
  <A HREF="" onClick="attachImport(); return false;">
    Import the style sheet <TT>importStyle.css</TT>
  </A></P>

  <P ALIGN=center>
  <A HREF="" onClick="disableLinked(); return false;">
    Disabled the style sheet <TT>linked</TT>
  </A></P>

  <P ALIGN=center>
  <A HREF="" onClick="addRule(); return false;">
    Add the rule<BR>
    <TT>BODY { font-weight: 900 }</TT><BR>
    to the defined style sheet
  </A></P>

  <SCRIPT>
    function attachImport()
    {
      document.styleSheets.defined.addImport("importedStyle.css");
    }

    function disableLinked()
    {
      document.styleSheets.linked.disabled = true;
    }
```

```
  function addRule()
  {
    document.styleSheets.defined.addRule("BODY", "font-weight: 900");
  }
</SCRIPT>

</BLOCKQUOTE>
</BODY>
</HTML>
```

Making Them Work Together

Manipulating style sheets in both Communicator 4.0 and IE4 is difficult at best. Because Communicator 4.0 makes no distinction between which style sheet a style rule originated from, the mechanisms used in IE4 to attach new style sheets and disable style sheets currently attached will not work in Communicator 4.0. Similarly, although IE4 provides a mechanism to add and remove style rules to and from a style sheet, it provides no method of determining the cumulative styles applying to a given element or group of elements.

Both Communicator 4.0 and IE4 *are* functionally capable of modifying styles applied to IDs, tags, or classes through defined, imported, and linked style sheets; however, scripts written to do so must perform a browser detect and use entirely browser-specific code. Scripts that only need to modify style properties defined using the inline STYLE attribute on page elements with the ID attribute, or styles defined by only one style rule in a style sheet, can use cross-browser code but must first correct for the differences in the object hierarchies of Communicator 4.0 and IE4. All other manipulations of style sheets are browser specific and cannot be scripted for cross-browser functionality.

The Event Model

The Event Model defines which events are generated, which page elements can generate events, and how events are delivered to the event handler that processes the event. It also defines an event object that provides information to event handlers about which event occurred, where it occurred, and other relevant information about the event. By defining the event handling capabilities of the browser, the Event Model determines the level of interactivity you can provide a user.

The Communicator 4.0 Approach

Communicator 4.0 implements an updated event model based on event capturing. Event capturing is a top-down approach, with events being delivered to page elements higher in the document structure before elements lower in the document structure. Events generated on a target element are captured first by the window object, then the document object, and then any layer objects before finally reaching the event handler of the target element. Capturing events at higher levels allows generic event handlers to be written for all elements on a page.

In addition to event capturing, the Communicator 4.0 Event Model implements the new events `dblClick`, `dragDrop`, `keyDown`, `keyUp`, `keyPress`, `mouseDown`, `mouseUp`, `mouseMove`, `move`, and `resize`. A new event object provides information to event handlers processing an event. Detailed information about this new event object, the new events, and event capturing can be found in Chapter 17, "The Communicator 4.0 Event Model: Event Capturing."

The IE4 Approach

IE4 implements an updated event model based on event bubbling. *Event bubbling* is a bottom-up approach in which events are generated by a target page element and then bubbled up through the document structure until they fall off the top. Events are first delivered to the target element, which can choose to continue the bubble—in which case, the event is delivered to the target element's parent element—or cancel the bubble—in which case, event delivery stops. By bubbling events to elements higher in the document structure, IE4 allows generic event handlers to be written for groups of elements contained within another element. The IE4 Event Model, by allowing every page element to receive events, also greatly increases the level of interaction you can provide the user through scripting.

Several new events have been added to the IE4 Event Model: `abort`, `afterUpdate`, `beforeUnload`, `beforeUpdate`, `bounce`, `dataAvailable`, `dataSetChanged`, `dataSetComplete`, `dblClick`, `dragStart`, `errorUpdate`, `filterChange`, `finish`, `help`, `keyDown`, `keyPress`, `keyUp`, `mouseDown`, `mouseMove`, `mouseUp`, `readyStateChange`, `resize`, `rowEnter`, `rowExit`, `scroll`, `scriptletEvent`, `select`, `selectStart`, and `start`. A new event object provides information to event handlers processing an event. Detailed information about this new event object, the new events, and event bubbling can be found in the Chapter 16, "The Internet Explorer 4.0 Event Model: Event Bubbling."

Making Them Work Together

The Communicator 4.0 and IE4 event models are compatible with respect to the functionality present in Navigator 3.0. Basic event handling through event handlers bound to the target element is supported in both IE4 and Communicator 4.0. However, because Communicator 4.0 generates events for only certain types of page elements, cross-browser code is restricted to handling events for only these types of elements. In addition, event handlers are restricted to handling the set of common events that exist in both browsers.

Advanced event handling techniques, such as event bubbling and event capturing, provide differing functionality and are not compatible between browsers. Under special circumstances, such as when a higher-level object is the sole object that will receive an event, advanced event handling techniques *can* be used to produce the same functionality. However, even in these circumstances, the code base for achieving the same effect remains completely different.

Although the event objects of Communicator 4.0 and IE4 appear to have many of the same properties, these properties are not always compatible for all events. The only property that consistently contains the same value for all events in both browsers is type. The x, y, screenX, and screenY position properties are compatible for mouse events, but for keyboard events, IE4 reports the mouse position in these properties, and Communicator 4.0 reports the position of the event's target element. Similarly, although the altKey, shiftKey, and ctrlKey properties in IE4 reflect the same information as the modifiers property in Communicator 4.0, the modifiers property is not set during mouse events in Communicator 4.0. And for key events, the keyCode property in IE4 uses UNICODE encoding, whereas the corresponding property in Communicator 4.0, which, uses ASCII encoding.

Page Updates

Whether a browser updates the page when a script makes a change to a page element's property determines how effective a DOM can be. A complete DOM with no page updating is the same as no DOM at all, because the user will never be able to see all the advanced scripting the DOM allows.

The Communicator 4.0 Approach

Communicator 4.0 updates the page under three circumstances: when a page is loading, when a property of a layer object is changed, and when the contents of a layer object are rewritten. Updating of the page during page loads is determined by the source order; that is, a page element's property must be changed earlier in the source code than the start tag for that element. When a page has completed loading, changes made to page element objects are made but are not rendered into the browser.

To update a page after it has finished loading requires layer objects. By changing the position properties of a layer object, a layer or positioned page element can appear, disappear, and move around a Web page. But the contents of a layer object are not updated unless they are rewritten using the document.write() functions. Using the document.write() function, the entire contents of a layer are wiped out and rewritten. When the document.close() function is executed on the layer object, the rendering of the layer object in the browser is updated.

The IE4 Approach

IE4 implements instantaneous page updating, meaning any change to a property of an element object that changes its appearance is instantly rendered in the browser window. Updates involve only those portions of the window that have changed. Page elements existing in the document flow that change size or disappear from the page completely cause the document to reflow—that is, adjust the layout of the page to accommodate the change in size of the element. Absolutely positioned page elements do not exist in the document flow and so are only updated within their clipping area.

Making Them Work Together

Communicator 4.0 and IE4 differ in how and when they update the rendering of a page in the browser window. IE4's instantaneous page updating is a superset of the page updating implemented in Communicator 4.0. Therefore, when designing scripts to be cross-browser, the following design principles, which take into account the Communicator 4.0 page updating methods, should be used:

- *Use positioned page elements.* After the page has finished loading, positioned page elements and layers are the only way to update the page in Communicator 4.0. Use regular page elements for static elements of a page and positioned page elements for anything that needs to be dynamic.

- *Change position, not properties.* Communicator 4.0 does not update the page when the properties of an element change after that element has been rendered. Design your dynamic effects to take advantage of moving elements rather than elements that change their appearance.

- *Use multiple page elements layered on top of one another.* By layering multiple page elements on top of one another and showing them one at a time, you can create the illusion of elements changing their properties.

Summary

With the release of Communicator 4.0 and IE4, Netscape and Microsoft have created two powerful new DOMs that empower authors to develop fully dynamic Web pages. However, the DOM implementations used by each browser are not always compatible with each other, interfering with the ability to easily script cross-browser DHTML pages.

The IE4 Object Model exposes all page elements, making it much more powerful than the Communicator 4.0 Object Model. However, for the most part, the Communicator 4.0 Object Model is a subset of the IE4 Object Model, allowing you to write cross-browser scripts by only using the functionality available in Communicator 4.0.

This is not true for scripts that involve attempting to manipulate style sheets in both browsers. The approaches taken in the Communicator 4.0 Style Sheet Object Model and the IE4 Style Sheet Object Model differ greatly between each browser. Although each browser implements powerful features for manipulating certain aspects of style sheets, these aspects overlap very little, making cross-browser style sheet manipulation very limited.

The Communicator 4.0 and IE4 Event Models are compatible up to the functionality included in Navigator 3.0. Both browsers implement advanced handling techniques, but these techniques are almost completely incompatible. And although at first glance the new events and event object implemented in Communicator 4.0 and IE4 seem similar, little functionality differences between the two browsers can quickly introduce bugs into cross-browser scripts trying to use these new features.

Overall, both Communicator 4.0 and IE4 implement new DOMs with many new powerful features. Unfortunately, these features are not always compatible. So until the DOMs converge in future versions of each browser, authors developing DHTML sites for use in both browsers must make compromises.

The Internet Explorer 4.0 Event Model: Event Bubbling

by Trevor Lohrbeer

IN THIS CHAPTER

Events are the engine behind all interactive HTML pages. They drive the scripts that react to a user's actions and determine the difference between a Dynamic HTML (DHTML) page that a user can watch and one the user can interact with. The Event Model is a crucial portion of the Document Object Model (DOM) because it determines how events are generated, delivered, and processed in DHTML.

The Internet Explorer 4.0 (IE4) Event Model implements a powerful form of event delivery called event bubbling. Event bubbling is an event delivery approach that allows parent elements of a page element the chance to react to an event by passing the event up along the document hierarchy. It integrates well with the IE4 Object Model by giving elements that are not the target of an event the capability to process the event.

In addition, the IE4 Event Model introduces several new events and a new event object. The new events provide precise information about a user's actions and add support for the new data binding functionality of IE4. The new event object enhances the capability of event handlers to react to events by storing detailed information about the characteristics of an event.

What Is Event Bubbling?

Event bubbling is an advanced event delivery mechanism based on a bottom-up approach that delivers an event first to the target element for an event and then in sequence to each parent element along the document hierarchy. By giving parent page elements the capability to handle an event, event bubbling helps to support backward-compatibility with the Internet Explorer 3.0 (IE3) and Netscape Navigator 3.0 object models, promotes cleaner and more portable code creation, and provides flexibility in creating event handers.

The Bottom-Up Approach

Event bubbling is a bottom-up approach to event delivery, meaning events start at the bottom of the document hierarchy and travel up along the hierarchy until the HTML element is reached. The page element that is the focus of the action causing the event to be generated is called the *target element* or *source element*. This element begins the *event path*, the sequence of page elements an event is delivered to on its way from the target element to the HTML element.

Event handlers can be attached, or bound, to a page element at any point along the event path. Event handlers are bound to a specific type of event and can only react to events of that type. Unless an event's bubbling is canceled, every event handler along the event path is called when an event of that type is generated by a child element.

When the event reaches the highest element in the hierarchy, the HTML element, it falls off the top and the default action is taken for the target element. The *default action* is the action normally taken by the browser in reaction to an unhandled event. For instance, the default action for the link element is to load the document specified by the HREF attribute.

Why Bubble Events?

Traditionally, when a user performed an action that triggered an event on a page element, the event was processed by the event handler specified for that element. If a page element had no event handler for that type of event, the event was processed by the browser, and the default action for that type of event was taken on the page element. Page elements could only react to events triggered on themselves, not to events triggered on any child elements the page element might have had.

For Navigator 3.0 and IE3, this was not a problem. The elements exposed in the Navigator 3.0 and IE3 object models did not contain child elements that reacted to the same type of events. The document object could contain a link element, but it could not bind click, mouseOver, and mouseOut events, so it did not matter that those events never reached the document object.

In the IE4 Object Model, all page elements are exposed, so the event model of events being handled only by the page element that triggered the event no longer works. Code previously written with the assumption that certain child elements do not have the capability to receive events will break when those elements begin to receive those events.

For instance, the link element often contains additional elements that change the style of the link. To make a link stand out more, the B element is often used like this:

```
<A HREF="home.html" onMouseOver="status='Return to Home';"><B>Home</B></A>
```

In older browsers this worked because the B element was not exposed to scripting and could not receive events. However, with the IE4 DOM, the B element is exposed and can receive events, including the mouseOver event. If event bubbling was not implemented in IE4, the B element would receive the event and, having no event handler, pass the event to the browser to be processed; the link element would never receive the event. Event bubbling enables the event to be passed along to the parent link element, where it can be processed.

Retaining backward compatibility with previous event models is not the only reason to implement event bubbling. By enabling page elements other than the target element to receive events, generic event handlers can be written that handle events for an entire group of page elements. Event handlers can also be bound higher in the document hierarchy, resulting in cleaner, more efficient code.

Listing 16.1 shows the HTML source for a menu that uses mouseOver and mouseOut events to create a rollover effect. The code does not utilize event bubbling and so requires each page element to bind both events. Listing 16.2 shows the same code using event bubbling. The mouseOver and mouseOut events are bound to the BODY element and allowed to bubble up from each link element. The result is code that is cleaner, easier to read, and more easily expanded. From now on, all new links added to the page will automatically have their mouseOver and mouseOut events handled.

Listing 16.1. Menu rollovers without event bubbling.

```
<BODY>

<A HREF="company.html" onMouseOver="highlightOption();"
                       onMouseOut="unhighlightOption();">Company</A>
<A HREF="products.html" onMouseOver="highlightOption();"
                        onMouseOut="unhighlightOption();">Products</A>
<A HREF="support.html" onMouseOver="highlightOption();"
                       onMouseOut="unhighlightOption();">Support</A>
<A HREF="solutions.html" onMouseOver="highlightOption();"
                         onMouseOut="unhighlightOption();">Solutions</A>

</BODY>
```

Listing 16.2. Menu rollovers with event bubbling.

```
<BODY onMouseOver="highlightOption();" onMouseOut="unhighlightOption();">

<A HREF="company.html">Company</A>
<A HREF="products.html">Products</A>
<A HREF="support.html">Support</A>
<A HREF="solutions.html">Solutions</A>

</BODY>
```

How Does Event Bubbling Work?

The process of event bubbling involves more than simply passing events up along the document hierarchy. Before an event can bubble, it must be generated and delivered to the target element. If the event bubbles and the event handler for the target element does not cancel the event bubble, the event then bubbles up along the document hierarchy. When the event reaches the top of the hierarchy, it falls off the top, and the default action for the target element is performed.

Event bubbling can be summarized into a series of four steps. The first two steps are taken by every event, and the second two can each be canceled by setting a property of the event object. The four steps of event bubbling are as follows:

- Event generation
- Event delivery
- Event bubbling
- The default action

Event Generation

Events can be generated by either the user or the system. User-generated events occur when the user performs an action, and system-generated events are generated by objects to indicate a change in state. Examples of user-generated events include `click`, `keyPress`, `focus`, and `resize`. Examples of system-generated events include `load`, `dataAvailable`, and `error`.

User-generated events are divided into low-level and high-level events. *Low-level events* are events triggered whenever the user performs a basic action, such as clicking or moving the mouse or pressing and releasing a key on the keyboard. *High-level events* are events generated by taking a series of low-level events in context, such as when a `mouseDown` event occurs over a piece of selected text and is followed by a `mouseMove` event to generate a `dragStart` event. In general, low-level user-generated events are triggered on every page element, whereas high-level user-generated events are triggered only on select page elements.

When an event is triggered, either by an action the user takes or a change in the state of an object, the event is generated. During the process of generation, the properties of the `event` object are set. Which of these properties are set and which values they contain depend on the type of event; this is discussed in detail in the section "New and Updated Events."

Event Delivery

After an event has been generated, the event is delivered to the target element. This target element can be either a page element or a system object to which the event applies. If the target element has bound an event handler for the type of event being delivered, that event handler is used to process the event.

Events can be bound to page elements using four different methods:

- Adding an *onEvent* attribute to the page element whose value contains a call to the event handler, like this, for instance:

```
<A ID=homeLink HREF="home.html" onMouseOver="highlight();">Home</A>
```

- Assigning the function to the *onevent* property of the page element object, like this, for instance:

```
document.forms[0].phone.onblur = "validatePhone();";
```

- Using the FOR and EVENT attributes of the SCRIPT element to bind an event for a specific page element, like this, for instance:

```
<SCRIPT FOR=homeLink EVENT=onmouseover>
  window.status = 'Return to Home';
</SCRIPT>
```

- In VBScript, naming the event handler *elementID_onEvent()*, like this, for instance:

```
Function homeLink_onMouseOver
  window.status = 'Return to Home';
End Function
```

After the event handler returns, or if no event handler was bound to the target element, the event continues along the event bubbling process. If the event is a bubbling event, it is delivered to the parent object of the target element. If the event is non-bubbling, it proceeds directly to the default action for the target element.

Event Bubbling

The normal action of events in the IE4 Event Model is to bubble up the document hierarchy. Typically, when an event has been delivered to the target element, it is passed along to the target's parent element. This parent element then executes any event handlers bound to it that match the event type and, when finished, passes the event to its parent element. Events travel up the document hierarchy being processed by any matching event handlers bound to page elements in the event path. When the event handlers for the HTML element have finished, the event falls off the top of the hierarchy and, if not canceled, the default action occurs.

Figure 16.1 and Listing 16.3 show the path an event takes from a B element inside a paragraph all the way up to the HTML element. Each element along the way has bound an event handler that adds its element's tag to the eventPath variable. By the time the event falls off the top of the hierarchy, the entire path is displayed.

FIGURE 16.1.

The event path taken by a bubbling event.

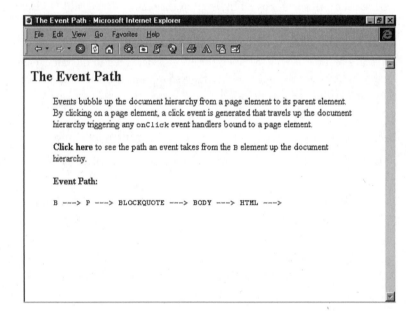

Listing 16.3. HTML source for Figure 16.1.

```
<HTML onClick="displayEventSource(this);">
<HEAD>
  <TITLE>The Event Path</TITLE>

  <SCRIPT>
    function displayEventSource(element)
    {
      if (element == event.srcElement)
        eventPath = "";
```

```
        eventPath += element.tagName + " --> ";
        document.all.results.innerHTML = eventPath;
    }

  </SCRIPT>
</HEAD>

<BODY onClick="displayEventSource(this);">
  <H2>The Event Path</H2>

  <BLOCKQUOTE onClick="displayEventSource(this);">
    <P>
    Events bubble up the document hierarchy from a page element
    to its parent element.  By clicking on a page element, a
    click event is generated that travels up the document
    hierarchy triggering any <TT>onClick</TT> event handlers
    bound to a page element.
    </P>

    <P onClick="displayEventSource(this);">
      <B onClick="displayEventSource(this);">
       Click here
      </B>
      to see the path an event takes from the <TT>B</TT> element
      up the document hierarchy.
    </P>

    <P><B>Event Path:</B><BR>
      <PRE ID=results>
      </PRE>
    </P>
  </BLOCKQUOTE>

</BODY>
</HTML>
```

Although this is the typical journey of an event, not all events follow this path, because, first, not all events bubble and, second, events that do bubble can have their bubble canceled.

An event bubbles because it has meaning not only to its target element but to its target's parent element. Some events, however, apply strictly to the target element and have little or no meaning to parent elements. The blur event, for instance, is generated when the focus is switched from one form element to another. However, just because a form element has lost focus and triggered a blur event does not mean the form itself has lost focus. Therefore, the blur event does not bubble. Conversely, if a user clicks on a word in a paragraph, it *is* true that the user has clicked on the paragraph as well, so the click event does bubble.

In some cases, events are non-bubbling for backward compatibility reasons. The load event in Navigator 3.0 can be generated by either an IMG element or the BODY element. If the event were to bubble in IE4, the BODY element's onLoad event handler in scripts written for Navigator 3.0 would be executed each time an IMG element fired a load event, subsequently breaking the script.

Although the capability of events to bubble up the document hierarchy can be convenient at times, other times it can be inconvenient. For example, when writing event handlers that perform a different function depending upon which context they are in, the bubbling of events is a disadvantage. Listing 16.4 demonstrates the use of the help event to display context-sensitive help. Unless the help event is stopped from bubbling, when the user requests help in the password field, both the general help and the password help will be displayed. To produce the desired effect of context-sensitive help, the event must be prevented from bubbling.

Listing 16.4. Handling the help event within a form.

```
<FORM onHelp="displayHelp('general');">

<P>Login:
  <INPUT TYPE=text SIZE=20></P>

<P>Password:
  <INPUT TYPE=password SIZE=20 onHelp="displayHelp('password');"><P>

</FORM>
```

By setting the cancelBubble property of the event object to true, an event ceases to continue to travel along the normal event path to the top of the document hierarchy and instead proceeds directly to the default action. Whether the default action occurs depends upon the value of the returnValue property of the event object.

Listing 16.5 demonstrates the use of the cancelBubble property in the displayHelp() event handler used in Listing 16.4. By canceling the bubble for the help event, only the help that applies to the element that generated the event is displayed.

Listing 16.5. Event handler for the help event.

```
function displayHelp(topic)
{
  if (topic == 'general')
    window.status = 'Enter values into the form.';

  if (topic == 'password')
    window.status = 'Enter your user password in this field.';

  event.cancelBubble = true;
  event.returnValue = false;
}
```

The Default Action

Some page elements have what is called a default action. The *default action* is the action normally performed by the browser when an element receives an event of a certain type. For instance, the default action for a Submit button is to send the information over the Internet using the method specified in the FORM element. Likewise, the default action of a link element is to load the page specified by the HREF attribute.

Canceling the default action allows a script the flexibility to redefine the results of a user's actions. Although a link normally might take the user to the location specified by the HREF attribute, by canceling the default action, the user can make the link display a dialog box instead, or disable it entirely.

The default action is canceled by setting the returnValue property of the event object to false. It can also be canceled by returning false from the last event handler that processes an event before it falls off the top of the document hierarchy. If the value stored in the returnValue property conflicts with the value returned by the last event handler, the returnValue property is used to determine if the default action occurs.

The canceling of the default action is not tied to the canceling of the event bubble. A default action can be canceled, yet the event can continue to bubble up the document hierarchy. And likewise, the event bubble can be canceled, yet the default action is still performed.

Listing 16.5 shows how the returnValue property is used to prevent the standard IE4 help window from opening.

The Event Object

The event object makes information about an event available to event handlers. It contains properties that store information about the event source, mouse position, and keys pressed. Properties also exist determining whether the event will continue to bubble and whether it will activate the default action for an element. All these properties are useful in advanced error handling.

Event Source Properties

The event source can be used by generic event handlers to determine which code should be executed. They specify the elements involved in the scope of the event and which type of event was generated by the actions taken toward these elements.

type and srcElement

The type property stores a string specifying the type of event that occurred. This string is the name of the event in all lowercase, such as *click* and *mouseover*. The source element, sometimes known as the event target, is referenced through the srcElement property that stores a reference to the page element object that generated the event. Both properties are used when creating generic event handlers that handle events of more than one type or are triggered by more than one page element.

fromElement and toElement

The fromElement and toElement properties are used during mouseOver and mouseOut events to specify which element the mouse was moving out of and which element it was moving to. This information can be used in mouseOver and mouseOut event handlers bound to a page element to prevent unwanted results from extraneous mouseOver and mouseOut events bubbling up from child elements.

Listing 16.6 demonstrates how the toElement and fromElement properties are used to prevent extraneous mouseOver and mouseOut events from being executed when the mouse moves from a paragraph element to one of its child B or TT elements. Within the highlight() function, a test is made to see if the element from which the mouse moved to cause the mouseOver event is a child of the element that called the highlight() function, the P element. If the element is not a child element, the mouseOver event occurred because the mouse moved from an element outside into the P element and the P element is highlighted; otherwise the highlighting is left alone. The reverse logic applies to the unhighlight() function and prevents the mouseOut events from the TT and B elements from removing the paragraph highlighting.

Listing 16.6. Using the fromElement and toElement properties to handle extraneous mouseOver and mouseOut events.

```
<HTML>
<HEAD>
  <TITLE>Handling mouseOver and mouseOut Events</TITLE>

  <SCRIPT>
    function highlight(callingElement)
    {
      if (!callingElement.contains(event.fromElement))
        callingElement.style.backgroundColor = "yellow";
    }

    function unhighlight(callingElement)
    {
      if (!callingElement.contains(event.toElement))
        callingElement.style.backgroundColor = "white";
    }
  </SCRIPT>
</HEAD>

<BODY BGCOLOR=white>
<P ID=text onMouseOver="highlight(this);" onMouseOut="unhighlight(this);">
  When the cursor moves from normal text within a paragraph to
  <B>bold text</B>, a <TT>mouseOut</TT> event is generated by the
  <TT>P</TT> element and a <TT>mouseOver</TT> event is generated by
  the <TT>B</TT> element. This causes the paragraph highlighting to
  blink. The cursor, however, has not moved out of the boundaries
  of the <TT>P</TT> element, simply onto one of its child elements.
</P>
</BODY>
</HTML>
```

Event Position Properties

For most events, the position of the mouse when the event is triggered is stored in a series of position properties that provide the mouse position relative to a series of different coordinate systems.

x, y, clientX, and clientY

The x, y, clientX, and clientY properties of the event object store the position of the mouse relative to the upper-left corner of the client area of the browser window. These properties can be used in event handlers to move positioned page elements on the basis of the mouse position, to respond to events generated within absolute areas of the screen, and to track mouse movement.

Figure 16.2 and Listing 16.7 demonstrate the use of the x and y properties of the event object to display a context-sensitive menu whenever the mouse button is pressed with the control key held down. By moving an absolutely positioned DIV element containing the menu to the location of the mouseDown event stored in x and y, the menu is displayed wherever the mouse is clicked. When the mouse button is released, the menu disappears again.

FIGURE 16.2.

Displaying context-sensitive menus using the x and y event properties.

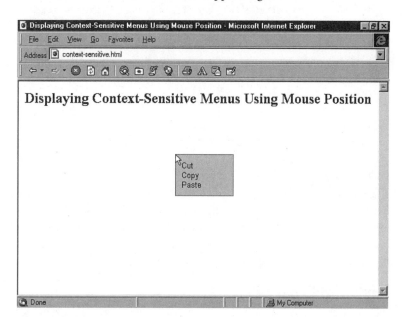

Listing 16.7. HTML source for Figure 16.2.

```
<HTML>
<HEAD>
  <TITLE>Displaying Context-Sensitive Menus Using Mouse Position</TITLE>
  <STYLE>
    .contextMenu  { position: absolute; background-color: #CCCCCC;
                    font-family: arial, helvetica, sans-serif;
                    font-size: 10pt; margin: 10; border: solid 1 gray; }
  </STYLE>

  <SCRIPT>
    function showDefaultMenu()
    {
```

continues

Listing 16.7. continued

```
      if (event.ctrlKey)
      {
        document.all.defaultMenu.style.left = event.x;
        document.all.defaultMenu.style.top = event.y;
        document.all.defaultMenu.style.display = "";
      }
    }

    function hideDefaultMenu()
    {
      document.all.defaultMenu.style.display = "none";
    }
  </SCRIPT>
</HEAD>

<BODY onMouseDown="showDefaultMenu();" onMouseUp="hideDefaultMenu();">
<H2>Displaying Context-Sensitive Menus Using Mouse Position</H2>

<DIV ID=defaultMenu CLASS=contextMenu STYLE="display: none; width: 100;">
Cut<BR>
Copy<BR>
Paste<BR>
</DIV>

</BODY>
</HTML>
```

offsetX, offsetY, screenX, and screenY

The offsetX, offsetY, screenX, and screenY properties also store the mouse position whenever an event is generated. However, they each use a different coordinate system. The offsetX and offsetY properties measure the position of the mouse relative to the upper-left corner of the parent block level element in the document hierarchy, and the screenX and screenY properties measure the position of the mouse relative to the upper-left corner of the screen.

Keyboard Properties

Four properties exist within the event object that store information related to the keyboard status during an event. Though they are primarily used for keyboard events, the shiftKey, altKey, and ctrlKey properties are set for all mouse and keyboard events.

keyCode

The keyCode property is used to store relevant information about which keys on the keyboard are pressed during a keyboard event. However, the information the keyCode property stores depends on the keyboard event being generated. For the keyDown and keyUp events, the keyCode property stores the key code of the key being pressed. The *key code* is a value that uniquely identifies the key with respect to the other keys on the keyboard, for instance, the key code for the "A" key is 65. Every key, including special keys such as INSERT and ALT, has one and only one key code.

During a keyPress event, the keyCode contains the character generated by the combination of pressed keys. The character generated is derived from the character key pressed and any modifier keys held down at the time. The keyCode property stores the generated character using the two-byte UNICODE encoding.

Listing 16.8 shows how the keyCode property can be used to restrict form input to numbers only. By binding this function to a text input field for the keyPress event, only keys pressed whose keyCode is within the range from '0' to '9' are displayed in the field.

Listing 16.8. Restricting input to numbers only using the keyCode property.

```
function inputNumbers()
{
  // Keycode of character '0' is 48, of character '9' is 57.
  if (event.keyCode >= 48 && event.keyCode <= 57)
    return true;
  else
    return false;
}
```

shiftKey, altKey, and ctrlKey

The shiftKey, altKey, and ctrlKey properties of the event object store the state of the Shift, Alt, and Control modifier keys during an event. Each property contains a boolean value that is true if the key was pressed when the event was generated or false if the key was not pressed. These properties are set for all mouse and keyboard events.

Event Action Properties

Two properties of the event object control the action an event takes within a script: The returnValue and cancelBubble properties determine whether an event bubbles up the document hierarchy and whether, when it reaches the top, it triggers the default action.

returnValue

The returnValue property determines whether the default action for a page element will take place in response to the event. If this property is set to false, the default action is canceled; if it is set to true, the default action for the page element is performed after an event finishes bubbling. This property overrides the return value of the last event handler to execute before the event falls off the document hierarchy.

cancelBubble

The cancelBubble property allows the bubbling of an event to be canceled. If you set the cancelBubble property to true within an event handler, event handlers further up the document hierarchy will not receive the event. Instead, the default action, if not canceled, will be executed by the browser and the event's life cycle will end.

New and Updated Events

The IE4 Event Model adds a slew of new events and updates many others to provide IE4 with powerful new tools to respond to the user. In addition to adding and updating several mouse, keyboard, and system events, IE4 has added eight new data binding events to support its new data binding functionality.

Mouse Events

The mouseDown, mouseUp, and mouseMove events provide low-level information about what the user is doing with the mouse. The mouseDown event is generated whenever the user presses down any of the mouse buttons, unless this action occurs immediately following a click event. Similarly, the mouseUp event is generated whenever the user releases a mouse button. mouseMove events are generated continuously while the mouse is moving over an element. The number of mouseMove events generated depends on the speed at which the mouse is moved; slow movement of the mouse will generate more events, and fast movement will generate fewer events.

The click event has been updated to work with the mouseDown and mouseUp events and the new ACCESSKEY page element attribute. It is generated when the user performs one of the following actions:

- Pressing and releasing the left mouse button once over any element.
- Pressing and releasing any mouse button once over an A element.
- Pressing the space bar while a radio, checkbox, submit, reset, or button form element has the focus.
- Pressing the Enter key while any form element except TEXTAREA has the focus. This action also changes the focus to the submit button. If the submit button is missing from the form, the click event is only generated when the Enter key is pressed on a button form element.
- Pressing the Esc key while a checkbox, radio, or select form element has the focus. This action also changes the focus to the reset form element. If the reset button is missing from the form, no click events are generated.
- Pressing the key specified by the ACCESSKEY attribute for a checkbox, radio, or button form element. A click event is also generated when the access key for an A element is pressed. Access keys for the select form element and all text form elements transfer focus to that element but do not generate a click event.

The dblClick event is generated when the user performs a double click, as defined by the local system. During a double click, before the dblClick event is generated, a series of mouseUp, mouseDown, and click events are generated. The sequence for these events during a double click is as follows:

```
mouseDown --> mouseUp --> click --> mouseUp ----> dblClick
```

Notice that the second pressing down of the mouse button does not generate an event. Mouse-down actions performed immediately after a `click` event do not generate a `mouseDown` event. The `dblClick` event is only generated for the left mouse button.

The `mouseOver` and `mouseOut` events have been updated to provide detailed information about the event to the event object. For these events, the `fromElement` property of the event object stores a reference to the element that the mouse was previously over, and the `toElement` property stores a reference to the element the mouse moved to.

All mouse events record the x and y position of the mouse in the position properties of the event object. Likewise, the state of the Shift, Control, and Alt keys is recorded for all mouse events. For `mouseDown` and `mouseUp` events, the `button` property stores which button was pressed.

Keyboard Events

The `keyUp` and `keyDown` events provide low-level information about the movement of the keys on the keyboard. The `keyDown` event is generated whenever a user presses any key on the keyboard, and the `keyUp` event is generated when the key is released. Every key on the keyboard—including special keys like CAPS LOCK, BACKSPACE, and SHIFT—trigger `keyUp` and `keyDown` events. However, not all keys generate a `keyPress` event.

The `keyPress` event occurs when a series of `keyUp` and `keyDown` events generate a character. The character represents the result of any modifier keys being pressed in conjunction with a character key. Special keys like BACKSPACE, TAB, and CTRL do not generate `keyPress` events. The only exception is the ESC key, which generates a `keyPress` event with a `keyCode` of 27.

The `help` event is a new event generated when the user presses the help key, as defined by the system (F1 on Windows-based machines). It is generated immediately after the `keyDown` event for the help key, before the `keyUp` event occurs. The default action of the help event is to open a help window.

All key events store the position of the mouse during the event in the position attributes of the event object. The `altKey`, `shiftKey`, and `ctrlKey` properties store the status of the modifying keys for all events except `keyUp`. For the `keyUp` and `keyDown` events, the `keyCode` property stores which key on the keyboard was pressed, and for the `keyPress` event, this property stores the character code for the resulting key combination pressed.

Selection Events

New to IE4 are two selection events that fire when the user selects text with the mouse and drags it to be pasted elsewhere. The `selectStart` event is generated when the user first begins making a selection by pressing down the left mouse button over a piece of text and dragging the mouse, or selecting text with the keyboard. When text has been selected, the `dragStart` event is generated as the user attempts to drag the selection elsewhere.

Load and Unload Events

The load event has been updated to fire on several new page elements, and the unload event remains the same as in IE3. A new beforeUnload event has been added, allowing a script to confirm with the user before unloading a page. If a string is returned as the return value for an onBeforeUnload event handler, a dialog box is displayed with the string giving the user the option to remain on the page.

Figure 16.3 and Listing 16.9 demonstrate the use of the beforeUnload event to ensure that a user understands that leaving the Web page cancels an order. If the user clicks the Cancel button on the dialog displayed, he or she remains on the order page; if the OK button is clicked, the page continues to unload.

> **NOTE**
>
> It is impossible to trap a user on a Web page using the beforeUnload event. If any value other than a string is returned from the onBeforeUnload event handler, the page continues to unload. Otherwise, the user is given the option of unloading the page or remaining on the page through a dialog that displays the string returned from the event handler.

FIGURE 16.3.

Using the beforeUnload *event to confirm leaving an online order form.*

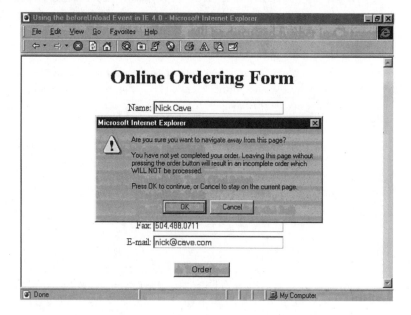

Listing 16.9. HTML source of Figure 16.3.

```
function confirmExit()
{
  if (!orderSubmitted)
  {
    message = "";
    message += "You have not yet completed your order. Leaving ";
    message += "this page without pressing the order button will ";
    message += "result in an incomplete order which WILL NOT be ";
    message += "processed.";

    return message;
  }
  else
    return null;
}
```

IE4 introduces two new events for handling errors, both called `error`. The first `error` event can be bound only to the `window` object and works the same as the `error` event in Navigator 3.0, being generated whenever an error in a script occurs. The second `error` event is generated whenever an error occurs loading one of several different page elements. For the `IMG` element, this second `error` event can be suppressed by setting the `onerror` property of the image's page element object to null.

The `load`, `unload`, and `beforeUnload` events use only the type property of the event object. The `error` event uses both the `type` and `srcElement` properties. None of these events are bubbling events.

General User Events

IE4 introduces the events `scroll` and `resize` to enable scripts to react when a user attempts to use a scrollbar or resize a window. The `scroll` event is triggered continuously while the scrollbar on an element or the browser window is moving. If the movement is sudden, such as when the spacebar is used to scroll the active window or when a user adds a line to a `TEXTAREA` element, only one `scroll` event is generated. The `scroll` event is a non-bubbling event, and its default action cannot be canceled.

The `resize` event is generated whenever a sized element changes its size. For the `IMG` element, this occurs when the source image is replaced or the `width` and `height` properties of the `IMG` element are changed. For the window object, the `resize` event is generated when the user changes the size of the window.

To provide compatibility with the Navigator 3.0 Event Model, the `abort` and `reset` events have been added to the IE4 Event Model. The `abort` event is generated when the user aborts the load of an image by either clicking a link or pressing the stop button while the `reset` event is generated when the reset button on a form is pressed. In addition to including the `reset` event, IE4 continues to support the `submit` event for forms.

The blur and focus events have been expanded in IE4 beyond forms. The blur event is now triggered when a page element loses the focus when the user tabs to another element, clicks on the background of the page, or switches to another application. Likewise, the focus event is triggered on certain page elements when they receive the focus by being tabbed to or the window containing the element receives focus again. Neither the blur nor focus events bubble, nor can their default actions be canceled.

Page Element Events

The filterChange, readyStateChange, scriptletEvent, start, finish, and bounce events all are triggered in response to a change in the state of a page element object. The filterChange event is generated when a filter attached to a page element via the filter style property changes state or finishes its transition. This event can be used to sequence a series of page element transitions.

The readyStateChange event is generated when a page element changes its readyState. The readyState of a page element measures how ready an element is to participate in a page. For IMG elements, readyState can take on the values of uninitialized, loading, or complete. For objects referenced with the APPLET, EMBED, or OBJECT elements, the readyState can also have the value of interactive.

The scriptletEvent event is generated by scriptlets to pass custom events to the page containing the scriptlet. Event handlers written to handle the scriptletEvent event take two parameters, *eventName* and *eventObject*. The first parameter, *eventName*, is a string assigned by the scriptlet, usually containing the name of the custom event. The second parameter, *eventObject*, is a reference to an object within the scriptlet, and can be anything from the page element within the scriplet that generated the event to a custom event object created by the scriptlet.

Finally, the start, finish, and bounce events are triggered only on the MARQUEE element and do not bubble. The start event is generated whenever a loop begins, and the finish event is generated once when all looping ends. The bounce event is generated whenever the marquee changes direction for elements where the BEHAVIOR attribute is set to alternate.

Data Binding Events

IE4 implements eight new data binding events to support its new data binding functionality. The first three—the dataSetChange, dataSetComplete, and dataAvailable events—are triggered by the data source to indicate the availability of data. The dataSetChange event is generated when the data first becomes available from the data source and any time the data set changes, such as when filters are applied. When all the data is available from the data source, the dataSetComplete event is generated. For data sources that receive data asynchronously, the dataAvailable event is generated whenever new data arrives. None of these three events can be canceled.

The rowExit and rowEnter events are generated directly before and after the current row for a data source is changed. The rowExit event is triggered to indicate that the data source is about to change the current row, and the rowEnter event is generated when the current row has changed. If the default action for the rowExit event is canceled, the data set does not change, and the rowEnter event is not generated.

When making changes to data bound to form elements, the beforeUpdate, afterUpdate, and errorUpdate events are used to indicate when an update to the data source occurs and if it was successful. The beforeUpdate event is generated by the form element whose data is being changed. It occurs immediately after the change has been committed to the form element by the element losing focus and immediately before the changed data set is updated with the data source. The afterUpdate event is generated when the data has been updated. If the default action for the beforeUpdate event is canceled, no update is made to the data source, and the errorUpdate event is generated instead.

All the data binding events bubble and are only triggered when both a data provider and a data consumer exist within a document. For more information about data binding and the events related to it, see Part V, "Data Awareness."

Summary

Based on the advanced event delivery technique of event bubbling, the IE4 Event Model provides powerful new tools for developing interactive DHTML pages. Event bubbling is a technique in which events generated by a specific page element are passed up along the document hierarchy to be processed by applicable event handlers bound to parent elements. This technique allows generic event handlers to be written for documents and promotes cleaner and easier-to-read code.

By including a new and expanded set of events and a new event object, the IE4 Event Model provides the Web designer with additional resources to dynamically respond to a user's actions. The new event object provides detailed information about the event to event handlers, and the new events enable scripts to react to low-level user-generated events for finer control over the user experience.

Together, the new events, new event objects, and advanced event delivery mechanism provide the Web designer with everything he or she needs to develop Web pages that truly interact with the user.

The Communicator 4.0 Event Model: Event Capturing

by Trevor Lohrbeer

IN THIS CHAPTER

CHAPTER 17

The Communicator 4.0 Event Model is one of the truly enabling aspects of the Communicator 4.0 Document Object Model (DOM). By using the new event delivery system, new events, and new event object, Web pages can be designed that react more effectively to users' actions and deliver an interactive experience to the user.

One of the most powerful aspects of the new event model, the event capturing mechanism, allows events to be delivered to objects other than the target object. By first delivering events to the browser window, then to each object successively lower in the object hierarchy, event capturing enables event handlers to be written that react to the page as a whole rather than separate parts each with its own event handlers.

Enhancing event handling capabilities even more, the Communicator 4.0 Event Model implements a new event object and several new and updated events. The new event object provides detailed information about the event to event handlers, while the new and updated events extend the ability of a document to react to user actions.

What Is Event Capturing?

Event capturing is an advanced event delivery mechanism based on a top-down approach that allows objects higher in the document hierarchy to capture events before they reach their intended target. By capturing events, generic event handlers can be written that process events for groups of elements, allowing code to be written that is cleaner and more portable.

The Top-down Approach

Event capturing is a top-down approach to event delivery, meaning events start at the top of the object hierarchy and are passed to elements lower in the hierarchy until the event target is reached. The *event target* is the page element or system object that caused the event to occur. The sequence of objects an event passes on its way to the event target is called the *event path*.

In event capturing, before an object can begin to capture an event, it must bind an event handler for that type of event. *Binding* is the process of specifying which event handler should handle events of a certain type for an object. Once an object has bound an event handler for an event type, it can begin to capture events of that type. Events targeted to objects lower in the document structure than an object capturing events are first handled by the capturing object's event handler. The event handler can then choose whether to pass the event further down the object hierarchy to another object within the page or directly to the default action. An object that no longer needs to handle events of a certain type can release those events. Released events are no longer captured by the object and proceed normally to the event target's event handler.

Why Capture Events?

Event capturing provides greater flexibility in the event handling capabilities of a script. By capturing events at a higher level in the object hierarchy, you can create event handlers that handle events for a group of page elements, redefine the meaning of events within a document, or provide multiple event handlers for an event.

The HTML source for a menu that uses mouseOver and mouseOut events to create a rollover effect is shown in Listing 17.1. The code does not utilize event capturing, so each page element is required to bind and handle both events. Listing 17.2 shows the same code with the mouseOver and mouseOut events captured by the surrounding layer object. The layer object captures and processes the events for all link objects within the layer, allowing new links added to the menu to have their mouseOver and mouseOut automatically handled. By capturing events at a higher level, the code is not only significantly cleaner, but easily expandable.

Listing 17.1. Menu rollovers without event capturing.

```
<LAYER ID=mainMenu>
  <A HREF="company.html" onMouseOver="highlightOption(event);"
                         onMouseOut="unhighlightOption(event);">
    <IMG NAME=company SRC="company-off.gif"></A>

  <A HREF="products.html" onMouseOver="highlightOption(event);"
                          onMouseOut="unhighlightOption(event);">
    <IMG NAME=products SRC="products-off.gif"></A>

  <A HREF="support.html" onMouseOver="highlightOption(event);"
                         onMouseOut="unhighlightOption(event);">
    <IMG NAME=support SRC="support-off.gif"></A>
</LAYER>
```

Listing 17.2. Menu rollovers with event capturing.

```
<LAYER ID=mainMenu>
  <A HREF="company.html">
    <IMG NAME=company SRC="company-off.gif"></A>

  <A HREF="products.html">
    <IMG NAME=products SRC="products-off.gif"></A>

  <A HREF="support.html">
    <IMG NAME=support SRC="support-off.gif"></A>
</LAYER>

<SCRIPT>
  document.mainMenu.captureEvents(Event.MOUSEOVER | Event.MOUSEOUT);
  document.mainMenu.onmouseover = highlightOption;
  document.mainMenu.onmouseout = unhighlightOption;
</SCRIPT>
```

How Does Event Capturing Work?

Event capturing works by implementing a series of distinct steps that can be taken to prepare objects to receive events, to allow event handlers to pass events along to other event handlers, and to release events from being captured once event handlers are no longer needed to handle the event. Event capturing, by performing these tasks using object methods, provides a great deal of flexibility in the capturing, routing, handling, and releasing of events.

Event capturing has five distinct techniques that are used together to create advanced event handling. The first two techniques are required for event capturing to work properly, whereas the last three are optional, depending on the needs of the event handlers being written. The five techniques used in event capturing are

- Binding events
- Capturing events
- Routing events
- Handling events
- Releasing events

Binding Events

Event binding is the process of specifying an event handler to handle a particular type of event for a page element or system object. Unless a page element or system object has bound an event handler for an event type, it cannot process events of that type. In Communicator 4.0, there are two ways to bind events to page elements and one way to bind events to system objects.

To bind an event to either a page element or a system object, a reference to the event handler function is assigned to the `onevent` property of the object. For instance, the following code binds the function `validatePhone()` to the `blur` event of the `phone` form element:

```
document.forms[0].phone.onblur = validatePhone;
```

Event handlers bound in this fashion are required to take either the event object as their sole parameter or no parameters at all. Unlike traditional binding where a JavaScript string specifies which event handler to call, it is not possible to assign a string containing JavaScript code to the `onevent` property of the page element or system object.

The second way to bind an event to a page element is to add an `onEvent` attribute to the element tag. The value of the `onEvent` attribute is a string containing JavaScript code that calls the event handler. For instance, the following code binds the function `highlight()` to the `mouseOver` event of the `homeLink` link element:

```
<A ID=homeLink HREF="home.html" onMouseOver="return highlight(event);">Home</A>
```

The `onEvent` attribute acts like a miniature function and can contain any valid JavaScript code. Any return values from event handlers called must be passed along to the browser using the `return` statement. Unlike assigning the event handler to an `onevent` property, event handlers bound using an `onEvent` attribute can take as many parameters as needed. However, except in certain circumstances with the `BODY` element and the `window` and `document` objects, system objects cannot bind event handlers using this method.

Capturing Events

Normally, events are delivered to the event handler bound to the event target. The event handler processes the event and returns a value of `true` or `false` that determines whether the default action for the event target is taken. However, for more advanced event handling, events need to be delivered to objects other than the event target. The Communicator 4.0 Event Model achieves this by capturing events as they fall down the object hierarchy toward the event target.

Events are captured with the `captureEvents()` method. The `captureEvents()` method is a common method of the `window` and `document` objects and any `layer` objects within a document. It activates the event handler for the object and begins interception of all events whose event target lies further down the object hierarchy. The syntax for using the `captureEvents()` method is

```
object.captureEvents(eventTypes);
```

The *object* is the `window` object or `document` object, or a `layer` object within the document. The *eventTypes* parameter is a list of the types of events that the object is capturing. Each event type is specified using the name of the event type in all uppercase scoped to the `Event` core object. Multiple event types can be specified in the same `captureEvents()` statement by performing a bitwise `OR` operation between each event type. For example, to capture the `mouseDown` and `mouseUp` events on the `window` object, the following notation would be used:

```
window.captureEvents(Event.MOUSEDOWN ¦ Event.MOUSEUP);
```

> **NOTE**
>
> The `Event` core object is different from the event object. The `Event` core object is an abstract object used by JavaScript to define the properties, methods, and constants of an event in general. The event object is a specific instance of the `Event` core object whose properties contain values related to a specific event.

Routing Events

After events have been captured, they are no longer delivered immediately to their target element. Instead, the event is passed down the object hierarchy until it reaches an object that is capturing events of the event type. The event is passed to the event handler bound to that object, at which point the event handler processes the event and performs one of four actions:

■ **Return `false`**

Returning `false` from the event handler cancels the default action and stops the event from continuing down the object hierarchy.

■ **Return `true`**

Returning `true` from the event handler causes the default action to execute immediately. The event does not continue down the object hierarchy.

■ **Call `routeEvent()`**

Calling `routeEvent()` from within the event handler executes the event handler of the next object down in the object hierarchy that is capturing events of that type.

■ **Call** `handleEvent()`

Calling `handleEvent()` from within the event handler bypasses the object hierarchy and sends the event directly to the event handler of the object calling `handleEvent()`.

By immediately returning either `true` or `false` within the event handler, the event stops traveling down the object hierarchy and immediately proceeds to execute the default action or end its life cycle. In order for the event to continue down the object hierarchy, the `routeEvent()` method must be called. The `routeEvent()` method passes the event to the next event handler in the event path. This process of passing the event to each successive event handler in the event path is called *routing*.

The `routeEvent()` method is called, usually at the end of an event handler, to pass the event to any event handlers bound to objects capturing the event further down the event path. If no other objects are capturing the event, the event handler bound to the event target is called.

Listing 17.3 demonstrates how the `routeEvent()` method is used at the end of the `window` object and `document` object event handlers to pass the event to the next event handler. The resulting path shown in Figure 17.1 illustrates how the event is first passed to the event handler for the `window` object, then to the `document` object's event handler and finally to the event handler of the target element. The event paths for both the `link` and `layer` elements are shown.

Figure 17.1.

Capturing an event with the window *and* document *objects.*

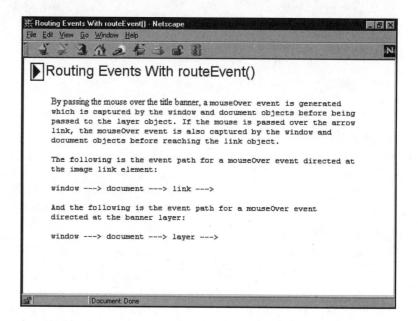

Listing 17.3. HTML source for Figure 17.1.

```
<HTML>
<HEAD>
  <TITLE>Routing Events With routeEvent()</TITLE>
```

```
<STYLE>
  #banner          { font-family: arial, helvetica, sans-serif;
                     font-size: 18pt; }
</STYLE>

<SCRIPT>
  eventText = "";
  capturingObject = "";

  function displayEvent(event)
  {
    eventText += capturingObject + " --> ";

    if (event.target.constructor == Layer)
      resultLayer = document.layerResults;
    else
      resultLayer = document.linkResults;

    resultLayer.document.writeln("<P><TT>");
    resultLayer.document.writeln(eventText);
    resultLayer.document.writeln("</TT></P>");
    resultLayer.document.close();
  }

  function handleWindow(event)
  {
    eventText = "";
    capturingObject = "window";
    displayEvent(event);
    return routeEvent(event);
  }

  function handleDocument(event)
  {
    capturingObject = "document";
    displayEvent(event);
    return routeEvent(event);
  }

  function handleLayer(event)
  {
    capturingObject = "layer";
    displayEvent(event);
  }

  function handleLink(event)
  {
    capturingObject = "link";
    displayEvent(event);
  }

  function initialize()
  {
    window.captureEvents(Event.MOUSEOVER);
    window.onmouseover = handleWindow;
    document.captureEvents(Event.MOUSEOVER);
    document.onmouseover = handleDocument;
  }
```

continues

Listing 17.3. continued

```
  </SCRIPT>

</HEAD>


<BODY onLoad="initialize();">

<LAYER ID=banner onMouseOver="handleLayer(event);">
  <A HREF="home.html" onMouseOver="handleLink(event);">
    <IMG SRC="arrow.gif" ALIGN=left>
  </A>

  Routing Events With <TT>routeEvent()</TT>
</LAYER>

<BR><BR>
<BLOCKQUOTE>
<P>By passing the mouse over the title banner, a <TT>mouseOver<TT>
event is generated which is captured by the window and document
objects before being passed to the layer object.  If the mouse is
passed over the arrow link, the <TT>mouseOver</TT> event is also
captured by the window and document objects before reaching the
link object.</P>

<P>The following is the event path for a <TT>mouseOver</TT> event
directed at the image link element:</P>

<LAYER ID=linkResults></LAYER>

<BR><BR>
<P>And the following is the event path for a <TT>mouseOver</TT> event
directed at the banner layer:</P>

<LAYER ID=layerResults></LAYER>
</BLOCKQUOTE>

</BODY>
</HTML>
```

Routing events to the next event handler in the object hierarchy is useful when an object higher up in the hierarchy must perform a general action for each event, yet still allow the event handler for a target element to perform its action. A typical application of this would be to implement a rollover effect on menu items by capturing the mouseOver and mouseOut events on a containing layer, then routing the event to each menu item's event handler to change the window status bar appropriately.

Although routeEvent() appears to simply pass the event down the object hierarchy, subtleties exist with how routeEvent() works that require special techniques when doing advanced event routing.

The routeEvent() method passes the event down the object hierarchy to a second event handler not by ending the first event handler and calling the second one, but by calling the second event handler within the first one. This means that once the second event handler ends, and execution begins again within the first event handler. This has two implications for designing event handlers.

First, because the execution continues in the first event handler, code can be written after the `routeEvent()` method that will be executed after the event finishes traveling down the rest of the object hierarchy. This allows event handlers higher in the object hierarchy to react to the actions taken by event handlers lower in the hierarchy.

Figure 17.2 and Listing 17.4 use this technique to simulate event bubbling using the event capturing mechanism of Communicator 4.0. By calling `routeEvent()` in the beginning of the event handler, the event is first passed all the way down to the target element's event handler. Once `routeEvent()` returns, the `cancelBubble` variable is checked to determine whether the bubble has been canceled. If the bubble has not been canceled, the code for handling the event is executed; otherwise, this code is skipped. Finally, the event handler returns with the return value passed to it from further down in the object hierarchy.

FIGURE 17.2.

Simulating event bubbling using event capturing.

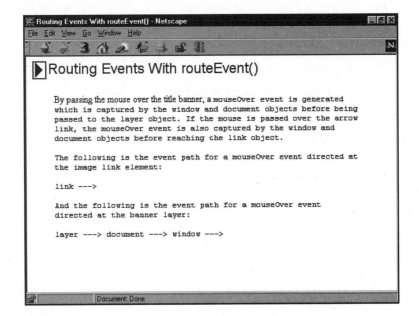

Listing 17.4. HTML source for Figure 17.2.

```
<HTML>
<HEAD>
  <TITLE>Simulating Event Bubbling With Event Capturing</TITLE>

  <STYLE>
    #banner          { font-family: arial, helvetica, sans-serif;
                        font-size: 18pt; }
  </STYLE>
```

continues

Listing 17.4. continued

```
<SCRIPT>
  eventText = "";
  capturingObject = "";

  function displayEvent(event)
  {
    eventText += capturingObject + " --> ";

    if (event.target.constructor == Layer)
      resultLayer = document.layerResults;
    else
      resultLayer = document.linkResults;

    resultLayer.document.writeln("<P><TT>");
    resultLayer.document.writeln(eventText);
    resultLayer.document.writeln("</TT></P>");
    resultLayer.document.close();
  }

  function handleWindow(event)
  {
    // Initialize event
    cancelBubble = false;
    eventText = "";

    // Send event down event hierarchy
    var returnValue = routeEvent(event);

    // If bubble hasn't been cancelled,
    // execute window event handler code
    if (!cancelBubble)
    {
      capturingObject = "window";
      displayEvent(event);
    }

    // Return return value for default action
    return returnValue;
  }

  function handleDocument(event)
  {
    // Send event down event hierarchy
    var returnValue = routeEvent(event);

    // If bubble hasn't been cancelled,
    // execute window event handler code
    if (!cancelBubble)
    {
      capturingObject = "document";
      displayEvent(event);
    }

    // Return return value for default action
    return returnValue;
  }
```

```
    function handleLayer(event)
    {
      capturingObject = "layer";
      displayEvent(event);
    }

    function handleLink(event)
    {
      capturingObject = "link";
      displayEvent(event);
      cancelBubble = true;
    }

    function initialize()
    {
      window.captureEvents(Event.MOUSEOVER);
      window.onmouseover = handleWindow;
      document.captureEvents(Event.MOUSEOVER);
      document.onmouseover = handleDocument;
    }
  </SCRIPT>

</HEAD>


<BODY onLoad="initialize();">

<LAYER ID=banner onMouseOver="handleLayer(event);">
  <A HREF="home.html" onMouseOver="handleLink(event);">
    <IMG SRC="arrow.gif" ALIGN=left>
  </A>

  Routing Events With <TT>routeEvent()</TT>
</LAYER>

<BR><BR>
<BLOCKQUOTE>
<P>By passing the mouse over the title banner, a <TT>mouseOver<TT>
event is generated which is captured by the window and document
objects before being passed to the layer object.  If the mouse is
passed over the arrow link, the <TT>mouseOver</TT> event is also
captured by the window and document objects before reaching the
link object.</P>

<P>The following is the event path for a <TT>mouseOver</TT> event
directed at the image link element:</P>

<LAYER ID=linkResults></LAYER>

<BR><BR>
<P>And the following is the event path for a <TT>mouseOver</TT> event
directed at the banner layer:</P>

<LAYER ID=layerResults></LAYER>
</BLOCKQUOTE>

</BODY>
</HTML>
```

The second implication for designing event handlers is that the return values of event handlers further down the object hierarchy must be passed back up the hierarchy for the default action to be cancelled by one of these event handlers. This is because the default action is determined not by the return value of the event handler of the target element, but by the return value of the event handler that called the first `routeEvent()`. Typically return values are passed back up the hierarchy by calling `routeEvent()` within the `return` statement. For example:

```
return routeEvent(event);
```

Another subtlety of routing events is that `routeEvent()`, when there are no more objects capturing the event type further down in the object hierarchy, passes the event to the event handler bound to the target element. If this event handler then calls `routeEvent()`, an infinite recursion is created where the target element's event handler continually passes the event to itself.

FIGURE 17.3.

An event handler bound to the target element that uses `routeEvent()` *causes infinite recursion to occur.*

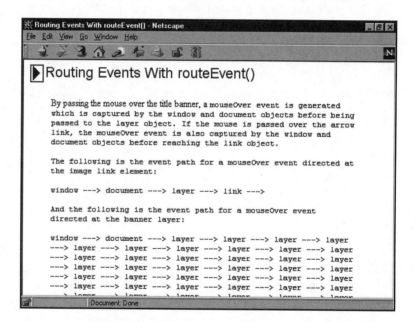

Figure 17.3 illustrates this recursion using the code from Listing 17.3 with the following two lines added to enable capturing of events for the layer object:

```
document.banner.captureEvents(Event.MOUSEOVER);
document.banner.onmouseover = handleLayer;
```

By testing the `layerHandled` variable before executing the event handler, Listing 17.5 shows how the `handleLayer()` function can be updated to prevent the recursion shown in Figure 17.3. The `layerHandled` variable is set to `true` once the event handling code for the `layer` object has been executed once, ensuring that if the `handleLayer()` function is called again by the `routeEvent()` method, the event handler code will not execute a second time.

Listing 17.5. Preventing recursion due to `routeEvent()`.

```
function handleLayer(event)
{
  if (layerHandled)
    return true;

  capturingObject = "layer";
  displayEvent(event);

  layerHandled = true;
  var returnValue = routeEvent(event);
  layerHandled = false;

  return returnValue;
}
```

Handling Events

Instead of being passed down the object hierarchy, events can be sent directly to the event handler of a specific page element or system object. The page element or system object an event is sent to does not have to reside further down the object hierarchy, allowing for a great deal of flexibility by bypassing the normal event path.

The `handleEvent()` method is a common method of every object that can bind event handlers, except `layer` objects. By calling this method within an event handler, the event is passed to the event handler bound to the calling object. For instance, the following notation passes the event to the event handler bound to the `window` object:

```
window.handleEvent(event);
```

Listing 17.6 demonstrates the use of the `handleEvent()` method to imitate the IE 4.0 functionality of the Enter and Escape keys within a form. Whenever a `keyUp` event is generated, it is captured by the `window` object. The `window_onKeyUp` event handler then passes the event directly to the event handler bound to either the submit or reset button, depending on which key was pressed. If neither of these keys was pressed, the event is routed to any event handlers further down the object hierarchy.

Listing 17.6. Using `handleEvent()` to submit a form when the Enter key is pressed and reset a form when the Escape key is pressed.

```
function submit_onKeyUp(event)
{
  document.forms.order.submitButton.focus();
  document.forms.order.submitButton.click();
}

function reset_onKeyUp(event)
{
  document.forms.order.resetButton.focus();
  document.forms.order.resetButton.click();
```

continues

Listing 17.6. continued

```
}

function window_onKeyUp(event)
{
  // The ENTER key is 13, which submits the form and
  // the ESC key is 27, which resets the form. Otherwise,
  // the event is routed to other event handlers.
  if (event.which == 13)
    document.forms.order.submitButton.handleEvent(event);
  else if (event.which == 27)
    document.forms.order.resetButton.handleEvent(event);
  else
    return routeEvent(event);
}

function initialize()
{
  document.forms.order.submitButton.onkeyup = submit_onKeyUp;
  document.forms.order.resetButton.onkeyup = reset_onKeyUp;

  window.captureEvents(Event.KEYUP);
  window.onkeyup = window_onKeyUp;
}
```

Similar to `routeEvent()`, advanced event handling techniques can be developed using the subtleties of the `handleEvent()` method. Because the `handleEvent()` method returns to the calling event handler, additional code can be executed after the call to `handleEvent()`. This code can react to the actions taken by the event handler called by `handleEvent()` or go on to route the event by calling `routeEvent()`.

Releasing Events

Many times an event handler does not need to be reacting to an event the entire time a user is viewing a page. The event is captured at some point after the page loads and is later released before the page unloads. The `releaseEvents()` method is used in these circumstances to stop the capturing of an event for an object. The notation for the `releaseEvents()` method is

```
object.releaseEvents(eventTypes);
```

The `object` parameter is the `window`, `document`, or `layer` object that previously was capturing events. The `eventTypes` parameter is a list of the types of events the object is releasing. Each event is specified in the same manner as when capturing events, by using the name of the event in all uppercase scoped to the `Event` core object. Multiple event types can be released in the same `releaseEvents()` statement by performing a bitwise OR operation between each event type. Only those events released with the `releaseEvents()` method stop being captured by the object; other events previously captured with the `captureEvents()` method remain captured.

The event Object

The Communicator 4.0 Event Model defines an event object that stores the characteristics of an event for access by event handlers. The event object exists only during an event, storing the event source and position, which keys were pressed and any additional information relevant to the type of event. Event handlers receive the event object as their sole parameter and use the information contained within its properties to process the event. By using the event source, event position, keyboard, and additional properties available in the event object, advanced event handlers can be written that react to an event based on the full context of the event.

Event Source Properties

The event source properties of the event object provide information to event handlers regarding the type of event and the event target. Using this information, event handlers can be written that react to multiple types of events, or that react differently depending on which type of object the event occurred.

type

The `type` property records a string specifying the type of event generated. This string is the name of the event in all lowercase, such as *click* and *keydown*.

target

The `target` property stores a reference to the page element or system object that is the target of the event. It can be used to write generic event handlers that react differently to different event targets, or to route an event differently depending on the event target. Listing 17.7 shows how the recursion problem discussed in the section "Routing Events" can be corrected by routing the event only when the event target is not a `layer` object.

Listing 17.7. Routing an event differently based on the event target.

```
function handleLayer(event)
{
  capturingObject = "layer";
  displayEvent(event);

  if (event.target.constructor != Layer)
    return routeEvent(event);
  else
    return true;
}
```

Event Position Properties

The event position properties record information about the location of an event with respect to several different coordinate systems. For most events, the values stored in the event position properties reflect the position of the mouse; however, when form elements are the target of an event, some events store the position of the upper-left corner of the form element in these properties.

x, y, layerX, layerY

The x, y, layerX, and layerY properties of the event object store the position of the event relative to the upper-left edge of the layer or window within which the event occurred. Because the upper-left edge disappears off the top of the browser viewing area as the page scrolls, the values of the x and y properties continue to increase as the page is scrolled down or to the right. The values of these properties correspond to the left and top properties for absolutely positioned elements within the same layer.

Listing 17.8 and Figure 17.4 show how the x and y properties of the event object can be used to create a context-sensitive menu that is displayed whenever a mouse button is clicked while the Control key is held down. Whenever the mouseDown event is generated in the client window, the showDefaultMenu() function is called to reposition an absolutely positioned DIV element containing the menu using the x and y properties. The menu remains until a mouseUp event is generated, when the hideDefaultMenu() function is called to hide the DIV element.

Figure 17.4.

Creating a context-sensitive menu, using the x and y event properties that appear when a mouse button is clicked while the control key is held down.

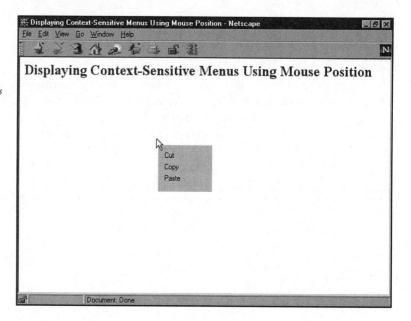

Listing 17.8. HTML source for Figure 17.4.

```
<HTML>
<HEAD>
  <TITLE>Displaying Context-Sensitive Menus Using Mouse Position</TITLE>
  <STYLE TYPE="text/css">
    .contextMenu  { background-color: #CCCCCC; font-size: 9pt;
                    font-family: ms sans serif, helvetica, sans-serif;
```

```
                    line-height: 1.5em; padding: 10px;
                    border-style: solid; border-width: 1;
                    border-color: white; }
    </STYLE>

    <SCRIPT>
      function showDefaultMenu(event)
      {
        if (event.modifiers & Event.CONTROL_MASK)
        {
          document.defaultMenu.left = event.x;
          document.defaultMenu.top = event.y;
          document.defaultMenu.visibility = "show";
        }
      }

      function hideDefaultMenu(event)
      {
        document.defaultMenu.visibility = "hide";
      }

      document.captureEvents(Event.MOUSEDOWN | Event.MOUSEUP);
      document.onmousedown = showDefaultMenu;
      document.onmouseup = hideDefaultMenu;
    </SCRIPT>
</HEAD>

<BODY>
<H2>Displaying Context-Sensitive Menus Using Mouse Position</H2>

<DIV ID=defaultMenu CLASS=contextMenu
     STYLE="position: absolute; visibility: hide; width: 100; ">
  Cut<BR>
  Copy<BR>
  Paste
</DIV>

</BODY>
</HTML>
```

pageX, pageY

The pageX and pageY properties of the event object store the position of the event relative to the upper-left edge of the client window. Similar to the layerX and layerY properties, the value of the pageX and pageY properties continue to increase as the page is scrolled. However, the pageX and pageY properties always reflect the position of the event relative to the window, regardless of which layer or window the event was generated in.

screenX, screenY

The screenX and screenY properties of the event object store the position of the event relative to the upper-left edge of the user's screen. However, unlike the other position properties, the values of the screenX and screenY properties never exceed the width and height of the screen, regardless of scrolling within the browser window.

Keyboard Properties

The event object records the status of the keys on the keyboard in the keyboard properties. These properties reflect which key generated a certain event and any significant keys that might have been pressed at the time of the event that would change how the key was interpreted.

which

The which property of the event object stores relevant information about which keys or mouse buttons were pressed during an event. For keyboard events, the which property contains the ASCII value of the key which generated the event. This value takes into account any modifier keys that were pressed during the event, returning the value 97 for an event generated by pressing A, while returning the value 65 for an event generated by pressed Shift+A. Keys that generate an event, but which have no ASCII character value return a value of 0 in the which property.

For mouse events using the which property, it contains a number representing which mouse button was clicked during the event. The left mouse button is represented by the value 1, whereas the right mouse button is represented by the value 3. For mouse events in which no mouse button was clicked, the which property stores the value 0.

Listing 17.9 shows how the which property can be used to restrict form input to numbers only. The inputNumbers() function checks whether the ASCII value of the key pressed is within the range of ASCII values used for numerical digits and returns true if it is, false otherwise. This determines whether the form element that has bound this function to the keyPress event performs the default action of displaying the result of the keypress.

Listing 17.9. Using the which property to restrict a text input to numbers only.

```
function inputNumbers(event)
{
  // The ASCII value for '0' is 48 and for
  // '9' is 57.
  if (event.which >= 48 && event.which <= 57)
    return true;
  else
    return false;
}
```

modifiers

The modifiers property of the event object stores the state of any modifier keys that were pressed during an event. *Modifier keys* are keys that do not generate a character or perform an action on their own, but rather modify how other keys on the keyboard are interpreted by programs. On most Windows-based machines the modifier keys are Shift, Control and Alt, while on Mac OS-based machines the modifier keys are Shift, Control, Option (also known as Alt), and Command.

To determine which modifier keys were pressed, masks must be applied to the `modifiers` property using the bitwise AND operation. For instance, the following notation returns `true` if the Shift key was pressed and `false` if it was not:

```
(event.modifiers & Event.SHIFT_MASK)
```

The four masks that are currently defined for modifier keys are `SHIFT_MASK`, `CONTROL_MASK`, `ALT_MASK`, and `META_MASK`.

Listing 17.10 shows how the `modifiers` property can be used to create a series of boolean properties in the `event` object that correspond to the properties of the IE 4.0 event object. Event handlers calling the `setModifiers()` function can then use cross-browser code when they need to determine which modifier keys were pressed during an event.

Listing 17.10. Decoding the `modifiers` property into a set of boolean variables.

```
function setModifiers(event)
{
  event.altKey = false;
  event.shiftKey = false;
  event.ctrlKey = false;
  event.metaKey = false;

  if (event.modifiers & Event.ALT_MASK)
    event.altKey = true;
  if (event.modifiers & Event.SHIFT_MASK)
    event.shiftKey = true;
  if (event.modifiers & Event.CONTROL_MASK)
    event.ctrlKey = true;
  if (event.modifiers & Event.META_MASK)
    event.metaKey = true;
}
```

Additional Properties

The `event` object contains a `data` property for storing additional information about an event. Currently, the `data` property is only set when a `dragDrop` event occurs during which the URLs of the dropped objects are stored in an array referenced by the `data` property. However, to maintain forward-compatibility with future versions of Communicator, this property should not be set in event handlers because it is very likely this property will be used for other events in the future.

New and Updated Events

The Communicator 4.0 Event Model provides a series of new events that provide a finer granularity to detecting actions taken by the user. It also updates several events existing in the Navigator 3.0 Event Model to take advantage of the new event object and event capturing.

Mouse Events

The mouse events provide detailed information about actions taken with the mouse. The mouseDown, mouseUp, and mouseMove events provide low-level information about what the user is specifically doing with the mouse, while the click, dblClick, mouseOver, and mouseOut events provide high-level information about the user's actions with the mouse.

mouseDown, mouseUp, mouseMove

The mouseDown, mouseUp, and mouseMove events provide low-level information about the state of the mouse. The mouseDown event fires whenever one of the mouse buttons is pressed while the mouseUp event fires when the button is released. The mouseMove event is generated continuously while the mouse moves over an element. The number of mouseMove events generated depends on the speed at which the mouse is moved; slow movement of the mouse will generate more events while fast movement will generate fewer events.

The position of the mouse during mouseDown, mouseUp, and mouseMove events is stored in the event position properties of the event object. For the mouseDown and mouseUp events, the mouse button involved is recorded in the which property and any modifier keys that were being held down during the event are stored in the modifiers property. The mouseMove event stores a value of 0 in both the which and modifiers properties, regardless of which keys or buttons are held down while the mouse is moving.

The mouseDown and mouseUp events are generated for both the left and the right mouse buttons. They are not generated, however, within text, password, select, or textarea form elements. Unlike other events though, they *are* generated on image page elements. The mouseMove event is generated only for objects that capture the event using the captureEvents() method. All three events store a reference to the event target within the target event property.

click

The click event is generated to indicate that the user has selected an object. It is generated when the user clicks the left mouse button or when the spacebar or Enter keys are pressed while a link element or a radio, checkbox, submit, reset, or button form element has the focus. It does not occur over text or images not contained within a link element, or within the boundaries of the block defined by the FORM element. However, it is generated on the window object when the mouse is clicked on empty space not contained within a FORM element.

When not generated on a form or link element, the event position properties of the event object during a click event record the position of the cursor. The which property stores a value of 1 while the modifiers property stores a value of 0. Within form elements, the click event stores the value 0 in all the position properties and a value of 1 in the which property. For click events generated by the mouse within a form element, the modifying keys pressed during the click are recorded in the modifiers property. The modifiers property is not set for click events generated using the keyboard.

Likewise, for `click` events generated on a link element using the mouse, the event position properties contain the position of the mouse. For `click` events generated using the keyboard, the event position properties contain the absolute position of the link on the page.

For all `click` events generated with the mouse, `mouseDown` and `mouseUp` events are generated before the `click` event. The sequence of these events is:

```
mouseDown --> mouseUp --> click
```

The `mouseDown` and `mouseUp` events are not generated before `click` events generated with the keyboard.

dblClick

The `dblClick` is generated when the user performs a double-click with the mouse, as defined by the local system. It is only generated for the left mouse button and is generated everywhere except in form elements that do not generate a `click` event. However, to be generated on a `link` object, the preceding `click` events must return `false` to prevent the page specified in the `HREF` attribute from being loaded before the `dblClick` event is generated.

For the `dblClick` event, the event position properties always contain the position of the mouse. The `which` property contains a value of 1 indicating that the left mouse button generated the double-click, while any modifier keys that were held down during the double-click are recorded in the `modifiers` property.

The `dblClick` event is composed of a series of low-level events that are generated each time a `dblClick` event occurs. The sequence of these events during a `dblClick` event is:

```
mouseDown --> mouseUp --> mouseDown --> click --> mouseUp --> dblClick --> click
```

However, because the `dblClick` event can be generated in locations where the `click` event is not generated, for instance, over text or images, the `click` events in the above sequence may not be generated. For `dblClick` events occurring in locations where the `click` event does not fire, the sequence of events is:

```
mouseDown --> mouseUp --> mouseDown --> mouseUp --> dblClick
```

mouseOver, mouseOut

The `mouseOver` and `mouseOut` events are fired whenever the mouse passes over a link, area, layer, image, or form element. When a `mouseOver` or `mouseOut` occurs, the event position properties store the position of the mouse where it crossed over or out of the element. The `modifiers` and `which` properties both contain the value 0 during these events.

NOTE

Many implementation issues relate to the mouseOver and mouseOut events. If the mouse is moved too fast, mouseOver and mouseOut events for elements that were passed over may not be generated. Similarly, mouseOver and mouseOut events are not generated while a mouse button is being held down.

Keyboard Events

The keyboard events provide detailed information about actions taken with the keyboard. The keyDown and keyUp events provide low-level information about the state of keys on the keyboard, while the keyPress event is triggered each time a user presses and releases a key.

keyDown, keyUp

The keyDown and keyUp events provide low-level information about the state of the keys on the keyboard. The keyDown event is generated whenever a key is initially pressed, while the keyDown event is generated once the key is released. For both the keyDown and keyUp events the which property of the event object contains the ASCII value of the key involved, while the modifiers property contains the modifying keys that were held down during the event.

Within a form element, the event position properties store the position of the upper-left corner of the form element, while the target property stores a reference to the form element that generated the event. When the keyDown or keyUp events are generated outside a form, the event position properties store the position of the mouse and the target property contains a reference to the page element that was underneath the mouse cursor.

The keyDown and keyUp events are not generated the same everywhere. Within forms, the keyDown and keyUp events are only generated in text, password, and textarea form elements. Within these form elements, the keyDown event is not generated for Shift, Ctrl, or special keys of any kind except Backspace and Enter. Outside a form element, the keyDown event is generated for all special keys except Esc, F1, F2, F3, F6, F10, Alt, and Tab. Similarly, the keyUp event is generated both within and outside form elements for every key except Alt, F1, and F10.

When special keys generate keyDown and keyUp events, the modifiers and which properties are set differently than for other keys. All special keys except Esc, Tab, Enter, and Backspace store a value of 0 in the which property. Similarly, all special keys, except modifier keys store a value of 0 in the modifiers property. For the modifying key to be stored in the modifiers property during a keyUp event, the key must remain down throughout the entire event; for this reason, keyUp events involving the release of a single modifier key store a value of 0 in the modifiers property.

keyPress

The keyPress event is generated when a sequence of keyDown and keyUp events occurs anywhere on a page or within a text, password, or textarea form element. Multiple keyPress events occur when the key is held down after the initial keyDown event. During a keyPress event, the which property stores the ASCII value of the key pressed, while the modifiers property stores any modifier keys that were held down.

For keyPress events occurring outside a form element, the event position properties store the position of the mouse while the target property stores a reference to the page element underneath the mouse cursor. Within a form, the keyPress event stores the absolute position of the form element in the event position properties and a reference to the form element object in the target property. This is the same functionality as with the keyDown and keyUp events.

Likewise, the restrictions on which keys generate keyDown and keyUp events apply to the keyPress event as well. Within a form element, the keyPress event is not generated for Shift, Ctrl, or special keys of any kind except Backspace and Enter, while outside a form element, the keyPress event is generated for all special keys except Esc, F1, F2, F3, F6, F10, Alt, and Tab. The which property stores a value only for the Enter and Backspace special keys; however, the modifiers property is set normally.

Window Events

The window events provide information about what actions are taken with the window. The move and resize events are generated when the user moves or resizes the window using the native operating system while the dragDrop event is generated when the user performs a drag-and-drop operation onto the browser window. The load event is generated by the browser to indicate certain items have finished loading.

move

The move event is generated continuously while the user moves the window about the screen. It is also generated during minimize and restore operations, most maximize operations, and whenever a toolbar is collapsed, hidden, shown, or expanded. During the move event, the x/y, layerX/layerY, and screenX/screenY properties contain the position of the window, while the pageX/pageY properties contain the value 0. A reference to the window object being moved is stored in the target property of the event object.

resize

The resize event is generated once after the user has finished resizing a window or frame, or whenever the size of the window or frame changes. During the resize event, the x/y and layerX/layerY properties of the event object contain the new width and height of the window. The target property contains a reference to the window or frame object which is being resized.

dragDrop

The dragDrop event is generated whenever a file or URL is dragged into the browser window and dropped. During the dragDrop event, the target property contains a reference to the window object and the screenX and screenY properties contain the location of where the object was dropped. Any modifier keys that were held down during the dragDrop event are recorded in the modifiers property. The default action of the dragDrop event is to load the file specified by the object dropped. Drag-and-drop operations can be disabled in a browser by capturing this event and returning false from the onDragDrop event handler.

load

The load event is generated when the browser finishes loading a document or an image. Although it is generated under the same circumstances as Navigator 3.0, when the load event is generated on a window object in Communicator 4.0, the x/y and layerX/layerY properties of the event object store the inner width and height of the window. The unload event remains the same as in Navigator 3.0 and does not use the event object.

Summary

The new Communicator 4.0 Event Model implements an advanced event delivery based on event capturing. Event capturing allows elements higher in the object hierarchy to capture events before they are delivered to the event target. By using the techniques provided by event capturing, code is cleaner and more efficient. In addition, more advanced event handlers can be created that react to the page as a whole rather than as separate elements each with its own custom event handler.

By adding a new event object, Communicator 4.0 provides event handlers with more information to process an event. This new information about an event allows for finer control over how an event handler reacts to an event. By also adding new events, the scope of user actions that can be reacted to in a document is greatly increased.

Although event capturing provides a greater level of control over how events are delivered to event handlers, the Communicator 4.0 Event Model suffers drawbacks with its lack of consistency in implementing the properties of its event object and the generation of events within a page. It is this inconsistency that makes using the advanced capabilities of the Communicator 4.0 Event Model difficult. However, after its quirks are mastered, the Communicator 4.0 Event Model is a powerful tool for creating interactive dynamic Web pages.

V

PART

Data Awareness

CHAPTER 18

Presenting Your Data with Dynamic HTML

by Craig Eddy

IN THIS CHAPTER

This chapter begins the trek into what I consider to be the coolest feature provided by Dynamic HTML: data binding. With data binding, your Web pages can be bound to a data source, can retrieve data from that data source at load time, and can manipulate the data on the client side without making a round-trip to the server.

For your site's visitors, this means that they'll be able to access and manipulate data much more quickly. For your network engineers, it means less of a load on your network and on the Web server itself. For the Web page designer, data binding provides a way to make your pages more informative and user specific. Everyone wins!

Part V, "Data Awareness," consists of four chapters:

- Chapter 18, "Presenting Your Data with Dynamic HTML," discusses the basics of setting up and utilizing data binding.
- Chapter 19, "Client-side Data Manipulation," provides techniques for allowing the users of your site to manipulate the data provided by your data-bound Web pages.
- Chapter 20, "Updating the Data," examines how you can allow your users to have a live connection to the data source by utilizing Microsoft's Remote Data Services.
- Finally, Chapter 21, "Summing Up—A Practical Application," provides a working example of a baseball trading card database implemented entirely with DHTML Web pages.

Data binding is made possible by two enhancements to Internet Explorer 4.0 (IE4): data source objects (DSOs) and HTML extensions. The DSOs provide the connection to the physical data source. The HTML extensions are a series of additional HTML elements that allow you to connect the Web document's elements to the DSO. This chapter explores both of these additions to the Internet Explorer browser.

> **CAUTION**
>
> As of this writing, data source objects and data binding were available only in Microsoft Internet Explorer 4.0. These technologies are not yet supported by Netscape Navigator 4.0.

Introducing Data Source Objects

DSOs provide the base upon which data-bound DHTML pages are written. The DSO, written as either an ActiveX component or a Java applet, supplies the data to the template provided by the HTML in the Web page. The browser can then merge the data with the template to produce the HTML page. This way, the data is completely removed from the HTML itself and will not even display if you use the View Source feature of the browser.

DSOs render their data asynchronously to the page itself. Similar to interlaced GIF files, this means that the page will be displayed and updated as data is pulled from the data source. This is particularly useful in situations in which there are large amounts of data. Unlike server-based solutions, where you must wait for all the necessary data to be retrieved from the data source, the DHTML data binding provides almost immediate response to the browser.

DSOs define the following features:

- The transport mechanism (HTTP, for example)
- The data specification mechanism, such as SQL
- Supported data manipulations functions such as sorting, filtering, and record pointer manipulation
- Support for updating the data
- An object model for scripting.

In this section I introduce you to three currently available DSOs: the Tabular Data Control, the JDBC Data Provider, and the Microsoft Remote Data Services. The Tabular Data Control is automatically installed when you install IE4. The other DSOs must be downloaded from Microsoft's Web site.

The Tabular Data Control

The Tabular Data Control (TDC) is so named because it reads data from a tabular data file, not because it's limited to displaying its data in an HTML table. The TDC does not provide data update capabilities but does provide sorting and filtering.

The data source for the TDC is a delimited text file that resides on the same host as the page containing the TDC instance (this is a security feature of the TDC). If the first line of the file contains field names, you can utilize this information when creating the HTML template. Otherwise, the field names default to `Column1`, `Column2`, and so on. Also, you can specify the field's data type in order to assist the TDC in sorting and filtering the data. On date fields, you can also specify what order the year, month, and day display in the date data.

We see a lot more of the TDC in the section "Creating the Data File for the Tabular Data Control."

The JDBC Data Provider

The Java Database Connector (JDBC) Data Provider is a Java applet that you can download from Microsoft's Web site (`http://www.microsoft.com/gallery/files/datasrc/JDBCapplet/JDBC.htm`). This applet allows you to connect your data-bound Web page to any ODBC-compliant data source.

To use the JDBC Data Provider to access the data, the client must have the ODBC data source specified in the applet's properties defined on its system. In an intranet or local situation, this is probably not much of a restriction, but for general Internet usage, this DSO leaves something to be desired.

Like the TDC, the JDBC Data Provider that you download from the Microsoft Web site does not give you the capability to update data. The Java source code, however, can also be downloaded from the Web site, and you can enhance the applet to provide such capability.

We won't spend any time using this DSO, but if you're a Java programmer interested in creating your own DSO, this is a great place to start.

The Microsoft Remote Data Services

The Remote Data Services (RDS, formerly known as the Advanced Data Connector) provide you with a data-bound connection to remote database systems. I'll introduce the RDS in this section, but we won't put them to heavy use until we get to Chapters 19 and 20. Additional information can be found on Microsoft's Web site at `http://www.microsoft.com/msdn/sdk/inetsdk/help/rds/default.htm`.

Unlike the other DSOs mentioned here, the RDS include the capability to update the data in those databases. However, this DSO requires both a server-side component and the client-side DSO.

Using the RDS provides all of the advantages of data source objects, plus the following:

- You can create Web-based, three-tiered applications using data-bound HTML elements on the client tier; the Web server and, optionally, ActiveX business objects as the middle tier; and the DBMS as the third tier.

- You can utilize Microsoft ODBC and OLE DB technologies to provide a consistent interface to the back-end data source, regardless of its format.

- The ODBC data source is set up on the Web server machine, not the client's machine. This makes your application easier to set up and maintain.

- You can use Secured Socket Layer technology to provide secured access to your database. This is an optional feature.

On the client side of the RDS is the `AdvancedDataControl` object. This is the RDS equivalent of the TDC. It provides the data binding to the elements on your Web page as well as the communication to the middle-tier Web server. It has all of the properties necessary to connect to the default middle-tier RDS business object, the `AdvancedDataFactory` object.

On the middle tier, the `AdvancedDataFactory` object is provided as a default business object. This object is where the actual work of reading and writing to the specified ODBC data source takes place. You can replace the `AdvancedDataFactory` object with a business object of your own creation. This allows you to encapsulate business logic and data validation into a server-side object.

The DBMS resides on the third tier. This can be any ODBC-compliant database to which the Web server machine has access.

Creating Your Own Data Source Objects

As with most Microsoft technologies, DSOs are built using an open specification. This means that, if you wish, you can write your own DSO.

Because DSOs are simply COM objects or Java applets, you can write your DSO in a myriad of development environments, including Visual Basic. You simply implement the required interfaces so that Internet Explorer and other DSO-enabled applications can recognize your object as a DSO data provider.

> **NOTE**
>
> When talking about DSOs, the term *data provider* refers to the DSO and the terms *data consumer* and `DataSourceListener` refer to the bound controls or HTML elements that utilize the DSO.

The first method you must implement is defined (in type library–speak) as follows:

```
HRESULT msDataSourceObject( [in] BSTR qualifier ,
                            [out,retval] IUnknown **ppUnk);
```

This method receives a string as the `qualifier` parameter and returns an interface pointer to one of the supported data interfaces. The `qualifier` parameter is used when the DSO supports access to multiple data sets. The value in this parameter specifies which set of data to access. However, IE4 will always invoke this method with `msDataSourceObject(0)` because it only supports DSOs that provide a single set of data.

In addition to the `msDataSource` function, your DSO should provide a method of notifying the data consumers that the underlying data has changed. This is accomplished by the data consumer registering itself through the following method:

```
HRESULT addDataSourceListener( [in] DataSourceListener *pEvent );
```

The `DataSourceListener` interface (which is implemented by a data consumer) is defined as follows:

```
[ local,
  object,
  version(1.0)
  uuid(7c0ffab2-cd84-11d0-949a-00a0c91110ed)
]
interface DataSourceListener : IUnknown
{
    HRESULT dataMemberChanged([in] BSTR qualifier);
    HRESULT dataMemberAdded([in] BSTR qualifier);
    HRESULT dataMemberRemoved([in] BSTR qualifier);
}
```

For example, when data changes, your DSO should call the `dataMemberChanged` method of the `DataSourceListener` to notify the data consumer of the modification to the data. The `qualifier` parameter is the same `qualifier` we saw with `msDataSourceObject`.

For more information on creating a DSO, visit Microsoft's Web site at `http://www.microsoft.com/msdn/sdk/inetsdk/help/inet3081.htm`.

Utilizing a Data Source Object

In a Web page, DSOs are inserted using the `<OBJECT>` tag. The values of the DSO properties can be specified using `PARAM` attributes. You must give each DSO a unique `ID` attribute in order for bound HTML elements to specify the DSO to which it is bound.

For example, to add the TDC to a Web page, use the following HTML:

```
<object id="quotelist"
        classid="clsid:333C7BC4-460F-11D0-BC04-0080C7055A83"
        border="0" width="0" height="0">
  <param name="DataURL" value="quotes.txt">
  <param name="UseHeader" value="True">
</object>
```

To insert the Remote Data Service's `AdvancedDataControl`, use something similar to the following:

```
<OBJECT CLASSID="clsid:9381D8F2-0288-11D0-9501-00AA00B911A5"
  ID="AdvancedDataControl"
  CODEBASE="HTTP://MyServer/MSADC/msadc11.cab#version=1,1,0000,0">
    <PARAM NAME="Bindings" VALUE="ControlNames;">
    <PARAM NAME="Connect" VALUE="DSN=DSNName; UID=usr;PWD=pw;">
    <PARAM NAME="Server" VALUE="http://awebsrvr">
    <PARAM NAME="SQL" VALUE="QueryText">
</OBJECT>
```

Note the reference to the `CODEBASE` attribute. One of the first steps toward using the RDS is to install the server-side components. This installation process includes installing the CAB file for the client-side `AdvancedDataControl`. Using the `CODEBASE` attribute informs the Web browser of the location of an installable version of the object. This way, you won't have to install the `AdvancedDataControl` on every PC that might connect to your RDS pages; the browser will do that work for you!

HTML Extensions Supporting Data Binding

To create a simple mechanism by which Web page authors could bind elements on their Web pages to a data source, Microsoft has proposed several HTML extensions. These extensions consists of four new HTML attributes: `DATASRC`, `DATAFLD`, `DATAFORMATAS`, and `DATAPAGESIZE`. (This section serves as a reference for each of these attributes. In the section "Tabular Data Source Properties and Methods," we'll look at specific examples of using the attributes.)

DATASRC

The DATASRC attribute specifies the ID of the DSO instance on the page. DSOs are added to a page using the <OBJECT> tag, which provides an ID attribute. The ID specified in the DATASRC attribute must match the ID of a valid data source object.

The format for the DATASRC attribute is as follows, where *IDref* is the ID of the DSO:

DATASRC="#*IDref*"

The DATASRC attribute is also an inherited attribute. This means that if you have data-bound elements contained within the element where the DATASRC attribute is specified, they will inherit the DATASRC value. This is how you build data-bound tables, as you'll see in the section "Creating a Data-Bound Table."

The DATASRC attribute can be used with any of the following HTML tags: TABLE, DIV, SPAN, SELECT, TEXTAREA, MARQUEE, INPUT, OBJECT, PARAM, IMG, A, FRAME, IFRAME, BUTTON, and LABEL.

DATAFLD

The DATAFLD attribute specifies the name of the column to which the HTML element should be bound. This attribute is used in conjunction with the DATASRC attribute to qualify the reference to the data. The format for the attribute is as follows, where *fieldname* is the name of the column to which the current element is to be bound:

DATAFLD=*fieldname*

The DATAFLD attribute can be used with the DIV, SPAN, SELECT, TEXTAREA, MARQUEE, INPUT, OBJECT, PARAM, IMG, A, FRAME, IFRAME, BUTTON, and LABEL elements.

DATAFORMATAS

The DATAFORMATAS attribute instructs the browser as to what format to expect the bound data to be returned. The valid values and their meanings follow:

text	Data will be provided in textual format.
html	Data will be provided as HTML, which might be parsed prior to display.
none	Data is supplied in raw format, as in the case of numeric data.

The default value, if the DATAFORMATAS attribute is not supplied, is text.

The DATAFORMATAS attribute can be used with the DIV, SPAN, MARQUEE, BUTTON, and LABEL HTML elements.

DATAPAGESIZE

When using a <TABLE> element to display the bound data, you can specify the number of rows to be displayed by specifying a value for the DATAPAGESIZE attribute. This allows you to do recordset paging and display data one page at a time. To move to a different page, you would use the nextPage and previousPage methods of the DHTML TABLE object. (We examine how this is done in Chapter 19.)

Tabular Data Source Properties and Methods

Like all ActiveX objects, the Tabular Data Source object provides the script writer with many properties and methods that affect its behavior and the data that it returns to the bound controls. This section serves as a reference to those properties and methods. (We'll put the information found in this section to use in both this chapter and in Chapter 19, where you'll see more in-depth examples of using the TDC to its fullest capabilities.)

As shown earlier in "Utilizing a Data Source Object," the class ID for the TDC is 333C7BC4-460F-11D0-BC04-0080C7055A83.

The AppendData Property

AppendData is a boolean property that affects how data from the data source is added to any existing data that is cached in the TDC. The default value for this property is False. This means that whenever the value of DataURL is changed and the Reset method is invoked, the new data will replace the existing cached data.

If AppendData is set to True and the DataURL value is changed, the new data will be appended to the cached data whenever Reset is invoked. The TDC assumes that the new data is in the exact same format as the existing data and will ignore the header line in the data source's text file. If the data of a column is different in the new data source file, its data is converted to string data (thus affecting the sort order of the column).

Setting AppendData to True can be useful in sequential searching operations, in which the client does not want to lose the results of the previous searches.

The CharSet Property

The CharSet property specifies the character set that was used in creating the data file. The property takes a string describing the character set used. The default value is latin1.

Typically, the value of this property is set at design time and not modified. Changing the value of this property within script code will not affect the data currently cached by the TDC. However, if the DataURL property is modified and Reset invoked, the data will be interpreted based on the current setting of the CharSet property.

The DataURL Property

The DataURL property specifies the location of the data file that will be used to populate the TDC's recordset. The value of this property is specified in standard URL format and can include http:, ftp:, and file: protocols. There is no default value, and this property is the TDC's only required property.

This property is typically set at design time but can be modified by script code. Data from the new data source will either overwrite or be appended to existing cached data, depending on the setting of the AppendData property, when the Reset method is invoked.

Examples include the following:

```
DataURL="elements.txt"
```

```
DataURL=ftp://myserver.com/data/elements.txt
```

```
DataURL=file://\\fileserver\data\elements.txt
```

In the section "Creating the Data File for the Tabular Data Control," you'll learn how to format the data file.

The EscapeChar Property

This property is used to specify an escape character. An *escape character* is a character that will be used in the data file to signify that the character following the escape character is part of the data, not a field delimiter. This is useful if your data contains the same characters that are used to delimit either the fields or the records in the data file.

For example, a common means of delimiting records is to use commas and double-quotes, as in the following:

```
"Eddy, Craig","Sr. Developer","Pipestream Technologies, Inc."
```

The double quote is used as part of the field delimiter, so if you needed to place a double quote within the data itself, you would have to use an escape character. For example, if EscapeChar were set to \ in the following code, Column1 would evaluate to The name of the work is "Dynamic HTML Unleashed" (note the double quotes in the data):

```
"The name of the work is \"Dynamic HTML Unleashed\"","SAMS.Net"
```

The FieldDelim Property

The FieldDelim property specifies the character or characters that separate the fields in the data file. The default value is a comma (,).

You can set the FieldDelim property to a nonprintable character. The syntax used to do so depends upon the context in which the property is set. If you're setting the property in the initial object tag for the TDC, use the following format:

```
<PARAM NAME="FieldDelim" VALUE="&#09;">
```

If you're setting it using VBScript, you can use the following, where *object* is the ID of a TDC:

```
object.FieldDelim = Chr(9)
```

The Filter Property

The Filter property is a string property that defines the criteria to be used to filter the data cached in the TDC's recordset. The default value for this property is an empty string, which means that no filter is applied to the recordset.

You can provide initial filtering of the data by setting the Filter property in the object tag. You can also set the property in script code and invoke the Reset method to cause the new filter to take effect. Because data is fetched from the data source only once, this is a very efficient method of modifying what data is displayed.

The syntax of the Filter property allows you to combine comparison operators and logical operators such as AND (&) and OR (¦), as in the following code:

```
(Column1 > 10) & (Column2 = 0)
```

The syntax of the property is defined as follows:

```
Complex ::== Simple
  ::== Simple '&' Simple [ '&' Simple ... ]
  ::== Simple '¦' Simple [ '¦' Simple ... ]
Simple ::== '(' Complex ')'
  ::== Atom Relop Atom
Relop ::== '=' ¦ '>' ¦ '>=' ¦ '<' ¦ '<=' ¦ '<>'
Atom ::== Characters up to a (, ), >, <, =, & or ¦
```

Note that AND and OR have equal precedence when evaluated and therefore must be surrounded by parentheses if both are combined in a single criteria.

We'll delve more into the Filter property in Chapter 19, when we discuss manipulating the data returned by the TDC.

The Language Property

This property specifies the language used to create the data file. This includes how numeric formats will be interpreted, as in the case of the decimal separator for floating point numbers. The property is a string expression whose values are the HTML standard language codes as defined in the ISO 369 document. The default value is eng-us.

The RowDelim Property

The RowDelim property specifies the character or characters that mark the end of a record. The default is the newline character. Typically, there is no reason to deviate from this value, but if your data file must use some other character or set of characters to mark the end of a record, this property is available.

The Sort and SortColumn Properties

These properties, though named differently, are in fact the same property. For simplicity, I will refer only to the Sort property in these chapters.

Using the Sort property, you can specify the order in which the data is returned from the TDC. You can specify multiple fields as well as the sort order to be used. Separate field names with a semicolon (;). Use a minus sign in front of the field name to specify descending sort order. For example, the following code specifies that data should be sorted by Column1 in ascending order and Column2 in descending order:

```
<PARAM NAME="Sort" VALUE="Column1; -Column2">
```

You can provide initial filtering of the data by setting the Sort property in the object tag. You can also set the property in script code and invoke the Reset method to cause the new sort order to take effect.

The TextQualifier Property

The TextQualifier property specifies a single optional character that can be used to surround the fields in the data file. The default value is the double quote (") character.

If the data file uses the comma as the field separator and the value of a data field also contains a comma, you should surround the field value with the TextQualifier character to eliminate the possibility that the fields might be read incorrectly. The property can also be useful if your data contains newline characters, which are typically used to mark the end of a record.

The UseHeader Property

The UseHeader property is a boolean property that specifies whether the first line of the data file contains field name and optional data type information. The default value is False. (We'll learn more about the header line in the upcoming section "Creating the Data File for the Tabular Data Control.")

The Recordset Property

The Recordset property returns the underlying ActiveX Data Object (ADO) recordset that the TDC provides. You can use the properties and methods defined by the recordset object as long as they are supported by the TDC. For example, the AddNew and Update methods are not supported because the TDC does not support updating of the data file. (As we'll see in the upcoming section "Using Data-Bound HTML Elements," the only ADO methods of real value when using the TDC are the recordset navigation methods.)

The Reset Method

The Reset method has two uses: First, it can cause the TDC to sort and/or filter the data based on the current settings of the Sort and Filter properties; and second, if any value is set in the DataURL field or the underlying data has changed, invoking this method will cause the data to be fetched again. Even if the value of the DataURL does not change when it is set, the data will still be fetched again simply by setting the property. This is a way you can implement a refresh button on your TDC pages.

Creating the Data File for the Tabular Data Control

Now that you've probably read all you care to about the technology behind DSOs and how to use them, it's about time to do some real work. In this section I describe ways to format the data file that is used by the TDC. The eventual goal of this part of the book is to build a baseball trading card database application (in Chapter 20, "Updating the Data"), so here we'll build a data file containing information about some of my baseball cards.

The data file is a simple text file that resides in a location reachable via a URL. Locations can include a Web server (using the `http:` protocol), an FTP server (using the `ftp:` protocol), or the machine's file system (using the `file:` protocol). One of the original security features of the TDC required the host name in the URL to match the host name of the page containing the TDC, but by the time you read this, that restriction may have been relaxed or replaced with a more complicated security scheme. (For the purposes of this chapter, we'll just be creating a local text file and placing it in the same folder as the HTML page containing the TDC.)

The first question that must be answered when creating the data file is, "How will fields and records be delimited?" The answer to this question will determine what value, if any, to place in the TDC's `FieldDelim`, `RowDelim`, and `TextQualifier` properties. For our purposes, we'll delimit the fields using commas and double quotes, and each record will appear on its own line. Not only does this make the most sense given the data we'll be placing in the data file, but these values also correspond to the defaults for the TDC properties. We won't have to worry about any of these properties when we create our tabular data source pages.

The second question we must answer is, "Will we use a header line?" The answer to this question, unless there's no way to avoid it, should be a resounding "Yes!" By providing a header line, you can not only specify intelligent field names, but you can also inform the TDC what data types are present in the file. This allows the TDC to intelligently sort data. Without knowing that a field is numeric, for example, the field will sort as a character field, meaning the 10 will sort before 2 when the sort order is ascending. Obviously, this would be a mistake for numeric data.

The format of the header line is as follows, where `fieldname` is the name to use for the field and `type` is an optional value that specifies the data type of the field:

```
fieldname:type, fieldname:type, ...
```

Possible values for type are as follows:

String	Textual data (default)
Date	Calendar dates
Boolean	Logical data (`True`/`False`, `Yes`/`No`, `0`/not `0`)
Int	Integers
Float	Floating point numbers

For the `Date` data type, you can also specify how the date data is interpreted by the TDC by placing the letters D (day), M (month), and Y (year) in the required order following the `Date` type and a space, as in the following:

```
birthday:Date MDY
```

The final, and most important, question is, "What data fields will be present in our data file?" The answer to this question determines which fields will be available to the TDC and the data-bound HTML page.

For our baseball trading cards, we'll have fields for year, `issuer`, `card set name`, `card number`, `description`, `condition` (also known as grade), and `card value`. The year field will be integer as opposed to a date, because we don't care about day and month. The `card number` field will also be an integer to allow proper sorting and filtering. The `card value` field will be a float because it represents a currency value.

Our header line, then, will look like this:

```
year:Int, issuer, setname, cardnumber:Int, description, grade, value:float
```

Following the header line, we'll enter one line for each card in our collection. Any data containing commas should be surrounded by double quotes. Listing 18.1 provides the data for a file we'll name `cards.txt` for use with our data-bound HTML pages. This file is also available on the Sams.net Dynamic HTML Guru Web site at `http://www.htmlguru.com`. There's not an overwhelming amount of data, but there is enough to make use of the features of the TDC throughout the remainder of this chapter.

18

PRESENTING YOUR DATA WITH DYNAMIC HTML

Listing 18.1. Contents of CARDS.TXT.

```
year:Int, issuer, setname, cardnumber:Int, description, grade, value:float
1977,Topps,1977 Topps,450,Pete Rose,NR MT,18.00
1977,Topps,1977 Topps,287,Reds Team (Sparky Anderson),NR MT,2.00
1976,Topps,1976 Topps,240,Pete Rose,EX,15.00
1975,Topps,1975 Topps,70,Mike Schmidt,EX,35.00
1976,Topps,1976 Topps,616,Buck Martinez,EX,0.75
1977,Topps,1977 Topps,1,"Batting Leaders (George Brett, Bill Madlock)",EX,1.40
1976,Topps,1976 Topps,66,"Father & Son (Buddy Bell, Gus Bell)",MT,1.00
1975,Topps,1975 Topps,421,"Mets Team (Yogi Berra)",EX,1.45
1975,Topps,1975 Topps,560,Tony Perez,EX,1.25
```

Using Data-bound HTML Elements

Thus far in this chapter we've seen how to utilize the HTML extensions and the TDC to build a data-bound HTML page. We've also created a small but useful data file that we can use to populate our HTML page. All that's left is to actually build a data-bound HTML page. We'll do so using Notepad.

Our first example will be to use what's known as *current record binding*. With current record binding, the HTML elements on a page are bound to the current record in the TDC's recordset object.

Only a single record is displayed at a time, so you must provide some means of navigating the recordset. There are no navigational methods of the TDC object itself, but the recordset object does provide MoveFirst, MoveLast, MoveNext, and MovePrevious methods. Simply placing Next and Previous buttons is sufficient to demonstrate the power of current record binding.

Listing 18.2 provides the HTML for our data-bound page. Save this file in the same folder as the CARDS.TXT file. This file is also found on the Sams.net Dynamic HTML Guru Web site at http://www.htmlguru.com.

Listing 18.2. The current record binding example.

```html
<html>
<head><title>Baseball Card Collection</title></head>

<body>

<h1 align="center"><font face="Arial">Baseball Card Collection</font></h1>

<p>
<object id="cards" classid="clsid:333C7BC4-460F-11D0-BC04-0080C7055A83"
width="77" height="49">
  <param name="DataURL" value="cards.txt">
  <param name="UseHeader" value="1">
  <param name="Sort" value="year; cardnumber">
</object>
</p>
<div align="center"><center>

<table border="0" cellpadding="0" height="195" cellspacing="0" width="524">
  <tr>
    <td align="right" valign="top"><font face="Arial">Year:</font></td>
    <td width="10" align="right"></td>
    <td valign="top"><input type="text" size="20" datafld="year"
                    datasrc="#cards"></td>
  </tr>
  <tr>
    <td align="right" valign="top"><font face="Arial">Issuer:</font></td>
    <td width="10" align="right"></td>
    <td valign="top"><input type="text" size="20" datafld="issuer"
                    datasrc="#cards"></td>
  </tr>
  <tr>
    <td align="right" valign="top"><font face="Arial">Set Name:</font></td>
    <td width="10" align="right"></td>
    <td valign="top"><input type="text" size="20" datafld="setname"
                    datasrc="#cards"></td>
  </tr>
  <tr>
    <td align="right" valign="top"><font face="Arial">Card Number:</font></td>
```

```
      <td width="10" align="right"></td>
      <td valign="top"><input type="text" size="20" datafld="cardnumber"
                        datasrc="#cards"></td>
    </tr>
    <tr>
      <td align="right" valign="top"><font face="Arial">Description:</font></td>
      <td width="10" align="right"></td>
      <td valign="top"><input type="text" size="36" datafld="description"
                        datasrc="#cards"></td>
    </tr>
    <tr>
      <td align="right" valign="top"><font face="Arial">Value:</font></td>
      <td width="10" align="right"></td>
      <td valign="top"><input type="text" size="20" datafld="value"
                        datasrc="#cards"></td>
    </tr>
  </table>
</center></div>

<p> </p>
<div align="center"><center>

<table border="0">
  <tr>
    <td><input type="button" value="Previous" onclick="previousrecord()"></td>
    <td><input type="button" value="Next" onclick="nextrecord()"></td>
  </tr>
</table>
</center></div>

<script language="VBScript">

sub previousrecord()
  if (cards.recordset.AbsolutePosition > 1) then
    cards.recordset.movePrevious
  else
    MsgBox "Already at first element"
  end if
end sub

sub nextrecord()
  if (cards.recordset.AbsolutePosition <> cards.recordset.RecordCount) then
    cards.recordset.moveNext
  else
    MsgBox "Already at last element"
  end if
end sub

sub refresh()
  cards.DataURL="cards.txt"
  cards.Reset
  cards.recordset.movefirst
end sub

</script>
</body></html>
```

Now open this page with IE4. You'll see the page shown in Figure 18.1. Use the Next and Previous buttons to walk through all of the records. Click the Refresh button to reload the data. Cool, huh?

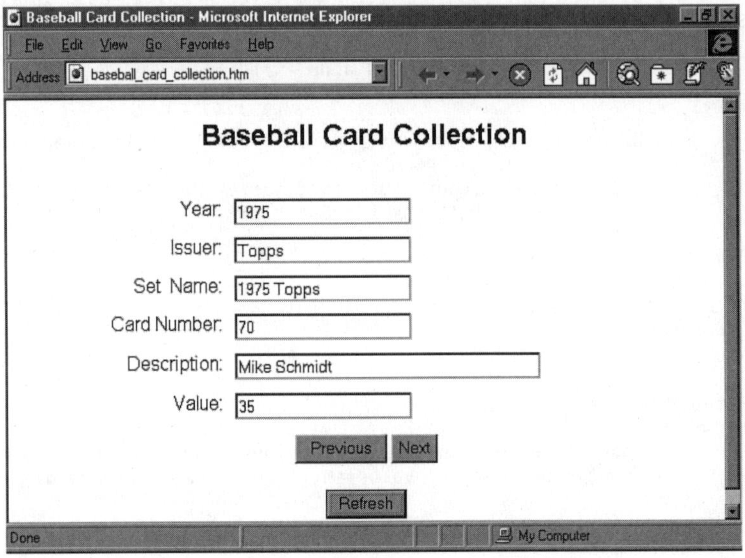

FIGURE 18.1.

An example of using data-bound HTML elements.

Here's how this page works. Of course, the <OBJECT> tag contains the TDC. We've named it cards, specified cards.txt as its data source (using the DataURL property), and told it to sort by the year and cardnumber fields.

Next we specify a borderless table to contain our bound controls. The table has three columns, using the middle column for spacing. The left column is used for field labels.

The right column is where the data-bound text boxes are placed. The text boxes are specified with the <INPUT> tag, as in the following:

```
<input type="text" size="20" datafld="value" datasrc="#cards">
```

As you can see, we've specified both the DATAFLD and DATASRC properties. This binds the text box to the specific field in the TDC's recordset.

Next we come to the three buttons: Previous, Next, and Refresh. These buttons, when clicked, invoke VBScript subroutines, which are defined in the <SCRIPT> tag found after the buttons.

The previousrecord and nextrecord procedures use the properties and methods of the TDC's recordset object to navigate the data. If you've reached the beginning or the end of the recordset, you'll get a message box informing you that you've done so.

The refresh routine causes the TDC to fetch the data from the text file. This is done by setting its DataURL property and then invoking the Reset method. The record pointer is then set back to the beginning of the recordset using the recordset's `MoveFirst` method. You can test this button by loading the page, modifying the data file, and clicking the Refresh button to view the modified data.

You can also verify that data is not fetched with each movement of the record pointer by changing the data file and navigating to the modified record without having clicked the Refresh button. Indeed, the TDC only fetches data when it's supposed to.

Creating a Data-bound Table

Next we'll look at creating a data-bound table. Using data-bound tables requires far fewer HTML elements than does current record binding. The table definition serves as a template for how the data will be displayed in the table.

Listing 18.3 shows the HTML for a data-bound table.

Listing 18.3. A data-bound table example.

```
<html>
<head>
<title>Baseball Cards</title></head>

<body bgcolor="#FFFFFF">
<OBJECT ID="cards" ondatasetcomplete="dataloaded()"
 CLASSID="CLSID:333C7BC4-460F-11D0-BC04-0080C7055A83">
  <PARAM NAME="DataURL" VALUE="cards.txt">
  <PARAM NAME="UseHeader" VALUE="1">
  <PARAM NAME="Sort" VALUE="year; cardnumber">
</OBJECT>

<table border="1" datasrc="#cards" align="center">
    <THEAD><tr>
        <td align="left">Year</td>
        <td align="left">Card Number</td>
        <td align="left">Issuer</td>
        <td align="left">Description</td>
        <td align="left">Value</td>
    </tr></THEAD>
    <tr>
        <td><div datafld="year"</DIV></td>
        <td><div datafld="cardnumber"</DIV></td>
        <td><div datafld="issuer"</DIV></td>
        <td><div datafld="description"</DIV></td>
        <td><div datafld="value" dataformatas="none"</DIV></td>
    </tr>
</table>
<P>
<H2 align=center ID=TotalText>Total Value: </H2>

<SCRIPT language="VBScript">

sub dataloaded()
```

continues

Listing 18.3. continued

```
while not(cards.recordset.eof)
   total = total + cards.recordset("value")
   cards.recordset.movenext
wend
document.all.totaltext.innertext = "Total Value: " & total

end sub

</SCRIPT>
</body></html>
```

The `<OBJECT>` tag is identical for either current record binding or data-bound tables. In Listing 18.3, however, I've added a bonus: the `ondatasetcomplete` event. This event fires whenever the TDC has completed fetching the data from the data file. In this case, we're going to call the `dataloaded` procedure that appears at the bottom of the page in the `<SCRIPT>` tag. This procedure steps through the recordset one record at a time and calculates the total value of the card collection. Then, using dynamic content, it updates the `innertext` tag to display the total value.

With data-bound tables, the `DATASRC` attribute is specified only in the `<TABLE>` tag. Then, all references to the `DATAFLD` attribute will inherit the `DATASRC` value to use as the data source. Each row containing a `DATAFLD` attribute will be repeated for each record in the data file.

If we had specified a `DATAPAGESIZE` attribute in the `<TABLE>` tag, only that number of rows would appear in the table. This feature, called table paging, will be discussed further in Chapter 19.

Figure 18.2 shows how the page looks in IE4.

Figure 18.2.

An example of using a data-bound table.

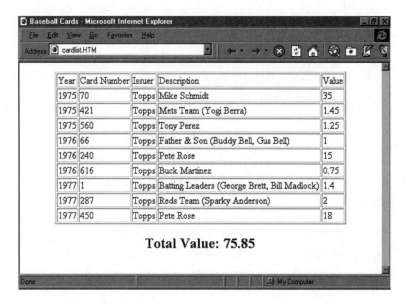

Summary

This chapter provides you with all the details necessary to create data-bound HTML pages. DSOs are ActiveX objects or Java applets that you can embed in your HTML pages to connect to a data source. The TDC is a simple DSO that can read a text file and provide the contents of that file in the form of a recordset object. Using the TDC, we created two HTML pages. The first is an HTML page that uses current record binding, displaying a single record at a time and providing recordset navigation buttons. The second utilizes a data-bound table that displayed all of the records on a single page and also used the TDC's recordset to tally up the total value of the baseball card collection.

In Chapter 19, we'll continue this discussion using the TDC. You'll learn how to use table paging, how to sort the data, and how to filter the data on-the-fly.

Client-side Data Manipulation

by Craig Eddy

IN THIS CHAPTER

CHAPTER 19

In Chapter 18, "Presenting Your Data with Dynamic HTML," you were introduced to the data-binding capabilities of DHTML. This chapter's introduction includes the following:

■ Data source objects (DSOs), which are ActiveX objects or Java applets that allow you to bind HTML elements to a data source

■ Extensions to the HTML specification necessary to support data binding

■ The Tabular Data Control (TDC), which is a simple ActiveX object that allows you to connect your DHTML page to a delimited text file

In this chapter, you'll learn more about using the TDC to allow the people browsing your HTML pages to manipulate the data that's presented to them. As you'll recall from Chapter 18, this includes sorting and filtering the data source. However, the TDC does not support editing and updating of the data. We'll save that discussion for Chapter 20, "Updating the Data," where I discuss the Remote Data Services in depth.

This chapter also discusses how you can use the table paging features of DHTML to display data in pages, limiting the number of records visible at a particular time to a manageable number.

Reviewing the Trading Card Database

For the sake of completeness, let's review the database we'll use for the examples in this chapter. The database is designed to hold information about a baseball trading card collection. I introduced the database in Chapter 18, but we'll briefly review the structure of the database now.

The database contains fields for `year`, `issuer`, `card set name`, `card number`, `description`, `condition` (also known as `grade`), and `card value`. The `year` field is formatted as an integer, because day and month aren't tracked for trading cards. The `card number` field will also be an integer, and the `card value` field will be a float, because it represents a currency value.

Listing 19.1 provides the data for the file. Name the file `CARDS.TXT`. This file is also available on the Sams.net Dynamic HTML Guru Web site at `http://www.htmlguru.com`. (Listing 19.1 contains a great deal more data than is used in Chapter 18.)

Listing 19.1. Contents of CARDS.TXT.

```
year:Int, issuer, setname, cardnumber:Int, description, grade, value:float
1977,Topps,1977 Topps,450,Pete Rose,NR MT,18.00
1977,Topps,1977 Topps,287,Reds Team (Sparky Anderson),NR MT,2.00
1976,Topps,1976 Topps,240,Pete Rose,EX,15.00
1975,Topps,1975 Topps,70,Mike Schmidt,EX,35.00
1976,Topps,1976 Topps,616,Buck Martinez,EX,0.75
1977,Topps,1977 Topps,1,"Batting Leaders (George Brett, Bill Madlock)",EX,1.40
1976,Topps,1976 Topps,66,"Father & Son (Buddy Bell, Gus Bell)",NR MT,1.00
1975,Topps,1975 Topps,421,"Mets Team (Yogi Berra)",EX,1.45
1975,Topps,1975 Topps,15,Jose Cardenal,EX,0.30
1975,Topps,1975 Topps,38,Buddy Bell,VG,0.60
```

```
1975,Topps,1975 Topps Mini,29, Dave Parker,VG,6.00
1975,Topps,1975 Topps,430,Luis Tiant,VG,0.30
1975,Topps,1975 Topps,437,Al Cowens,EX,0.40
1976,Topps,1976 Topps,300,Johnny Bench,EX,5.00
1976,Topps,1976 Topps,150,Steve Garvey,NR MT,9.00
1976,Topps,1976 Topps,268,Dell Unser,EX,0.16
1976,Topps,1976 Topps,295,Dave Cash,NR MT,0.30
1976,Topps,1976 Topps,321,Jose Crux,NR MT,0.70
1976,Topps,1976 Topps,550,Hank Aaron,NR MT,14.00
1976,Topps,1976 Topps,430,Jose Cardenal,EX,0.20
1978,Topps,1978 Topps,500,George Foster,NR MT,1.40
1978,Topps,1978 Topps,580,Rod Carew,EX,2.50
1978,Topps,1978 Topps,450,Tom Seaver,NR MT,2.50
1978,Topps,1978 Topps,201,"Batting Leaders (Rod Carew, Dave Parker)",EX,3.50
1978,Topps,1978 Topps,1,Record Breaker (Lou Brock),NR MT,4.00
1978,Topps,1978 Topps,5,Record Breaker (Pete Rose),NR MT,4.00
1978,Topps,1978 Topps,60,Thurmon Munson, EX,2.50
1975,Topps,1975 Topps,560,Tony Perez,EX,1.25
```

Save this file into the folder you'll be using to store your DHTML documents. As mentioned, you should name this file cards.txt, because this is the name that I'll use for the DataURL property in the examples in this chapter.

Sorting the Database

If you can do nothing else with regard to letting users manipulate the data on your Web pages, you must at least allow them to sort it. Sorting is perhaps the most used feature of any data viewing application, and data-bound DHTML pages should be no exception.

The method used to sort the data varies depending on the DSO used to bind the page to the data source. For the purposes of this chapter we'll be using the Tabular Data Control. This control was discussed in depth in Chapter 17. I'll discuss the TDC's Sort property next; review the section "Tabular Data Source Properties and Methods" of Chapter 17 for further details about the TDC.

Using the TDC's Sort Property

The Sort property allows you to specify the order in which the data is returned from the data file to the data-bound page. Multiple fields are specified by separating the field names with a semicolon (;).

Use a minus sign (-) in front of the field name to specify descending sort order. For example, the following code specifies that data should be sorted by the year field in ascending order and by the value field in descending order:

```
<PARAM NAME="Sort" VALUE="year; -value">
```

By setting the Sort property in the object tag of the TDC, you can provide an initial sort order. You can also set the property in script code. After doing so, invoke the Reset method to cause the new sort order to take effect.

The remainder of this section provides two examples of using the `Sort` property in your data bound pages.

Providing the User Interface for Sorting Data

Of course, if the users of your DHTML pages don't know how to sort the data you provide them, you might as well not provide the capability. This section discusses some ways to provide the user interface for data sorting. We'll discuss how to indicate that a column is sorted as well as how the user might specify which column(s) to sort with.

If you're using a table to display the data, as shown in Figure 19.1, you can use the column headers to indicate sort order. As you can see in Figure 19.1, the data is sorted by the year and card number. This is indicated by the plus sign (+) in front of the column name.

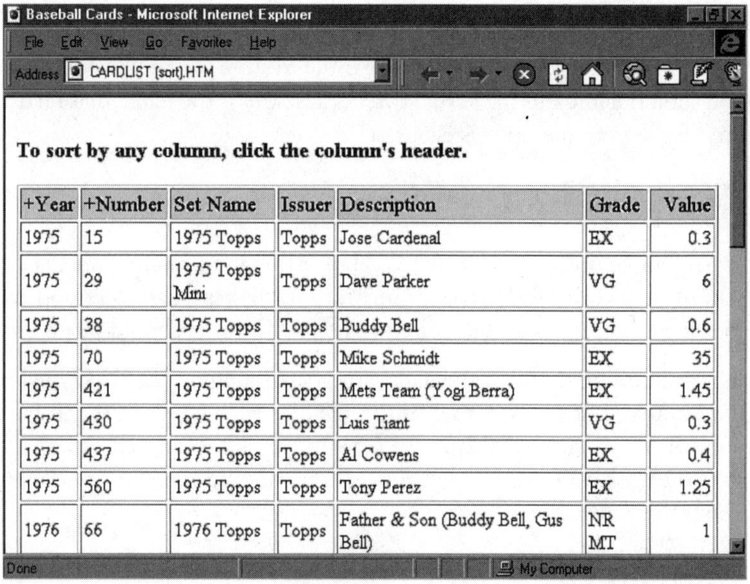

+Year	+Number	Set Name	Issuer	Description	Grade	Value
1975	15	1975 Topps	Topps	Jose Cardenal	EX	0.3
1975	29	1975 Topps Mini	Topps	Dave Parker	VG	6
1975	38	1975 Topps	Topps	Buddy Bell	VG	0.6
1975	70	1975 Topps	Topps	Mike Schmidt	EX	35
1975	421	1975 Topps	Topps	Mets Team (Yogi Berra)	EX	1.45
1975	430	1975 Topps	Topps	Luis Tiant	VG	0.3
1975	437	1975 Topps	Topps	Al Cowens	EX	0.4
1975	560	1975 Topps	Topps	Tony Perez	EX	1.25
1976	66	1976 Topps	Topps	Father & Son (Buddy Bell, Gus Bell)	NR MT	1

FIGURE 19.1.
An example of a sorted DHTML table.

You can also indicate sort order by using graphics, providing a different background color for the column, or using a check box or option group in a separate row, among other ways. The key is to make sure the user is aware of why the column looks different. If you're using color to indicate the sort order, you'll probably want to provide a color legend of some sort.

Using the dynamic content features provided by DHTML makes it extremely easy to indicate sort order to the user. To create the page shown in Figure 19.1, I used the `innerText` and `innerHTML` properties to change the text shown in the column header, adding plus and minus signs where appropriate. If you were to use an image to indicate sort order, you'd modify the `src` property of the appropriate `<IMAGE>` element to change the displayed image, again using dynamic content functionality.

Now that we've discussed ways to indicate that a column is sorted, let's look at ways to allow the user to specify which columns to sort. There are many ways to provide the user with this capability. Again, the key is to make sure the user knows how to sort the data. If it's not obvious based on the user interface you choose, you should provide some text indicating how to sort the data, as you can see in Figure 19.1.

The most common means for users to sort data that's displayed in tabular format is to click the column's header. This is the actual standard for data displayed in any of Microsoft's products that provide list or table views of information. To trap the click on an HTML table cell, simply place the attribute onclick="*clickroutine()*" in the cell's <TD> tag. Of course, *clickroutine* must be a valid VBScript or JScript subroutine, and you can also specify any parameters you wish. In Listing 19.2, I use some very simplistic VBScript and DHTML to accomplish the column header click.

Listing 19.2. Using column header clicks to sort data.

```
<!DOCTYPE HTML PUBLIC "-//IETF//DTD HTML//EN">
<html><head>
<meta http-equiv="Content-Type" content="text/html; charset=iso-8859-1">
<title>Baseball Cards</title></head>
<body bgcolor="#FFFFFF">
<p>
<object id="cards" ondatasetcomplete="dataloaded()"
classid="CLSID:333C7BC4-460F-11D0-BC04-0080C7055A83" width="192" height="192">
  <param name="DataURL" value="cards.txt">
  <param name="UseHeader" value="1">
  <param name="Sort" value="year; cardnumber">
</object>
</p>

<H3>To sort by any column, click the column's header.</H3>

<table border="1" datasrc="#cards" align="center" cellpadding="2">
<THEAD>
  <tr>
    <td align="left" id="year" onclick="tableclick('year')"
        bgcolor="#00FFFF"><big>+Year</big></td>
    <td align="left" id="CardNumber" onclick="tableclick('cardnumber')"
        bgcolor="#00FFFF"><big>+Number</big></td>
    <td align="left" id="setname" onclick="tableclick('setname')"
        bgcolor="#00FFFF"><big>Set Name</big></td>
    <td align="left" id="issuer" onclick="tableclick('issuer')"
        bgcolor="#00FFFF"><big>Issuer</big></td>
    <td align="left" id="description" onclick="tableclick('description')"
        bgcolor="#00FFFF"><big>Description</big></td>
    <td align="left" id="grade" onclick="tableclick('grade')"
        bgcolor="#00FFFF"><big>Grade</big></td>
    <td align="right" id="value" onclick="tableclick('value')"
        bgcolor="#00FFFF"><big>Value</big></td>
  </tr>
</THEAD>
  <tr>
```

19

continues

Listing 19.2. continued

```
        <td><div datafld="year"></div></td>
        <td><div datafld="cardnumber"></div></td>
        <td><div datafld="setname"></div></td>
        <td><div datafld="issuer"></div></td>
        <td><div datafld="description"></div></td>
        <td><div datafld="grade"></div></td>
        <td width="50" align="right"><div datafld="value"></div></td>
    </tr>
<TFOOT>
    <tr>
        <td colspan="6" align="right" height="40" bgcolor="#000080">
        <font color="#FF0000" size="4"><strong>Total:</strong></font></td>
        <td valign="center" align="right" bgcolor="#000080">
        <font color="#FF0000" size="4">
        <strong><div id="TotalText"></div></strong></font></td>
    </tr>
</TFOOT>
</table>

<p>
<script language="VBScript"><!--

sub tableclick(columnname)

if columnname <> "year" and (left(document.all.item("year").innertext,1)
➡       = "+"
➡    or left(document.all.item("year").innertext,1) = "-") then
        document.all.item("year").innerHTML = "<big>" +
➡            mid(document.all.item("year").innertext,2) + "</big>"
end if

if columnname <> "cardnumber" and
➡    (left(document.all.item("cardnumber").innertext,1) = "+" or
➡    left(document.all.item("cardnumber").innertext,1) = "-") then
        document.all.item("cardnumber").innerHTML = "<big>" +
➡            mid(document.all.item("cardnumber").innertext,2) + "</big>"
end if

if columnname <> "setname" and
➡    (left(document.all.item("setname").innertext,1) = "+" or
➡    left(document.all.item("setname").innertext,1) = "-") then
        document.all.item("setname").innerHTML = "<big>" +
➡            mid(document.all.item("setname").innertext,2) + "</big>"
end if

if columnname <> "issuer" and
➡    (left(document.all.item("issuer").innertext,1) = "+" or
➡    left(document.all.item("issuer").innertext,1) = "-") then
        document.all.item("issuer").innerHTML = "<big>" +
➡        mid(document.all.item("issuer").innertext,2) + "</big>"
end if

if columnname <> "description" and
➡    (left(document.all.item("description").innertext,1) = "+" or
➡    left(document.all.item("description").innertext,1) = "-") then
        document.all.item("description").innerHTML = "<big>" +
➡        mid(document.all.item("description").innertext,2) + "</big>"
end if
```

```
if columnname <> "grade" and
➥   (left(document.all.item("grade").innertext,1) = "+" or
➥    left(document.all.item("grade").innertext,1) = "-") then
        document.all.item("grade").innerHTML = "<big>" +
➥          mid(document.all.item("grade").innertext,2) + "</big>"
end if

if columnname <> "value" and
➥   (left(document.all.item("value").innertext,1) = "+" or
➥    left(document.all.item("value").innertext,1) = "-") then
        document.all.item("value").innerHTML = "<big>" +
➥          mid(document.all.item("value").innertext,2) + "</big>"
end if

if left(document.all.item(columnname).innertext,1) = "+" then
    document.all.item(columnname).innerHTML =   "<big>-" +
➥      mid(document.all.item(columnname).innertext,2) + "</big>"
    cards.sort = "-" + columnname
elseif left(document.all.item(columnname).innertext,1) = "-" then
    document.all.item(columnname).innerHTML = "<big>+" +
➥      mid(document.all.item(columnname).innertext,2) + "</big>"
    cards.sort = columnname
else
    document.all.item(columnname).innerHTML = "<big>+" +
➥      document.all.item(columnname).innertext + "</big>"
    cards.sort = columnname
end if

cards.reset

end sub

sub dataloaded()

while not(cards.recordset.eof)
    total = total + cards.recordset("value")
    cards.recordset.movenext
wend
document.all.totaltext.innertext =  total

end sub

--></script> </p>
</body></html>
```

Notice first that I've specified an initial sort order for the data. This is done in the <OBJECT> tag by setting the Sort property to year; cardnumber. I've also used the plus sign in the table header cells for these fields.

After the DSO is specified, the definition of the data-bound table begins. In the <THEADER> section, you'll find the column headers. (The <THEADER> tag informs the parser to exclude this section from being repeated for each data row found in the data file.) Each of the <TD> tags contains a reference to a subroutine named tableclick. This subroutine is where the sorting and column header text modification takes place. You'll find it near the bottom of Listing 19.2, immediately following the <SCRIPT> tag.

The `tableclick` subroutine's first task is to fix up the column header text. There are more eloquent uses of the DHTML object model than the one I've chosen here, but I think this method gets the point across a little better.

The first section of code (all of the `if columnname <> ...` constructs) is responsible for changing the header text of any previously sorted columns back to the original text. Remember, the `onclick` event occurs on a single column header. This is done by comparing the `columnname` parameter with each of the known column names. If the user hasn't clicked a particular column header, its text is reset (removing any plus or minus signs).

Next, we check to see if the column is already sorted. This is done by examining the text of the column header. If it contains a plus sign, we change the text to a minus sign and change the `Sort` property to have a minus sign preceding the column name (forcing a descending sort). If the text contains a minus sign, we do the same but leave off the minus sign on the `Sort` property to force an ascending sort. Finally, if neither character is displayed, we use the plus sign and an ascending sort order.

After the column headers and `Sort` property have been set, we use the `Reset` method to force the TDC to apply the new sort order.

Another Example of Sorting Data

You can also use other HTML elements to allow the user to specify how to sort the data. You could use a drop-down list box that has a choice for each useful sort order. Or, you could place some pushbuttons on the page, label them appropriately, and use the `onclick` event to modify the sort order. This is exactly what I've done to create the page shown in Figure 19.2.

Figure 19.2.

An example of a DHTML table sorted using multiple columns.

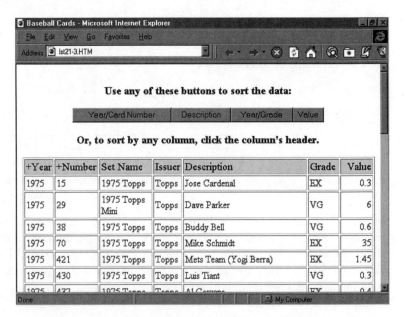

For this page, I've left the column header click in place and added some buttons to allow the user to quickly specify some extended sort orders. With the simple column heading click, for example, you cannot sort by year and grade at the same time. Using the pushbuttons we can specify any sort order we wish. The code for this page, provided in Listing 19.3, is identical to Listing 19.2, with the addition of the buttons and the `buttonclick` subroutine.

Listing 19.3. Using push-button clicks to sort data.

```
<!DOCTYPE HTML PUBLIC "-//IETF//DTD HTML//EN">
<html><head>
<meta http-equiv="Content-Type" content="text/html; charset=iso-8859-1">
<title>Baseball Cards</title></head>
<body bgcolor="#FFFFFF">
<p>
<object id="cards" ondatasetcomplete="dataloaded()"
classid="CLSID:333C7BC4-460F-11D0-BC04-0080C7055A83" width="192" height="192">
  <param name="DataURL" value="cards.txt">
  <param name="UseHeader" value="1">
  <param name="Sort" value="year; cardnumber">
</object>
</p>

<!-- START modified from Listing 19.2 -->
<h3 align="center">Use any of these buttons to sort the data:</h3>
<p align="center"><input type="button" value="Year/Card Number" name="B1"
onclick="buttonclick(1)"><input type="button" value="Description" name="B2"
onclick="buttonclick(2)"><input type="button" value="Year/Grade" name="B3"
onclick="buttonclick(3)"><input type="button" value="Value" name="B4"
onclick="buttonclick(4)"></p>
<h3 align="center">Or, to sort by any column, click the column's header.</h3>
<!-- END modified from Listing 19.2 -->

<table border="1" datasrc="#cards" align="center" cellpadding="2">
<THEAD>
  <tr>
    <td align="left" id="year" onclick="tableclick('year')"
        bgcolor="#00FFFF"><big>+Year</big></td>
    <td align="left" id="CardNumber" onclick="tableclick('cardnumber')"
        bgcolor="#00FFFF"><big>+Number</big></td>
    <td align="left" id="setname" onclick="tableclick('setname')"
        bgcolor="#00FFFF"><big>Set Name</big></td>
    <td align="left" id="issuer" onclick="tableclick('issuer')"
        bgcolor="#00FFFF"><big>Issuer</big></td>
    <td align="left" id="description" onclick="tableclick('description')"
        bgcolor="#00FFFF"><big>Description</big></td>
    <td align="left" id="grade" onclick="tableclick('grade')"
        bgcolor="#00FFFF"><big>Grade</big></td>
    <td align="right" id="value" onclick="tableclick('value')"
        bgcolor="#00FFFF"><big>Value</big></td>
  </tr>
</THEAD>
  <tr>
    <td><div datafld="year"></div></td>
    <td><div datafld="cardnumber"></div></td>
    <td><div datafld="setname"></div></td>
```

19

CLIENT-SIDE DATA
MANIPULATION

continues

Listing 19.3. continued

```
      <td><div datafld="issuer"></div></td>
      <td><div datafld="description"></div></td>
      <td><div datafld="grade"></div></td>
      <td width="50" align="right"><div datafld="value"></div></td>
  </tr>
<TFOOT>
  <tr>
    <td colspan="6" align="right" height="40" bgcolor="#000080">
    <font color="#FF0000" size="4"><strong>Total:</strong></font></td>
    <td valign="center" align="right" bgcolor="#000080">
    <font color="#FF0000" size="4">
    <strong><div id="TotalText"></div></strong></font></td>
  </tr>
</TFOOT>
</table>

<p>
<script language="VBScript"><!--

sub tableclick(columnname)

if columnname <> "year" and
➥    (left(document.all.item("year").innertext,1) = "+"
➥    or left(document.all.item("year").innertext,1) = "-") then
       document.all.item("year").innerHTML = "<big>" +
➥           mid(document.all.item("year").innertext,2) + "</big>"
end if

if columnname <> "cardnumber" and
➥    (left(document.all.item("cardnumber").innertext,1) = "+" or
➥    left(document.all.item("cardnumber").innertext,1) = "-") then
       document.all.item("cardnumber").innerHTML = "<big>" +
➥           mid(document.all.item("cardnumber").innertext,2) + "</big>"
end if

if columnname <> "setname" and
➥    (left(document.all.item("setname").innertext,1) = "+" or
➥    left(document.all.item("setname").innertext,1) = "-") then
       document.all.item("setname").innerHTML = "<big>" +
➥           mid(document.all.item("setname").innertext,2) + "</big>"
end if

if columnname <> "issuer" and
➥    (left(document.all.item("issuer").innertext,1) = "+" or
➥    left(document.all.item("issuer").innertext,1) = "-") then
       document.all.item("issuer").innerHTML = "<big>" +
➥        mid(document.all.item("issuer").innertext,2) + "</big>"
end if

if columnname <> "description" and
➥    (left(document.all.item("description").innertext,1) = "+" or
➥    left(document.all.item("description").innertext,1) = "-") then
       document.all.item("description").innerHTML = "<big>" +
➥        mid(document.all.item("description").innertext,2) + "</big>"
end if
```

```
        if columnname <> "grade" and
➡️        (left(document.all.item("grade").innertext,1) = "+" or
➡️        left(document.all.item("grade").innertext,1) = "-") then
              document.all.item("grade").innerHTML = "<big>" +
➡️                mid(document.all.item("grade").innertext,2) + "</big>"
        end if

        if columnname <> "value" and
➡️        (left(document.all.item("value").innertext,1) = "+" or
➡️        left(document.all.item("value").innertext,1) = "-") then
              document.all.item("value").innerHTML = "<big>" +
➡️                mid(document.all.item("value").innertext,2) + "</big>"
        end if

        if left(document.all.item(columnname).innertext,1) = "+" then
              document.all.item(columnname).innerHTML =   "<big>-" +
➡️                mid(document.all.item(columnname).innertext,2) + "</big>"
              cards.sort = "-" + columnname
        elseif left(document.all.item(columnname).innertext,1) = "-" then
              document.all.item(columnname).innerHTML = "<big>+" +
➡️                mid(document.all.item(columnname).innertext,2) + "</big>"
              cards.sort = columnname
        else
              document.all.item(columnname).innerHTML = "<big>+" +
➡️                document.all.item(columnname).innertext + "</big>"
              cards.sort = columnname
        end if

        cards.reset

        end sub

<!-- START modified from Listing 19.2 -->
sub buttonclick(button)

if (left(document.all.item("year").innertext,1) = "+" or
➡️    left(document.all.item("year").innertext,1) = "-") then
        document.all.item("year").innerHTML = "<big>" +
➡️            mid(document.all.item("year").innertext,2) + "</big>"
end if

if (left(document.all.item("cardnumber").innertext,1) = "+" or
➡️    left(document.all.item("cardnumber").innertext,1) = "-") then
        document.all.item("cardnumber").innerHTML = "<big>" +
➡️            mid(document.all.item("cardnumber").innertext,2) + "</big>"
end if

if (left(document.all.item("setname").innertext,1) = "+" or
➡️    left(document.all.item("setname").innertext,1) = "-") then
        document.all.item("setname").innerHTML = "<big>" +
➡️            mid(document.all.item("setname").innertext,2) + "</big>"
end if

if (left(document.all.item("issuer").innertext,1) = "+" or
➡️    left(document.all.item("issuer").innertext,1) = "-") then
        document.all.item("issuer").innerHTML = "<big>" +
➡️            mid(document.all.item("issuer").innertext,2) + "</big>"
end if
```

19

CLIENT-SIDE DATA
MANIPULATION

continues

Listing 19.3. continued

```
if (left(document.all.item("description").innertext,1) = "+" or
➥    left(document.all.item("description").innertext,1) = "-") then
       document.all.item("description").innerHTML = "<big>" +
➥          mid(document.all.item("description").innertext,2) + "</big>"
end if

if (left(document.all.item("grade").innertext,1) = "+" or
➥    left(document.all.item("grade").innertext,1) = "-") then
       document.all.item("grade").innerHTML = "<big>" +
➥          mid(document.all.item("grade").innertext,2) + "</big>"
end if

if (left(document.all.item("value").innertext,1) = "+" or
➥    left(document.all.item("value").innertext,1) = "-") then
       document.all.item("value").innerHTML = "<big>" +
➥          mid(document.all.item("value").innertext,2) + "</big>"
end if

select case button
case 1
   document.all.item("year").innerHTML = "<big>+" +
➥              document.all.item("year").innertext + "</big>"
   document.all.item("cardnumber").innerHTML = "<big>+" +
➥              document.all.item("cardnumber").innertext + "</big>"
   cards.sort = "year; cardnumber"
case 2
   document.all.item("description").innerHTML = "<big>+" +
➥              document.all.item("description").innertext + "</big>"
    cards.sort = "description"
case 3
   document.all.item("year").innerHTML = "<big>+" +
➥              document.all.item("year").innertext + "</big>"
   document.all.item("grade").innerHTML = "<big>+" +
➥              document.all.item("grade").innertext + "</big>"
   cards.sort = "year; grade"
case 4
   document.all.item("value").innerHTML = "<big>+" +
➥              document.all.item("value").innertext + "</big>"
   cards.sort = "value"
end select

cards.reset
end sub
<!-- END modified from Listing 19.2 -->

sub dataloaded()

while not(cards.recordset.eof)
   total = total + cards.recordset("value")
   cards.recordset.movenext
wend
document.all.totaltext.innertext =  total

end sub
--></script> </p>
</body></html>
```

In the `buttonclick()` subroutine, we first clear all the column headers any sort order indicator. Then, based on the `button` parameter passed to the routine, we set the appropriate column header text and the `Sort` property of the TDC. Then we invoke the TDC's `Reset` method to apply the new sort order.

As you can see, using pushbuttons or a drop-down list is a very intuitive way to allow the user to specify a sort order.

Filtering the Returned Data

The second most useful data manipulation feature you can provide your users is the capability to filter the displayed data. Doing so allows the user to view only the data in which he or she is interested at the time.

Most DSOs will provide the capability of filtering the data. The method used to filter data varies depending on the DSO used to bind the page to the data source. As mentioned previously, the Tabular Data Control is the DSO we're using for this chapter. This control is discussed in depth in Chapter 17. I'll discuss the TDC's `Filter` property next; review the section "Tabular Data Source Properties and Methods" of Chapter 17 for further details about the TDC.

Using the TDC's `Filter` Property

`Filter` is a string property that defines the criteria that will be used to filter the data cached in the TDC's recordset. The default value for this property is an empty string, which means that no filter is applied to the recordset.

You can provide initial filtering of the data by setting the `Filter` property in the TDC's `<OBJECT>` tag. You can also set the property in script code and invoke the `Reset` method to cause the new filter to take effect.

The syntax of the `Filter` property allows you to combine comparison operators and logical operators such as AND (&) and OR (¦), as in the following:

```
(year = 1976) & (value > 5)
```

The syntax of the property is defined as follows:

```
Complex ::== Simple
 ::== Simple '&' Simple [ '&' Simple ... ]
 ::== Simple '¦' Simple [ '¦' Simple ... ]
Simple ::== '(' Complex ')'
 ::== Atom Relop Atom
Relop ::== '=' ¦ '>' ¦ '>=' ¦ '<' ¦ '<=' ¦ '<>'
Atom ::== Characters up to a (, ), >, <, =, & or ¦
```

Note that AND and OR have equal precedence when evaluated and, therefore, must be surrounded by parentheses if both are combined in a single criteria.

A Data-Filtering Example

To provide filtering capabilities to your users, you must provide some sort of user interface that can be used to build the value for the `Filter` property. This can consist of any of the HTML input elements—including text boxes, drop-down lists, or pushbuttons. You should also provide a pushbutton or image that the user must click in order to apply the filter. Without a separate button, the user will have a hard time constructing a filter combining multiple criteria.

Figure 19.3 shows an example of using a text box and pushbuttons to build a filter based on the year field. The user simply enters the year of interest and clicks the Filter button. Entering 1978 and clicking Filter produces the results shown in Figure 19.4. To clear the text box and reset the data to the complete result set, click the Reset button.

FIGURE 19.3.

An example of a filter construction form.

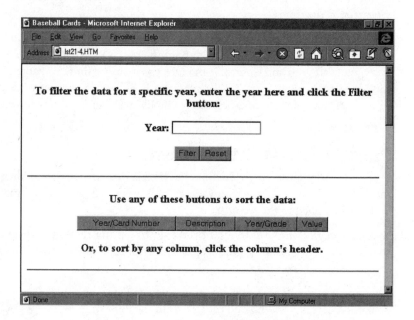

To create this page, use the code in Listing 19.4. I've again simply extended the page constructed in Listing 19.3. The modified sections in Listing 19.4 are marked with HTML comments within the listing. I've added the HTML form that contains the text box and buttons for constructing the filter and, of course, the VBScript code that actually performs the filter.

FIGURE 19.4.

The results of a filter based on year = 1978.

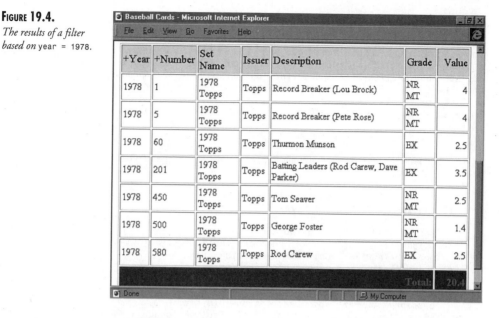

Listing 19.4. Using pushbutton clicks to sort data.

```
<!DOCTYPE HTML PUBLIC "-//IETF//DTD HTML//EN">
<html><head>
<meta http-equiv="Content-Type" content="text/html; charset=iso-8859-1">
<title>Baseball Cards</title></head>
<body bgcolor="#FFFFFF">
<p>
<object id="cards" ondatasetcomplete="dataloaded()"
classid="CLSID:333C7BC4-460F-11D0-BC04-0080C7055A83" width="192" height="192">
  <param name="DataURL" value="cards.txt">
  <param name="UseHeader" value="1">
  <param name="Sort" value="year; cardnumber">
</object>
</p>

<!-- START modified from Listing 19.3 -->
<h3 align="center">
To filter the data for a specific year, enter the year here and click the
Filter button:</h3>
<form id="filterform">
  <div align="center"><center><h3>Year:
    <input type="text" name="FilterYear" size="20"></h3>
  </center></div>
  <div align="center"><center><h3>
  <input type="submit" value="Filter" name="B1" onclick="filteryear(0)">
  <input type="reset" value="Reset" name="B2" onclick="filteryear(1)">
  </h3></center></div>
</form>
<hr>
```

continues

Listing 19.4. continued

```
<h3 align="center">Use any of these buttons to sort the data:</h3>
<p align="center"><input type="button" value="Year/Card Number" name="B1"
onclick="buttonclick(1)"><input type="button" value="Description" name="B2"
onclick="buttonclick(2)"><input type="button" value="Year/Grade" name="B3"
onclick="buttonclick(3)"><input type="button" value="Value" name="B4"
onclick="buttonclick(4)"></p>
<h3 align="center">Or, to sort by any column, click the column's header.</h3>
<hr>
<!-- END modified from Listing 19.3 -->

<table border="1" datasrc="#cards" align="center" cellpadding="2">
<THEAD>
  <tr>
    <td align="left" id="year" onclick="tableclick('year')"
        bgcolor="#00FFFF"><big>+Year</big></td>
    <td align="left" id="CardNumber" onclick="tableclick('cardnumber')"
        bgcolor="#00FFFF"><big>+Number</big></td>
    <td align="left" id="setname" onclick="tableclick('setname')"
        bgcolor="#00FFFF"><big>Set Name</big></td>
    <td align="left" id="issuer" onclick="tableclick('issuer')"
        bgcolor="#00FFFF"><big>Issuer</big></td>
    <td align="left" id="description" onclick="tableclick('description')"
        bgcolor="#00FFFF"><big>Description</big></td>
    <td align="left" id="grade" onclick="tableclick('grade')"
        bgcolor="#00FFFF"><big>Grade</big></td>
    <td align="right" id="value" onclick="tableclick('value')"
        bgcolor="#00FFFF"><big>Value</big></td>
  </tr>
</THEAD>
  <tr>
    <td><div datafld="year"></div></td>
    <td><div datafld="cardnumber"></div></td>
    <td><div datafld="setname"></div></td>
    <td><div datafld="issuer"></div></td>
    <td><div datafld="description"></div></td>
    <td><div datafld="grade"></div></td>
    <td width="50" align="right"><div datafld="value"></div></td>
  </tr>
<TFOOT>
  <tr>
    <td colspan="6" align="right" height="40" bgcolor="#000080">
    <font color="#FF0000" size="4"><strong>Total:</strong></font></td>
    <td valign="center" align="right" bgcolor="#000080">
    <font color="#FF0000" size="4">
    <strong><div id="TotalText"></div></strong></font></td>
  </tr>
</TFOOT>
</table>

<script language="VBScript"><!--
sub tableclick(columnname)

if columnname <> "year" and
➥    (left(document.all.item("year").innertext,1) = "+"
➥    or left(document.all.item("year").innertext,1) = "-") then
      document.all.item("year").innerHTML = "<big>" +
➥          mid(document.all.item("year").innertext,2) + "</big>"
end if
```

```
if columnname <> "cardnumber" and
➥   (left(document.all.item("cardnumber").innertext,1) = "+" or
➥   left(document.all.item("cardnumber").innertext,1) = "-") then
      document.all.item("cardnumber").innerHTML = "<big>" +
➥         mid(document.all.item("cardnumber").innertext,2) + "</big>"
end if

if columnname <> "setname" and
➥   (left(document.all.item("setname").innertext,1) = "+" or
➥   left(document.all.item("setname").innertext,1) = "-") then
      document.all.item("setname").innerHTML = "<big>" +
➥         mid(document.all.item("setname").innertext,2) + "</big>"
end if

if columnname <> "issuer" and
➥   (left(document.all.item("issuer").innertext,1) = "+" or
➥   left(document.all.item("issuer").innertext,1) = "-") then
      document.all.item("issuer").innerHTML = "<big>" +
➥        mid(document.all.item("issuer").innertext,2) + "</big>"
end if

if columnname <> "description" and
➥   (left(document.all.item("description").innertext,1) = "+" or
➥   left(document.all.item("description").innertext,1) = "-") then
      document.all.item("description").innerHTML = "<big>" +
➥        mid(document.all.item("description").innertext,2) + "</big>"
end if

if columnname <> "grade" and
➥   (left(document.all.item("grade").innertext,1) = "+" or
➥   left(document.all.item("grade").innertext,1) = "-") then
      document.all.item("grade").innerHTML = "<big>" +
➥        mid(document.all.item("grade").innertext,2) + "</big>"
end if

if columnname <> "value" and
➥   (left(document.all.item("value").innertext,1) = "+" or
➥   left(document.all.item("value").innertext,1) = "-") then
      document.all.item("value").innerHTML = "<big>" +
➥        mid(document.all.item("value").innertext,2) + "</big>"
end if

if left(document.all.item(columnname).innertext,1) = "+" then
   document.all.item(columnname).innerHTML =  "<big>-" +
➥      mid(document.all.item(columnname).innertext,2) + "</big>"
   cards.sort = "-" + columnname
elseif left(document.all.item(columnname).innertext,1) = "-" then
   document.all.item(columnname).innerHTML = "<big>+" +
➥      mid(document.all.item(columnname).innertext,2) + "</big>"
   cards.sort = columnname
else
   document.all.item(columnname).innerHTML = "<big>+" +
➥      document.all.item(columnname).innertext + "</big>"
   cards.sort = columnname
end if

cards.reset
```

continues

Listing 19.4. continued

```
end sub

sub buttonclick(button)

if (left(document.all.item("year").innertext,1) = "+" or
➥    left(document.all.item("year").innertext,1) = "-") then
        document.all.item("year").innerHTML = "<big>" +
➥            mid(document.all.item("year").innertext,2) + "</big>"
    end if

if (left(document.all.item("cardnumber").innertext,1) = "+" or
➥    left(document.all.item("cardnumber").innertext,1) = "-") then
        document.all.item("cardnumber").innerHTML = "<big>" +
➥            mid(document.all.item("cardnumber").innertext,2) + "</big>"
    end if

if (left(document.all.item("setname").innertext,1) = "+" or
➥    left(document.all.item("setname").innertext,1) = "-") then
        document.all.item("setname").innerHTML = "<big>" +
➥            mid(document.all.item("setname").innertext,2) + "</big>"
    end if

if (left(document.all.item("issuer").innertext,1) = "+" or
➥    left(document.all.item("issuer").innertext,1) = "-") then
        document.all.item("issuer").innerHTML = "<big>" +
➥            mid(document.all.item("issuer").innertext,2) + "</big>"
    end if

if (left(document.all.item("description").innertext,1) = "+" or
➥    left(document.all.item("description").innertext,1) = "-") then
        document.all.item("description").innerHTML = "<big>" +
➥            mid(document.all.item("description").innertext,2) + "</big>"
    end if

if (left(document.all.item("grade").innertext,1) = "+" or
➥    left(document.all.item("grade").innertext,1) = "-") then
        document.all.item("grade").innerHTML = "<big>" +
➥            mid(document.all.item("grade").innertext,2) + "</big>"
    end if

if (left(document.all.item("value").innertext,1) = "+" or
➥    left(document.all.item("value").innertext,1) = "-") then
        document.all.item("value").innerHTML = "<big>" +
➥            mid(document.all.item("value").innertext,2) + "</big>"
    end if

select case button
case 1
    document.all.item("year").innerHTML = "<big>+" +
➥                document.all.item("year").innertext + "</big>"
    document.all.item("cardnumber").innerHTML = "<big>+" +
➥                document.all.item("cardnumber").innertext + "</big>"
    cards.sort = "year; cardnumber"
case 2
    document.all.item("description").innerHTML = "<big>+" +
➥                document.all.item("description").innertext + "</big>"
    cards.sort = "description"
```

```
case 3
   document.all.item("year").innerHTML = "<big>+" +
➥             document.all.item("year").innertext + "</big>"
   document.all.item("grade").innerHTML = "<big>+" +
➥             document.all.item("grade").innertext + "</big>"
   cards.sort = "year; grade"
case 4
   document.all.item("value").innerHTML = "<big>+" +
➥             document.all.item("value").innertext + "</big>"
   cards.sort = "value"
end select

cards.reset
end sub

<!-- START modified from Listing 19.3 -->
sub filteryear(reset)

if reset then
   fstring = ""
else
   fstring = "year = " + document.forms("filterform").item("filteryear").value
end if

cards.filter = fstring
cards.reset

end sub
<!-- END modified from Listing 19.3 -->

sub dataloaded()

while not(cards.recordset.eof)
   total = total + cards.recordset("value")
   cards.recordset.movenext
wend
document.all.totaltext.innertext = total

end sub
--></script>
</body></html>
```

Let's start by looking at the form I've added. The form and text box are given an ID because we'll need to reference them in order to get the value that the user entered into the text box. The two pushbuttons both have their onclick event set to filteryear(), each with a different parameter.

The code for filteryear() is found, of course, within the <SCRIPT> tag at the bottom of the listing. This routine's parameter, reset, is used to determine whether the filter criteria should be cleared or should be derived from the form's text box. The code for this routine is very straightforward, consisting only of an If...Then...Else statement, an assignment to the TDC's Filter property, and the invocation of the TDC's Reset method.

Notice the total value row at the bottom of the table. As you can see in Figure 19.4, the data has changed to show the total value of the cards included in the filter instead of all the cards. This further demonstrates the usefulness of the filter property: You can summarize data across differing criteria by applying multiple filters to the data prior to each summarization.

Using Table Paging

The sample data file we've been using in this chapter doesn't contain an overwhelming amount of data. But what if our trading card collection was enormous, with thousands of cards? We certainly wouldn't want to display all of those cards on a single page. For this reason, DHTML includes a feature known as *table paging*. The biggest advantage of using table paging as opposed to some CGI or Active Server paging mechanism is that, after the data is loaded by the DSO, there won't be any further trips to the server to gather data. The DSO, even with table paging enabled, still has all the data cached locally.

Using table paging allows you to specify how many records will appear on each page. Table paging doesn't rely on the DSO to get its job done. Instead, the <TABLE> element is also extended to include the necessary elements. These extensions are discussed in the following two sections.

The third section explains how to extend the pages we've already built to include table paging. As you'll see, adding table paging to your pages is a snap.

The DATAPAGESIZE Attribute

One of the extensions of the <TABLE> element is the DATAPAGESIZE attribute. When the table is being used to display bound data (that is, when it has a valid DATASRC attribute specified), the DATAPAGESIZE attribute specifies the number of rows to be displayed on each page. By specifying an integer value for this attribute, you're instructing the DHTML parser to display only that number of records on each data page.

The table object in the DHTML object model includes a dataPageSize property. This means that you can change the page size at runtime. You might have a text box or drop-down list that allows the user to specify a desired page size. Setting the dataPageSize property in script code causes the table to be rendered again with the new dataPageSize value.

To remove the table paging, simply set the dataPageSize property to 0. This will cause the table to be re-rendered with all the data from the data source (obeying the filter, of course).

The nextPage and previousPage Methods

In addition to the dataPageSize property, the table object also includes two methods, nextPage and previousPage, which scroll the table's contents through the data source's data. As you might expect, nextPage moves the displayed data window to the next set of records, and previousPage moves the displayed data window to the previous set of records.

A Table-Paging Example

Listing 19.5 provides the code that was used to create the page you see in Figure 19.5. This page is built by adding to the code in Listing 19.4. The modified sections are marked with HTML comments within the listing.

Listing 19.5. Using table paging.

```
<!DOCTYPE HTML PUBLIC "-//IETF//DTD HTML//EN">
<html><head>
<meta http-equiv="Content-Type" content="text/html; charset=iso-8859-1">
<title>Baseball Cards</title></head>
<body bgcolor="#FFFFFF">
<p>
<object id="cards" ondatasetcomplete="dataloaded()"
classid="CLSID:333C7BC4-460F-11D0-BC04-0080C7055A83" width="192" height="192">
  <param name="DataURL" value="cards.txt">
  <param name="UseHeader" value="1">
  <param name="Sort" value="year; cardnumber">
</object>
</p>

<h3 align="center">
To filter the data for a specific year, enter the year here and click the
Filter button:</h3>
<form id="filterform">
  <div align="center"><center><h3>Year:
    <input type="text" name="FilterYear" size="20"></h3>
  </center></div>
  <div align="center"><center><h3>
  <input type="submit" value="Filter" name="B1" onclick="filteryear(0)">
  <input type="reset" value="Reset" name="B2" onclick="filteryear(1)">
  </h3></center></div>
</form>
<hr>
<h3 align="center">Use any of these buttons to sort the data:</h3>
<p align="center"><input type="button" value="Year/Card Number" name="B1"
onclick="buttonclick(1)"><input type="button" value="Description" name="B2"
onclick="buttonclick(2)"><input type="button" value="Year/Grade" name="B3"
onclick="buttonclick(3)"><input type="button" value="Value" name="B4"
onclick="buttonclick(4)"></p>
<h3 align="center">Or, to sort by any column, click the column's header.</h3>
<hr>

<!-- START modified from Listing 19.4 -->
<table border="1" datasrc="#cards" datapagesize=5
 align="center" cellpadding="2">
<!-- END modified from Listing 19.4 -->
<THEAD>
  <tr>
    <td align="left" id="year" onclick="tableclick('year')"
        bgcolor="#00FFFF"><big>+Year</big></td>
    <td align="left" id="CardNumber" onclick="tableclick('cardnumber')"
        bgcolor="#00FFFF"><big>+Number</big></td>
    <td align="left" id="setname" onclick="tableclick('setname')"
        bgcolor="#00FFFF"><big>Set Name</big></td>
```

continues

Listing 19.5. continued

```
      <td align="left" id="issuer" onclick="tableclick('issuer')"
          bgcolor="#00FFFF"><big>Issuer</big></td>
      <td align="left" id="description" onclick="tableclick('description')"
          bgcolor="#00FFFF"><big>Description</big></td>
      <td align="left" id="grade" onclick="tableclick('grade')"
          bgcolor="#00FFFF"><big>Grade</big></td>
      <td align="right" id="value" onclick="tableclick('value')"
          bgcolor="#00FFFF"><big>Value</big></td>
  </tr>
</THEAD>
  <tr>
    <td><div datafld="year"></div></td>
    <td><div datafld="cardnumber"></div></td>
    <td><div datafld="setname"></div></td>
    <td><div datafld="issuer"></div></td>
    <td><div datafld="description"></div></td>
    <td><div datafld="grade"></div></td>
    <td width="50" align="right"><div datafld="value"></div></td>
  </tr>
<TFOOT>
  <tr>
    <td colspan="6" align="right" height="40" bgcolor="#000080">
    <font color="#FF0000" size="4"><strong>Total:</strong></font></td>
    <td valign="center" align="right" bgcolor="#000080">
    <font color="#FF0000" size="4">
    <strong><div id="TotalText"></div></strong></font></td>
  </tr>
</TFOOT>
</table>

<!-- START modified from Listing 19.4 -->
<hr>
<p id="pagesizetext" align="center">Page Size: 5</p>
<p align="center"><strong><input type="button" value="Previous Page" name="B1"
onclick="scrollpage(0)"> <input type="button" value="Next Page" name="B1"
onclick="scrollpage(1)"> </strong></p>

<p align="center"><input type="button" value="Decrease Page Size" name="B1"
onclick="pagesize(0)"><strong>
<input type="button" value="Increase Page Size" name="B1"
onclick="pagesize(1)"></strong></p>

<p align="center"><input type="button" value="Disable Table Paging" name="B1"
onclick="pagesize(2)"></p>
<!-- END modified from Listing 19.4 -->

<script language="VBScript"><!--
sub tableclick(columnname)

if columnname <> "year" and
➥    (left(document.all.item("year").innertext,1) = "+"
➥    or left(document.all.item("year").innertext,1) = "-") then
       document.all.item("year").innerHTML = "<big>" +
➥         mid(document.all.item("year").innertext,2) + "</big>"
end if
```

```
if columnname <> "cardnumber" and
➡   (left(document.all.item("cardnumber").innertext,1) = "+" or
➡   left(document.all.item("cardnumber").innertext,1) = "-") then
      document.all.item("cardnumber").innerHTML = "<big>" +
➡         mid(document.all.item("cardnumber").innertext,2) + "</big>"
end if

if columnname <> "setname" and
➡   (left(document.all.item("setname").innertext,1) = "+" or
➡   left(document.all.item("setname").innertext,1) = "-") then
      document.all.item("setname").innerHTML = "<big>" +
➡         mid(document.all.item("setname").innertext,2) + "</big>"
end if

if columnname <> "issuer" and
➡   (left(document.all.item("issuer").innertext,1) = "+" or
➡   left(document.all.item("issuer").innertext,1) = "-") then
      document.all.item("issuer").innerHTML = "<big>" +
➡         mid(document.all.item("issuer").innertext,2) + "</big>"
end if

if columnname <> "description" and
➡   (left(document.all.item("description").innertext,1) = "+" or
➡   left(document.all.item("description").innertext,1) = "-") then
      document.all.item("description").innerHTML = "<big>" +
➡         mid(document.all.item("description").innertext,2) + "</big>"
end if

if columnname <> "grade" and
➡   (left(document.all.item("grade").innertext,1) = "+" or
➡   left(document.all.item("grade").innertext,1) = "-") then
      document.all.item("grade").innerHTML = "<big>" +
➡         mid(document.all.item("grade").innertext,2) + "</big>"
end if

if columnname <> "value" and
➡   (left(document.all.item("value").innertext,1) = "+" or
➡   left(document.all.item("value").innertext,1) = "-") then
      document.all.item("value").innerHTML = "<big>" +
➡         mid(document.all.item("value").innertext,2) + "</big>"
end if

if left(document.all.item(columnname).innertext,1) = "+" then
   document.all.item(columnname).innerHTML =  "<big>-" +
➡      mid(document.all.item(columnname).innertext,2) + "</big>"
   cards.sort = "-" + columnname
elseif left(document.all.item(columnname).innertext,1) = "-" then
   document.all.item(columnname).innerHTML = "<big>+" +
➡      mid(document.all.item(columnname).innertext,2) + "</big>"
   cards.sort = columnname
else
   document.all.item(columnname).innerHTML = "<big>+" +
➡      document.all.item(columnname).innertext + "</big>"
   cards.sort = columnname
end if

cards.reset
```

continues

Listing 19.5. continued

```
end sub

sub buttonclick(button)

if (left(document.all.item("year").innertext,1) = "+" or
➥  left(document.all.item("year").innertext,1) = "-") then
    document.all.item("year").innerHTML = "<big>" +
➥        mid(document.all.item("year").innertext,2) + "</big>"
end if

if (left(document.all.item("cardnumber").innertext,1) = "+" or
➥  left(document.all.item("cardnumber").innertext,1) = "-") then
    document.all.item("cardnumber").innerHTML = "<big>" +
➥        mid(document.all.item("cardnumber").innertext,2) + "</big>"
end if

if (left(document.all.item("setname").innertext,1) = "+" or
➥  left(document.all.item("setname").innertext,1) = "-") then
    document.all.item("setname").innerHTML = "<big>" +
➥        mid(document.all.item("setname").innertext,2) + "</big>"
end if

if (left(document.all.item("issuer").innertext,1) = "+" or
➥  left(document.all.item("issuer").innertext,1) = "-") then
    document.all.item("issuer").innerHTML = "<big>" +
➥        mid(document.all.item("issuer").innertext,2) + "</big>"
end if

if (left(document.all.item("description").innertext,1) = "+" or
➥  left(document.all.item("description").innertext,1) = "-") then
    document.all.item("description").innerHTML = "<big>" +
➥        mid(document.all.item("description").innertext,2) + "</big>"
end if

if (left(document.all.item("grade").innertext,1) = "+" or
➥  left(document.all.item("grade").innertext,1) = "-") then
    document.all.item("grade").innerHTML = "<big>" +
➥        mid(document.all.item("grade").innertext,2) + "</big>"
end if

if (left(document.all.item("value").innertext,1) = "+" or
➥  left(document.all.item("value").innertext,1) = "-") then
    document.all.item("value").innerHTML = "<big>" +
➥        mid(document.all.item("value").innertext,2) + "</big>"
end if

select case button
case 1
    document.all.item("year").innerHTML = "<big>+" +
➥            document.all.item("year").innertext + "</big>"
    document.all.item("cardnumber").innerHTML = "<big>+" +
➥            document.all.item("cardnumber").innertext + "</big>"
    cards.sort = "year; cardnumber"
case 2
    document.all.item("description").innerHTML = "<big>+" +
➥            document.all.item("description").innertext + "</big>"
    cards.sort = "description"
```

```
case 3
    document.all.item("year").innerHTML = "<big>+" +
➥            document.all.item("year").innertext + "</big>"
    document.all.item("grade").innerHTML = "<big>+" +
➥            document.all.item("grade").innertext + "</big>"
    cards.sort = "year; grade"
case 4
    document.all.item("value").innerHTML = "<big>+" +
➥            document.all.item("value").innertext + "</big>"
    cards.sort = "value"
end select

cards.reset
end sub

sub filteryear(reset)

if reset then
    fstring = ""
else
    fstring = "year = " + document.forms("filterform").item("filteryear").value
end if

cards.filter = fstring
cards.reset

end sub

<!-- START modified from Listing 19.4 -->
sub scrollpage(direction)

if direction = 0 then
    mytable.previouspage
else
    mytable.nextpage
end if

end sub

sub pagesize(direction)

if direction = 0 and mytable.datapagesize > 1 then
    mytable.datapagesize = mytable.datapagesize - 1
    document.all.pagesizetext.innertext = "Page Size: "
➥        + cstr(mytable.datapagesize)
elseif direction = 1 then
    mytable.datapagesize = mytable.datapagesize + 1
    document.all.pagesizetext.innertext = "Page Size: "
➥        + cstr(mytable.datapagesize)
elseif direction = 2 then
    mytable.datapagesize = 0
    document.all.pagesizetext.innertext = "Table paging disabled"
end if

end sub
<!-- END modified from Listing 19.4 -->
```

19

CLIENT-SIDE DATA MANIPULATION

continues

Listing 19.5. continued

```
sub dataloaded()

while not(cards.recordset.eof)
   total = total + cards.recordset("value")
   cards.recordset.movenext
wend
document.all.totaltext.innertext = total

end sub
--></script>
</body></html>
```

FIGURE 19.5.

The results of using data paging.

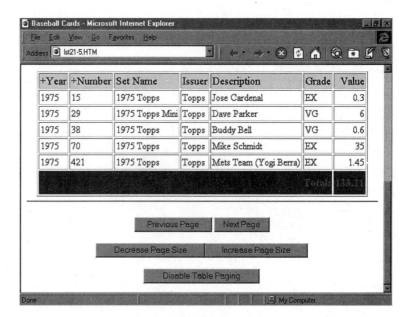

The first modification is to add the DATAPAGESIZE attribute to the <TABLE> tag. I initially set this to 5, meaning that the table will show, at most, five records at a time.

Immediately following the close of the <TABLE> tag is a text label and series of buttons. The text label will inform the user, using dynamic content, of the current table page size. The buttons will be used to scroll the pages as well as affect the dataPageSize property of our data-bound table. The code for these buttons is found within the <SCRIPT> tag, right where you'd expect it to be.

The code to move from page to page is pretty simple. There is no property for the table object that will let you know which page you're currently viewing, so there's no bounds checking. As a matter of fact, the previousPage and nextPage methods won't even produce errors if you attempt to go beyond the first or last pages. So, we simply invoke the appropriate method, depending on which button was clicked.

For the page size buttons, the code is found in the `pagesize()` routine. We have three choices: decrease, increase, or disable. If the user decides to decrease the page size, we first verify that the value is greater than 1. If it is, we'll decrease it; otherwise, we simply ignore the button click. We allow the user to increase the page size to whatever value he or she wishes. To disable the table paging, the `dataPageSize` property is set to `0`. For any button click, the text displayed in the `pagesizetext` element is modified to show the current state of the `dataPageSize` property.

As you can see, it's a relatively trivial task to add table paging to your DHTML pages. You'll probably want to include the option of table paging on every data-bound page you write.

Summary

This chapter covers the three most important aspects of client-side data manipulation: sorting, filtering, and paging. Using these techniques, you're well on your way to creating professional data–browsing HTML pages. Prior to DHTML and DSOs, all these techniques required some sort of round-trip to the Web server in order to retrieve new data for each action performed. Now, not only are you not required to make such a round-trip, but you also don't even need a Web server to serve these pages to you. DHTML takes care of all this for you.

In Chapter 20, "Updating the Data," we'll discuss the next step in creating a database application with DHTML: editing and updating data. Although the TDC does not directly support the updating of data, I'll show you how you can combine HTML forms with a back-end process (either CGI or Active Server Pages) to update the TDC's data file.

This method, while fine for single-user applications, falls on its face if multiple users attempt to update the data at the same time. For that reason, we'll also examine the Remote Data Services, which combine a client-side DSO with some server-side objects to provide two-way connections to an ODBC data source.

Updating the Data

by Craig Eddy

IN THIS CHAPTER

CHAPTER 20

Chapters 18, "Presenting Your Data with Dynamic HTML," and 19, "Client-side Data Manipulation," deal with presenting data on DHTML pages and providing some rudimentary data manipulation features, such as sorting and filtering. In this chapter we'll look at providing data-updating capabilities in your DHTML pages.

There are two possible locations for data updating: on the client (that is, at the page's display point) and on the server. Prior to DHTML and data source objects (DSOs), the server-side approach was the only approach available to the site developer. With DHTML, the possibility of client-side data updating is opened up.

The server-side approach requires some application, such as a CGI application or Perl script, to exist on the HTTP server machine. Microsoft introduced Active Server Pages, which can execute server-side VBScript, including accessing any ActiveX component that is installed on the HTTP server. This allows Active Server Pages to access the ActiveX Data Objects (a technology similar to, and built on the same platform as, DSOs) to both retrieve and update data contained in ODBC data sources. Even with Active Server Pages, though, you're relying exclusively on the capabilities and resources of the HTTP server machine.

Using DSOs, you can provide the capability of updating data through DHTML pages. To do so, though, you must be using a DSO that allows you to update the database. The Tabular Data Control (TDC) does not allow data updating. The Advanced Data Control (ADC), which is part of Microsoft's Remote Data Services (RDS) platform and is automatically installed with Internet Explorer 4.0 (IE4), does allow data updating. The ADC must work in conjunction with a server-side piece of the RDS but still provides you with all of the benefits of client-side data manipulation and caching.

This chapter briefly discusses using Active Server Pages and the ActiveX data objects to update data on the server side. The remainder of the chapter covers using the functionality provided by ADC and RDS. The examples in this chapter are built using a database created from the TDC data file used in Chapter 19. The database was created in Microsoft Access and the file, `cards.mdb`, is included on the Companion Web site at `http://www.htmlguru.com`.

Creating an ODBC Data Source

Both the Active Server Page and RDS solutions to updating data require the use of ODBC. To open a connection to an ODBC data source, you must first have a data source to open. The data source used must be a system data source that is accessible by your Web server machine.

To create such a data source, you'll need a few key pieces of information:

■ The database management system (DBMS) on which the data resides. Examples are SQL Server, Oracle, and Microsoft Access.

■ The name of the database and, if applicable, the name of the server on which the database resides.

■ Any required login credentials, such as username and password, required to open and validate a connection to the data source.

When you've gathered the necessary information, you can create the data source. The steps vary depending on the needs of the DBMS and the ODBC driver that connects to it, as well as the version of the ODBC driver manager you have installed, but they'll probably follow the general path presented here:

1. Start the Control Panel application by clicking the Windows Start button and selecting Settings and then Control Panel.

2. Double-click the 32-bit ODBC icon. The ODBC Data Source Administrator application is displayed, as shown in Figure 20.1.

FIGURE 20.1.

The ODBC Data Source Administrator.

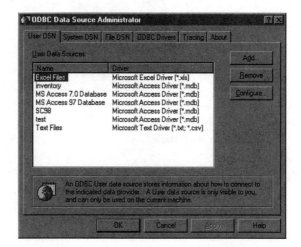

3. Select the System DSN tab. You must create a system DSN as opposed to a user DSN because the Web server runs as a system service, not as a logged-in user. A system DSN is valid for every user of the particular system as well as any service running on the system.

4. Click the Add button. The Create New Data Source dialog, shown in Figure 20.2, is displayed. The drivers shown in the list box are the ODBC drivers that have been installed on the system. If the driver you need is not present, you must install it on the system before it can be used. The installation process depends on the individual driver.

5. In the list box, select the ODBC driver that matches the database to which you're connecting. Then click the Finish button.

6. The ODBC data source setup dialog for the driver chosen in step 5 is displayed. Although this dialog is different for each driver, they all have two things in common: a data source name and a database location. Some drivers might require additional

information to complete the definition of the data source. If you need help defining the data source, click the Help button. The driver-specific help file will be displayed.

7. After you've entered the necessary information, click the OK button to save the data source information and return to the ODBC Data Source Administrator.

FIGURE 20.2.

The Create New Data Source dialog.

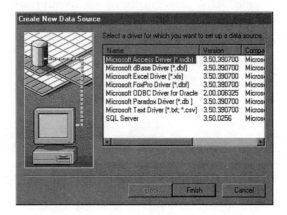

Now that you've created the data source, you can use it with Active Server Pages containing ActiveX Data Objects or with the RDS.

Server-side Data Updates

To update data using a server-side process, you must have an application or Active Server Page that runs on the Web server machine. This application requires server resources and network bandwidth in the process of retrieving the data changes from the user and modifying the underlying data source. (This section discusses using Active Server Pages in combination with ADO to update the data.)

Active Server Pages, which are installed with Microsoft's Internet Information Server, combine server-side VBScript, JScript, or any other Active Script language with server-side components. If you're familiar with VBScript (or Visual Basic itself) or JScript, you won't have any trouble picking up Active Server Page programming. The scripting code is parsed by the Web server before the page is returned to the browser. None of the Active Server Page script code is actually returned to the user. This allows you to hide the implementation details from the browser, thus making both your code and your data more secure. In addition, because Active Server scripting can access and manipulate ActiveX components, you can further encapsulate your code by creating an ActiveX component.

The ActiveX Data Objects (ADO) are a set of data-access objects contained with an ActiveX component installed with Active Server Pages. Using the ADO is very similar to using its cousins, Remote Data Objects (RDO) and Data Access Objects (DAO). Both of these technologies will be familiar to you if you've done any database programming using Visual Basic.

Creating an Active Server Page

Active Server Pages combine HTML with server-side scripting. The script code is delimited from the HTML using the characters `<%` and `%>` to mark the start and end of server-side script. The HTTP server executes this script code as it parses the page for return to the browser. (For the purposes of this chapter, I'll work only with VBScript.)

After you have the Active Server Page system files installed on your Web server, you must create a Web-accessible directory with executable permission to house them. You can then use a text editor or any HTML editor that supports scripting to create the Active Server Page files. If you'll be doing a great deal of Active Server Page coding, I recommend investing in a copy of Microsoft Visual InterDev. InterDev is a complete Web server programming environment that includes the Visual Data Tools, a set of handy tools for creating database tables, queries, stored procedures, and triggers, as well as manipulating the data itself.

You can place script code either in line or within procedures. Placing the script in line allows you to alter the HTML that is returned to the browser based on the code's execution. For example, the following snippet will place the current date into the page:

```
<H2>Today's date is <%= Date() %>.</H2>
```

The marker `<%=` instructs the parser to output the results of the expression to follow in place of the marker. If you use this construct, make sure your expression returns a value that can be displayed properly by the parser.

Or, for a more complicated example, the following uses an `If...Then` statement to control the browser output:

```
<% If rs("date") = Date() then %>
<H2>This appointment is for Today.</H2>
<% elseif rs("date") < Date() then %>
<H2>This appointment is for a date in the past.</H2>
<% else %>
<H2>This appointment is for a date in the future. </H2>
<% end if %>
```

When this code is executed by the Active Server Page parser, only one of the `<H2>` lines will be returned to the browser. Viewers of the page, even if they use View Source, won't have any idea how the line was placed onto the page.

Script code does not necessarily have to return HTML or anything at all. It can simply be executed. This will be necessary for accomplishing data updates using Active Server Pages. The code is still executed as it is stumbled upon by the parser. If no HTML is returned, nothing is placed in the output page for that section of code. The following section discusses how to use the ADO to actually update data provided by an HTML form.

The Active Server Page system has several built-in objects, including `server`, `request`, and `response`. The `server` object provides access to several utility functions available on the Web server. This includes the all-important `CreateObject` method, which is used to create instances of ActiveX components installed on the server. The `request` object provides access to the data

20

UPDATING THE DATA

passed from the Web browser to the Web server during the HTTP request. This includes any data passed either within the page's URL or within an HTTP POST request message (such as from an HTML form). The response object is used to specify the data and server properties that will be returned to the Web browser in the HTTP response message.

Introducing the ActiveX Data Objects

The ADO components are high-speed, lightweight data-access objects specifically designed for use with Microsoft OLE DB providers such as ODBC. The ADO, as you'll see in this chapter, has a very flat object model. This makes it particularly easy to program in the Active Server environment because you do not have to traverse an entire object model to get your database work accomplished.

The ADO includes only six objects of any significance: connection, recordset, field, command, error, and parameter (see Figure 20.3).

FIGURE 20.3.

The ADO object model.

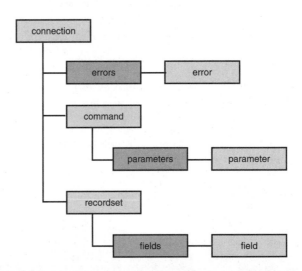

NOTE

For more information on the ADO, please refer to *Microsoft Visual InterDev Unleashed* by Sams.net Publishing where you'll find a chapter titled "Integrating ActiveX Database Components."

The connection object is used to establish the physical connection to the data source. The recordset object contains the properties and methods we'll use in updating the database. The other objects, though they serve useful purposes elsewhere, won't be necessary for our purposes here.

To use a `connection` object to access a data source, you'll use code similar to the following:

```
<%
set conn = Server.CreateObject("ADODB.Connection")
conn.open "DSN=AdvWorks;", "sa", "secret"
%>
```

This code creates a new object named `conn` using the `CreateObject` method of the `Server` object. The `Server` object is a built-in object that is always available to Active Server Page code. The method's parameter specifies the programmatic class identifier of the object being created. In this case we're creating an ADO `connection` object.

To open a recordset using this connection, you can code the following:

```
<%
set rs = Server.CreateObject("ADODB.recordset")
rs.Open "Products", conn, 1, 3, 2
%>
```

The first parameter of the `Open` method is the table name. The second parameter is the `Connection` object that was opened on the database. The third and fourth are the cursor type and lock type to be used when accessing the data in the table. The last parameter specifies that the first parameter is a table name. (The first parameter could also have been a SQL statement, a stored procedure name, or any other command supported by the data provider.)

After the recordset is successfully opened, you can navigate its records or use any of the methods available to the `recordset` object. We'll see an example of this in the section "The Advanced Data Control," but first let's examine how to create an ODBC data source you can use to open the connection in the first place.

Updating Data with the ActiveX Data Objects

Now that we've seen how to create `recordset` objects and ODBC data sources, it's time to put that knowledge to use. The `recordset` object provides you with access to the fields in the underlying data source. If the recordset was opened using an updatable cursor and lock type, you can modify any updatable field and use the object's `Update` method to store the changes back to the data source.

Remember that because this is a server-side activity, you must have some means of submitting any data modifications to the Web server. For this example we'll use an HTML form with a submit button that activates an Active Server Page file. This file outputs the data for a given card onto the form. The code for this Active Server Page file is provided in Listing 20.1. The ODBC data source used in these files points to the `cards.mdb` file created for the trading card database. The data could also have been provided by a DHTML DSO that can access ODBC data sources.

20

UPDATING THE
DATA

Listing 20.1. Active Server Page to retrieve data into an HTML form.

```
<html><head><title>Data Editing Form</title></head>

<body>
<%set conn = server.createobject("ADODB.connection")
conn.open "DSN=Cards"

set rs = Server.createobject("ADODB.recordset")
rs.open "Select * from Cards where CardID = " + request("CardID"), conn, 3, 1, 1
%>

<form method="POST" action="update.asp?CardID=<%=request("CardID")%>">
  <p>Year: <input type="text" name="Year" size="20" value="<%=rs("Year")%>"></p>
  <p>Issuer: <input type="text" name="Issuer" size="20"
  value="<%=rs("Issuer")%>"></p>
  <p>Set Name: <input type="text" name="SetName" size="20"
  value="<%=rs("SetName")%>"></p>
  <p>Card Number: <input type="text" name="CardNumber" size="20"
  value="<%=rs("CardNumber")%>"></p>
  <p>Description: <input type="text" name="Description" size="50"
  value="<%=rs("Description")%>"></p>
  <p>Grade: <input type="text" name="Grade" size="20"
  value="<%=rs("Grade")%>"></p>
  <p>Value: <input type="text" name="Value" size="20"
  value="<%=rs("Value")%>"></p>
  <p><input type="submit" value="Submit Changes" name="B1">
  <input type="reset" value="Reset"
  name="B2"></p>
</form>
</body></html>
```

As you can see, this is a pretty straightforward piece of code. A connection object and a recordset object are opened to retrieve the data from the database. Then an HTML <FORM> tag is started. The action for this form is another Active Server Page, which takes posted data from the form as well as a URL parameter specifying the value for the CardID field. Then a text box is output for each field that can be updated. The initial value for each text box is taken from the recordset opened earlier in the page (this is specified in the VALUE element of each <INPUT> tag). Finally, the form's buttons are placed onto the page.

The update.asp file referenced in the <FORM> tag's ACTION element is shown in Listing 20.2.

Listing 20.2. Active Server Page to update data received from the HTML form.

```
<html><head><title>Submit Changes</title></head>
<body>
<%set conn = server.createobject("ADODB.connection")
conn.open "DSN=Cards"

set rs = Server.createobject("ADODB.recordset")
rs.open "Select * from Cards where CardID = " + request("CardID"), conn, 1, 2, 1

rs("Year") = request("Year")
rs("Issuer") = request("Issuer")
rs("SetName") = request("SetName")
```

```
rs("CardNumber") = request("CardNumber")
rs("Description") = request("Description")
rs("Grade") = request("Grade")
rs("Value") = request("Value")

on error resume next
rs.Update

if err then %>
<h2 align="center">An error occurred updating the database:</h2>
<h3 align="center"><%= err.description %></h3>
<% else %>
<h2 align="center">Updates successful!</h2>
<% end if %>
</body></html>
```

Again, the code opens a connection and a recordset object. The recordset's fields are then updated with the data passed from the HTML form in the request object. The request object is referenced using the NAME element from the form's <INPUT> elements. The recordset's Update method is then invoked, and the result of the method is output to the browser.

This is all well and good, you're probably thinking, but what has this got to do with DHTML? To be honest, the only thing it has to do with DHTML is to serve as a stark contrast to the method used with DHTML. Using the Active Server Page approach requires several trips to the server: one trip to retrieve the data placed on the HTML form and a round-trip to post the updated data to the database and to determine whether the update was successful.

Using DSOs, as we'll see in the next section, does not require an HTTP round-trip. Instead, the client-side DSO caches the data and communicates updates directly with the server-side RDS components. This lightens the load on the Web server and provides a much more efficient data access mechanism.

Introducing the Remote Data Services

Microsoft's Remote Data Services (RDS) provide the capability to update data contained in ODBC-compliant data sources using a client-side DSO. The RDS provides complete database connectivity to your Internet and intranet applications. By combining the RDS with ActiveX components, HTML, and VBScript, you can quickly and easily port existing Visual Basic applications to Web-based applications.

With the RDS, you can do the following:

- Bind data-aware controls, including DHTML elements, to data on remote servers.
- View, edit, and update this remote data.
- Utilize the DSO's client-side data caching capabilities, thereby reducing the required number of round-trips to the HTTP or database server.
- Create three-tiered systems using the Web server or server-based ActiveX components as the middle tier.

■ Secure the data using the Secured Sockets Layer technologies available with Internet Information Server.

All these benefits are extremely useful to Web site developers, both for Internet and intranet applications. The RDS provides you with a complete platform upon which to develop data-aware Web-based applications.

To use RDS, you'll need the following software configuration on your Web server machine:

■ Microsoft Windows NT Server, version 4.0 Service Pack 3 or later, or Windows 95.

■ Internet Information Server (IIS) 3.0 or Windows 95 Personal Web Server, both with Microsoft Active Server Pages installed.

■ An ODBC Level 2–compliant data source, such as Microsoft SQL Server 6.5 or Microsoft Access 97. (See the earlier section "Creating an ODBC Data Source" for details on setting up a data source.)

To install the server-side RDS system files to your IIS machine, download the necessary files from the Microsoft Web site at `http://www.microsoft.com/data`. As of this writing, the latest version of RDS was a beta of version 1.5.

The client side of RDS, the Advanced Data Control, is installed automatically when IE4 is installed. As of this writing, the ADC had not been successfully tested with the Netscape Navigator 4.0.

More information regarding the RDS can be obtained from Microsoft's Internet Client Software Developer's Kit, downloadable from `http://www.microsoft.com/workshop/prog/inetsdk/`.

The Advanced Data Control

The ADC is the first tier of the RDS's three-tiered data access approach. The ADC provides all of the capabilities of the TDC (discussed in Chapters 18 and 19), plus the capability to access remote data and to update that data.

The class ID for the ADC is `BD96C556-65A3-11D0-983A-00C04FC29E33`. To insert an ADC into a Web page, use the following syntax:

```
<OBJECT CLASSID="clsid:BD96C556-65A3-11D0-983A-00C04FC29E33"
        ID="AdvancedDataControl">
</OBJECT>
```

You can also specify the initial values for properties such as `Connect`, `Server`, and `SQL` in `<PARAM>` tags within the `<OBJECT>` tag. We'll examine the properties and methods of the ADC in the following sections.

Properties

The ADC has many of the same properties that the TDC has. Several properties, such as those involving sorting and filtering, provide the same functionality as the TDC but use different (often more straightforward) script code.

Connect

The Connect property sets or returns the ODBC data source's connection string. This string is made up of the name given to the data source as well as any user authentication information necessary to complete the connection to the data source. The format for this string is as follows, where *user* is the name of a valid user on the database and *password* is that user's database login password:

```
DSN=DataSourceName;UID=user;PWD=password
```

This property can be set at runtime using VBScript code or at design time using the <PARAM> tag found in the object's <OBJECT> tag.

ExecuteOptions

The ExecuteOptions property's setting controls asynchronous operation of the ADC. Left at its default value (0), no asynchronous operation takes place. The property can also be set to adAsyncExecute or adAsyncFetch, in which case data is retrieved asynchronously. You can check the value of the State property after a Refresh or Reset method to verify whether a query is still executing (adStateExecuting), an error has occurred (adStateClosed), or the fetch has completed (adStateOpen).

> **NOTE**
>
> The values for the constants mentioned (such as adAsyncExecute) can be obtained from the file ADCVBS.INC, which is installed in the C:\Program Files\Common Files\System\MSADC folder when the RDS system files are installed.

FilterColumn, FilterCriterion, and FilterValue

FilterColumn, FilterCriterion, and FilterValue, in combination with the Reset method, allow you to filter the data available in the ADC's recordset. The FilterColumn property holds the name of the field to be used to evaluate the filter. The FilterCriterion property holds the evaluation operator to be used when evaluating the filter. Valid values for this string property are <, <=, >, >=, =, and <> (not equal). The FilterValue property is a string property that holds the value used to filter the data. After these properties have been set, invoking the Reset method executes the filter and replaces the current recordset with a read-only recordset containing only records matching the filter.

For example, to filter the cards.mdb database for cards whose year field equals 1976, the following code would be used:

```
Cards.FilterColumn = "year"
Cards.FilterCriterion = "="
Cards.FilterValue = "1976"
Cards.Reset
```

By invoking `Reset(True)`, you can filter the data available from a previous filter. If you specify `Reset(False)` or do not provide this optional parameter, the original data set is considered for the filter evaluation. For example, to view only those cards from 1976 having a `value` field greater than $10, you would use the following code:

```
Cards.FilterColumn = "year"
Cards.FilterCriterion = "="
Cards.FilterValue = "1976"
Cards.Reset

Cards.FilterColumn = "value"
Cards.FilterCriterion = ">"
Cards.FilterValue = "10"
Cards.Reset(True)
```

Recordset and SourceRecordset

`Recordset` and `SourceRecordset` are ActiveX Data Object recordsets that provide you with a means of accessing the ADC's underlying data. The `Recordset` property is read-only and will be the most often used of these two. This is the recordset provided by the default RDS system (that is, without using custom ActiveX components in the middle tier).

The `SourceRecordset` property is a write-only property that you will set to the `recordset` object returned by a custom ActiveX component (also known as a *business object*). Creating business objects for use with RDS is an advanced topic best left for an entire book on the subject of RDS. Microsoft's Web site has plenty of information on creating these objects as well. Visit `http://www.microsoft.com/data/rds/rds_doc/default.htm` to view the Remote Data Services documentation.

Server

The `Server` property, which can be set in a `<PARAM>` tag or at runtime, specifies the name of the HTTP server machine as well as the protocol used to communicate with that machine (`http:` or `https:`). This property is necessary for the ADC to connect with the server-side components of the RDS system.

SQL

The `SQL` property, which can be set in a `<PARAM>` tag or at runtime, specifies the query string used to retrieve data from the data source. This property should be set to a valid SQL-92 syntax SQL statement such as `Select * From Cards`. Unless you're using a custom business object for the middle tier, this property is required in order for the ADC to retrieve any data.

You are not limited to SQL statements that return data. You can also execute any action queries, such as SQL `UPDATE`, that are supported by the ODBC driver for the data source that the ADC is using. We'll see an example of updating data with this method in the section "Updating Data Using the ADC."

SortColumn and SortDirection

The SortColumn property specifies the name of the field to be used to sort the recordset's data. The SortDirection property specifies the order of the sort. Setting SortDirection to True indicates an ascending sort order; setting it to False indicates descending sort order. After these properties are set, invoke the Reset method to enact the new sort specification.

State

The State property returns the current state of the ADC's recordset object. The possible values follow:

State	Description
adStateClosed	The recordset is closed.
adStateOpen	The recordset is open.
adStateExecuting	The ADC is executing asynchronously.
adStateFetching	The ADC is fetching data asynchronously.

If an error occurs, the value of State changes to adStateClosed.

Methods

The ADC provides several methods similar to the TDC and two important methods that aren't provided by the TDC: CancelUpdate and SubmitChanges.

Cancel

The Cancel method, when invoked, cancels the current asynchronous operation. If the ADC was asynchronously fetching records, the fetch is canceled. The State property is immediately set to adStateClosed, and Recordset will evaluate to the value Nothing.

CancelUpdate

The CancelUpdate method discards any changes that have been made to the client-side copy of the data. The values of the recordset's fields are set to their values at the last Refresh method call. Any data-bound controls have their data restored to the original values as well.

CreateRecordset

This method, another of the advanced features provided for use with custom middle-tier business objects, allows you to create a new recordset object and specify its layout (that is, information about the fields it contains).

MoveFirst, MoveLast, MoveNext, and MovePrevious

MoveFirst, MoveLast, MoveNext, and MovePrevious, used mostly with current record binding, are used to navigate the ADC's recordset object. Typically, pages that use current record binding will provide buttons for navigating forward and backward through the data, as well as moving to the first or last record. These methods provide the muscle behind those buttons.

Refresh

The Refresh method causes the ADC to query the data source, fetch a fresh copy of the data set, and to discard any changes that have not been saved. The Server, Connect, and SQL properties must be set prior to invoking Refresh. This method differs from the Reset method in that it actually goes out to the remote data source and retrieves the data again. After Refresh is called, the first record in the recordset is made the current record.

Reset

The Reset method executes the sort or filter specified by the SortColumn, SortDirection, FilterValue, FilterCriterion, and FilterColumn properties. This operation acts on the cached copy of the recordset, thus preventing a round-trip to the server.

This method has an optional parameter that specifies whether the filter should be applied to the current filtered data (pass True) or to the original copy of the recordset before any previous filters were applied (leave the parameter off or set to False).

SubmitChanges

The SubmitChanges method is used to save the modified data to the underlying data source. The Server, Connect, and SQL properties must be set prior to invoking SubmitChanges.

You do not have to invoke this method each time a record is updated. Instead, you can allow the user to update a "batch" of records and then invoke SubmitChanges. Using this method, either all updates succeed or all updates fail.

This method cannot be used if you're using a custom business object on the middle tier.

Updating Data Using the ADC

Now that we've learned all about the properties and methods of the ADC, let's put that knowledge to use. We've already seen how to update data using Active Server Pages. This involves several Active Server Page files and several round-trips between the browser, the Web server, and the database.

Using the ADC, the number of round-trips will be cut dramatically, thanks to the client-side data caching. For example, there will only be a single round-trip made to retrieve the data and editing page. Subsequently, data will be retrieved from the client-side data cache instead of having to open an Active Server Page file such as the one in Listing 20.1.

This section discusses two methods of updating the data: using a SQL UPDATE statement and using the ADC's SubmitChanges method.

Creating a Data Editing Page

The first step is to create a DHTML page to be used when updating the database. We'll use current record binding and place text boxes on the page to hold the field values. We could also use a data-bound grid to allow editing of many records at once.

Figure 20.4 shows the page we'll use to edit the data. The First, Prev, Next, and Last buttons are used to move the record pointer through the recordset. The Requery button forces a refresh of the data cache, and the Save Changes button stores the data to the database. The HTML for this page is shown in Listing 20.3.

FIGURE 20.4.

The Trading Card Database Editor page.

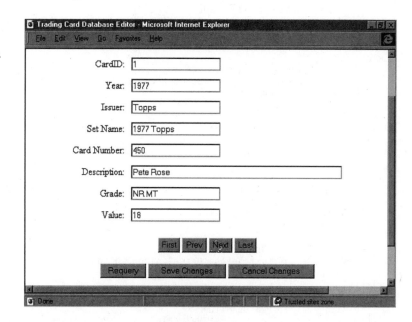

Listing 20.3. The HTML for the Trading Card Database Editor page.

```html
<html><head><title>Trading Card Database Editor</title></head>
<body
bgcolor="ffffff" text="000000" link="000080" language="VBS" onload="Init">

<object classid="clsid:BD96C556-65A3-11D0-983A-00C04FC29E33"
        id="ADC" height="1" width="1">
</object>

<h1 align="center">Trading Card Database Editor</h1>

<p align="center"><br>
<br>
</p>
<div align="center"><center>

<table border="0" cellpadding="5">
  <tr>
    <td align="right">CardID:</td>
    <td><input type="text" name="CardID" size="20" datasrc="#ADC"
        datafld="CardID"></td>
  </tr>
  <tr>
    <td align="right">Year:</td>
```

continues

Listing 20.3. continued

```
      <td><input type="text" name="YearFld" size="20" datasrc="#ADC"
          datafld="year"></td>
  </tr>
  <tr>
    <td align="right">Issuer:</td>
    <td><input type="text" name="Issuer" size="20" datasrc="#ADC"
        datafld="Issuer"></td>
  </tr>
  <tr>
    <td align="right">Set Name:</td>
    <td><input type="text" name="SetName" size="20" datasrc="#ADC"
        datafld="SetName"></td>
  </tr>
  <tr>
    <td align="right">Card Number:</td>
    <td><input type="text" name="CardNumber" size="20" datasrc="#ADC"
        datafld="CardNumber"></td>
  </tr>
  <tr>
    <td align="right">Description:</td>
    <td><input type="text" name="Description" size="50" datasrc="#ADC"
        datafld="Description"></td>
  </tr>
  <tr>
    <td align="right">Grade:</td>
    <td><input type="text" name="Grade" size="20" datasrc="#ADC"
        datafld="Grade"></td>
  </tr>
  <tr>
    <td align="right">Value:</td>
    <td><input type="text" name="ValueFld" size="20" datasrc="#ADC"
        datafld="CardValue"></td>
  </tr>
</table>
</center></div>

<p align="center"><input type="BUTTON" name="First" value="First"
onclick="MoveFirst"> <input type="BUTTON" name="Prev" value="Prev"
onclick="MovePrev"> <input type="BUTTON" name="Next" value="Next"
onclick="MoveNext"> <input type="BUTTON" name="Last" value="Last"
onclick="MoveLast"> <br>
<br>
<input type="BUTTON" name="Run" value="Requery" onclick="Requery">
<input type="BUTTON" name="Update" value="Save Changes" onclick="Update">
<input type="BUTTON" name="Cancel" value="Cancel Changes" onclick="Cancel"> </p>

<p>SQL UPDATE:<br>
<input type="text" name="SQL" size="100"></p>

<script language="VBScript" onload="Init"><!--

SUB MoveFirst
    ADC.Recordset.MoveFirst
END SUB

SUB MoveNext
  On Error Resume Next
```

```
    ADC.Recordset.MoveNext
    IF ERR.Number <> 0 THEN
      ADC.Recordset.MoveLast   'If already at end of recordset stay at end.
    END IF
END SUB

SUB MovePrev
  On Error Resume Next
  ADC.Recordset.MovePrevious
  IF ERR.Number <> 0 THEN
    ADC.Recordset.MoveFirst   'If already at start of recordset stay at top.
  END IF
END SUB

SUB MoveLast
  ADC.Recordset.MoveLast
END SUB

'Submits edits made and pull a clean copy of the new data.
SUB Update
  ssql = "Update Cards Set "
  ssql = ssql + "Year = " + yearfld.value + ", "
  ssql = ssql + "Issuer = '" + issuer.value + "', "
  ssql = ssql + "SetName = '" + setname.value + "', "
  ssql = ssql + "CardNumber = " + cardnumber.value + ", "
  ssql = ssql + "Description = '" + description.value + "', "
  ssql = ssql + "Grade = '" + grade.value + "', "
  ssql = ssql + "CardValue = " + valuefld.value + " "
  ssql = ssql + "WHERE CardID = " + CardID.Value

  SQL.value = ssql

  ADC.SQL = ssql
  ADC.Refresh

    ADC.SQL = "Select * from Cards"
    ADC.Refresh

END SUB

'Cancel edits and restores original values.
SUB Cancel
  ADC.CancelUpdate
END SUB

SUB Requery
  ADC.Server = "http://<%=Request.ServerVariables("SERVER_NAME")%>"
  ADC.Connect = "DSN=Cards"
  ADC.SQL = "Select * from Cards"
  ADC.Refresh

END SUB

SUB Init
  ADC.Server = "http://<%=Request.ServerVariables("SERVER_NAME")%>"
  ADC.Connect = "DSN=Cards"
  ADC.SQL = "Select * from Cards"
```

20

UPDATING THE
DATA

continues

Listing 20.3. continued

```
 ADC.Refresh

END SUB

--></script>
</body></html>
```

The first major item in this page is the ADC's <OBJECT> tag. None of the design-time parameters are set. Instead, a procedure named Init is used to initialize the ADC control. Each of the
buttons also has its own procedure that is executed in response to the onclick event for each
button. The Update procedure is where most of the action takes place. We'll discuss this procedure in the next two sections.

Updating with SQL

As mentioned in the section "Updating Data Using the ADC," there are two ways to update a
record using the ADC: You can execute an SQL UPDATE statement, or you can use the
SubmitChanges method. I stumbled upon the SQL statement method in response to a bug in
the beta version of RDS that prevented updates to Microsoft Access data sources. It seems that
the current beta of version 1.5 would not actually update the database but also wouldn't provide any indication that it hadn't updated the data.

For this reason I needed to come up with an alternative method of updating the database. The
Update procedure provided in Listing 20.3 utilizes the SQL UPDATE method. The UPDATE state-
ment is generated by retrieving the value of each text box on the form with the exception of the
CardID field, which is not an editable field. The SQL statement is then assigned to the ADC's
SQL property, and the Refresh method is invoked. Immediately following this, the original
recordset is restored by resetting the SQL property to its original value and once again invoking
Refresh.

There are a few drawbacks to using this method:

- You cannot batch the updates as you can with the SubmitChanges method.
- Every field's value is included in the UPDATE statement, not just the fields that have
  been updated. Although not significant, this does result in a few more bytes being sent
  over the wire to the RDS server machine.

For the present time, however, this method does have the major advantage of actually working
with an Access data source. For now, this advantage greatly outweighs the two disadvantages.
By the time you read this chapter, we hope that the RDS's SubmitChanges method (discussed
in the following section) will have been fixed to work properly with Access data source.

Using the `SubmitChanges` Method

To use the `SubmitChanges` method, you simply need to replace the `Update` procedure in Listing 20.3 with the procedure found in Listing 20.4.

Listing 20.4. The `Update` method utilizing `SubmitChanges`.

```
SUB Update
        ADC.SubmitChanges
    ADC.Refresh
END SUB
```

As you can see, this method requires significantly less code. It also overcomes the two disadvantages of the previous method.

Summary

This chapter presented two methods of updating data in an ODBC data source. The Active Server Page method, which uses ActiveX Data Objects, is an inefficient means of updating data because it requires several round-trips to the Web server in order to accomplish the update.

On the other hand, using DHTML and the RDS, you can create powerful, efficient Web-based database applications. The RDS takes advantage of a DHTML client-side DSO, the ADC, to provide the caching and client-side data-manipulation efficiency necessary for large-scale Web-based database applications.

In Chapter 21, "Summing Up—A Practical Application," we'll build a complete application based upon the RDS, the ADC, and our trading card database.

20

UPDATING THE DATA

CHAPTER 21

Summing Up—A Practical Application

by Craig Eddy

IN THIS CHAPTER

In Chapters 18–20 you learned a great deal about all the basics of data binding using Dynamic HTML (DHTML). This section starts with Chapter 18, "Presenting Your Data with Dynamic HTML," and the most essential part of data binding—providing a means to display the data to the user. This is followed by Chapter 19, "Client-side Data Manipulation," which discusses ways you can use DHTML to allow users to rearrange how they view the available data. Finally, Chapter 20, "Updating the Data," shows you how to use the Remote Data Services (RDS) to allow browsers to update the data in your ODBC databases.

In this chapter, I present the culmination of the work done thus far. The chapter builds on the database and examples used throughout the other three chapters of Part V, "Data Awareness." In fact, many of the pages used in previous chapters will be repeated with some enhancements for this chapter. The text discussing these pages will only cover the differences in the rendition of the pages here. I provide a reference to the original discussion of these pages for you to review if necessary.

The application created is based completely on DHTML and the Microsoft RDS. All the programming is done with DHTML and VBScript. You won't need to utilize any other programming environment to make this application work. You will need a Web server application, though, as discussed in the "Software Requirements" section.

After I list the software you'll need, I show you how to set up the Web site used to house the application. Finally, we'll review the database being used to store the trading card data.

After all this setup information is covered, I'll get into the meat of the chapter—the actual Web files that make the application tick. These sections present the complete listing for each page and then provide some discussion about how these pages function. The pages as well as the database are also provided in the Web site at `http://www.htmlguru.com`.

Software Requirements

The software requirements for this application are the basic requirements for Microsoft's RDS. These are introduced in Chapter 20, but I'll repeat them here. I'll also let you know which one I use in this chapter if there's a choice available. The requirements are as follows:

- Microsoft Windows NT Server, version 4.0 Service Pack 3 or higher, or Windows 95.
- Internet Information Server (IIS) 3.0 or Windows 95 Personal Web Server (PWS), both with Microsoft Active Server Pages (ASPs) installed. For this chapter I use the PWS.
- Microsoft Internet Explorer 4.0.
- Microsoft Remote Data Services version 1.5 or higher. The files and installation instructions are available for download at `http://www.microsoft.com/data`.
- An ODBC Level 2–compliant data source, such as Microsoft SQL Server 6.5 or Microsoft Access 97. For this chapter I use Access 97.

In addition to these, you'll also need an editor if you plan to enter or edit the pages yourself. I'd recommend using either Microsoft FrontPage (which is what I used to develop the application) or Visual InterDev.

Setting Up the Web

Because this application uses the RDS, you'll need a Web server and a Web site onto which you'll deploy the application. By *site* I simply mean a directory that the Web server recognizes as housing the application's files. You'll create the pages in this directory. When the pages are viewed by the browser, the URL will include the virtual directory name you assign to the site, not the physical pathname you see in Windows Explorer for this directory.

In this section I'll walk you through how to create the site using the PWS. The steps are very similar for the IIS Web server, so I'll only cover the PWS here. In fact, if you use the HTML Administration features of IIS instead of the IIS Server Manager, the steps will be practically identical.

After you have PWS installed and running on your machine, follow these steps to create the directory to house the application:

1. Run Control Panel by using the Start menu's Settings | Control Panel menu item. Double-click the Personal Web Server icon.

2. On the Personal Web Server Properties dialog, select the Administration tab. Click the Administration button.

3. Internet Explorer will load and display the Internet Services Administrator page, as shown in Figure 21.1.

FIGURE 21.1.

The Internet Services Administrator start page.

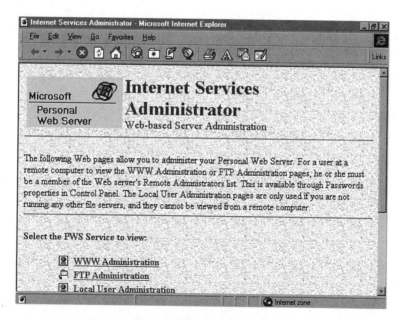

4. Click the WWW Administration link. On the page that is displayed, click the Directories tab.

5. A page similar to the one shown in Figure 21.2 is displayed. Scroll this page, if necessary, until you see a link labeled Add... in the Action column. Click this link.

Figure 21.2.

The Internet Services Administrator Directories page.

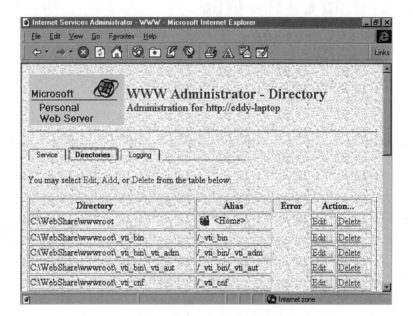

6. The Directory Add page, shown in Figure 21.3, is displayed. If you've already created the directory you'll use to store the pages, enter the directory's path in the Directory text box. If you haven't created the directory yet or can't remember the pathname, click the Browse button. The page that is displayed contains a tree showing the directory structure on the machine. There's also a text box for entering the name of a new subdirectory. Navigate to the location you want to use for the site. If you're creating a new directory, enter a directory name in the New Directory text box and click the Create Directory button.

7. After the Directory text box on the Directory Add page contains a valid directory path, enter cards in the Directory Alias text box of the Virtual Directory section of the page. Then, check the Execute checkbox in the Access section. Click the OK button.

8. The Directories page is loaded again, now showing the cards virtual directory. If you've made a mistake entering the settings for the directory, you can click the Edit link next to the cards directory to modify the settings.

9. Close Internet Explorer. The site is now ready to use.

Summing Up—A Practical Application

CHAPTER 21

461

21

SUMMING UP—A
PRACTICAL
APPLICATION

FIGURE 21.3.

*The Internet Services
Administrator
Directory Add page.*

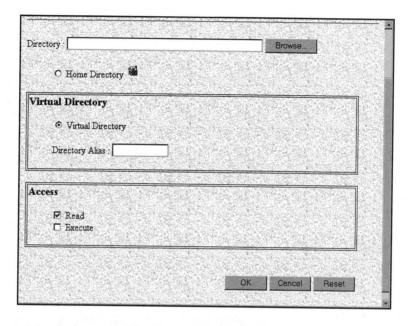

Setting Up the Trading Card Database

Although we used the database in Chapter 20, I'll cover how to set up the database here as well. You'll also need to create an ODBC data source for the database. Instructions for doing so are covered in the section "Creating an ODBC Data Source" in Chapter 20.

The database consists of a single table, Cards, that holds the data for the trading cards in my collection. The design of this table is shown in Table 21.1.

Table 21.1. Design of the Cards table.

Field Name	Data Type	Field Size
CardID	AutoNumber	Long Integer
Year	Number	Integer
Issuer	Text	50
SetName	Text	50
CardNumber	Number	Integer
Description	Text	50
Grade	Text	10
CardValue	Currency	

That's all there is to it. You can create this database in any database platform you want to use, as long as it provides an ODBC driver.

After you've created the database, create an ODBC data source for the database. Name the data source Cards to match the pages of this chapter. If this name is already used by another data source, you can choose a different name. You can then use the Setup page (discussed in the section "The Application Setup Page") to change the data source name that the application uses or change all the code to use the alternate data source name.

Creating the Home Page

The home page serves as the launching pad for the application. You give the home page a filename that matches the Default Document setting for your Web server. For the PWS, the value of this setting is found on the Directories tab of the WWW Administration page. The default value is default.htm.

The home page for the trading card application, shown in Figure 21.4, provides links to the other pages in the application as well as a form that can be used to search for cards.

Figure 21.4.

The home page for the trading card applica-tion.

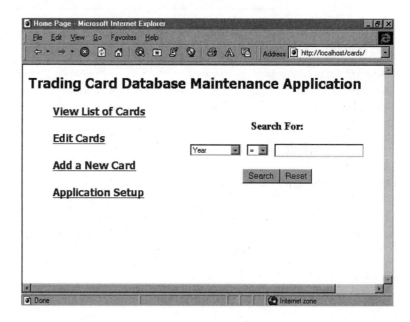

The search form allows the user to select a field to search, an operator to use in the search, and a value to search on. The information entered here will be provided to an ASP, list.asp, which is discussed in the section "The Card List Page." list.asp uses this information to populate the FilterColumn, FilterCriterion, and FilterValue properties of the Advanced Data Control (see the section "The Advanced Data Control" in Chapter 20 for more details on these properties).

Summing Up—A Practical Application

CHAPTER 21

463

21

SUMMING UP—A
PRACTICAL
APPLICATION

The code for default.htm is provided in Listing 21.1.

Listing 21.1. HTML for the home page (default.htm).

```html
<html>
<head><title>Home Page</title></head>
<body>
<h2><font face="Tahoma">Trading Card Database Maintenance Application</font>
</h2>
<blockquote>
  <form method="POST" action="list.asp">
    <table border="0" width="100%">
      <tr>
        <td width="29%"><h3><a href="list.asp"><font face="Tahoma">
View List of Cards</font></a></h3></td>
        <td width="71%" align="center" rowspan="4"><h3>Search For:</h3></td>
        <h3><select name="FilterColumn" size="1">
          <option selected value="Year">Year</option>
          <option value="Issuer">Issuer</option>
          <option value="SetName">Set Name</option>
          <option value="CardNumber">Card Number</option>
          <option value="Description">Description</option>
          <option value="Grade">Grade</option>
          <option value="CardValue">Card Value</option>
        </select>  <select name="FilterCriterion" size="1">
          <option selected value="=">=</option>
          <option value="&lt;">&lt;</option>
          <option value="&gt;">&gt;</option>
          <option value="&lt;=">&lt;=</option>
          <option value="&gt;=">&gt;=</option>
          <option value="&lt;&gt;">&lt;&gt;</option>
        </select>  <input type="text" name="FilterValue" size="20"></h3>
        <h3><input type="submit" value="Search" name="B1">
<input type="reset" value="Reset"
        name="B2"></h3>
        </td>
      </tr>
      <tr>
        <td width="29%"><h3><a href="editor.asp"><font face="Tahoma">
Edit Cards</font></a></h3>
        </td>
      </tr>
      <tr>
        <td width="29%"><h3><a href="addnew.asp"><font face="Tahoma">
Add a New Card</font></a></h3>
        </td>
      </tr>
      <tr>
        <td width="29%"><h3><a href="setup.asp"><font face="Tahoma">
Application Setup</font></a></h3>
        </td>
      </tr>
    </table>
  </form>
</blockquote>
</body></html>
```

The Application Setup Page

The Application Setup page, shown in Figure 21.5, allows you to specify values for some of the variables used in the application. The Submit button activates an ASP (`submitprfs.asp`) that stores the entered values in the browser's cookie file.

FIGURE 21.5.

The Application Setup page.

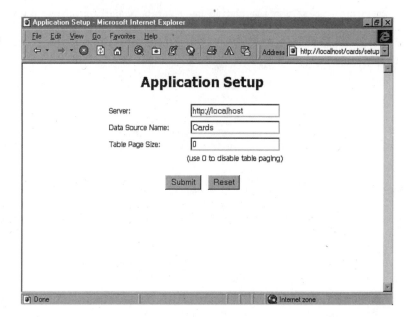

You can enter the protocol and machine name of the database server. This is necessary if the database server is not on the same machine as the Web server or if you're using a protocol other than HTTP to access the RDS.

If you've used a name other than `Cards` for the database's ODBC data source, enter that in the `Data Source Name` text box.

Finally, the default value for the `DATAPAGESIZE` element of any data-bound tables is entered in the final text box. This element controls table paging, first introduced in the section "Using Table Paging" of Chapter 19. If `0` is entered, table paging is disabled. Otherwise, the value entered will be the number of records displayed in each table page.

When the Submit button is clicked, `submitprfs.asp` stores the form's data in the browser's cookie file. The ASP code then redirects the browser back to the home page.

The code for `setup.asp` is provided in Listing 21.2. The code for `submitprfs.asp` is provided in Listing 21.3.

Listing 21.2. ASP source code for the Application Setup page (setup.asp).

```
<html>
<head><title>Application Setup</title></head>

<body>
<% servername = request.cookies("servername")
   if len(servername)=0 then
     servername = "http://" + Request.ServerVariables("SERVER_NAME")
   end if
   datapagesize = request.cookies("pagesize")
   if len(datapagesize) = 0 then
     datapagesize = "0"
   end if
   dsn = request.cookies("dsn")
   if len(dsn) = 0 then
     dsn = "Cards"
   end if
%>

<h2 align="center"><font face="Tahoma">Application Setup</font></h2>

<form method="POST" action="submitprfs.asp" align="center">
  <div align="center"><div align="center">
<center>
<table border="0" style="font-family: Tahoma; font-size: 9pt" width="325">
  <tr>
    <td width="109">Server: </td>
    <td width="208" align="center"><input type="text" name="server" size="20"
    value="<%=servername%>"></td>
  </tr>
  <tr>
    <td width="109">Data Source Name: </td>
    <td width="208" align="center">
    <input type="text" name="dsn" size="20" value="<%=dsn%>"></td>
  </tr>
  <tr>
    <td width="109">Table Page Size: </td>
    <td width="208" align="center">
    <input type="text" name="pagesize" size="20" value="<%=datapagesize%>">
    </td>
  </tr>
  <tr>
    <td width="109"></td>
    <td width="208" align="center">(use 0 to disable table paging)</td>
  </tr>
</table>
  </center></div><div align="center"><center><p>
  <input type="submit" value="Submit" name="B1">
   <input type="reset" value="Reset" name="B2"> </p>
  </center></div></div>
</form>
</body></html>
```

Listing 21.3. ASP source code for the setup submission page (`submitprfs.asp`).

```
<%
response.cookies("servername") = request("server")
response.cookies("dsn") = request("dsn")
response.cookies("pagesize") = request("pagesize")
response.redirect "default.htm"
%>
<html>
<head><title>Submit Setup</title></head>
<body>
<p align="center">
If you're viewing this page, your browser doesn't support redirection. </p>
<p align="center">
Click <a href="default.htm">here</a> to go to the Home Page. </p>
</body></html>
```

The Editing and New Card Pages

The editing page, shown in Figure 21.6, is the same page introduced in Chapter 20's "Updating Data Using the ADC" section, with a minor change or two. The code for this page, `editor.asp`, is provided in Listing 21.4.

The page uses current record binding (first introduced in the section "Using Data-bound HTML Elements" of Chapter 18) to display a single record from the data source object. There are buttons that are used to navigate the recordset, plus buttons used for updating the data.

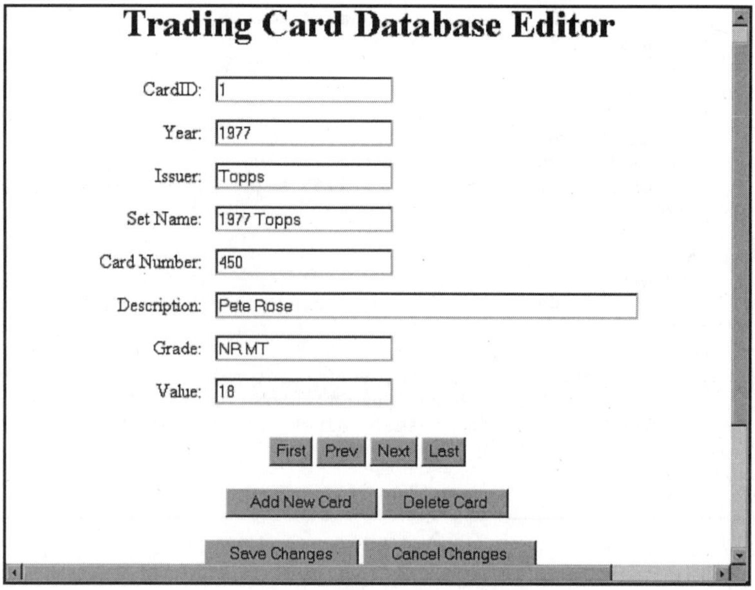

FIGURE 21.6.
The Database Editor page.

Trading Card Database Editor

CardID:	1
Year:	1977
Issuer:	Topps
Set Name:	1977 Topps
Card Number:	450
Description:	Pete Rose
Grade:	NR MT
Value:	18

First | Prev | Next | Last

Add New Card | Delete Card

Save Changes | Cancel Changes

Summing Up—A Practical Application

CHAPTER 21

467

21

SUMMING UP—A
PRACTICAL
APPLICATION

The first difference is apparent at the top of the listing. The page's server-side code first retrieves the setup page options stored in the cookie file and assigns them to local variables that will be used later in the page. Another addition to this page is the Add New Card button. This button invokes a procedure that uses the window.navigate method to load the Add New Card page.

This page also sports a Delete button, which will delete the current record.

> **NOTE**
>
> The code behind the Update and Delete buttons uses SQL instead of the methods provided by the ADC to perform the operations. This was done because, at the time of this writing, the beta version of the Advanced Data Control (ADC) did not have complete support for updates functioning properly.

Listing 21.4. ASP source code for the Database Editor page (`editor.asp`).

```
<html>
<% servername = request.cookies("servername")
   if len(servername)=0 then
     servername = "http://" + Request.ServerVariables("SERVER_NAME")
   end if
   dsn = request.cookies("dsn")
   if len(dsn) = 0 then
     dsn = "Cards"
   end if
%>

<head><title>Trading Card Database Editor</title></head>

<body bgcolor="ffffff" text="000000" link="000080" language="VBS"
 onload="init">

<h1 align="center">Trading Card Database Editor</h1>
<div align="center"><center>

<table border="0" cellpadding="5">
  <tr>
    <td align="right">CardID:</td>
    <td>
    <input type="text" name="CardID" size="20"
     datasrc="#ADC" datafld="CardID">
    </td>
  </tr>
  <tr>
    <td align="right">Year:</td>
    <td>
    <input type="text" name="YearFld" size="20"
     datasrc="#ADC" datafld="year">
    </td>
  </tr>
```

continues

Listing 21.4. continued

```html
<tr>
  <td align="right">Issuer:</td>
  <td>
  <input type="text" name="Issuer" size="20"
   datasrc="#ADC" datafld="Issuer">
  </td>
</tr>
<tr>
  <td align="right">Set Name:</td>
  <td>
  <input type="text" name="SetName" size="20"
   datasrc="#ADC" datafld="SetName">
  </td>
</tr>
<tr>
  <td align="right">Card Number:</td>
  <td>
  <input type="text" name="CardNumber" size="20"
   datasrc="#ADC" datafld="CardNumber">
  </td>
</tr>
<tr>
  <td align="right">Description:</td>
  <td>
  <input type="text" name="Description" size="50"
   datasrc="#ADC" datafld="Description">
  </td>
</tr>
<tr>
  <td align="right">Grade:</td>
  <td>
  <input type="text" name="Grade" size="20"
   datasrc="#ADC" datafld="Grade">
  </td>
</tr>
<tr>
  <td align="right">Value:</td>
  <td>
  <input type="text" name="ValueFld" size="20"
   datasrc="#ADC" datafld="CardValue">
  </td>
</tr>
</table>
</center></div>

<p align="center">
<input type="BUTTON" name="First" value="First" onclick="MoveFirst">
<input type="BUTTON" name="Prev" value="Prev" onclick="MovePrev">
<input type="BUTTON" name="Next" value="Next" onclick="MoveNext">
<input type="BUTTON" name="Last" value="Last"
onclick="MoveLast"></p>

<p align="center"><input type="button" name="AddNew" value="Add New Card"
onclick="AddNewCard"> <input type="button" name="Delete" value="Delete Card"
onclick="DeleteCard"></p>

<p align="center"> <input type="BUTTON" name="Update" value="Save Changes"
```

```
onclick="Update"> <input type="BUTTON" name="Cancel" value="Cancel Changes"
onclick="Cancel"> </p>

<p align="center">
<input type="BUTTON" name="Run" value="Requery" onclick="Requery"></p>

<p>SQL UPDATE:<br>
<input type="text" name="SQL" size="100"></p>

<p>
<object classid="clsid:BD96C556-65A3-11D0-983A-00C04FC29E33"
id="ADC" height="1" width="1">
</object>
</p>
<script language="VBScript" onload="Init"><!--


SUB MoveFirst
   ADC.Recordset.MoveFirst
END SUB

SUB MoveNext
   On Error Resume Next
   ADC.Recordset.MoveNext
   IF ERR.Number <> 0 THEN
      ADC.Recordset.MoveLast
   END IF
END SUB

SUB MovePrev
   On Error Resume Next
   ADC.Recordset.MovePrevious
   IF ERR.Number <> 0 THEN
      ADC.Recordset.MoveFirst
   END IF
END SUB

SUB MoveLast
   ADC.Recordset.MoveLast
END SUB

SUB Update
   ssql = "Update Cards Set "
   ssql = ssql + "Year = "
   if isnumeric(yearfld.value) then
      ssql = ssql + yearfld.value + ", "
   else
      ssql = ssql + "0, "
   end if
   ssql = ssql + "Issuer = "
   if len(issuer.value) > 0 then
      ssql = ssql + "'" + issuer.value + "', "
   else
      ssql = ssql + "NULL, "
   end if

   ssql = ssql + "SetName = "
   if len(setname.value) > 0 then
```

continues

Listing 21.4. continued

```
      ssql = ssql + "'" + setname.value + "', "
   else
      ssql = ssql + "NULL, "
   end if
   ssql = ssql + "CardNumber = "
   if isnumeric(cardnumber.value) then
      ssql = ssql + cardnumber.value + ", "
   else
      ssql = ssql + "0, "
   end if
   ssql = ssql + "Description = "
   if len(description.value) > 0 then
      ssql = ssql + "'" + description.value + "', "
   else
      ssql = ssql + "NULL, "
   end if
   ssql = ssql + "Grade = "
   if len(grade.value) > 0 then
      ssql = ssql + "'" + grade.value + "', "
   else
      ssql = ssql + "NULL, "
   end if

   ssql = ssql + "CardValue = "
   if isnumeric(valuefld.value) then
      ssql = ssql + valuefld.value + ""
   else
      ssql = ssql + "0"
   end if

   ssql = ssql + "WHERE CardID = " + CardID.Value

   SQL.value = ssql

   ADC.SQL = ssql
   ADC.Refresh

   ADC.SQL = "Select * from Cards"
   ADC.Refresh

END SUB

SUB DeleteCard
   ssql = "DELETE FROM Cards WHERE CardID = " + CardID.Value
   SQL.value = ssql

   ADC.SQL = ssql
   ADC.Refresh

   ADC.SQL = "Select * from Cards"
   ADC.Refresh
end sub

'Cancel edits and restores original values.
SUB Cancel
   ADC.CancelUpdate
END SUB
```

Summing Up—A Practical Application

CHAPTER 21

471

21

SUMMING UP—A
PRACTICAL
APPLICATION

```
SUB Requery
   ADC.Server = "<%=servername%>"
   ADC.Connect = "DSN=Cards"
   ADC.SQL = "Select * from Cards"
   ADC.Refresh

END SUB

Sub AddNewCard
   window.navigate "addnew.asp"

end sub

SUB Init
   ADC.Server = "<%=servername%>"
   ADC.Connect = "DSN=<%=dsn%>"
   ADC.SQL = "Select * from Cards"
   adc.refresh
END SUB

--></script>
</body></html>
```

The Add Card page (`addcard.asp`) is shown in Figure 21.7 and its listing is provided in Listing 21.5. This page is very similar to the Database Editor page; however, it has only three buttons: Save Changes, Cancel Changes, and Add Another New Card. The Save Changes button fires off a procedure that performs an SQL INSERT statement, inserting a new record with the information entered on the form. If the INSERT is successful, the user is prompted as to whether he or she wants to add another card. If the answer is yes, the page is reloaded. If no, the home page is loaded.

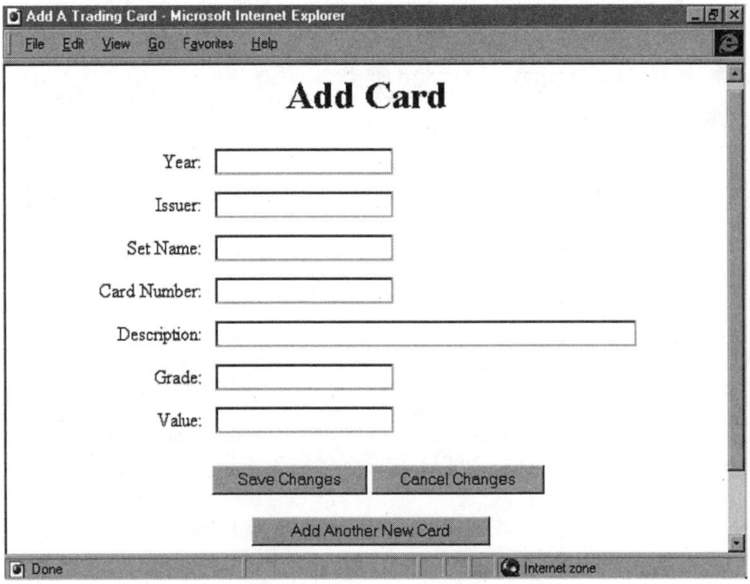

FIGURE 21.7.

The page used to add cards to the database.

Listing 21.5. ASP source code for the Add Card page (addcard.asp).

```
<html>
<head><title>Add A Trading Card</title></head>

<body
bgcolor="ffffff" text="000000" link="000080" language="VBS" onload="init">
<% servername = request.cookies("servername")
   if len(servername)=0 then
     servername = "http://" + Request.ServerVariables("SERVER_NAME")
   end if
   dsn = request.cookies("dsn")
   if len(dsn) = 0 then
     dsn = "Cards"
   end if
%>

<h1 align="center">Add Card</h1>
<div align="center"><center>

<table border="0" cellpadding="5">
  <tr>
    <td align="right">Year:</td>
    <td><input type="text" name="YearFld" size="20"></td>
  </tr>
  <tr>
    <td align="right">Issuer:</td>
    <td><input type="text" name="Issuer" size="20"></td>
  </tr>
  <tr>
    <td align="right">Set Name:</td>
    <td><input type="text" name="SetName" size="20"></td>
  </tr>
  <tr>
    <td align="right">Card Number:</td>
    <td><input type="text" name="CardNumber" size="20"></td>
  </tr>
  <tr>
    <td align="right">Description:</td>
    <td><input type="text" name="Description" size="50"></td>
  </tr>
  <tr>
    <td align="right">Grade:</td>
    <td><input type="text" name="Grade" size="20"></td>
  </tr>
  <tr>
    <td align="right">Value:</td>
    <td><input type="text" name="ValueFld" size="20"></td>
  </tr>
</table>
</center></div>

<p align="center">    <input type="BUTTON" name="Update"
value="Save Changes" onclick="Update"> <input type="BUTTON" name="Cancel"
value="Cancel Changes" onclick="Cancel"></p>

<p align="center"> 
<input type="button" name="AddNew" value="Add Another New Card"
 onclick="AddNewCard"></p>
```

```
<p> </p>

<p>
<object classid="clsid:BD96C556-65A3-11D0-983A-00C04FC29E33"
id="ADC" height="1" width="1">
</object>
</p>
<script language="VBScript" onload="Init"><!--

SUB Update

    ssql = "Insert Into Cards (Year,Issuer,SetName,CardNumber, "
    ssql = ssql + "Description, Grade, CardValue) VALUES ( "
    if isnumeric(yearfld.value) then
        ssql = ssql + yearfld.value + ", "
    else
        ssql = ssql + "0, "
    end if
    if len(issuer.value) > 0 then
        ssql = ssql + "'" + issuer.value + "', "
    else
        ssql = ssql + "NULL, "
    end if
    if len(setname.value) > 0 then
        ssql = ssql + "'" + setname.value + "', "
    else
        ssql = ssql + "NULL, "
    end if
    if isnumeric(cardnumber.value) then
        ssql = ssql + cardnumber.value + ", "
    else
        ssql = ssql + "0, "
    end if

    if len(description.value) > 0 then
        ssql = ssql + "'" + description.value + "', "
    else
        ssql = ssql + "NULL, "
    end if
    if len(grade.value) > 0 then
        ssql = ssql + "'" + grade.value + "', "
    else
        ssql = ssql + "NULL, "
    end if
    if isnumeric(valuefld.value) then
        ssql = ssql + valuefld.value + ")"
    else
        ssql = ssql + "0)"
    end if

    ADC.SQL = ssql
    ADC.Refresh
    if err = 0 then
        if Msgbox("Add another card?",4) = 6 then
            location.reload
        else
            window.navigate "default.htm"
        end if
```

continues

Listing 21.5. continued

```
    else
        msgbox "An error occurred."
    end if

END SUB

SUB Cancel
    ADC.CancelUpdate
    yearfld.value = ""
    issuer.value = ""
    setname.value = ""
    cardnumber.value = ""
    description.value = ""
    grade.value = ""
    valuefld.value = ""

END SUB

Sub AddNewCard
    window.location.href = "addnew.asp"
end sub

SUB Init
    ADC.Server = "<%=servername%>"
    ADC.Connect = "DSN=<%=dsn%>;"
    ADC.SQL = "Select * from Cards"

END SUB

--></script>
</body></html>
```

The Card List Page

The Card List page, shown in Figure 21.8, is first introduced in Chapter 19. The code for this rendition is provided in Listing 21.6.

The sorting and filtering features of this page have been modified to match the properties and methods available for the ADC. These properties and methods are introduced in the section "Using the Advanced Data Control" in Chapter 20.

The page also checks the ASP request object to see whether any filter information was provided when the page was loaded. The home page, as you'll recall from the section "Creating the Home Page," provides this information to the page if the user enters it and clicks its Search button. If this information is provided in the request object, the Init procedure sets the ADC's filter properties, thus causing the data presented to the user to match the search criteria entered on the home page.

21
SUMMING UP—A
PRACTICAL
APPLICATION

FIGURE 21.8.

The page used for displaying a list of trading cards.

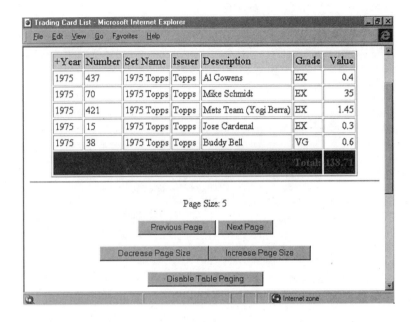

Listing 21.6. ASP source code for the Card List page (`list.asp`).

```
<!DOCTYPE HTML PUBLIC "-//IETF//DTD HTML//EN">
<html>
<% servername = request.cookies("servername")
   if len(servername)=0 then
     servername = "http://" + Request.ServerVariables("SERVER_NAME")
   end if
   datapagesize = request.cookies("pagesize")
   if len(datapagesize) = 0 then
     datapagesize = "0"
   end if
   dsn = request.cookies("dsn")
   if len(dsn) = 0 then
     dsn = "Cards"
   end if
   filtercolumn = request("filtercolumn")
   filtercriterion = request("filtercriterion")
   filtervalue = request("filtervalue")
%>

<head>
<title>Trading Card List</title>
</head>

<body bgcolor="#FFFFFF" language="vbs" onload="init">

<p> </p>

<p>
<object classid="clsid:BD96C556-65A3-11D0-983A-00C04FC29E33"
id="ADC" height="1" width="1"
```

continues

Listing 21.6. continued

```
ondatasetcomplete="dataloaded()">
</object>
</p>

<p> </p>

<table id="MyTable" border="1" datasrc="#ADC" datapagesize="<%=datapagesize%>"
align="center" cellpadding="2">
<thead>
   <tr>
     <td onclick="tableclick('year')" align="left"
       id="year" bgcolor="#00FFFF"><big>+Year</big></td>
     <td align="left" bgcolor="#00FFFF" onclick="tableclick('cardnumber')"
id="CardNumber"><big>+Number</big></td>
     <td align="left" onclick="tableclick('setname')" id="setname"
      bgcolor="#00FFFF"><big>Set Name</big></td>
     <td align="left" onclick="tableclick('issuer')" id="issuer"
      bgcolor="#00FFFF"><big>Issuer</big></td>
     <td align="left" onclick="tableclick('description')"
      id="description" bgcolor="#00FFFF"><big>Description</big></td>
     <td align="left" onclick="tableclick('grade')"
      id="grade" bgcolor="#00FFFF"><big>Grade</big></td>
     <td align="right" onclick="tableclick('cardvalue')"
      id="Cardvalue" bgcolor="#00FFFF"><big>Value</big></td>
   </tr>
</thead>
   <tr>
     <td><div datafld="year"></div></td>
     <td><div datafld="cardnumber"></div></td>
     <td><div datafld="setname"></div></td>
     <td><div datafld="issuer"></div></td>
     <td><div datafld="description"></div></td>
     <td><div datafld="grade"></div></td>
     <td width="50" align="right"><div datafld="cardvalue"></div></td>
   </tr>
<tfoot>
   <tr>
     <td colspan="6" align="right" height="40" bgcolor="#000080">
      <font color="#FF0000" size="4"><strong>Total:</strong></font></td>
     <td valign="center" align="right" bgcolor="#000080"><strong>
      <font color="#FF0000" size="4"><div id="TotalText"></div></font></strong></td>
   </tr>
</tfoot>
</table>

<hr>
<% if datapagesize = 0 then %>

<p id="pagesizetext" align="center">Table paging disabled.</p>
<% else %>

<p id="pagesizetext" align="center">Page Size: 5</p>
<% end if %>

<p align="center"><strong><strong><input type="button"
value="Previous Page" name="B1"
onclick="scrollpage(0)"> <input type="button" value="Next Page" name="B1"
```

Summing Up—A Practical Application

CHAPTER 21

477

21

SUMMING UP—A
PRACTICAL
APPLICATION

```
onclick="scrollpage(1)"> </strong></strong></p>

<p align="center"><input type="button" value="Decrease Page Size" name="B1"
onclick="pagesize(0)"><strong>
<input type="button" value="Increase Page Size" name="B1"
onclick="pagesize(1)"></strong></p>

<p align="center"><input type="button" value="Disable Table Paging" name="B1"
onclick="pagesize(2)"></p>

<p> </p>
</strong>

<h3 align="center">
To filter the data for a specific year, enter the year here and click
the Filter button:</h3>

<h3 align="center">Year: <input type="text"
  name="FilterYearTxt" size="20"></h3>

<h3 align="center">
<input type="button" value="Filter" name="B1" onclick="filteryear(0)">
<input type="reset" value="Reset" name="B2" onclick="filteryear(1)"></h3>

<hr>

<h3 align="center">To sort by any column, click the column's header.</h3>

<hr>

<p><strong><script language="VBScript"><!--

sub tableclick(columnname)

if columnname <> "year" and
➡(left(document.all.item("year").innertext,1) = "+"
➡or left(document.all.item("year").innertext,1) = "-") then
   document.all.item("year").innerHTML = "<big>" +
      ➡mid(document.all.item("year").innertext,2) + "</big>"
end if

if columnname <> "cardnumber" and
➡(left(document.all.item("cardnumber").innertext,1) = "+"
➡or left(document.all.item("cardnumber").innertext,1) = "-") then
   document.all.item("cardnumber").innerHTML = "<big>" +
      ➡mid(document.all.item("cardnumber").innertext,2) + "</big>"
end if

if columnname <> "setname" and
➡(left(document.all.item("setname").innertext,1) = "+" or
➡left(document.all.item("setname").innertext,1) = "-") then
   document.all.item("setname").innerHTML = "<big>" + ➡
      ➡mid(document.all.item("setname").innertext,2) + "</big>"
end if

if columnname <> "issuer" and
➡(left(document.all.item("issuer").innertext,1) = "+"
➡or left(document.all.item("issuer").innertext,1) = "-") then
```

continues

Listing 21.6. continued

```
      document.all.item("issuer").innerHTML = "<big>" +
         ➥mid(document.all.item("issuer").innertext,2) + "</big>"
   end if

   if columnname <> "description" and
➥(left(document.all.item("description").innertext,1) = "+" or
➥left(document.all.item("description").innertext,1) = "-") then
      document.all.item("description").innerHTML = "<big>" +
         ➥mid(document.all.item("description").innertext,2) + "</big>"
   end if

   if columnname <> "grade" and
➥(left(document.all.item("grade").innertext,1) = "+" or
➥left(document.all.item("grade").innertext,1) = "-") then
      document.all.item("grade").innerHTML = "<big>" +
         ➥mid(document.all.item("grade").innertext,2) + "</big>"
   end if

   if columnname <> "cardvalue" and
➥(left(document.all.item("cardvalue").innertext,1) = "+" or
➥left(document.all.item("cardvalue").innertext,1) = "-") then
      document.all.item("cardvalue").innerHTML = "<big>" +
         ➥mid(document.all.item("cardvalue").innertext,2) + "</big>"
   end if

   if left(document.all.item(columnname).innertext,1) = "+" then
      document.all.item(columnname).innerHTML =   "<big>-" +
         ➥mid(document.all.item(columnname).innertext,2) + "</big>"
      ADC.sortcolumn = columnname
      ADC.sortdirection = false
   elseif left(document.all.item(columnname).innertext,1) = "-" then
      document.all.item(columnname).innerHTML = "<big>+" +
         ➥mid(document.all.item(columnname).innertext,2) + "</big>"
      ADC.sortcolumn = columnname
      ADC.sortdirection = true
   else
      document.all.item(columnname).innerHTML = "<big>+" +
         ➥document.all.item(columnname).innertext + "</big>"
      ADC.sortcolumn = columnname
      ADC.sortdirection = true
   end if

   adc.reset

end sub


sub filteryear(resetfilter)

if resetfilter then
   adc.refresh
else
   adc.filtercriterion = "="
   adc.filtercolumn = "year"
   adc.filtervalue = filteryeartxt.value
   adc.reset(false)
end if
```

Summing Up—A Practical Application

CHAPTER 21

479

21

SUMMING UP—A
PRACTICAL
APPLICATION

```
      end sub

      sub scrollpage(direction)

      if direction = 0 then
         mytable.previouspage
      else
         mytable.nextpage
      end if

      end sub

      sub pagesize(direction)

      if direction = 0 and mytable.datapagesize > 1 then
         mytable.datapagesize = mytable.datapagesize - 1
         document.all.pagesizetext.innertext =
      ➡"Page Size: " + cstr(mytable.datapagesize)
      elseif direction = 1 then
         mytable.datapagesize = mytable.datapagesize + 1
         document.all.pagesizetext.innertext =
      ➡"Page Size: " + cstr(mytable.datapagesize)
      elseif direction = 2 then
         mytable.datapagesize = 0
         document.all.pagesizetext.innertext = "Table paging disabled"
      end if

      end sub

      sub dataloaded()

      while not(adc.recordset.eof)
         total = total + adc.recordset("cardvalue")
         adc.recordset.movenext
      wend
      document.all.totaltext.innertext =  total

      end sub

      sub init
        Adc.Server="<%=servername%>"
        adc.Connect="DSN=<%=dsn%>"
        adc.SQL="Select * from Cards"
   <% if len(filtercriterion) > 0 and len(filtercolumn) > 0 and
        ➡len(filtervalue) > 0 then %>
        adc.filtercolumn = "<%=filtercolumn%>"
        adc.filtercriterion="<%=filtercriterion%>"
        adc.filtervalue="<%=filtervalue%>"
   <% end if %>
        adc.refresh

      end sub
      --></script> </strong></p>
      </body></html>
```

Summary

This chapter served as the summary for Part V, "Data Awareness." Although most of the Web pages are repeats from previous chapters, this is the first time I've combined them into a cohesive unit, creating a usable, extendible Web-based database application.

Using these pages as a base, you can easily create any data-bound DHTML application to suit your needs. Part VI, "Other Dynamic Techniques," introduces you to many cool features available when using DHTML. These include transition effects, layers, and multimedia effects. After you've completed Part VI, you might want to return to this chapter and spice up the pages using these features.

VI

PART

Other Dynamic Techniques

Using Layers

by Ryan Peters

IN THIS CHAPTER

CHAPTER 22

Layers aren't a new concept. Desktop publishing and graphics packages have been using layers for years, but only recently has this technology started to appear in Web technology. With the release of Netscape Navigator and Communicator 4.0, layering has made a huge splash on the Web. Whereas prior releases required the developer to use a complex layout of HTML tables, graphics, and text, 4.0 brings the ease of simplicity that only layering makes possible. In this chapter we examine HTML layers, their acceptance in the industry among competing standards, and simple ways to implement them. You'll learn

- What layers are and which browsers support them
- How to create single- and multi-layered documents
- The difference between cascading style sheets (CSS) and layers
- How to safely use layers in your pages

An Introduction to Layers

For those of you familiar with applications such as Adobe Photoshop or Microsoft Publisher, layers are nothing new. The concept of assigning an element a position above or below other elements within a document makes layered documents extremely flexible when it comes to any type of publishing. HTML layers are poised to create a new breed of Web page: faster, cleaner, more dynamic—a revolution in the way we look at an online document. With an easy-to-use HTML syntax, layering is a technology for everyone. Add the capability to control those layers through JavaScript, and you have the basis for some pretty interactive Web sites.

A Divergence in Standards

The browser wars have been escalating over the past year, bringing a wealth of new technologies to our desktops. Prior to the release of the 4.0 browsers from Microsoft and Netscape, you've enjoyed some model of compatibility between the two. With layering, that compatibility goes right out the door. Microsoft's view of layers focuses on the CSS document model, which allows a group of page elements to be grouped together in a CSS and any of those elements to be manipulated through JScript or VBScript. Although Netscape 4.0 supports CSS, it supports a slightly different implementation and extends the style sheet's properties in the document object model through JavaScript—hence, JSS, or JavaScript style sheets.

To create layered page elements under an Internet Explorer browser, one simply modifies the properties of a style sheet. Netscape's browser offers an entirely new markup tag, <LAYER>, to create layered documents. Internet Explorer does not recognize this tag; it simply ignores it and processes any embedded HTML elements.

What About the Other Guys?

Currently, the only browser that supports the <LAYER> tag is the Netscape Navigator/ Communicator 4.0 and higher. Although some market studies say that Netscape still holds more than 70 percent of the market share, some of that percentage are still older versions of the

Navigator software. When you're thinking about implementing a layer-enhanced site, unless you know that your target user group is sure to use the latest and greatest from Netscape, it's best to use layers to augment or complement existing work. I consider myself a tremendous Netscape advocate, yet I'd be somewhat hesitant to deploy an entire site based on this technology.

It's important to note that a lot of the functionality in layers can be duplicated, although not as easily, in Microsoft's Internet Explorer 4.0 (IE4) using CSS. Microsoft's version of Dynamic HTML (DHTML) is similar in function to Netscape's but accomplishes absolute positioning, animation and movement effects, and other tactics in a matter not completely compatible with Netscape's implementation of DHTML. The point is that similar tricks can be pulled off in either browser, but not using the same code.

Creating Your First Layer

At first glance, JavaScript layers can be even more daunting than the first time you looked at tables. My first quick peek at a multi-layered Netscape HTML document had me running for cover, back to the safety and comfort of version 3.0. But, like the rest of you, curiosity got the better of me, and late one night (or was it early in the morning?) I went back for a closer look. I forget the exact page—it was buried somewhere on Netscape's DevEdge site `http://developer.netscape.com/`—but I was determined to get a handle on it. After printing out the source code and staring relentlessly back and forth at the piece of paper in my hand and the screen, it dawned on me how much sense layers actually made. If you look at a complex table layout, it's pretty easy to get lost among the <td> and <tr> shuffle. A closer look at the layers' syntax showed that things that used to take an incredible amount of code or some artwork to pull off were now relatively simple to do.

The jump into the realm of layers starts with a really quick page for this killer new design firm called XYZ Webcrafters. XYZ is a pretty new company, so they've gone online with a really basic page—no advanced design elements. Outside of some specific fonts, it's pretty much the same under about any browser out there. Being the new company that they are, XYZ doesn't have the resources yet to get a graphics guru, so even the logo is plain text. The source is shown below in Listing 22.1. Simple enough? Take a look at Figure 22.1 and decide for yourself.

Listing 22.1. XYZ home page HTML source (as shown in Figure 22.1).

```
<html>
<head>
<title>XYZ webcrafting</title>
</head>
<body bgcolor="#000000" text="#ffffff">
<center>
<font color="gray" face="Tahoma, Arial" size=+4><b>X Y Z</b></font><br>
<font color="aqua" face="Arial" size=+1><b>w e b c r a f t i n g</b></font>
</center>
<blockquote>
<font face="Tahoma, Arial" size=-1>
```

continues

Listing 22.1. continued

```
<p>don't the burden of building a presence online get to
you? innovation comes easy at XYZ.  we pride ourselves
on being at the very forefront of technology, incorporating
the latest in web design components.  just contact us for
all your javascript, java, and dynamic html needs</p>
</font>
</blockquote>
</body>
</html>
```

> **NOTE**
>
> Some of you looking at the source might wonder why I switch back and forth between RGB
> color values ("#ffffff") and color names ("aqua"). The named values work in most newer
> browsers that support font color assuagements and are much easier to remember than all
> the RGB codes. I mean, who can remember the RGB code for "salmon"? :-)

FIGURE 22.1.

XYZ Webcrafting: the first round.

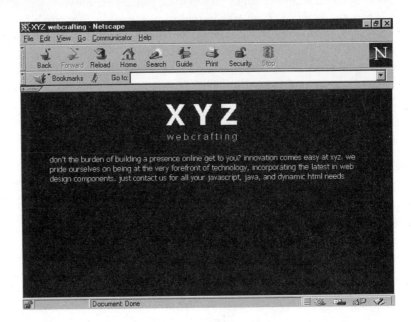

With that tiny tidbit of a Web page, XYZ is only sort of ready for business. But how can they be at the forefront of technology when their page can be viewed under just about anything with no difference in appearance? It's the enhanced pages that set the edge guys like us apart from the rest of the pack, right?

Without the budget for a graphics person, artwork is out of the question. Multimedia stuff like Shockwave or RealAudio clips both require either expensive server or developer software. Got it...time to trick it out with a little splash of DHTML à la Netscape!

Like I said, layers just make sense when you look at them closely. The syntax for most of the layers' basic properties is the same as other HTML elements. Each layer has a width, a height, a background or bgcolor, the layer SRC or source, and some layer-specific attributes. The only layer-specific attributes needed now are the top, visibility, and id properties. The top property specifies how many pixels from the top of the page the layer should be, the id is an optional attribute specifying the name of the layer, and the visibility controls whether the layer is displayed. The redesign starts with taking the word *Webcrafting* and throwing it into a separate layer; then we just move it to a specific spot on the page. How? Check out the new source in Listing 22.2. It's easier than you think!

Listing 22.2. XYZ home page HTML source: Round 2 (as shown in Figure 22.2).

```
<html>
<head>
<title>XYZ webcrafting</title>
</head>
<body bgcolor="#000000" text="#ffffff">
<center>
<font color="gray" face="Tahoma, Arial" size=+4><b>X Y Z</b></font><br>
<layer top=36 id="subheading" visibility=show>
<center>
<font color="aqua" face="Arial" size=+1><b>w e b c r a f t i n g</b></font>
</center>
</layer>
</center>
<blockquote>
<font face="Tahoma, Arial" size=-1>
<p>don't the burden of building an online presence get to
you? innovation comes easy at xyz.  we pride ourselves
on being at the very forefront of technology, incorporating
the latest in web design components.  just contact us for
all your javascript, java, and dynamic html needs</p>
</font>
</blockquote>
</body>
</html>
```

See the change? It only took four small lines of code to add a simple layer to the XYZ page. Now, without graphics or artwork, we have a superimposed effect on the company name. Check the result in Figure 22.2, and compare it with the original. Although it's a simple effect, pulling this trick off without layers would've required either the use of graphics (which is out of XYZ's budget for now) or some type of special plug-in. In either case, the end result would have probably taken a bit longer to load than our little layer hack.

FIGURE 22.2.

*XYZ Webcrafting gets
layered.*

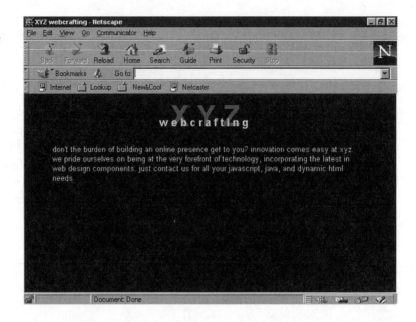

This chapter briefly touches on using layers in conjunction with CSS technology. Accomplishing this is pretty straightforward, much like using a style anywhere else in a document. Looking back on XYZ again, notice that the subtitle appears centered, lowercase, and in an aqua color. Taking those attributes, it's easy to create a simple style and apply it to the subtitle text. The result is pretty much identical to the previous iteration, except now you have access to that same style across anything in the document, if needed.

Listing 22.3. Style sheets used with layers.

```
<html>
<head>
<title>XYZ webcrafting</title>
</head>
<style type="text/css">
all.subtitle {
font-family:Arial;
font-weight:bold;
font-size:14pt;
color: aqua;
textAlign:center;
}
</style>
<body bgcolor="#000000" text="#ffffff">
<center>
<font color="gray" face="Tahoma, Arial" size=+4><b>X Y Z</b></font><br>
<layer top=36 name="subheading" visibility=show>
<span class="subtitle">w e b c r a f t i n g</span>
</layer>
</center>
```

```
<blockquote>
<font face="Tahoma, Arial" size=-1>
<p>don't the burden of building an online presence get to
you? innovation comes easy at xyz.  we pride ourselves
on being at the very forefront of technology, incorporating
the latest in web design components.  just contact us for
all your javascript, java, and dynamic html needs</p>
</font>
</blockquote>
</body>
</html>
```

That's about the most one can do with that one layer, so it's time to start getting a little more in depth. You should know that because its designers used DHTML, XYZ Webcrafting is now gaining notoriety in the development community. Bigger budgets are on the horizon, so let's attack this page with a little more effort in the next section.

Adding More Layers

Now that you've mastered the concept of adding a simple layer to a page, it's time to get down to business. XYZ's site has gotten a bit bland with the recent flood of layer-enhanced sites onto the Web. I'll run through the more advanced concepts behind layers, look at how the properties and parameters for layers work, and create XYZ's first-quarter DHTML-enabled newsletter.

The Lowdown on Layering

To get rolling with the new project (the XYZ DHTML newsletter), we need to get deep into the trenches of layering. In the section "Creating Your First Layer," you were introduced to some basic layer parameters, or properties. The first examples used three parameters in the last few XYZ revisions: top, id, and visibility. Take a look at the triple-layer setup listed in Listing 22.4. The first layer (ID main) is the parent or container layer for the other two layers (IDs sub1 and sub2). The top attribute specified in the main layer is relative to the document window. Because the other two layers were coded within the main layer, their top parameter is relative to their parent layer. It's pretty close to working with <frameset> tags, so those of you familiar with setting up frames should be able to get nested layers down fairly quickly.

Listing 22.4. Source HTML for three nested layers.

```
<layer id=main bgcolor=red top=50 left=50 height=210 width=200>
   <p align=center>Parent Layer</p>
   <layer id=sub1 bgcolor=blue top=20 left=10 height=40 width=180>
   <p align=center>Child Layer 1</p>
   </layer>
   <layer id=sub2 bgcolor=silver top=70 left=10 height=130 width=180>
   <p align=center>Child Layer 1</p>
   </layer>
</layer>
```

The id parameter is that layer's unique name. An optional parameter, this comes in handy when you're manipulating your layers through JavaScript. You notice we used a `left` parameter in Listing 22.4; this acts exactly the same as the `top` parameter except on the position from the left side of the window or parent layer. Check out the end result of these nested layers in Figure 22.3.

FIGURE 22.3.

Nested layers using relative positioning.

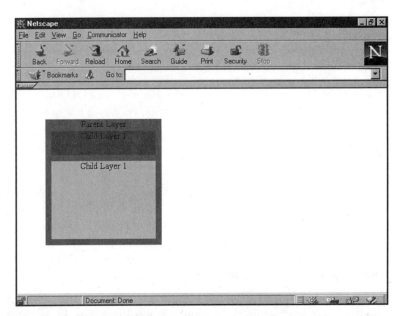

> **TIP**
>
> When you're working with layers and assigning each layer an `id` parameter, naming conventions can be a nightmare with large numbers of layers on the same document. You can circumvent this by using the same `id` for child layers within separate parent layers. So long as no two layers in a container (whether that container is a parent layer or the document) have the same `id`, you can save yourself some time!

Visibility is cool, especially when you're scripting your layers. There are three flavors to choose from when it comes to deciding whether a layer is visible. The first, `show`, means that the layer is visible within the browser. Setting the `visibility` parameter to `hide` makes it invisible to the user but still accessible using JavaScript. My personal favorite is setting `visibility` to `inherit`, meaning that it follows the lead of its parent layer. You'll see briefly in the section "Layers and Their Properties" and much more in Chapter 23, "Transition Effects," how inherited visibility makes work easy when scripting layer effects.

Those are the parameters you've touched on so far. You've seen how setting up parent/child layers and basic positioning work. In the next section, you'll see some of the other possible attributes of a layer. You'll be amazed at what you can pull off with a layer and a little ingenuity, so let's forge ahead!

Layers and Their Properties

In the previous sections I used a few of the core properties behind layers, but to take the project to the next level, you need to harness all the power of the `<layer>` tag. For those of you familiar with the CSS syntax, some of this will be a review. Believe it or not, CSS and layers share a lot of similar parameters, making the learning curve for the "other" technology a breeze. Table 22.1 shows each of the parameters used in a `<layer>` tag and gives a brief description of how it affects that layer.

Table 22.1. Parameters for the `<layer>` tag.

Property	Values	Description
position	absolute/relative	Defines whether a layer's position is absolute when compared to the parent document or relative to where it is in the flow of the HTML.
id	(any string value)	A name for the layer, the id can be anything but must begin with an alphabetic character.
left and top	number of pixels	Specifies the horizontal and vertical position of the upper-left corner of a layer in relation to the top-left corner of its parent container, which can be either the page or another layer.
width	number of pixels or percentage	Specifies the layer's width. The percentage value is based on the parent container's width.
height	number of pixels or percentage	Specifies the layer's height. The percentage value is based on the parent container's height.
pageX and pageY	number of pixels or percentage	Specifies the position of a layer's top-left corner, in relation to the X and Y pixels of the Web page. The top-left corner of the Web page translates to 0 and 0 for both values.

continues

22

USING LAYERS

Table 22.1. continued

Property	Values	Description
visibility	show/hide/inherit	The visibility attribute controls whether the layer is shown. Setting it to inherit means that it follows the lead of its parent layer.
z-index	positive number	The z-index allows you to control the z-order, or stacking order of your layers. Higher z-index value layers are above lower ones. (If one layer had a z-index of 1 and the second had a z-index of 2, the second layer would be above the first.)
above and below	a layer ID	Setting an above or below parameter is an alternate way to control the stacking order of layers. Let's say you have three layers, with IDs of lay1, lay2, and lay3. You can make sure that lay1 is below lay3 by setting the below attribute on lay1 to below='lay3' or the above attribute on lay3 to above='lay1'. You can only use one of the three (above, below, or z-index) parameters when working with the z-order on your layers.
clip	"#,#,#,#" or "#,#"	The clip property sets a visible rectangle area of a layer. By default, a layer's clipped area is determined by its height and width or content. The numbers correspond to the left value, top value, right value, and bottom value. If you just set two numbers, this affects the left and top values of the visible rectangle. As a suggestion, if you don't use the quotes, make sure there are no spaces between any numbers.
src	URL to file	The src attribute loads an external file into a layer.

Property	Values	Description
bgcolor	RGB or color name	Just as you set the background color for a Web page or table, you can specify the background color for a layer. If you omit the bgcolor attribute, the HTML layer defaults to having a transparent background.
background	URL to file	The background property functions exactly like the background for a Web page. If you specify a background, that layer will load a tiled version of the image pointed to by that URL.

Most of the <layer> tag's attributes are optional, so you can keep them simple at first, adding more advanced properties as needed. Now that you have an idea of what the attributes are, let's start looking at using them for XYZ's newsletter. At this point, you can see how using layers gave us increased flexibility in the layout of the "XYZ Webcrafting" logo, saving the trouble, expense, and bandwidth of creating a graphical logo. Now that you've got a handle on multiple layers and understand how their properties work, it's time to take XYZ a little further along the road to Internet glory.

Listing 22.5. XYZ's layered newsletter (as shown in Figure 22.4).

```
<html>
<head>
<title>XYZ webcrafting</title>
</head>
<!-- these are the styles we'll be using in this document -->
<style type="text/css">
<!--
all.subtitle {
font-family:Arial;
font-weight:bold;
font-size:14pt;
color:aqua;
textAlign:center;
}

all.menus {
font-family:Tahoma;
font-weight:bold;
font-size:16pt;
color:white;
text-decoration:none;
}
```

continues

Listing 22.5. continued

```
all.verbage{
font-family:Tahoma,Arial;
font-size:10pt;
color:white;
textAlign:justify;
}

all.gtitle {
font-family:Tahoma,Arial;
font-weight:bold;
font-size:xx-large;
color:gray;
textAlign:center;
}

all.stitle {
font-family:Tahoma,Arial;
font-weight:bold;
font-size:xx-large;
color:silver;
textAlign:center;
}

-->
</style>
<body bgcolor="#000000" text="#ffffff">

<!-- This is the container layer for the entire newsletter -->
<layer z-index=1 left=25 top=25 height=250 width=500 id="title_block">

<!-- These three layers make up the "x", "y", and "z" of the logo -->
<layer left=0 top=0 height=65 width=40 id="main_x">
<span class="gtitle">X</span>
</layer>
<layer z-index=3 left=30 top=12 height=65 width=40 id="main_y">
<span class="stitle">Y</span>
</layer>
<layer z-index=1 left=60 top=0 height=65 width=40 id="main_z">
<span class="gtitle">Z</span>
</layer>

<!--These two layers create the thin blue lines used to  -->
<!--outline the top-left of the newsletter -->
<layer z-index=2 bgcolor="blue" left=50 top=5 height=240 width=1 id="div0">
</layer>
<layer z-index=2 bgcolor="blue" left=0 top=35 height=1 width=500 id="div1">
</layer>

<layer z-index=3 left=310 top=25 id="sub_title" visibility=show>
<span class="subtitle">w e b c r a f t i n g</span>
</layer>

<layer z-index=2 left=125 top=55 width=375 id="title_block">
<p class="verbage">don't the burden of building an online presence get to
you? innovation comes easy at xyz.  we pride ourselves
```

```
on being at the very forefront of technology, incorporating
the latest in web design components.  just contact us for
all your javascript, java, and dynamic html needs</p>
</layer>
</layer>
</body>
</html>
```

TIP

Keep in mind that layers don't have to be just text. In the newsletter example, there are two simple layers with blue backgrounds to create thin intersecting lines, seemingly weaving in and out through the letters that make up the company name. Fast and low-bandwidth, layers like these can help draw attention to important page elements, so get creative!

FIGURE 22.4.

XYZ gets rolling with multiple layers.

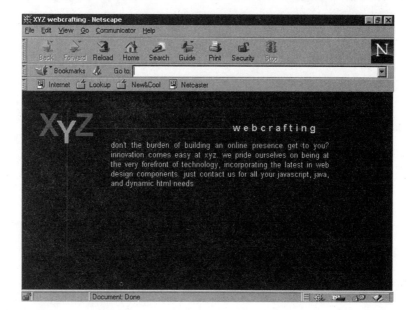

JavaScript Layers Versus CSS

CSS and layers are similar in syntax and implementation, offering the developer two possible routes for positioning HTML content. Layers have the advantage of not requiring any pre-defined parameters, and I personally find them somewhat more flexible for creating animation effects with graphics. Style sheets, in my humble opinion, tend to be geared more toward text style, positioning, and layout, and certainly have their place in the future of the Web. Layers and CSS can be used in conjunction to easily apply a style to the content of a layer.

Contingency Plans: <NOLAYER>

Like any other advanced Web creation, your layered pages might occasionally be trafficked by nonsupported browsers. Remember the big uproar when frames came out a few years ago, and people were adding frame-based navigation to a page without handling the users who hadn't upgraded? The same thing is bound to happen with a document using the <LAYER> tag, and you run the risk of scaring off potential visitors.

The simplest way to tackle the non-Netscape crowd is to include a set of tags that display alternate text to those users. Placing either another, layerless copy of the content or a "Please Upgrade Your Browser" message between a set of <NOLAYER> and </NOLAYER> tags will display that information to the user. It takes a few minutes to set up, but it encourages further use of your site and can help deter any nasty "I came to your page, but nothing came up on my screen!" messages you might receive.

When developing a layer-specific page, it's important to remember that any text or images within your layer are shown to older browsers without the layer-specific formatting.

Look at the example in Listing 22.6, showing a few colored layers containing nothing but text with a <NOLAYER> tag set at the end of the document. The resulting document is shown in Figure 22.5.

Listing 22.6. Layers versus no layers.

```
<html>
<head>
<title>My Layers</title>
</head>
<body bgcolor="white" text="black">
<layer id="lower" bgcolor="blue" top=100 left=100 width=100 height=40>
<b>This is the 'lower' layer.</b>
</layer>
<layer id="upper" bgcolor="red" top=10 left=10 width=100 height=40>
<b>This is the 'upper' layer.</b>
</layer>
<nolayer>Requires Netscape 4!</nolayer>
</body>
</html>
```

Looking at the code, notice how the flow of the document doesn't match what's slated to be shown to the layer-ready browser. However, because of the beauty of being able to specify exactly where to display a layer, HTML flow isn't a concern when targeting the Netscape 4 browser. But look at that same code under an older version of Internet Explorer in Figure 22.6.

FIGURE 22.5.
Simple layers.

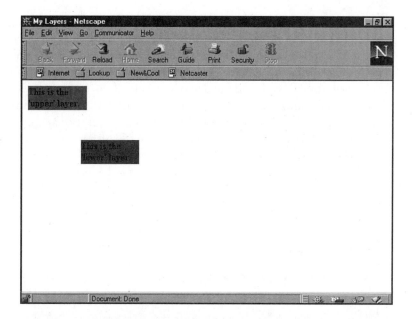

FIGURE 22.6.
Layers viewed under an incompatible browser.

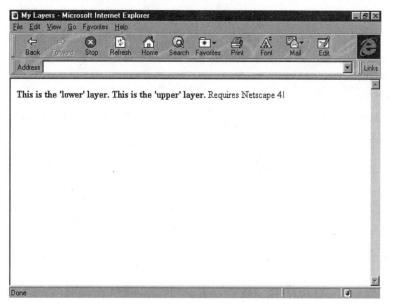

22

USING LAYERS

Placing the `<nolayer>` and `</nolayer>` tags in the document did nothing more than append that text to other senseless text. Know that your layered document could contain an incredible amount of scripting, resulting in larger file sizes and longer download times to view essentially nothing. The easiest way to get around this inconvenience is to create a document containing all your layer-specific code and call that document in as an external source file from your page. Using the same code listed in Listing 22.6 as a separate document named `layers.htm`, you could create a page that loads `layers.htm` as the source for a layer with an unassigned size. The code in Listing 22.7 provides you with the flexibility to add extremely comprehensive older browser code to the parent document, enclosing it in the `<nolayer>` and `</nolayer>` tags, which ensures that visitors are looking at the page you want to be seen.

Listing 22.7. Writing "safe" layered pages.

```
<html>
<head>
<title>My Layers</title>
</head>
<body bgcolor="white" text="black">

<layer src="layers.htm">
</layer>

<nolayer>
non-Layer HTML code goes here….
</nolayer>

</body>
</html>
```

FIGURE 22.7.

Safe layers under non-layered browsers.

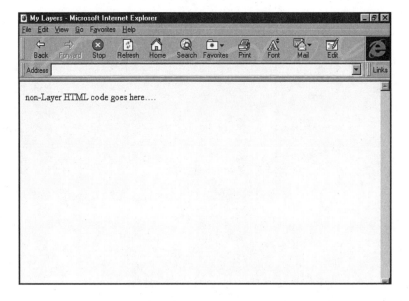

So it is possible to create a page that supports layer- and non–layer-capable browsers at the same time. With the advances made possible in Netscape Navigator/Communicator 4.0 and IE4 and a little creative coding, you can create pages that take full advantage of the best both versions of DHTML have to offer.

Summary

Layers and style sheets are revolutionizing content on the Web, giving you the ability to define exactly how you want your Web site to appear. The dimension added to online publishing by layers can help you create faster, more effective Web sites in less time than more conventional methods.

By now, you should have a fairly decent idea of what layers are and how to create and position them and have a basic grasp on what their properties are. In Chapter 23, you'll see how you can utilize JavaScript to create animations and transition effects and manipulate your Web creations in an effort to grab and hold your user's attention.

22

USING LAYERS

Transition Effects

by Ryan Peters

IN THIS CHAPTER

Web pages with layers can make people open their eyes to what you really can do with the Web. Page elements are placed exactly where the developer intended them to be. Text and images flow fluidly throughout the document. This translates into a much more attractive browsing experience, as the Web finally gets a much-needed facelift. Of course, the Web is much more than a place to read text and look at pretty pictures. Today's users expect multimedia, sound, video, interaction, and more.

There is a formula for fast, interactive, compelling Web sites. Layers + JavaScript = Cooler Pages. Sure, absolute positioning is nice, and having more control over text elements and layouts is okay, but this chapter takes you to the next level. You'll learn

- Core scripting concepts for layer transitions
- Low-bandwidth layer animations using layers
- High impact layer animation effects for your site
- How to avoid overdoing it

Core Scripting Concepts

You've seen how each layer has a set of properties that define its width, height, visibility, clipping area and position on the screen. By taking control of these attributes with JavaScript, you can easily create seemingly complex animations, transitions, and movements with a relatively small amount of code. Smaller code means smaller file sizes, less transfer time, and most important, faster pages. There's nothing more frustrating to someone on the Web than having to wait an eternity for a page to load all its plug-ins, applets, controls, and animations.

Accessing Layers with JavaScript

Along with other page elements in a document, Netscape Communicator exposes the *Layers Array* for your control. For those unfamiliar with arrays, think of it as a type of Rolodex, with each layer translating into a specific card in the bunch. These layers, referred to as *elements* of the document's layer array, can be accessed by either their name (the ID property) or their index within the document (the first layer is layer 0, the second one is layer 1, and so on) via your script. Take a look at the code in Listing 23.1, and you'll see how you can use this JavaScript to play with some of the attributes of each layer in a document.

Listing 23.1. Playing with layer arrays.

```
<html>
<head>
<title>Playing With The Layers Array</title>
</head>
<script language="JavaScript1.2">
<!--//

var currentLayer;
```

```
//-------loadLayer function--------
//this function populates a <select> input box with the array of layers on the
//page...

function loadLayers(obj) {
  var n = 0;
  var el;
  for(n=1;n<document.layers.length;n++) {
      el = new Option('document.layers[' + n + ']', n);
      obj.mylayers.options[n] = el;
  }
}


//-------getLayer function--------
//if you've selected a layer from the select list (mylayers) this function
//populates the form with information about the layer, then moves the layer into
//the table for your inspection and manipulation...

function getLayer(obj) {
   if (obj.mylayers.selectedIndex > 0) {
      var selLayer = obj.mylayers.options[obj.mylayers.selectedIndex].value;
      if ((currentLayer != selLayer) && (currentLayer)) {
          document.layers[currentLayer].left = (20 + ((currentLayer -1) * 40));
          document.layers[currentLayer].top = 10;
          document.layers[currentLayer].width = 40;
      }
      currentLayer = selLayer;
      document.layers[currentLayer].left = 380;
      document.layers[currentLayer].top = 113;
      obj.layername.value = document.layers[currentLayer].id;
   } else {
      alert('No Layer Selected!');
   }
}
```

```
//-------getValue function--------
//if you're looking at a layer, the JavaScript statement in the control box has a
//dropdown list of several layer properties.  Selecting one of them will auto-fill
//that attribute's property in the form...

function getValue(obj) {
      if (currentLayer) {
          var gv = obj.att.options[obj.att.options.selectedIndex].value
          var cl = document.layers[currentLayer]
          if (gv == 'top') obj.setting.value = cl.top;
          if (gv == 'left') obj.setting.value = cl.left;
          if (gv == 'visibility') obj.setting.value = cl.visibility;
          if (gv == 'src') obj.setting.value = cl.src;
      } else {
          alert('No Layer Was Selected!');
      }
}
```

continues

Listing 23.1. continued

```
//-------resetLayers function--------
//this just clears the form, and moves all layers back to their original
//positions...

function resetLayers(obj) {
   if (currentLayer) {
        document.layers[currentLayer].left = (20 + ((currentLayer -1) * 40));
        document.layers[currentLayer].top = 10;
        document.layers[currentLayer].width = 40;
        currentLayer = null;
        obj.layername.value = '';
        obj.setting.value = '';
        obj.att.options[0].selected = true;
   } else {
      alert('No Active Layer Selected!');
   }
}

//-------setValue function--------
//once you're viewing a layer, and have selected an attribute, you can change its
//value and click the 'set' button to assign that value to the selected property.
//Keep in mind that the page is showing the actual JavaScript syntax that could
//be run to control that selected layer...

function setValue(obj) {
     if ((currentLayer) && (obj.setting.value != '')){
         var gv = obj.att.options[obj.att.options.selectedIndex].value;
         var cl = document.layers[currentLayer];
         if (gv == 'top') cl.top = obj.setting.value;
         if (gv == 'left') cl.left = obj.setting.value;
         if (gv == 'visibility') cl.visibility = obj.setting.value;
         if (gv == 'src') cl.src = obj.setting.value;
     } else {
         alert('No Layer or Attribute Was Selected!');
     }
}

//-->
</script>
<body bgcolor="white">
<layer z-index=1 id="redblock" width=40 bgcolor="red" top=10 left=20><h1>[1]</h1>
➥</layer>
<layer z-index=2 id="blueblock" width=40 bgcolor="blue" top=10 left=60><h1>[2]
➥Easier and Faster Animations 0
</h1></layer>
<layer z-index=3 id="silverblock" width=40 bgcolor="silver" top=10
➥left=100><h1>[3]</h1></layer>
<layer z-index=4 id="yellowblock" width=40 bgcolor="yellow" top=10
➥left=140><h1>[4]</h1></layer>
<layer z-index=5 id="greenblock" width=40 bgcolor="green" top=10 left=180><h1>[5]
➥Easier and Faster Animations 0
</h1></layer>
<layer z-index=0 name="control" width=550 height=70 left=20 top=65>
<form>
<table width=550>
<tr><td colspan=3 align=center>
<b>Control Center</b> ( document.layers[0] )
</td></tr>
```

```
<tr><td valign=top width=150>
<select name="mylayers" size=6>
<option value="">----Layers Array----
</select>
</td><td valign=middle align=center width=100>
<input type="button" value="Load Array" onClick="loadLayers(this.form)">
<input type="button" value="Properties " onClick="getLayer(this.form)">
<input type="button" value="    Reset   " onClick="resetLayers(this.form)">
</td><td bgcolor="black" width=250>
 
</td></tr>
<tr><td align=center valign=top colspan=3 width=500>
<br>
<tt>document.layers['<input type="text" name="layername"
   size=12>']</tt>.<select name="att" onChange="getValue(this.form)">
<option value=" ">
<option value="top">top
<option value="left">left
<option value="visibility">visibility
<option value="src">src
</select> = <input type="text" size=15 name="setting">
<input type=button value="set" onClick="setValue(this.form)"><br>
</table>
</form>
</layer>
</body>
</html>
```

FIGURE 23.1.

Working with the Layers Array.

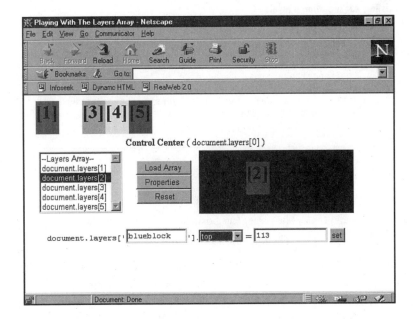

23

TRANSITION EFFECTS

This code presents your browser with six layers. The five small color-keyed blocks are manipulated through the form in the "Control Center," housed in the first layer. The page, shown in Figure 23.1, allows you to dynamically set the position and visibility of a layer through the use of a form and some simple JavaScript. In the example, referring to the layer can be done in one of two ways: either `document.layers[1]` or `document.layers['redblock']`. Add a property to the end of either one of those objects, assign a value, and you've changed that attribute.

Easier and Faster Animations

One of the points I've stressed is that layers can be used to create fast-loading animations. Conventional Web-based animations range from simple GIF89a images to complex streaming video clips, many of which can range in size from 25K to several megabytes for higher quality content. You can move, clip, and hide or show layers on demand to create complex animations that don't even come close to using the bandwidth consumed by standard means.

Animating Layers with JavaScript

As you saw in the example in Listing 23.1, you can assign the position to a layer on-the-fly. How can you create animations using this idea? Simple! Take a look at the `slideTo` function in Listing 23.2 to see how you can progressively move a layer to a destination.

Listing 23.2. Sliding a layer.

```
function slideTo(targetLayer, targetTop, targetLeft) {
    if((targetLayer.top != targetTop) || (targetLayer.left != targetLeft)) {
        if (targetLayer.top < targetTop) targetLayer.top = targetLayer.top  + 1;
        if (targetLayer.top > targetTop) targetLayer.top = targetLayer.top  - 1;
        if (targetLayer.left < targetLeft) targetLayer.left = targetLayer.left  + 1;
        if (targetLayer.left > targetLeft) targetLayer.left = targetLayer.left  - 1;
        setTimeout('slideTo(document.layers["'+targetLayer.name+'"],'+targetTop+',
        ➡'+targetLeft+')',1);
    }
}
```

The `slideTo` function accepts three arguments:

- `targetLayer`—A reference to the layer to be moved
- `targetTop`—The target top position of the moving layer
- `targetLeft`—The target left position of the moving layer

By setting a timer event in the function, the movement of the layer is slowed down somewhat, so it appears to be sliding across the screen to that position. When both conditions are finally met for the `while` loop, the function clears the time-out event and exits. In Chapter 9, "Using JavaScript with Dynamic HTML," you learned how JavaScript 1.2 allows you to capture and route events. By capturing the `mouseUp` event and routing it to the `slideTo` function, you can create a layer that "follows" the user's instructions on your Web page.

How about using it to tell a virtual puppy to obey your commands? Check out Listing 23.3 for a glimpse at how the page featured in Figure 23.2 handles this animation based on where you click.

Listing 23.3. Basic layer animation.

```html
<html>
<head>
<title>Walk The Dog</title>
</head>
<body bgcolor="white">
<script language="JavaScript1.2">
<!--//

//first off, the page sets itself to capture the
//MOUSEDOWN event and route it to the moveLayer handler

window.captureEvents(Event.MOUSEDOWN);
window.onmousedown = moveLayer;


//The moveLayer function takes the mousedown event, and throws
//where the user clicked to the slideTo function.  It also moves
//the cartoon style 'blurb' layer to where the mouse was clicked,
//changing it to visible, and releases the MOUSEDOWN event.

function moveLayer(e) {
    slideTo(document.layers['slider'], e.pageY, e.pageX);
    document.layers['blurb'].moveTo(e.pageX, e.pageY);
    document.layers['blurb'].visibility = true;
    window.releaseEvents(Event.MOUSEDOWN);
}

//the only thing added to this iteration of the slideTo function
//was an 'else' block, that hides the 'blurb' layer, then re-enables
//capturing of the MOUSEDOWN event.  The reason I release the event
//is to avoid confusing the script by recursively calling the slideTo
//function with different coordinates.

function slideTo(targetLayer, targetTop, targetLeft) {
    if((targetLayer.top != targetTop) || (targetLayer.left != targetLeft)) {
        if (targetLayer.top < targetTop) targetLayer.top = targetLayer.top  + 1;
        if (targetLayer.top > targetTop) targetLayer.top = targetLayer.top  - 1;
        if (targetLayer.left < targetLeft) targetLayer.left = targetLayer.left  + 1;
        if (targetLayer.left > targetLeft) targetLayer.left = targetLayer.left  - 1;
        setTimeout('slideTo(document.layers["'+targetLayer.name+'"],'+targetTop+
        ➥',' +targetLeft+')',1);
    } else {
        window.captureEvents(Event.MOUSEDOWN);
        document.layers['blurb'].visibility = false;
    }
}
}
//-->
</script>
<body bgcolor="white">
```

continues

Listing 23.3. continued

```
<!-- the 'slider' layer holds the picture of the puppy -->
<layer z-index=2 id="slider" height=50 width=50 top=0 left=0>
<img src="puppy.gif" border=0 height=50 width=50>
</layer>
<!-- the 'blurb' layer is invisible until the user clicks on the page -->
<!-- when it is moved to the spot clicked, and shown -->

<layer z-index=1 visibility=hide id="blurb" width=50 height=50 top=100 left=100>
<img width=50 height=50 src="cartoon.gif">
</layer>
</body>
</html>
```

Shown in Figure 23.2, the entire Walk The Dog page, animation, graphics, and HTML, is only around 5KB. Something that small is sure to load fast, even over a dial-up connection. If you'd attempt to duplicate just the moving dog itself, with any other technology, the file sizes and transfer times would increase accordingly.

FIGURE 23.2.

Walk The Dog: simple layer animation.

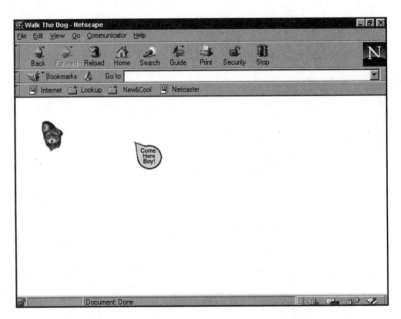

You probably noticed the bit of code in the function moveLayer document.layers['blurb']. moveTo(e.pageX, e.pageY); that controlled the "blurb" layer. When moving a layer, you have several different layer methods at your disposal. The moveTo method, which was touched on in Chapter 22, "Using Layers," accepts two arguments: the x or top position of the layer, and the y or left position of the layer. These coordinates are in relation to its parent container, in this case the document. As an alternative, you could use the moveBy method, which accepts the same x and y arguments as the moveTo method, but the values are the number of pixels to move in either direction.

How Layers Stack Up

Another thing to keep in mind when scripting layer movement is the layer's position in the stack. Think of the stacking order of layers like a deck of cards. The King may be over the Ace, which is under the Jack. Confused? Look at the page in Figure 23.3, which has a total of four layers.

FIGURE 23.3.

Over, under, above, and below: ordering layers.

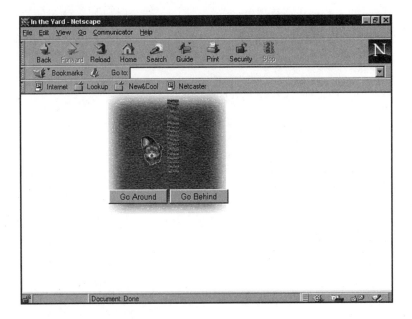

The grass, tree, dog, and form buttons are each contained on separate layers. The source code is available in Listing 23.4, and you can see how each of the layers has a z-index attribute specified. When working with the z-Order of layers on a Web page, higher numbers mean that those layers are above any lower-numbered layers. The base layer (yard) has a z-index of 1, and all the other layers fall above that in the stacking order. The "tree" layer has a z-index of 3, allowing the "puppy" layer to have a z-index of 2 so it can move behind the tree.

It's easy to set up a layered page with the correct order, but changing the z-index of layers on-the-fly to create layers that move above and behind one another requires JavaScript. Notice the walkDog function in Listing 23.4. Passed an argument of a single number (the argument (d), either a 1 or 0), the walkDog function determines whether the "puppy" layer is below or above the "tree" layer. Based on that argument, either the moveBelow or moveAbove method is used on the layer. Both of these methods accept a reference to a layer as their single argument. The code dl.moveBelow(document.layers['tree']) re-assigns dl (object variable that got set to document.layers['puppy'] in the first line of the function) to be below document.layers['tree'] in the z-Order.

From that point it's pretty straightforward. The first if... else... block checks to make sure that the "puppy" layer is either at the start or end position of the movement cycle, making sure that the layer isn't trying to move in multiple directions at once. The last if... else conditional determines whether the puppy is on the right or left, and fires off the slideTo function to move the layer in the opposite direction.

Listing 23.4. Controlling the z-Order.

```
<html>
<head>
<title>In the Yard</title>
</head>
<body bgcolor="white">
<script language="Javascript1.2">
<!--//

function walkDog(d) {
    var dl = document.layers['puppy'];
    if ((dl.left == 270) || (dl.left == 200)) {
        if (d == 1) {
            dl.moveBelow(document.layers['tree']);
        } else {
            dl.moveAbove(document.layers['tree']);
        }
        if (dl.left == 200) {
            slideTo(dl, 70, 270);
        } else if (dl.left == 270) {
            slideTo(dl, 70, 200);
        }
    }
}

function slideTo(targetLayer, targetTop, targetLeft) {
    if((targetLayer.top != targetTop) || (targetLayer.left != targetLeft)) {
        if (targetLayer.top < targetTop) targetLayer.top = targetLayer.top  + 1;
        if (targetLayer.top > targetTop) targetLayer.top = targetLayer.top  - 1;
        if (targetLayer.left < targetLeft) targetLayer.left = targetLayer.left  + 1;
        if (targetLayer.left > targetLeft) targetLayer.left = targetLayer.left  - 1;
        setTimeout('slideTo(document.layers["'+targetLayer.name+'"],'+targetTop+
        ➥',' +targetLeft+')',1);
    }
}
//-->
</script>
<body bgcolor="white">

<layer z-index=2 id="grass" background="grass.gif" height=200 width=200 top=0
➥left=150></layer>

<layer z-index=4 id="tree" background="tree.gif" height=124 width=20 top=10
➥left=250></layer>

<layer z-index=3 id="puppy" height=50 width=50 top=70 left=200>
<img src="puppy.gif" border=0 height=50 width=50>
</layer>
```

```
<layer name="commands" top=120 left=0>
<form>
<input type="button" value="Go Around" width=100 onClick="walkDog(0)"><br>
<input type="button" value="Go Behind" width=100 onClick="walkDog(1)">
</form>
</layer>

</body>
</html>
```

> **NOTE**
>
> I must apologize for the overabundance of the dog in this section. While I had originally written the examples with a smiley face, our puppy paid a visit to my office and became the victim of my digital camera. Besides, with the name Packet, he fits perfectly in an Internet-related book.

Dynamically Creating Animated Layers

Until this point, all the layers in the examples were written right into the HTML. The bulk of the time, documents have their layers predefined, but occasionally, you need to create new layers on demand. By using the new operator, you can use JavaScript to create new layers on-the-fly.

When generating new layers, there are several key things to keep in mind. First, any new layer you create has a visibility of false until you set it. That was enough to make me pull my hair out for hours trying to figure out why everything was fine, no errors were generated, but my new layers were missing in action. Second, once you create a layer, it's a blank canvas; you have to either write content to it, or use the load method to bring in an external source file. Third and most important, just remember that you can't create new layers until the page has finished loading.

The page shown in Figure 23.4 starts off with one simple layer in the upper-left corner and is set to capture the MOUSEDOWN event. Viewing the code in Listing 23.5, you can see that when the event happens, it's routed to the buildLayer function. A new layer is created, and its source is written using the document.write method. The script can determine exactly where the user clicked on the page. Passing a reference to the new layer along with the coordinates determined by e.pageY and e.pageX, the slideTo function can move the new layer to where the click took place.

In the interest of saving time on generating and moving these new layers, the slideTo function was slightly modified to move the layer at a faster pace. The function shown in Listing 23.5 increments the layer's position by 15 pixels, and rather than check to see if the layer is at the exact point the user clicked, it loops until the position of the layer is greater than the spot that was clicked.

FIGURE 23.4.

New layers on demand.

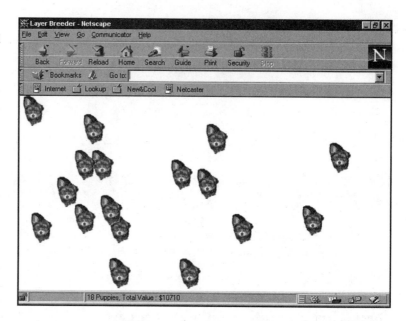

Just for kicks, when the new layer is moved into position and the MOUSEDOWN event is recaptured, the script updates the status bar with the total number of puppies, and a running total of what they're worth. With the ability to create new layers, almost anything is possible. You could have a menu of news items in a page, and clicking on one of them would create a new layer with the article and move it to a prespecified destination. Because these layers are created on demand, you wouldn't have to write new layers into the parent document, just script an event handler that creates the new layer, and load an external source file into it that contains the article.

Listing 23.5. Creating layers with JavaScript.

```
<html>
<head>
<title>Layer Breeder</title>
</head>
<body bgcolor="white">
<script language="Javascript1.2">
<!--//

//capture MOUSEDOWN events, routing them to the buildLayer function
window.captureEvents(Event.MOUSEDOWN);
window.onmousedown = buildLayer;

//The buildLayer function takes the mousedown event, and starts
//by creating a new layer object.  After dynamically writing the
//html needed for the 'puppy.gif' image, it makes the new layer
//visible, and starts a modified slideTo function that moves it
//to where the user clicked. Again, the MOUSEDOWN event is released
//to ensure that you don't end up overloading your browser with
//fifty or so layers moving at once.
```

```
function buildLayer(e) {
   var newPup = new Layer(50);
   newPup.document.write("<img src='puppy.gif' width=50 height=50>");
   newPup.document.close();
   newPup.moveTo(0,0);
   newPup.visibility=true;
   slideTo(newPup, e.pageY, e.pageX);
   window.releaseEvents(Event.MOUSEDOWN);
}

//This modified slideTo function, in the interest of building new layers
//as fast as possible, just fires until the layer is beyond
//the target coordinate on the screen.  Just for kicks, because it's a
//Yorkshire Terrier, and those dogs aren't cheap, it also keeps a running
//tally of your total amount in dogs in the status line by
//multiplying the number of layers in the layers array by $595 :)

function slideTo(targetLayer, targetTop, targetLeft) {
   if((targetLayer.top <= targetTop) || (targetLayer.left <= targetLeft)) {
      if (targetLayer.top <= targetTop) targetLayer.top = targetLayer.top  + 15;
      if (targetLayer.left <= targetLeft) targetLayer.left = targetLayer.left  +
15;
      setTimeout('slideTo(document.layers["'+targetLayer.name+'"],'+targetTop+
      ',' '+targetLeft+')',1);
   } else {
      window.captureEvents(Event.MOUSEDOWN);
      n = document.layers.length;
      self.status = n + ' Puppies, Total Value : $' + (n * 595);
   }
}
//-->
</script>
<body bgcolor="white">

<layer id="puppy" height=50 width=50 top=0 left=0>
<img src="puppy.gif" border=0 height=50 width=50>
</layer>

</body>
</html>
```

23

TRANSITION
EFFECTS

Changing and Creating Layer Content

The previous example briefly touched on writing content to a layer, and I had mentioned in passing the ability to load external source files into a layer. It shouldn't come as any surprise that with JavaScript, you have complete control over what's shown in any layer in your document. Every layer can have an external source file, which is defined in the <layer> tag by the src attribute. But, by using the load method of a layer, you can load in a new source file, even if one had not been used previously.

The load method takes two arguments, the first of which is a string containing either a full or relative path to the source document, the second is a number used to resize the width of the layer. For example, document.layers[0].load("myfile.html", 300) loads the specified file into the first layer in the layer array and resizes its width to 300 pixels. This is perfect for instances where you may be regularly updating specific content, and allows you to make drastic changes to that content with no revisions to the parent page.

The other way to change the content, which was used on one of the previous examples, is by using the document.write() method. The code in Listing 23.6 shows how it's possible to give the appearance of an image resizing on-the-fly by looping through a function until the picture reaches a specified size.

Listing 23.6. Writing to a layer with JavaScript.

```
<html>
<head>
<title>Dynamic Layer Content</title>
</head>
<body bgcolor="white">
<script language="Javascript1.2">
<!--//

//The growPic and shrinkPic functions resize the layers and
//use the document.write() method to replace the layer's content
//with the same image, width larger or smaller height and width
//values.

function growPic(targetLayer, img, height, width) {
    if((targetLayer.clip.height <= height) ¦¦ (targetLayer.clip.width <= width)) {
       if (targetLayer.clip.height <= height) targetLayer.clip.height =
➡targetLayer.clip.height + 1;
       if (targetLayer.clip.width <= width) targetLayer.clip.width =
➡targetLayer.clip.width  + 1;
          targetLayer.document.write("<img src='" + img + "'
➡width="+targetLayer.clip.width+" height="+targetLayer.clip.height+">");
       targetLayer.document.close();
       setTimeout('growPic(document.layers["'+targetLayer.name+'"],"'+img+'",'+height+
➡','+width+')',1);
    }
}

function shrinkPic(targetLayer, img, height, width) {
    if((targetLayer.clip.height >= height) ¦¦ (targetLayer.clip.width >= width)) {
       if (targetLayer.clip.height >= height) targetLayer.clip.height =
➡targetLayer.clip.height - 1;
       if (targetLayer.clip.width >= width) targetLayer.clip.width =
➡targetLayer.clip.width  - 1;
          targetLayer.document.write("<img src='" + img + "'
➡width="+targetLayer.clip.width+" height="+targetLayer.clip.height+">");
       targetLayer.document.close();
       setTimeout('shrinkPic(document.layers["'+targetLayer.name+'"],"'+img+'",'
➡+height+','+width+')',1);
    }

}

//-->
</script>
<body bgcolor="white">
<layer id="control" height=40 width=100 top=4 left=0>
<!--- notice how the script is called 'parent.window.document' -->
<!--- this is used to call scripts in other windows and other -->
```

```
<!--- child layers within the document. A necessary evil sometimes.-->
<form>
<input type="button" value="Grow"
   onClick="growPic(parent.window.document.layers['puppy'],
➥'puppy.gif',100,100)"><input
   type="button" value="Shrink"
   onClick="shrinkPic(parent.window.document.layers['puppy'], 'puppy.gif',25,25)">
</form>
</layer>
<layer id="puppy" height=50 width=50 top=44 left=0>
<img src="puppy.gif" border=0 height=50 width=50>
</layer>
</body>
</html>
```

Advanced Scripting Concerns

Layers give you the ability to place multiple documents at specified locations on the page. For graphic artists around the world, this means online content gets prettier. As their counterparts in the Web programmer division get these pages full of nested layers and external content files, you can almost hear agonizing groans from their offices. Countless "'someFunction()' is not defined" error messages, browser crashes, and material that just doesn't do what it should do are likely. With a little foresight and patience you can work around some of the common problems that stem from using layered documents. In many cases, you can use those same features that create problems for some programmers to your advantage.

Scripts Within Layers

Accessing scripts within other layers can create major headaches for developers. Before layers, if a script was on a page, you called it, passing any necessary arguments, and it worked. With nested layers, just because a script is coded into the same page doesn't mean that the JavaScript interpreter can even find it.

The concept is easy to grasp. Take a peek at the HTML in Listing 23.7, which is for a page that has a nested layer setup up to three layers deep. There are two separate scripts on the page, both of them called usrMessage. The first one, which is accessible from any layer in the document by calling usrMessage() is located before the <body> tag. The second usrMessage() is within the layer named "first", and can be used by any layer, but must be called with the relative full document object path to that layer (document.layers['first'].usrMessage()) to work.

Listing 23.7. Scripting nested layers.

```
<html>
<head>
<title>Script Dilemma</title>
</head>
   <script>
   <!--//
```

continues

23

TRANSITION
EFFECTS

Listing 23.7. continued

```
    function usrMessage(st) {
        return prompt('Parent Window\n' + st, '');
    }
    //--->
    </script>
<body bgcolor="white">
<layer id="first" width=100 height=40 top=0 left=0>
    <script>
    <!--//
    function usrMessage(st) {
        return prompt('document.layers[\'first\'].document.layers[\'firstsub\'].\n'
➥+ st, '');
    }
    //--->
    </script>
</layer>

<layer id="second" width=100 height=40 top=45 left=0>
    <layer id="secondsub" width=96 height=36 top=2 left=2>
        <layer id="subchild1" width=50 height=30 top=3 left=3>
        <!--this one calls the usrMessage in the first document layer -->
        <a href="javascript:alert('Hi ' +
➥document.layers['first'].usrMessage('What\'s Your Name?')+'!')">CLICK</a>
        <!--this one calls the usrMessage at the head of the document -->
        <a href="javascript:alert('Hi ' + usrMessage('What\'s Your
➥Name?')+'!')">HERE</a>
        </layer>
    </layer>
</layer>

</body>
</html>
```

So, you have both global and local scripts to work with. Each layer can act as a separate document, and that layer can have its own scripts that it calls with the function name. Those scripts are accessible from other layers in the document, but must be called with the layer object's name added to the beginning of the function call.

Animating layers is easy to do with JavaScript, and hopefully with these examples under your belt, you can start envisioning the next revision of your Web site. In the next section, you'll see some practical uses of animations, and gain some insight into how you can incorporate similar components into your projects.

Using Animations

Just as image onMouseOver tricks quickly took hold as a standard on the Web, layered menus and documents are sure to follow the same path. This section will show you some real-world examples that can be easily integrated into site work you may be doing. From drag-and-drop to sliding menus and content layers, I've attempted to annotate the source code as much as possible, and make the function calls fairly broad to facilitate faster integration with your ideas.

You'll find all the source code used in this chapter located in the HTML Guru Companion Site at http://www.htmlguru.com, so feel free to copy, paste, and hack to your heart's content.

Real-World Dynamic HTML

Animations are great, and dogs are man's best friends, but what about using Dynamic HTML on a mainstream Web site? The possibilities are endless and limited only by your imagination as a developer. You've learned in the past chapters how to create, place, and control layers. You have a decent understanding of JavaScript 1.2 and Netscape's Document Object Model. Putting these pieces together on your site is pretty much up to you.

This section shows one simple way to use DHTML to create an interactive menu system for your Web pages. Similar to toolbars in Windows 95, the toolbar used in the example has an auto-hide feature, and allows you to access any page from this chapter with the click of a button. Extensive use of JavaScript, layers, and forms combine to give you a menu system that's smaller than 5KB in size. To get started, check out the source code in Listing 23.8.

Listing 23.8. DHTML Site Navigator.

```
<html>
<head>
<title>DHTML Site Navigator</title>
</head>

<!-- small style sheet to set the font properties on the menu -->
<style type="text/css">
<!--
all.mnuTxt{
text-decoration:none;
color:black;
font-family:Tahoma,Arial,Helvetica;
font-size:10pt
}
-->
</style>

<script language="JavaScript1.2">
<!--//

//initialize the global variables immediately...
var seed = 1;
var lastPage = '';
var timerID = null;
var timerRunning = false;

//A throwback to my days with JavaScript 1.0 under Netscape 2.0, the ParseArray
//function builds an arrays on the fly, based on the number of arguments passed to
it.  Occasionally, this type //of script is useful for when you're not too clear on
how many elements are going to be in the //array.  Added bonus code! It works on
any JavaScript-compliant browser!
function ParseArray() {
```

continues

Listing 23.8. continued

```
    this.length = ParseArray.arguments.length;
    for (var i = 0; i < this.length; i++) {
        this[i+1] = ParseArray.arguments[i]
    }
}


//A slideTo variant that uses the global variable 'seed' to increase the movement
//of the target layer.
function slideTo(targetLayer, targetTop) {
    seed = seed * 1.2;
    if((targetTop >= 0) &&  ((targetLayer.top + seed * 1.2) < targetTop)) {
        if (targetLayer.top < targetTop) targetLayer.top = targetLayer.top + seed;
        setTimeout('slideTo(document.layers["'+targetLayer.name+'"],
        ➡'+targetTop+')',1);
    } else if((targetTop < 0) &&  ((targetLayer.top - seed * 1.2) > targetTop)) {
        if (targetLayer.top > targetTop) targetLayer.top = targetLayer.top - seed;
        setTimeout('slideTo(document.layers["'+targetLayer.name+'"],
        ➡'+targetTop+')',1);
    } else {
        //make sure the layer is exactly at its target position and reset the 'seed'
//variable.
        seed = 1;
        targetLayer.top = targetTop;
    }
}


//The fun really starts here... two arrays are created to hold the titles and urls
//for the menu bar, and initialize the clock.  The init() function is called by the
//onLoad event of the document.
function init() {
//The sTitles array holds the titles of the pages on the select menu.
    var sTitles = new ParseArray('Current News',
                                 'Site Help',
                                 'Company Info',
                                 'Feedback');

//The sUrls array holds the filenames for the pages in the select list.
    var sUrls = new ParseArray('content1.htm',
                               'content2.htm',
                               'content3.htm',
                               'content4.htm');

//This for loop cycles through the sUrls and sTitles arrays, and populates the
//DHTML menu's select box with the page names and URLs to use.  To add a new page
//to the menu, you'd simply add or change elements in the two arrays above.
    for (var s = 1; s <= sUrls.length; s++) {
        var nPage = new Option(sTitles[s], sUrls[s]);
        document.layers['sysmenu'].layers['lock'].document.forms[0].pages.options[s]
➡= nPage;
    }
    //One of the buttons on the menu bar is a clock, so when the page is loaded,
    //the clock is set and fired up to keep track of the current time for the user.
    stopclock()
    showtime()
}
```

```
//Which way to go?  The showMenu() function determines the menu bar's current top
//position and fires off the slideTo function to handle the animation.  Most
//importantly, notice the first if... block that checks to see if the Auto Hide
checkbox is clear before activating any movement.
function showMenu(layerName) {
    if (document.layers['sysmenu'].layers['lock'].document.forms[0].hold.checked !=
➥false) {
        if (document.layers[layerName].top <= -32) {
            slideTo(document.layers[layerName], 0);
        } else if(document.layers[layerName].left >= 0) {
            slideTo(document.layers[layerName], -32);
        }
    }
}

//This function stops the clock if necessary.  Guards against dreaded memory leaks!
function stopclock(){
        if(timerRunning)
            clearTimeout(timerID)
        timerRunning = false
    }

//A quick hack of the classic showtime() function, this function formats a string
//with the current time, and tacks an 'am' or 'pm' onto it. The big switch from
//some of the older clock functions out there is that it changes the text on a
//button as opposed to the text in a simple text box.
function showtime(){
        var now = new Date();
        var hours = now.getHours();
        var minutes = now.getMinutes();
        var timeValue = "" + ((hours > 12) ? hours - 12 : hours);
        timeValue  += ((minutes < 10) ? ":0" : ":") + minutes;
        timeValue  += (hours >= 12) ? " pm" : " am";
        //notice how the button is referred to via the complete layer hierarchy
        document.layers['sysmenu'].layers['lock'].document.forms[0].clock.value =
➥timeValue;
        timerID = setTimeout("showtime()",1000);
        timerRunning = true;
}

//the openPage function grabs the value of the current selection from the 'pages'
//select object and loads it into the 'contentLayer' layer.  By loading the
//external document into an existing layerA quick hack of the classic showtime()
//function, this function formats a string with the current time, and tacks an 'am'
//or 'pm' onto it.  The big switch from some of the older clock function
openPage(obj) {
    if (obj.pages.selectedIndex > 0) {
        lastPage = document.layers['contentLayer'].src;
        document.layers['contentLayer'].src=obj.pages.options[obj.pages.
        ➥selectedIndex].value;
    }
}

//-->
</script>
```

continues

Listing 23.8. continued

```html
<body onLoad="init()" bgcolor="black">

<!-- the first layer uses mouseover and mouseout events to determine whether the
➥layer -->
<!-- is shown or hidden. It also serves as the parent layer for the rest of the
menu. -->
<layer id="sysmenu"
    onMouseOver="showMenu('sysmenu')"
    onMouseOut="showMenu('sysmenu')" bgcolor="silver" width=99% height=34 left=0
➥top=0>


<!-- Graphics? Not here!  The shadow is a 1 pixel tall layer in a darker shade of
➥gray. -->
<layer bgcolor="gray" width=100% height=1 left=0 top=33></layer>

<!-- The menu is held within the 'lock' layer's document.  I used a table here to
➥simplify -->
<!--the task of keeping the form elements lined up. -->
<layer id="lock" width=100% height=27 left=5 top=3>
<table cellspacing=0 cellpadding=0 border=0 width=100%>
<tr>
<form name="locker"><td align=center valign=middle>
<span class="mnuTxt"><input type="checkbox" name="hold">Auto Hide   ¦
<input type="button" value="Home"
➥onClick="parent.window.document.layers['contentLayer'].src='content0.htm'" > ¦
<select size=1 name="pages">
<option value=""> ---- Site Quick Navigator ----
<option value="">
<option value="">
<option value="">
<option value="">
</select> <input type="button" value="Open"
    onClick="openPage(this.form)"> ¦
<input type="button" name="clock" value=" 00:00    "> ¦
<input type="button" value="Exit" onClick="self.close()" >

</span>
</td></form>
</tr>
</table>
</layer>

</layer>

<!--this layer serves as the screen, or canvas that the other pages are loaded in.
➥-->
<layer top=45 left=200 id="contentLayer" height=245 width=400 src="content0.htm">

</layer>

</body>
</html>
```

The concept behind the example is simple: Create a constant navigation system for the user. Think of the code shown in Listing 23.8 as a television, with the menu bar controlling the channels on the screen (the `contentLayer` layer) and the external files referenced in the `sTitles` and `sUrls` arrays as channels. The page makes a great starting point for a wide variety of Dynamic HTML projects.

Some of the possible uses are an online catalog, a real estate property showcase, a news center, or just a cooler way to view your site. To modify the framework, customize the HTML in Listing 23.8, adding whatever artwork, graphics, and links that you see fit. Pay careful attention to the size and position of the `contentLayer` layer. You need to make sure that your external files fit in the width defined by this layer. As an alternative, you could even create another layer behind `contentLayer`, allowing your HTML to appear over the image of a monitor screen, theater, or stage.

Adding your own pages to the menu requires a simple modification to the code in Listing 23.8. Toward the top of the script, in the `init()` function, are two calls that create arrays based on a list of URLs and Web page titles. These two lists should be exactly the same length (that is, if you have four URLs, you should have four titles) so the list shows the correct information. After plugging in this information about your pages, save and reload the page. Your new Web documents are easily accessible, and will load in the same area as the other content. To change the start page of the site, modify the `src` attribute of `contentLayer`. In a few simple steps, you have a new, innovative Dynamic HTML interface to your creation.

Avoiding Overload

There are some things to be aware of when creating Dynamic HTML-driven sites. It's quite easy to overload the user (and possibly their browser) with too many animations at any given point. Extensive use of `setTimeout()` functions is a common mistake, resulting in animations that may work fine for the first 30 seconds or so, but generate errors after that point. Also, when attempting to use the maximum screen area possible as the canvas for your creation, it's important to remember that people are viewing your site in a wide range of resolutions and color depths. I personally use a 1024×768 resolution on my desktop, and either a 640×480 or 800×600 resolution on my laptop. Just as having access to older browsers makes sense to ensure that the folks out there who haven't upgraded yet get some semblance of a normal page when hitting your site, it's imperative to view the work under various screen resolutions.

Summary

As you've seen, Netscape's layer implementation makes it incredibly easy to create high impact, low bandwidth animation and transition effects. The material covered in this chapter is very Netscape-specific, and is meant to show how to use the `<layer>` tag to enhance or replace more conventional navigation and multimedia effects that you may use in everyday development. The next chapter will cover the other side of the coin, and delve into doing animations, transitions, and filters through syntax and objects unique to Internet Explorer 4. You can support both browsers on the same page through the use of careful scripting, external content files, and the <nolayer> tag.

Building a Web site with Dynamic HTML content takes careful planning, a grasp of the various elements used, and a fairly decent understanding of what people are using to access your pages. I can't stress enough that deciding which Dynamic HTML path to follow should depend on what your visitors are using. With research, and some decent statistics from your server's log files, you can decide for yourself on which side of the fence your Web site's Dynamic HTML tricks should fall.

CHAPTER 24

IE 4.0 Multimedia Effects with Dynamic HTML

by John J. Kottler

IN THIS CHAPTER

In the world of the Internet, users have become accustomed to technology that changes quickly. Within the past year we have witnessed many changes in Internet computing and have been introduced to some new technologies. There was a time when the Internet was simply a collection of static pages, linked in some fashion to other related information around the world. Within just the past year, however, we have seen how the Internet is turning into a true computing platform. This can be seen by the number of online database systems, E-Commerce, and other applications that are becoming more apparent. But even more interesting is the heightened approach in marketing and interaction between the user and the Web site.

In an attempt to make the Internet even more appealing, one of the most exciting areas of computing is being further enhanced on the Internet: multimedia. Although arguably multimedia has existed on the Internet in one fashion or another for quite some time, with the introduction of new browsers such as Microsoft's Internet Explorer 4.0, truly rich yet practical multimedia experiences can be created for the first time on the Internet. With Internet Explorer 4.0 creating multimedia sites becomes a reality, because many multimedia-rich functions are built into and included with the Internet Explorer 4.0 client.

What does this combination of Internet Explorer and multimedia features mean? From the user's perspective the advantage is simple: A user can enjoy all the richness of multimedia sites that the Internet has to offer without needing to obtain and install ActiveX controls, plug-ins, or other inconvenient objects to display content. The necessary multimedia controls are available immediately and the user does not need to endure long delays while controls are downloaded from the Internet. From the developer's perspective, because many multimedia features are included with Internet Explorer 4.0, the developer simply needs to optimize a Web site for Internet Explorer and can be assured that visitors will be able to receive the content as it was intended.

Where Multimedia Has Been

Multimedia has many definitions. Usually a multimedia application is one that consists of animation, video, and sound. On the Internet, the world of multimedia has progressed slowly. In the beginning, multimedia on the Internet consisted of hyperlinks that pointed to audio or video files that could be painstakingly downloaded by the user and played by a separate program. To help Web developers control the appearance of video, Shockwave animations, or other rich data types within their pages, plug-ins were added to the Web browser that displayed this content within regions that the developer specified. In addition, new streaming technologies were soon introduced to help relieve the burden of downloading a large video file. Animated GIFs soon became the optimal approach for creating simply animated pictures. But even with all these improvements, there was still a lack of interactivity on Web pages. Only true embedded applications such as Java applets or ActiveX controls could provide the interactive multimedia applications that designers craved.

Where Multimedia Is Headed

Let's face it, until recently the only way to create truly interactive Web pages was to include Java applets or ActiveX controls, either of which required much more programming experience. Throughout this book, you have seen that Dynamic HTML is capable of offering features similar to those found in application development environments such as Java. Therefore, the future of multimedia on the Internet includes and relies heavily upon the use of Dynamic HTML.

There are many ways to accomplish multimedia effects using Internet Explorer 4.0 and DHTML. Internet Explorer is rich with multimedia capabilities and its Document Object Model, which has been proposed to the World Wide Web Consortium for standardization, makes the manipulation of objects on an HTML form simple. This simplicity is important because one possible method for creating multimedia animation is to simply move objects via script commands on a page.

Another more impressive feature of Internet Explorer 4.0 is its capability to render special effects or filters on objects or sets of objects within a Web page. With this capability it is possible to create special effects on static information on a page, or programmatically control these effects to create even more stunning presentations. Some of these effects, which will be covered later in the section "The Filter List," include `Blur`, `Alpha Channel`, `Chroma Key`, `Glow`, `Shadow`, `Waves`, and `Stage Lights` to name a few.

In addition to the scripting and effect filters offered by Internet Explorer, the capability to perform transition effects on a Web page is also included. Transition effects are segues from one image or text block to another. These transitions are the same as those found in typical presentation software packages such as Microsoft PowerPoint. Transition effects such as fade to black, wipe left or right, vertical blinds, and checkerboard are just a few examples. These effects can be applied to the enter Web page or to individual objects within the Web page. They can even be used to span multiple Web pages, providing a visually appealing transition between pages in a site or a cue for when a user has clicked on a link that leads outside the site.

Finally, as appealing as these special effects and transitions are for creating multimedia sites, there is still room for improvement when it comes to complex multimedia. To accommodate for this need, Microsoft is bundling its Direct Animation control with Internet Explorer 4.0. This ActiveX object works with DirectX technologies to provide accelerated and complex animations. Some of the capabilities that Direct Animation provides include 3D and polygon rendering, animation paths, sprite manipulation, and direct control over audio. However, an incredibly powerful multimedia tool, covering Direct Animation completely, is beyond the scope of this chapter. Instead, we will concentrate on multimedia capabilities included in Internet Explorer 4.0 that are exposed directly through standard DHTML without special ActiveX controls.

24

IE 4 MULTIMEDIA EFFECTS WITH DYNAMIC HTML

Up, Up, and Away

Throughout this book, you have witnessed how DHTML and scripting can dramatically improve the usability of a Web page. Likewise, scripting can change the position of DHTML-controlled objects to create movement, change the object's size, or perform many other manipulations. In this section, we will investigate how to move objects, size objects, and change their layering behind or in front of other objects.

To understand how scripting can aid in animating objects, let's first take a look at a sample Web page. Figure 24.1 demonstrates a basic Web page with two images of balloons. Although these images are static in the figure, they actually float around the screen. When they hit the sides of the screen, they bounce in the opposite direction. Additionally, the blue balloon becomes larger as it nears the center of the screen and shrinks back to normal size as it moves away from the center. Notice that the Swap Blue/Green Z-Order button toggles which balloon is on top of the other.

FIGURE 24.1.

Using DHTML and scripting commands, it is possible to move and size objects to create animation.

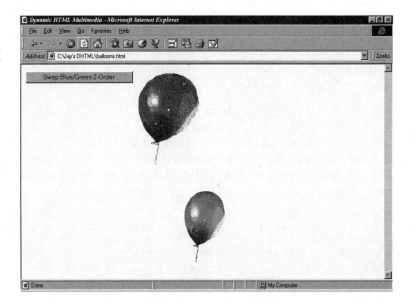

Previously, this type of animation was only possible using plug-ins such as Macromedia Shockwave or Java applets. But now it is possible to do the same animation techniques with DHTML and scripting languages. To begin to understand how these flying balloons are animated in Figure 24.1, let's take a look at the source code for the page. Listing 24.1 contains the Web page file necessary to create the animated balloons.

Listing 24.1. Using VBScript, cascading style sheets, and DHTML, it is possible to create complex animations.

```
<HTML>
<HEAD>
<TITLE>
Dynamic HTML Multimedia
</TITLE>
</HEAD>

<SCRIPT LANGUAGE="VBScript">
dim dir1_x, dir1_y, dir2_x, dir2_y

'Set some initial x,y directions for Balloon1
dir1_x=5
dir1_y=-2

'Set some initial x,y directions for Balloon2
dir2_x=-3
dir2_y=4

sub window_onload()
    'Start a timer.  Every 100ms (1/10 second), call the
    'function that updates the balloon positions.
    window.settimeout "moveBalloons()",100
end sub

sub swapZOrder()
    'Z-Order for the balloons initially are 0 and 1.
    'Doing a "NOT" will toggle state of zIndex property
    'between 0 and 1. This treats the property as boolean
    '     ie: not 1 = 0, not 0 = 1

    balloon1.style.zIndex = not balloon1.style.zIndex
    balloon2.style.zIndex = not balloon2.style.zIndex
end sub

sub moveBalloons()
    bal1_x = balloon1.style.posLeft
    bal1_y = balloon1.style.posTop
    bal2_x = balloon2.style.posLeft
    bal2_y = balloon2.style.posTop

    'If balloon goes off the sides of the screen,
    'Change the balloon's direction.
    if bal1_x<0 or bal1_x>500 then
        dir1_x = -1 * dir1_x
    end if

    if bal1_y<0 or bal1_y>400 then
        dir1_y = -1 * dir1_y
    end if

    if bal2_x<0 or bal2_x>500 then
        dir2_x = -1 * dir2_x
    end if
```

24

**IE 4 MULTIMEDIA
EFFECTS WITH
DYNAMIC HTML**

continues

Listing 24.1. continued

```
        if bal2_y<0 or bal2_y>400 then
            dir2_y = -1 * dir2_y
        end if

        'We want the balloon to shrink or expand when in the middle,
        'depending on the direction of the balloon.
        if bal1_x>200 and bal1_x<300 then
            balloon1.style.posWidth=balloon1.style.posWidth + dir1_x
            balloon1.style.posHeight=balloon1.style.posHeight + dir1_x
        end if

        'We want the balloon to shrink or expand again past the middle,
        'depending on the direction of the balloon.
        if bal1_x>300 and bal1_x<400 then
            balloon1.style.posWidth=balloon1.style.posWidth - dir1_x
            balloon1.style.posHeight=balloon1.style.posHeight - dir1_x
        end if

        balloon1.style.posleft = bal1_x + dir1_x
        balloon1.style.posTop = bal1_y + dir1_y

        balloon2.style.posLeft = bal2_x + dir2_x
        balloon2.style.posTop = bal2_y + dir2_y

        'Call this function again to create a loop, to continuously move.
        window.settimeout "moveBalloons()",100
end sub

</SCRIPT>

<BODY>
<INPUT TYPE=BUTTON
        VALUE="Swap Blue/Green Z-Order"
        onClick="swapZOrder()">

<img id=balloon1
     style="position:absolute;
            left:0px;
            top:100px;
            width:92px;
            height:164px;
            z-index:1"
     src="balloon1.gif">

<img id=balloon2
     style="position:absolute;
            width:92px;
            height:164px;
            left:500px;
            top:50px;
            z-index:0"
     src="balloon2.gif">

</BODY>

</HTML>
```

> **NOTE**
>
> Although Listing 24.1 is written using VBScript, any other scripting language such as JavaScript could be used. The scripting code simply performs some logical conditions and then updates properties of the image objects. Be careful, however, to check on other implementations of the Document Object Model in other browsers until a standard becomes available.

Moving Objects

When defining images using cascading style sheets (CSS), you may specify numerous properties. In our balloon example, we place the images of the balloons at absolute positions and indicate their layering position on top of each other. It is important to notice that when we use absolute positioning, it will be possible for us to return the exact pixel location later in our movement script. We can then modify that position easily by adding or subtracting values. For example, to move the image right, we can simply add a value to the present *left* location of the image. To move the image left, we can subtract (or add a negative value) to the image's present *left* location.

To start the animation process we need a timer, some form of conductor that keeps the event of moving objects going. This timer event can be emulated using the `setTimeOut` function. This function causes the browser to wait a given number of milliseconds and then call a function, in this case the `moveBalloons` function.

Within the `moveBalloons` function, the script starts by assigning local variables to the various left and top positions of the two balloon images. Although this is not necessary, it makes life easier later in the script when we need to constantly reference these values. Instead of typing the complete line `balloon1.styles.posLeft`, we can simply use `bal1_x`. This will actually save computational time as well, because the position information used in the conditional statements can be retrieved as fast variables instead of invoking the actual image objects each time.

After setting variables and before actually updating the image's properties, we need to do some checking. This checking verifies the current position of the objects to make certain that they won't go far off the screen. Each item is checked to see whether its position is less than the left side or top of the screen. Each is also checked to see whether its position is greater than the right side or bottom of the screen. If any of these cases occurs, the direction for the object in question is reversed to create a "bouncing off the wall" effect.

> **TIP**
>
> Although the use of global variables is not traditionally good practice, in certain circumstances, such as animation, they can be particularly useful. In Listing 24.1, the direction of each balloon is held in a global variable so that it does not get lost between function calls.

After performing all the conditional checks, we can update the actual positions of the objects. This update is accomplished by changing the posLeft or posTop properties of the style attribute for each object. The actual change is accomplished by taking the previous posLeft or posTop properties and adding an amount to it. In this example it is important to notice that we are using the posLeft and posTop properties of the style sheet, not the left and top properties. Although the left and top properties specify the X and Y location for the top-left corner of an object, these values are stored as strings. Also, because style sheets allow developers to position objects using a variety of units of measurement, these string values are followed by characters that indicate what unit is being used. For instance in our balloon example, the balloon images are loaded and placed at exact pixel (px) locations.

When attempting to update actual numeric values of these properties, we do not want the trailing unit of measure to get in the way. When we add five pixels, we want the *value* of the property to be increased; we do not want the string "5" added to the end of the current position, such as "20px5". To avoid the use of string converters that change these strings to values, you can simply reference the posTop, posLeft, posWidth, posHeight properties. The prefix pos returns the property values for a style sheet as true numbers, not strings.

Blowing Up Balloons

Already you can see the power of scripting languages for creating multimedia animations. With the scripting language and the power of DHTML, it is possible to change any object's property value at any time. Additionally, you can create more interesting effects by changing these values continuously over time or adding logic to the changes that are made.

For purely demonstration purposes, the blue balloon in Figure 24.1 becomes larger, or is "blown up," as it passes through the center of the page. This dynamic scaling is accomplished in a similar manner as the balloons are moved. If we look back at the moveBalloons function again, you will notice that there are some additional checks being performed toward the end of the function. These validations simply determine the location of the blue balloon (balloon1) and whether it is in the middle, expands, or contracts the balloon accordingly. This change in size can be easily accomplished by tweaking the width and height parameters for the image.

Although we could simply just double the amount of both the width and height of the image to double the overall size of the image, we want to make the balloon appear to grow. Therefore, the script will cause these values to change progressively. You may also notice that the script in Listing 24.1 uses the dir1_x and dir1_y variables to update the size of the balloon. This is simply for ease of scripting instead of introducing separate variables. We want the balloon to expand just to the left of the center and collapse to the right of center while the balloon is heading to the right. If the balloon is heading left, we want the same effects to occur, but in reverse order. Because the direction variables are already set to positive or negative values depending on the direction the balloon is headed, we can cheat and use those values in the width and height to achieve the desired effect.

You Before Me, Except After Z

To complete this flying balloons example, you'll remember that Figure 24.1 demonstrates a pushbutton in the top-left corner of the page that toggles the "Z-Order" (zIndex) of the balloon objects on the page. Pressing this button will toggle the green balloon on top of the blue balloon, or vice versa. The zIndex property specifies how far behind or in front of other objects a particular object should be. The lower the number specified in an object's zIndex, the further back that object will be. The appearance achieved is that objects with a lower Z-Order will be drawn underneath other objects on the screen, while objects with higher Z-Order values will be drawn on top. Therefore, although the balloon example uses 0 and 1 for each object's zIndex, it is possible to use any positive or negative integer value.

> **TIP**
>
> You can think of Z-Order as the depth between objects. Just as you think of X as horizontal position or width and Y as vertical position or height, Z is the depth of an object. You can think of each object on a Web page as being drawn on separate transparent pages of notebook paper. If you want to move one object in front of another, you would move that page forward. Moving objects forward programmatically simply means adding positive values to their zIndex. Moving objects backward is the exact opposite.

To provide this functionality in the balloon example, the standard intrinsic HTML button triggers the swapZOrder function via its onClick event. Whenever a user clicks on the button, the swapZOrder function is called, which adjusts the zIndex properties of each balloon by performing boolean operations. Figure 24.2 illustrates how the Z-Order of objects appear.

FIGURE 24.2.

With the zOrder *property it is possible to control whether the green balloon appears in front of or in back of the blue balloon.*

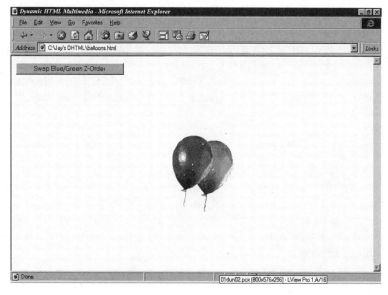

Adding Special Effects

Nowadays, no blockbuster movie would be complete without some incredible special effects. With the newest capabilities of Internet Explorer 4.0, soon no Web site will be without special effects as well. True, the special effects we're talking about here in Internet Explorer are not three-dimensional dinosaurs, but they are quite useful for creating sites with visual impact that no longer require separate images. Figure 24.3 demonstrates all the new special effect filters that are included with Internet Explorer 4.0. Although many of these filters are illustrated on images, they can be equally applied to other HTML objects such as text or buttons.

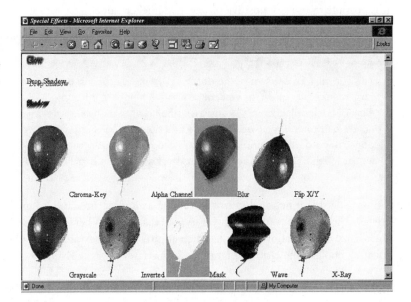

These special effects found in Internet Explorer 4.0 can be applied to any rectangular defining object in HTML. Therefore, they can be applied to objects such as BODY, BUTTON, IMG, INPUT, MARQUEE, TABLE, TH, TD, TR, THEAD, TFOOT, and TEXTAREA. These filters also can be used in conjunction with the DIV and SPAN tags as long as specific width and height properties are assigned for those tags.

Applying Filters

The filter techniques displayed in Figure 24.3 are defined and changed via cascading style sheets and the STYLE attribute for an HTML object. Therefore, you can set the filters for an object just as easily as you would specify an object's absolute position. Additionally, you can choose to change these filters dynamically using scripting languages and the Document Object Model to address filter properties for an object. Listing 24.2 demonstrates how to apply styles such as blur to an object.

Listing 24.2. Special effects are easily incorporated using style sheets syntax or by modifying property values.

```
<IMG SRC="balloon1.gif"
    STYLE="position:static;
           width:92;
           height:164;
           filter:blur(direction=135,strength=1)"
    ID=balloon1>

<SCRIPT LANGUAGE="VBScript">
    for z=1 to 150
        balloon1.filters.blur.direction = z
    next
</SCRIPT>
```

NOTE

Although filters can be set via the STYLE attribute, you do not need to use the STYLE property with the object that has a filter applied in script. The FILTERS property is associated directly with an object and any filter used with that object can be addressed by name, following the FILTERS property. Likewise, the actual value that you want to change within a filter can be addressed by name as well.

You will notice immediately that some filters contain additional properties of their own that can adjust the overall effect of the filter. For example, in Listing 24.2 the blur filter can be changed in both strength and the direction of the blur. These properties can be set via the STYLE attribute as comma-separated, name-value pairs. You can include as many specific properties as you like. Where no specific values are supplied, the default will be used.

Of course, you can address these properties equally as well using scripting commands. There is a collection of filters available for each object of the Web page. Each filter defined increases the total number of items in this collection. An individual filter applied on an object can be addressed one of three ways, mainly to accommodate for differences in languages and coding practices induced by languages such as VBScript and JavaScript:

- As an object of the FILTERS collection, such as `myObject.filters.alpha`
- By name, such as `myObject.filters["alpha"]`
- By index value, such as `myObject.filters[0]`

Chaining Filters Together

Most of these filters are useful and cool by themselves; however, it will become necessary at times to combine filters. For instance, you might find it necessary to apply an alpha channel filter to an object so that it appears semitransparent, but you may also need the blur effect to make it look like it is streaking across the screen as it moves.

Chaining filters together is relatively simple. You simply define as many filters as you would like to apply to an object in that object's STYLE tag. Each filter that you define must simply be separated by a space within the tag. When using multiple filters, the technique for referencing them by name becomes exceedingly important so that you can programmatically change the right filter at the right time. However, referencing these same filters by number is also useful for applying similar values to a set of filters that can be iterated easily with a loop in script. In this case, the order in which filters can be referenced by a number is directly related to the order in which multiple filters are defined using the STYLE tag for that object.

> **TIP**
>
> Be considerate with the use of filters. It is very easy to overdo the use of filters and make pages *less* appealing because special effects were used just for the sake of having them. Consider what you are trying to accomplish with filters and do not overuse them. Remember they should be used creatively to *enhance* your site, not be the focus of it.

The Filter List

To apply filters in Internet Explorer 4.0, you need to know the name of the filter as well as any additional properties that can be set on an individual filter. The following is a list of all the filters available in Internet Explorer 4.0 and the effects they produce.

> **TIP**
>
> You can group objects together within grouping tags such as a single DIV tag and affect all those objects at once with a single filter for the group tag.

Alpha(opacity, finishOpacity, style, startX, startY, finishX, finishY)

This filter allows you to specify the opacity of an object. In addition to simply making the object more or less opaque, you may also introduce opacity progressively from one point of the object to another. The following properties may be set for the Alpha filter:

- **opacity**—The level of opacity to be applied to an object. A value of 100 indicates that the object is to be painted entirely opaque, whereas 0 indicates a transparent object.

- **finishOpacity**—Because an object can be more opaque in one portion and less opaque in another, this value indicates how opaque the final position should be rendered. For instance, you could set the initial opacity to 100 and the finishOpacity to 0. The object would get progressively more transparent between the start and end points.

■ `style`—Because a gradient will be constructed to create the progressive opacity between the start and end points, you can choose what style of gradient you would like to use. The following table illustrates the values available:

0	None
1	Linear
2	Radial
3	Rectangular

■ `startX`/`startY`—These two values identify the starting X and Y positions for the opacity gradient that will be used.

■ `finishX`/`finishY`—Like `startX` and `startY`, these two values identify X and Y positions for the opacity gradient. They indicate the ending position of the gradient and do not necessarily have to be to the lower-right of the starting position.

Blur(add, direction, strength)

To make the appearance of quick movement, you can use the blur filter to streak pixels in a given direction with a specific strength.

■ `add`—After streaking the image, the original image will be blurry and unreadable. If you would like to redraw the original image at its original location, you can set this value to 1 for `true`; otherwise, set the value to 0 for `false`.

■ `direction`—Streaking can occur in any direction. This property allows you to specify that direction by supplying a value between 0 and 360 degrees in 45-degree increments, where zero is straight up.

■ `strength`—As the image streaks, you can specify how many pixels the filter will extend with this property.

Chroma(color)

Often images created will require a transparent color so that background information will pass through the image. This effect, often implemented via GIF89a graphic format files, can be added dynamically using the `Chroma` filter.

■ `color`—This property specifies the color in the image that you want to treat as transparent. This color is identified using the hexadecimal HTML red, green, and blue color pairs: `#000000` to `#FFFFFF`.

DropShadow(color, offX, offY, positive)

Usually graphics artists like to create the illusion of depth by adding a drop shadow to the lower-right corner of an image or text. The effect is essentially an all-gray version of the original image, copied behind the original image and moved slightly to the bottom right. This same effect can be accomplished easily with the `DropShadow` filter and numerous properties can be tweaked.

- **color**—Although most drop shadows are gray in color, they do not have to be. This property allows you to identify a color using the hexadecimal HTML red, green, and blue color pairs: #000000 to #FFFFFF.

- **offX/offY**—Common drop shadows can be found to the lower right, but you can change the amount of this offset and the direction by changing these properties. The offX property specifies the number of pixels to the left or right that the shadow should be offset. Likewise, the offY property specifies the number of pixels to offset above or below the image. Both values are identified in pixels and negative numbers can be used to indicate left or above offsets.

- **positive**—This property is set to 1 or true by default. Changing this value allows you to specify whether you would like to create a drop shadow for every nontransparent pixel (true or 1) in an image or for every transparent pixel (false or 0). If you set this property to 0, every transparent pixel in the original image will be used to make the shadow for the image. That shadow then will be drawn only within the non-transparent pixels of the original image. The end result is a shadow that is more like a mask that is rendered inside the image.

FlipH()

This is one of several filters that are available in Internet Explorer 4.0 that do not have additional properties. By adding this filter to an image, the image will be flipped horizontally. That is, the final image will appear as if you were holding up the image to a mirror.

FlipV()

Similar to the FlipH() filter, this filter does not require that any additional properties be set. Adding this filter to an object will flip the image vertically. This is equivalent to looking at the image upside down.

> **TIP**
>
> A good place to use the FlipH() and FlipV() filters is with animation. Let's assume that an object is moving to the left and the image for that object was drawn to face the left. If we want to move the image to the right, it then will appear that it is moving backward. By using the FlipH() filter, however, we can instantly change the direction of the graphic so that it is facing right.

Glow(color, strength)

Another interesting effect that is added to Web pages is the glow effect. This effect provides the illusion of a warm glow, cast off from the object itself. Graphics artists usually create this effect by applying a Gaussian blur to the image. This filter does not apply an actual Gaussian blur because that effect is too time-consuming. Instead, the blur is simulated to create a soft light that loses intensity as it moves away from the object.

- **color**—You can choose whatever color you want for the glow that emanates from behind the object. Like other filters, this color is identified using the standard HTML red, green, and blue color pairs: #000000 to #FFFFFF.

- **strength**—You may also specify the intensity for the glow effect ranging from 0 to 100, where 0 indicates no glow and 100 is maximum glow.

Gray()

This filter does not require any properties to be set in order to function. If you apply the Gray() filter to a color object, the filter will remove any color from the image and create a grayscale equivalent.

Invert()

The Invert() filter does not require any additional parameters. When this filter is invoked on an object, the colors in that object are inverted. This inversion reverses the hue, saturation, and brightness for each pixel within the colored object.

Mask(color)

The Mask() filter is very similar to the Chroma filter, but renders the opposite results. You will recall that the Chroma filter removes pixels of a particular color from an object and makes them transparent. The Mask filter removes all pixels from an object *except* those of a particular color. If our sample image is a balloon with a gray background, applying the Chroma filter for the gray color will remove the gray. But applying the Mask filter will "cut out" the balloon and leave just the surrounding gray image. This is particularly useful for creating "windows" to see only portions of objects behind the masked object.

- **color**—Similar to the Chroma filter, you must specify the HTML red, green, and blue color pairs (#000000 to #FFFFFF) for the color you would like to keep to form the mask.

Shadow(color, direction)

Not to be confused with DropShadow, the Shadow filter takes the original image and copies it as a specific color behind the original image at an offset position. What makes this filter different, however, is that the shadow streaks slightly behind the original image and its color intensity lightens as it moves away.

- **color**—Although most shadows are gray, they do not need to be. You can change the color of the shadow by changing this property to suitable HTML red, green, and blue color pairs (#000000 to #FFFFFF).

- **direction**—Shadows can be cast in any direction. To specify a direction, set this property to a degree between 0 and 360 in increments of 45 degrees. Again, like the Blur filter, a value of 0 indicates the shadow should be directly above the rendered image.

Wave(add, frequency, lightStrength, phase, strength)

To simulate sinusoidal waves within an image, you can use the Wave filter. This filter includes numerous properties for specifying the characteristics of the waves that run through an image.

- **add**—Similar to the Blur filter, you can set this property to 1 (true) to make a copy of the original image on top of the image that has been processed with the Wave filter. Usually the Wave filter will make the image somewhat illegible; this option allows the original image to be painted again without replacing the Wave effect entirely.

- **frequency**—This parameter is a number that indicates the number of waves that are to appear within the object that this filter acts upon. The higher this number is, the more waves are rendered.

- **lightStrength**—Because the waves are rendered, you can control the amount of light that should be projected on the rendered image. This strength can be controlled via this property as a percentage between 0 and 100, where 0 indicates no light.

- **phase**—This is the offset at which the waves will appear. Typically the waves begin at zero degrees, but by changing this value you can modify this amount. Valid values for this property are from 0 to 100 percent. In this case, 0 indicates 0 degrees and 100 specifies 360 degrees.

- **strength**—You can change how much of a ripple effect is caused by varying this filter's strength. This property is equivalent to the amplitude of a sine wave. The larger this amount, the larger ripples are caused to be rendered.

XRay()

This filter, like many others, does not need additional parameters to function. Applying this filter will decrease the color depth of an image and force it to grayscale. The final effect is an image that appears somewhat like an X ray of an object.

Light()

In addition to the usual filters that you have been introduced to, you have the ability to add rendered lighting effects on top of areas of the Web page. The lighting effects are being covered separately because they are the only filters that must be implemented using script. This is not necessarily bad, however, because the most dramatic lighting effects will be those that are animated, panning light across an object, for instance. In any case, the light filter requires that methods be invoked on the filter, not just the properties set. Because of these methods, you must use a call statement in VBScript to invoke the methods, as in this example:

```
call object.filters.light.addAmbient(R, G, B, strength)
```

Figure 24.4 illustrates a simple cone light added to the image of a balloon. To add a light filter to an object, you can use the same approach as with the other filters. The following is a list of the filter's methods.

FIGURE 24.4.
The balloon image is left dark except for the area to which a cone light is applied.

> **NOTE**
>
> Notice that in Figure 24.4 that the balloon appears black everywhere except where the light has been added. This is the default nature when you create light filters on an object. Everything within the object becomes dark (or black) until appropriate lights are displayed. If you want to show more of a blue balloon with a yellow highlight, consider adding an ambient light first to light the scene before a conical light.

AddAmbient(R, G, B, strength)

Ambient light is nondirectional light. Think of an incandescent lightbulb and the way it illuminates a room. You don't see the beams streaming out of the bulb in a single direction, but rather in all directions. By adding an ambient light to an object, you can change its color subtly. The light is similar to straight light, hitting your computer screen at a perpendicular angle.

- **R,G,B**—Together these parameters for the method indicate the color of the light being added to the scene. These parameters represent the amount of red, blue, and green light respectively. They are similar to the HTML color pairs that you are familiar with, but each integer value in this case ranges from 0 to 255.

- **strength**—Although you control the independent colors for a light, you can also adjust the light's overall intensity by modifying this parameter.

AddCone(x1,y1,z1,x2,y2,R,G,B,strength,spread)

To create more visual lighting effects, you will need to use lights other than ambient lights. The more stunning presentations come from directional light, in which you can see from where the light originates and the direction in which it scatters. Cone lights create directional light where the light cast forms the shape of a cone, tighter and brighter at its origin, and wider and dimmer as it spreads.

- **x1, y1, z1**—Because a cone light has an origin and an intended direction, you can specify the origin of the light with these first three parameters of the method. The parameters indicate where the origin of the light should exist horizontally, vertically, and depth-wise. Like Z-Order, higher values indicate that the light should be emanating from the front of the object, like a light behind you projecting at your computer display.

- **x2, y2**—Although conical light will spread, you can indicate the general direction in which you want it to be aimed. By modifying the x2 and y2 parameters, you can specify a point to which the light should be aimed.

- **R, G, B**—As usual, you can specify the unique color of each light. Again like ambient light, you adjust this color by specifying how much red, green, and blue you would like to mix into the light.

- **strength**—Just as with other lights, you can specify how bright you want the light to be by addressing this parameter in the method.

- **spread**—The conical shape rendered by the light method will spread as light emanates away from the origin. How much the light spreads is controlled by this method. The amount of spread is measured in degrees from 0 to 90.

AddPoint(x, y, z, R, G, B, strength)

Just as you can add other lights, you can also add another point light. These types of lights are similar to incandescent lightbulbs that radiate light in all directions. However, these lights can appear more as points within the scene, with light radiating off those points. An example of this would be a picture of the front of a car with lit headlights. These artificial lights could be enhanced with point lights to create a glow in the scene.

- **x, y, z**—Just as with the cone light, you can specify the exact location of a point light within the scene. These parameters specify the x, y, and z locations for the light.

- **R, G, B**—Also like the cone light, you can choose what color a point light should be. As with other lights, you can pick the color of the light by adjusting the red, green, and blue values with the R, G, and B parameters, respectively. Each value can be an integer between 0 and 255.

- **strength**—After specifying a location and color, you can adjust the light's intensity with the strength parameter.

ChangeColor(lightNumber, R, G, B, absolute)

After you have created your lights, you will continue to use methods to modify their values. The ChangeColor method, for instance, will allow you to change the color of a light after it has been created.

- **lightNumber**—Because multiple lights can be added for a single object, you can specify the number of the light you want to change. Lights are numbered by the order in which they are created.

- **R, G, B**—Because the method is named `ChangeColor`, obviously you will want to alter the color values for the light. These three parameters allow you to reset the amount of red, green, or blue to project from the light, respectively.

- **absolute**—The default value for this parameter is 1 (`true`). When set to `true`, the values you pass in for the R, G, and B parameters are the actual colors to change the light to. If you set this parameter to 0 (`false`), the R, G, and B parameters will indicate how much to change the color of the light. Therefore, if `absolute` is set to 0, you can set the B parameter to -15 to drop the value of the blue channel by 15.

ChangeStrength(lightNumber, strength, absolute)

Just as you can change light colors with the `ChangeColor` method, you can adjust the intensity of a light by modifying this parameter.

- **lightNumber**—Multiple lights can be assigned to a single object. Therefore, to determine which light is to be brightened or dimmed, a light's number must be passed as part of this method.

- **strength**—The actual intensity of the light can be set by this parameter.

- **absolute**—Similar to the `ChangeColor` method, you can choose whether you would rather change the intensity of the light directly to the `strength` parameter passed in or adjust how much to change the intensity of the light. If `absolute` is set to 0, you could set the `strength` parameter to -15 to reduce the intensity by 15.

Clear

If you want to remove all lights from a given object's light filter, you can simply call the `Clear` method. This method will remove *all* lights and the attributes of those lights from the object. You do not need to specify any additional parameters in order for this method to function.

MoveLight(lightNumber, x, y, z, absolute)

So far you have seen how to change the properties of the lights, but what if you wanted to reposition them? Fortunately the `MoveLight` method provides just this functionality.

- **lightNumber**—Because multiple lights may be assigned in a filter to an object, you must explicitly specify which light you want to move by number.

- **x, y, z**—Because you are changing the position of the light source, you must specify new x, y, and z coordinates for the light. For point lights, this is the location of the actual source of the light. For cone lights, only the x and y parameters are used to specify the direction to which the cone light is pointed.

Transitions

Another special type of filter that can be applied to elements of a Web page is transitions. These transitions, which you are already familiar with if you use presentation software such as Microsoft PowerPoint, allow you to do special segues between images, text, or other objects. Instead of simply changing presentation values of an object, you can change them gracefully with a transition. For instance, you can display an image on the page and then fade it out progressively until it is hidden.

You can also apply separate effects that will reveal portions of the destined image or text object until the entire object is displayed. The portions of the object that are revealed can be displayed in a variety of animation formats, including checkerboard, wipes, blinds, and much more. In Internet Explorer 4.0, the two types of transitions that are available are transitions that blend objects together and transitions that animate to reveal portions of objects. Figure 24.5 illustrates the transition between a green and blue balloon using the checkerboard transition. As you can see, the balloon on the right has the checkerboard effect across it. This effect is animated and each checkerboard square is elongated, revealing one balloon over another.

FIGURE 24.5.

Transition effects are useful for producing segues between images.

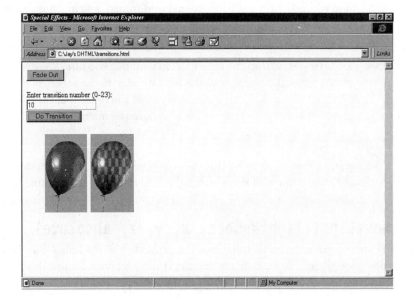

Using Transitions

To add transition capabilities to objects on a Web page, or to the Web page itself, you simply add either the `blendTrans` or `revealTrans` filters to the style attributes for the object or page. For example, the following code adds the `revealTrans` filter to an image on the page:

```
<IMG SRC="balloon1.gif"
     id=balloon2
```

```
STYLE="position:absolute;
       left:150;
       top:150;
       width:92;
       height:164;
       filter:revealTrans()">
```

Just like other filters, transition filters can also be modified by script. To reference a transition, you can simply use the `object.filters` syntax followed by the transition name. After the transition name, you can specify the transition property to change or the method that you want to invoke. For example, to play a transition via script you could use:

```
MyObj.filters.blendTrans.play()
```

Transition Properties

Both the `blendTrans` transition and the `revealTrans` transition contain similar properties and methods. The `main` transition property indicates the length of time allowed for the transition to occur. In addition to this, the `revealTrans` transition includes a second property for specifying exactly which transition to use.

- ■ **Duration**—The length of time for a transition to occur can be set via this property for a transition. This duration is measured in seconds, whereas a longer value indicates a slower transition.

- ■ **Transition**—With the `revealTrans` transition, the source object is replaced by the destination result by a progressive reveal. The nature in which the revealed areas of the object appear can be picked from one of 24 transition effects such as wipes or checkerboard. You can specify which transition to use by setting this property between the values of `0` and `24`. Table 24.1 lists all the transitions available to the `revealTrans` transition filter and their appropriate values.

Table 24.1. The `revealTrans` transition filter can create many effects similar to those found in presentation packages such as Microsoft PowerPoint.

Effect	Value
Box in	0
Box out	1
Circle in	2
Circle out	3
Wipe up	4
Wipe down	5
Wipe right	6
Wipe left	7

continues

Table 24.1. continued

Effect	Value
Vertical blinds	8
Horizontal blinds	9
Checkerboard across	10
Checkerboard down	11
Random dissolve	12
Split vertical in	13
Split vertical out	14
Split horizontal in	15
Split horizontal out	16
Strips left down	17
Strips left up	18
Strips right down	19
Strips right up	20
Random bars horizontal	21
Random bars vertical	22
Random	23

Transition Methods

Whether you use the `blendTrans` or the `revealTrans` transition, you will use three main methods. The combination of these methods instructs the browser which portions of the page are to be updated with new content and then executes the transition.

- **apply**—The `apply` method instructs the browser that the information following the `apply` method is to be updated in place of the object. Any information between the `apply` method and the `play` method will be considered new content to replace the original content. For instance, between the two methods you might want to hide the original object using a style sheet property. When the animated transition is played for that object, it will slowly disappear.

- **play**—After you have finished describing what you want to have happen to the objects after the transition, you can begin the transition. To start the transition, use the `play` method.

- **stop**—If you want to abort the transition and reveal the final result, you can stop the transition with this method.

Transition Example

Listing 24.3 illustrates transitions of Figure 24.5 in action. Notice that there are simply two subroutines invoked when buttons are clicked on the page. These subroutines perform either a blended transition or a revealed transition that uses the number in the text box as a transition effect identifier.

Listing 24.3. Transition effects can be easily created with filter style properties and manipulated by script.

```
<HTML>
<HEAD>
<TITLE>Special Effects</TITLE>

<SCRIPT LANGUAGE="VBScript">
sub doFade(obj)
    if obj.filters.blendTrans.status=0 then
        obj.filters.blendTrans.apply()
        obj.style.visibility="hidden"
    obj.filters.blendTrans.play()
    end if
end sub

sub doTrans(obj)
    if obj.filters.revealTrans.status=0 then
        obj.filters.revealTrans.apply()

        if right(obj.src,5)="1.gif" then
            obj.src="balloon2.gif"
        else
            obj.src="balloon1.gif"
        end if

        obj.filters.revealTrans.transition=TransType.value
        obj.filters.revealTrans.play()
    end if
end sub
</SCRIPT>
</HEAD>

<BODY>
<IMG SRC="balloon4.gif"
    id=balloon1
    STYLE="position:absolute;
            left:50;
            top:150;
            width:92;
            height:164;
            filter:blendTrans()">
<IMG SRC="balloon1.gif"
    id=balloon2
    STYLE="position:absolute;
            left:150;
            top:150;
            width:92;
            height:164;
            filter:revealTrans()">
```

continues

Listing 24.3. continued

```
<P>
<INPUT TYPE=BUTTON VALUE="Fade Out" onClick="doFade(balloon1)"></P>
Enter transition number (0-23):<BR>
<INPUT NAME=TransType TYPE=TEXT VALUE="0"><BR>
<INPUT TYPE=BUTTON VALUE="Do Transition" onClick="doTrans(balloon2)">
</BODY>

</HTML>
```

TIP

You can also cause transition effects to appear *between* pages as a user navigates your site. You can accomplish this via a META tag at the top of your HTML file. For example, to fade out a Web page as you leave it, you could use the following:

```
<META   HTTP-EQUIV="Page-Exit"
        CONTENT="blendTrans(duration=5)">
```

In addition to the Page-Exit HTTP-Equivalent, you may use Page-Enter, Site-Enter, and Site-Exit.

Summary

In this chapter you were introduced to the many new multimedia capabilities integrated within Internet Explorer 4.0. With the use of Dynamic HTML and scripting, filters, and transitions, you can create incredibly robust multimedia Web pages without incurring the cost of downloading large animation files, Java applets, or additional plug-in support. This chapter only touches the iceberg of multimedia on the Web in Internet Explorer 4.0. You are encouraged to check out Microsoft's Web site at http://www.microsoft.com/ie/ie40 to find out more about the multimedia capabilities included with Internet Explorer 4.0. For now, enjoy using the technology you have learned in this chapter to enhance your own pages.

Using Netscape Navigator's Canvas Mode

by Stephanos Piperoglou

IN THIS CHAPTER

CHAPTER 25

In this chapter, we examine a powerful new feature that first appeared in Netscape Communicator Preview Release 2 called *canvas mode.*

Canvas mode allows developers to open a browser window that contains only the *document canvas.* The document canvas is that part of the window in which the document is rendered.

When a window is in canvas mode, it has none of the normal identifying marks; a title bar, a menu bar, all the navigation icons, the status bar at the bottom, scrollbars, and so on are all missing. In this chapter, we examine how canvas mode works and how to use it, and suggest some possible applications. As a bonus, you get a glimpse of the procedure needed to sign your scripts in JavaScript for authenticity verification.

Why Use Canvas Mode?

The first question you have to ask yourself is whether you actually need canvas mode for an application. Displaying a real-size wall poster of yourself in .TGA format full-screen is hardly a good reason to get rid of all the user interface stuff in your Navigator. Why would you want to invoke canvas mode? I can think of some possible reasons, but you might require it for something else:

- *To have a simple, unadorned pop-up.* For instance, you might want to display an image in a separate window with nothing but the image showing.

- *To create a fancy dialog box.* You won't be the first to decide that your operating system's widget set doesn't appeal to your taste.

- *To create a separate window for output.* It's useful to have a little screen appear out of nowhere that can be manipulated from the parent page.

- *To briefly display a splash screen.* Netscape does it, Microsoft does it, why can't your Web page do it?

- *To disable as many Navigator features as possible.* For a specific application, you might not want users to have access to Back, Forward, Print, and View Source features, for instance. By removing the menu bar and icons (and, as you will see later, access to hotkeys), you can accomplish this.

- *To increase screen real estate.* All the gadgets that normally surround the canvas take up a lot of space that you usually do not care that much about, but many applications benefit from each pixel gained.

- *To get rid of the Navigator look.* If you're using Navigator for something such as navigating through a CD-ROM full of files or accessing your company's database over an intranet, you might not want all of the normal appearance that goes along with Navigator.

- *To have a uniform, cross-platform look.* Although canvas mode was exclusive to Navigator at the time of this writing, it may soon be adopted by other browsers. At such a time, you can use canvas mode to shed all the gadgets a browser may offer and supply your own.

As you can see, canvas mode can radically change the way Navigator operates. For this reason, all scripts that invoke canvas mode need to be signed for security. A lot of the features of canvas mode rely on the specifics of the operating environment, so you also have a couple of things to consider before using it on Web pages published on the Internet. For more on script signing and cross-browser issues, see the relevant sections later in this chapter.

How to Invoke Canvas Mode

You invoke canvas mode using the title-bar window feature of the open() method for window objects. In case you're not familiar with the window.open() method, we summarize the way it works in the next section.

The window.open() Method

You use the window.open() method to open a new Navigator window, similar to pressing Ctrl+N or selecting New Window from the File menu in Navigator. What the window.open() method can do that the New Window menu option can't is give the window special features. JavaScript 1.2 changed these special features, such as the title-bar feature, which invokes canvas mode.

Versions of Navigator earlier than 4.0PR2 do not recognize the special features. In these versions of Navigator, all you could do is make the menu bar, toolbar, location bar, status bar, and scrollbars disappear. Although this created a nice effect (and worked with Internet Explorer as well), you still had the title bar and window border tagging along (whether you could resize the window or not). Also, you could only specify the size of the whole window, meaning you had to make rough calculations about how thick the menu bar and window border would be to get the required dimensions for your canvas.

In Navigator 4.0, all this changed, and Dynamic HTML authors have absolute control over the window's appearance. The syntax for the window.open() method is as follows:

```
[variable = ]window.open("URL", "name", ["features"])
```

URL is, obviously, the URL you want the window to contain. This can be empty, indicating that you don't want anything in the window initially.

The optional *variable* in the beginning is an identifier used to refer to the window in your scripts, in contrast to the window's *name*, which is used to refer to the window in HTML and can be empty. For example, suppose you open a window for use as a dialog box with the following line of code:

```
winDialog = window.open("","dialog")
```

You want to put some data into it because you supplied no URL. You can use something such as this in JavaScript:

```
winDialog.document.write("<TITLE>Dialog Box</TITLE><P>This is a dialog box")
```

You can also have a link somewhere in an HTML document that puts the URL it mentions in the new window:

```
<A HREF="dialog1.html" TARGET="dialog">Dialog box contents</A>
```

Following this link puts `dialog1.html` in the new window. Notice that the first example refers to the new window as `winDialog`, which is the identifier you assigned to it, whereas the second example refers to it as `dialog`, which is the name you gave it in the parameters of the `open()` method.

> **TIP**
>
> You can use the same name for the identifier and the window name, so you don't have to worry about confusing the two later.

Now I come to the interesting part: the window features.

As you saw in the brief example, you don't have to supply any window features; they are purely optional. However, what is the point of opening a new window if you can't make it look good?

You can control many window features with the `window.open()` method. This chapter discusses most of them, and Table 25.1 includes a complete list. These window features work in JavaScript 1.1 and in older versions of Navigator (and Explorer).

Table 25.1. JavaScript 1.1 window features.

Feature	Default	Description
toolbar=yes¦no	No	Controls the display of the toolbar.
location=yes¦no	No	Controls the display of the location bar.
directories=yes¦no	No	Controls the display of the directories bar (or personal toolbar in Navigator 4.0).
status=yes¦no	No	Controls the display of the status bar.
menubar=yes¦no	No	Controls the display of the menu bar.
scrollbars=yes¦no	No	Controls the display of scrollbars if the document doesn't fit in the window.
resizable=yes¦no	No	Controls the capability to resize the new window, whether manually or using JavaScript methods.
width=*pixels* height=*pixels*	Parent window size	The width and height of the new window.

JavaScript 1.2 introduced the features in Table 25.2.

Table 25.2. JavaScript 1.2 window features.

Feature	Default	Description
alwaysLowered=yes¦no	No	If given a value of yes, the new window always remains below all other windows.
alwaysRaised=yes¦no	No	If given a value of yes, the new window always remains above all other windows.
dependent=yes¦no	No	If given a value of yes, the new window is a dependent window of the previous one, much like a dialog box. Like a dialog box, it closes if the original window is closed, and if you're running Windows, it does not show on the taskbar.
hotkeys=yes¦no	Yes	If given a value of no and the new window has no menu bar, the various hotkeys (for instance, Alt+Left Arrow for Back, Ctrl+N for New Window, and so on) do not work, except for the security and Quit hotkeys, as well as any OS-dependent hotkeys that Navigator can't change (such as Alt+Ctrl+Del in Windows).
innerHeight=*pixels* innerWidth=*pixels*	Parent window size	Specify the dimensions of the canvas. The rest of the window is sized so that the canvas has these dimensions. When a window is in canvas mode, this is the same as the window size.
outerHeight=*pixels* outerWidth=*pixels*	Parent window size	Specify the dimensions of the window. These features replace the width and height features in JavaScript 1.1. When a window is in canvas mode, this is the same as the canvas size.
screenX=*pixels* screenY=*pixels*	Arbitrary	Specify the offset of the window's top-left corner from the top-left corner of the screen.
titlebar=yes¦no	Yes	If given a value of no, the new window is in canvas mode, with only the document canvas displayed.
z-lock=yes¦no	no	If given a value of yes, the window does not rise when given the focus.

Confused a bit? Don't worry, an example in the section "Your First Canvas Mode Window" later in this chapter will make everything clear.

25

USING NETSCAPE NAVIGATOR'S CANVAS MODE

Many of these properties can be security risks for the user and thus require the use of signed scripts. The method for this is discussed in the section "Signing Your Scripts." You can also circumvent this requirement using the procedure described in the following section. The properties that require signed scripts are `alwaysLowered=yes`, `alwaysRaised=yes`, all the width and height properties if they define a window smaller than 100×100 pixels, `screenX` and `screenY` if they place the window outside the visible screen, `titlebar=no`, and `z-lock=yes`.

Bypassing the Script Signing Requirement

Although the Web pages you publish on the Internet must contain signed scripts, script signing is a long and tedious process that you cannot follow each time you change something in your code. You can follow the procedure outlined in this section to make Navigator run your scripts without signing them.

CAUTION

This procedure makes your copy of Navigator, and only your copy of Navigator, run all scripts without requiring a digital certificate. Scripts that can potentially damage your system can be executed this way. Make sure to reverse the process when you don't need it anymore.

1. Quit all Communicator applications you are running.

2. In the directory that contains your Navigator user profile is a file called `prefs.js` or `preferences.js`, depending on your platform. This is your Netscape Preferences JavaScript file. Open it using a text editor, and you will find a number of lines containing your user preferences.

3. Go to the end of the file and append the following line:

```
user_pref("signed.applets.codebase_principal_support", true);
```

TIP

In Netscape Communicator 4.0PR2, you don't need to sign your scripts or use this workaround. All you have to do is start Communicator with the `-tb` command-line switch. Later versions do require the procedure or signed scripts, however.

Now Navigator will not require potentially dangerous scripts to be digitally signed. You will still receive a warning and be able to choose not to execute the scripts. Note that others will not be able to execute your scripts unless they make the same modification on their copies of Navigator.

Your First Canvas Mode Window

For a useful example of canvas mode, you create three HTML files: cmIndex.html (Listing 25.1), which is the primary page, cmWindow1.html (Listing 25.2), which is the initial content of the new window, and cmWindow2.html (Listing 25.3), which is shown in the window later.

Listing 25.1. cmIndex.html.

```
<!DOCTYPE HTML PUBLIC "-//W3C//DTD HTML 4.0 Transitional//EN">
<HEAD>
<TITLE>Canvas Mode Demo</TITLE>
<SCRIPT LANGUAGE="JavaScript1.2">
function cmWindowOpen() {
 netscape.security.PrivilegeManager.enablePrivilege("UniversalBrowserWrite");
 cmWindow=window.open("cmWindow1.html","Canvas",
➥ "titlebar=no,innerWidth=200,innerHeight=100,screenX=10,screenY=10");
}
</SCRIPT>
</HEAD>
<BODY>
<P>Welcome to your first canvas mode demo!
<P><A HREF="javascript:cmWindowOpen()">Click here to open the window</A>
<P><A HREF="cmWindow2.html" TARGET="Canvas">Click here
➥to put file cmWindow2.html inside the window</A>
<P><A HREF="cmWindow1.html" TARGET="Canvas">Click here
➥to put file cmWindow1.html back inside the window</A>
```

> **CAUTION**
>
> Watch the quotes on the open() method! Omitting them can cause really strange things to happen because Navigator may consider the window features to be JavaScript property assignments. For instance, window.open("","",innerHeight=100) would be interpreted as window.open("","",100) since innerHeight=100 is evaluated as window.innerHeight=100, which would change the *parent* window height to 100 and return the new value.

Listing 25.2. cmWindow1.html.

```
<!DOCTYPE HTML PUBLIC "-//W3C//DTD HTML 4.0 Transitional//EN">
<HEAD><TITLE>Canvas Mode Window - 1</TITLE></HEAD>
<BODY BGCOLOR=white TEXT=black LINK=blue ALINK=red VLINK=purple>
<P>This is a Canvas Mode Window
```

Listing 25.3. cmWindow2.html.

```
<!DOCTYPE HTML PUBLIC "-//W3C//DTD HTML 4.0 Transitional//EN">
<HEAD><TITLE>Canvas Mode Window - 2</TITLE></HEAD>
<BODY BGCOLOR=white TEXT=black LINK=blue ALINK=red VLINK=purple>
<P>Links can be followed in this window.
```

Load `cmIndex.html` in Navigator. Clicking the top link creates a new square window containing `cmWindow1.html`, as shown in Figure 25.1.

Figure 25.1.

Your first canvas mode window.

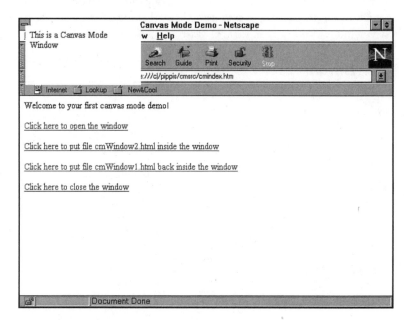

Clicking the second link puts `cmWindow2.html` in the window. You can try hotkeys in the new window; click inside it and then press Ctrl+LeftArrow. It will promptly move back in the history list and display `cmWindow1.html`.

What It All Meant

You might have noticed a new piece of code in the `cmWindowOpen()` function:

```
netscape.security.PrivilegeManager.enablePrivilege("UniversalBrowserWrite");
```

This line enables expanded Navigator privileges; you wouldn't be able to access canvas mode without it. This is the command that requires the script to be signed. `UniversalBrowserWrite` is called a *target*. There are several targets, but `UniversalBrowserWrite` is the only one you need to use for the examples in this chapter.

> **NOTE**
>
> Enabling expanded privileges works on a per-function basis. The new privileges only work in the function in which they were enabled. If you require them in other functions, you must re-enable them.

The `window.open()` method tells Navigator to open a new window with the name `Canvas` and the identifier `cmWindow`, containing `cmWindow1.html` in canvas mode at 200×100 pixels large and 10 pixels from the top and 10 pixels from the left of the screen.

By clicking the second link in `cmIndex.html`, you follow it to its tail (`cmWindow2.html`), which is shown in the canvas mode window because it's identified in the TARGET attribute. Clicking the third link follows a link to `cmWindow1.html`, putting that file in the new window instead.

> **TIP**
>
> To close this window, either use your OS-specific hotkeys (such as Alt+F4 in Windows) or the Quit hotkey.

Adding Spice to Your Window

You may have noticed, if your original window overlapped with the canvas mode window, that clicking the original window obscures the canvas window because the parent window is raised. This is where the `alwaysRaised` feature comes into play. You also discovered that hotkeys work in your new window, and this could have strange results in a finished application. Also, if you close the original window, the canvas window is still there, confusing users who won't know how to close it without a menu bar. Change this behavior by augmenting `cmMain.js`. Change the line that invokes `window.open()`:

```
cmWindow=window.open("cmWindow1.html","Canvas",
➥"titlebar=no,alwaysRaised=yes,dependent=yes,
➥hotkeys=no,innerWidth=200,innerHeight=100,screenX=10,screenY=10");
```

Playing around with the new window, you notice the following:

- The hotkeys don't work. Try the Security hotkey and the Quit hotkey; they still work. In fact, the Quit hotkey is the only way to actually close the window, unless your platform doesn't allow Navigator to capture all hotkeys. If you're running UNIX, Navigator will probably not be able to shut off your window manager's hotkeys. If you're using Windows, you can press Alt+Ctrl+Del to invoke the Task Manager and close the window.

- The window is always raised above all other windows, no matter where you click.

- If you're running Windows, the window doesn't show on the taskbar. Close the original Navigator window, and the canvas mode window will close along with it.

You obviously don't want people stuck figuring out how to close the window you just opened because you've taken away their hotkeys, so make up for it. Add the following line to the end of `cmWindow1.html` and `cmWindow2.html`:

```
<A HREF="javascript:window.close()">Close this window</A>
```

Try the demo again; clicking "Close this window" invokes the `window.close()` method, which by default closes the current window. You can also do this from the main window; add the following to `cmIndex.html`:

```
<P><A HREF="javascript:cmWindow.close()">Click here to close the window</A>
```

Using the `cmWindow` identifier, you can close the window from anywhere. Now you have a reliable way of closing the window no matter what happens to it.

I hear you crying, however, that I was talking about increasing screen real estate while working with a tiny 200×100 pixel window at one corner of the screen. When does that "taking over the screen" propaganda achieve fruition?

The answer comes with the new `screen` object in Navigator 4.0. This object has several properties, and two of them are `height` and `width`, which return the height and width of the user's screen. I think you get the picture; here's an updated script for `cmIndex.html`:

```
function cmWindowOpen() {
    netscape.security.PrivilegeManager.enablePrivilege("UniversalBrowserWrite");
    cmWinFtrs="titlebar=no,alwaysRaised=yes,dependent=yes,hotkeys=no";
    cmWinFtrs+=",screenX=0,screenY=0";
    cmWinFtrs+=",innerWidth="+screen.width+",innerHeight="+screen.height;
    cmWindow=window.open("cmWindow1.html","Canvas",cmWinFtrs);
}
```

This code is much "cleaner" than the previous example. All window features are concatenated into a string, `cmWinFtrs`, which contains the same features as before with two exceptions: `screenX` and `screenY` are `0`, putting the window at the top left of the screen, whereas `innerWidth` and `innerHeight` are equal to the `screen.width` and `screen.height` properties, giving the canvas the same exact dimensions as the screen.

Run the demo. Your screen should be full of nothing but `cmWindow1.html`. You can close it by clicking the "Close this window" link.

So far, you've learned how to open a window in canvas mode, resize it, give it the size of the user's screen, disable Navigator hotkeys, and keep it on top of other windows. Now it's time to put this into action and build an application. Before you can do that, you need to sign your scripts.

Signing Your Scripts

Scripts that cause strange things to happen to your Navigator can be security risks because people can use them to tamper with a user's system. Before requesting expanded privileges, a script must be signed with a digital certificate.

A digital certificate is issued by a certifying authority (or CA, for short), which verifies that the owner of the certificate is who he claims he is. This way, if someone does something bad with their signed scripts, they can be traced. Granted, it's not foolproof, but it's not up to you either.

Buying a Certificate

CAs offer many kinds of certificates. What you need here is an *object-signing certificate*. Here's the problem with object-signing certificates: They cost money. Because the certificate authorities have many expenses related to verifying the identities of certificate holders, they charge for certificates to make a living.

To order a certificate, follow these steps:

1. Open the Security window by clicking the padlock icon on the Navigator toolbar or selecting Window | Security Info.
2. Select Certificates | Yours.
3. Select Get a Certificate, which will take you to a page on one of Netscape's Web servers that lists current supported CAs. Pick one that matches your requirements and follow their instructions. Remember, you're looking for an object-signing certificate. Many CAs also offer company certificates that cost more but can be used by anyone in your organization.
4. After following all the required steps, you are given your certificate, and a dialog box appears so you can import it to Navigator's database. You can give it any name you want.

> **CAUTION**
>
> Do not use a complicated name for your certificate. A single word with no spaces or special characters is what you need because the tools you use to sign your scripts might have problems with other characters.

Congratulations! You are now several bucks poorer and one digital certificate richer.

What Can Be Signed

Script signing works by creating what is called a JAR archive, mainly because it has a file extension of `.jar`. A JAR archive is really just a Zip file that contains some special information.

First, it contains the public key to your certificate. If you're familiar with PGP or public key encryption in general, you'll understand what this is; it's the part of your certificate that identifies you to others. It also contains information on the content of your scripts, so that if a script is changed, it won't match this information, preventing people from signing harmless scripts and then changing them into malicious Trojan horses. It may also contain JavaScript `.js` script files, which is practical if you want to create a library of signed scripts.

A JAR archive is accessed using the ARCHIVE attribute to the SCRIPT element. If I have a script called `myScript.js`, which has been signed in archive `myArchive.jar`, you use code like this to access it:

```
<SCRIPT ARCHIVE="myArchive.jar" SRC="myScript.js">
</SCRIPT>
```

Note that myScript.js may be zipped in myArchive.jar or supplied separately. However, this element indicates that myScript.js is signed in myArchive.jar.

It's often useful to use inline scripts and almost essential to use inline event handlers. These can also be signed. What you need to do is put an ARCHIVE attribute on a SCRIPT element in your page. In fact, you need to include an ARCHIVE attribute only once in a page, unless you're using multiple archives, in which case you need multiple SCRIPT elements. Once you have an ARCHIVE attribute that points to the archive containing your signatures, you need to include unique ID attributes on every element that has an inline script or an event handler that refers Navigator to the corresponding entry in the JAR archive.

> **NOTE**
>
> You cannot sign javascript: URLs or JavaScript entities.

In other words, your HTML file will look something like this:

```
[...]
<SCRIPT ARCHIVE="myArchive.jar" SRC="myScript.js" LANGUAGE="JavaScript1.2">
</SCRIPT>
<SCRIPT LANGUAGE="JavaScript1.2" ID="sign1">
... inline script commands ...
</SCRIPT>
<SCRIPT SRC="myScript2.js" LANGUAGE="JavaScript1.2">
</SCRIPT>
[...]
<IMG SRC="someurl" onMouseDown="myfunction()" ID="sign2">
[...]
```

myArchive.jar is a JAR file that contains signatures for script files myScript.js and myScript2.js, the inline script with the ID sign1, and the inline event handler with the ID sign2. As you probably know, you can use any arbitrary string for an ID, as long as it is unique in a page.

> **CAUTION**
>
> You cannot use a mix of signed and unsigned or unsignable objects on a page. Either you sign everything or Navigator treats everything as unsigned.

Using Zigbert

Netscape currently offers two tools to sign your scripts. One is JAR Packager, a Java application that is quite suited to the task because it is written in Java and is a cross-platform tool. Unfortunately, it's still in prerelease and hideously broken. The other is JAR Packager Command Line, also known as *zigbert*, which I briefly examine.

Zigbert is written in Perl and is available for 32-bit Windows platforms (Windows 95 and NT) and IRIX only. You need a working Perl interpreter on your system to make zigbert work.

You can download zigbert from Netscape DevEdge Online at

```
http://developer.netscape.com/software/signedobj/jarpack.html
```

and install it on your system. Remember that you need a functioning Perl on your system as well.

Zigbert contains the zigbert executable, a pair of zip and unzip utilities that fit the requirements for the job, and a Perl script called signpages.pl, which is your main tool.

To sign a script, perform the following steps:

1. Create your HTML file as mentioned previously.
2. In your Netscape user profile directory are two files called cert7.db and key3.db, which contain your certificates. Identify the directory where they are located.
3. Install zigbert and make sure Perl, zigbert, and zip and unzip are in your search path.
4. Execute the following command:

   ```
   zigbert -d"dbdir" -1
   ```

   dbdir is the directory where your cert7.db and key3.db files are, if it is not the default ~/.netscape. You get a list of all keys in your database. Zigbert will put a star beside those that you can use to sign objects but will often be wrong about this. Identify the key that you purchased for object signing.
5. Execute the following:

   ```
   perl -- signpages.pl -d"dbdir" -k"keyname" myfile.html
   ```

You might have to point to the location of signpages.pl if it's not in the current directory. *dbdir* is the certificate database directory. *keyname* is the name of the certificate you plan to use and *myfile.html* is the HTML file you prepared earlier.

Zigbert creates a JAR archive, named as you named it in your HTML file, containing signatures for all your script files, inline scripts, and event handlers. As a bonus, it includes all script files that are linked via SRC attributes in your document. In other words, you're set! Give it a try, and you can proceed to create your first application that uses canvas mode.

A Portable Canvas Mode Image Zoomer

The "image gallery" is a popular kind of Web page, whether it's displaying the paragons of impressionism or your holiday snapshots. You must have seen the format; lots and lots of tiny thumbnails that link to large versions of the images. Listing 25.4 contains a typical example.

Listing 25.4. index.html.

```html
<!DOCTYPE HTML PUBLIC "-//W3C//DTD HTML 4.0 Transitional//EN">
<HTML>
<HEAD>
<TITLE>John Doe's Image Gallery</TITLE>
<STYLE TYPE="text/css">
BODY {
 font: normal 12pt/14pt Verdana, sans-serif;
 color: black; background-color: white;
}
H1 { font-weight: bold; font-size: 150%; text-align: center }
H2 { font-weight: bold; font-size: 120%; }
I { font-style: italic }
B { font-weight: bolder }
U { text-decoration: underline }
P.links { font-size: smaller; text-align: center }
P.images { text-align: center }
</STYLE>
</HEAD>
<BODY>
<H1>John Doe's Image Gallery</H1>
<P>Here are some pictures you might find interesting.
Follow the link on each Thumbnail to view the whole picture.
<P CLASS="images">
<A HREF="images/image01.gif"><IMG SRC="images/thumb01.gif"></A>
<A HREF="images/image02.gif"><IMG SRC="images/thumb02.gif"></A>
<A HREF="images/image03.gif"><IMG SRC="images/thumb03.gif"></A>
</P>
<HR>
<P CLASS="links"><A HREF="../index.html">[Home]</A> <A
HREF="mailto:johndoe@somewhere.org">[Mail]</A></P>
</BODY>
</HMTL>
```

This page displays three thumbnails, `thumb01.gif` through `thumb03.gif`, with links to three full-size images, `image01.gif` to `image03.gif`. Following each link gives you the image, making you press the Back button to return to the thumbnails page (see Figure 25.2).

Enter the canvas mode script. This script uses event capturing, discussed in Chapter 17, "The Communicator 4.0 Event Model: Event Capturing" (you might want to take a look in case you don't remember the details), to capture all clicks on this page and create canvas mode windows with the images if the viewer clicks one of them.

Catch That Mouse!

The first thing you have to do is capture the `mouseDown` event in the document. You'll redirect it to a function called `clicker`, which will handle everything else from there. Before you do this, you have to make sure only Navigator 4.0 browsers execute the script. The most reliable way to do this at this time is to check for the existence of the `document.layers` object, which is exclusive to Navigator 4.0:

```
Nav40 = (document.layers) ? 1 : 0;
```

FIGURE 25.2.

John Doe's (typically boring) image gallery.

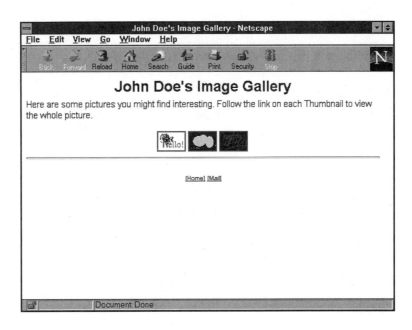

The `Nav40` variable is `true` only if the Web page is being viewed with Navigator 4.0. Introduce the event capturing as follows:

```
if (Nav40) {
 document.captureEvents(Event.MOUSEDOWN);
 document.onmousedown = clicker;
}
```

Non-Navigator 4.0 browsers behave normally because clicks are not captured; instead, clicking a thumbnail takes the user to the full-sized image. Navigator 4.0, on the other hand, invokes the `clicker` function. As you may remember, the function called when an event is captured accepts a single argument, the event. It's time to build the `clicker` function.

The `clicker` Function

First, you need to check whether an image is already open because you don't want the screen filling up with zoomed images. You'll introduce a global variable that keeps track of whether a canvas mode window is open:

```
cmWinOpen = false;
```

Start the `clicker` function. First, it checks for an open window and, if there is one, closes it. This way you can close any open window simply by clicking anywhere in the document:

```
function clicker(e) {
if (cmWinOpen) {
  cmClose();
  return false;
 }
}
```

Notice the `return false` line that tells Navigator that the event was captured and dealt with so it doesn't pass the click onto the document and also exits the `clicker` function. `cmClose()` is a function you define later that closes open windows.

Find That Click!

Now you need to see whether the click event actually happened on an image or elsewhere in the document. If it happened elsewhere, you release the event and let it execute its intended function.

One of the properties of the `event` object is `target`. Netscape claims this returns the recipient of the event. In fact, it doesn't. It returns the target of the recipient, *if the recipient is a hyperlink*. Otherwise, the property returns undefined.

Although it's supposed to be a string, the `target` property doesn't have string methods, so you need to use the `toString()` method on it to convert it to a string:

```
imURL = e.target.toString();
```

Now, you use string functions to find the extension of the file indicated by the hyperlink, if there is one:

```
imExt = imURL.substring(imURL.lastIndexOf(".") + 1, imURL.length);
```

What this line of code does is take the *last* occurrence of . in `imURL`, cut the rest of the characters after this occurrence, and put them into `imExt`, which is effectively the extension of the file if it is an image. You then test it to see if it is equal to `gif` or `jpg`. You can add other image types if you want:

```
isImage = ( imExt == "gif" || imExt == "jpg" );
```

Now, if `imExt` is equal to any of the image types, you call the `cmOpen` function that opens the window, passing to it the event:

```
isImage = ( imExt == "gif" || imExt == "jpg" );
 if (isImage) {
  cmOpen(e)
  return false;
 }
```

The `return false` line exits the function and tells Navigator not to pass the event on to the document. Now you add the `return true` that is executed only if `isImage` is `false`, releasing the `mouseDown` event and making the rest of the page functional. Here's the finished `clicker` function:

```
function clicker(e) {
 if (cmWinOpen) {
  cmClose();
  return false;
 }
 imURL = e.target.toString();
 imExt = imURL.substring(imURL.lastIndexOf(".") + 1, imURL.length);
```

```
isImage = ( imExt == "gif" || imExt == "jpg" );
if (isImage) {
 cmOpen(e)
 return false;
}
return true;
}
```

That's all for the `clicker` function. Move on to the actual window.

Open Sesame

Now it's time to actually open the window. The `cmOpen()` function, which you define for this purpose, will look familiar because it is a lot like the one in the first canvas mode demo.

First, enable the `UniversalBrowserWrite` target:

```
netscape.security.PrivilegeManager.enablePrivilege("UniversalBrowserWrite");
```

Now, open the window. Note the `resizable=yes` feature, without which you wouldn't be able to resize the window. Don't worry about users resizing the window manually because it has no border. You'll use the `screen.width` and `screen.height` properties again, this time to place the window conveniently offscreen:

```
cmWinProps="titlebar=no,alwaysRaised=yes,dependent=yes"
cmWinProps+=",hotkeys=no,resizable=yes";
cmWinProps+=",screenX=" + screen.width + ",screenY=" + screen.height;
cmWindow=window.open("","",cmWinProps);
```

Now you write the HTML to the window. You use CSS positioning to place the image at the top left of the canvas:

```
cmWindow.document.write('
<!DOCTYPE HTML PUBLIC "-//W3C//DTD HTML 4.0 Transitional//
➥EN"><HTML><HEAD><TITLE>Image</TITLE>
<STYLE TYPE="text/css">
#divIm { position: absolute; top: 0; left: 0 }
</STYLE>
<BODY><DIV ID="divIm"><IMG SRC="' + e.target + '"></DIV>');
cmWindow.document.close;
```

This document has only one image. Note that it is included in a DIV (required for the CSS positioning to work), so you get its width and height and assign them to the `innerHeight` and `innerWidth` properties of the window. Note that the window is still off-screen, hiding all this violent resizing from the user:

```
imWidth=cmWindow.document.divIm.document.images[0].width;
imHeight=cmWindow.document.divIm.document.images[0].height;
cmWindow.innerWidth=imWidth-4;
cmWindow.innerHeight=imHeight-4;
```

You may have noticed that you subtract 4 from the window's size. This is because, even though it should, Netscape doesn't make the window small enough and creates an ugly border of the background shining through around the edges if you don't.

Now you need to move the window into view. A nice place to put it is centered around the mouse pointer at the time of the click. You have the coordinates of the click and the size of the image, so you can use the moveTo window method to move it to the right spot:

```
cmWindow.moveTo(e.screenX - (imWidth / 2) , e.screenY - (imHeight / 2));
```

Lastly, you need an easy way to close the window, other than clicking the original page (which you already have taken care of at the beginning of the clicker() function). To do this, you use the enableExternalCapture window method, which allows other windows (in this case, the original window) to capture events in a window (here, the canvas mode window). Then you capture the mouseDown event in the new window and point it to the cmClose() function, and you shouldn't forget the cmWinOpen boolean that should be updated to indicate that a window is open:

```
cmWindow.enableExternalCapture;
cmWindow.captureEvents(Event.MOUSEDOWN);
cmWindow.onmousedown=cmClose ;
cmWinOpen = true;
```

Speaking of the cmClose() function, you should put it here somewhere:

```
function cmClose() {
 cmWindow.close();
 cmWinOpen = false;
}
```

That's it! Take a look at Listing 25.5 for zoomer.js, the portable canvas mode image zoomer.

Listing 25.5. zoomer.js, a portable canvas mode image zoomer.

```
//
// zoomer.js
// A Portable Canvas Mode Image Zoomer
//

// True if we're using Navigator 4.0
Nav40 = (document.layers) ? 1 : 0;

// True if a zoomed window is open
cmWinOpen = false;

// Capture Click events
if (Nav40) {
 document.captureEvents(Event.MOUSEDOWN);
 document.onmousedown = clicker;
}

function clicker(e) {
 // If an image is already showing, close the window
 if (cmWinOpen) {
  cmClose();
  return false;
 }

 // If the user clicked on a hyperlink that was one of our images,
```

```
 // open the image
 imURL = e.target.toString();
 imExt = imURL.substring(imURL.lastIndexOf(".") + 1, imURL.length);
 isImage = ( imExt == "gif" || imExt == "jpg" );
 if (isImage) {
  cmOpen(e)
  return false;
 }

 return true;
}

// A function that opens the canvas mode window
function cmOpen(e) {
 // Enable universal write target
 netscape.security.PrivilegeManager.enablePrivilege("UniversalBrowserWrite");

 // Set window features for Canvas Mode
 cmWinProps="titlebar=no,alwaysRaised=yes,dependent=yes
 cmWinProps+=",hotkeys=no,resizable=yes";

 // Put the window off-screen until it's resized
 cmWinProps+=",screenX=" + screen.width + ",screenY=" + screen.height;

 // Open the window
 cmWindow=window.open("","",cmWinProps);

 // Write the document to the new window
 cmWindow.document.write('<!DOCTYPE HTML PUBLIC "-//W3C//DTD HTML 4.0
➥Transitional//EN"><HTML><HEAD><TITLE>Image</TITLE><STYLE TYPE="text/css">#divIm {
➥position: absolute; top: 0; left: 0 }</STYLE><BODY><DIV ID="divIm"><IMG SRC="' +
➥e.target + '"></DIV>');
 cmWindow.document.close;

 // Get the width and height of the image and resize the window
 imWidth=cmWindow.document.divIm.document.images[0].width;
 imHeight=cmWindow.document.divIm.document.images[0].height;
 cmWindow.innerWidth=imWidth-4;
 cmWindow.innerHeight=imHeight-4;

 // Now move it into view, centered on the mouse pointer
 cmWindow.moveTo(e.screenX - (imWidth / 2) , e.screenY - (imHeight / 2));

 // Capture all mousedown events in it, so that a click will close it.
 cmWindow.enableExternalCapture;
 cmWindow.captureEvents(Event.MOUSEDOWN);
 cmWindow.onmousedown=cmClose ;

 // Update cmWinOpen so that we know an image is being displayed
 cmWinOpen = true;
}
// A function that simply closes the canvas mode window
function cmClose() {
 cmWindow.close();
 cmWinOpen = false;
}
```

Now all you have to do is add the following to your HTML file's HEAD:

```
<SCRIPT LANGUAGE="JavaScript1.2" SRC="zoomer.js" ARCHIVE="zoomer.jar">
</SCRIPT>
```

Run zigbert on the file so the scripts are signed, and off you go. The new page will look something like Figure 25.3.

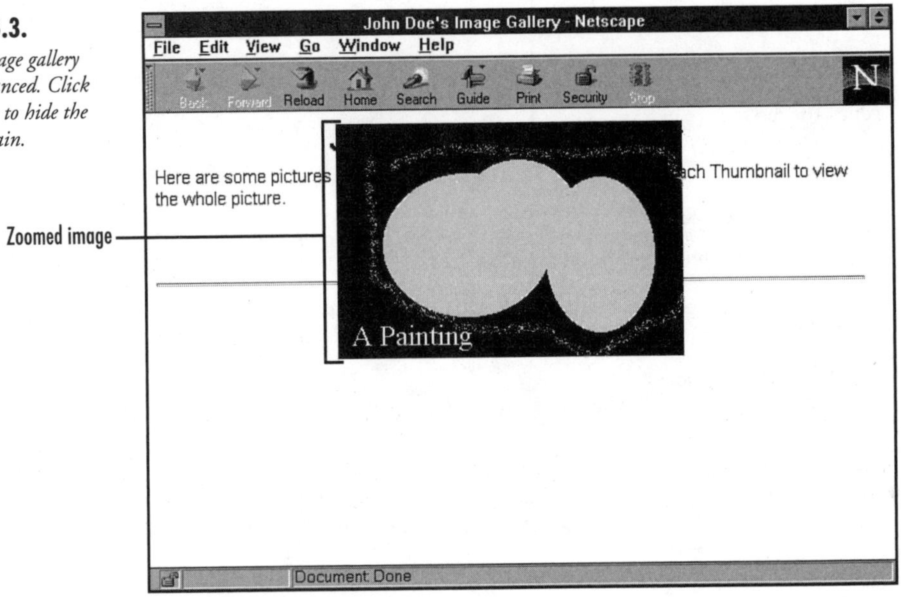

FIGURE 25.3.

John's image gallery now enhanced. Click anywhere to hide the image again.

Zoomed image

Any link on the page that leads to a GIF or JPEG image is displayed in a nifty little canvas mode window that disappears with a click, while keeping backwards compatibility for older browsers.

Build Your Own Navigator

In the last example, you create a "kiosk mode" application—a Navigator that occupies the whole screen and is used for a specific reason, without all the normal trimmings. This can be useful for a public access touch-screen terminal, a CD-ROM contents browser, or just for fun, to see what you would make Navigator look like if you had designed it.

The Launchpad

To start, you need a launchpad document that launches the new browser. What you do is create two windows, one occupying the top 100 pixels of the screen (which contains the navigation tools) and another occupying the rest of the screen (which contains the actual documents you browse).

You might be thinking of using frames instead of separate windows, but this is not advisable for several reasons. First, it is very easy for a link inside the documents you browse to have TARGET=_top and break out of the frameset. Second, JavaScript 1.2 offers many methods for windows that are difficult to replicate using frames. Our launchpad is described in Listing 25.6.

Listing 25.6. launchpad.html.

```html
<!DOCTYPE HTML PUBLIC "-//W3C//DTD HTML 4.0 Transitional//EN">
<HTML>
<HEAD>
<TITLE>MyScape Navigator Launchpad</TITLE>
<STYLE TYPE="text/css">
</STYLE>
<SCRIPT LANGUAGE="JavaScript1.2" ARCHIVE="myScape.js" ID="Launcher">
function myLaunch() {
  netscape.security.PrivilegeManager.enablePrivilege("UniversalBrowserWrite");
  navbarProps="titlebar=no,alwaysRaised=yes,hotkeys=no,";
  navbarProps+=",outerWidth=" + screen.width + ",outerHeight=100";
  navbarProps+=",screenX=0,screenY=0";
  window.open("navbar.html","",navbarProps);
}
</SCRIPT>
</HEAD>
<BODY>
<P><FORM><INPUT TYPE=SUBMIT VALUE=Click onClick="myLaunch()">
 to launch MyScape Navigator.</FORM>
```

You probably understand everything in Listing 25.6 by now. The navigation bar window is opened at the top of the screen, with width equal to the screen and height equal to 100 pixels; is always raised; and has hotkeys disabled. To open it, you click a button in the launchpad document. Now you must build your Navigator, which you will call MyScape.

MyScape Navigator

Create a nice-looking toolbar for MyScape, such as the one in Listing 25.7. It will have a lot of the usual trimmings of a toolbar. You'll use form buttons with onClick event handlers to access the functions in this example, but you can make the navigation bar look like anything you want, as long as it calls the same functions.

Listing 25.7. navbar.html.

```html
<!DOCTYPE HTML PUBLIC "-//W3C//DTD HTML 4.0 Transitional//EN">
<HTML>
<HEAD>
<TITLE>Myscape Navigator</TITLE>
<STYLE TYPE="text/css">
BODY {
 background-color: black;
 color: white;
 font: 10pt Times,serif;
 text-align: center
```

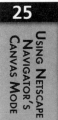

continues

Listing 25.7. continued

```
}
#Title {
 color: rgb(0%,100%,0%);
 font: bold 14pt Verdana,sans-serif
}
</STYLE>
<SCRIPT LANGUAGE="JavaScript1.2" SRC="myScape.js" ARCHIVE="myScape.jar">
</SCRIPT>
</HEAD>
<BODY>
<FORM NAME="Nav">
<SPAN ID="Title">MyScape Navigator</SPAN>, a Custom Browsing Environment
<BR>
<INPUT TYPE="SUBMIT" VALUE="<=" NAME="Back" onClick="myBack()">
<INPUT TYPE="SUBMIT" VALUE="=>" NAME="Forward" onClick="myForward()">
<INPUT TYPE="SUBMIT" VALUE="Home" NAME="Home" onClick="myHome()">
<INPUT TYPE="SUBMIT" VALUE="Reload" NAME="Reload" onClick="myReload()">
<INPUT TYPE="SUBMIT" VALUE="Stop" NAME="Stop" onClick="myStop()">
<INPUT TYPE="SUBMIT" VALUE="Exit" NAME="Exit" onClick="myExit()">
<BR>
<INPUT TYPE="TEXT" SIZE=10 VALUE="Enter Search String" NAME="String">
<INPUT TYPE="SUBMIT" VALUE="Find" NAME="Find" onClick="myFind()">
</FORM>
```

Now that you have everything set up, you will create the script that opens the canvas window and handles all the click events.

First, you define your own home page. You can even read Navigator's preferences for this, if you want, but you'll use Macmillan Publishing's home page for now. Insert the following:

```
homePageURL="http://www.mcp.com/"
```

Now you will open the canvas. It will start just below the navigation bar and occupy the rest of the window:

```
openCanvas()
```

```
function openCanvas() {
 netscape.security.PrivilegeManager.enablePrivilege("UniversalBrowserWrite");
 canvasProps="titlebar=no,alwaysRaised=yes,dependent=yes";
 canvasProps+=",outerWidth="+screen.width+",outerHeight="+(screen.height-100);
 canvasProps+=",screenX=0,screenY=100";
 canwin=window.open(homePageURL,"Canvas",canvasProps);
}
```

Now you have a page displaying; you can play around with it, follow links, scroll, and do anything you usually do with a Web page. What you do next is define the functions that are called by the click events in the navigation bar.

Remember that myScape.js is running from the Navigation bar window. Remember also that you need to refer to the canvas window by its name, canwin. The forward and back functions are covered by the similarly named window methods. Calling these methods is the same as clicking the back and forward buttons on the Navigator toolbar:

```
function myBack() { canwin.back() }
function myForward() { canwin.forward() }
```

For the Home and Reload functions, you'll use the location property of a window. By setting it, you can load any document in a window. Using its `reload()` method, you reload the document:

```
function myHome() { canwin.location=homePageURL }
function myReload() { canwin.location.reload() }
```

The Stop function is also a window method. For Exit, you will use the window `close()` method, but remember, you must close the navigation bar window, not the canvas window. Because the canvas window has `dependent=yes`, it will promptly close, too:

```
function myStop() { canwin.stop() }
function myExit() { parent.close() }
```

Finally, you need a function that reads a text string from the text input and performs a text search in the document. This is done using the `find()` window method and reading the value property of the element:

```
function myFind() {
 netscape.security.PrivilegeManager.enablePrivilege("UniversalBrowserRead");
 searchString=document.Nav.String.value;
 canwin.find(searchString);
}
```

Notice that you use a new privilege target, `UniversalBrowserRead`. This is required because a script in one window is making changes to a document in another window and has to have this privilege granted. The procedure to enable this target is the same as for the `UniversalBrowserWrite` target. The effect you expect (showcasing the previous example quite admirably) is the one shown in Figure 25.4.

Listing 25.7 contains the complete `myScape.js`.

Listing 25.7. myScape.js.

```
homePageURL="http://www.mcp.com/"

openCanvas()

function openCanvas() {
 netscape.security.PrivilegeManager.enablePrivilege("UniversalBrowserWrite");
 canvasProps="titlebar=no,alwaysRaised=yes,dependent=yes";
 canvasProps+=",outerWidth="+screen.width+",outerHeight="+(screen.height-100);
 canvasProps+=",screenX=0,screenY=100";
 canwin=window.open(homePageURL,"Canvas",canvasProps);
}

function myBack() { canwin.back() }
function myForward() { canwin.forward() }
function myHome() { canwin.location=homePageURL }
function myReload() { canwin.location.reload() }
function myStop() { canwin.stop() }
```

continues

Listing 25.7. continued

```
function myExit() { parent.close() }
function myFind() {
 netscape.security.PrivilegeManager.enablePrivilege("UniversalBrowserRead");
 searchString=document.Nav.String.value;
 canwin.find(searchString);
}
```

FIGURE 25.4.

MyScape Navigator, although not the latest in design style, is almost as functional as Netscape's design.

Navigation bar —

Document —

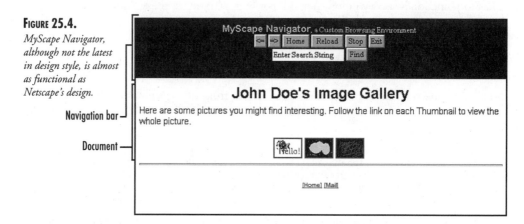

Congratulations! You have created a new Navigator, suited to your needs. If you want, you can get rid of the buttons and create images that fit your liking, place the navigation bar anywhere on the screen, or do anything else with the appearance of the window.

Summary

In this chapter, you've learned how to use canvas mode in Netscape Navigator 4.0 and created windows without the usual trimmings. You also learned how to digitally sign your scripts using zigbert and use scripts that haven't been signed yet. You then used canvas mode to create pop-up windows for zoomed images, and created a useful replacement for Navigator's interface suitable for use in a public access terminal or similar application.

VII
PART

Managing Dynamic HTML

Creating a Site for the 4.0 Browsers

by Jeff Rouyer

IN THIS CHAPTER

For a moment, if you can, just look straight at the little light at the tip of my pen. In a few seconds, you will see a flash and all your memories of past Web page meddling will be erased. If only it could be that simple to clear your mind and start out fresh before you begin building the next killer Dynamic HTML (DHTML) Web site. DHTML development requires a new perspective—a perspective that can challenge your ability to tell a story or provide an atmosphere to display information without bounds. One of the new and exciting aspects of DHTML is the ability to build a site that exists in both time and space. You may be familiar with the two-dimensional nature of standard HTML, as illustrated in Figure 26.1. Add to that the three-dimensional nature of overlapping layers and the four-dimensional nature of timed events, and you get a whole new world to deal with.

FIGURE 26.1.

This diagram illustrates the complexity of a DHTML Web site, which can contain two-dimensional HTML positioned in three-dimensional overlapping layers and can be made to interact over time.

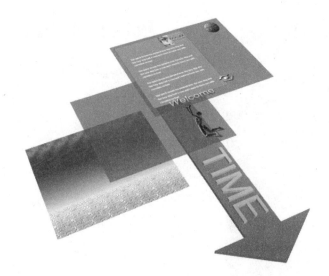

In this chapter, I discuss my discoveries in building the cross-browser compatible DHTML Guru Resource Web site located at `http://www.htmlguru.com`. The goal for the Guru Web site is to incorporate many cool programming techniques that make DHTML so interactive and immersive. I also want to introduce and inspire you to a new way of interface design and create an interesting place to be.

I was asked how I dreamed up the DHTML Guru Web site. I answered just that I dreamed it. Therein is the beauty of DHTML: It gives you the freedom to display your subconscious on the Net for the world to see, if you so choose (be careful, though). Although I encourage unbounded creative expression, I do believe that it is important to follow a systematic approach. The broad scope of DHTML, combined with cross-browser considerations, can conspire to boggle the mind, especially if your are new to JavaScript and style sheets. For the Guru Web site, I used a systematic approach to JavaScript coding combined with a multimedia metaphor of a stage production. Together they helped me follow a logical flow in blending design and

Creating a Site for the 4.0 Browsers

CHAPTER 26

575

26

CREATING A SITE
FOR THE 4.0
BROWSERS

functionality. I considered two main processes in a DHTML stage production: staging and choreography. These can simplify the planning and development of a highly interactive Web site.

Staging

Using our stage production metaphor, staging is the first thing you need to consider in building a DHTML Web site. Staging involves positioning and layering backgrounds, text, images, and navigational elements. Table 26.1 outlines six steps that can be used to stage a DHTML site. Although these steps are specific to the Guru site, they can be applied to your DHTML development project.

Table 26.1. Six steps in staging a DHTML Web site.

Description	Programming Method	Location
1. Create a canvas window	JavaScript	Home page window
2. Manage resolution-specific images	JavaScript	Canvas window
3. Layer HTML style sheets	HTML	Canvas window
4. Switch the document object model	JavaScript	Canvas window
5. Manage image loading	JavaScript	Canvas window
6. Position style sheet layers	JavaScript	Canvas window

Creating a Canvas Window

The Guru Web site exists across two windows. The first window displays Web site information and browser upgrade links for non-DHTML browsers. This poses the question: Do people actually upgrade their browsers because they came to your site? The answer is yes. I have had many people tell me that they did upgrade, but the trick is to include a screen shot so they get to see what they are missing. The second window is the canvas window that contains the framed DHTML page. There are considerations to make when displaying a new window, so it is up to you if you want to create a new window for your site. I find it incredibly refreshing not to have toolbar clutter all over my screen design, and for me, switching to the other window to browse elsewhere isn't a burden.

To begin, you need to pull out that well-worn browser sniffer routine. As shown in Listing 26.1, I get busy with a series of if...else statements to determine the visiting browser's name and version number. This is a cross-browser–compatible DHTML Web site, so I am only interested in the browser version numbers equal to or higher than 4.0 for displaying the canvas window. If the browser sniffer statement returns true for any of the 4.0 browsers, the nav variable is set to ver4; otherwise, it is set to ver3. All non-DHTML browsers display upgrade and site information text.

Script goals:

- Determine browser version
- Determine screen resolution
- Open new canvas window based on screen resolution
- Dynamically write a frameset HTML to the new canvas window

Listing 26.1. Creating a canvas window.

```
var nav = "";

if(navigator.appName == "Netscape" && navigator.appVersion.indexOf("X11") == -1) {
    if(parseInt(navigator.appVersion) >= 4) {
        nav = "ver4";
    } else if(parseInt(navigator.appVersion) == 3) {
        nav = "ver3";
    }
} else if (navigator.appName == "Microsoft Internet Explorer"
➥&& navigator.appVersion.indexOf("Macintosh") == -1) {
    if(parseInt(navigator.appVersion) >= 4) {
        nav = "ver4";
    } else if(parseInt(navigator.appVersion) == 3) {
        nav = "ver3";
    }
}
function openGuru() {
    if(nav == "ver4") {
        screen_width = screen.width-10;
        screen_height = screen.height-30;
        if (screen.height > 768) {
            screen_width = (1024-10);
            screen_height = (768-25);
        }
        var loading = '<HTML><BODY BACKGROUND="images/sky.jpg" BGCOLOR="#800000"
LINK="#00FFFF"
➥ALINK="#FFFF00" VLINK="#00FFFF"><BR><BR><BR><BR><BR><BR><BR><BR><BR><BR><CENTER>
➥<IMG SRC="images/closedeye.gif" BORDER="0"><BR><BR><FONT SIZE=5
COLOR="#ECD8AC">Loading
➥Guru...</FONT></CENTER></BODY></HTML>';

        var frames = '<HTML><HEAD><TITLE>Sams.net Dynamic HTML Guru Resource
</TITLE></HEAD>
➥<FRAMESET ROWS="0,*" FRAMEBORDER="0" FRAMESPACING="0" BORDER="0">';
            frames += '<FRAME SRC="about:blank" BORDER="0" MARGINHEIGHT="0"
MARGINWIDTH="0"
➥NAME="SNEAK" SCROLLING="NO">'
            frames += '<FRAME SRC="about:blank" BORDER="0" MARGINHEIGHT="0"
MARGINWIDTH="0"
➥NAME="GURU" SCROLLING="NO">'
            frames += '</FRAMESET></HTML>';

        var guruWindow =
➥window.open('','guruCanvas','width='+screen_width+',height='+screen_height+',top=0,
➥left=0');
        guruWindow.document.write(frames);
        guruWindow.document.close();
```

Creating a Site for the 4.0 Browsers

CHAPTER 26

577

26

CREATING A SITE
FOR THE 4.0
BROWSERS

```
          guruWindow.SNEAK.document.open();
          guruWindow.SNEAK.document.write(loading);
          guruWindow.SNEAK.document.close();

          guruWindow.GURU.document.open();
          guruWindow.GURU.document.write(loading);
          guruWindow.GURU.document.close();

          guruWindow.GURU.location.href = "interface/guru.htm";
     }
}
```

The canvas window is opened by the `openGuru()` function, which is triggered when the home page loads. This function also tests for the browser version by testing the `nav` variable with an `if...else` statement. If the browser passes the DHTML version test, then the screen resolution statements are initiated next. The width and height of the user's screen is determined by the statements `screen.width-10` and `screen.height-30`. I am subtracting a few pixels from the screen dimensions to account for the space that the window borders and title field take up. The Guru site uses images that are dependent on screen resolution, so I use a second `if` statement—`if(screen_height > 768)`—to trap any screen resolutions higher than 768 pixels. Now I know that the canvas window will not be greater than 768 pixels high, making the management of resolution-specific images easier. The next goal of the `openGuru()` function is to create a new window using the `screen_width` and `screen_height` variables in the `window.open()` statement. With the canvas window now opened, I can dynamically write frameset HTML to the window with the `guruWindow.document.write()` statement. The resulting framed page is shown in Figure 26.2.

FIGURE 26.2.

The Guru Web site in canvas mode showing the positioning of the two borderless frames making up the interface.

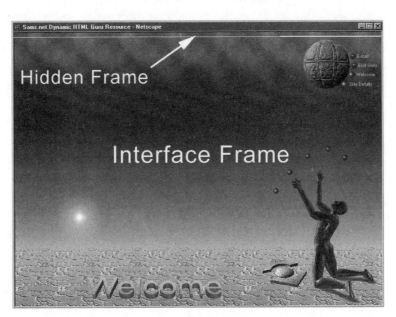

Users whose browsers are not 4.0 compatible get the joy of viewing a browser upgrade and Web site information page. To do this in a cross-browser and backward-compatible environment, place standard HTML between a pair of <NOSCRIPT></NOSCRIPT> tags. The <NOSCRIPT> tags will prevent DHTML-aware browsers from reading the unnecessary site information. For other JavaScript-aware browsers, the upgrade and site information has to be dynamically written using the document.write() method. In Chapter 27, "Degrading DHTML Gracefully," I expand on the browser-sniffing function to make your Web site look and feel the same across multiple browser technologies. In addition, I have included a backward-compatible DHTML template that you can use and experiment with for yourself.

LOADING EXTERNAL FILES

A major problem in building a multi-layered DHTML Web site is the style sheet limitation of not being able to load external HTML files into a layer. With the Netscape <LAYER> tag, you can dynamically change the HTML content of a layer at any time. Unfortunately, this is a browser-specific solution. As an alternative, you can pop up a secondary window, load whole new pages, or use a hidden frame as I did for the Guru site. The HTML in the hidden frame is stored in JavaScript variables. The HTML is then read into the Guru interface screen by JavaScript method when needed.

Managing Resolution-Specific Images

Now it is time to take care of the DHTML pages directly. As shown in Listing 26.2, I start out setting the screen resolution variables with the screen_height = screen.height and screen_width = screen.width statements. Setting the screen resolution variables is repeated in the canvas window because the two open windows are totally independent of each other.

Script goals:

- Use a chain of if...else statements to assign image URLs to resolution-specific image variables

Listing 26.2. Managing resolution-dependent images.

```
var screen_height = screen.height;
var screen_width = screen.width;

if (screen_height >= 768) {
    background_img = "images/horizon768.jpg";
    sun_img = "images/sun768.jpg";
    flare_img = "images/flare768.jpg";
    screen_width = 1024;
    screen_height = 768;
} else if (screen_height >= 624) {
```

Creating a Site for the 4.0 Browsers

CHAPTER 26

579

26

CREATING A SITE
FOR THE 4.0
BROWSERS

```
    background_img = "images/horizon624.jpg";
    sun_img = "images/sun624.jpg";
    flare_img = "images/flare624.jpg";
} else if (screen_height >= 600) {
    background_img = "images/horizon600.jpg";
    sun_img = "images/sun600.jpg";
    flare_img = "images/flare600.jpg";
} else if (screen_height >= 480) {
    background_img = "images/horizon480.jpg";
    sun_img = "images/sun480.jpg";
    flare_img = "images/flare480.jpg";
} else {
    background_img = "images/horizon600.jpg";
    sun_img = "images/sun600.jpg";
    flare_img = "images/flare600.jpg";
    screen_width = 640;
    screen_height = 480;
}
```

The Guru Web site is heavily dependent on screen resolution due to the nature of the vertical tiling desert background, sun, and sun flare images. Building images based on resolution allows for increased flexibility in screen design and layout, but it requires you to build additional images for each screen resolution supported. To set the image variables based on screen resolution, I use a chain of if...else statements to test the screen_height variable against known screen resolutions. If one of the statements rings true, the background_img, sun_image, and flare_img variables are set to the appropriate image URL. As you might guess, a consistent naming convention for your images comes in handy here. If no match is made, then the final else statement sets the image variables to a default screen solution of 640×480. Notice also that I am trapping vertical screen resolutions higher than 768 pixels. This corresponds to the maximum size of the window that I want to have opened. All image variables will be used later in the HTML portion of the Web page. For example, to use the background image variable, I use the following document.write() method to dynamically create the <BODY> tag using the resolution specific background image variable:

```
<SCRIPT>
    document.write('<BODY BACKGROUND=' + background_img + ' LINK="#00FFFF"
ALINK="#FFFF00"
➡ VLINK="#00FFFF" onLoad="preLoad()">');
</SCRIPT>
```

Layering HTML Style Sheets

The predominant force in DHTML is JavaScript controlling the document object model. The secondary force is that oddity of style sheets. Frankly, I find style sheets to be unintuitive by any measurement, but they represent the only cross-compatible method of building a layered site. Listing 26.3 shows all the layers that are used in the Guru interface page. All standard HTML tags go between the <DIV></DIV> tags, and the style sheet parameters are set as attributes of the <DIV> tag.

Listing 26.3. Creating style sheet layers.

```
<DIV ID="coreLyr" STYLE="position: absolute; width: 303px; height: 101px; clip:
rect (0 101 101 0); z-index: 4; visibility: hidden;">
    <IMG SRC="../images/core.gif" WIDTH="303" HEIGHT="101" BORDER="0">
</DIV>

<DIV ID="guruLyr" STYLE="position: absolute; width: 700px; height: 178px; clip:
rect (0 700 178 560); z-index: 5; visibility: hidden;">
    <IMG SRC="../images/guru.gif" WIDTH="700" HEIGHT="178" BORDER="0">
</DIV>

<DIV ID="legsLyr" STYLE="position: absolute; width: 140px; height: 120px; z-index:
7; visibility: hidden;">
    <IMG SRC="../images/legs.gif" WIDTH="140" HEIGHT="120" BORDER="0">
</DIV>

<DIV ID="pageLyr" STYLE="position: absolute; width: 400px; height: 48px; z-index:
9; visibility: hidden;"></DIV>

<DIV ID="titleLyr" STYLE="position: absolute; z-index: 10; visibility: hidden;">
    <IMG NAME="title_img" SRC="../images/blank.gif" SUPPRESS="TRUE" BORDER="0"
WIDTH="400" HEIGHT="48">
</DIV>
```

There are three areas to note in the use of the style sheet parameters for the Guru site. The first is the z-index ordering. If you have many layers, you will have a hard time finding out where that layer is in relation to the others, so you should order the layers on the page based on their z-index order. You might have noticed that all the visibility attributes of the layers are set to hidden. This is done for the Guru site because the layers are dependent on the screen resolution for their positioning. When the layers are positioned, their visibility attributes will be turned on and they will display in the right place at the right time. The third area of interest is the ID="layerName" attribute. Later I will refer to the ID names when I define the layer object variables, which will be used to dynamically position and animate the layers.

NAMING CONVENTIONS

Gone is the ability to name any HTML element what you want. Naming in style sheets has to fit a prescribed guideline. For example, naming a layer ID="my_layer" will not work. I found it safe to use alternating caps in naming layers, such as ID="myLyr". It is also a good idea to establish a naming convention, which will help you keep track of what is a layer, an object, or an image. I use the conventions of nameLyr for naming style sheet layers and nameObj for naming document object variables.

Creating a Site for the 4.0 Browsers
CHAPTER 26

581

26

CREATING A SITE
FOR THE 4.0
BROWSERS

Switching the Document Object Model

This is it, the big deal—switching the Document Object Model (DOM). Listing 26.4 is all that is needed to make the majority of functions in a DHTML Web site work across all 4.0 browsers.

Listing 26.4. Document Object Model switch.

```
if(navigator.appName == "Netscape") {
    nav = "ns4"
    doc = "document";
    sty = "";
} else {
    nav = "ie4"
    doc = "document.all";
    sty = ".style";
}
```

The DOM is switched by using the `if(navigator.appName == "Netscape")` statement to test the presence of Netscape. If the statement returns `true`, the three document object variables are set for Netscape; otherwise, they are set for Explorer. The `nav` variable is set with a string identifying the browser in use: `"ns4"` for Netscape or `"ie4"` for Explorer. The `nav` variable will be used later to differentiate the two browsers for dynamic clipping animations and referencing document objects in a framed window. The `doc` variable is set to reflect the differences of how the two browsers refer to document objects. Netscape refers to a document object with just `document.ObjectName`, whereas Explorer refers to the same document object as `document.all.objectName`. The third variable is required by Explorer only when referring to style sheet objects. Therefore, for Explorer, the variable `sty` is set to the string `".style"`, whereas for Netscape, it is set to nothing. The variables will be used later to construct object references useable by both browsers.

Managing Image Loading

With traditional HTML, it did not matter how and when images were loaded. In a DHTML site, it matters a lot, especially if parts of the same images are scattered across multiple layers to achieve a 3D effect. Listing 26.5 shows two functions that are called from a JavaScript `onload()` event handler located in the `<BODY>` tag of the Guru interface document. JavaScript statements in the `preLoad()` function will first create an image object for each image, and then assign an image URL to the object. After each image is loaded, the `onLoad` event handler is triggered for each image object and, in turn, calls the `loadCheck()` function.

Script goals:

- Define an image object and assign the image URL to the object
- Trigger the `onload` event handler and call the `loadCheck()` function to count the images that have been loaded
- Trigger the `positionLayers()` function when image count is reached

Listing 26.5. Managing image loading.

```
var count = 0;

function preLoad() {
    core = new Image();
    core.src = "../images/core.gif";
    core.onLoad = loadCheck();

    closedeye = new Image();
    closedeye.src = "../images/closedeye.gif";
    closedeye.onLoad = loadCheck();

    openeye = new Image();
    openeye.src = "../images/openeye.gif";
    openeye.onLoad = loadCheck();

    flare = new Image();
    flare.src = flare_img;
    flare.onLoad = loadCheck();

    guru = new Image();
    guru.src = "../images/guru.gif";
    guru.onLoad = loadCheck();

    legs = new Image();
    legs.src = "../images/legs.gif";
    legs.onLoad = loadCheck();

    sun = new Image();
    sun.src = sun_img;
    sun.onLoad = loadCheck();

    guide_off = new Image();
    guide_off.src = "../images/guide_off.gif";
    guide_off.onLoad = loadCheck();

    guide_on = new Image();
    guide_on.src = "../images/guide_on.gif";
    guide_on.onLoad = loadCheck();
}

function loadCheck() {
    count++;
    if(count == 9) {
        positionLayers();
    }
}
```

The job of the loadCheck() function is to count the number of images loaded. The if(count == 9) statement is used to check the state of the count variable. When the count variable reaches the count value of 9, the positionLayers() function is initiated. Using this method, you can control image loading and the flow of the next action from the time the page loads. For the Guru site, I want to load the images first, then position them based on screen resolution, and finally display them to the viewer.

Creating a Site for the 4.0 Browsers

CHAPTER **26**

583

26

CREATING A SITE
FOR THE **4.0**
BROWSERS

Positioning Style Sheet Layers

You can position style sheet layers in many ways. You can inline their absolute or relative positions directly into the <DIV> tag, or position them using the <STYLE> tag reference. This type of positioning is useless to anyone who needs to dynamically position elements based on screen resolution. Again, JavaScript comes to the rescue, beating back the evils of the style sheets to dynamically position layered elements. Listing 26.6 shows a segment of the positionLayers() function, which does the entire style sheet layer positioning for the Guru site.

Script goals:

- Create a layer object variable by constructing a layer object using the document switch variables
- Relocate the x and y screen position of a layer object in relation to screen resolution
- Turn on the layer object's visibility attribute

Listing 26.6. Dynamic layer positioning routines.

```
function positionLayers() {
    arrowImg = eval(doc + '["arrowLyr"]' + '.document');
    arrowObj = eval(doc + '["arrowLyr"]' + sty);
    arrowObj.left = (screen_width-270);
    arrowObj.top = (screen_height-140);

    pageObj = eval(doc + '["pageLyr"]' + sty);
    pageObj.left = 10;
    pageObj.top = 10;

    coreObj = eval(doc + '["coreLyr"]' + sty);
    coreObj.left = (screen_width-180);
    coreObj.top = (screen_height-408);

    flareObj = eval(doc + '["flareLyr"]' + sty);
    flareObj.left = (screen_width/2);
    flareObj.top = (screen_height-280);

    logoImg = eval(doc + '["pageLyr"]' + '.document');

    guruObj = eval(doc + '["guruLyr"]' + sty);
    guruObj.left = (screen_width-785);
    guruObj.top = (screen_height-338);

    infoObj = eval(doc + '["infoLyr"]' + sty);
    infoObj.visibility = "hidden";
    infoObj.left = (screen_width-230);
    infoObj.top = (screen_height-430);

    legsObj = eval(doc + '["legsLyr"]' + sty);
    legsObj.left = (screen_width-165);
    legsObj.top = (screen_height-160);
```

continues

Listing 26.6. continued

```
mainmenuImg = eval(doc + '["mainmenuLyr"]' + '.document');
mainmenuObj = eval(doc + '["mainmenuLyr"]' + sty);
mainmenuObj.left = (screen_width-258);
mainmenuObj.top = (screen_height-375);

submenuImg = eval(doc + '["submenuLyr"]' + '.document');
submenuObj = eval(doc + '["submenuLyr"]' + sty);
submenuObj.left = (screen_width-125);
submenuObj.top = 40;

sunObj = eval(doc + '["sunLyr"]' + sty);
sunObj.left = -120;
sunObj.top = (screen_height-280);

titleImg = eval(doc + '["titleLyr"]' + '.document');
titleObj = eval(doc + '["titleLyr"]' + sty);
titleObj.left = (screen_width-600)/2;
titleObj.top = (screen_height-95);

coreObj.visibility = "visible";
flareObj.visibility = "visible";
guruObj.visibility = "visible";
legsObj.visibility = "visible";
sunObj.visibility = "visible";

lensFlare();
}
```

The first goal is to define the document object for each layer that will be dynamically positioned. This is where the document object variables *doc* and *sty* defined earlier will come into play. Using the *layerObj* = eval(doc + '["*styleLyr*"]' + sty) expression, you can build the document object variable based on the visiting browser. When the document object variable has been defined, you can actually start doing cool stuff like positioning, animation, and toggling visibility. For example, I am positioning the Guru image layer referenced by the guruObj variable with the guruObj.left = (screen_width-785) statement. Notice the screen_width variable coming into play. The same routine is used for positioning the Guru image layer's top position with the guruObj.top = (screen_height-338) statement. The numbers being subtracted from the screen variables coincide with the width of the layers being positioned so that they display onscreen correctly. The next portion of the positionlayers() function is to set the layered object's visibility attribute. Remember that all visibility attributes were initially set to hidden. By this time, all the images have been loaded and the layers properly positioned, so it is time to make them visible. The *layerObj*.visibility = "visible" statement will do that in a snap. The last action of the positionLayers() function is to continue to manage program flow by triggering the lens flare animation.

It is important to review how the document object switch works to maintain cross-4.0-browser compatibility. Given a screen resolution of 800 × 600, Netscape will read the guruObj.left = (screen_width-785) statement as document.guruLyr.left = (800-785), whereas Explorer will

Creating a Site for the 4.0 Browsers

CHAPTER 26

585

26

CREATING A SITE
FOR THE 4.0
BROWSERS

read the same statement as `document.all.guruLyr.style.left = (800-785)`. All document object variables defined here are used heavily in the next phase of DHTML development involving choreography of movement.

Choreography

Consider choreography as the process of making your DHTML Web site come alive with interactivity and animation. As in a stage production, actors must wait for cues from others to start their roles. This analogy applies very well to interactive DHTML development, where flow control is very important. Table 26.2 lists six processes that can be used to choreograph interactivity and movement in a DHTML Web site.

Table 26.2. Six steps in choreographing a DHTML Web site.

Steps	Programming Method	Location
1. Layer animation	JavaScript	Canvas window
2. Imagemap resurrection	HTML/JavaScript	Canvas window
3. Sprite animation	JavaScript	Canvas window
4. Toggling visibility	JavaScript	Canvas window
5. Changing DHTML content	JavaScript	Canvas window
6. Scrolling layers	JavaScript	Canvas window

Layer Animation

Like animated GIFs of yore, an obligatory opening animation is almost a requirement for a DHTML Web site. I do not know why, but it fills some sort of psychological need for the Web developer. Opening animations can be practical, too, by keeping the eye busy as images continue to load in the background. For the Guru site, I open with a lens flare animation. This animation slides an image of a bright sun to the right while sliding an image of a lens flare in the opposite direction.

Overall, doing any kind of DHTML layer animation is easy with only minor cross-browser consideration. The general goal in a layer animation is to move a layer in a looping function so many pixels at a time until a predefined limit is reached. If you are good at math, you can extend these animations to mimic bouncing, twirling, or curved paths. Listing 26.7 shows the code for performing the lens flare animation, which starts out moving fast but slows at a linear rate. For example, the first statement defines a local variable `var sun_x_pos = parseInt(sunObj.left)` with the left position of the object you want to move. Before that happens, the object must be stripped of any text strings with the `parseInt()` function. This is only a consideration for Explorer as it returns a layer object position as a string, such as `356px`. This makes it difficult to compare and set limits that are based solely on numbers. Netscape returns the objects position as a real number.

Script goals:

- Get the sun layer's left position
- Get the lens flare layer's left position
- Reposition the sun layer one pixel to the right for each loop cycle until the limit is reached
- Reposition the flare layer one pixel to the left for each loop cycle until the limit is reached

Listing 26.7. Simple layer animation loop.

```
var timer_0 = null;
var flare_delta = 1;

function lensFlare() {
    var sun_x_pos = parseInt(sunObj.left);
    var flare_x_pos = parseInt(flareObj.left);
    if(sun_x_pos < 60) {
        sunObj.left = sun_x_pos+1;
        flareObj.left = flare_x_pos-1;
        timer_0 = setTimeout("lensFlare()", flare_delta);
        flare_delta++;
    } else {
        gurulogoObj.visibility = "visible";
    }
}
```

Layer animation is actually performed with methods defined within the if(sun_x_pos < 60) statement. For as long as the sun_x_pos variable is less than 60 pixels, the sun layer object will be moved to the right by one pixel with the sunObj.left = sun_x_pos+1 statement. The inverse happens for the lens flare object, which is moved to the left by one pixel with the flareObj.left = flare_x_pos-1 statement. The function will continue to loop with the timer_0 = setTimeout("lensFlare()", flare_delta) statement until the pixel limit is reached. Notice that the incrementing global variable flare_delta++ is in the setTimeout() function where static time in milliseconds would normally be. This is a cheap way of slowing the animation down as it gets closer to its predefined limit.

Imagemap Resurrection

You might have disliked imagemaps in the past, but they take on a new life in DHTML. Instead of using imagemaps to define areas of a large graphics and having them disappear as soon as you click, you can use them now for a precise navigational aid. In the Guru site, I use an imagemap exclusively to control the actions of the Guru's navigational system. It is accomplished by building a style sheet layer covering the same area and position of your navigational widget. Within that layer, you link a small transparent blank GIF image to an imagemap. The

Creating a Site for the 4.0 Browsers

CHAPTER 26

587

26

CREATING A SITE
FOR THE **4.0**
BROWSERS

result is a clear surface of predefined hot spots that can act to capture onMouseOver, onMouseOut, and onClick JavaScript events. In Listing 26.8, I have created a style sheet layer named guruLyr. Contained in the layer is a transparent GIF image positioned over the Guru interface. The GIF is linked to the guru_map imagemap. You can see the outline of the transparent imagemap superimposed over the Guru interface in Figure 26.3.

Listing 26.8. Imagemaps revisited.

```
<DIV ID="mainmenuLyr" STYLE="position: absolute; width: 230px; height: 120px;
z-index: 12;
➥visibility: hidden;">
    <IMG NAME="mainmenu_img" SRC="../images/guide_off.gif" WIDTH="230" HEIGHT="120"
➥USEMAP="#guru_map" BORDER="0">
</DIV>

<MAP NAME="guru_map">
    <AREA SHAPE=CIRCLE COORDS="17,103,13" HREF="JavaScript://"
➥onClick="getPage('../home/welcome.htm'); return false";
➥onMouseOver="mouseOver('down','<FONT FACE=\'ARIAL, HELVETICA, COURIER'
COLOR=#EEDD8E>
➥<B>Welcome</B></FONT><BR><FONT FACE=\'ARIAL, HELVETICA, COURIER' COLOR=#FFFFFF
SIZE=-1>
➥<B>What Guru is all about</B></FONT>')";
➥onMouseOut="mouseOut()"; ALT="">

    <AREA SHAPE=CIRCLE COORDS="47,63,13" HREF="JavaScript://"
➥onClick="getPage('../books/books.htm'); return false";
➥onMouseOver="mouseOver('up','<FONT FACE=\'ARIAL, HELVETICA, COURIER'
COLOR=#EEDD8E>
➥<B>Our Books</B></FONT><BR><FONT FACE=\'ARIAL, HELVETICA, COURIER' COLOR=#FFFFFF
SIZE=-1>
➥<B>Books from Sams.net</B></FONT>')";
➥onMouseOut="mouseOut()"; ALT="">

    <AREA SHAPE=CIRCLE COORDS="86,29,13" HREF="JavaScript://"
➥onClick="getPage('../ask/ask.htm'); return false";
➥onMouseOver="mouseOver('left','<FONT FACE=\'ARIAL, HELVETICA, COURIER'
COLOR=#EEDD8E>
➥<B>Ask A Guru</B></FONT><BR><FONT FACE=\'ARIAL, HELVETICA, COURIER' COLOR=#FFFFFF
SIZE=-1>
➥<B>Answers to your DHTML questions</B></FONT>')";
➥onMouseOut="mouseOut()"; ALT="">

    <AREA SHAPE=CIRCLE COORDS="131,14,13" HREF="JavaScript://"
➥onClick="getPage('../tutorials/tutorials.htm'); return false";
➥onMouseOver="mouseOver('center','<FONT FACE=\'ARIAL, HELVETICA, COURIER'
COLOR=#EEDD8E>
➥<B>Tutorials</B></FONT><BR><FONT FACE=\'ARIAL, HELVETICA, COURIER' COLOR=#FFFFFF
SIZE=-1>
➥<B>Get started with tutorials & templates</FONT></FONT>')";
➥onMouseOut="mouseOut()"; ALT="">
```

continues

Listing 26.8. continued

```
    <AREA SHAPE=CIRCLE COORDS="167,32,13" HREF="JavaScript://"
➥onClick="getPage('../resources/resources.htm'); return false";
➥onMouseOver="mouseOver('right','<FONT FACE=\'ARIAL, HELVETICA, COURIER'
COLOR=#EEDD8E>
➥<B>Resources</B></FONT><BR><FONT FACE=\'ARIAL, HELVETICA, COURIER' COLOR=#FFFFFF
SIZE=-1>
➥<B>Additional information to aid in your quest</FONT></B></FONT>')";
➥onMouseOut="mouseOut()"; ALT="">
</MAP>
```

Using an imagemap editor, I defined five hot spot areas that control the Guru interface. For each area, I have added JavaScript events that react to either an onMouseOver, onMouseOut, or onClick event. For the imagemap HREF parameter, I use the JavaScript:// URL. You might be unfamiliar with the JavaScript URL, which is used in place of an HTML file reference to allow for pure JavaScript control.

FIGURE 26.3.

Outline of the transparent imagemaps used to capture mouse events over predefined hot spots for the Guru Web site interface.

UNINTERRUPTED LOADING

If you use the JavaScript URL HREF="JavaScript://" and an onClick event, adding a return false statement to the event will allow images to finish loading even if you clicked something else. This method can prevent important images from being half-loaded.

Sprite Animation

There are three ways to do cross-browser animation with DHTML. You can use animated GIFs, dynamic image replacement, or dynamic clipping. Animated GIFs are hard to manage, because you cannot start or stop them programmatically. Dynamic image replacement is the process of replacing an image with another in real time without refreshing the whole browser page. This is fine for swapping a few images but is a burden if you want to animate many images. Dynamic clipping animation is the process of rapidly displaying a frame at a time from a single graphic. The advantage to this type of animation is that you only need to load a single image containing multiple frames, as shown in Figure 26.4.

FIGURE 26.4.

Dynamic clipping animation can take a strip of images and display one frame at a time. This screen shot shows the Guru site with dynamic clipping turned off.

The difficulty of using dynamic clipping animation is keeping track of all the changing clipping regions over time. In Listing 26.9, there are two functions that control the rotation of the spinning interface using dynamic clipping animation. The first function, coreAction(), uses setTimeout commands to call the spinCore() function. The spinCore() function is passed five variables that define the new position of the image and its new clipping region.

Listing 26.9. Quick and dirty dynamic clipping animation routine.

```
var rotation = true;

function coreAction() {
    if(rotation == true) {
        spinCore(screen_width-281, 0, 202, 101, 101);
        setTimeout("spinCore(screen_width-382, 0, 303, 101, 202)", 150);
```

continues

Listing 26.9. continued

```
        setTimeout("spinCore(screen_width-180, 0, 101, 101, 0)", 300);
        setTimeout("coreAction()", 450);
    }
}
function spinCore(left, cTop, cRight, cBottom, cLeft) {
    coreObj.left = left;
    if(nav == "ns4") {
        coreObj.clip.left = cLeft;
        coreObj.clip.right = cRight;
    } else {
        coreObj.clip = "rect(" + cTop + " " + cRight + " " + cBottom + " " + cLeft
+ ")";
    }
}
```

The `left` variable is used to move the image position along its x-axis. The `cTop` variable sets a new top boundary of the image's clipping region. The `cRight` variable sets a new right boundary of the image's clipping region. The `cBottom` variable sets a new bottom boundary of the image's clipping region. The `cLeft` variable sets a new left boundary of the image's clipping region. Here's how it works: The image is moved left the distance of a single frame. It then changes the clipping region from the first frame to the second frame, so only the second frame is displayed. It continues to move and clip until the last frame is reached. The clipping process is repeated in a looping function.

Dynamic clipping does have some cross-browser constraints that are best met by separating the browser-specific clipping methods between the two browsers. Netscape can dynamically clip a style sheet object by adding `clip.left`, `clip.right`, `clip.top`, or `clip.bottom` to the layer object, as in `coreObj.clip.right = cRight`. Explorer can only dynamically clip a layer object by assigning the whole clipping string, such as `coreObj.clip = "rect(0 140 100 0)"`.

I have used the simplest of possible functions to perform a dynamic image clipping animation. The functions can easily be extended to do complex image manipulation in both the x- and y-axes of direction and can include clipping regions that are stored into a data array.

Changing Dynamic HTML Content

Although DHTML has opened the floodgates to advanced Web development, it has some early-bird pitfalls. The biggest is the inability to load HTML content directly into an existing style sheet layer. This can destroy a plan of having a single interface that does not suffer from constant page refreshing. For the Guru site, I chose to use borderless frames to manage the loading of external HTML content in one hidden frame while the Guru interface stays put in another. The cool trick here is to manipulate HTML content in the main Guru interface frame by retrieving HTML stored in the hidden frame. For this to work, the HTML in the hidden frame is stored in the JavaScript variable `message`. To load new HTML into the hidden frame, the `getpage()` function is used as shown in Listing 26.10.

Creating a Site for the 4.0 Browsers

CHAPTER 26

591

26

CREATING A SITE
FOR THE 4.0
BROWSERS

Listing 26.10. Accessing HTML from a hidden frame.

```
function getPage(page) {
    if(page != "") {
        parent.SNEAK.location.href = page;
    }
}
```

The getpage() function is passed a Web page's URL by the Guru interface and loads that page into the hidden frame named SNEAK. After new HTML is loaded, the displayPage()function is initiated by an onLoad() event contained in the new page. The displayPage() function will read the HTML stored in the JavaScript variable message, and then dynamically display its content into the main content layer, pageLyr (see Listing 26.11). The displayPage() function does other interesting things before displaying the page. It first repositions the main content layer to its default starting point with the statement pageObj.left = 10 and pageObj.top = 10. Next an if...else statement is used to separate the two browsers from each other because they have entirely different ways of dynamically displaying HTML in a style sheet layer.

Listing 26.11. Dynamically displaying HTML.

```
function displayPage() {
    pageObj.left = 10;
    pageObj.top = 10;
if(nav == "ns4") {
        document.pageLyr.document.open();
        document.pageLyr.document.write(parent.SNEAK.message);
        document.pageLyr.document.close();
        pageObj.clip.top = 0;
        pageObj.clip.right = (screen_width-205);
        pageObj.clip.bottom = (screen_height-90);
        pageObj.clip.left = 0;
    } else {
        var cTop = 0;
        var cRight = screen_width-205;
        var cBottom = screen_height-90;
        var cLeft = 0;
        document.all.pageLyr.innerHTML = parent.SNEAK.message;
        pageObj.clip = "rect(" + cTop + " " + cRight + " " + cBottom + " " + cLeft
+ ")";
    }
    titleImg.title_img.src = parent.SNEAK.title;
    submenuImg.submenu_img.src = parent.SNEAK.submenu;
}
```

For Netscape, the document.pageLyr.document.write(parent.SNEAK.message) statement is used to write new HTML content to the main content layer. In addition, the dynamic clipping regions for the main content layer are also created. This keeps the page from overlapping Guru interface graphics. In Explorer, writing to the main content layer is accomplished by the document.all.pageLyr.innerHTML = parent.SNEAK.message statement. As it is for Netscape, dynamic clipping is achieved by Explorer-specific JavaScript methods. After new content has been loaded, clipped, and displayed into the Guru interface, it can be manipulated like any other DHTML object.

Scrolling Layers

The Guru site is set up to have the main content page scrollable by using the scroll page widget. When the scroll arrow widget is clicked, it passes a direction variable of either up or down to the scroll() function, as shown in Listing 26.12.

Script goals:

- Get the content layer's top position
- Move the content layer position up or down depending on the direction variable passed to the function

Listing 26.12. Scrolling DHTML content.

```
function scroll(dir) {
    var y_pos = parseInt(contentObj.top);
    if(dir == "up") {
        contentObj.top = (y_pos-60);
    } else {
        contentObj.top = (y_pos+60);
    }
}
```

The first portion of the script sets the local y_pos variable with the current top position of the content layer object. The contentObj.top is wrapped in the parseInt() statement to weed out the "px" string that Explorer will return. I only want the numerical value of the layer's position. Next, the if...else statement is used to check whether the content layer is to be scrolled up or down. The "up" or "down" variable is passed to this function by the scroll arrow widget imagemap. To move the content layer up, the top position of the content layer is relocated with the statement contentObj.top = (y_pos-60). Essentially, I am subtracting 60 pixels from the layer's current top position and resetting its location. To move the layer down, I am adding 60 pixels to the layer's current top position and repositioning to the layer. Extensions to this function can include a timed loop to automatically scroll the layer.

Summary

My adventures in building a cross-4.0-browser DHTML site took me along many interesting paths. Surprisingly, I found little difficulty in making the Guru site work the way I envisioned it, let alone function identically across both browsers. The basic philosophy I kept in my research was to look for the common denominator among both browsers and ignore the propaganda that either side of the browser war spits out. In the future, some of the minor pitfalls—such as the inability to dynamically load HTML content into style sheet layers—should be things of the past. In the meantime, please look to the Guru at http://www.htmlguru.com for the latest in cross-browser DHTML developments.

Degrading DHTML Gracefully

by Jeff Rouyer

IN THIS CHAPTER

CHAPTER 27

The path to building a backward-compatible Dynamic HTML site is strewn with stinging nettles, broken glass, pitfalls, and dead bodies. Understandably, it is a path not many Web developers care to take. As a result, many Web sites are crippled to cater to the most primitive Web technology or bisected into duel Web site development. These drawbacks were enough to motivate many Web developers through the path of degradability, and they were thoughtful enough to leave some crumbs in their wake for the rest of us to follow.

This chapter describes techniques on how to build a cross-browser backward-compatible Dynamic HTML Web site. Accompanying this chapter is a fully functional Web template to use as an example. The template is not a cheap set of basic HTML code, but a collection of advanced features built to be practical for most Web development applications. The template as shown in Figure 27.1 includes the following features:

- Cross browser Dynamic HTML functionality.
- Graceful backward compatibility across three generations of Web browser technologies.
- The ability to make single page edits viewable in all supported browsers.

The template is free for you to use any way you want, but please read the Terms of Use contained on the template pages. You can access the template from the Dynamic HTML Guru Web site at http://www.htmlguru.com. To make things complete and wholesome, the original Photoshop 4.0 source graphics are included for you to customize the template to your needs. So put on your best shoes and travel down the path of Web page degradation—and you may pick up a few crumbs along the way.

Grouping Browsers

The initial planning stage of building a backward-compatible Web site involves the process of grouping browsers in order of their support of Web technology. Table 27.1 shows the browsers grouped based on their support of HTML tables, borderless frames, and JavaScript.

Table 27.1. Grouping browsers based on their HTML and JavaScript support.

Browser	Tables	Frames	JavaScript	Grouping
Netscape 4.0	Yes	Yes	Yes (DHTML)	Group 4.0
Explorer 4.0	Yes	Yes	Yes (DHTML)	Group 4.0
Netscape 3.0	Yes	Yes	Yes	Group 3.0
Explorer 3.0	Yes	Yes	Yes	Group 3.0
Netscape 2.0	Yes	Yes*	Yes	Group 2.0
Opera 2.12	Yes	No	No	Group 2.0

* Does not support borderless frames.

FIGURE 27.1.

The home page of the backward-compatible Dynamic HTML Web site template as shown across six browsers.
(a) Netscape 4.0,
(b) Explorer 4.0,
(c) Netscape 3.0,
(d) Explorer 3.0,
(e) Netscape 2.0,
(f) Opera 2.12.

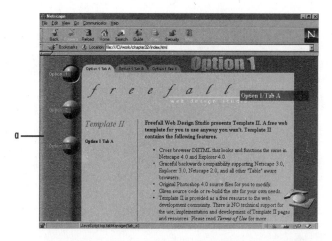

a

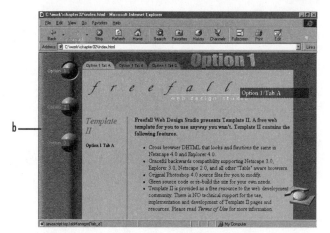

b

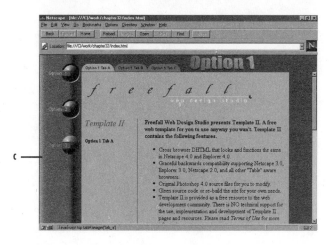

c

d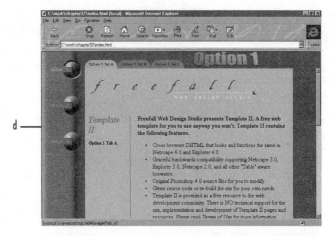

e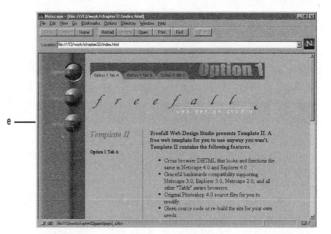

f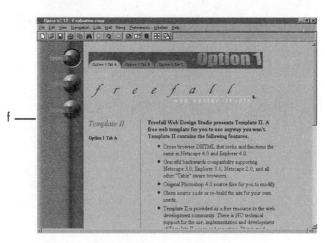

The first grouping, Group 4.0, contains the browsers that support advanced Dynamic HTML as well as tables and borderless frames.

The second grouping, Group 3.0, contains the browsers that support tables, borderless frames, and JavaScript, but the JavaScript support has limited Dynamic HTML capabilities.

The third group contains the browsers that support HTML tables only. Although Netscape 2.0 supports JavaScript and frames and can be added to the Group 3.0 browsers, it doesn't support borderless frames and, therefore, it's too ugly to use, so it is thrown to the dogs in the Group 2.0 category. Many other browsers not listed qualify to go under Group 2.0 based on their capability to support the full HTML spec for table formatting. With the grouping information, we can enter the next phase of development, which is to formulate a development flow.

Development Flow

Establishing a good development flow is crucial for building backward-compatible Web sites. With all the differing features and functionality of the various Web browsers, it can become confusing quick. The following list outlines the development flow used for the template site. The general rule is to build for the high-end browsers first and then work your way down to the low-end bottom-dwelling browsers.

A. Build the Control Page (`index.html`)

> Step 1: Add Document Object Switch JavaScript code for Group 4.0 and 3.0 browsers.

> Step 2: Add Dynamic Frame Setting JavaScript code for Group 4.0 and 3.0 browsers.

B. Build the Main Menu Page (`menu.htm`)

> Step 1: Add the Main Menu HTML and graphics for Group 4.0 and 3.0 browsers.

> Step 2: Add JavaScript event handlers to the Main Menu buttons for button animation and other mouse-over events for Group 4.0 and 3.0 browsers.

> Step 3: Add the corresponding JavaScript functions to the Control document to handle the Main Menu events for Group 4.0 and 3.0 browsers.

C. Build the Tab Menu Page (`tabs.htm`)

> Step 1: Add the Tab Menu HTML and graphics for Group 4.0 and 3.0 browsers.

> Step 2: Add JavaScript event handlers to the Tab Menu buttons for button animation and other mouse-over events for Group 4.0 and 3.0 browsers.

> Step 3: Add the corresponding JavaScript functions to the Control document to handle the Tab Menu events for Group 4.0 and 3.0 browsers.

D. Build the Main Content Page (`page.htm`)

> Step 1: Add JavaScript header event handlers for Group 4.0 and 3.0 browsers.

> Step 2: Add Main Menu and Tab Menu HTML and graphics code contained in `<NOSCRIPT>` tags for Group 2.0 browsers.

27

DEGRADING DHTML GRACEFULLY

Step 3: Add standard HTML body code for all browser groups.

Step 4: Add the Style Sheet layer code to all content pages for Group 4.0 browsers.

In the development flow for the template site, there are four essential areas. These areas include building a control document page first, the main menu page second, the tabs menu page third, and finally, the main content page. As you can see from the list, building a backward-compatible Web site is not a linear process. That means you will come back to the control page to add corresponding JavaScript that reflects events you added to other documents. This non-linear process continues for each step of the development flow. Making the site suitable for Group 2.0 browsers is handled in the last phase of the development flow as you build the main content page.

The idea behind this whole scheme is to have the template show up as frames for Group 4.0 and 3.0 browsers and as only table formatting for Group 2.0 browsers. A motivating force to building a site this way is that you only have to edit a content page once to have it show up nicely across six or more different browsers.

The Control Page (`index.html`)

The job of the Control document is to serve as the mother to all other Web pages by filling three major roles. The first role of the control page is to dynamically create a `<FRAMESET>` and load the `menu.htm`, `tabs.htm`, and `blank.htm` pages.

The second role of the control page is to display a standard table formatted page for the Group 2.0 browsers.

The third role of the control document is to serve as the central source of all JavaScript functions. The next few sections focus on this central role beginning with setting up browser-specific variables.

Document Object Switch

The document object switch is used to smooth out some of the major JavaScript differences between the 4.0 browsers and the way Netscape and Explorer display frames. The object switch is built by combining the standard browser sniffing code and setting variables for each browser, as shown in Listing 27.1. The switching code will be used through all JavaScript functions to separate code between browsers or allow the ability to write a single line of JavaScript that will work for both 4.0 browsers.

Script goals:

- Determine browser version.
- Set browser-specific variables for building frames.
- Set browser-specific variables differing document object models.

Listing 27.1. Browser sniffing code used for setting document object switches.

```
if(navigator.appName == "Netscape" && parseInt(navigator.appVersion) == 2) {
    nav = "ns2";
} else if (navigator.appName == "Netscape" && parseInt(navigator.appVersion) == 3){
    nav = "ns3";
    scroll = "AUTO";
    rowSpace = 50;
} else if (navigator.appName == "Netscape" && parseInt(navigator.appVersion) >= 4){
    nav = "ns4";
    scroll = "NO";
    rowSpace = 50;
    doc1 = "document";
    doc2 = ".document";
    sty = "";
    screen_height = screen.height;
    screen_width = screen.width;
} else if (navigator.appName == "Microsoft Internet Explorer" &&
➥parseInt(navigator.appVersion) == 2) {
    nav = "ie3";
    scroll = "AUTO";
    rowSpace = 46;
} else if (navigator.appName == "Microsoft Internet Explorer" &&
➥parseInt(navigator.appVersion) >= 4) {
    nav = "ie4";
    scroll = "NO";
    rowSpace = 46;
    doc1 = "document.all";
    doc2 = "";
    sty = ".style";
    screen_height = screen.height;
    screen_width = screen.width;
}
```

The script used five `if else` statements to test the presence and version of Netscape and Explorer. If the statement returns `true` for a particular browser, then several variables are set. The `nav` variable is set with a string identifying the browser type and version, such as `ns2` for Netscape 2.0 or `ie3` for Explorer 3.0. The `nav` variable will be used extensively to differentiate JavaScript code among browsers.

The `scroll` variable will be used to turn on or off frame scrolling when we dynamically create a `<FRAMESET>`. Similarly, the `rowSpace` variable will be used in the `<FRAMESET>` to adjust the row height to account for display differences between Netscape and Explorer.

The `doc1` variable is set to reflect the differences of how the two 4.0 browsers refer to style sheet layers. Netscape refers to a style sheet layer with the *document.layerName* statement, while Explorer refers to the same document object as *document.all.layerName.sty*. The `sty` variable is set to the string "style" for Explorer only.

The `doc2` variable is similar to the `doc1` variable but it is used to differentiate how the 4.0 browsers access named objects within a style sheet layer. Netscape refers to document image objects in a style sheet layer by the *document.layerName.document.imageName.src* statement, while Explorer refers to the same document image object, as *document.all.layerName.imageName.src*.

The variables defined in the object switch script will be used to construct single JavaScript statements useable by both browsers for DHTML manipulation. In the next section, you will see how the scroll and rowSpace variables are used for dynamically creating a <FRAMESET>.

Dynamic Frame Setting

The dynamic frame setting technique is the first culling of browser technology. It separates the browsers that support borderless frames from browsers that only support HTML table layout. Listing 27.2 shows the frame setting code used in the template site. Once the code is initiated by the browsers, it will create a new <FRAMESET> and load the appropriate pages into it.

Script goals:

- Test the nav variable and allow browsers that support borderless frames to execute the code.

- Dynamically create a <FRAMESET> using the scroll and rowSpace variables.

Listing 27.2. Dynamic frame setting code for 4.0 and 3.0 browsers.

```
if (nav == "ns3" || nav == "ns4" || nav == "ie3" || nav == "ie4") {
    var frames = '<HTML><FRAMESET COLS="124,*" FRAMEBORDER="0" FRAMESPACING="0"
    ➡BORDER="0">';
        frames += '<FRAME SRC="interface/menu.htm" BORDER="0" MARGINHEIGHT="0"
        ➡MARGINWIDTH="0"
        ➡NAME="MENU" SCROLLING="NO">';
        frames += '<FRAMESET ROWS="' + rowSpace + ',*">';
        frames += '<FRAME SRC="interface/tabs.htm" BORDER="0" MARGINHEIGHT="0"
        ➡MARGINWIDTH="0"
        ➡NAME="TABS" SCROLLING="NO">';
        frames += '<FRAME SRC="interface/blank.htm" BORDER="0" MARGINHEIGHT="0"
        ➡MARGINWIDTH="0"
        ➡NAME="MAIN" SCROLLING="' + scroll + '">';
        frames += '</FRAMESET>';
        frames += '</FRAMESET></HTML>';
    document.write(frames);
    document.close();
}
```

In the frame setting code, the nav variable is used to filter out browsers that do not support borderless frames. The scroll variable is used to turn off window scrolling for the 4.0 browsers or turn on window scrolling for the 3.0 browsers. The rowSpace variable is used to set the row height to account for differences in how Netscape and Explorer render frame dimensions. The variables are inserted in the frame setting HTML code, which is stored in the variable frames. The statements document.write(frames) and document.close() write the HTML stored in the frames variable to the window.

Notice that one of the pages loaded is named `blank.htm` and contains no content. This is done to allow for the correct synchronization of page loading.

Preload Manager

The synchronization of the framed Web pages is important, especially if you use DHTML. It is possible for a page to load in one frame that calls a function in another frame that does not exist. The Preload Manager routine tries to manage the loading of pages as well as preload images for real-time image animation. Listing 27.3 shows the two functions that comprise the Preload Manager routine.

Script goals:

- ■ Create an image object and assign an image URL to it.
- ■ Use the image object's `onLoad` event handler to update the `loadCheck()` function.
- ■ Once a specified count is reached in the `loadCheck()` function, initiate the loading of the final page.

Listing 27.3. Using the `preLoad()` and `loadCheck()` functions to check the status of loading images and Web pages.

```
var count = 0;
if(nav == "ie4" || nav == "ns3" || nav == "ns4") {
    btn1_up = new Image();
    btn1_up.src = "images/btn1_up.gif";
    btn1_up.onLoad = loadCheck();

    btn1_dn = new Image();
    btn1_dn.src = "images/btn1_dn.gif";
    btn1_dn.onLoad = loadCheck();

    btn2_up = new Image();
    btn2_up.src = "images/btn2_up.gif";
    btn2_up.onLoad = loadCheck();

    btn2_dn = new Image();
    btn2_dn.src = "images/btn2_dn.gif";
    btn2_dn.onLoad = loadCheck();

    btn3_up = new Image();
    btn3_up.src = "images/btn3_up.gif";
    btn3_up.onLoad = loadCheck();

    btn3_dn = new Image();
    btn3_dn.src = "images/btn3_dn.gif";
    btn3_dn.onLoad = loadCheck();
}
function loadCheck() {
    if(nav == "ie4" || nav == "ns3" || nav == "ns4") {
        count++;
        if(count == 8) {
```

continues

Listing 27.3. continued

```
            parent.MAIN.location.href = "../page1/page1_a.htm"
        }
    } else if (nav == "ie3") {
        count++;
        if(count == 2) {
            parent.MAIN.location.href = "../page1/page1_a.htm"
        }
    }
}
```

As with most of the functions used at the template site, the nav variable is used again in the preLoad() function to filter out Web browsers that do not support the JavaScript image object required for preloading images. The first statements in the preLoad() function will create an image object for each image and then assign an image URL to the object. After each image is loaded, the onLoad event handler is triggered and in turn, calls the loadCheck() function.

The job of the loadCheck() function is to count the number of images loaded. The if(count == 8) statement is used to check the state of the count variable. When the variable reaches the count value of eight, the parent.MAIN.location.href="../page1/page1_a.htm" statement is initiated to load the final page replacing the blank page. The count variable is only incremented to eight when the menu.htm and tabs.htm pages are loaded. On each of these pages resides the onLoad="top.loadCheck()" event handler that calls the loadCheck() function directly. To further complicate the Preload Manager process, Internet Explorer has to be filtered out with the nav variable because it does not support the JavaScript image object, but it does support borderless frames. The count variable for Explorer 3.0 is incremented to two by the menu.htm and tabs.htm pages before loading the first content page.

> **TIP**
>
> In the template site, the majority of the JavaScript functions are stored on the index.html control page. In a framed window environment, Web pages in one frame may need to call JavaScript in another frame. To make a JavaScript reference to a function in the control window, you would use the top.functionName() reference. To reference a function in another window, you would reference it as parent.windowName.function() reference. It is a good idea to keep all your functions in the index.html control page because that document is always present. Once all the pages and images have loaded according to plan, it is safer to perform cross-window JavaScript functions, such as dynamic image replacement.

Dynamic Image Replacement

Dynamic image replacement is the process of replacing an image with another in real time without having to refresh the whole Web page. In the template site, it is used to animate the main menu buttons as well as the scroll arrow images for the 4.0 browsers. For browsers that support the image object, it is an easy JavaScript solution. For browsers that do not support the image object, such as Explorer 3.0, it can be simulated with dynamic page creation. Listing 27.4 shows the code used in the template site, which is responsible for the toggle effect used for the main menu button animation.

Script goals:

■ Filter out the browsers that support the image object.

■ Reset all button images to their up position using the preloaded image variables.

■ Filter for Explorer 3.0 and assign images to variable names used to build the dynamically created menu page.

■ Display the dynamically created page every time the button is selected in Explorer 3.0.

Listing 27.4. The `toggle()` function used for dynamic image replacement and dynamic page creation for Explorer 3.0.

```
var selected = "btn1_img";
function toggle(imageName, fileName) {
    if(nav == "ie4" ¦¦ nav == "ns3" ¦¦ nav == "ns4") {
        parent.MENU.document.btn1_img.src = btn1_up.src;
        parent.MENU.document.btn2_img.src = btn2_up.src;
        parent.MENU.document.btn3_img.src = btn3_up.src;
        parent.MENU.document.images[imageName].src = eval(fileName + ".src");
        selected = imageName;
    } else if(nav == "ie3") {
        var btn1 = "btn1_up.gif";
        var btn2 = "btn2_up.gif";
        var btn3 = "btn3_up.gif";
        if(imageName == "btn1_img") {
            btn1 = "btn1_dn.gif";
        } else if(imageName == "btn2_img") {
            btn2 = "btn2_dn.gif";
        } else if(imageName == "btn3_img") {
            btn3 = "btn3_dn.gif";
        }

        var menuPage = '<HTML><BODY BACKGROUND="../images/menu.jpg"
        ➡BGCOLOR="#D9C9B5">
➡<TABLE BORDER="0" CELLPADDING="0" CELLSPACING="0" WIDTH="115" HEIGHT="300">';

        menuPage += '<TR><TD ALIGN=RIGHT><A HREF="../page1/page1_a.htm"
        ➡TARGET="MAIN"
➡onClick="top.toggle(\'btn1_img\', \'btn1_dn\')"><IMG NAME="btn1_img"
➡SRC="../images/' + btn1 + '" SUPPRESS="TRUE" WIDTH="108" HEIGHT="53"
➡BORDER="0"></A>
➡</TD></TR>';

        menuPage += '<TR><TD ALIGN=RIGHT><A HREF="../page2/page2_a.htm"
        ➡TARGET="MAIN"
```

continues

27

DEGRADING
DHTML
GRACEFULLY

Listing 27.4. continued

```
➡onClick="top.toggle(\'btn2_img\', \'btn2_dn\')"><IMG NAME="btn2_img"
➡SRC="../images/' + btn2 + '" SUPPRESS="TRUE" WIDTH="108" HEIGHT="53"
➡BORDER="0"></A>
➡</TD></TR>';

       menuPage += '<TR><TD ALIGN=RIGHT><A HREF="../page3/page3_a.htm"
       ➡TARGET="MAIN"
➡onClick="top.toggle(\'btn3_img\', \'btn3_dn\')"><IMG NAME="btn3_img"
➡SRC="../images/' + btn3 + '" SUPPRESS="TRUE" WIDTH="108" HEIGHT="53"
➡BORDER="0"></A>
➡</TD></TR>';

       menuPage += '</TABLE></BODY></HTML>';
       parent.MENU.document.write(menuPage);
       parent.MENU.document.close();
    }
}
```

Image replacement for browsers that support the image object is simple. It just requires JavaScript to point to an image object's name on the Web page and then replace it with a preloaded image as shown in the `parent.MENU.document.btn1_img.src = btn1_up.src` statement. You can simulate image replacement for Explorer 3.0 by dynamically writing a new Web page to the frame every time a button is clicked. To do this, you use the nav variable to isolate the JavaScript code for Explorer 3.0. Next, you set a local variable with several `if else` statements to the name of the image being selected, such as `btn1 = "btn1_dn.gif"`. Once set, the variables containing the image names are used to build HTML representing the `menu.htm` page and stored in the `menuPage` variable. The statements `parent.MENU.document.write(menuPage)` and `parent.MENU.document.close()` are used to write the HTML stored in the `menuPage` variable to the MENU window. For Explorer 3.0, a dynamically created page is written to the MENU window every time a main menu button is clicked. It is not as smooth as dynamic image replacement, but it's better than loading a new menu page to represent a button being pushed down. The Dynamic image replacement process is repeated for the changing tab menu also.

Info Box Widget

If you view the template in the 4.0 browsers, you will notice the pop-up info box describing where your mouse is as you float over a menu item. Using the pop-up text box is a way to help your audience navigate the site as they have more information on what a particular link is about. Creating the info box is easy, but it requires JavaScript code separation between Netscape 4.0 and Explorer 4.0 as shown in Figure 27.5.

Script goals:

■ Filter for the 4.0 browsers and query the windowStatus variable to see whether it is okay to execute the pop-up code.

- Create a style sheet layer object to reference the style sheet layer by both browsers.
- Dynamically write the HTML to the style sheet layer named info layer.

Listing 27.5. Pop-up info box routine for displaying floating tool tips or help screens.

```
var windowStatus = false;
function displayInfo(info) {
    if(nav == "ie4" || nav == "ns4" && windowStatus == true) {
        infoObj = eval("parent.MAIN." + doc1 + '["infoLyr"]' + sty);
        infoObj.left = screen_width-350;
        infoObj.top = 50;

        infoMsg = eval("parent.MAIN." + doc1 + '["infoLyr"]' + doc2);

        var msg = '<TABLE BORDER="0" BACKGROUND="../images/screen1.gif"
        ➥CELLPADDING="4"
➥CELLSPACING="0" WIDTH="200"><TR><TD VALIGN="TOP">' + info + '</TD></TR></TABLE>';
        if(nav == "ns4") {
            infoMsg.open();
            infoMsg.write(msg);
            infoMsg.close();
        } else    if(nav == "ie4") {
            infoMsg.innerHTML = msg;
        }
        infoObj.visibility = "visible";
    }
}

function hideInfo() {
    if(nav == "ie4" || nav == "ns4" && windowStatus == true) {
        infoObj.visibility="hidden";
    }
}
```

The first process in the `displayInfo()` function is to filter out all non–4.0 browsers using the nav variable. In addition to the browser sniffing, the `&& windowStatus == true` statement is used to test the state of the `windowStatus` variable. If true, the rest of the function is initiated. The `windowStatus` variable is set to `true` or `false` by an `onLoad` event handler found on every content page. Since the info box is a style sheet layer found on each content page, it is important to prevent the pop-up script from working until the content page is fully loaded. The info box style sheet layer is described in more detail later is this chapter.

The next step of the `displayInfo()` function is to define the style sheet layer object. Using the `doc1`, and `sty` variables set earlier in the browser switch routine, you can build an object variable that points to the style sheet layer using the `infoObj = eval("parent.MAIN." + doc1 + '["infoLyr"]' + sty)` statement. Once the layer object variable has been defined, its position can be manipulated with the `infoObj.left = 50` statement. The layer's visibility attribute can be turned on or off with the `infoObj.visibility = "visible"` method.

As noted earlier, Explorer and Netscape have two different ways of writing HTML to a style sheet layer. Netscape uses the statement, `infoMsg.document.write(msg)`, whereas Explorer uses the statement `infoMsg.innerHTML = msg`. To account for these document object model differences, you have to create another style sheet layer object using the `doc1` and `doc2` variables, as shown in the statement `infoMsg = eval("parent.MAIN." + doc1 + '["infoLyr"]' + doc2)`. Once defined, you can use the new style sheet object reference to repeatedly write HTML to the info box layer.

Page Scroller Widget

The page scroller widget can be seen only in the 4.0 browsers. It replaces the standard scrolling window bar you turned off in the dynamic frame setting code. Depending on what part of the cursor you click, the widget will either scroll the main content window up or down. As with the info box pop-up, the page scroller widget is contained in a hidden layer on every content page. Figure 27.6 shows the JavaScript code responsible for moving the content window up, down, or returning it to its top position.

Script goals:

■ Test for browser compatibility and test the `windowStatus` variable.

■ Define the style sheet page object used for positioning the main content layer.

■ Set the `pageTop` variable with the current top position of the style sheet layer.

■ Use `if else` statement to control whether the page should be scrolled up, down, or returned to top of the screen.

Listing 27.6. The `pageScroll()` function is used to move the main content page up or down.

```
function pageScroll(dir) {
    if(nav == "ie4" || nav == "ns4" && windowStatus == true) {
        var pageObj = eval("parent.MAIN." + doc1 + '["pageLyr"]' + sty);
        var pageTop = parseInt(pageObj.top);
        if(dir == "up") {
            pageObj.top = (pageTop-50);
        } else if(dir == "down") {
            if(pageTop >= 0) {
                pageObj.top = 0;
                displayInfo('<FONT COLOR=#FFFFE1 SIZE=4>You are at the top
                ➡</FONT>');
            } else {
                pageObj.top = (pageTop+50);
            }
        } else if(dir == "top") {
            pageObj.top = 0;
        }
    }
}
```

The first part of the pageScroll() function uses the nav variable to isolate the DHTML specific code for the 4.0 browser. The next step in the function is to define the style sheet layer object using the var pageObj = eval("parent.MAIN." + doc1 + '["pageLyr"]' + sty) statement. The next action of the function is to assign the main content page's top position with the var pageTop = parseInt(pageObj.top) statement. With the pageObj and the pageTop variables defined, you can move the layer up or down using a series of if else statements that match the command being passed to the function. For example, the page layer is moved up 50 pixels with the pageObj.top = (pageTop-50) statement.

Main Content Page

Up until now, we have been discussing how the template's navigational buttons, tabs, and arrows are made to function across multiple browsers, but the real backward compatibility starts here with the main content page. The main content page includes all the HTML pages that display content in a framed environment, as well as in a nonframed environment. Every content page is divided into seven sections consisting of JavaScript code, NOSCRIPT HTML code, standard HTML code, and style sheet code. Depending on the visiting browser, these seven sections are either revealed or hidden enabling the page to be viewed across multiple browsers. Each content page includes three style sheet layers. The first layer displays the main text area of the page. The second layer displays the pop-up info box, and the third layer displays the page scroller widget. The functionality of the style sheet layers is only visible to the 4.0 browsers.

JavaScript Header

At the top of every content page is a JavaScript header that contains code that can be executed only in browsers that support borderless frames. As shown in Listing 27.7, the header script is responsible for setting a window status variable and dynamically writing the <BODY> tag.

Script goals:

- Set the windowStatus to false.

- Dynamically write the <BODY> tag for a browser supporting borderless frames.

- Initiate an onLoad event handler that will call a function to change the tab menu button items as well as set the windowStatus variable to true.

Listing 27.7. JavaScript header found at the top of every content page.

```
<HEAD><SCRIPT LANGUAGE="JavaScript"><!--
top.windowStatus = false;
// --></SCRIPT></HEAD>
<SCRIPT LANGUAGE="JavaScript"><!--
if(navigator.appName == "Netscape" && parseInt(navigator.appVersion) != 2 ||
➡navigator.appName == "Microsoft Internet Explorer" &&
```

continues

Listing 27.7. continued

```
➥parseInt(navigator.appVersion) != 1) {
    document.write('<BODY BACKGROUND="../images/main.jpg" TEXT="#000000"
    ➥LINK="#0000FF"
➥VLINK="#0000FF" ALINK="#FF0000" onLoad="top.pageManager(1, \'a\');
➥top.windowStatus = true"; onUnload="top.windowStatus = false">');
}
// --></SCRIPT>
```

In the header script, the windowStatus variable is first set to false before anything else is loaded. This is done to prevent the info box widget from popping up before the page is loaded. The next step of the header script is to filter out browsers that don't support borderless frames and then dynamically write the <BODY> tag for those that do. The script also creates the onLoad event handler that is triggered when the page is fully loaded. The event handler calls the top.pageManager(1, \'a\') function, passing to it two variables. The variables tell the pageManager() function what page is being loaded, in this case, page1_a. The pageManager() function takes that information and displays the appropriate tab menu graphic and hyperlinks. The second part of the event handler sets the windowStatus variable to true, making it safe for the info box and page scroller widget to appear.

A second onUnload event handler resets the windowStatus variable to false with the statement onUnload="top.windowStatus = false" when the page is replaced by another. This trick seems to work most of the time, except in Internet Explorer, which is slow at triggering onUnload events.

Main Content Page Layer

The main content page style sheet layer is used to encapsulate the HTML of the content page and separate it from the info box and page scroller layers. It takes a single tag to create a style sheet layer, as shown in Listing 27.8.

Listing 27.8. Style sheet layer syntax for the main content page.

```
<DIV ID="pageLyr" STYLE="position: absolute; left: 0; top: 0; z-index: 2;
➥visibility: visible;">
```

The first attribute of the style sheet layer is the ID label, which is used to identify the layer by name. All functions that will manipulate this layer will refer to the layer's name.

The second style attribute of significance to the template site is the layer's z-index order. This tells the browser what order in three-dimensional space to place the layer relative to the other layers. With a z-index of 1, the main content layer is placed farthest away from the viewer, so any subsequent layers will float on top of it. The third style sheet layer attribute of importance is the layer's visibility setting. This setting either enables the layer to be viewed or not. For the main content page, the layer is set to visible by default.

JavaScript Table Header

The JavaScript table header is used to avoid a nonframes browser from displaying a table background such as the Opera 2.12 browser. As shown in Listing 27.9, the JavaScript table header is a standard document.write() statement that writes the opening <TABLE> tag to the main content page.

Script goal:

■ Dynamically write the opening <TABLE> tag for browsers supporting borderless frames.

Listing 27.9. Using document.write to create a table header for 3.0 and 4.0 browsers.

```
<SCRIPT LANGUAGE="JavaScript"><!--
if(navigator.appName == "Netscape" && parseInt(navigator.appVersion) != 2 ||
➥navigator.appName == "Microsoft Internet Explorer" &&
➥parseInt(navigator.appVersion) != 1) {
        document.write('<TABLE BACKGROUND="../images/page.jpg" BGCOLOR="#CAD2BB"
        ➥BORDER="0"
➥CELLPADDING="10" CELLSPACING="0" WIDTH="90%">');
}
// --></SCRIPT>
```

The table being created in this script is nearly identical to the table header used for 2.0 browsers, but it includes the BACKGROUND="../images/page.jpg" attribute to create a background for the table viewable in a framed window.

<NOSCRIPT> Navigation Menus

Consider the <NOSCRIPT> tag your savior in building backward-compatible sites. Any HTML contained in the <NOSCRIPT> tag is automatically ignored by the 3.0 and 4.0 browsers. This means you can load an alternative interface suitable for viewing in a no-frames environment. As shown in Listing 27.10, the <NOSCRIPT> tag is used to set up a table with vertical main menu buttons as well as a horizontal tab menu to come as close as possible to the navigational scheme in the framed page environment.

Listing 27.10. Using the <NOSCRIPT> tag to build an alternative interface for browsers that only support table formatting.

```
<NOSCRIPT>
<BODY BACKGROUND="../images/menu_bg2.jpg" TEXT="#000000" LINK="#0000FF"
➥VLINK="#0000FF"
➥ALINK="#FF0000">
<TABLE BORDER="0" CELLPADDING="10" CELLSPACING="0" WIDTH="90%">
<TR>
<TD ALIGN=LEFT VALIGN=TOP ROWSPAN="10">
<A HREF="../page1/page1_a.htm"><IMG SRC="../images/btn1_dn.gif" WIDTH="108"
➥HEIGHT="53"
➥BORDER="0"></A><BR><BR>
```

continues

27

DEGRADING
DHTML
GRACEFULLY

Listing 27.10. continued

```
<A HREF="../page2/page2_a.htm"><IMG SRC="../images/btn2_up.gif" WIDTH="108"
➥HEIGHT="53"
➥BORDER="0"></A><BR><BR>

<A HREF="../page3/page3_a.htm"><IMG SRC="../images/btn3_up.gif" WIDTH="108"
➥HEIGHT="53"
➥BORDER="0"></A></TD>
</TR>

<TR>
<TD COLSPAN="3" VALIGN=TOP><A HREF="../page1/page1_a.htm"><IMG SRC="../images/
➥tab1a_up.gif"
➥WIDTH="94" HEIGHT="46" BORDER="0"></A><A HREF="../page1/page1_b.htm">
➥<IMG SRC="../images/tab1b_dn.gif" WIDTH="94" HEIGHT="46" BORDER="0"></A>
➥<A HREF="../page1/page1_c.htm"><IMG SRC="../images/tab1c_dn.gif" WIDTH="94"
➥HEIGHT="46"
➥BORDER="0"></A><IMG SRC="../images/option1.gif" WIDTH="216" HEIGHT="46"
➥BORDER="0"></TD>
</TR>

</NOSCRIPT>
```

Notice that the <BODY> and the header <TABLE> tags are included in the <NOSCRIPT> zone. These tags are there to hide from the 3.0 and 4.0 browsers. The 3.0 and 4.0 browsers use the JavaScript document.write() method to hide their version of the <BODY> and <TABLE> tags from the 2.0 browsers.

> **CAUTION**
>
> By using the standard <DIV></DIV> tags to contain our style sheet layer and having the layer contained in a nested table for backward compatibility introduces potential HTML formatting conflicts. Avoid using the <P> paragraph separator tags in the HTML in the style sheet HTML. Use multiple <BR> tags instead. Remember that we use the <DIV> tag simply as a style sheet container and not for its traditional HTML formatting abilities.

Standard Table Body

Use the standard HTML syntax to create table rows and table data cells that can be viewed in all browsers supporting tables. As shown in Listing 27.11, the standard HTML table syntax is used to build a table row containing an image.

Listing 27.11. Standard HTML viewable by all browsers supporting table formatting.

```
<TR>
<TD COLSPAN="3" VALIGN=TOP><IMG SRC="../images/freefall.gif" SUPPRESS="TRUE"
➥WIDTH="480"
```

```
➥HEIGHT="60" VSPACE="20" BORDER="0"></TD>
</TR>
...
</TABLE>

</DIV>
```

When you are done with the main content page, you then need to close the layer container with the closing </DIV> tag.

Page Scroller Widget Layer

The page scroller widget layer is used to display the scroll arrow image on top of the main content page. As shown in Listing 27.12, the scroller layer uses the same style sheet parameters as in the main content layer.

Listing 27.12. The page scroller layer and imagemap responsible for scrolling the main content page.

```
<DIV ID="arrowLyr" STYLE="position: absolute; z-index: 2; visibility: hidden;">
    <IMG NAME="arrow_img" SRC="../images/blank.gif" USEMAP="#arrow_map"
    ➥SUPPRESS="TRUE" WIDTH="90" HEIGHT="66" BORDER="0" ALT="">
</DIV>

<MAP NAME="arrow_map">
    <AREA SHAPE=POLY COORDS="0,27,89,7,90,0,0,0,27"
➥HREF="JavaScript:top.pageScroll('up')";
➥onMouseOver="top.arrowToggle('up'); top.displayInfo('<FONT COLOR=#FFFFE1 SIZE=4>
➥Scroll Page Up</FONT>')"; onMouseOut="top.hideInfo(); top.arrowToggle('center')";
➥ALT="">

    <AREA SHAPE=POLY COORDS="0,28,90,8,90,30,0,50,0,28"
➥HREF="JavaScript:top.pageScroll('top')";
➥onMouseOver="top.arrowToggle('center'); top.displayInfo('<FONT COLOR=#FFFFE1
➥SIZE=4>
➥Return Page</FONT>')"; onMouseOut="top.hideInfo(); top.arrowToggle('center')";
➥ALT="">

    <AREA SHAPE=POLY COORDS="0,51,90,31,89,68,0,68,0,51"
➥HREF="JavaScript:top.pageScroll('down')";
➥onMouseOver="top.arrowToggle('down'); top.displayInfo('<FONT COLOR=#FFFFE1
SIZE=4>
➥Scroll Page Down</FONT>')"; onMouseOut="top.hideInfo();
➥top.arrowToggle('center')"; ALT="">
</MAP>
```

The scroll arrow image is linked to an imagemap that triggers several functions depending on whether the mouse is clicked, moved over an imagemap hotspot, or moved out of an imagemap hotspot. On a mouse click event, the top.pageScroll('top') function is called and is passed the direction command 'top'. The pageScroll() function evaluates the direction command and either scrolls the page up, down, or returns the page to its top position.

On an `onMouseOver` event, two functions are called. The first function, `top.arrowToggle('center')` is passed the position variable "center", which the `arrowToggle()` function uses to dynamically swap out the current arrow image with the one being specified by the position variable. This gives the arrow the appearance of movement depending on where your mouse falls on the imagemap. The second function called by the `onMouseOver` event is the `top.displayInfo('<FONT COLOR=#FFFFE1 SIZE=4>Return Page</FONT>` function and is passed the HTML string that will be displayed in the pop-up window.

On an `onMouseOut` event, two more functions are called. The first function, `top.hideInfo()`, is used to hide the pop-up window when the mouse leaves the imagemap hotspots. The second function is the `top.arrowToggle('center')` function, which resets the arrow image back to the center image when the mouse leaves the imagemap.

As you can see, the use of image maps to trigger a JavaScript event can be a powerful DHTML interface tool.

Info Box Layer

The info box layer is used to provide space to display Dynamic HTML as created by the `displayInfo()` function. Because all content will be dynamically written to the info box layer, the layer is created as an empty style sheet layer, as shown in Listing 27.13.

Listing 27.13. The empty info box layer ready to accept Dynamic HTML.

```
<DIV ID="infoLyr" STYLE="position: absolute; z-index: 3; visibility: visible;">
➥</DIV>
```

The main consideration to this layer is its `z-index` order. In the template site, the info box layer should float on top of all other layers, therefore it has a `z-index` order of 3.

Summary

Making a cross browser, backward-compatible Dynamic HTML Web site can be a killer. In the process of building such a beast, you will undoubtedly end up with glass in your feet, and you will have fallen in a few pitfalls. Have faith. After you accomplish this art form the first time, it will get easier, especially when someone builds a free template for you to exploit any way you want. Soon it will become second nature to build a fully backward-compatible Web site for every Web project you do. However, please continue to harass people who refuse to upgrade their old world, flat earth society browsers.

Netcasting Your DHTML Site

by Brian Gallagher and Jeff Rouyer

IN THIS CHAPTER

CHAPTER 28

In this chapter, we will walk through the processes involved in creating a Netcaster channel, what exactly a channel is, and why you would want one. Perhaps more importantly, we will illustrate how to modify an existing cross-browser DHTML Web site into an effective channel. Our trials of making a Netcaster channel are made real as we use the Dynamic HTML Guru Resource Web site as an example throughout this chapter. Before we go any further, be aware this technology is Netscape specific and as such may be victim of a volatile life span. Given the potential benefits associated with "push" technology and the current bandwidth limitations likely to persist for the foreseeable future, it is likely that Netcaster-type or channel-type content will endure in one form or another as the Web matures.

In a nutshell, a Netcaster channel is a form of Web content that is downloaded to a cache on the client machine and can be accessed online or offline. Channels are supposed to contain a timely collection of information such as business briefs, stock quotes or profiles, tutorials, or other timely, interactive material necessitating frequent viewing. One of the biggest complaints about the infantile Netcaster channels available today is that they remain little more than glorified, interactive spam. When you build your channel, strive to make it not only enticing, but also worthwhile, and by all means, keep it up-to-date.

To keep up on the latest updates to the Dynamic HTML Guru Resource Web site, you can subscribe to the Guru Netcaster channel. Simply log in to the Guru site at `http://www.htmlguru.com` and navigate to the Guru channel section. Remember that you must have the Netcaster component installed on your system. The Netcaster interface shown in Figure 28.1 requires you to be running Communicator version 4.02 or later.

FIGURE 28.1.

The Netcaster component showing a list of predefined channels.

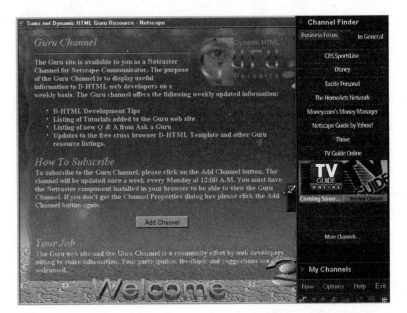

The Guru channel is updated every Monday at 12:00 a.m. The channel offers the DHTML developer community the latest updates to the Guru Web site, including weekly DHTML tips, weekly DHTML tutorials, a listing of new DHTML questions answered by a gaggle of Web gurus, and the latest collection of valuable links and literature available for high-end Web developers today.

What Is a Channel?

Channels are just what the name implies, a channel for the flow of information. They contain HTML and JavaScript and are delivered to subscribers at predefined intervals. Channels can be delivered as standards-based Web-server channels or Castanet channels. We will focus on the easy-to-build, standards-based HTML and JavaScript channels for this introduction.

Channels allow subscribers to personalize the information delivered to their desktop and can be viewed in window mode or in the Netcaster-specific Webtop mode.

What Is a Webtop?

Simply put, a Webtop is a means for displaying content that covers the entire screen of a user's display—fixed to what would be the wallpaper in the Windows OS. Because Webtops are the interface for a user's interaction with your channel, and as such will be viewed for hours at a time, be sure to make your Webtop as uncluttered and as elegant as possible so as not to fatigue users. Webtop links should open windows, not change the backdrop of the Webtop itself, and a Webtop display should not require scrolling. (However, text within the Webtop may be scrolled.)

Also, because a Webtop is the interface through which you display information to users, you need to be sure to include full navigational controls in the Webtop itself and make those controls standout. For example, you can use the highlight effect on buttons when the mouse passes over them. The Guru Webtop, as shown in Figure 28.2, uses many multimedia features of Dynamic HTML such as layer animation, sprite animation, dynamic content, and audio.

Because downloads are presumably done in the background, and therefore more content can be transferred to a client than in traditional Web sites, adding sound (including audio files in your channel "crawl" or download) is acceptable and effective. Be careful not to overdo it.

In the Windows OS, cached or crawled files are downloaded to a client machine here:

```
C:\Program Files\Netscape\Users\userName\
```

In the Macintosh OS, cached or crawled files are downloaded to a client machine here:

```
System Folder/Preferences/Netscape/
```

Upon completion of crawling a channel's content, Netcaster creates a file listing the URLs of the channel files that were downloaded and cached successfully. The file can be opened by any text editor and is titled *N*.dat where *N* is a number. Each line in the file represents a URL designated by either an L for a link, I for an image, or R for anything else.

FIGURE 28.2.

The Guru channel in Netcaster Webtop mode.

Channel Components

Channels are built of the same building blocks used to create Dynamic HTML pages; they include HTML, JavaScript, style sheets, and Java applets. To convert an existing Web site, such as the Guru Web site, to provide channel content, you must take into consideration several factors. First of all, users need a way to add your channel to the Netcaster channel finder, and you as a developer need to be sure that their subscription will contain all the files, and only the files, the subscriber requests. Keep in mind that Netcaster channels are designed to be viewed online or offline and as such require some special design considerations.

Adding a Netcaster channel involves the following three steps:

- Creating an Add Channel button
- Creating the Channel Definition function
- Optimizing existing HTML and JavaScript code in your channel page's site to work in the Netcaster environment

The first step is necessary when a user subscribes to a Netcaster channel. He or she "adds" the channel through the Netcaster channel finder or more likely through an Add Channel button. The second step is building the JavaScript Channel Definition function that describes the parameters of the channel. The third step involves optimizing JavaScript and HTML formatting to best fit in the Netcaster performance model.

Add Channel Button

One of the first steps you need to take toward getting your Web site channel ready is one of the obvious steps: You need to make a control enabling a user to add the channel. For the Guru Web site, you do this by calling the `defineChannel()` function with the HTML and JavaScript code shown in Listing 28.1. The script's goal is to use an `onClick` event to call the `defineChannel` function within a form button.

Listing 28.1. Add Channel form button and JavaScript.

```
<FORM>
<INPUT TYPE="BUTTON" VALUE="Add Channel" onClick="defineChannel(\'DHTML Guru
➥Resource\', \'http://www.iex.net/rouyer/channel/index.html\')">
</FORM>
```

The Add Channel button is a form with the input type equal to `"BUTTON."` Within the `FORM` element is the JavaScript `onClick` event handler that triggers the `defineChannel()` function when the button is clicked. Passed to the `defineChannel()` function are two variables. The first variable is the name of the Netcaster channel because it appears in the channel finder. The second variable is the URL to the HTML source of the channel itself. The `onClick` event handler is not restricted to a `FORM` element because it can be applied to image and text links as well.

Now that you have a way to get the channel to your users, called "subscribers" in Netcaster lingo, you have to tell Netcaster what to expect. To do this, you need to identify the channel components, one of the cornerstones of what makes a channel work.

Channel Definition Function

Identifying the channel to the channel finder is accomplished through the Channel Definition function. Listing 28.2 shows the `defineChannel()` function used to set up the Guru channel. The function is called from the Add Channel HTML element and passed the channel name and channel URL.

Script goals:

- Create a channel object `nc` using the Netcaster component and make it active.
- Test the active state of channel object and if it's true, continue to define the channel.
- Import two Netcaster component methods.
- Define channel attributes and initiate the Add Channel method.

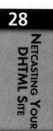

28

NETCASTING YOUR
DHTML SITE

Listing 28.2. The defineChannel() function used to define a Netcaster channel.

```
function defineChannel(name, url) {
    var nc = components["netcaster"];
    nc.activate();
    if(nc.active == true) {
        import nc.getChannelObject;
        import nc.defineChannel;
        channel = getChannelObject();
        channel.url = (url || "URL");
        channel.name = (name || "Name");
        channel.desc = name;
        channel.intervalTime = -6;
        channel.absoluteTime = 1440;
        channel.estCacheSize = -1;
        channel.maxCacheSize = 1024000;
        channel.depth = 2;
        channel.active = 1;
        channel.topHint = screen.availTop;
        channel.leftHint = screen.availLeft;
        channel.widthHint =  600;
        channel.heightHint = 391;
        channel.mode="webtop";
        channel.type=1;
        channel.cardURL = '';
        addChannel(channel);
        }
    }
}
```

The first action of the function is to create and activate the channel object nc with the var nc = components["netcaster"] and nc.activate() statements. Once activated, the nc channel object is assigned two Netcaster specific methods, getChannelObject and defineChannel, which access the Netcaster component. The next step of the function is to use the if(nc.active == true) statement to ensure the Netcaster component is active. Once the component is active, it is safe to import the Netcaster-specific methods with the following two statements:

```
Import components["Netcaster'].getChannelObject;
Import components["Netcaster"].defineChannel;
```

Now that you have access to the channel, you must define the channel object attributes. The first three attributes define the channel URL of the top channel page, the channel name, and the channel description that is shown in the channel finder list. The channel name is used as the description for the channel.

The second set of channel attributes deal with the page refresh request times. As with programming a VCR, the interval time refers to the minute, hourly, daily, or weekly schedule on which the channel is updated. Values include any positive integer representing minutes. Special negative integers serve as default schedule times as follows:

-2   Every 15 minutes

-3   Every 30 minutes

-4	Every hour
-5	Every day
-6	Once a week

In a Netcaster channel, time is represented in minutes by an integer value that starts at midnight Sunday and is used to set the absolute time attribute. Adding 1440 minutes for each day from Sunday, a developer who wants to download on Wednesday at 1:00 a.m. would use the value `4260` ($3 \times 1440 + 60$) for the channel `channel.absoluteTime`.

For the Guru channel definition, the `Interval` attribute is set to `-6` for a daily schedule and the absolute time is set to `1440`, representing Monday. The channel is programmed to seek new updates every Monday at 12:00 a.m.

The next set of attributes deal with the caching parameters that may be required for the channel. The estimated cache size attribute `channel.estCacheSize = -1` is your guess about how much cache space Netcaster should allocate for storing your channel. If you don't know how much to estimate, use `-1`; otherwise, you enter a value in bytes between the range of 1 and 1,047,527,424.

The maximum cache size attribute indicated by the `channel.maxCacheSize = 1024000` statement represents the largest amount of space Netcaster will cache for the channel. For the Guru channel, you request the maximum cache size to be 1MB; otherwise, you use an integer value between the range of 1 and 1,047,527,424.

The last attribute dealing with caching system is the channel depth attribute represented by the `channel.depth = 2` statement. The channel depth property refers to the levels of link hierarchy to be downloaded into the client cache. Although channel depth is not used in Netcaster 1.0, it is important to build Netcaster channels with no more than two layers. When channels are cached on a client machine, they are downloaded through a process called "crawling," whereby successive links from the top-level HTML pages are downloaded to a user-specified depth.

The remaining attributes of the channel definition set the width and height of the channel window. Because the Guru channel uses Webtop mode, the width and height values are ignored. Alternatives to the Webtop mode are window mode and full mode. Window mode is defined by the top, left, width, and height hints. Full mode is similar to Webtop mode in that it occupies the whole display area, but it is not anchored to the screen, and it does not show the Netcaster toolbar. The final method of the channel definition triggers the `addChannel` method using the channel attributes in the `addChannel(channel)` statement.

After all HTML pages are cached, the images in those pages are cached in the same manner, and the embedded objects such as Java applets and individually referenced JavaScript scripts are downloaded. By caching information in this manner, you can preserve much of the functionality and information in a channel if the connection is terminated for whatever reason.

28

NETCASTING YOUR
DHTML SITE

Channel Code Optimization

Although you have defined your Netcaster channel and added it to the channel finder, you might still have some details to manage. With the Guru channel, we had to clean up the code to make sure we had no external links while the channel is in Webtop mode, as well as make sure that all animated images were preloaded. Listing 28.3 shows the preLoad() function we used to preload all images into cache before they are used by DHTML in the channel. The script's goal is to create an image object and assign an image URL to it to store the image into cache.

Listing 28.3. Image preloading functions used to store images into cache before they are displayed.

```
function preLoad() {
    bloom = new Image();
    bloom.src = "../images/bloom.jpg";

    core = new Image();
    core.src = "../images/core.gif";

    flare = new Image();
    flare.src = flare_img;

    guru = new Image();
    guru.src = "../images/guru.gif";

    legs = new Image();
    legs.src = "../images/legs.gif";

    sun = new Image();
    sun.src = sun_img;

    guide_off = new Image();
    guide_off.src = "../images/guide_off.gif";

    guide_on = new Image();
    guide_on.src = "../images/guide_on.gif";
}
```

The first statements in the preLoad() function create an image object for each image with the guide_on = new Image() statement. The next step is to assign an image URL to the object such as guide_on.src = "../images/guide_on.gif". Once loaded into cache, the images can be referenced by their object names and used for dynamic animations.

> **TIP**
>
> If you do not want a Web page or image to cache, do not refer to the image in an HREF tag. Refer to it with a JavaScript link instead because it will not cache.

> **TIP**
>
> Be sure to define height and width image attributes to optimize offline viewing.

Full Media Immersion

Netcaster channels especially in Webtop mode tend to be developed as a full-fledged multimedia experience. The Guru channel uses layer animation, dynamic content, music, and sound to make exploring the channel a bit more interesting. You must consider several design options to develop a channel in Webtop mode. The biggest consideration is resolution-specific images. The Webtop will adjust to the size of the screen and so must the accompanying images and positional HTML elements. The code in Listing 28.4 is used in the Guru channel to switch between different sizes of background images to match the screen resolution. The script's goal is to use a chain of `if...else` statements to assign image URLs to resolution-specific image variables.

Listing 28.4. Multiple resolution image management.

```
var screen_height = screen.height;
var screen_width = screen.width;

if (screen_height >= 768) {
    background_img = "../images/horizon768.jpg";
    sun_img = "../images/sun768.jpg";
    flare_img = "../images/flare768.jpg";
    screen_width = 1024;
    screen_height = 768;
} else if (screen_height >= 624) {
    background_img = "../images/horizon624.jpg";
    sun_img = "../images/sun624.jpg";
    flare_img = "../images/flare624.jpg";
} else if (screen_height >= 600) {
    background_img = "../images/horizon600.jpg";
    sun_img = "../images/sun600.jpg";
    flare_img = "../images/flare600.jpg";
} else if (screen_height >= 480) {
    background_img = "../images/horizon480.jpg";
    sun_img = "../images/sun480.jpg";
    flare_img = "../images/flare480.jpg";
} else {
    background_img = "../images/horizon600.jpg";
    sun_img = "../images/sun600.jpg";
    flare_img = "../images/flare600.jpg";
    screen_width = 800;
    screen_height = 600;
}
```

28

NETCASTING YOUR DHTML SITE

To set the image variables based on screen resolution, we use a chain of `if...else` statements to test the `screen_height` variable against known screen resolutions. If one of the statements rings true, the `background_img`, `sun_image`, and `flare_img` variables are set to the appropriate image URL. As you may have guessed, you have to create a separate image for each resolution support. It is actually not a difficult task when you are dealing with backgrounds and a few images. For the browser to display the dynamically chosen images, the image can use the `document.write()` method as shown in displaying the background image for the Guru site:

```
<SCRIPT>
    document.write('<BODY BACKGROUND=' + background_img + ' BGCOLOR=
"#B56A6A" LINK="#00FFFF" ALINK="#FFFF00" VLINK="#00FFFF"
onLoad="preLoad()" TEXT="#FEE4B6">');
</SCRIPT>
```

The clean canvas is ready for creative minds to manipulate. Webtop designers need to use the full breadth of tools available to them, including style sheets, Dynamic HTML, and the JavaScript event model, allowing for drag-and-drop functionality and dramatic animations.

Obligatory Animations

Go for it! The user has downloaded all the images to your channel a while ago, so why not treat him or her to a show with the obligatory intro animation? Listing 28.5 shows the code for performing the opening sequence lens flare animation for the Guru channel. The sun and lens flare start out moving fast toward each other but slow at a linear rate.

Script goals:

- ■ Get the sun layer's left position.

- ■ Get the flare layer's left position.

- ■ Reposition the sun layer one pixel to the right for each loop cycle until the limit is reached.

- ■ Reposition the flare layer one pixel to the left for each loop cycle until the limit is reached.

Listing 28.5. Sample JavaScript layer animation.

```
var timer_0 = null;
var flare_delta = 1;

function lensFlare() {
    var sun_x_pos = parseInt(sunObj.left);
    var flare_x_pos = parseInt(flareObj.left);
    if(sun_x_pos+125 < flare_x_pos) {
        sunObj.left = sun_x_pos+2;
        flareObj.left = flare_x_pos-2;
        timer_0 = setTimeout("lensFlare()", flare_delta);
        flare_delta++;
    } else {
        upCore();
    }
}
```

The first statement defines a local variable var `sun_x_pos = parseInt(sunObj.left)` with the left position of the object you want to move. Layer animation is actually performed with methods defined within the `if(sun_x_pos < 60)` statement. As long as the `sun_x_pos` variable is less than `flare_x_pos`, the sun layer object will be moved to the right by two pixels with the `sunObj.left = sun_x_pos+2` statement. The inverse happens for the lens flare object, which is moved to the left by two pixels with the `flareObj.left = flare_x_pos-2` statement. The function will continue to loop with the `timer_0 = setTimeout("lensFlare()", flare_delta)` statement until the right edge of the sun image reaches the left edge of the lens flare image. Using the incrementing global variable `flare_delta++` in the `setTimeout()` function is a cheap way of slowing the animation down as the two moving images come close to each other.

Audiophile Pages

Audio is used two ways in the Guru channel. It is first used to play the *2001: A Space Odyssey* theme song with an embedded MIDI file. It is then used to play mouse-over and mouse-click sounds as the user investigates the Guru interface. The following script in Listing 28.6 shows the two JavaScript routines we used for controlling audio using the LiveAudio multimedia plug-in. The script's goal is to use an `onClick` event to call the `defineChannel` function within a form button.

Listing 28.6. LiveAudio JavaScript used to control the playing of sound and music in the Guru channel.

```
function audioEnabled(plug_in) {
    for (var i = 0; i < navigator.plugins.length; i++) {
        if (navigator.plugins[i].name.toLowerCase() == plug_in.toLowerCase()) {
            for (var j = 0; j < navigator.plugins[i].length; j++) {
                if (navigator.plugins[i][j].enabledPlugin) {
                    return true
                }
            }
            return false
        }
    }
    return false
}

function playAudio(cmd) {
    if (audioEnabled("LiveAudio")) {
        if (cmd == "2001") {
            document.MIDI.play(false);
        }
    }
}
```

All audio is controlled by the `playAudio()` function. JavaScript event handlers triggered by `onMouseOver` and `onClick` events pass to this function a command variable such as `"2001"`. A series of `if...else` statements is used to match the command and execute the LiveAudio play method. Before any command is initiated, the `if (audioEnabled("LiveAudio"))` statement is used to test the presence of the LiveAudio plug-in. If it's `true`, the LiveAudio methods are free to run.

To play an audio file, it is necessary to use the `<EMBED>` tag as shown for the MIDI file `2001.mid`. Referring to an embedded audio file using LiveAudio methods is done by referencing the `NAME` attribute of the embedded sound file in the `document.MIDI.play(false)` statement.

Security Considerations

Because Netcaster caches channels on a client's hard drive, you must consider serious security concerns whenever a Netcaster channel is added (or subscribed to) by a user. To accommodate the very understandable concerns involved with push, or server-initiated, technology, the Netcaster designers created the object-signing protocol. This protocol steps the user through various levels of requested access to potentially harmful actions by a typical Netcaster caching operation. At each interval, the user is prompted to either grant or deny the requested Netcaster operation.

The key strengths of the object-signing protocol are

- Provides a sequential interface for access privileges
- Limits the code under its jurisdiction
- Locks access to the duration of the call in which access was granted

Some actions requiring user approval include writing to the hard disk, providing the unconditional capability to close browser window, setting a property on an event, getting data from a `DragDrop` event, and submitting a form to a mailto or news URL.

To Bot or Not to Bot

An information channel such as a news service with a broad spectrum of material is a great place for a Web search engine *robot* to visit. Robots visit Web sites on a scheduled basis and busily index all the pages in Web sites. Lycos and Hotbot are two major search engine robots that do this. In many cases, it is a bad idea for a robot crawler to index Web pages associated with a Netcaster channel due to the fact these pages may be unreadable by a browser accessing the pages via a robot search engine, thereby circumventing the Netcaster software. You can control how the robot search engines index your site by creating a simple `robot.txt` file. When encountered by a crawler the `robot.txt` file is read first, delivering instructions to the crawler as to which files are cached and which are not. The following code provides a good idea of what a `robot.txt` file looks like:

```
# /robot.txt for http://www.htmlguru.com/
User-agent: CAST
Disallow: /channel/index.html
```

This robot instructs the crawler to not cache `index.html` in the `/channel` folder. In the event a crawler does not encounter a `robot.txt` file, it proceeds to crawl and index all pages in the site with no restrictions.

Push? Pull? Oh, Please!

Despite the fact that casting technology at this point is largely referred to as "push" technology and sometimes referred to as "pull" technology, the reality is that it is "scheduled" content—updating, crawling, caching, downloading, whatever you want to call it, only at predefined, scheduled times.

You cannot really talk about new technology and Web advances without addressing the Microsoft question. Currently Microsoft supports what it calls Webcasting, using the Channel Definition Format, or CDF. The Microsoft effort is similar to Netcaster in many aspects, including file caching, offline viewing, pursuing enriched content through "push" or "pull" content, and even providing a Webtop equivalent–theater mode. However, like many other Microsoft-based Web initiatives, Microsoft channels carry the Active prefix and along with it the baggage of proprietary licensing and incompatibility with currently accepted standards. As of this writing, the software giant maintains that it supports a "pending HTML standard."

Much of what makes Netcaster and the Webtop interface work has to do with the new extensions built into JavaScript 1.2 and supported by Netscape Communicator. A good resource for JavaScript 1.2 and Netcaster extensions can be found at `http://developer.netscape.com`.

Summary

Numerous other nuances involved with Netcaster channels have yet to be implemented in the current iteration of the software, but some things are clear even at this stage. The Webtop interface is truly a new medium to be explored by the best and the brightest the Web has to offer. Tailor-made newspapers, tutorial programs, and even university-accredited courses become more of a reality.

Combined with the ongoing advancements in processor speed and memory capacity, Netcaster content is likely to become some of the richest and most interactive the Net has to offer. Although the technology evolves, we have some suggestions that can make "casting" as popular a method of information retrieval as browsing. For starters, integrating the dialer with Netcaster for modem users would allow those with serial access to the Net to enjoy the benefits of casting technology. As it is, the home user with modem access to the Internet must first log on and start a channel crawl before he can view the channel content he desires. Also, to make it easier to download, real-time compression on the server end would be nice; it would allow more channels to be cached faster, while leaving more room on a hard drive for additional channel content.

We wait, watch, and work through yet another of the latest features the Web has to offer. At this stage, we are still on top of the iceberg, casting our nets into the ether of ocean that is the Web, always wondering what it is we will catch tomorrow.

CHAPTER 29

Debugging Your Dynamic HTML

by William Royere

IN THIS CHAPTER

In previous chapters, you learned how to create powerful and dynamic Web content using DHTML. In this chapter, you will learn how to debug that content.

What Is Debugging?

Debugging is both a diagnostic and problem-solving process. With it, you identify and eliminate errors within your code that produce unpredictable or undesirable behavior. The programming community refers to these errors as *bugs*. The following are good examples of bugs:

- Pages fail to load correctly
- The user's browser crashes
- The user's monitor explodes (just kidding)

In this chapter, you will learn to avoid these problems by writing clean code. An inherent part of that process is *debugging*, or the art of getting the bugs out.

This chapter is broken into three sections:

- Basic concepts of debugging
- Common tools and techniques
- Hands-on debugging

Why Is Debugging Important?

Debugging is important because without it, your site might not function correctly. To understand why, consider the major difference between DHTML and standard HTML: DHTML relies heavily on scripting languages. Such languages enforce certain limitations on how you can express your code, called *language conventions*. If you fail to observe these language conventions, your code could malfunction. To understand how this climate differs from standard HTML development, consider the following example.

Standard HTML Enforces No Special Limitations

Standard HTML can be written any way you like. In all but the most extraordinary circumstances, it will still execute cleanly. For example, consider the following code:

```
<HTML>
<HEAD>
</HEAD>
<BODY bgcolor = #FFFFFF><br><br><br><br><br><center>
<form>
<input type = "button"
Value =
"Any Problems?"
onClick = "alert('No Problems Here')">
</form>
</center>
</BODY>
</HTML>
```

Note that elements within the FORM structure have been broken into separate lines:

```
<form>
<input type = "button"
Value =
"Any Problems?"
onClick = "alert('No Problems Here')">
</form>
```

This code is poorly written. Elements within the form structure should have been written on one continuous line. However, because of the way most browsers work, it doesn't really matter (see Figures 29.1 and 29.2).

FIGURE 29.1.

The resulting page loads without error.

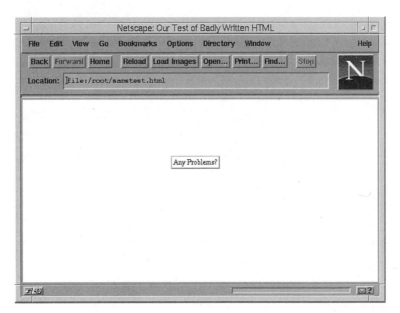

As you can see, the code works just fine despite the haphazard style in which it was written.

DHTML and Scripting Languages Require Clean Code

In contrast, when you incorporate complex scripting into your Web pages, your style cannot be so laid-back. To demonstrate why, I will expand (and slightly complicate) the previous example.

Suppose that when the user clicks the button, you want to display a message window instead of an alert. To do so, you employ a scripting language. (I will use JavaScript.)

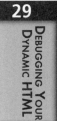

FIGURE 29.2.

The alert box executes without error.

I start with a function called `sams_pop_up_window()`. This function will draw my message window. Here is the code:

```
<script language = JavaScript>
function sams_pop_up(){

//First, define the window's attributes and dimensions
msg=open('','NewWindow','toolbar=no,location=no,directories=no,
➥status=no,menubar=no,scrollbars=yes,resizable=no,copyhistory
➥=yes,width=255,height=150');

//Next, define the document's general characteristics
msg.document.write('<HEAD><TITLE>Nope!...Everything is Fine
➥Here!</TITLE><HEAD><BODY BGCOLOR =
➥#ffffff></BODY>');

//Lastly, write the message
msg.document.write('<font face = arial,
➥helvetica size = -1><center>The Script Works Well</center><ul
➥type = square><li>We see no error messages<li>The browser did
➥not freeze<li>The monitor did not blow
➥up<br><br><center></ul><form><input type = button value =
 ➥Okay! onClick = window.close();></form></center></p>');          } //JavaScript
➥Ends -->
</script>
```

Next, I add an event handler to trigger it, like this:

```
<form>
<input type = "button" Value = "Any Problems?" onClick =
➥sams_pop_up(this.form);">
</form>
```

The results are shown in Figure 29.3.

FIGURE 29.3.

The message window loads without error.

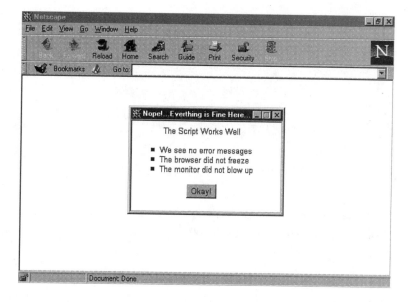

Take another look at the `sams_pop_up_window()` code. Note that the script is broken into three sections. Each section is segregated from the next, and each is expressed as a continuous, unbroken line of code. The code is therefore clean and well organized.

Suppose, however, that I had written this code in the same haphazard fashion as the HTML you saw in the first example. Would my message window still launch correctly? Let's look at Figures 29.4 and 29.5.

FIGURE 29.4.

The message window script fails in Netscape Navigator.

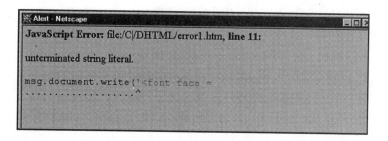

As you can see, something went terribly wrong. Both Netscape Navigator and Internet Explorer spawned error windows, telling us that the script was flawed. What could have happened and how can we find out? Answer—we apply the first and most important rule of debugging: Carefully review any error message you receive.

FIGURE 29.5.

The message window script fails in Internet Explorer.

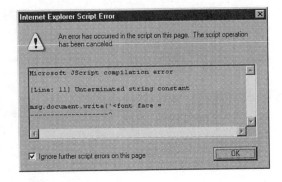

How Error Messages Can Help You

Error messages are tremendously helpful. For example, in this case, the error message began as follows:

```
unterminated string literal
```

This tells us that code expressed within the second `msg.document.write` instruction (part 3 of the script) was not a continuous line. Instead, it was broken where the FONT attributes were set. We know this because the error message identifies the precise point at which the line was broken. But it tells us much more than this. We simply have to interpret the information.

Interpreting Error Message Content

To demonstrate how to interpret error messages, I want to break one down, line by line. For this, I will use the error message example shown in Figure 29.4. Here again is the full message, reproduced from Netscape Communicator:

```
unterminated string literal
msg.document.write('font face =
. . . . . . . . . .^
```

This error message is composed of three lines. Each relates something different about the error:

- Line 1 reports that the error was caused by a broken line. In other words, it reports *why* the error occurred.
- Line 2 explains that the error occurred within the `msg.document.write` instruction. Thus, it identifies *where* the error occurred.
- Line 3 reports that the error occurred immediately after the code `font face =` appeared. It thus tells us *when* the error occurred during execution of the code.

In the debugging process, these are questions you must continually ask: Why, where, and when did your code go wrong? In most instances, error messages will answer these questions.

Important points made so far, then, are these:

- Debugging is the art of finding and eliminating errors in your code.
- DHTML must be debugged because it relies on scripting languages.
- When you debug your DHTML, you want to know why, where, and when the code went wrong.
- Error messages will generally assist you in this process.

If you remember these points, debugging will soon become second nature. That said, we now explore the options available to you.

Methods of Debugging Your DHTML

There are two methods of debugging your DHTML:

- Debugging by hand—This involves using a text-based editor or other rudimentary editing tool. When employing this technique, you work exclusively in text-only mode.
- Debugging with special tools—This involves using software designed specifically for debugging DHTML. Those few tools that exist can be enormously helpful.

Debugging by Hand

Debugging by hand is a formidable task. For example, the only clues you receive about errors in your script come from the browser. At a minimum, therefore, you must know how to interpret these error messages.

Nevertheless, debugging by hand does not have to be an unpleasant experience. There are plaintext HTML editors that can streamline the process. On the Microsoft Windows platform, I prefer to use Acadia Infuse (see Figure 29.6). In fact, I use Infuse for the hands-on example in the section "A Staff Directory Example.")

Acadia Infuse

Acadia Infuse provides DHTML authors with several amenities:

- Syntax color-coding—Infuse identifies functions, variables, and statements by text color. By default, for example, function and variable declarations appear in blue text, whereas script closing tags appear in red. This feature enables you to instantly identify blocks of code. (You can also customize the color scheme.)
- Script navigation—When Infuse starts, two panels are displayed on the left side of the screen (see Figure 29.7). One houses the Script Navigator, which graphically displays functions and objects within your document. To go to one such function or object, simply double-click its icon. This will immediately position the cursor at the code in question.

FIGURE 29.6.

The Acadia Infuse opening screen: Starting a new document.

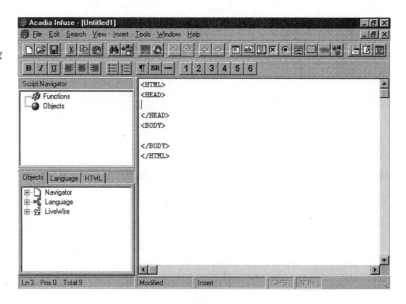

FIGURE 29.7.

The Acadia Infuse panel: Script Navigator and other tools.

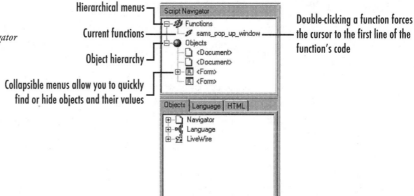

Hierarchical menus

Current functions

Object hierarchy

Collapsible menus allow you to quickly find or hide objects and their values

Double-clicking a function forces the cursor to the first line of the function's code

■ Prefabricated language components—Infuse also provides prefabricated language components, including operators, loops, and conditional statement blocks. This feature is located at the second tab on the lower panel (see Figure 29.8). You can place these components by either dragging them to your document or double-clicking them.

Together, these features provide a powerful debugging environment. To demonstrate why, let's review the `sams_pop_up_window()` function. This time, we will look at a screen capture of it in Acadia Infuse, as shown in Figure 29.9.

FIGURE 29.8.

The Acadia Infuse panel: The language components tool.

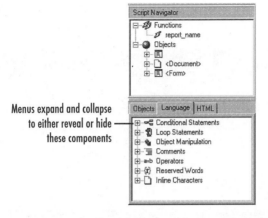

Menus expand and collapse to either reveal or hide these components

FIGURE 29.9.

The sams_pop_up_window() code in Acadia Infuse.

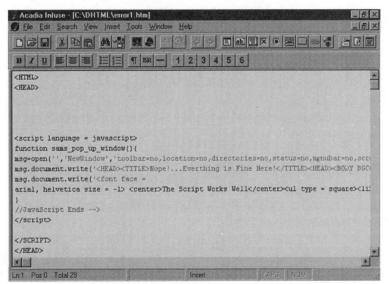

As noted, the flaw in the sams_pop_up_window() function was an unterminated string literal, beginning with the code font face =. As you look at Figure 29.9, you can see that the line is broken. The broken line appears as follows:

```
msg.document.write('<font face =
```

The instruction is truncated. Its remaining statements are continued (erroneously) on the next line:

```
arial, helvetica size = -1>
```

In Acadia Infuse, this is immediately clear because string literals by default appear in gray text. Thus, the beginning of the instruction appears in gray while the remaining text (erroneously positioned on the next line) appears in black. This warns you that there is a truncated line. The main value of color coding, therefore, is that it trains you to quickly spot common errors.

> **NOTE**
>
> Acadia Infuse also contains a complete JavaScript Object Model reference. At any time, you can right-click a language component and a tutorial window will be displayed. This object model reference can often provide clues on what mistakes you have made.

Debugging Using Special Tools

Another approach is to use tools specifically designed for debugging DHTML. These are rare, largely because DHTML is a new technology. However, two such tools do exist, and both are superb: Microsoft's Script Debugger and Netscape Communications' JavaScript Debugger.

There is no point in speculating about which is the better product. Each is the best in its class; they are simply designed to serve different purposes. Microsoft's product is geared chiefly toward debugging JScript and VBScript, and Netscape's product is for debugging JavaScript. Be that as it may, the products do share certain characteristics. For example, both are finely integrated with their corresponding browser. Both also have the look and feel of traditional debugging environments.

Microsoft Script Debugger

Microsoft Script Debugger was released in July 1997 and is available as freeware. (The license never expires.) It can be downloaded at `http://www.microsoft.com/intdev/scriptIE/ie302dbg.exe`.

> **NOTE**
>
> There are system requirements for Microsoft Script Debugger. At a minimum, you must have Microsoft Internet Explorer 3.02 or higher. If you fail to acquire 3.02 or higher, Microsoft Script Debugger will not install.

After you have installed Microsoft Script Debugger, perform these steps:

1. Open Microsoft Internet Explorer.
2. Open the page containing the script you intend to debug.
3. Choose View|Source on the menu bar.

These steps will launch Microsoft Script Debugger (see Figure 29.10).

FIGURE 29.10.

Starting the Microsoft Script Debugger on the page to debug.

Debug menu —

Project Explorer —

Source window —

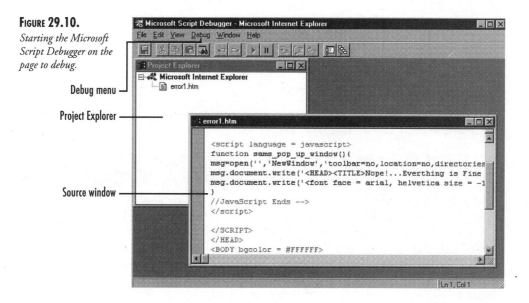

On examining Figure 29.10, you might recognize similarities between Microsoft Script Debugger and Acadia Infuse. By default, one window panel holds the source to be debugged. The other (the Project Explorer Window) graphically displays objects contained within the source document. This approach is valuable because it trains you to visualize the components, logic, and program flow of your code.

Microsoft's Script Debugger has other amenities. One is that you can debug scripts by steps, a common feature in debuggers for many programming languages. It allows you to set *breakpoints* in the script, or areas where particular functions occur. Think of a breakpoint as a bookmark. When you set a breakpoint, you can later return to it on demand. This allows you to selectively test different blocks of code, independently of one another. In this way, you can incisively identify problems, without having to run all functions within the page.

NOTE

If you debug a script nested within the HEAD structure of a document, you must first choose the Break at Next Statement command. You can do this in either Microsoft Internet Explorer (Edit | Break at Next Statement) or Microsoft Script Debugger (Debug | Break at Next Statement). If you fail to do so, you will be unable to set breakpoints on that script. This is especially so if the script is called using the onLoad event handler, because such code executes when the document is loaded. Therefore, the functions have already been completed even before Script Debugger loads.

29

DEBUGGING YOUR DYNAMIC HTML

In closing, Microsoft Script Debugger is an excellent tool, particularly for power users. If your JScript or VBScript project entails numerous functions of high complexity, this tool is perfect for you.

Netscape JavaScript Debugger

Netscape's JavaScript Debugger is a new product, available for download at `http://developer.netscape.com/software/jsdebug_license.html`.

> **NOTE**
>
> As of this writing, JavaScript Debugger is available only for Windows 95, Windows NT, Macintosh PPC, and select flavors of UNIX (SunOS, Solaris, and IRIX). Moreover, it requires 16MB of RAM on PC platforms and a minimum of 32MB of RAM on UNIX. Most important, it requires Netscape Communicator. It will not work with any other browser.

JavaScript Debugger is tightly integrated with (and can be launched directly from) Netscape's Visual JavaScript. Like Microsoft Script Debugger, Netscape's JavaScript Debugger is a bona fide debugging environment. Figure 29.11 shows Netscape's JavaScript Debugger.

Figure 29.11.

Starting the Netscape JavaScript Debugger.

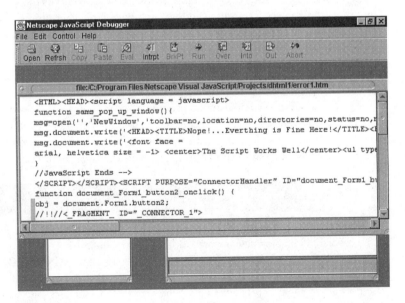

The Netscape JavaScript Debugger is geared mainly toward professional Web developers. Its features are endless. (It even has support for manipulation of JavaBeans and other complex components.) In short, it contains everything you will need to debug your DHTML, provided that JavaScript is your preferred language.

Summary of These Tools

Both Microsoft's Script Debugger and Netscape's JavaScript Debugger are powerful applications. Both employ the use of breakpoints and watchpoints, devices that can streamline debugging from an organizational and procedural point of view.

> **NOTE**
>
> *Watchpoints* are used to debug a script while it is running. Their purpose is to notify you as you pass through each function. For example, suppose you have three functions in a script, and these are designed to execute one after the other. To isolate which function has errors, you assign watchpoints either at the beginning or end of each function. These watchpoints notify you as you successfully pass through each function. This notification is also user definable. For example, you could define watchpoints that write to the status bar of your browser. As you pass through the first function, a message would appear in your status bar, reporting that "You cleared function number 1 without errors." This tells you that function number 1 is fine. However, if an error occurs before your second watchpoint reports a successful pass, you know that function number 2 is flawed. You then jump to the breakpoint for function 2 and inspect the code. In this respect, watchpoints and breakpoints can greatly enhance your ability to debug your DHTML.

In this chapter, however, we will debug our DHTML by hand. My reason for this is simple: I want you to fully understand each step. Later, when you develop sites with complex DHTML, you will appreciate this experience.

A Staff Directory Example

It is now time to put these tools and concepts to work. To do so, we will make use of a fictional situation.

This morning, we were contacted by a company called Knuckleheads, Incorporated. The company has a Web site but no shell account access. Therefore, it is unable to employ traditional CGI to serve data to its Web site visitors. This poses a unique problem.

It wants to publish a staff directory on its site. At present, only a handful of employees have e-mail addresses, but that is expected to change. Therefore, the company wants a user-friendly DHTML routine that can accommodate this ever-expanding list. They suggest a "pop-up box" in which visitors can browse staff e-mail addresses. What do we do?

Building and Debugging the Staff Directory Visual Interface

We begin by visualizing the Staff Directory. We want the interface to look like the Staff Directory window in Figure 29.12.

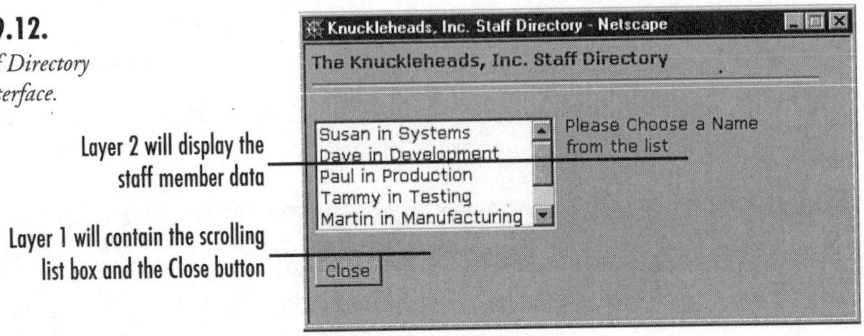

FIGURE 29.12.

The Staff Directory visual interface.

Layer 2 will display the staff member data

Layer 1 will contain the scrolling list box and the Close button

To create the interface, we use two separate `layer` objects. The first will house the scrolling list. The second will dynamically display vital information about each employee, including their name, function, location, telephone number, e-mail address, and Web URL.

Here is the code for the interface:

```
<HTML>
<TITLE>Knuckleheads, Inc. Staff Directory</TITLE>
<HEAD>
</HEAD>

<BODY BGCOLOR = "#33CCFF"></BODY>
<layer name = "formlayer" top = "5" left = "5" bgcolor = #33ccff>

<font face = verdana size = -1>
<b>The Knuckleheads, Inc. Staff Directory</b>
<hr>
<form name = "thelist">
<select name="telename" size = "5">
<option>Susan in Systems</option>
<option>Dave in Development</option>
<option>Paul in Production</option>
<option>Tammy in Testing</option>
<option>Martin in Manufacturing</option>
<option>Richard in Repairs</option>
<option>Laura in Legal</option>
</select>
</form>

<form>
<input type = button value = Close onClick=window.close()>
</form>

</layer>

<layer name="username" top="55" left="200" bgcolor = "#33ccff">
<font face = verdana size =-1>
Please Choose a Name<br>
from the list</font>
</layer>

</BODY>
</HTML>
```

We then test the code to ensure that the positioning of our layers is correct (see Figure 29.13).

Figure 29.13.

The positioning of the layers appears to be correct.

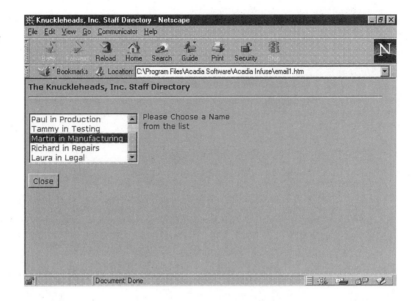

The positioning appears to be correct, so we continue. We define a function on the client's Web page that will launch the Staff Directory window. The page from which the code will launch is displayed in Figure 29.14.

Figure 29.14.

The page that will load the Staff Directory.

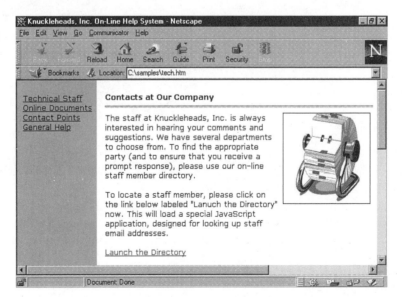

At a minimum, the new loading function must have the following elements:

- The attributes of the new window
- The dimensions of the new window

Suppose, then, that we write our function like this:

```
<script language = javascript>
function directory(form){
msg=open('','NewWindow','toolbar=no,location=no,directories=no,
➥status=no,menubar=no,scrollbars=yes,resizable=no,
➥copyhistory=yes,width=420,height=210');
}
</script>
```

Then suppose we add the appropriate event handler:

```
<a href = "javascript:directory('this.form')">Launch the Directory</a>
```

We then save the document and launch the Staff Directory. Did everything work as planned? See Figure 29.15.

FIGURE 29.15.

No error message appears, but the window is empty!

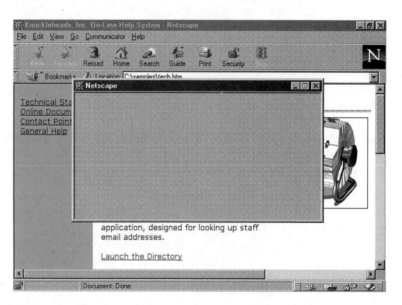

Something has gone wrong. What could have happened? Because there is no error message (a contingency that sometimes arises), we must discover on our own what caused the problem. To find out, we must reexamine our code and all relevant language references.

Finding the Error

The script uses the open() method of the window object. To double-check that all options and values were included, we refer to the JavaScript Object Model Reference in Acadia Infuse (see Figure 29.16).

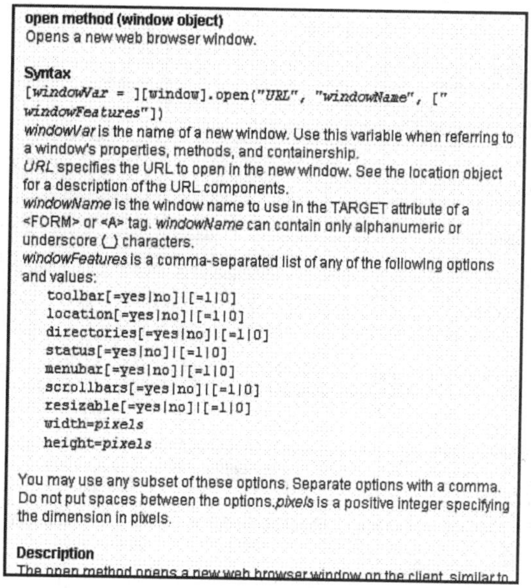

FIGURE 29.16.

The JavaScript Object Model Reference pop-up in Acadia Infuse.

```
open method (window object)
Opens a new web browser window.

Syntax
[windowVar = ][window].open("URL", "windowName", ["
windowFeatures"])
windowVar is the name of a new window. Use this variable when referring to
a window's properties, methods, and containership.
URL specifies the URL to open in the new window. See the location object
for a description of the URL components.
windowName is the window name to use in the TARGET attribute of a
<FORM> or <A> tag. windowName can contain only alphanumeric or
underscore (_) characters.
windowFeatures is a comma-separated list of any of the following options
and values:
    toolbar[=yes|no]|[=1|0]
    location[=yes|no]|[=1|0]
    directories[=yes|no]|[=1|0]
    status[=yes|no]|[=1|0]
    menubar[=yes|no]|[=1|0]
    scrollbars[=yes|no]|[=1|0]
    resizable[=yes|no]|[=1|0]
    width=pixels
    height=pixels

You may use any subset of these options. Separate options with a comma.
Do not put spaces between the options. pixels is a positive integer specifying
the dimension in pixels.

Description
The open method opens a new web browser window on the client, similar to
```

Here, we review syntax and options for the open() method. On closer examination, the problem immediately becomes clear. When using the open() method, we provided a series of options and values. Most of these defined visual attributes of the window being opened. In this case, the script was perfect with the exception of one minor detail: The URL of our Staff Directory document was missing. Armed with this knowledge, we reopen the document and insert the URL. The updated code looks like this:

```
<script language = javascript>
function directory(form){
msg=open('tele.htm','NewWindow','toolbar=no,location=no,directories=no,
➡status=no,menubar=no,scrollbars=yes,resizable=no,
➡copyhistory=yes,width=420,height=210');
}
</script>
```

Next, we save the document and try again. This time, the code executes perfectly. The resulting window looks exactly like the one in Figure 29.12. Excellent. The DHTML that generates the visual interface of the Staff Directory has just been debugged.

29

DEBUGGING YOUR DYNAMIC HTML

NOTE

The task described here defines the debugging process perfectly. You debug your code one step at a time. After each function is created, you test it. If there are bugs, you identify and eliminate them. You continue this process until each function executes flawlessly. When (and only when) you have debugged all functions separately, you then begin the task of

continues

continued

debugging them in concert. Here is why: Functions or scripts that work perfectly by themselves can often cause problems when coupled (or coexisting) with others. When debugging scripts in concert, follow the same pattern: Add one at a time. Thus, if you had a total of ten scripts embedded within the document, you would start by running only two of them in concert, then three, four, five, and so forth. You continue this refining process until every function and every script works flawlessly with its counterparts.

Writing and Debugging the Data Manipulation Routine

Let's return to the Staff Directory. We now have a clean visual interface that loads without error. What remains is to dynamically display a staff member's information when his or her name is selected from the list. The first step is to decide where that data will be stored. In this example, we will store it in the select object telename. That way, we can access our data through the select object's options array.

> **NOTE**
>
> Storing data in the select object is preferable to assigning each staff member's information to a variable within a script. String formatting performed purely in JavaScript is more difficult and prone to error. Moreover, we need not create a new array as one already conveniently exists.

The first step is to embed each staff member's data within the value of their corresponding option. Here is an example:

```
<option value = "<font face = verdana size = -1>
➥Susan in Systems<br>Room 204<br>555-0204<br>
➥<a href =mailto:suzy@knuckleheads.com>
➥Suzie@knuckleheads.com</a>
➥<br><a href =http://www.knuckleheads.com/>
➥http://www.knuckleheads.com
➥</a></font>>Susan in Systems</option>
```

After we have completed this task, we save the document and reload the Contacts at Our Company page. Again, we launch the directory, hoping that no errors occur. For the results, examine Figure 29.17 closely.

Bad news. We encountered problems with our visual interface again. Apparently, the HTML code we inserted between the option tags is flawed. To identify the error, we trace our steps back, examining each character within our code. Take a moment now to do just that. Do you see the problem? It occurred near the end:

```
</a></font>>Susan in Systems</option>
```

FIGURE 29.17.

The results of embedding each staff member's data in the value of their corresponding option: Our once perfect visual interface is now mangled.

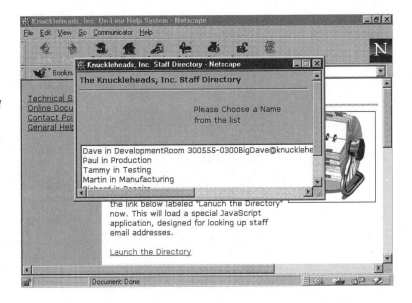

There is no closing quotation mark following the closed font tag. Because of this, the option's value absorbed excess HTML. In fact, it absorbed everything up until the next closed quotation mark! Note that this error did not affect the output of the JavaScript function that opened the window. All window parameters remained intact. However, this error severely distorted the contents of that window. In any event, it is a small problem. If we add the quotation mark and reload, our visual interface returns to normal.

NOTE

Errors like the one we just corrected are insidious, because they leave few clues to their origin. That brings us to an important point: When you are debugging DHTML, you will be debugging not only your scripts, but your HTML.

Now comes the interesting part. Our next task is to transplant the option's value into the second layer of the document. We do this with JavaScript, employing a function called report_name(). To clarify this process, I graphically illustrate its components in Figure 29.18.

From Figure 29.18, You can see the relationships of objects to one another. Our task is a simple one: Drill down into the select object, capture the value of the current option, and print it. The report_name() function will take three steps to perform this task:

- Find the data stored within the option value
- Open the document and write the data to Layer 2
- Close the document

29

DEBUGGING YOUR
DYNAMIC HTML

FIGURE 29.18.

The relationship of objects and data in this example.

> **Master Document**
>
> The master document contains the JavaScript function directory(). This function will drill down and capture staff data from the select options array.

> **Layer Object**
>
> Serves as container for the select object.

> **Select Object**
>
> Serves as container for the select options.

> **Option**
>
> Serves as container for staff data.

> **Layer Object 2**
>
> Serves as container for dynamic content, which the directory function derives from the select object's options array. In other words, whatever information is contained within the options array will be displayed here. The script opens this layer, writes to it, and closes this layer again.

Before we actually draft the report_name() function, we first assign an event handler to it. (We do this so we can test it from the start. After all, we might write the script perfectly the first time around.) Because we have used a select object, we choose the onChange event handler. Our code looks like this:

```
<select name="telename" size = "5" onChange="report_name
➥(this.form, this.form.telename.selectedIndex)">
```

Next, we write the function:

```
<script language = javascript>
function report_name(form, i) {
document.username.document.write(form.telename.options[i].text);
document.username.document.close();
}
</script>
```

Finally, we test it. Again, we load the Contacts at Our Company page and launch the Staff Directory. We then choose the first name on the list (Susan in Systems). Did our script work? See Figure 29.19.

Again, we encounter problems. This time, however, the error is of a different character. Instead of an error message (or a deformed visual interface), we are confronted with the wrong information. In other words, the script works fine, it just does something different from what we had intended. Can you guess why the wrong information was displayed? Let's take another look at our code:

```
<script language = javascript>
function report_name(form, i) {
document.username.document.write(form.telename.options[i].text);
```

```
document.username.document.close();
}
</script>
```

FIGURE 29.19.

The wrong information has been displayed.

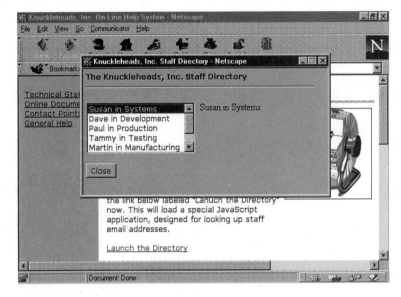

The error relates only to what information was displayed, so we can discard the rest of the code. Instead, we examine only one line:

```
document.username.document.write(form.telename.options[i].text);
```

We travel along that line, looking for mistakes. First, we know that the initial method (`write`) is correct, because data (albeit the wrong data) was written to Layer 2. Our problem, then, is clearly related to the variable we used to represent that data. So, we can even discard the beginning of the line. Our problem code, therefore, is this:

```
form.telename.options[i].text
```

We continue our process of elimination, looking for the error point. As we do so, keep in mind the results we had when we first tested the script. We know, for example, that when we chose Susan in Systems, the following information was displayed:

```
Susan in Systems
```

This text string is indeed part of the `select` object `telename`, so we can be certain that we called the right object. (The right object in this case being `telename`.) We even know that we are reaching the right area of `telename`, because we grabbed a value within its `options` array. Therefore, we can discard all the code except this snippet:

```
options[i].text
```

We now have a definitive answer. The problem is that we pulled the wrong value from the `options` array. We instructed JavaScript to grab the `text` value from the `options` array when what we really need is the `value` value. So, we update our code accordingly:

```
<script language = javascript>
function report_name(form, i) {
document.username.document.write(form.telename.options[i].value);
document.username.document.close();
}
</script>
```

We save our document, reload, and launch the Staff Directory. Did everything work properly? See Figure 29.20.

FIGURE 29.20.

Susan's data is displayed in Layer 2.

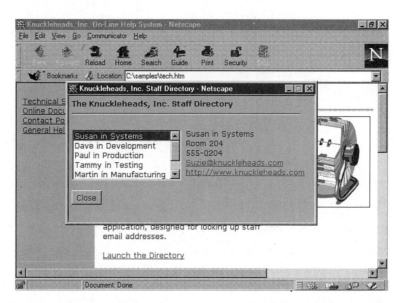

Everything worked perfectly. Susan's name, department, room number, telephone number, e-mail address, and Web URL are displayed. Moreover, her e-mail address and Web URL are hyperlinks. Therefore, visitors can now travel to Susan's Web page or even send her e-mail.

Summary of the Staff Directory Example

Before we move on, let's summarize the important points of this example. First, we review points that relate to technique:

- Debugging is a refining process that should be performed procedurally. Take it one step at a time.

- To streamline this process, read your code in a hierarchical fashion. Eliminate from your search any code that appears to have executed cleanly.

- Always have your preferred language's object model on hand. Without it, you are lost.

Moreover:

- When debugging DHTML, you might encounter errors not only in your scripting language but also in your HTML.
- When errors occur within HTML, you might not be notified. (In other words, the browser might not catch the error.)
- In such situations, examine the code character by character. It could be the only way to find the error.

Types of Errors You Will Encounter

Now, it is time to expand our view. In this section, we examine common errors that you will encounter. There are three basic types of error, explained in Table 29.1.

Table 29.1. The types of errors you will encounter.

Type of Error	Explanation
Errors on Load	Errors on load occur when the document loads and before the page is drawn. These can be fatal (the page fails to load) or serious (the page loads but content and functions fail). You saw such an on-load error in Figure 29.14.
Errors at Runtime	Runtime errors occur only when the script is active. Generally, unless the entire document is dependent on the script, runtime errors are fatal only to functions within the script. You saw such a runtime error in Figure 29.16.
Errors in Logic	Errors in logic are seldom identified by a browser. They occur when the script works but does something different from what you intended. You saw such a logic error in Figure 29.18.

Now that we have established the types of errors you will encounter, I want to discuss common reasons for them.

On-load errors most commonly occur for two reasons:

- You called a function or script using the onLoad event handler. The target function or script is not defined, the language is not supported, or the target function or script is flawed. Check that the target function actually exists and that you spelled its name correctly. If this is not the problem (and the language is supported), examine the function itself, character by character.
- The browser does not support the function you called. You have been a naughty, lazy programmer. Go back and design a script that first identifies the user's browser and then conditionally loads (or does not load) your opening script, depending on the browser type.

Runtime errors most commonly result for the following reasons:

■ You made a typographical error. Somewhere in the script, you have misspelled the name of a function, variable, or object. Go back and check your spelling.

■ You erroneously assigned an incompatible type. For example, you tried to convert a string literal to an object value that does not support this type of assignment. Compare this assignment with those provided in your language reference.

■ You omitted a vital portion of a script's structure, such as a closing bracket, parenthesis, quotation mark, comma, semicolon, operator, or closing `</script>` tag. Examine the code, find the error, and insert the missing element.

Logic errors typically occur for the following reasons:

■ You used an improper operator. Review your language reference to see whether what you are trying to do is even possible. If it is possible, review the operators necessary to do it. Are all of them present? If so, did you implement them properly? If not, find the flawed implementation and repair it.

■ You wrote a loop that provides no break or exit. Go back and examine the loop. Is there a condition that you did not provide for? If so, write some code to cover that contingency.

■ You coupled the right logic with the wrong object. For example, you wrote a script that validates form data. If the user does not enter his or her name before pressing the button to continue, an alert pops up. If that button is of the type `submit`, the empty form data will be submitted anyway, even though the alert is displayed. Change the button type and write a small routine that conditionally submits the data.

The only way to become proficient at debugging your DHTML is by experience. And if you plan to do heavy DHTML development, you will get more experience than you bargained for. For example, for purposes of clarity, I took you through errors in the Staff Directory one by one. However, in practice, you could encounter load, runtime, and logic errors all at once. This is quite an experience. Depending on your browser or scripting language, you may be confronted with as many as ten error message windows.

Advanced Techniques and Special Circumstances

What remains is to discuss advanced techniques. The rules of how you write your code can change under special circumstances. One such special circumstance is where your DHTML is integrated with CGI. I will not kid you about this. Integrating DHTML with CGI is probably the most difficult task you will ever face. In the following section, I demonstrate why.

Incorporating DHTML Techniques with CGI

CGI is commonly performed using the Practical Extraction and Report Language (Perl), created by Larry Wall. I will therefore use Perl in the following example.

When using Perl, user input is stored within variables declared in your HTML. Here is an example:

```
<form name = "myform" action = "get_user_input.cgi">
<input type = "text" name = "user_input">
</form>
```

This code makes two statements:

- User input will be encased in the variable `user_input`.
- The value of `user_input` will be passed to a Perl script named `get_user_input.cg`.

That is on the client side. On the server side, the Perl script would look something like this:

```
#!/usr/bin/perl
if ($ENV{'REQUEST_METHOD'} eq 'POST') {
read(STDIN, $buffer, $ENV{'CONTENT_LENGTH'});
@pairs = split(/&/, $buffer);
foreach $pair (@pairs) {
($name, $value) = split(/=/, $pair);
$value =~ tr/+/ /;
$value =~ s/%([a-fA-F0-9][a-fA-F0-9])/pack("C", hex($1))/eg;
$value =~ tr/,/ /;
$FORM{$name} = $value;
    }
}

print "$FORM{'user_input'}\n";
```

This Perl script performs three relevant functions:

- It reads the `user_input` value into `STDIN`.
- It strips any illegal characters from this input.
- It prints the value of `user_input` on a new page.

In essence, you are using Perl to write the resulting page. For several years now, this has been the standard way of doing things. However, when you add DHTML into this equation, the process becomes more complicated. To understand why, consider the following hypothetical example.

Suppose a client requests that you write a help system for its Web site. This help system will employ DHTML, JavaScript, pop-up windows, and more. Suppose further that your client wants this help system to be available on every viewable page. (Including those that are written by CGI processes.) You now have a problem.

Here is why: I explained in the section "Why Is Debugging Important?" that programming languages impose certain conventions. These conventions dictate the way your code can be written. Perl, despite its amazing text-formatting capabilities, is no exception to this rule. If you instruct Perl to print data received from a Web page, that data must be encased within quotation marks, like this:

```
print "$FORM{'user_input'}\n";
```

This technique is not problematic when employing standard HTML. However, with DHTML (or any HTML carrying scripts), this introduces a unique situation: Your scripting language might also require that certain elements be enclosed in quotation marks. Hence, you could find yourself encasing quoted JavaScript or JScript inside an already quoted `print()` instruction in Perl.

On the surface, this does not seem to be a particularly menacing problem. For example, you could perform this quoting in a hierarchical fashion. Using this approach, you would employ double quotes to open and close the Perl `print()` instruction and single quotes around quoted script elements. But, what if within your script—inside already double-quoted Perl and single-quoted script elements—you must again encase something in either single or double quotes? Clearly, you run out of permissible quotation marks. This is fatal both to your Perl CGI script and your embedded DHTML script. The result will be a "Server Has Encountered an Error" message.

A similar situation arises when you use WYSIWYG HTML development tools in conjunction with CGI. A good example would be Fusion by NetObjects, often referred to as the PageMaker of the World Wide Web. Such tools write the code for you, allowing you to construct Web pages as precisely as you would construct a word processing document. The problem is, these tools make liberal use of quotation marks to define properties and values. Therefore, your code could look like this:

```
<TR VALIGN="top" ALIGN="left">
<TD COLSPAN=3></TD>
<TD COLSPAN=2 ROWSPAN=2 WIDTH=221>
<P>This is the plain text</TD>
<TD COLSPAN=3 HEIGHT=3></TD>
</TR>
```

Notice that values are assigned using quotation marks. Alas, when you use Perl to write this out, the quotation marks must be removed. If they are not removed, Perl will exit on error. It is therefore an immutable rule that when integrating DHTML with CGI, all quotation marks around HTML elements be removed.

> **NOTE**
>
> Removing quotation marks around HTML elements does not affect the visual appearance of your page, nor is the task of removing them a difficult one. In addition, this does not mean that you must avoid such products. It simply means that after you have graphically constructed the page, you must dump the source into a text editor that can perform Find and Replace functions. There, you can replace all quotes with white space. This process—which takes less than a minute—will save you many hours of heartache.

Therefore, if you intend to incorporate your DHTML with CGI, observe these rules:

■ Eliminate quotation marks in scripts wherever possible. Where this is not possible, always use single quotation marks.

■ If using a WYSIWYG HTML editor, eliminate all quotation marks within the resulting source.

■ In eliminating these quotation marks, use an editor that does not line wrap.

■ Debug your DHTML thoroughly before embedding it within any CGI script.

Summary

This chapter is a short introduction to debugging DHTML; as such, the examples are rudimentary. However, they are designed to illustrate the theory and practice of debugging. Armed with these concepts, you can now experiment with various techniques and tools.

What remains is to explore the final step in deploying your DHTML: publishing and managing your content. Chapter 30, "Publishing and Managing Your Content," covers these issues.

Publishing and Managing Your Content

by William Royere

IN THIS CHAPTER

In previous chapters, you learned how to create stunning Web sites by using DHTML. In this chapter, you will learn how to publish and manage those sites.

This chapter is broken into three sections. These sections cover the following topics:

- Publishing concepts
- Management concepts
- Tools

Publishing Concepts

Web publishing has changed radically since HTML was first developed. What began as a method of displaying simple text and graphics has blossomed into an art form. Indeed, few activities demand such a peculiar mix of technical expertise, imagination, and creativity. Although this brave new world is a virtual paradise for the user, it has presented the Web author with many practical problems.

The craft of Web authoring is constantly evolving. In that evolutionary process, new technologies sometimes demand that publishing techniques are changed. In this chapter, you will explore how DHTML will influence your publishing technique.

DHTML Publishing Is Unique

You might think that DHTML publishing differs little from standard HTML publishing. After all, the mechanical process is the same: You write your code and upload it. Indeed, in this limited way, DHTML publishing and regular HTML publishing are quite similar. However, that is where the similarity ends.

DHTML (with its scripting languages, layers, and other amenities) demands not only greater organization, but also a more generic style of publishing. To demonstrate why, let's examine how Web publishing has changed over the years.

Traditional Web Publishing: The Olden Days

A poem can sum up this section:

```
In days of old
when authors were bold
and WYSIWYG wasn't invented,
they wrote their code
in plain text mode
and this is how it was presented.
```

I am a horrible poet, true, but that little bit of poetry expresses the situation perfectly. Traditional Web publishing was bare-bones, requiring only minimal organization on the author's part. Text and graphics were often kept in the same directory, for example. Because these were the only types of media to display, this technique was sufficient. Advanced publishing theory had not yet emerged because it wasn't needed.

Similarly, the tools required to publish Web content were primitive. (I refer to those dark years as the Stone Age of Web publishing). HTML was written in a plain text editor, validation was performed by viewing the result, and publishing was achieved via classic FTP. For those of us that favor UNIX, these were the good old days.

Alas, those good old days are now long gone. As the Internet grew in popularity, this climate changed drastically. Commercial developers discovered the Web and sought to maximize its potential. To that end, they created new forms of media and new techniques of data manipulation. In the face of these emerging technologies, traditional Web publishing quickly became outmoded. The final result was a double-edged sword.

On one hand, the Web became a more functional medium for distributing information. On the other hand, the process of publishing that information became infinitely more complex. Thus, it wasn't long before developers realized that a more intelligent approach was needed.

Modern HTML Publishing Methods

To satisfy this demand for a more intelligent approach, developers created a new generation of HTML editors. These new tools were more powerful than their predecessors and streamlined the publishing process. I am referring here to the birth of WYSIWYG HTML editors.

WYSIWYG HTML editors enable you to construct a Web page in precisely the same manner as you would construct a word processor document. You can drop and drag objects (such as images) on a page. You can specify page size, color, and resolution with a click of the mouse. In essence, you draw the page and the editor writes the code—the underlying HTML.

These new editors also solved a multitude of formatting problems. Prior to their introduction, for example, you could not perform absolute positioning of objects. To solve this problem, these new editors employed invisible table structures to manipulate object placement. The process worked as follows: you dropped an image on the page and dragged it to the desired position. For each image (or other object) that you positioned this way, the HTML editor wrapped invisible table structures around it (see Figure 30.1).

Note the shaded areas marked as invisible tables. These hem in the picture of Spot and the accompanying text. At view time, these tables (though invisible), still occupy the space allocated for them. The invisible tables, therefore, form an invisible barrier around the visible objects. In this way, they force the objects to an absolute position on the page, as shown in Figure 30.2.

FIGURE 30.1.

*Invisible table
structures surround
visible objects.*

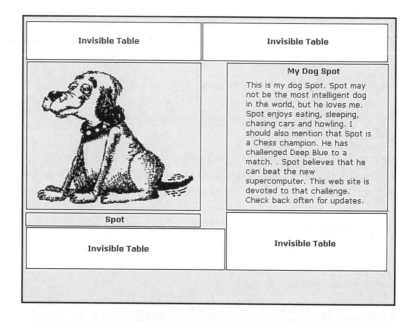

FIGURE 30.2.

*The objects are forced to
an absolute position on
the page.*

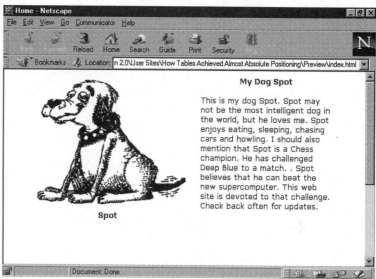

Although the finished result looks neat and clean, the code is complex and unwieldy. Take a look:

```
<!DOCTYPE HTML PUBLIC "-//W3C//DTD HTML 3.2//EN">
<HTML>
<HEAD>
<TITLE>Home</TITLE>
</HEAD>
```

```
<BODY BGCOLOR="#FFFFFF" LINK="#0000FF" VLINK="#800080" TEXT="#000000">
  <TABLE BORDER=0 CELLSPACING=0 CELLPADDING=0 WIDTH=602><TR VALIGN="top"
➥ALIGN="left">
    <TD COLSPAN=1 WIDTH=37><IMG SRC="./assets/images/dot_clear.gif"
➥WIDTH=37 HEIGHT=1 BORDER=0></TD>
    <TD COLSPAN=1 WIDTH=1><IMG SRC="./assets/images/dot_clear.gif"
➥WIDTH=1 HEIGHT=1 BORDER=0></TD>
    <TD COLSPAN=1 WIDTH=267><IMG SRC="./assets/images/dot_clear.gif"
➥WIDTH=267 HEIGHT=1 BORDER=0></TD>
    <TD COLSPAN=1 WIDTH=2><IMG SRC="./assets/images/dot_clear.gif"
➥WIDTH=2 HEIGHT=1 BORDER=0></TD>
    <TD COLSPAN=1 WIDTH=23><IMG SRC="./assets/images/dot_clear.gif"
➥WIDTH=23 HEIGHT=1 BORDER=0></TD>
    <TD COLSPAN=1 WIDTH=225><IMG SRC="./assets/images/dot_clear.gif"
➥WIDTH=225 HEIGHT=1 BORDER=0></TD>
    <TD COLSPAN=1 WIDTH=47><IMG SRC="./assets/images/dot_clear.gif"
➥WIDTH=47 HEIGHT=1 BORDER=0></TD>
    <TD COLSPAN=1 WIDTH=0><IMG SRC="./assets/images/dot_clear.gif"
➥WIDTH=0 HEIGHT=1 BORDER=0></TD>
</TR>

    <TR VALIGN="top" ALIGN="left">
    <TD COLSPAN=1></TD>
    <TD COLSPAN=3 ROWSPAN=1 WIDTH=270 ALIGN="center" VALIGN="middle">
<IMG HEIGHT=222 WIDTH=270 SRC="file:///C:/chapter2/spot.GIF"
➥BORDER=0  ALT="Picture" ></TD>
    <TD COLSPAN=1></TD>
    <TD COLSPAN=1 ROWSPAN=2 WIDTH=225>
<P ALIGN="CENTER"><B><FONT SIZE="-1" FACE="Verdana, Frutiger">My Dog Spot</B>
➥</FONT></P>
<P><FONT SIZE="-1" FACE="Verdana, Frutiger">This is my dog Spot.
➥Spot may not be the most intelligent dog in the world,
➥but he loves me. Spot enjoys eating, sleeping, chasing
➥cars and howling. I should also mention that Spot is a
➥Chess champion. He has challenged Deep Blue to a match.
➥Spot believes that he can beat the new supercomputer.
➥This web site is devoted to that challenge. Check back
➥often for updates. </FONT></TD>

    <TD COLSPAN=2 HEIGHT=222></TD>
    </TR>
    <TR VALIGN="top" ALIGN="left">
    <TD COLSPAN=5></TD>
    <TD COLSPAN=2 HEIGHT=2></TD>
    </TR>
    <TR VALIGN="top" ALIGN="left">
    <TD COLSPAN=8 HEIGHT=1></TD>
    </TR>
    <TR VALIGN="top" ALIGN="left">
    <TD COLSPAN=2></TD>
    <TD COLSPAN=1 ROWSPAN=1 WIDTH=267>
<P ALIGN="CENTER">
<B><FONT SIZE="-1" FACE="Verdana, Frutiger">Spot</B></FONT></TD>
    <TD COLSPAN=5 HEIGHT=16></TD>
    </TR>
    <TR VALIGN="top" ALIGN="left">
    <TD COLSPAN=8 HEIGHT=284></TD>
    </TR>
```

```
  <TR VALIGN="top" ALIGN="left">
   <TD COLSPAN=8 HEIGHT=0></TD>
  </TR>
 </TABLE></BODY>
</HTML>
```

This seems like a lot of code just to place a picture and two blocks of text. However, before DHTML emerged, this was the only way to perform absolute positioning.

The preceding example brings you to an important point. Using such an editor to generate DHTML is very difficult. To understand why, consider this: One major advantage of DHTML is that you can employ layers. Take another look at the previous code. Suppose that you wanted to isolate Spot in one layer and his story in another. Where, within the code, would you insert your layers? This presents a serious problem. The values of the invisible tables were generated for a page without layers. If you attempt to incorporate layers into this code, the results turn ugly (see Figure 30.3).

FIGURE 30.3.

When layers are incorporated, positioning changes.

Thus, under certain conditions, features in WYSIWYG editors that once streamlined Web authoring may now inhibit it. If you have been using such a WYSIWYG tool to generate your Web pages, you may want to reconsider. In many instances, arbitrarily inserting DHTML routines into auto-generated code produces disastrous results.

NOTE

Inserting DHTML routines into auto-generated code is not impossible. Rather, the time necessary to experiment with this combination may be costly. Much depends on the type of

> code that the WYSIWYG editor generates. If it looks like the code in the previous example, expect problems.

That said, we will now explore available publishing options.

Techniques of Publishing Your DHTML

You can publish your DHTML in two ways:

- By using integrated publishing tools
- By using nonintegrated publishing tools

The method you choose depends on your personal situation. In the following section, I will look at the advantages and disadvantages of each.

Integrated Publishing Tools

Integrated publishing tools are typically large, powerful packages. These may range from a few megabytes in size (Netscape's Composer) to almost 30 megabytes (Microsoft FrontPage 98). All such tools share these common characteristics:

- Support for scripting languages
- Support for at least minimal debugging
- A means of publishing your data

These tools are often touted as complete solutions because they provide a graphical environment for design, object model-based language support, and some degree of logical directory mapping. In addition, many such applications enable you to update your Web site selectively. (For example, you can update only those components that have changed since your last edit.) These are all key advantages.

Integrated publishing tools also have disadvantages. These tools often incorporate proprietary tags or code into your project. Thus, in certain situations, you can use these tools only to generate and upload a rough draft of your site. After completing this process, you may be forced to apply more incisive, hands-on techniques to achieve the desired result (removing quotation marks, eliminating proprietary code, altering paths and so on).

NOTE

Integrated publishing tools have other practical pitfalls. Suppose, for example, that you belong to a Web development team and that members of this team are located in different

continues

---

continued

buildings, or even in different cities. For all members to update or contribute to your work, each must have the same program. Moreover, each must re-create a directory structure on his local drive that is identical to your own.

At day's end, the chief value of integrated publishing tools is this: They offer you a holistic development environment. Within this environment, you can access most of the tools you need to create and deploy a site. Three good examples of integrated publishing tools follow:

- Fusion by NetObjects
- Microsoft FrontPage 98
- Macromedia Backstage

These integrated publishing tools have become extremely advanced. Some, such as FrontPage and Backstage, even offer Web servers and management utilities. In this way, they offer an integrated solution to authoring, viewing, debugging, publishing, and managing Web content.

Nonintegrated Publishing Tools

Nonintegrated publishing tools are specialized tools, often designed to serve a single purpose. Good examples of nonintegrated tools are

- An FTP client
- A link validator
- A script authoring application

When using nonintegrated tools, you may have to employ as many as 10 applications to complete your published Web site. On first examination, it may seem that using integrated publishing tools is a more desirable approach. For example, why use 10 applications when you can use just one? By using nonintegrated tools, you can perform changes more incisively. You, therefore, gain greater control over your code.

Remember the example with my dog Spot? In that case, the code was generated automatically in a WYSIWYG editor. Building that page took only seconds. However, the time gained by using a WYSIWYG tool was later lost, when the layers couldn't be integrated into the code.

Which Is the Better Choice?

Perhaps a combination of these tools is the best choice. By combining the best attributes of each, you can employ an assembly-line approach to development. This assembly-line approach can dramatically streamline your work and can also help you prepare for management of your site.

The easiest way to explain this assembly-line approach is to describe it in stages. At each stage of the process, you will be introduced to one or more tools or concepts that can help you. Assume that you are about to build a site with DHTML, but you have not yet written your first line of code.

The Power of Visualization

DHTML projects are usually complex. This complexity—unless coupled with strict organization—can make maintenance a difficult task. Therefore, tools that help you visualize the logic and structure of your site are extremely valuable.

In fact, visualization is a requisite when developing complex sites because human beings can only remember so much. By applying visualization to your site, you can easily identify snares in logic, common coding mistakes, and other problems. Thus, at the inception of your project, you must conceive (and visualize) two important elements:

- The logic of your site
- The structure of your site

These two qualities are quite different, but each reveals something important about the project.

Visualizing Site Logic

The *logic* of your site reveals how the user will interface with it. In reviewing site logic, you seek to determine the relationship of objects along a given data path. For an example, examine Figure 30.4.

FIGURE 30.4.
*A help data path
illustrated.*

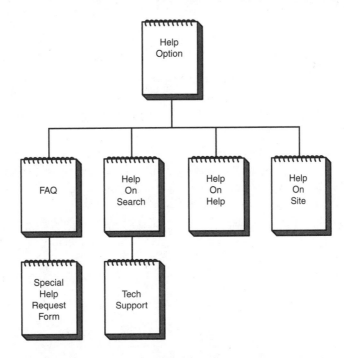

Figure 30.4 illustrates a help data path. The beginning of that path is the initial Help option. The end of that path (where the user runs out of links) is the Tech Support page. In complex DHTML sites, you may have data paths composed of 20 pages or more. Remembering their logical relationship is difficult unless you employ visualization.

If you map the logic of your site prior to building it, management will be very easy. This is the first rule of advanced Web publishing theory.

Two types of tools can help you with visualization. The first type is used before any code has been written. The second type is employed when a site already exists (where you inherit a site and are charged with updating it). For the first type, something such as Web Modeler works effectively.

Web Modeler

Manufacturer: Web Modeler Corporation
Location: `http://www.webmodeler.com/`
Status: Commercial ($499.00) Demo Version is Available
System Requirements: Windows 95, Windows NT 4.0

Web Modeler is an extraordinary tool, which can assist you in storyboarding your site. *Storyboarding* is the process of logically laying out the site, page by page. Employing this method, you can visualize data paths that a user can take. Web Modeler helps you do this within a graphical environment (see Figure 30.5).

NOTE

Storyboarding reportedly originated in the animation field. Each frame was presented on a poster board. This would enable the director to visualize the scene about to be filmed.

When you start a new Web Modeler project, you are presented with an empty screen. Using your mouse, you can place blank, unnamed pages on the drawing area. You label each page (assigning its properties, including name, purpose, and so on) and position it on the drawing canvas.

As you add pages to the canvas, you can draw links between them. These links can be either normal links (page to page) or *sequential* links. Use sequential links to lock the user into a series of sequential pages; for example, if you are displaying an article that has four pages. Sequential links enable the user to move forward (next) or backward (previous) through the article.

The amazing thing is that Web Modeler doesn't just perform layout so you can visualize the site; it actually writes the pages and links to disk. Thus, before you even start coding your DHTML, you can lay out the general logic of the site. Having done this, you can then incisively add your DHTML scripts to each page.

FIGURE 30.5.

The Web Modeler graphical interface.

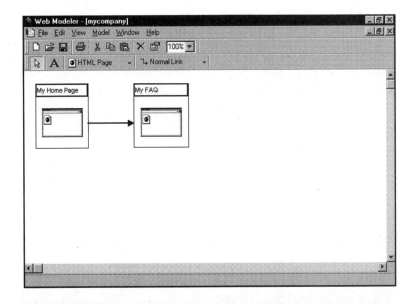

NOTE

A special note about Web Modeler: It generates clean HTML, has support for multiple browsers and editors, and provides tools to model image maps and frames.

What If the Site Already Exists?

You might need to work with a site that has already been built. If so, storyboarding tools will not help you (at least, not in the short run). Instead, you need something that can scan the current site and build a model of the logic already there. For this, try Astra SiteManager or PowerMapper.

Astra SiteManager

Manufacturer: Mercury Interactive Corporation
Location: http://www.merc-int.com/
Status: Commercial ($495.00) Demo Version is Available
System Requirements: Windows 95, Windows NT 4.0

Astra SiteManager is probably the most comprehensive site visualization tool currently available. It has several key advantages over its competitors, including the following:

- Support for all objects, including CGI scripts, Java applets, images and more.
- Comparison maps (before and after) of changes in the site.
- Recognition and indexing of external links.

This information can display in several ways, the most useful of which is a graphical, relational layout, as shown in Figure 30.6.

FIGURE 30.6.

Astra SiteManager maps the logic of your site.

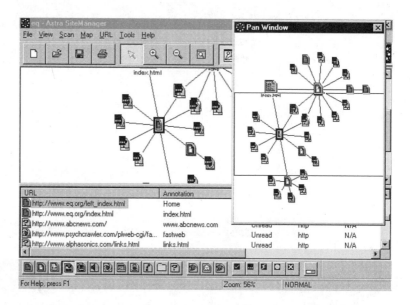

The top of the screen sports a detailed map of the site. Each object (file, link, and so on) can be examined separately. Each is identified by its file type, the protocol used, and whether it has been accessed by users. This information is further supplemented by important statistics, such as the number of incoming and outgoing links, number of broken links, date of last modification, and more. Finally, you can view the site link logic in a number of ways, focusing on a single page or file and examining the rest of the site in relation to that object.

PowerMapper

Manufacturer: Electrum Multimedia
Location: `http://www.electrum.co.uk/`
Status: Commercial ($99.00) Demo Version is Available
System Requirements: Windows 95, Windows NT 4.0

PowerMapper is easy to use. You simply specify a site (either local or remote) and let the application do its job. PowerMapper opens each file on the target site, analyzes the links there, and builds a graphic illustration of data paths (see Figure 30.7).

Using this utility, you can quickly identify logic flaws. You can also observe the relationship of each page to all others on the site. In addition, PowerMapper reveals malformed or dead links, as long as these links are local. When bad links are found, the missing page is represented as a page with a large, red X in the middle.

FIGURE 30.7.

PowerMapper maps the logic of your site.

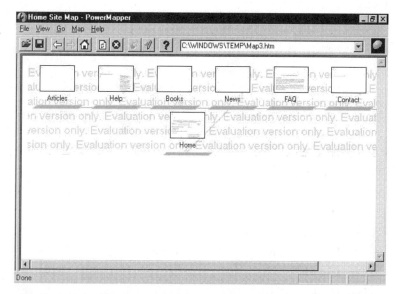

NOTE

PowerMapper scrupulously observes Robot Exclusion Standard rules. Therefore, it cannot be used to hammer away against sites that restrict robot access. You cannot use PowerMapper to either verify or follow external links. (For this, you may need to get other, more aggressive spiders.)

Visualizing Site Structure

By visualizing site logic, you can understand how the user will interface with the project. This will help enormously in preparing your site for management. Next, you must address the structure of your site.

The *structure* of your site refers to the logical organization of objects within it. As you will learn momentarily, you should group similar file types together, depositing all images of a given type into one directory. This way, you can quickly find them—as opposed to searching frantically through a directory that also houses video, audio, HTML, scripts, and other file objects.

If you properly organize your site, you can use any garden-variety FTP tool to visualize site structure. Some tools, such as Fusion by NetObjects, automatically map site structure for you. By briefly examining how Fusion maps directory structure, you can understand the process. Examine Figure 30.8.

FIGURE 30.8.

The Fusion opening screen—a graphical HTML editor.

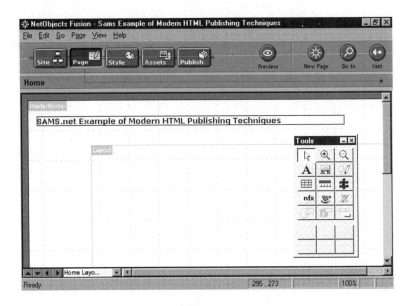

Fusion operates much like an advanced word processor. You can perform absolute positioning of objects, integrate Java applets, and even draw freehand, all with a click of the mouse. Fusion is a powerful Web development environment; however, the real intelligence built into Fusion operates behind the scenes.

Fusion creates an organized directory structure to house your work. This structure isolates different objects and media types. To see this technique in action, examine Figure 30.9.

FIGURE 30.9.

The typical directory structure of a Fusion project.

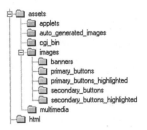

Notice that each data type has been assigned its own directory; therefore, you can easily understand the site's structure. Table 30.1 explains the significance of each directory.

Table 30.1. The significance of each directory in a Fusion project.

Directory	Purpose
assets	The top-level directory. Data elements (such as images and applets) are referred to as assets.

Directory	Purpose
`applets`	Houses Java applets.
`auto_generated_images`	Houses image map transparencies, rectangles, and other generic images automatically generated by Fusion.
`cgi-bin`	Houses CGI scripts.
`images`	Houses image files.
`multimedia`	Houses video and sound files.
`html`	Houses all HTML pages (except `index.html`).

Upon completing your project, you instruct Fusion to publish the site. During this process, Fusion imposes the preceding directory structure on the remote server. From that point on, even when you are using a rudimentary FTP client, you can easily recognize data types and their locations. This is important, because as your project grows, it becomes more difficult to manage.

In this respect, the folks at NetObjects (and other companies selling similar software) were on the right track. Good site organization is the key to successful HTML publishing and management.

DHTML publishing, however, demands even greater organization. To understand why, think back to our Staff Directory example in Chapter 29, "Debugging Your Dynamic HTML." In that example, the script function was embedded within the Web page; the code was written that way to simplify the example. However, in practice, you may often employ server-side scripts as well. If so, these scripts will be housed in external source files.

To manage a site designed this way, you must seriously consider the organization and structure, even prior to building the site.

Following are some suggestions to help you begin:

- Isolate external source files so that their logical relationship to the project is obvious. Thus, external source files called from `sales.html` should be placed in a `/sales` directory hierarchy.

- Group similar objects together. You might place scripts in a `/scripts` directory hierarchy, for example. In this way, you can quickly identify their location.

- Group server-side scripts by language. Consider placing JavaScript source files in a directory named `/my_javascript`. In this way, you can quickly ascertain a script's language dependencies.

- Script names should reflect their purpose. Thus, a JavaScript source file containing the function `report_status()` should be named `report_status.js`. This way, you can easily determine a script's function.

When you build your site, you should do it in a manner that will make future management as simple as possible. By adhering to the suggested rules, you ensure that you can instantly examine any object and know the following:

■ The object's logical relation to the project.

■ The type of object at which you are looking.

■ If the object is a script, the language in which it is written.

■ What the script does.

For instance, examine the following path:

```
/sales/scripts/my_javascript/report_status.js
```

This path immediately tells you everything you need to know about the object:

1. This object was called from a sales presentation.
2. This object is a script.
3. This script is written in JavaScript.
4. This script reports the status of the company's sales.

These measures will greatly enhance your ability to automate management and updating, especially if you develop large sites that are compatible with multiple browsers. (Or where your client requests that the site support a wide variety of technologies, for example, a Java version, a DHTML version, a plain text version, and so on.)

Important points of this section are the following:

■ DHTML publishing demands that you carefully organize your project, even from its inception. Visualization can greatly assist you in doing this, enabling you to see your site's logic.

■ By grouping data, language, and file types, you achieve better structural organization.

■ Better organization means easier management.

Adding Reusable Code

After you determine the generic structure of your site, your next step is to place reusable code or components. These are snippets of code that you probably use on all your sites. Good examples of reusable code are

■ A pop-up help function

■ A scrolling status bar

■ Links to a credits page

Some of these reusable components may appear in (or be embedded within) all viewable pages; for example, in a menu bar. Perhaps this menu bar highlights each menu choice as the user's mouse passes over it. Manually dropping this routine into all viewable pages is time-consuming. For this task, I recommend HTML Sniplets by IslandSoft.

HTML Sniplets by IslandSoft

Manufacturer: IslandSoft
Location: `http://www.lava.net/~islesoft/`
Status: Shareware ($14.95)
System Requirements: Windows, Windows 95, Windows NT

HTML Sniplets enables you to store and index blocks of reusable code. Code snippets can be as large as 3,277 characters in length. Each can be given a unique name (for example, `Highlight Button Script`). These can be instantly retrieved and pasted into your current project. (See Figure 30.10.)

FIGURE 30.10.

HTML Sniplets.

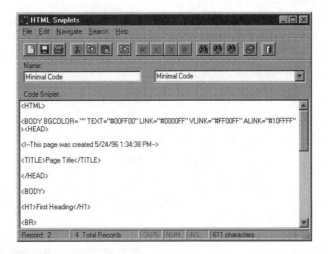

The usefulness of this little application is not apparent at first glance. However, suppose that you are designing a site in which each page must have the same header, footer, timestamp, mail link, and pop-up help routine. Suppose further that of these same pages, a handful will also have links to an index, bibliography, sitemap, and members area. You, therefore, have two tasks. First, you have to impose certain links on all pages. Second, you must go back and insert special links on just a few. Doing this by hand would take a long time; Doing this with HTML Sniplets will take seconds.

Checking for Errors

After having placed reusable code, your next step is to write some DHTML. However, it is now time to review an obscure point in Chapter 29.

During the process of debugging your DHTML, you can easily recognize when your scripts fail to work properly. The browser usually warns you by hurling a series of errors windows across your screen. (Subtleness is not an issue when an error is caught by a browser). However, errors

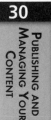

in HTML syntax may not be so obvious. Thus, after mapping the logic and structure of your site, placing reusable code, and writing DHTML, you should follow by checking HTML syntax and links. As you probably suspect, this process can also be automated (just another step in the assembly-line process).

Syntax and Link Validators

During HTML validation, you subject both syntax and links to quality control. On sites empowered with DHTML, doing this by hand is too difficult. Instead, you should employ automated tools. For this, I recommend either HTML PowerTools or CSE 3310 HTML Validator.

HTML PowerTools

Manufacturer: OppoSite Software
Location: `http://www.opposite.com/`
Status: Commercial ($59.95) Demo is Available
System Requirements: Windows, Windows 95, Windows NT

HTML PowerTools is a suite of applications that manipulate and validate HTML. It includes many useful programs, such as

- An image scanner
- An HTML validator (HTML 3.2, IE 3.0, and Netscape 3.0 extensions)
- An HTML to plain-text converter
- A powerful search-and-replace application

Here, you are concerned only with the HTML PowerAnalyzer, the validation tool. HTML PowerAnalyzer is fast, compact, and hearty. The program is simple but effective. Check out Figure 30.11.

FIGURE 30.11.
*The HTML
PowerAnalyzer opening
screen.*

To start a new project, choose Select Project. This prompts you for a project name and code. (The code is arbitrary; you can make it anything you like.) You then specify a directory or list of files, and the program does the rest. It begins by analyzing the target files for errors (see Figure 30.12).

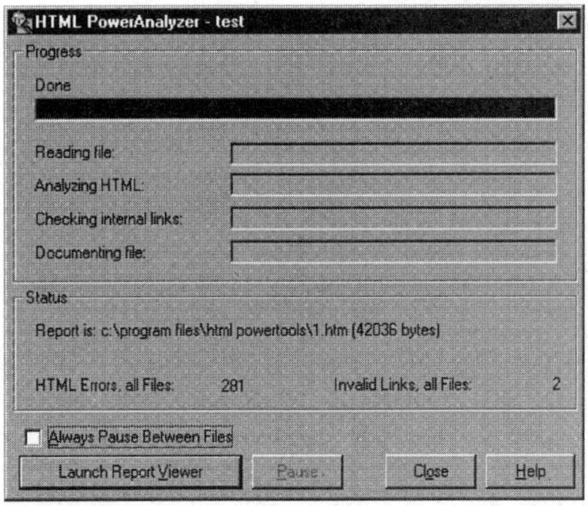

FIGURE 30.12.

*HTML PowerAnalyzer
analyzes the code.*

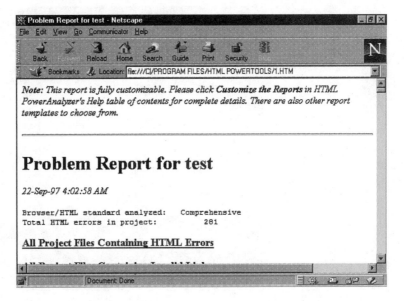

After the analysis is complete, HTML PowerAnalyzer reports the number of errors and invalid links. To get a comprehensive report, choose Launch Report Viewer. This causes HTML PowerAnalyzer to load a comprehensive report within your browser, as shown in Figure 30.13.

FIGURE 30.13.

*HTML PowerAnalyzer
loads a comprehensive
report in your browser.*

The report produced by HTML PowerAnalyzer is extremely detailed. It reports the line at which the error occurred, the type of error it was, and prints the code that contains the error. A typical error report follows:

```
(52) Line 449: Invalid use of quote marks in parameter value:
➥<font size=4 face="Tahoma,Arial,Helvetica,Geneva,
➥Bookman,Times" color=$black">
```

This error message reports that in line 449 of the file, a quotation mark has either been omitted or misused. The errant code is this:

```
color=$black"
```

Think of HTML PowerAnalyzer as a debugging utility for HTML.

CSE 3310 HTML Validator

Manufacturer: AI Internet Solutions
Location: `http://www.htmlvalidator.com/htmlval/orderinfo.html`.
Status: Commercial ($39.95) Demo is Available
System Requirements: Windows, Windows 95, Windows NT

CSE 3310 HTML Validator is for the DHTML author who wants to control every aspect of the validation process. The program offers a rules editor that probably contains every HTML tag, escape sequence, and character notation ever devised. You can manipulate how these values are treated during the validation process by using the HTML Configuration Editor. (See Figure 30.14.)

FIGURE 30.14.

CSE 3310 HTML Validator's HTML configuration editor.

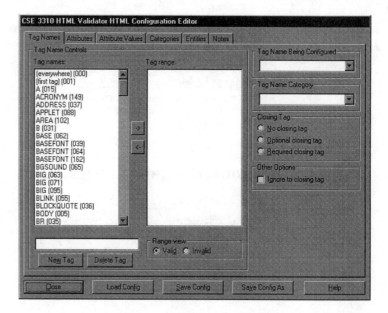

Most important, this application also addresses all tags used in generating DHTML. The following are a few of the extensions with which this application can work:

- Microsoft Internet Explorer 4.0
- Netscape Navigator 4.0
- Cold Fusion
- Style Sheets

Using CSE 3310 HTML Validator, you can tailor your HTML debugging to the extreme. I highly recommend this application.

> **NOTE**
>
> You do not need to use local tools to perform HTML validation. A number of online services will validate your HTML free of charge. WebLint gateways are a good example. WebLint is a Perl script that cleans HTML. (Its name was derived from Lint, the extremely popular debugger for C and C++ programmers.) Because the application was written in Perl, it was easily adapted to the WWW. WebLint gateways (WWW interfaces to WebLint) now exist at many locations, such as `http://www.fal.de/cgi-bin/WeblintGateway`. You simply specify your page URL and wait. The WebLint gateway will generate a report in your browser.

Publishing Your Material

Moving along through the assembly-line process, we have thus far covered the following subjects:

- Visualizing site logic and structure
- Generating site logic and structure
- Placing reusable code or objects
- Validating URLs and syntax

As you can see, this is a graded process. You first address the big picture—for example, the concept, logic, and structure of your site. To handle this big picture, you use a tool that performs generalized functions (such as imposing the desired directory structure system-wide). Such a tool could be likened to a shotgun. The blast is wide and covers a lot of ground. Gradually, you use tools that perform more and more incisive tasks, until you reach the debugging process. (At that stage, your tools are more like scalpels.) Finally, you will be ready to publish your site.

To perform this publishing, you can use any FTP client. (Or equally, perhaps you use an integrated package that uploads the entire work automatically.) Thus, it's not necessary to cover that aspect of the publishing process. However, somtimes it might be necessary to use specialized tools. This section addresses one such situation: the three-party FTP transfer.

Whether you're a professional Web developer or hobbyist, sooner or later you will be faced with a grueling task: moving a complete and functional Web site from one remote server to another (or perhaps, to several others). This can be time-consuming. The following tools can automate that process.

Cupertino

Manufacturer: H. Sean Hu
Location: `http://tucows.tierranet.com/files/Cupertino.zip`
Status: Beta
System Requirements: Windows 95, Windows NT

Cupertino allows transfers between one or more remote hosts, which means that you can transfer files from Site A to Sites B, C, and D. It is not required that the files be located on your local drive. As illustrated in Figure 30.15, Cupertino's interface is quite intuitive. It fully supports drag-and-drop transfers among multiple FTP hosts.

FIGURE 30.15.

The Cupertino FTP client.

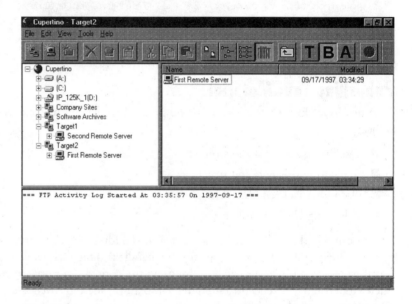

One word of caution: Cupertino performs this practical task by transparently downloading the files to your hard disk drive and then back up to the target hosts. Therefore, if you transfer a very large site to several other servers, be sure you have adequate disk space.

JavaFTP

Manufacturer: Dave Ragones, Joe Ross and Dr. Fred Douglis
Location: `http://tucows.tierranet.com/files/Cupertino.zip`
Status: Freeware
System Requirements: Any Platform with full-fledged Java support

A platform-independent FTP client, JavaFTP is intriguing for several reasons. First, the source code is available with the distribution. Second, it runs on any platform with a Java virtual machine. Third (and most importantly), it can handle FTP transfers across multiple servers.

JavaFTP accomplishes this task through the use of a tabbed interface (see Figure 30.16). The program is fast and efficient. Perhaps most incredible of all, however, this application takes very little disk space.

FIGURE 30.16.

The JavaFTP client.

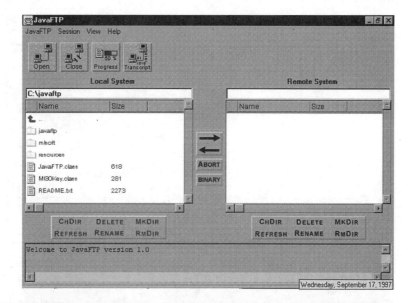

For JavaFTP to function correctly, you must include the `JavaFTP.class` directory into your `CLASSPATH`. Windows users can do this by editing the `autoexec.bat` and inserting the appropriate directory. This can be done as follows:

```
SET CLASSPATH=.;C:\javaftp;%CLASSPATH%
```

UNIX users must do this by using either the `SET` or `SETENV` commands (for example, `SET CLASSPATH=/classdirectory/`).

Mirror for Macintosh

Manufacturer: Alastair Rankine, Progmatics Pty Ltd
Location: `ftp://progmatics.seagull.net/mirror-10.sit.bin`
Status: Free for non-commercial use
System Requirements: System 7.0+, MacTCP, Open Transport

This utility was created for the purpose of mirroring Web sites. As such, it has the capability to transfer files between two remote sites. Management of such transfers is easy and intuitive (see Figure 30.17).

This application is very well coded, providing support for either partial automation (from within Mirror itself) or full automation (using AppleScript). You can not only use this utility to perform mirroring, you can also automate the entire process.

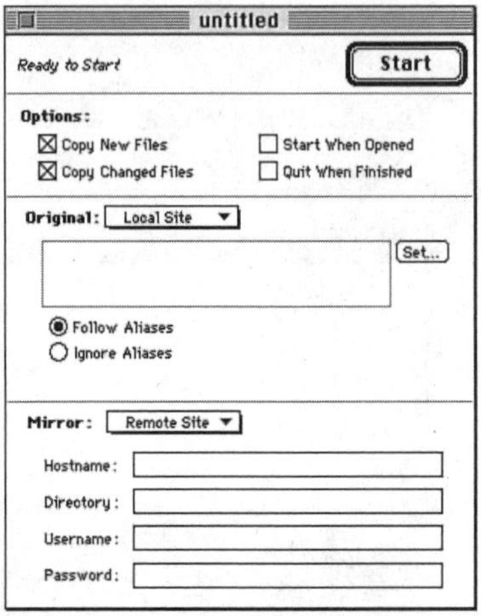

Figure 30.17.

Mirror for Macintosh.

Management Concepts

Earlier in this chapter, you learned that good site organization leads to easier management. This section proves it.

Most management tasks involve changing or updating information. Often, this process demands that you make global changes to a certain class of file. Perhaps you want to include additional functionality to one of your DHTML routines. If you are a dedicated author, you probably created code that will work with multiple browsers. These routines are almost certainly written in different languages. If you organized your site as previously explained, updating or changing that code is easy; your source files are indexed by their language dependency and function.

Changing the information can now be automated. To do so, you must take three steps:

- Write the new routine (or include additional functionality to an existing routine).
- Identify the files that contain the old routine.
- Replace the old routine with the new one.

This process sounds easy enough, and it is, as long as your approach to publishing is well organized. For example, you should have stored your scripts somewhere. If you were truly organized, you already have these scripts stored in HTML Snippets or a similar indexing tool. If so, you can immediately call up the old script. After you have the text for both the old and new scripts, you can perform a global search and replace, as explained in the next section.

Automating URL and Script Updates

In Web publishing, you will often face the task of updating URLs or scripts. On a small site, this is not a problem. However, sites that employ DHTML may contain many URLs or scripts. Worse still, these may be embedded in files with different extensions, including

- HTML, HTM, CSS, ASP, and SHTML
- JS, PL, and CGI

If you are a Perl or shell language guru, this is no problem; you simply write a script to scan directories recursively. The script opens each file fitting the criteria and changes the information. However, what if you have no UNIX programming experience? The following utilities solve this problem.

> **NOTE**
>
> These utilities can be used to search and replace links or even entire scripts. For example, you may have a script that is embedded in every viewable page on your server. If so, you can use these utilities to quickly update or delete that script system-wide.

Search and Replace

Manufacturer: Funduc Software Inc.
Location: `http://ourworld.compuserve.com/homepages/funduc/`
Status: Shareware
System Requirements: Windows, Windows 95

Search and Replace will open files across multiple directories and replace text strings. Figure 30.18 shows the opening screen.

Search and Replace has several important features. It supports multiple file masks. Therefore, you can simultaneously update URLs in files bearing different extensions. Also, the application ships with a script language, which is implemented with a script editor (see Figure 30.19).

The script editor enables you to store automated search and replace functions for later use. No Web developer should be without such a tool.

SR-HTML32

Manufacturer: Ellipse Data Systems
Location: `http://www.ellipse-data.com/freestuff.shtml`
Status: Freeware
System Requirements: Windows, Windows 95

SR-HTML32 is a simple but powerful application. It does not sport the scripting functionality of Search and Replace, but it is extremely fast. Also, all functions are available from a single screen (see Figure 30.20).

FIGURE 30.18.
Search and Replace opening screen.

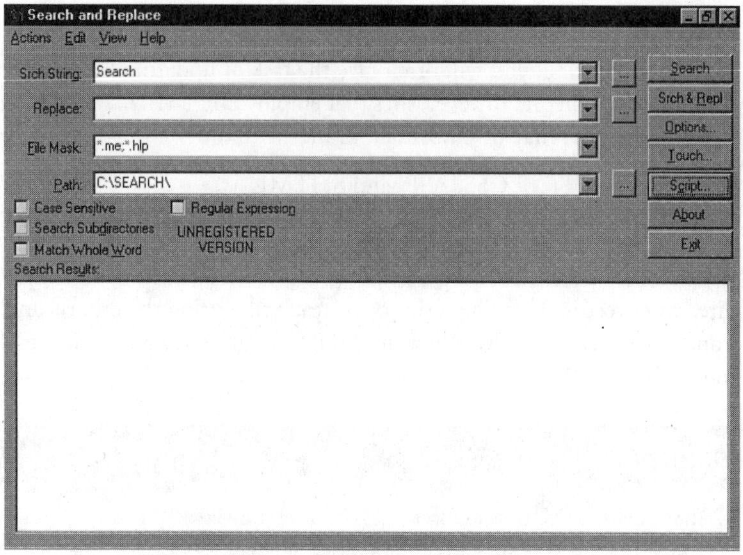

FIGURE 30.19.
The Search and Replace script editor.

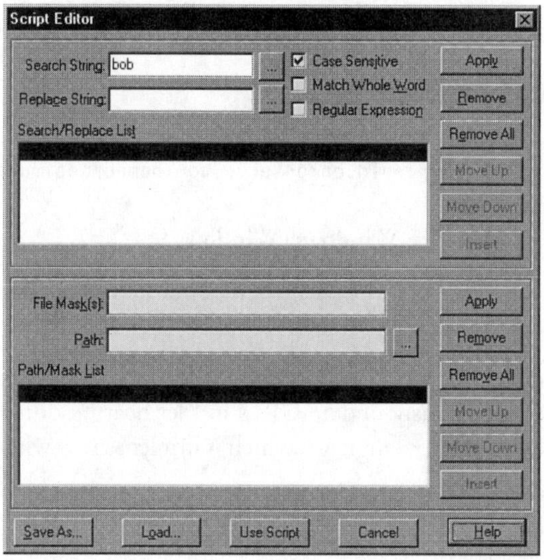

Updating Time-Based Information

Sometimes, you create a page that contains time-based information, or information that will eventually expire. Sites of this nature require your constant attention because when such information does expire, it should either be removed or marked as dated. To perform this process by hand is unpleasant and time-consuming. For this, you need Xpire Plus.

FIGURE 30.20.

SR-HTML32 main screen.

Xpire Plus

Manufacturer: Bungalow Systems, Chris Lindell
Location: `http://www.kagi.com/bungalow/`
Status: Shareware ($20.00)
System Requirements: Windows, Windows 95, Windows NT

Xpire Plus is a tool that will find and replace old information with new information and is designed specifically for Web developers. (See Figure 30.21.)

FIGURE 30.21.

The Xpire Plus main screen.

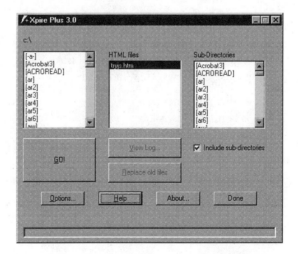

Xpire Plus can dramatically reduce the time you spend performing searching and replacing; in fact, it can automate the entire process. Xpire Plus also can recursively scan directories, so you can perform update procedures on an entire Web site with the click of a button.

Collecting and Analyzing Site Statistics

One major aspect of management is the task of collecting and analyzing site statistics. Your clients will want to know who is using the site, where they are coming from, how often they visit, and more. This type of data collection can often be revealing. For example, you can track the success (or lack thereof) of advertising campaigns. Or you can isolate sections of your site that generate more interest than others. By studying such statistics, you may discover why.

In any event, up until recently, generating site statistics was a complex task. At least, this was a complex task for anyone without UNIX shell language or Perl experience.

> **NOTE**
>
> Most Web servers house the access and error logs in plain-text format. Perl is therefore incredibly well-suited for generating site statistics. Log files generally separate fields by white space. Using the `split()` function in Perl, one can catch these fields and manipulate them. If you use a UNIX system, I highly recommend using Perl for this task.

Thankfully, developers have introduced statistical data-gathering solutions for the rest of the computing community. Today, many tools are designed expressly for this purpose. I will offer only one: NetIntellect.

NetIntellect

Manufacturer: WebManage Technologies
Location: `http://www.webmanage.com/`
Status: Commercial ($199.00) Demo Download is Available
System Requirements: Windows 95, Windows NT

Every so often, a killer app emerges. A *killer app* is any application that performs its tasks so well that it fulfills (and exceeds) all expectations of the user. NetIntellect is one such tool.

NetIntellect is a utility for generating and analyzing site statistics. It analyzes many types of log files, such as

- NCSA
- CERN
- Microsoft Internet Information Server
- WebStar
- O'Reilly
- Oracle

In all, NetIntellect can analyze 14 types of log files on disparate platforms, including Windows 95, Windows NT, Novell, UNIX, MacOS, and more. This in itself is quite extraordinary. However, although NetIntellect's multiplatform, multiformat support is impressive, the granular data it culls from such log files is dumbfounding.

When the application first opens, it looks unimpressive. It prompts for a log file and does nothing more. (See Figure 30.22.)

FIGURE 30.22.

The NetIntellect opening screen.

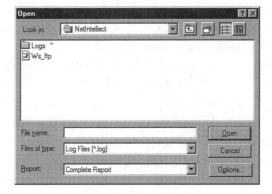

After you provide a log file, however, NetIntellect immediately goes to work. Within seconds, it slurps up the data and begins formatting it. Final results can be viewed either within NetIntellect's interface (my preference) or within your browser. (NetIntellect generates a comprehensive report in HTML, along with links to various portions of the report.) Examine Figure 30.23.

FIGURE 30.23.

A NetIntellect comprehensive report.

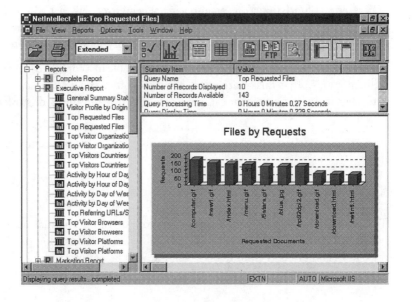

30

PUBLISHING AND
MANAGING YOUR
CONTENT

As you can see from Figure 30.23, the screen is split into three parts. On the extreme left, you can choose from a variety of report formats, including

- Technical Report
- Executive Report (Summary)
- Marketing Report
- Complete Report

In Figure 30.23, I chose the Executive Report and highlighted the Top Files by Request option. This option reports which files were most requested and how often. In the upper-right window, the information appears in plain-text. In the lower-right window is a graph that enables you to visualize the general status of the top-requested files. If you want exact numbers from the graph, you simply pass your mouse cursor over the desired record, and the exact number appears.

Unfortunately, we do not have enough space here for a list of all the data that NetIntellect gathers, but following are some of the most interesting queries you can perform:

- **By Region:** List connections by the country from which they came. This option reveals the provider (or IP) from which the request came. This can be mapped to cities.

- **Peaks of Activity:** Tells you the peak traffic times, including by month, week, day, day of the week, and hour.

- **Client and Server Side Errors:** Gives you a comprehensive report on all errors that occurred within a specified time range. This option can also reveal errors by category, how often they occurred, and which hosts experienced them.

- **General Statistics:** You can also get a general overview that will report highest traffic times, total number of visits, average visits per day, total bytes transferred, average number of bytes transferred, most active day of the week, and more.

This is only a small portion of the information available in a complete NetIntellect report. This utility not only offers this information, but it also offers you a way to automate the process of gathering it. In addition, you can automate the distribution of this information by using e-mail.

In short, NetIntellect offers a very complete solution to the problem of gathering statistical data.

Summary

This chapter took you through basic concepts of publishing and managing your site. It is not necessary that you use the tools presented. Rather, this information provides an overview of these tasks and presents an order in which they can be performed.

In closing, organization is everything. If you apply good organizational techniques to your site from the beginning, management will be a snap. If you fail to implement such techniques, management will be very difficult.

Publishing and managing sites developed with DHTML is a formidable task, but that's okay. In the process of learning DHTML, you have transcended the identity of Web author and entered the realm of Web developer. Learning organizational techniques is a small price to pay in exchange for such power.

I

INDEX

X-Z

A   V I A C O M   S E R V I C E

The Information SuperLibrary™

Bookstore	**Search**	**What's New**	**Reference**	**Software**	**Newsletter**	**Company Overviews**
Yellow Pages	**Internet Starter Kit**	**HTML Workshop**	**Win a Free T-Shirt!**	**Macmillan Computer Publishing**	**Site Map**	**Talk to Us**

CHECK OUT THE BOOKS IN THIS LIBRARY.

You'll find thousands of shareware files and over 1600 computer books designed for both technowizards and technophobes. You can browse through 700 sample chapters, get the latest news on the Net, and find just about anything using our massive search directories.

All Macmillan Computer Publishing books are available at your local bookstore.

We're open 24-hours a day, 365 days a year.

You don't need a card.

We don't charge fines.

And you can be as **LOUD** as you want.

The Information SuperLibrary
http://www.mcp.com/mcp/   ftp.mcp.com

MACMILLAN COMPUTER PUBLISHING USA

A VIACOM COMPANY

Technical
Support:

If you cannot get the CD/Disk to install properly, or you need assistance with a particular situation in the book, please feel free to check out the Knowledge Base on our Web site at **http://www.superlibrary.com/general/support**. We have answers to our most Frequently Asked Questions listed there. If you do not find your specific question answered, please contact Macmillan Technical Support at **(317) 581-3833**. We can also be reached by email at **support@mcp.com**.